17th Workshop on Innovative Use of NLP for Building Educational Applications (BEA 2022)

Online
15 July 2022

ISBN: 978-1-7138-5624-5

Printed from e-media with permission by:

Curran Associates, Inc.
57 Morehouse Lane
Red Hook, NY 12571

Some format issues inherent in the e-media version may also appear in this print version.

Association for Computational Linguistics
209 N. Eighth Street
Stroudsburg, Pennsylvania 18360

Phone: 1-570-476-8006
Fax: 1-570-476-0860

acl@aclweb.org

Additional copies of this publication are available from:

Curran Associates, Inc.
57 Morehouse Lane
Red Hook, NY 12571 USA
Phone: 845-758-0400
Fax: 845-758-2633
Email: curran@proceedings.com
Web: www.proceedings.com

BEA 2022

17th Workshop on Innovative Use of NLP for Building Educational Applications

Proceedings of the Workshop

July 15, 2022

The BEA organizers gratefully acknowledge the support from the following sponsors.

Gold Level

duolingo NBME ETS iLexIR

Order copies of this and other ACL proceedings from:

Association for Computational Linguistics (ACL)
209 N. Eighth Street
Stroudsburg, PA 18360
USA
Tel: +1-570-476-8006
Fax: +1-570-476-0860
acl@aclweb.org

Introduction

This year marks the 17th edition of the *Workshop on Innovative Use of NLP for Building Educational Applications*. We received an impressive number of 66 submissions, from which we accepted 4 papers as oral and 27 as poster presentations, for an overall acceptance rate of 47 percent. We in the Organizing Committee were excited to see so many truly diverse and excellent submissions and selecting the ones to be presented at the workshop was often a hard decision. The papers accepted were selected on the basis of several factors, including the relevance to a core educational problem space, the novelty of the approach or domain, and the strength of the research. As always, excellence in research was one of the main factors considered. Each paper was reviewed by at least three members of the Program Committee who we believed to be most appropriate for the paper. As in the previous years, we also continue to have a strong policy to deal with conflicts of interest and double submission policy.

Being a long-running workshop, we are glad to see novel research and publications from the regular BEA authors. At the same time, we are also very happy to welcome our new authors who are publishing their work with BEA for the first time this year. We hope the new authors will become active members of the BEA and the SIGEDU communities. We also hope that with our relatively high acceptance rate, we were able to include a diverse set of papers on a variety of topics and from a wide set of institutions, which is itself a clear indicator of the growing variety of research interests in the field of educational applications.

In addition to oral and poster presentation, BEA 2022 is hosting two invited talks: by Klinton Bicknell, a staff research scientist at Duolingo, where he co-leads the Learning AI Lab, and by Alexandra I. Cristea, Professor, Deputy Head, Director of Research and Head of the Artificial Intelligence in Human Systems research group in the Department of Computer Science at Durham University. As in the previous years, we are also hosting an ambassador paper talk from one of the sister societies from the International Alliance to Advance Learning in the Digital Era (IAALDE). This year, the talk will be given by James Fiacco (Carnegie Mellon University) from the International Society of the Learning Sciences (ISLS).

This year, a number of authors released their data and code for the benefit of the educational community; we list these resources below. The papers present a wide variety of approaches: from traditional NLP and ML models to the state-of-the-art techniques applied to the educational applications. In addition, it is exciting to see a variety of domains and applications addressed in this year's papers – from language learning to engineering and math education. Last but not least, this year's submissions represent a wide variety of applications developed for languages other than English. Three papers address applications to German: Rietsche *et al.* introduce an automatic peer-to-peer feedback classification model; Weiss and Meurers present a new state-of-the-art readability assessment model for German L2 readers; and Laarmann-Quante *et al.* explore acceptability of spelling variants in free-text answers to listening comprehension prompts. In addition, Moner and Volodina introduce a synthetic error dataset for Swedish; Chang *et al.* perform automatic short answer assessment on texts written in Finnish; while Reyes *et al.* present a baseline readability model for Cebuano; and Ahumada *et al.* introduce a tool aimed at supporting educational activities in Mapuzugun. It is exciting to see educational applications developed for such a wide variety of languages, many of which are traditionally considered to be low resource, and we hope to see even more publications addressing other languages in the coming years.

The BEA 2022 workshop has presentations on a variety of topics, including automated writing evaluation, item generation, readability, discourse analysis, dialogue, annotation, speech, grammatical error detection and correction, feedback, and multi-modal approaches.

Automated Writing Evaluation (AWE) and Grading: Four papers address this topic. Bexte *et al.* introduce an architecture that efficiently learns a similarity model for content scoring and find that results on the standard ASAP dataset are on par with a BERT-based classification approach. Takano and

Ichikawa present a BERT-based automated scoring model for short-answer questions that benefits from pre-training on a large amount of general text data. Chang *et al.* investigate the grouping of short textual answers, which is approached as a paraphrase identification task and evaluated on a dataset consisting of textual answers from various disciplines written in Finnish. Jalota *et al.* discuss debiasing approaches to mitigate the impact of an author's L1 on automated CEFR classification.

Automated Item Generation (AIG): Four papers present various approaches to automated item generation. Zou *et al.* propose an unsupervised True / False Question Generation approach (TF-QG) that automatically generates questions from a given passage for reading comprehension and show that this approach can generate valuable testing items. Keim and Littman explore a novel approach that leverages large language models to select inline challenges and automatically generate context cloze items that discourage skipping during reading. Rathod *et al.* propose a new Multi-Question Generation task aimed at generating multiple semantically similar but lexically diverse questions assessing the same concept in reading comprehension and report preliminary results from sampling multiple questions from their model. Heck and Meurers present a tool that builds on a language-aware search engine that helps identify suitable texts for readers and generates practice exercises from authentic texts.

Reading and Text Complexity: In addition to the papers that generate testing items for reading comprehension, three more focus on readability assessment models. Reyes *et al.* present the first baseline readability model for the Cebuano language, the second most used native language in the Philippines with about 27.5 million speakers. Weiss and Meurers present a new state-of-the-art sentence-wise readability assessment model for German L2 readers and make a number of insightful conclusions about this model. Finally, North *et al.* investigate the performance of binary comparative Lexical Complexity Prediction (LCP) models for complex word identification applied to CompLex 2.0 dataset that was used in SemEval-2021 Task 1.

Discourse and dialogue: This year, a number of papers focused on various aspects of discourse analysis in educational contexts and on dialogue and conversational systems. Among them, Suresh *et al.* investigate the feasibility of using enriched contextual cues to improve model performance on the classification of talk moves – discursive strategies used by teachers and students to facilitate conversations in classrooms; they apply their models to the publicly available TalkMoves dataset and report new state of the art over previously published results on this task. Alic *et al.* propose the task of computationally detecting funneling and focusing questions in classroom discourse, create and release an annotated dataset of teacher utterances, and introduce a range of approaches to differentiate between these questions. Ding *et al.* explore the role of topic information in student essays from an argument mining perspective and show that, given the same amount of training data, prompt-specific training performs better than cross-prompt training. Fiacco *et al.* propose a state-of-the-art method for automated analysis of structure and flow of writing and lay a foundation for a generalizable approach to automated writing feedback related to these aspects. Ganesh *et al.* introduce a new task called response construct tagging (RCT), in which student responses to tailored survey questions are automatically tagged for six constructs measuring transformative experiences and engineering identity of students. Finally, Tyen *et al.* make an initial foray into adapting open-domain dialogue generation for second language learning, propose and implement decoding strategies that can adjust the difficulty level of the chatbot according to the learner's needs, and evaluate these strategies using judgements from human examiners trained in language education.

Speech: Speech processing and assessment, as usual, are very popular topics at BEA. This year, we have six presentations in these areas. Kwako *et al.* investigate potential biases of transformer-based models for automated English speech assessment and report that no statistically significant difference that can be related to biases was found in their preliminary experiments. Chen *et al.* report on their first effort of using deep learning to evaluate L2 learners' reduced form pronunciations, which are useful in training ASR applications. Laarmann-Quante *et al.* present a corpus study in which they analyze human acceptability decisions in a high stakes listening test for German; they show that spelling variants are harder to score consistently than other answer variants and examine how the decision can be operationalized using features that could be applied by an automatic scoring system. Skidmore and Moore explore the application of laughter as a feature for incremental disfluency detection in spoken learner English and show that, combined with silence, these features reduce the impact of learner errors on model precision and lead to an overall improvement of model performance. Kyle *et al.* introduce and release a dependency treebank of spoken L2 English that is annotated with part of speech (Penn POS) tags and syntactic dependencies (Universal Dependencies) and then evaluate the impact of this treebank on training models for POS and UD annotation tasks. The work by Dutta *et al.* explores the fusion of conversational speech and real-time location in the context of cognitive development in children and provides preliminary evidence that the use of speech technology in educational settings supports early childhood intervention.

Grammatical Error Detection (GED) and Correction (GEC): Remarkably, two more papers at BEA are at the intersection of speech and grammatical error correction. Specifically, the work by Lu *et al.* focuses on the assessment and development of spoken grammatical error correction (SGEC) systems and discusses evaluation metrics, the problem of error propagation in cascaded approaches, and the importance of accurate feedback for learners. In the same vein, Bannò and Matassoni address the task of automatically predicting proficiency scores for spoken test responses of English as a second language learners by training models on written data and using the presence of grammatical errors as a feature; they investigate the impact of the feature extractor on spoken proficiency assessment and conclude that their approach can be beneficial for assessing spoken language proficiency.

Feedback: The topic of feedback generation in learning environments also attracted a lot of attention this year. For intstance, Jia *et al.* present a new paradigm, which they call incremental zero-shot learning (IZSL), to tackle the problem of lacking sufficient historical data for the task of peer assessment, which is an effective pedagogical strategy for delivering feedback to learners. Rietsche *et al.* present an automatic classification model to measure sentence specificity in written peer-to-peer feedback; they train and test their models on student feedback texts written in German, and their results suggest that specificity of feedback sentences weakly correlates with perceptions of helpfulness. Wambsganss *et al.* present a novel tool to support and engage English language learners with feedback on the quality of their argument structures, which automatically detects claim-premise structures and provides visual feedback to learners to prompt them to repair any broken argumentation structures.

Annotation: Moner and Volodina generate a synthetic error dataset for Swedish by replicating errors observed in the authentic error-annotated dataset.

Multi-modal approaches: Loginova and Benoit propose an adaptation of NLP techniques from the field of machine comprehension to the area of mathematical educational data mining; they show that incorporating syntactic information can improve performance in predicting exercise difficulty.

Resources: Reyes *et al.* open-source the code and data used to develop the baseline readability model for the Cebuano language. The language tool presented by Ahumada *et al.* for Mapuzugun is also publicly available through an online interface in both Mapuzugun and Spanish. Tyen *et al.* release the code and demo of their controllable complexity chatbot. Moner and Volodina release for public use fakeDaLAJ (S-FinV), synthetic error dataset generated using error labels based on linguistic analysis of real-life error-annotated learner data. Kyle *et al.* make their SL2E Treebank publicly available for non-commercial purposes. Rietsche *et al.* release both code and annotated data used for their peer-to-peer feedback evaluation model. Bexte *et al.* make their code for the S-BERT similarity-based content scoring publicly available. Ding *et al.* release their code and clustering results for argument identification in student writing. Rathod *et al.* release the code for their Multi-Question Generation model for reading comprehension. Annotated data and code for distinguishing between funneling and focusing questions is also released by *Alic et al.* Finally, Ganesh *et al.* release the data, code and models for the Response Construct Tagging task.

To conclude, we would like to thank everyone who showed interest and submitted a paper this year – all of the authors for their contributions, the members of the Program Committee for their valuable feedback and thoughtful reviews, and everyone who is attending the workshop. We hope to see many of you at the workshop, both remotely and in person in Seattle.

Ekaterina Kochmar, University of Bath
Jill Burstein, Duolingo
Andrea Horbach, FernUniversität in Hagen
Ronja Laarmann-Quante, FernUniversität in Hagen
Nitin Madnani, Educational Testing Service
Anaïs Tack, Stanford University
Victoria Yaneva, National Board of Medical Examiners
Zheng Yuan, King's College London
Torsten Zesch, FernUniversität in Hagen

Organizers

Jill Burstein, Duolingo
Andrea Horbach, FernUniversität in Hagen
Ekaterina Kochmar, University of Bath
Ronja Laarmann-Quante, FernUniversität in Hagen
Nitin Madnani, Educational Testing Service
Anaïs Tack, Stanford University
Victoria Yaneva, University of Wolverhampton; National Board of Medical Examiners
Zheng Yuan, King's College London
Torsten Zesch, Computational Linguistics, FernUniversität in Hagen

Program Committee

Tazin Afrin, University of Pittsburgh
David Alfter, UCLouvain
Jason Angel, Instituto Politécnico Nacional
Piper Armstrong, Brigham Young University
Timo Baumann, Ostbayerische Technische Hochschule Regensburg
Lee Becker, Pearson
Beata Beigman Klebanov, Educational Testing Service
Lisa Beinborn, Vrije Universiteit Amsterdam
Kay Berkling, Cooperative State University, Karlsruhe
Marie Bexte, FernUniversität in Hagen
Daniel Brenner, Educational Testing Service
Christopher Bryant, University of Cambridge
Andrew Caines, University of Cambridge
Dumitru-Clementin Cercel, University Politehnica of Bucharest
MeiHua Chen, Department of Foreign Languages and Literature, Tunghai University
Guanliang Chen, Monash University
Zhiyu Chen, University of California, Santa Barbara
Leshem Choshen, IBM, Hebrew University Jerusalem Israel
Mark Core, University of Southern California
Scott Crossley, Georgia State University
Kordula De Kuthy, SFB 833, Universität Tübingen
Yuning Ding, FernUniversität in Hagen
Rahul Divekar, Educational Testing Service
Yo Ehara, Tokyo Gakugei University
Mariano Felice, University of Cambridge
Michael Flor, Educational Testing Service
Thomas François, UCLouvain, CENTAL
Jennifer-Carmen Frey, EURAC Research
Michael Gamon, Microsoft Research
Lingyu Gao, Toyota Technological Institute at Chicago
Samuel González-López, Technological University of Nogales
Cyril Goutte, National Research Council Canada
Na-Rae Han, University of Pittsburgh
Jiangang Hao, Educational Testing Service

Nicolas Hernandez, Nantes University
Chung-Chi Huang, Frostburg State University
Yi-Ting Huang, Academia Sinica
Joseph Marvin Imperial, National University, Manila, Philippines
Radu Tudor Ionescu, University of Bucharest
Richard Johansson, University of Gothenburg
Lis Kanashiro Pereira, Ochanomizu University
Elma Kerz, RWTH Aachen University
Ekaterina Kochmar, University of Bath
Mamoru Komachi, Tokyo Metropolitan University
Ritesh Kumar, Dept. of Linguistics, Dr. Bhimrao Ambedkar University, Agra
Kristopher Kyle, University of Oregon
Ji-Ung Lee, UKP Lab Technische Universität Darmstadt
Yudong Liu, Western Washington University
Anastassia Loukina, Educational Testing Service
Lieve Macken, Ghent University
Irina Maslowski, OSS360
Sandeep Mathias, Presidency University
Janet Mee, National Board of Medical Examiners
Detmar Meurers, Universität Tübingen
Alessio Miaschi, Institute for Computational Linguistics A. Zampolli, ILC-CNR
Masato Mita, RIKEN AIP
Diane Napolitano, The Associated Press
Kamel Nebhi, Education First
Hwee Tou Ng, National University of Singapore
Huy Nguyen, Amazon
Mengyang Qiu, University at Buffalo
Martí Quixal, University of Tübingen
Vipul Raheja, Grammarly
Lakshmi Ramachandran, Amazon Search
Hanumant Redkar, Indian Institute of Technology Bombay
Frankie Robertson, University of Jyväskylä
Alla Rozovskaya, Queens College, City University of New York
C. Anton Rytting, University of Maryland College Park
Katherine Stasaski, University of California at Berkeley
Helmer Strik, Centre for Language and Speech Technology (CLST), Centre for Language Studies (CLS), Radboud University Nijmegen
Anaïs Tack, Stanford University
Shalaka Vaidya, IIIT Hyderabad
Giulia Venturi, Institute of Computational Linguistics Antonio Zampolli (ILC-CNR)
Carl Vogel, Trinity College Dublin
Elena Volodina, University of Gothenburg
Hongfei Wang, Tokyo Metropolitan University
Xinyu Wang, Riiid Labs
Zarah Weiss, University of Tübingen
Michael White, The Ohio State University
David Wible, National Central University
Alistair Willis, The Open University
Yunkai Xiao, North Carolina State University
Yiqiao Xu, North Carolina State University
Zheng Yuan, King's College London

Marcos Zampieri, Rochester Institute of Technology
Klaus Zechner, ETS
Fabian Zehner, DIPF | Leibniz Institute for Research and Information in Education
Torsten Zesch, Computational Linguistics, FernUniversität in Hagen
Robert Östling, Department of Linguistics, Stockholm University
Jan Švec, NTIS, University of West Bohemia

Keynote Talk: ML and NLP for Language Learning at Scale

Klinton Bicknell
Duolingo

Abstract: As scalable learning technologies become ubiquitous, it generates a large amount of student data, which can be used with machine learning and NLP to develop new instructional technologies, such as personalized practice schedules and adaptive lessons. Additionally, machine learning and NLP are uniquely poised to solve the problems inherent in scaling language instruction to a large number of languages and courses. In this talk, I will describe several projects illustrating these two uses of ML and NLP in language learning at scale at Duolingo – the world's largest language education platform with over 100 courses and around 40 million monthly active learners.

Keynote Talk: Aspects of Learning Analytics

Alexandra I. Cristea
Durham University

Abstract: My favourite definition of Learning Analytics (LA) is Eric Duval's: LA means "collecting traces that learners leave behind and using those traces to improve learning.", and I'll tell you more about why during my talk. Whilst the term LA was coined relatively recently (2011), it is a growing area of interest, with immediate practical application, albeit a growing research area at the same time, bringing together many classic as well as cutting edge methodologies, such as statistics, data mining, machine learning (including deep learning), network analysis and visualisation. This talk will bring together an understanding of LA as an emerging discipline and research area, as well as new research directions in LA, such as applications in gamification, explainable AI, predicting certification of students, urgent instructor intervention (where we do use a bit of NLP), and further predict the development and maturity of this area as a whole.

Keynote Talk: Taking Transactivity to the Next Level

James Fiacco
Carnegie Mellon University, USA

Ambassador paper presentation from the 2021 Annual Meeting of the ISLS (International Society of the Learning Sciences), a member society of the IAALDE (International Alliance to Advance Learning in the Digital Era)

Abstract: Transactivity is a valued collaborative process, which has been associated with elevated learning gains, collaborative product quality, and knowledge transfer within teams. Dynamic forms of collaboration support have made use of real time monitoring of transactivity, and automation of its analysis has been affirmed as valuable to the field. Early models were able to achieve high reliability within restricted domains. More recent approaches have achieved a level of generality across learning domains. In this study, we investigate generalizability of models developed primarily in computer science courses to a new student population, namely, masters students in a leadership course, where we observe strikingly different patterns of transactive exchange than in prior studies. This difference prompted both a reformulation of the coding standards and innovation in the modeling approach, both of which we report on here.

Table of Contents

Using Item Response Theory to Measure Gender and Racial Bias of a BERT-based Automated English Speech Assessment System

Alexander Kwako
University of California, Los Angeles
akwako@ucla.edu

Elaine Wan
University of California, Los Angeles
elaine1wan@ucla.edu

Jieyu Zhao
University of Maryland, College Park
jieyuz@umd.edu

Kai-Wei Chang
University of California, Los Angeles
kwchang@cs.ucla.edu

Li Cai
University of California, Los Angeles
cai@cresst.org

Mark Hansen
University of California, Los Angeles
markhansen@ucla.edu

Abstract

Recent advances in natural language processing and transformer-based models have made it easier to implement accurate, automated English speech assessments. Yet, without careful examination, applications of these models may exacerbate social prejudices based on gender and race. This study addresses the need to examine potential biases of transformer-based models in the context of automated English speech assessment. For this purpose, we developed a BERT-based automated speech assessment system and investigated gender and racial bias of examinees' automated scores. Gender and racial bias was measured by examining differential item functioning (DIF) using an item response theory framework. Preliminary results, which focused on a single verbal-response item, showed no statistically significant DIF based on gender or race for automated scores.

1 Introduction

Automated speech assessment systems have become prominent at the K-12 and post-secondary levels (Collier and Huang, 2020; Educational Testing Service, 2005). Scores produced by automated systems are used for high stakes decisions, such as allocating public funds and determining university admissions decisions. Compared to human raters, automated assessments may be more efficient and affordable (Evanini et al., 2017), and they may improve reliability (Zechner, 2020). Yet automated assessments have a unique set of challenges (Williamson et al., 2012), and it is important that test developers and researchers continue to improve the overall enterprise of automated speech assessment.

Researchers have recently begun applying transformer-based models (Devlin et al., 2018) to English speech assessment. Largely, these research efforts have been directed towards improving the accuracy of automated scoring systems. For instance, Ormerod et al. (2021) has conducted research on BERT-based methods in automated essay scoring. In English speech assessment, Wang et al. (2021) compared the performance of BERT and XLNet for the purpose of scoring examinees' transcribed responses. Results have demonstrated that transformer-based models are highly accurate and correlate strongly with human ratings.

Although transformer-based models can produce accurate scores, less attention has been devoted to examining the biases of these models. In the field of English speech assessment, no such analyses have been conducted to date. In the broader field of natural language processing (NLP), research has demonstrated that transformer-based models can propagate and, in some cases, exacerbate gender and racial prejudice (e.g. Zhao et al., 2017; Kiritchenko and Mohammad, 2018). Biased scoring models certainly have the potential to cause allocational harms (Blodgett et al., 2020), underscoring the importance of conducting detailed analysis prior to implementation.

Beyond text modeling, there are additional sources of potential bias in audio processing. Audio speech recognition (ASR), in particular, may be

Proceedings of the 17th Workshop on Innovative Use of NLP for Building Educational Applications (BEA 2022), pages 1 - 7

less accurate for certain language-minority groups (e.g. Koenecke et al., 2020). Less accurate transcripts, in turn, could lead to biased scores.

There are multiple ways to measure bias, and the most appropriate method varies depending on the specific research context. Most techniques, however, are similar in that they deteremine the extent to which language modeling outputs—whether word embeddings (e.g. Dev et al., 2020) or inferences (e.g. Zhang et al., 2020)—conform to pro-stereotype expectations. This study takes a similar overall approach, but is unique in using measurement tools from educational assessment.

This study examines a type of bias known as differential item function (DIF), which is defined as the systematic difference (in scores) between a reference group and a focal (minority) group, while controlling for overall proficiency (Angoff, 1993). Although bias and fairness are conceptually distinct in educational testing, detection of DIF may provide evidence for a larger claim about fairness for certain groups of examinees (Camilli, 2006). Although analysis of DIF is common in educational assessment, it has not been applied to studies of bias in NLP.

In order to detect DIF, we use the Improved Wald Test, which is rooted in item response theory (IRT) (Cai, 2012). There are a variety of methods used to detect DIF but, in general, IRT tends to offer the most statistical power (Osterlind and Everson, 2009). The Improved Wald Test, in particular, has gained widespread adoption because it is sensitive to small group differences, holding constant examinees' overall proficiency (Woods et al., 2013).

The research design of this study involves three principal components: (1) constructing an ASR system, (2) training a transformer-based scoring model, and (3) investigating potential gender and racial bias based on these automated scores. Our analyses focus on a single speaking item. Although we found no statistically significant result in the automated scores for this item, analyses will soon be expanded to a larger pool of items and multiple grade bands which may be more susceptible to automated scoring bias.

2 Methods

Below, we describe the key methodological aspects of the research project. These include (1) the source of data used in analyses, (2) the design and development of our automated English speech assessment system, and (3) the statistical techniques used to measure gender and racial bias.

2.1 Data

This study draws on data from the English Language Proficiency Assessment for the Twenty-First Century (ELPA21), a collaborative of 7 state education agencies in the United States (Huang and Flores, 2018). Approval for this research project was granted by the consortium and the a university institutional review board. Confidentiality agreements and ethical considerations prevent sharing test items or student-level data publicly.

For test items in the speaking domain, students speak into a microphone, and their responses are recorded and subsequently sent to a third party to be scored. Currently, all verbal responses are scored by human raters.

For this study, we selected a single speaking item that was administered to students in grade 2-3. This particular item elicited responses that were short in duration (median response length = 4.8 seconds). Responses were scored 0, 1, or 2, with the highest score being given to examinees who correctly answered the question, even if small grammatical mistakes were made. A score of 0 indicated that the question was not addressed at all.

Home language was used as an indicator of race because it afforded several advantages. First, it was more fine-grained, i.e., included more categories, than the alternative indicator of race. Second, it was more related to examinees' speech, which was a focal point of the study. Home language does not necessarily indicate cultural identity, however, or native language. Respondents whose home language had fewer than 200 responses were removed from analysis.

2.2 Automated Speech Assessment

Chen et al. (2018) enumerate four components of automated speaking assessment systems. These include (1) an automated speech recognition (ASR) system, which includes speech-to-text transcription, (2) the extraction of linguistic features from audio and text data, (3) a filter model to remove non-scorable responses, and (4) a scoring model to combine linguistic features into a single score. Below, we discuss each of these components in turn.

ASR System We compared the performance of several ASR systems, based on both accuracy and efficiency (see Appendix A for details). Ultimately,

	n	%
GENDER		
Male	$4,988$	52.5
Female	$4,517$	47.5
LANGUAGE		
Spanish	$6,881$	72.4
Russian	858	9.0
Vietnamese	440	4.6
Chinese	420	4.4
Ukrainian	381	4.0
Arabic	321	3.4
Persian	204	2.1

Table 1: Descriptive Statistics of the Sample

we opted to use Google's speech-to-text service to generate text transcripts from examinees' speech. Of the $10,147$ total responses, Google produced $9,505$ non-blank transcripts, all of which were included in analyses. Descriptive statistics of the sample, disaggregated by gender and home-language, are presented in Table 1.

To assess Google's transcription accuracy for young, non-native speakers, we sampled 100 responses, listened to examinees' audio recordings, and manually transcribed them. Treating our own annotations as ground truth, we measured the word error rate (WER) of the Google-generated transcripts. We determined the average WER to be 22.3%—close to human parity for non-native speech, which typically ranges from 15-20% (Zechner, 2009).

Feature Extraction Linguistic features were not manually specified, but were embedded latently in the BERT scoring model.

Filtering Blank transcripts were not included in model training or analysis of bias. In some cases, blank transcripts were the result of silent audio files; in other cases, however, Google returned blank transcripts when it failed to detect speech (e.g. when examinees whispered into the microphone). 642 blank transcripts were removed from analyses.

Scoring Model We compared BERT and RoBERTa as two potential scoring models. Selection of the scoring model was based on the accuracy of models' predictions of examinees' scores on the test dataset. Because the particular speaking item that we studied was imbalanced (e.g., 76.6% of responses were scored a 2), we chose to use a cross-entropy loss function, weighted inversely to the marginal frequency of the scores. Scoring models were trained for 10 epochs. Batch size, dropout ratio, and learning rate were set to 128, 0.1 and $2 \cdot 10^{-5}$, respectively. Data were split 80%/20% for training and testing sets.

Averaged across 3 random seeds, the most accurate model was the BERT model. Test set accuracy for BERT was 88.85%, marginally higher than RoBERTa. Figure 1 presents the confusion matrix of true and predicted scores using the above scoring model for the test dataset. Details regarding the series of experiments to optimize model performance may be found in Appendix B.

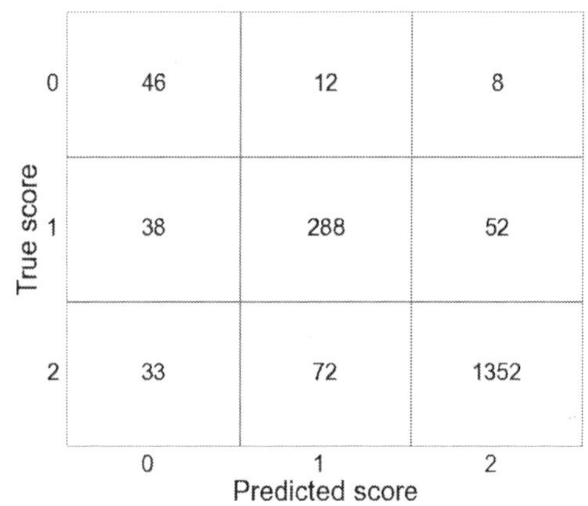

Figure 1: BERT Confusion Matrix.

The automated scoring model was found to be slightly more consistent than human raters. The Spearman Correlation Coefficient among human raters was calculated to be $\rho = 0.81$ (based on $n = 1,929$ doubly-scored responses). By comparison, the Spearman Correlation Coefficient of 2 BERT models, whose starting values and test-train splits were determined by 2 different random seeds, was found to be $\rho = 0.88$ (based on all $9,505$ responses).

2.3 Measurement of Bias

To measure bias, we used the Improved Wald Test to examine differential item functioning (DIF) using an item response theory (IRT) framework (Cai, 2012; Woods et al., 2013). In IRT, the Wald Test is used to measure and compare differences in item parameters between two groups of examinees. For the particular test item examined in this paper, IRT parameters included one discrimination parameter, a, and two item difficulty parameters, b. The discrimination parameter captures the variability of scores, whereas the item difficult parameters capture how difficult the item is (in this case, how difficult it is for examinees to receive a score of 1 or 2). See Cai et al. (2016) for a review of the Graded 2PL model, which was used to model this item. When weighted by the inverse of the variance-covariance matrix, the difference in a (or $\mathbf{b}$) is asymptotically distributed as χ^2.

If there is a statistically significant difference between groups' item parameters based on χ^2 values, this may indicate that scores are biased against certain groups of examinees, holding constant examinees' proficiency (Holland et al., 1993; Osterlind and Everson, 2009). In mathematical notation, DIF is present (i.e. bias against examinees is present) if and only if

$$P(correct\,response|\theta, g = 0) > \\ P(correct\,response|\theta, g = 1),$$

where $g = 0$ refers to the reference group, $g = 1$ refers to the focal group, and θ is overall proficiency. For multiple-group comparisons, multiple pairs are tested separately against the same reference group.

To take an example, if the automated system was excessively harsh toward female examinees, we would see higher $\mathbf{b}$ for female examinees (as compared to male examinees). If the automated system was less reliable for female examinees, then we would see higher a (as compared to male examinees). Since these scaled differences are distributed as χ^2, we can calculate observed p-values for each comparison.

The false discovery rate of multiple comparisons was controlled using the Benjamini-Hochberg technique (Benjamini and Hochberg, 1995), which has been shown to limit Type 1 errors to the nominal level while also maximizing statistical power (Williams et al., 1999). This approach is common in analysis of DIF using IRT (Edwards and Edelen, 2009).

3 Results

Table 2 shows the results of DIF for automated scores of one speaking item, based on gender and race differences. Reference groups were "Male" and "Spanish" as these were the two majority groups for gender and race, respectively. Results were originally ordered in decreasing value of p-observed ($\mathbf{p_{obs.}}$), as required by the Benjamini-Hochberg adjustment; however, for ease of interpretation, rows have been rearranged. In no comparison was $\mathbf{p_{obs.}}$ found to be lower than p-critical ($\mathbf{p_{crit.}}$), which indicates that none of the comparisons were statistically significant.

Two Wald Tests were conducted for each DIF comparison: one to test the significance of the discrimination parameter, a, and the other to test the significance of the difficulty parameters, $\mathbf{b}$. $\mathbf{b}$ is written in bold to indicate that it is a vector of difficulty parameters. There are two degrees of freedom for tests of differences of $\mathbf{b}$, corresponding to the two difficulty parameters. Observed p-values were calculated based on χ^2 and df.

Critical p-values were determined a-priori using the Benjamini-Hochberg adjustment. Although not shown, p-values would have been significant if any $\mathbf{p_{obs.}}$ had been lower than its corresponding $\mathbf{p_{crit.}}$. Although not presented here, there were also no significant differences found in human-rated scores, based on gender or race.

4 Conclusion and Next Steps

Transformer-based models have gained widespread attention due to their highly accurate predictions and correlations with human ratings, yet it is important that issues of fairness be addressed concurrently. Our study constitutes a step forward in automated English speech assessment by examining bias in BERT-based scoring models. Our study also demonstrates how item response theory can be used to identify differential item functioning (DIF) in the context of automated scoring—a practice that is common in educational assessment, yet uncommon in the field of natural language processing.

Although our analysis did not find any gender or race DIF in automated scores produced by our BERT-based model, we refrain from drawing general conclusions about the bias of such models for English speech assessment. In this instance, we found no evidence of bias, yet it is possible that such biases are more prominent in lengthier speaking items, for older groups of examinees, or for different language minorities. Indeed, based on research of implicit bias (Spencer et al., 2016), we might expect more bias in lengthier items or for older students. The next step of our research project is to take up these challenges by expanding DIF analyses to different types of speaking items, multiple age groups, and respondents with different home-languages.

Attribute	Ref. Group	Focal Group	Parameter	χ^2	df	$p_{obs.}$	$p_{crit.}$
Gender	Male	Female	a	0.0	1	0.8438	0.0232
			b	4.4	2	0.1082	0.0107
Language	Spanish	Persian	a	0.0	1	0.9500	0.0250
			b	9.1	2	0.0104	0.0036
		Ukrainian	a	4.9	1	0.0262	0.0071
			b	1.4	2	0.5055	0.0214
		Arabic	a	5.1	1	0.0241	0.0054
			b	2.2	2	0.3396	0.0196
		Vietnamese	a	1.0	1	0.3186	0.0179
			b	11.9	2	0.0025	0.0018
		Chinese	a	2.0	1	0.1555	0.0125
			b	2.8	2	0.2523	0.0161
		Russian	a	1.8	1	0.1747	0.0143
			b	6.8	2	0.0327	0.0089

Table 2: Differential Item Functioning of Automated Scores by Gender and Language

In addition to expanding the scope of the current analysis, next steps also include experimenting with a wider variety of transformer-based models and ASR systems. Incorporating audio data into the scoring model, for instance, may improve accuracy yet also change the behavior of the automated scoring system. If biases are detected, then there will be further opportunities to explore sources of bias and to apply debiasing techniques that have been developed for other applications of transformer-based models (Sun et al., 2019).

References

William H. Angoff. 1993. Perspectives on Differential Item Functioning Methodology. In Paul W. Holland and Howard Wainer, editors, *Differential Item Functioning*, pages 3–23. Lawrence Erlbaum Associates, Inc., Hillsdale, NJ.

Yoav Benjamini and Yosef Hochberg. 1995. Controlling the false discovery rate: a practical and powerful approach to multiple testing. *Journal of the Royal statistical society: series B (Methodological)*, 57(1):289–300. Publisher: Wiley Online Library.

Su Lin Blodgett, Solon Barocas, Hal Daumé III, and Hanna Wallach. 2020. Language (technology) is power: A critical survey of" bias" in nlp. *arXiv preprint arXiv:2005.14050*.

L. Cai. 2012. flexMIRT: Flexible multilevel item factor analysis and test scoring [Computer software]. *Seattle, WA: Vector Psychometric Group, LLC.*

Li Cai, Kilchan Choi, Mark Hansen, and Lauren Harrell. 2016. Item response theory. *Annual Review of Statistics and Its Application*, 3:297–321. Publisher: Annual Reviews.

Gregory Camilli. 2006. Test fairness. *Educational measurement*, 4:221–256.

Lei Chen, Klaus Zechner, Su-Youn Yoon, Keelan Evanini, Xinhao Wang, Anastassia Loukina, Jidong Tao, Lawrence Davis, Chong Min Lee, Min Ma, Robert Mundkowsky, Chi Lu, Chee Wee Leong, and Binod Gyawali. 2018. Automated scoring of nonnative speech using the¬†speechratersm v. 5.0 engine. *ETS Research Report Series*, 2018(1):1–31.

Jo-Kate Collier and Becky Huang. 2020. Test Review: Texas English Language Proficiency Assessment System (TELPAS). *Language Assessment Quarterly*, 17(2):221–230. Publisher: Taylor & Francis.

Sunipa Dev, Tao Li, Jeff M. Phillips, and Vivek Srikumar. 2020. On measuring and mitigating biased inferences of word embeddings. *Proceedings of the AAAI Conference on Artificial Intelligence*, 34(05):7659–7666.

Jacob Devlin, Ming-Wei Chang, Kenton Lee, and Kristina Toutanova. 2018. Bert: Pre-training of deep bidirectional transformers for language understanding. In *Proceedings of the 2019 Conference of the North American Chapter of the Association for Computational Linguistics: Human Language Technologies*.

Educational Testing Service. 2005. Test and Score Data Summary: 2004-05 Test Year Data Test of English as a Foreign Language. Technical report.

Michael C. Edwards and Maria Orlando Edelen. 2009. Special topics in item response theory. *The SAGE handbook of quantitative methods in psychology*, pages 178–198. Publisher: Sage Publications New York, NY.

Keelan Evanini, Maurice Cogan Hauck, and Kenji Hakuta. 2017. Approaches to automated scoring of speaking for k‚Äì12 english language proficiency assessments. *ETS Research Report Series*, 2017(1):1–11.

Paul W. Holland, Howard Wainer, and William H. Angoff. 1993. *Perspectives on Differential Item Functioning Methodology*, page 3–23. Lawrence Erlbaum Associates.

Becky H. Huang and Belinda Bustos Flores. 2018. The English language proficiency assessment for the 21st century (ELPA21). *Language Assessment Quarterly*, 15(4):433–442. Publisher: Taylor & Francis.

Svetlana Kiritchenko and Saif M. Mohammad. 2018. Examining gender and race bias in two hundred sentiment analysis systems. *arXiv preprint arXiv:1805.04508*.

Allison Koenecke, Andrew Nam, Emily Lake, Joe Nudell, Minnie Quartey, Zion Mengesha, Connor Toups, John R. Rickford, Dan Jurafsky, and Sharad Goel. 2020. Racial disparities in automated speech recognition. *Proceedings of the National Academy of Sciences*, 117(14):7684–7689. Publisher: National Acad Sciences.

Christopher M. Ormerod, Akanksha Malhotra, and Amir Jafari. 2021. Automated essay scoring using efficient transformer-based language models. *arXiv preprint arXiv:2102.13136*.

Steven J. Osterlind and Howard T. Everson. 2009. *Differential item functioning*. SAGE.

Daniel Povey, Arnab Ghoshal, Gilles Boulianne, Lukas Burget, Ondrej Glembek, Nagendra Goel, Mirko Hannemann, Petr Motlicek, Yanmin Qian, Petr Schwarz, Jan Silovsky, Georg Stemmer, and Karel Vesely. 2011. The kaldi speech recognition toolkit. In *IEEE 2011 Workshop on Automatic Speech Recognition and Understanding*. IEEE Signal Processing Society. IEEE Catalog No.: CFP11SRW-USB.

Steven J. Spencer, Christine Logel, and Paul G. Davies. 2016. Stereotype threat. *Annual review of psychology*, 67:415–437. Publisher: Annual Reviews.

Tony Sun, Andrew Gaut, Shirlyn Tang, Yuxin Huang, Mai ElSherief, Jieyu Zhao, Diba Mirza, Elizabeth Belding, Kai-Wei Chang, and William Yang Wang. 2019. Mitigating gender bias in natural language processing: Literature review. *arXiv preprint arXiv:1906.08976*.

Xinhao Wang, Keelan Evanini, Yao Qian, and Matthew Mulholland. 2021. Automated Scoring of Spontaneous Speech from Young Learners of English Using Transformers. In *2021 IEEE Spoken Language Technology Workshop (SLT)*, pages 705–712. IEEE.

Valerie SL Williams, Lyle V. Jones, and John W. Tukey. 1999. Controlling error in multiple comparisons, with examples from state-to-state differences in educational achievement. *Journal of educational and behavioral statistics*, 24(1):42–69. Publisher: Sage Publications.

David M. Williamson, Xiaoming Xi, and F. Jay Breyer. 2012. A framework for evaluation and use of automated scoring. *Educational measurement: issues and practice*, 31(1):2–13. Publisher: Wiley Online Library.

Carol M. Woods, Li Cai, and Mian Wang. 2013. The Langer-improved Wald test for DIF testing with multiple groups: Evaluation and comparison to two-group IRT. *Educational and Psychological Measurement*, 73(3):532–547. Publisher: Sage Publications Sage CA: Los Angeles, CA.

Klaus Zechner. 2009. What did they actually say? Agreement and disagreement among transcribers of non-native spontaneous speech responses in an English proficiency test.

Klaus Zechner. 2020. Summary and Outlook on Automated Speech Scoring. In Klaus Zechner and Keelan Evanini, editors, *Automated Speaking Assessment: Using Language Technologies to Score Spontaneous Speech*, volume 3 of *Innovations in Language Learning and Assessment at ETS*, pages 192–204. Routledge, New York, NY.

Haoran Zhang, Amy X. Lu, Mohamed Abdalla, Matthew McDermott, and Marzyeh Ghassemi. 2020. Hurtful words: quantifying biases in clinical contextual word embeddings. In *proceedings of the ACM Conference on Health, Inference, and Learning*, pages 110–120.

Jieyu Zhao, Tianlu Wang, Mark Yatskar, Vicente Ordonez, and Kai-Wei Chang. 2017. Men also like shopping: Reducing gender bias amplification using corpus-level constraints. In *Proceedings of the 2017 Conference on Empirical Methods in Natural Language Processing, EMNLP 2017, Copenhagen, Denmark, September 9-11, 2017*, pages 2979–2989. Association for Computational Linguistics.

A ASR Systems Comparison

We explored two different approaches to the automated speech recognition (ASR) task. First, we looked into publicly-accessible transcribing services provided by Cloud computing platforms. Specifically, we tried services provided by Amazon Web Service (AWS) and Google Cloud Platform (GCP). Second, we considered implementing our own ASR system, trained on our own audio data. We experimented with the Librispeech ASR Chain 1d model, a pre-trained Factorized Deep Tensor Neural Network (DTNN-F)-based chain model specifically targeting speech recognition tasks provided by Kaldi, an open-source speech recognition toolkit for speech recognition and signal processing tasks (Povey et al., 2011). Based on accuracy and speed of transcription, we opted to use Google's speech-to-text service to generate text transcripts based on examinees' speech.

B Scoring Model Optimization

We divided cleaned data into train and test datasets with proportions of 0.8 and 0.2 using sickit-learn's train-test split function for training and evaluating the NLP model. In order to get a better sense of the generality of model performance, we experimented with three different random seeds—0, 1, and 2.

We trained uncased, medium-sized BERT and RoBERT models for 10 epochs with three different random seeds during the training process. Hyperparameters batch size, dropout ratio and learning rate were set to 128, 0.1 and $2 \cdot 10^{-05}$, respectively. Accuracy on test set and training loss were averaged across the 3 different random seeds.

Model Name	**Seed**	**Test Acc (%)**	**Train Loss**
BERT	0	89.58	7.77
	1	88.74	9.47
	2	88.22	7.76
	Average	**88.85**	**8.33**
RoBERTa	0	88.69	10.24
	1	88.80	11.58
	2	88.22	10.47
	Average	88.57	10.76

Table 3: Model Performance on Score-stratified Dataset Split with Seed 0

According to Table 3, BERT performed (marginally) better than RoBERTa on both test accuracy and training loss. Overall accuracy of BERT, averaged across 3 different random seeds, was found to be 88.85% with training loss of 8.33 (compared to 88.17% and 12.42 for RoBERTa).

Therefore, we choose to use the uncased BERT base model for scoring examinees' transcripts in further experiments.

Automatic scoring of short answers using justification cues estimated by BERT

Shunya Takano, Osamu Ichikawa
Faculty of Data Science, Shiga University
Hikone, Japan
pppublic2020@gmail.com, osamu-ichikawa@biwako.shiga-u.ac.jp

Abstract

Automated scoring technology for short-answer questions has been attracting attention to improve the fairness of scoring and reduce the burden on the scorer. In general, a large amount of data is required to train an automated scoring model. The training data consists of the answer texts and the scoring data assigned to them. It may also include annotations indicating key word sequences. Many previous studies have created models with large amounts of training data specific to each question. This paper aims to achieve equivalent performance with less training data by utilizing a BERT model that has been pre-trained on a large amount of general text data not necessarily related to short answer questions. On the RIKEN dataset, the proposed method reduces the training data from the 800 data required in the past to about 400 data, and still achieves scoring accuracy comparable to that of humans. Annotating 400 data is still costly, but it is beneficial to reduce the number of data needed.

1 Introduction

Automatic short answer scoring (SAS) system using natural language processing technology has several advantages, such as the immediate return of scoring results and the ability to submit answers from any location over networks. To realize such interactive learning, a lot of research has been done on ASAP-SAS data. Assuming amount of scored short answers are available as training data, semantic similarity (Sultan et al. 2016) or machine learning (Zhao et al. 2017) is used for the score prediction. Also, as an attempt using deep learning, CNN and LSTM have been configured on top of word embedding to predict the holistic score directly (Riordan et al. 2017; Taghipour et al. 2016).

Unfortunately, predicting holistic scores directly from word sequences is not very promising because there are too big a leap between words and scores. With this background, RIKEN Center for AIP provided SAS dataset with analytic scores and annotations (justification cues) as well as holistic scores in public to help with research activities. The dataset includes sample responses from 2,100 students for each of the six readings comprehension test prompts (RIKEN 2020). RIKEN Center also developed automatic scoring technology using deep learning for the dataset. Mizumoto et al. proposed a bidirectional LSTM model integrating a supervised attention mechanism estimating the justification cue for scoring (Mizumoto et al. 2019). The model was evaluated with various sizes of training data. It is reported that approximately 800 training data per question are needed to achieve the same accuracy as humans. However, we know it is difficult to prepare 800 training data manually in actual schools.

Therefore, we consider using BERT model (Devlin et al. 2019) pre-trained with a large amount of general text not necessarily related to short answer questions, so to reduce the amount of specific training data required. Several research institutes provide pre-trained BERT models. They are well-trained with huge general corpus and supposed to be fine-tuned with small amount of specific corpus.

Instead of using supervised attention in Mizumoto et al. 2019, this study uses BERT to annotate word sequences as the justification cues. The justification identification model is created by fine-tuning one of the pre-trained BERT models with a specific data set.

Proceedings of the 17th Workshop on Innovative Use of NLP for Building Educational Applications (BEA 2022), pages 8 - 13

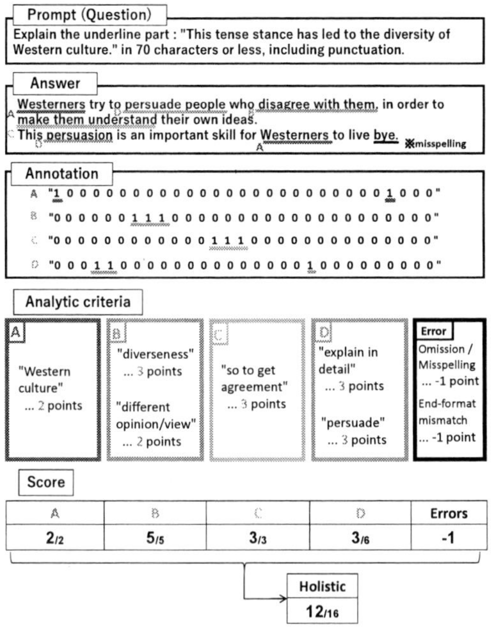

Figure 1: Example of data in Riken dataset (Translated from Japanese). Note this study does not consider point deductions based on the "error" criterion.

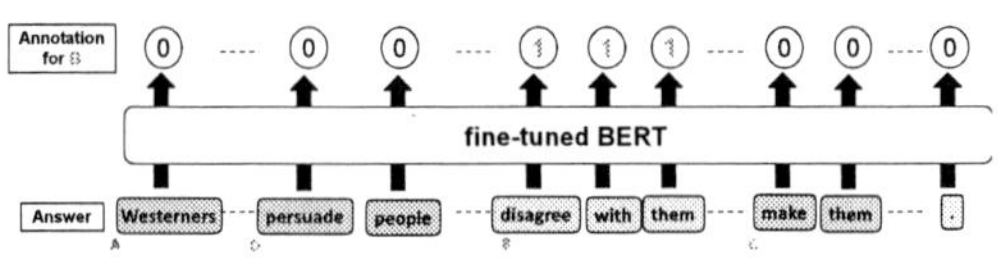

Figure. 2: Image of the justification identification model.

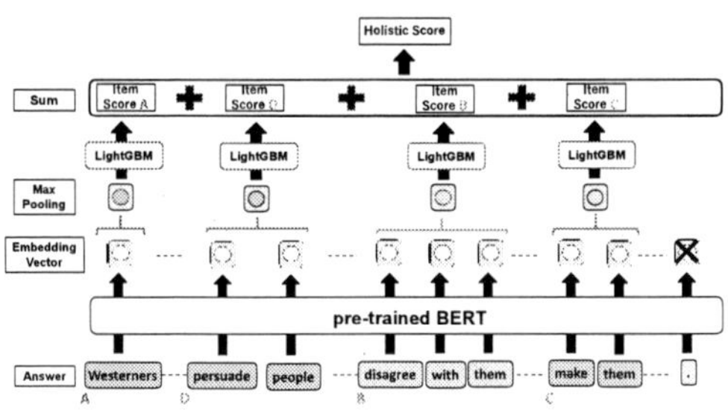

Figure 3: Image of the score prediction model.

2 RIKEN dataset for short answer assessment

Our study compares the performance and the required data size with the previous method by Mizumoto et al. 2019. Therefore, the same RIKEN dataset was used. This data was obtained by annotating and scoring the answers to Japanese writing questions in the mock examinations for high school students conducted by Yoyogi Seminar from 2014 to 2015 according to a predefined rubric. Answers are approximately 50 to 70 characters long (in Japanese). As shown in Figure 1, each answer is annotated with a "1" for words that contribute to the score and a "0" for words that do not. The overall score is calculated as the sum of the individual scores. In the example shown in Figure 1, there are four analytic criteria, A, B, C, and D, and annotations are assigned to each of them. Each item is then scored using this annotation as a justification cue. The overall score is calculated by summing the item scores and subtracting points for spelling errors and bad sentence endings etc.

3 Proposed Method

3.1 Justification prediction

The RIKEN dataset includes justification cues (annotations) indicating the words in the answer text that support each of the analytic criteria, such as A, B, C, and D in Figure 1. Justification cues were integrated in the scoring model as supervised attention in the previous method (Mizumoto et al. 2019). As our approach uses them to select embedding vectors, they must be explicitly predicted by a separate model.

Figure 2 shows our proposed justification prediction model. The pre-trained BERT model is fine-tuned with the answer text as input, and the "0" and "1" annotations as teacher signal. In this figure, taking scoring criterion B as an example, "1" annotations are output for words that support B.

Note that prompt phrases are not used to predict annotations. The performance of the justification identification model solely depends on the quality of the annotated answer text used for training.

3.2 Analytic score and holistic scores predictions

Figure 3 shows the proposed model. First, the answer is divided into units of strings called tokens, which are converted into IDs and passed through the pre-trained BERT model. The tokens are then converted into 768-dimensional embedding vectors. It should be noted that the embedding vector of BERT is context-aware unlike the one of Word2Vec and etc. This is one of the advantages of using BERT. For each scoring criterion, we collect the embedding vectors of the word tokens that are annotated with "1", which indicating these words support the analytic criteria. A new 768-dimensional vector is generated by taking the maximum value for each dimension of the collected vectors. Using the vectors as features, analytic scores for each item are predicted by the respective LightGBM model trained on the same data used in the justification identification model.

If the annotations are all "0", the score for the corresponding item is set to 0 because there is no vector to feed the score prediction model. Finally, the holistic score is calculated by summing up all the item scores.

4 Experiments

The following experiments were conducted to evaluate the performance of the proposed method. Our experiments used the Japanese pre-trained BERT model published by the Inui-Suzuki Laboratory at Tohoku University (Inui Laboratory 2021).

4.1 Settings

RIKEN Dataset for short answer assessment was used for the experiments. As in the previous study (Mizumoto et al. 2019), we used 6 out of 9 test prompts. They are denoted by Q1 through Q6 in the tables in this paper. There are 2100 answer sheets for each prompt. The holistic score was calculated by summing up all the item scores. In this study, deduction for errors of misspellings, omissions, sentence endings etc. was not considered.

To evaluate the performance of the models, we created several test cases with different sizes of training data such as 100, 200, 400, 800 and 1600. For example, in 100-training case, 100 answers were used as training data and the remaining 2000 answers as test data. Similarly, in 400-training case, 400 answers were used as training data and the remaining 1700 answers as test data. Each case consisted of five sets of training data selected to have as little overlap as possible between the sets, and performance was measured by the average of the five sets.

[1] Quadratic Weighted Kappa (QWK) is an evaluation metric for multi-class classification. It takes a value from 0 to 1, with a higher value indicating a better fit of the prediction. In this study, we convert the predicted overall scores into integers by rounding off fractions and treat the integer scores as classes for QWK.

	Q1	Q2	Q3	Q4	Q5	Q6
100 train	0.97	0.96	0.91	0.89	0.93	0.94
200 train	0.98	0.97	0.94	0.91	0.95	0.96
400 train	0.98	0.98	0.95	0.93	0.96	0.96
800 train	0.99	0.98	0.96	0.94	0.96	0.97
1600 train	0.99	0.98	0.95	0.95	0.97	0.97
Human	0.96	0.94	0.76	0.84	0.82	0.90

Table 1: QWK with correct justification cue given.

	Q1	Q2	Q3	Q4	Q5	Q6
100 train	0.77	0.59	0.31	0.61	0.65	0.63
200 train	0.81	0.71	0.38	0.66	0.70	0.70
400 train	0.85	0.77	0.44	0.71	0.74	0.74
800 train	0.87	0.82	0.47	0.73	0.77	0.77
1600 train	0.90	0.84	0.53	0.75	0.79	0.79

Table 2: QWK without using justification cue.

	Precision	Recall	F-measure
Current	0.848	0.895	0.866
Mizumoto	0.837	0.703	0.758

Table 3: Performance of justification identification (100 training data case)

100 train		Q1	Q2	Q3	Q4	Q5	Q6
Analytic criteria	A	0.970	0.928	0.867	0.936	0.839	0.809
	B	0.912	0.914	0.840	0.859	0.883	0.891
	C	0.937	0.973	0.746	0.885	0.954	0.819
	D	0.922	0.844	0.468	—	—	—

Table 4: F-measure of annotation (100 train).

400 train		Q1	Q2	Q3	Q4	Q5	Q6
Analytic criteria	A	0.982	0.954	0.902	0.965	0.869	0.910
	B	0.940	0.949	0.890	0.872	0.896	0.923
	C	0.956	0.980	0.820	0.910	0.960	0.853
	D	0.942	0.869	0.724	—	—	—

Table 5: F-measure of annotation (400 train).

4.2 (Preliminary Experiment) Automatic scoring with / without correct justification cues

To investigate the upper bound of the performance of the score prediction model shown in Section 3.2, we predict the item score and holistic scores with using the correct justification cues given by the dataset. Also, we investigated the lower bound without using any justification cues. Quadratic Weighted Kappa (QWK)[1] (Cohen 1960) was used as evaluation metrics for the holistic score, and the mean values calculated on the five sets are shown in Table 1 and Table 2. Table 1 also shows the human scoring accuracy in QWK, which was reported in Mizumoto et al. 2019.

4.3 (Experiment 1) Justification identification

We evaluated the performance of the justification identification model shown in Section 3.1. Although Figure 2 shows only scoring criterion B, we trained 21 BERT models to predict the annotations for all analytic criteria for each test prompt.

The BERT models were prepared by fine-tuning the pre-trained BERT models with the number of epochs set to 10, batch size set to 16, optimization algorithm set to Adam, and loss function set to cross-entropy function.

Table 3 outlines the performance of justification identification for the case of 100-training data. It also shows the supervised attention case reported in Mizumoto et al. 2019 which also reports 100-training data case. Table 4 and Table 5 provide breakdowns of all analytic criteria in the 100-training case and the 400-training case. Please note each of the six test prompts, from Q1 to Q6, has its own analytic criteria from A to D (or C).

4.4 (Experiment 2) Automatic scoring using automatically predicted justification cues

We evaluated the performance by combining both models shown in Section 3. The justification cues were predicted by the model shown in Section 3.1, and the item and holistic scores were predicted by the model shown in Section 3.2, using the predicted justification cues and embedding vectors. QWK was used as evaluation metrics, and the mean values[2] of the five sets of the metric are shown in Table 6.

4.5 Discussion of the experimental results

As shown in Table 1, given the correct justification cues, the accuracy in QWK of automatic scoring by the proposed model is much higher than human scoring for all questions, even when using only 100 training data. On the other hand, accuracy was poor when justification cues were not used. This indicates that justification cues are critically important in SAS, especially in our model proposed in Section 3.2.

[2] The values have been updated since our last report in domestic meeting of FIT 2021, due to the calculation errors Also, we found increasing epochs from 3 to 10 in fine-tuning of BERT significantly improved the accuracy of justification cue prediction.

	Q1	Q2	Q3	Q4	Q5	Q6
100 train	0.94	0.88	0.65	0.80	0.82	0.83
200 train	0.96	0.91	0.74	0.83	0.85	0.87
400 train	0.97	0.92	0.77	0.85	0.86	0.89
800 train	0.97	0.95	0.80	0.87	0.88	0.91
1600 train	0.98	0.95	0.83	0.88	0.88	0.92
Human	0.96	0.94	0.76	0.84	0.82	0.90

Table 6: QWK with predicted justification cue.

	100	200	400	800	1600
No cues	0.590	0.659	0.706	0.737	0.766
Given cues	0.934	0.950	0.959	0.965	0.969
Predicted cues	0.820	0.857	0.877	0.894	0.906
Mizumoto	0.776	0.827	0.856	0.876	0.892

Table 7: QWK summaries of all experiments and references for training data of various sizes.

With respect to the accuracy of justification identification, Table 3 shows that our fine-tuned BERT model can identify cues much better than the supervised attention model reported in Mizumoto et al. 2019. Table 5 provides the details in F-measure in 400-training data case. The BERT model worked well, with high accuracy on most items. One exception is criterion D of Q3, which concerns human emotions such as "frustration" and "distress", unlike the other analytic criteria. Even BERT may not be able to properly translate human emotions into numeric vectors.

The performance of our proposed method integrating the two models is shown in Table 6. With 400 training data, the QWK values are quite close to human scoring. This means our justification identification model successfully selected the BERT embedding vectors that form the input to the analytic scoring model of LightGBM. However, comparing Table 6 and Table 1, the upper bound results using given correct justification cues are still much better. This suggests further refinement in justification identification model would be desirable in the future.

Table 7 summarizes the experimental results for various sizes of training data. Given the correct justification cues, the performance degradation when training data is small is very small. As the proposed method improved cue prediction, it performed better than the comparative method (Mizumoto et al. 2019), especially when training data was small, such as 100 or 200 training data.

5 Conclusion

This paper proposed the combined model of justification prediction and analytic scoring model. It includes fine-tuning of pre-trained BERT model that predicts justification cues (annotations), which are crucial for automatic scoring. BERT embedding vectors of annotated words are subsequently passed to LightGBM model (Ke et al. 2017) for scoring. The proposed model uses a BERT model that has been pre-trained with a large corpus of text in a general domain. As shown in Table 7, this helped automated scoring on specific data sets and showed that the accuracy of scoring on the RIKEN dataset can be comparable (0.88) to that of human scorers (average 0.873) with training data of only 400 answers per prompt. Compared to the comparative method (Mizumoto et al. 2019) which showed an accuracy of 0.87 with 800 answers, almost 50% reduction of training data has been achieved.

Acknowledgments

In this paper, we used "RIKEN Dataset for Short Answer Assessment" provided by RIKEN via IDR Dataset Service of National Institute of Informatics. This work was supported by JSPS KAKENHI (Grant Numbers JP19K02999).

References

ASAP-SAS. 2012. Scoring short answer essays. ASAP short answer scoring competition system description.

Md Arafat Sultan, Cristobal Salazar and Tamara Sumner. 2016. Fast and easy short answer gradingwith high accuracy. *Proceedings of the 2016 Conference of the North American Chapter of the Association for Computational Linguistics: Human Language Technologies (NAACL-HLT)*, pages 1070–1075.

Siyuan Zhao, Yaqiong Zhang, Xiaolu Xiong, Anthony Botelho and Neil Heffernan. 2017. A memory-augmented neural model for automated grading. *Proceedings of Fourth ACM Conference on Learning @ Scale*, pages 189–192.

Brian Riordan, Andrea Horbach, Aoife Cahill, Torsten Zesch and Chungmin Lee. 2017. Investigating neural architectures for short answer scoring. *Proceedings of the 12th Workshop on Building Educational Applications Using NLP (BEA)*, pages 159-168.

Kaveh Taghipour and Hwee Tou Ng. 2016. A neural approach to automated essay scoring. *Proceedings of the 2016 Conference on Empirical Methods in Natural Language Processing*, pages 1882-1891.

RIKEN. 2020. RIKEN Dataset for Short Answer Assessment. *Informatics Research Data Repository, National Institute of informatics.* Dataset: https://doi.org/10.32130/rdata.3.1

Tomoya Mizumoto, Hiroki Ouchi, Yoriko Isobe, Paul Reisert, Ryo Nagata, Satoshi Sekine and Kentaro Inui. 2019. Analytic score prediction and justification identification in automated short answer scoring. *Proceedings of the Fourteenth Workshop on Innovative Use of NLP for Building Educational Applications (BEA 14)*, pages 316-325.

Jacob Devlin, Ming-Wei Chang, Kenton Lee and Kristina Toutanova. 2019. BERT: pre training of deep bidirectional transformers for language understanding. *Proceedings of the 2019 Conference of the North American Chapter of the Association for Computational Linguistics: Human Language Technologies*, pages 4171-4186.

Guolin Ke, Qi Meng, Thomas Finley, Taifeng Wang, Wei Chen, Weidong Ma, Qiwei Ye and Tie-Yan Liu. 2017. LightGBM: a highly efficient gradient boosting decision tree. *Advances in Neural Information Processing Systems*, pages 3149-3157.

Inui Laboratory, Tohoku University. 2021. Pretrained Japanese BERT models. https://github.com/cl-tohoku/bert-japanese (referred on June 10, 2021.)

Jacob. Cohen. 1960. A coefficient of agreement for nominal scales. *Educational and Psychological Measurement*, 20 (1): 37–46.

Mitigating Learnerese Effects for CEFR classification

Rricha Jalota*, Peter Bourgonje+, Jan van Sas+, and Huiyan Huang+

*Universität des Saarlandes
+Morningsun Technology GmbH

Abstract

The role of an author's L1 in SLA can be challenging for automated CEFR classification, in that texts from different L1 groups may be too heterogeneous to combine them as training data. We experiment with recent debiasing approaches by attempting to devoid textual representations of L1 features. This results in a more homogeneous group when aggregating CEFR-annotated texts from different L1 groups, leading to better classification performance. Using iterative null-space projection, we marginally improve classification performance for a linear classifier by 1 point. An MLP (e.g. non-linear) classifier remains unaffected by this procedure. We discuss possible directions of future work to attempt to increase this performance gain.

1 Introduction

The need for automated methods in establishing both the readability of a piece of text and the level of linguistic proficiency of its author has been recognised decades before most students started writing essays, compositions and other homework assignments on computers. Motivations for creating such automated methods are diverse. Seminal work by Page (1966) focused on alleviating work load of language teachers and fast turn-around of writing feedback to language students. Since then, much progress has been made, and a comprehensive overview of original and still standing challenges in this field is presented by Beigman Klebanov and Madnani (2020). Related to this is the line of research on grammatical error correction (Leacock et al., 2010; Bryant and Ng, 2015), accompanied by a number of shared tasks (Ng et al., 2013, 2014; Bryant et al., 2019).

Much of the work in this sub-field of NLP is usually aggregated under the label *Automated Essay Scoring*[1]. Scoring an essay, however, depends on a number of factors related to the background of the author and moreover is not just about grading the quality of language usage, but usually also about the quality of content. The same essay about basic concepts of quantum physics may receive a high grade when written by a child in elementary school, but a considerably lower grade when written by a post-graduate physics student. A framework focusing solely on second language (L2) level skills, attempting to propose an objective (i.e., independent of native language) six-point scale is represented by the CEFR[2] levels. Since our use case is establishing the proficiency level of L2 language learners and providing them with feedback on how to improve, we experiment with CEFR classification.

While the nature of the influence of one's native language (L1) on Second Language Acquisition (SLA) is a topic of ongoing debate (Richards and Rodgers, 2014) and the terms being used are dependent on the assumed framework (*interference* (Weinreich, 2010), *transfer* (Lado, 1957; Selinker, 1969), *influence* (Smith and Kellerman, 1986)) the fact that there is interaction is uncontroversial. This L1 interaction is problematic in the sense that a classifier trained on texts written by native speakers of Chinese may perform poorly on texts written by native speakers of Portuguese, for example.

Inspired by recent successes in debiasing embeddings-based representations for particular traits (Manzini et al., 2019; Sun et al., 2019; Ravfogel et al., 2020; Karimi Mahabadi et al., 2020; Chowdhury et al., 2022), we set out to dispose the representations that feed into the classifier of traits that can be taken as signs of L1 influence, to train a single CEFR classifier -devoid of L1 features (i.e. *learnerese*)- that improves its performance when trained on aggregated data from different native

[1] Or variations thereof: Automated Essay Grading, Automated Writing Evaluation, etc.

[2] `https://www.coe.int/en/web/common-european-framework-reference-\languages/level-descriptions`

Proceedings of the 17th Workshop on Innovative Use of NLP for Building Educational Applications (BEA 2022), pages 14 - 21

speaker groups.

The rest of this paper is structured as follows: Section 2 discusses earlier work on both CEFR classification and debiasing strategies. Section 3 explains the data we used in our experiments. Section 4 explains the classification setup. Section 5 discusses our results and provides pointers to future work. Finally, Section 6 sums up our main findings.

2 Related Work

The task of Automated Essay Scoring itself has received a fair amount of attention over the last decades, see Beigman Klebanov and Madnani (2020) for a comprehensive overview of the current state of the art. Individual sub-tasks that can be taken as indicative for proficiency in a given language, such as Grammatical Error Correction (GEC), have been accompanied by a number of popular shared tasks (Ng et al., 2013, 2014; Bryant et al., 2019). The task of CEFR classification itself however, seems to have received fewer attention. Among the studies that address this problem for various languages are Santucci et al. (2020) (Italian), Hancke and Meurers (2013) (German), Vajjala and Lõo (2014) (Estonian) and Volodina et al. (2016) (Swedish). Earlier work on English (our language of interest) is represented by Tack et al. (2017), who create their own annotated corpus and experiment with automated classification using several classification algorithms.

In this paper, we interpret the influence of L1 as an issue of bias in the embeddings-based representation of the English texts. Particular word order, article- or gender-based preferences or errors that can be traced back to the native language of the author, are likely to be more ubiquitous within the same group of native speakers. To the best of our knowledge, the CEFR classification problem has not been combined before with methods attempting to debias embeddings for L1 features.

Bias in NLP has attracted a lot of interest recently (Bender et al., 2021; Costa-jussa et al., 2021; Bokstaller et al., 2021; Garrido-Muñoz et al., 2021), and the specific mitigation approach that we follow in our work is that of Ravfogel et al. (2020), who propose **INLP** - an iterative nullspace projection algorithm to debias gender stereotypes in text. Unlike previous approaches (Bolukbasi et al., 2016; Dev and Phillips, 2019) that solely rely on a contrastive wordlist to identify a linear direction for debiasing, INLP debiases all linearly present gender directions in a data-driven manner. Considering that a classification task relies on a certain feature that we want to remove, INLP iteratively trains a series of probing (linear) classifiers to predict that feature until the probing classifier is confounded. For more details, we encourage the readers to read the original paper. In Chowdhury et al. (2022), the potential of this approach was explored for debiasing translation artifacts (which carry similar stylistic differences as learnerese) in human/machine-translated documents. Building upon this work, we employ the algorithm for our use-case.

3 Data

Our first experiments were done on the International Corpus Network of Asian Learners of English (ICNALE) (Ishikawa, 2019), a data set comprising essays from 2.800 authors from over 10 different native speaker groups, annotated for different metrics indicating skill levels (TOEIC, TOEFL, IELTS, etc.), including CEFR labels. When aggregating all data from non-native English speakers, using a vanilla BERT (Devlin et al., 2019) classifier, we obtained a classification accuracy of 0.51, for 2.600 essays[3]. For individual native language groups, however, we achieved comparable performance while using considerably fewer training instances (for example, 0.50 on just 200 essays whose authors are from Indonesia). At the same time, some native speaker groups in ICNALE are heavily imbalanced, resulting in simple majority vote classifiers outperforming the trained classifier for those native speaker groups. While these preliminary findings initially inspired us to apply debiasing strategies, we decided to use a larger, less imbalanced corpus for the majority of the experiments reported on in this paper.

We extracted a subset of the EF-Cambridge Open Language Database (EFCAMDAT) (Geertzen et al., 2014), consisting of 191,969 texts from authors from China, Japan and Korea. Since all texts in EFCAMDAT are from language learners, we combined this with 200 texts from native English speakers from ICNALE to get debiasing directions. Furthermore, EFCAMDAT only provides information on the author's country of origin. Information on native language would be more accurate, but unfortunately is not specified in

[3]In a 10-fold cross-validation setup.

the corpus. For the purpose of this paper, we will assume the country of origin and native language to align. Table 1 summarises the key figures of the subsets of EFCAMDAT and ICNALE we used in our experiments.
In addition to the aforementioned English-L2 datasets, we conducted experiments on a subset of the MERLIN (Boyd et al., 2014) corpus, specifically the subset with German-L2 learners (henceforth called MERLIN_DE). This subset consists of 652 learner texts from 13 known nationalities and 275 Target Hypotheses (i.e. texts expected from the native speakers and written by annotators.) Due to the skewness of this dataset, we only consider data from the top three represented nationalities. Table 2 summarises the subset of the MERLIN_data we used for our experiments.

4 Method & Results

As mentioned in Section 3, we were initially inspired by the fact that adding more training data did not seem to improve classification performance. In addition, earlier work indicated that classifying the country of origin of an author based on their English text provides good results, with Tang et al. (2021) reporting an accuracy of 87% on all of ICNALE for this task. We argue that this points at signals of L1 in the English learner texts that a classifier can pick up on, and that consequently, finding a way to make input text more homogeneous to a classifier through debiasing (Section 4.1) can lead to CEFR classification performance gains (Section 4.2).

4.1 Country of Origin Classification and Debiasing

To classify the country of origin of the author of a learner text, we use multiple binary classifiers (for example, China vs. EN, Japan vs. EN, Korea vs. EN). In particular, we first derive BERT document-level representations (by mean-pooling the token-level embeddings) of the text and then feed them to a Logistic Regression classifier for the binary classification task. Recall that country of origin classification is just an intermediate step in order to find directions to debias our embeddings. For this task, we randomly sample 200 texts from China, Japan and Korea to compare against the 200 from native English speakers (to keep the data balanced) and we used a static train/dev/test split of 70/15/15, respectively. Following Ravfogel et al. (2020), we proceed to get rid of any signals (in the embeddings) that the classifier exploits to base its decision on and found that this works surprisingly well. After 300 iterations for null-space projection, the perfect performance of 100 for country of origin classification for all three language pairs (to be compared to 87% for all of ICNALE as reported by Tang et al. (2021)) drops to approximately random performance after debiasing (Table 3).
We follow similar steps for the country of origin classification for the MERLIN_DE dataset. Recall that in this setup, the direction for native-German comes from Target Hypotheses (TH) and the number of Target Hypotheses (275) exceeds the number of text samples coming from the three nationalities. In order to achieve a balanced dataset for the binary classification, we randomly sample TH texts equal to the number of Russian-DE, Polish-DE and Spanish-DE texts, respectively. Thereafter, we apply INLP for 7 iterations on all three language pairs and achieve classification accuracies as shown in Table 4.

4.2 CEFR classification

As illustrated in Table 1, our data is fairly unbalanced, with most texts belonging to the A1 category. A majority vote classifier would result in an accuracy of 55%. To improve over this, as a baseline, we apply a multinomial Logistic Regression classifier and an MLP classifier having a hidden layer of 256-dimensions.

We then attempt to improve over this baseline by applying debiasing conditional on the country of origin of the author. BERT-encoded document-level representations of native-EN and L2-EN[4] (200 each) are fed to the INLP algorithm for bias removal. As stated earlier in section 4.1, to carry out this procedure, the data are first combined and shuffled, and then split into train, test and dev (70/15/15), followed by 12 iterations of INLP. By applying the INLP procedure on the training split, as one of the three outputs, we get the nullspace projection, which is devoid of any learnerese-signal. So, we simply project this nullspace onto the whole of respective L2-EN BERT embeddings to get debiased L2-EN embeddings.

We combine all data (i.e. BERT embeddings) from China, Japan and Korea for EFCAMDAT_NATIVE_EN, and for Russian, Polish and

[4]Where L2 corresponds to Japan/Korea/China.

	A1	*A2*	*B1*	*B2*	*C1*	*C2*	total
China	94,494	48,564	17,613	3,946	504	51	**165,162**
Japan	8,567	6,396	4,390	1,601	395	25	**21,374**
Korea	1,966	1,697	1,277	379	103	11	**5,433**
EN	-	-	-	-	-	-	**200**
total	*105,027*	*56,657*	*23,280*	*5,916*	*1,002*	*87*	

Table 1: Number of texts in native speaker groups and skill levels in EFCAMDAT_NATIVE_EN dataset.

	A1	*A2*	*B1*	*B2*	*C1*	*C2*	total
Russia	7	35	45	48	8	0	143
Polish	1	22	27	41	5	0	96
Spanish	3	23	31	27	1	0	85
total	11	80	103	116	14	0	**324**

Table 2: Number of texts in native speaker groups and skill levels in MERLIN_DE dataset.

	before debiasing		**after debiasing**	
	LR	**MLP**	LR	MLP
China	100	100	48.33	95.00
Japan	100	100	46.47	93.34
Korea	100	100	40.00	96.67

Table 3: EFCAMDAT_NATIVE_EN dataset: Accuracy for country of origin classification.

	before debiasing		**after debiasing**	
	LR	**MLP**	LR	MLP
Russia	83.72	93.02	51.16	53.48
Polish	89.66	93.10	65.52	82.76
Spanish	84.61	92.31	57.69	73.07

Table 4: MERLIN_DE dataset: Accuracy for country of origin classification.

Spanish for MERLIN_DE, and proceed to classify the CEFR levels. The results are illustrated in Table 5, where in the *after debiasing* column, the debiased embeddings, conditional on the author's country of origin, are used in classification. The numbers are the result of 5-fold cross-validation.

As shown in Table 5, the debiasing strategy improves performance by 1 point for the Linear Regression classifier, whereas the Multi-Layer Perceptron classifier remains unaffected for the EFCAMDAT_NATIVE_EN dataset. The performance of both classifiers drops for the MERLIN_DE dataset. We refer to Appendix A.1 for hyper-parameter settings. In the next section, we discuss these results, discuss promising directions for future work and summarise our main findings.

		before debiasing	after debiasing
EN-CEFR	LR	82	83
	MLP	96	96
DE-CEFR	LR	58	43
	MLP	73	63

Table 5: Weighted F1-scores for CEFR classification.

5 Discussion

For the EFCAMDAT_NATIVE_EN dataset, we observe a marginal performance gain when using a linear classifier (LR), but not when using a non-linear classifier (MLP). This can be explained from the results in Table 3, wherein the accuracy for MLP drops only marginally after debiasing. This means the non-linear classifer is still able to tell whether a sample comes from native or non-native speaker. The effects of debiasing on linearly separable vs. non-linearly separable problems is also discussed in Ravfogel et al. (2020), who state that their method is designed for *"removal of linear information regarding a protected attribute"*. This may explain why our setup with an MLP classifier shows no difference. Furthermore, the MLP classifier having better performance in the baseline setup already may suggest that the specific surface realisations of learnerese may be less prone to linear separation. Alternatively, Ravfogel et al. (2020) focus on guarding the classifier against gender and race. These dimensions might be expected to correlate to individual words or short phrases. The effects of learnerese may surface more on syntactic (phrase- or sentence-) level, which may just need more training data than we have available to us. As for hyperparameter settings; we have experimented with various different numbers of iterations (ranging from 8 to 300) for finding the directions for debiasing, but beyond a certain point (12 for EFCAMDAT_NATIVE_EN and 7 for MERLIN_DE) the INLP classifier started to overfit and the quality of embeddings start to decrease.

Furthermore, in the EFCAMDAT data, there appears to be a strong correlation between sentence length and CEFR level, with the average text length in words for levels A1 to C2 being, respectively, 45, 74, 97, 128, 161 and 164. This may be a strong indicator to the classifier, and one we have not compensated for. We decided against simply sampling individual sentences from the different CEFR levels, as we argue that (the ability to implement) overall text coherence is an important part of mastering a language. Any such text structure or coherence features would in most cases be lost when considering individual sentences. We consider experimenting with more sophisticated techniques to compensate for the differences in text length an important part of future work.

As illustrated in Table 1, we only have 200 native English texts to find directions for debiasing. This works surprisingly well (Table 3), but we get a comparatively small performance gain of 1 point for CEFR classification. Perhaps the ICNALE essays are easily distinguishable from the EFCAMDAT ones on other grounds (lay-out, topic, length) than just native vs. non-native. The EFCAMDAT corpus contains data from English-speaking countries, but since these originate from language learners, it is a heterogeneous L1 group. Using this would thus result in finding, for example, Chinese-specific vs. many-different-L1-specific traits, as opposed to finding Chinese-specific vs. native English-specific traits. In order to find out if the additional data (42,442 texts from authors from the USA and Great Britain from EFCAMDAT, compared to 200 from ICNALE) would compensate for the heterogeneity in L1 background however, we experimented with this setup too and got comparable results to the ones reported on in Table 5.

Compared to earlier work, the overall performance of our system scores well. Tack et al. (2017) also work on English and report an accuracy of 53% on their data set[5]. In other related work however, performance seems to depend highly on the specific data set (and language), with reported accuracy figures between 64.5% (Hancke and Meurers, 2013) and 79% (Vajjala and Lõo, 2014).

[5]Moreover, they aggregate the C1 and C2 levels, resulting in 5-way classification, compared to 6-way in our setup.

From Table 5, both the CEFR classifiers perform poorly on MERLIN_DE corpus. This comes as no surprise since we had only a few hundred samples for training and the data-class ratio was too skewed to begin with. Even though in Table 4, the accuracies of country-classifiers drop significantly after debiasing, it does not translate to a performance gain during CEFR-classifation and instead has the opposite effect. This means that the directions that are being removed by INLP are rather significant and perhaps to achieve gains on the downstream CEFR-classification task, INLP requires lot more training samples to find more reliable learnerese directions.

Unfortunately, we suspect that the majority of freely available datasets for CEFR-classification are too small (in the order of 10^2 or 10^3) to see any improvements from debiasing with INLP.

In future work, besides experimenting with other debiasing approaches, we plan to address this bottleneck by curating data for language-families (instead of considering languages in isolation for debiasing) and investigating if a combined debiasing approach on aggregated data from the same language family works better.

6 Conclusion

In this paper, we experiment with compensating for L1 influence in CEFR classification by applying a debiasing approach, the idea being to debias the embeddings for learnerese features in any specific L1-related direction. By doing so, we obtain a small performance improvement with a linear classifier. CEFR classification performance seems to be highly dependent on the particular corpora/data used, with earlier work reporting accuracy figures between 53% and 79%. On the EFCAMDAT dataset, results look promising - best weighted F1-score of 83 via Logistic Regression and even higher (96) with MLP classifier without any debiasing. Our code is available on GitHub[6].

References

Beata Beigman Klebanov and Nitin Madnani. 2020. Automated evaluation of writing – 50 years and counting. In Proceedings of the 58th Annual Meeting of the Association for Computational Linguistics, pages 7796–7810, Online. Association for Computational Linguistics.

[6]https://github.com/mst-sb/AES

Emily M. Bender, Timnit Gebru, Angelina McMillan-Major, and Shmargaret Shmitchell. 2021. On the dangers of stochastic parrots: Can language models be too big? In Proceedings of the 2021 ACM Conference on Fairness, Accountability, and Transparency, FAccT '21, page 610–623, New York, NY, USA. Association for Computing Machinery.

Jonas Bokstaller, Georgios Patoulidis, and Aygul Zagidullina. 2021. Model bias in NLP - application to hate speech classification using transfer learning techniques. CoRR, abs/2109.09725.

Tolga Bolukbasi, Kai-Wei Chang, James Y Zou, Venkatesh Saligrama, and Adam T Kalai. 2016. Man is to Computer Programmer as Woman is to Homemaker? Debiasing Word Embeddings. Advances in Neural Information Processing Systems, 29:4349–4357.

Adriane Boyd, Jirka Hana, Lionel Nicolas, Detmar Meurers, Katrin Wisniewski, Andrea Abel, Karin Schöne, Barbora Štindlová, and Chiara Vettori. 2014. The MERLIN corpus: Learner language and the CEFR. In Proceedings of the Ninth International Conference on Language Resources and Evaluation (LREC'14), pages 1281–1288, Reykjavik, Iceland. European Language Resources Association (ELRA).

Christopher Bryant, Mariano Felice, Øistein E. Andersen, and Ted Briscoe. 2019. The BEA-2019 shared task on grammatical error correction. In Proceedings of the Fourteenth Workshop on Innovative Use of NLP for Building Educational Applications, pages 52–75, Florence, Italy. Association for Computational Linguistics.

Christopher Bryant and Hwee Tou Ng. 2015. How far are we from fully automatic high quality grammatical error correction? In Proceedings of the 53rd Annual Meeting of the Association for Computational Linguistics and the 7th International Joint Conference on Natural Language Processing (Volume 1: Long Papers), pages 697–707, Beijing, China. Association for Computational Linguistics.

Koel Dutta Chowdhury, Rricha Jalota, Cristina España-Bonet, and Josef van Genabith. 2022. Towards debiasing translation artifacts.

Marta Costa-jussa, Hila Gonen, Christian Hardmeier, and Kellie Webster, editors. 2021. Proceedings of the 3rd Workshop on Gender Bias in Natural Language Processing. Association for Computational Linguistics, Online.

Sunipa Dev and Jeff Phillips. 2019. Attenuating bias in word vectors. In The 22nd International Conference on Artificial Intelligence and Statistics, pages 879–887. PMLR.

Jacob Devlin, Ming-Wei Chang, Kenton Lee, and Kristina Toutanova. 2019. BERT: Pre-training of deep bidirectional transformers for language understanding. In Proceedings of the 2019 Conference of the North American Chapter of the Association for Computational Linguistics: Human Language Technologies, Volume 1 (Long and Short Papers), pages 4171–4186, Minneapolis, Minnesota. Association for Computational Linguistics.

Ismael Garrido-Muñoz , Arturo Montejo-Ráez , Fernando Martínez-Santiago , and L. Alfonso Ureña-López . 2021. A Survey on Bias in Deep NLP. Applied Sciences, 11(7).

Jeroen Geertzen, Theodora Alexopoulou, and Anna Korhonen. 2014. Automatic linguistic annotation of large scale l2 databases: The ef-cambridge open language database (efcamdat). In Selected Proceedings of the 2012 Second Language Research Forum: Building Bridges between Disciplines, pages 240–254.

Julia Hancke and Detmar Meurers. 2013. Exploring CEFR classification for German based on rich linguistic modeling. pages 54–56.

Shin'ichiro Ishikawa. 2019. The ICNALE Spoken Dialogue: A New Dataset for the Study of Asian Learners' Performance in L2 English Interviews. English teaching, 74:153–177.

Rabeeh Karimi Mahabadi, Yonatan Belinkov, and James Henderson. 2020. End-to-end bias mitigation by modelling biases in corpora. In Proceedings of the 58th Annual Meeting of the Association for Computational Linguistics, pages 8706–8716, Online. Association for Computational Linguistics.

Robert Lado. 1957. Linguistics across cultures: Applied linguistics for language teachers. University of Michigan press.

Claudia Leacock, Martin Chodorow, Michael Gamon, and Joel Tetreault. 2010. Automated Grammatical Error Detection for Language Learners. Morgan and Claypool Publishers.

Thomas Manzini, Lim Yao Chong, Alan W Black, and Yulia Tsvetkov. 2019. Black is to criminal as caucasian is to police: Detecting and removing multiclass bias in word embeddings. In Proceedings of the 2019 Conference of the North American Chapter of the Association for Computational Linguistics: Human Language Technologies, Volume 1 (Long and Short Papers), pages 615–621, Minneapolis, Minnesota. Association for Computational Linguistics.

Hwee Tou Ng, Siew Mei Wu, Ted Briscoe, Christian Hadiwinoto, Raymond Hendy Susanto, and Christopher Bryant. 2014. The CoNLL-2014 shared task on grammatical error correction. In Proceedings of the Eighteenth Conference on Computational Natural Language Learning: Shared Task, pages 1–14, Baltimore, Maryland. Association for Computational Linguistics.

Hwee Tou Ng, Siew Mei Wu, Yuanbin Wu, Christian Hadiwinoto, and Joel Tetreault. 2013. The CoNLL-2013 shared task on grammatical error correction. In Proceedings of the Seventeenth Conference on Computational Natural Language Learning: Shared Task, pages 1–12, Sofia, Bulgaria. Association for Computational Linguistics.

Ellis B. Page. 1966. The imminence of... grading essays by computer. The Phi Delta Kappan, 47(5):238–243.

Shauli Ravfogel, Yanai Elazar, Hila Gonen, Michael Twiton, and Yoav Goldberg. 2020. Null it out: Guarding protected attributes by iterative nullspace projection. In Proceedings of the 58th Annual Meeting of the Association for Computational Linguistics, pages 7237–7256, Online. Association for Computational Linguistics.

Jack C Richards and Theodore S Rodgers. 2014. Approaches and methods in language teaching. Cambridge university press.

Valentino Santucci, Filippo Santarelli, Luciana Forti, and Stefania Spina. 2020. Automatic classification of text complexity. Applied Sciences, 10(20).

Larry Selinker. 1969. Language transfer. General linguistics, 9(2):67.

M Sharwood Smith and Eric Kellerman. 1986. Crosslinguistic influence in second language acquisition: An introduction. Crosslinguistic Influence in Second Language Acquisition, New York: Pergamon.

Tony Sun, Andrew Gaut, Shirlyn Tang, Yuxin Huang, Mai ElSherief, Jieyu Zhao, Diba Mirza, Elizabeth Belding, Kai-Wei Chang, and William Yang Wang. 2019. Mitigating gender bias in natural language processing: Literature review. In Proceedings of the 57th Annual Meeting of the Association for Computational Linguistics, pages 1630–1640, Florence, Italy. Association for Computational Linguistics.

Anaïs Tack, Thomas François, Sophie Roekhaut, and Cédrick Fairon. 2017. Human and automated CEFR-based grading of short answers. In Proceedings of the 12th Workshop on Innovative Use of NLP for Building Educational Applications, pages 169–179, Copenhagen, Denmark. Association for Computational Linguistics.

Zixin Tang, Prasenjit Mitra, and David Reitter. 2021. Are BERTs sensitive to native interference in L2 production? In Proceedings of the Second Workshop on Insights from Negative Results in NLP, pages 36–41, Online and Punta Cana, Dominican Republic. Association for Computational Linguistics.

Sowmya Vajjala and Kaidi Lõo. 2014. Automatic CEFR level prediction for Estonian learner text. In Proceedings of the third workshop on NLP for computer-assisted language learning, pages 113–127, Uppsala, Sweden. LiU Electronic Press.

Elena Volodina, I. Pilán, and David Alfter. 2016. Classification of Swedish learner essays by CEFR levels.

Uriel Weinreich. 2010. Languages in Contact: Findings and Problems. De Gruyter Mouton.

A Appendix

A.1 Hyper-parameter settings

LinearSVC (iterative debiasing):

- penalty='l2'
- C=0.01
- fit_intercept=True
- class_weight=None
- dual=False

Logistic Regression (country of origin):

- penalty = 'l2'
- warm_start = True
- solver="saga"
- random_state=23
- max_iter=7

Logistic Regression (CEFR):

- penalty = 'l2'
- warm_start = True
- solver="saga"
- random_state=23
- max_iter=7
- multi_class='multinomial'
- fit_intercept=True

MLP (CEFR):

- hidden_layer_sizes = 256
- activation = relu

Automatically Detecting Reduced-formed English Pronunciations by Using Deep Learning

Lei Chen[1], Chenglin Jiang, Yiwei Gu, Yang Liu[2], Jiahong Yuan[3]
[1]Rakuten Institute of Technology (RIT)
[2]Alexa AI, Amazon
[3]Baidu Research
LAIX Inc. Shanghai China

Abstract

Reduced form pronunciations are widely used by native English speakers, especially in casual conversations. Second language (L2) learners have difficulty in processing reduced form pronunciations in listening comprehension and face challenges in production too. Meanwhile, training applications dedicated to reduced forms are still few. To solve this issue, we report on our first effort of using deep learning to evaluate L2 learners' reduced form pronunciations. Compared with a baseline solution that uses an ASR to determine regular or reduced-formed pronunciations, a classifier that learns representative features via a convolution neural network (CNN) on low-level acoustic features, yields higher detection performance. F-1 metric has been increased from 0.690 to 0.757 on the reduction task. Furthermore, adding word entities to compute attention weights to better adjust the features learned by the CNN model helps increasing F-1 to 0.763.

1 Introduction

The term "reduced forms" refers to the phenomenon of phonological simplification and variation commonly observed in connected speech of native speakers (Brown and Kondo-Brown, 2006; Khaghaninezhad and Jafarzadeh, 2014; Cangemi et al., 2018). In phonetic reduction, "segments may be shorter, less clearly articulated, or absent compared to canonical or dictionary forms" (Cangemi et al., 2018). Reduced-formed pronunciations appear in daily English communication among native speakers (Johnson, 2004).

On one hand, the existence of reduced form challenges second language (L2) learners in their listening comprehension (Norris, 1995). On the other hand, L2 learners often face great challenges on producing reduced forms so that they can sound more close to native speakers. English as a second language (ESL) teachers have realized the importance of specially training L2 learners on understanding reduced form pronunciations to improve their listening comprehension skills. (Yeh et al., 2017) is such an effort of designing an app to train students accordingly. Compared to the emphasis on reduced forms when training the listening comprehension skills, the effort on training the specific skills on the production of reduced forms is still limited. Most computer aided language learning (CALL) tools focus on training regular form pronunciations and do not provide adequate supports to L2 learners' demands on the production of reduced forms.

Hence, in this paper, we will report on our initial effort of using a deep learning based classification method to detect L2 learners' reduced form productions. Note that the detection is the first required step for creating a training tool that can generate feedback and provide interventions to cultivate L2 learners' specific skills.

2 Previous research

Reduced forms have been actively investigated in phonetics. For example, (Ernestus and Warner, 2011) introduced reduced-formed pronunciation variant phenomenal in phonetics. It pointed out that such variations are quite common in different languages in their casual conversation conditions. (Jurafsky et al., 1998) investigated English function words' reduced forms in the Switchboard corpus and found that a high percentage of reduced forms appears in the telephone conversations. Also, the authors investigated possible reasons causing reduced forms, such as words' frequencies.

(Wong et al., 2017) examined the role of the perception of reduced forms (e.g., contraction, elision, assimilation) of English words in connected speech comprehension and the phonological skills underpinning reduced forms perception. This study

[0]The work was conducted while Lei, Jiahong, and Yang were working in LAIX Silicon Valley AI Lab

Proceedings of the 17th Workshop on Innovative Use of NLP for Building Educational Applications (BEA 2022), pages 22 - 26

delivers a clear message to ESL teachers that the ability of perceiving reduced pronunciation variants is important for L2 listening comprehension skills. There are some emerging technical works on helping L2 learners' perception of reduced forms. For example, (Yeh et al., 2017) reports on an Android App to use authentic native connected speeches as material to teach.

Reduced forms sometimes are produced as variants to formal forms. Based on this fact, methods that can distinguish pronunciation variants in ASR can be used to detect the existence of reduced forms. (Strik and Cucchiarini, 1999) systematically surveyed the methods for recognizing pronunciation variants. In a widely used approach, extended recognition network (ERN) (Qian et al., 2016; Harrison et al., 2009), extra decoding paths are added to represent pronunciation variants on top of the regular paths built on formal forms' pronunciations. However, reduced forms can sometimes occur without pronunciation variants. Hence, solutions working on broader cases are worth investigating.

3 Data

In this paper, we focused on the two types of reduced forms, i.e., *reduction* and *liaison*. The first refers to changing pronunciation from its formal form on individual words while the second term refers to co-articulation among adjacent words.

In 2019, Company-X released a new product for training various specific pronunciation skills, including reduction and liaison, in its main English learning mobile App. This product has already been used by a large number of Chinese English learners. From the audio samples collected in this product, we built up our own research data set. We sampled speech files from a large group of English learners from different locations in China. When sampling L2 learners' spoken responses, we used pronunciation scores automatically rated by Company-X AI-based pronunciation scoring system to include learners from diverse levels.

On $8,570$ practice audio samples for the reduction skill, $seven$ human raters annotated whether learners produce correct reductions or not on the required words. During rating, the annotators considered three aspects, including energy, rhythm (duration and its connection to context words), and pronunciation variations. These raters are high-level non-native English speakers and doing linguistics and phonetics annotation as their full-time jobs. For each audio sample, if at least four raters agree on one label, this label will be used to be the sample's final decision. Otherwise, the sample will be treated to be too challenging for human annotators and will be excluded from the experiments. The entire rating was done in two stages by using two groups of double raters. For each stage, a kappa set was used to measure two raters' rating consistence. In the first stage, the rating agreement was $\kappa = 0.63$. Then, raters obtained more training on understanding the rating guideline before going to the second stage of rating. The agreement measurement on the second stage has been increased to $\kappa = 0.79$. Figure 1 shows the annotation interface in Praat software. We can see that for selected words, e.g., "you", "have", "to", and "me", human raters used annotation tiers to label their decisions. "1" denotes reduction while "0" denotes formal form.

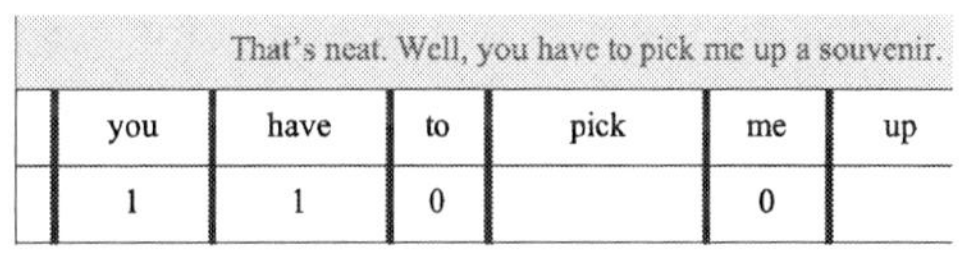

Figure 1: Annotation interface for reductions in Praat

On $4,027$ practice audio samples for the liaison skill, three human annotators marked whether some word pairs are spoken as liaisons or not. Figure 2 shows the annotation interface in Praat. For the word pairs "big living" and "will a", annotators mark 1 indicating two words are spoken in a connected way or use 0 indicating two words are spoken in their formal forms. For each audio sample, the majority voting results among the three annotators were used as final labels. Among the three raters, their between-rater agreement values are 0.74, 0.81, and 0.82 respectively. This shows that judging liaison is relatively easy compared to judging reductions. Table 1 summaries the label counts of the two data sets.

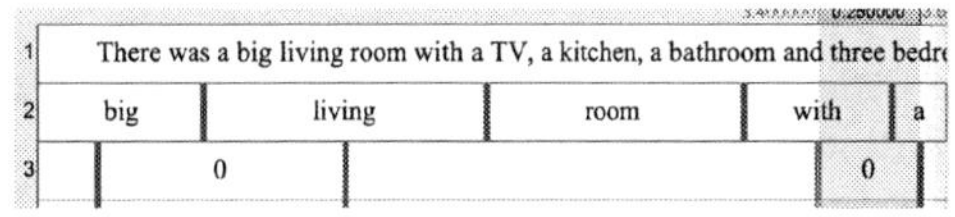

Figure 2: Annotation interface for liaison detection in Praat

Reduced form type	#Yes	#No	#Total
reduction	$3,610$	$7,953$	$11,563$
liaison	$1,334$	$2,693$	$4,027$

Table 1: Statistics of the two reduced form data sets

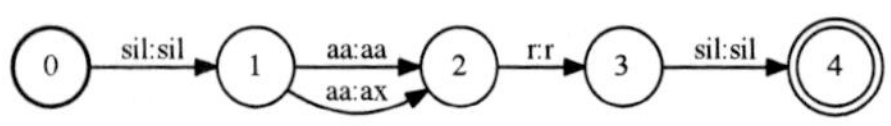

Figure 3: Decoding network for the word "are" with formal form /ar/ and reduced form /r/

4 Models

4.1 ASR based method

For words (including single words or multi-word with reduced forms, e.g. "got you" to "gotcha") with pronunciation variations, a typical solution is using an ASR system with two distinct pronunciation entries in its dictionary to determine real pronunciation on the fly. For example, "are" can be pronounced as its formal form /ar/ or its reduced form /r/. Here, we first use a forced alignment step to locate words being considered. Then, a recognition network with paths mapping to two pronunciation forms is used to decode the audio portion to find the more possible path. Figure 3 shows one concrete example of a decoding network for the word "are".

The automatic speech recognition (ASR) system was built with the Kaldi open-source toolkit. This model is a 9-layer time delayed neural network (TDNN) using Mel frequency cepstrum coefficient (MFCC) acoustic features from the current frame plus the previous and following 5 context frames. The ASR model was trained on our in-house read-aloud corpus containing about $2,500$ hours of native and non-native speech files. The ASR system achieved a word error rate (WER) of 9% on learners' speech.

4.2 CNN based method

ASR based method was based on an assumption that pronunciation variations always occur in the reduced forms. However, some reduced forms may only show in low energy levels and shorter duration. To address this limitation, we investigated building a classifier to predict a audio segment's pronunciation form directly,

Pronunciation in a reduced form is a complicated process. To obtain effective representations, we conducted an automatic feature learning by utilizing a convolution neural network (CNN) model (Abdel-Hamid et al., 2014). For the reduction detection task, we used MFCC feature sequence over each audio segment being considered. For the liaison detection task, we used the MFCC feature sequence starting from the last phoneme of the starting word to the first phoneme of the ending word in each adjacent word pair being considered. Also, these two phonemes were connected to form a token to be the "word entity" associated with this word pair. In each reduced form detection task, all of the audio portions were padded to the same length. For example, for the reduction detection task, all portions were padded to 0.5 second long.

The **librosa** (McFee et al., 2015) V0.7 audio signal processing Python package was used to extract MFCC ($n = 40$) features. For example, in the reduction detection task, each input feature (on a word) takes a shape of 16×40. Then, we sent these tensors to two CNN blocks, each block contains a 1D CNN (filters numbers are 128 and 256 respectively) and a batch normalization (BN) (Ioffe and Szegedy, 2015) layer. From the second CNN block's output, global max pooling and Dropout (Srivastava et al., 2014) layers were used to convert learned features to be vectors with a dimension of 256. At last, the learned features went through a fully connected (FC) layer using a sigmoid activation function to obtain reduced form prediction binary output.

All of the audio clips used in this study were collected from learners when they practiced on a set of pre-defined words. We noticed that learners' reduction production varied among these word entities. Therefore the word entity's prior information is expected to be useful for modeling learners' production behaviors. To incorporate word entity cues in the reduced form prediction, we utilized word entities one-hot representations to compute feature attention weights so that for each specific word entity, a different feature weighting plan can be learned in our CNN model. The learned feature from CNNs is denoted as $\mathbf{F} = \{\mathbf{f_t}\}$ where $0 <= t <= 255$. $\mathbf{V_i}$ is the one-shot encoding vector for the word w_i among all $|V|$ pre-defined words for testing L2 speakers' reduction production capabilities. We use a linear mapping $\mathbf{W}$, which is learned during model training, and a softmax activation to compute attention weights α_t. Then, an adjusted feature vector $\mathbf{S}$ is obtained by applying the attention weights on $\{\mathbf{f_i}\}$ element-wise.

$$A_i = \{a_t\} = W \times V_i \quad (1)$$

$$\alpha_\mathbf{t} = \frac{\exp(\mathbf{a_t})}{\sum_{\mathbf{k}=0}^{255} \exp(\mathbf{a_k})} \quad (2)$$

$$\mathbf{S} = \{\alpha_\mathbf{t}\mathbf{f_t}\} \quad (3)$$

Figure 4 depicts our CNN models in details. Note that the left panel shows the model only considering audio information while the right panel shows how word entities were used to compute attention weights to adjust the learned features dynamically. The model was implemented by using Keras package (Chollet et al., 2015) on TensorFlow (Abadi et al., 2015).

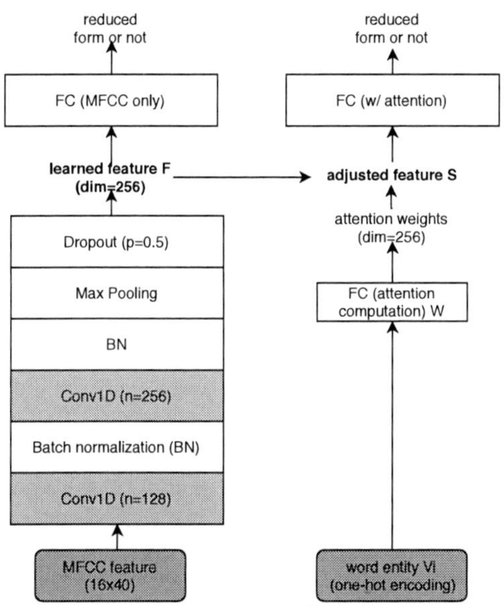

Figure 4: Using 1D CNN to learn features from MFCC for predicting whether a reduced form pronunciation occurs or not. The learned feature can be directly used (as in the left side) or adjusted by using attention weights based on word entities (as shown in the right side)

5 Experiments

Using the entire data set, we run our ASR based method to obtain reduced form predictions. When evaluating our classification based methods, we run cross-validation experiments. To compensate non-deterministic effects of using neural networks, we repeated our CV experiments 5 times and reported average performance among.

Regarding evaluating methods, we used standard metrics when evaluating binary classification, i.e., accuracy and F-1 score weighted by label percentage. The higher measurement metrics, the better the methods.

Method	Accuracy	F-1 (mean)
ASR	70.38%	0.690
CNN	76.19%	0.757
CNN + ATTN	77.01%	0.763

Table 2: Reduction detection results measured in both accuracy and F-1 score on different methods

Method	Accuracy	F-1 (mean)
ASR	70.85%	0.692
CNN	71.49%	0.719
CNN + ATTN	72.11%	0.720

Table 3: liaison detection performance measured in both accuracy and F-1 score on different methods

Table 2 reports on the experiment for the reduction detection task. CNN model shows improvements over the baseline ASR model, suggesting that CNN can automatically learn more indicative features from audio signals. When using attentions based on word entities to adjust the learned features, we can find further performance improvements (F-1 from 0.757 to 0.763).

Table 3 reports on the experiment result for the liaison detection task. Similar to what we found on the reduction task, the two methods using a CNN model to learn features automatically show improved performance than the method based on ASR decoding. Also, using attention weights computed based on phoneme-pairs is helpful.

6 Discussion

Reduced forms are commonly used by native speakers in their casual conversations. Because L2 learners mostly face formal forms in their language learning, perception and production of reduced forms in fact greatly challenges learners' listening comprehension and speaking capabilities. With a goal of building a training application on producing reduced-formed pronunciations, we conducted a research on automatically detecting reduced forms with a high accuracy. Following on the work of recognition of pronunciation variants, we firstly utilized an ASR decoding method to distinguish formal vs. reduced forms. To cope with reduced forms without obvious pronunciation variations, we then explored using a CNN model to learn distinguishable features from learner speech directly.

Our experiment results show that CNN method has improved performance over the ASR decoding method. Using word entities in the CNN model to compute attention weights to adjust the learned features is proven to be useful. Overall, on the two reduced form types, i.e., reduction and liaison, our CNN model has F-1 measurement about 0.763 and 0.720 respectively.

We envision that there are several research directions in future. Firs, so far, we only used CNNs to encode MFCC feature sequence, it is worthwhile trying some new encoding method, like Transformer. Second, human annotation on reduction still have a room to improve. We are hoping to continue increasing rating agreement to provide a even more solid research base. At last, a training module has been added into LAIX Liulishuo App. Based on real user data, it is worthwhile tracking whether provided training helps on learners' mastery of reduced forms.

References

Martın Abadi, Ashish Agarwal, Paul Barham, Eugene Brevdo, Zhifeng Chen, Craig Citro, Greg S. Corrado, Andy Davis, Jeffrey Dean, and Matthieu Devin. 2015. Tensorflow: Large-scale machine learning on heterogeneous distributed systems.

Ossama Abdel-Hamid, Abdel-rahman Mohamed, Hui Jiang, Li Deng, Gerald Penn, and Dong Yu. 2014. Convolutional neural networks for speech recognition. *Audio, Speech, and Language Processing, IEEE/ACM Transactions on*, 22(10):1533–1545.

J. D. Brown and K. Kondo-Brown. 2006. Testing reduced forms. In *Perspectives on teaching connected speech to second language speakers*, pages 247–264.

Francesco Cangemi, Meghan Clayards, Oliver Niebuhr, Barbara Schuppler, and Margaret Zellers. 2018. Rethinking reduction: Interdisciplinary perspectives on conditions, mechanisms, and domains for phonetic variation.

François Chollet et al. 2015. Keras. `https://keras.io`.

Mirjam Ernestus and Natasha Warner. 2011. An introduction to reduced pronunciation variants. *Journal of Phonetics*, 39(SI):253–260.

Alissa M. Harrison, Wai-Kit Lo, Xiao-jun Qian, and Helen Meng. 2009. Implementation of an extended recognition network for mispronunciation detection and diagnosis in computer-assisted pronunciation training. In *International Workshop on Speech and Language Technology in Education*.

Sergey Ioffe and Christian Szegedy. 2015. Batch Normalization: Accelerating Deep Network Training by Reducing Internal Covariate Shift. In *Proceedings of the 32nd International Conference on Machine Learning*, volume 37 of *Proceedings of Machine Learning Research*, pages 448–456, Lille, France. PMLR.

Keith Johnson. 2004. Massive reduction in conversational american english. *Yoneyama, K and Maekawa, K. (Eds), Spontaneous Speech: Data And Analysis*.

Daniel Jurafsky, Alan Bell, Eric Fosler-Lussier, Cynthia Girand, and William Raymond. 1998. Reduction of English function words in Switchboard. In *Fifth International Conference on Spoken Language Processing*.

Mohammad Saber Khaghaninezhad and Ghasem Jafarzadeh. 2014. Investigating the Effect of Reduced Forms Instruction on EFL Learners' Listening and Speaking Abilities. *English Language Teaching*, 7(1):159–171.

Brian McFee, Colin Raffel, Dawen Liang, Daniel PW Ellis, Matt McVicar, Eric Battenberg, and Oriol Nieto. 2015. librosa: Audio and music signal analysis in python. In *Proceedings of the 14th python in science conference*, volume 8.

Robert W. Norris. 1995. Teaching reduced forms: Putting the horse before the cart. In *English Teaching Forum*, volume 33, pages 47–50.

Xiaojun Qian, Helen Meng, and Frank Soong. 2016. A two-pass framework of mispronunciation detection and diagnosis for computer-aided pronunciation training. *IEEE/ACM Transactions on Audio, Speech and Language Processing (TASLP)*, 24(6):1020–1028.

Nitish Srivastava, Geoffrey Hinton, Alex Krizhevsky, Ilya Sutskever, and Ruslan Salakhutdinov. 2014. Dropout: a simple way to prevent neural networks from overfitting. *The journal of machine learning research*, 15(1):1929–1958.

Helmer Strik and Catia Cucchiarini. 1999. Modeling pronunciation variation for ASR: A survey of the literature. *Speech Communication*, 29(2-4):225–246.

Simpson WL Wong, Peggy PK Mok, Kevin Kien-Hoa Chung, Vina WH Leung, Dorothy VM Bishop, and Bonnie Wing-Yin Chow. 2017. Perception of native English reduced forms in Chinese learners: Its role in listening comprehension and its phonological correlates. *TESOL Quarterly*, 51(1):7–31.

Hsin-Yu Yeh, Yu-Tzu Tsai, and Chih-Kai Chang. 2017. Android app development for teaching reduced forms of EFL listening comprehension to decrease cognitive load. In *2017 International Conference of Educational Innovation through Technology (EITT)*, pages 316–321. IEEE.

A Baseline Readability Model for Cebuano

Lloyd Lois Antonie Reyes, Michael Antonio Ibañez, Ranz Sapinit, Mohammed Hussien, Joseph Marvin Imperial
National University
Manila, Philippines
jrimperial@national-u.edu.ph

Abstract

In this study, we developed the first baseline readability model for the Cebuano language. Cebuano is the second most-used native language in the Philippines with about 27.5 million speakers. As the baseline, we extracted traditional or surface-based features, syllable patterns based from Cebuano's documented orthography, and neural embeddings from the multilingual BERT model. Results show that the use of the first two handcrafted linguistic features obtained the best performance trained on an optimized Random Forest model with approximately 87% across all metrics. The feature sets and algorithm used also is similar to previous results in readability assessment for the Filipino language—showing potential of crosslingual application. To encourage more work for readability assessment in Philippine languages such as Cebuano, we open-sourced both code and data[1].

1 Introduction

The proper identification of the difficulty levels of reading materials is a vital aspect of the language learning process. It enables teachers and educators alike to assign appropriate materials to young learners in which they can fully comprehend, preventing boredom and disinterest (Guevarra, 2011). However, assessing readability presents challenges, particularly when you have a large corpus of text to sift through. Manually extracting and calculating a wide range of linguistic features can be time-consuming and expensive and can lead to subjectivity of labels due to human errors (Deutsch et al., 2020). To tackle this problem, more and more research in the field have focused on experimenting with automated methods for extracting possible linguistic predictors to train models for readability assessment.

While automating readability assessment is a challenge itself, one of the original problem in the field starts with data. In the Philippines, the Mother-Tongue Based Multilingual Education (MTB-MLE) scheme was introduced by the Department of Education (DepEd) in 2013. With this initiative, there were little to no available tool for automatically assessing readability of reading resources, instructional materials, and grammatical materials in mother tongue languages aside from Filipino such as Cebuano, Hiligaynon, and Bikol (Medilo Jr, 2016). To answer this challenge, in this paper, we investigate various linguistic features ranging from traditional or surface-based predictors, orthography-based features from syllable patterns, and neural representations to develop a baseline readability assessment model for the Cebuano language. We use an array of traditional machine learning algorithms to train the assessment models with hyperparameter optimization. Our results show that using non-neural features are enough to produce a competitive model for identifying the readability levels of children's books in Cebuano.

2 Previous Work

Readability assessment has been the subject of research of linguistic experts and book publishers as a method of measuring comprehensibility of a given text or document. Villamin and de Guzman (1979) pioneered a readability assessment for the Filipino language in 1979. Hand-crafted indices and surface information from texts, such as hand counts of words, phrases, and sentences, are used in these formula-based techniques. An equivalent technique of traditional formula was applied on to Waray language (Oyzon et al., 2015) to complement the DepEd's MTB-MLE program in certain regions of the Philippines such as in Samar and Leyte. While traditional featured formulas relied on linear models, recent studies on readability research assessment have shifted their focus on ex-

[1]The resources can be found using this link: https://github.com/imperialite/cebuano-readability.

Proceedings of the 17th Workshop on Innovative Use of NLP for Building Educational Applications (BEA 2022), pages 27 - 32
July 15, 2022

panding the traditional method to more fine-grained features. Guevarra (2011) and Macahilig (2014) introduced the use of a logistic regression model trained with unique word counts, total word and sentence counts, and mean log of word frequency. A few years later, lexical, syllable patterns, morphology, and syntactic features were eventually explored for readability of Filipino text by works of Imperial and Ong (Imperial and Ong, 2021a, 2020, 2021b).

3 The Cebuano Language

Cebuano (CEB) is an Austronesian language mostly spoken in the southern parts of the Philippines such as in major regions of Visayas and Mindanao. It is the language with the second highest speaker count[2] in the country with 27.5 million, just after Tagalog, where the national language is derived from, with 82 million speakers. Both Cebuano and Tagalog languages observe linguistic similarities such as in derivation, prefixing, disyllabic roots, and reduplication (Blake, 1904). On the other hand, differences are seen in syntax such as use of particles (*ay*, *y*), phonetic changes, and morphological changes on verbs. Figure 1 illustrates a portion of the Philippine language family tree emphasizing on where Cebuano originated. Cebuano is part of the Central Philippine subtree along with Tagalog and Bikol which can be attributed to their similarities and differences as mentioned. The full image can be viewed at Oco et al. (2013).

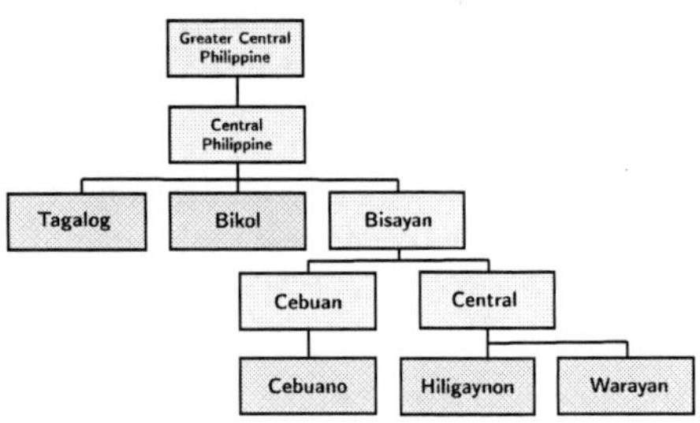

Figure 1: Right portion of the Philippine language family tree highlighting origin of Cebuano.

3.1 Cebuano Readability Corpus

We compiled the first Cebuano text corpus composed of 277 expert-annotated literary pieces uniform to the first three grade levels (L1, L2, and L3) of the Philippine primary education. For comparison to international grading systems, the standard age range for each level is 6-7, 7-8, and 8-9 respectively. We collected the materials from three online, open-sourced book repositories online: **Let's Read**, **Bloom Library**, and **DepEd Commons**. All materials are licensed under Creative Commons BY 4.0 allows redistribution in any medium or format provided proper attribution. Table 1 shows the distribution of the collected corpus.

Corpus	L1	L2	L3	Total
Let's Read	6	21	50	82
Bloom	50	50	25	125
DepEd	22	1	4	27
Total	**76**	**72**	**79**	**227**

Table 1: Distribution of compiled text passages in Cebuano.

Let's Read. Let's Read[3] is an initiative by the The Asia Foundation to open-source culturally friendly children's books in diverse themes, characters, and settings. The resource materials from this repository are mostly sourced from BookLabs and translated by local volunteers across multiple languages including Cebuano. Let's Read covers a wide variety of genre such as gender equality, environment, understanding and empathy, and science and technology. We collected 82 Cebuano children's books from this website for our corpus.

Bloom. The Bloom Library[4] is also an free repository of diverse children's books resources funded and maintained by the Summer Institute of Linguistics (SIL International). Similar to Let's Read, local volunteers can also upload high-quality and validated translations of book resources or original pieces to the platform. We collected 125 Cebuano children's books from this website for our corpus.

DepEd Commons. The Commons Library[5] is an initiative by the Department of Education in the Philippines to grant free access to literature in various Philippine languages for students and

[2] https://www.ethnologue.com/language/ceb

[3] https://www.letsreadasia.org/

[4] https://bloomlibrary.org/

[5] https://commons.deped.gov.ph/

teachers during the COVID-19 pandemic. We collected 27 Cebuano children's books from this website for our corpus.

4 Linguistic Features

In this study, we extracted three linguistic feature groups from our Cebuano text corpus: **traditional or surface-based features**, **orthography-based features**, and **neural embeddings**. To the best of our knowledge, no study has ever been conducted to assess and explore the readability assessment of Cebuano text using these features.

4.1 Traditional Features (TRAD)

Traditional or surface-based features are predictors that were used by experts for their old readability formulas for Filipino such as sentence and word counts in Guevarra (2011). Despite the claims that these features insufficiently measures deeper text properties for readability assessment (Redish, 2000), since this is the pioneering study for Cebuano, we still considered these features for our baseline model development. In this study, we adapted the seven features of traditional features from existing works in Filipino (Imperial and Ong, 2020, 2021a,b) such as *number of unique words, number of words, average word length, average number of syllables, total number of sentences, average sentence length* and *number of polysyllable words*.

4.2 Syllable Pattern (SYLL)

Orthography-based features measure character-level complexity of texts through combinations of various syllable patterns (Imperial and Ong, 2021b). Same as in Filipino, we adapted syllable patterns as features for the baseline model development but used only seven recognizable consonant-vowel combinations linguistically documented in the Cebuano language (Blake, 1904). We used *consonant clusters* and syllable pattern combinations of *v, cv, cc, vc, cvc, ccv, ccvc* normalized by the number of words.

4.3 Substitute Features using Neural Embeddings (NEURAL)

The use of Transformer-based language model embeddings have shown to be an effective *substitute* for handcrafted features in low-resource languages (Imperial, 2021). Probing tasks have shown that these representations contain information such as semantic and syntactic knowledge (Rogers et al., 2020) which can be useful in readability assessment. For this study, we extracted embedding representations with dimension size of 768 from the multilingual BERT model (Devlin et al., 2019) as features for each instance from the Cebuano corpus. According to the training recipe of multilingual BERT, Cebuano data in the form of Wikipedia dumps was included in its development which makes the model a viable option for this study.

Feature	Acc	Prec	Rec	F1
TRAD	**0.789**	**0.754**	**0.749**	**0.750**
SYLL	0.544	0.546	0.559	0.551
TRAD + SYLL	0.719	0.721	0.722	0.718
NEURAL	0.754	0.759	0.766	0.757
Combination	0.737	0.714	0.729	0.714

Table 2: Performance of finetuned Logistic Regression model.

Feature	Acc	Prec	Rec	F1
TRAD	0.718	0.728	0.685	0.676
SYLL	0.649	0.648	0.648	0.646
TRAD + SYLL	0.789	0.787	0.791	0.784
NEURAL	**0.807**	**0.813**	**0.812**	**0.811**
Combination	0.789	0.788	0.789	0.793

Table 3: Performance of finetuned Support Vector Machines model.

Feature	Acc	Prec	Rec	F1
TRAD	0.842	0.843	0.842	0.842
SYLL	0.579	0.579	0.586	0.580
TRAD + SYLL	**0.873**	**0.852**	**0.858**	**0.852**
NEURAL	0.772	0.776	0.761	0.763
Combination	0.825	0.801	0.804	0.799

Table 4: Performance of finetuned Random Forest model.

5 Experiment Setup

The task at hand is a multiclass classification problem with three classes being the aforementioned grade levels. We specifically chose traditional learning algorithms such as Logistic Regression, Support Vector Machines, and Random Forest for building the baseline models for post-training interpretation techniques described in the succeeding sections. To reduce bias, a k-fold cross validation where $k = 5$ was implemented. For the intrinsic evaluation, we used standard metrics such as accuracy, precision, recall and macro F1-score. In addition, we also used grid search to optimize the following model-specific hyperparamters: solver and regularization penalties for Logistic Regression, kernel type, maximum iterations, and regularization penalties for Support Vector Machines, and number of estimators, maximum features, and maximum depth for Random Forest.

6 Results

To assess the effectiveness of the proposed framework in the experimentation, we examined model performances on three different ablation studies: (a) linguistic features only, (b) neural embeddings only, and (c) combination of the two via concatenation. The results of each fine-tuned model utilizing the given evaluation metric are showed in Tables 2, 3, and 4.

Across the board, the best performing model and feature combination for Cebuano achieved approximately 87.3% for all metrics using the combination of TRAD and SYLL features with Random Forest. This top performing model makes used of 100 tree estimators, automatically adjusted maximum features, and a max depth of 20. Interestingly, the feature combination and the algorithm of choice is also the *same* for Filipino readability assessment as seen in the work ofImperial and Ong (2021b). This may suggest that, despite language differences and similarities, the use of surface-based features such as counts and syllable patterns are accepted for both Filipino and Cebuano languages in the readability assessment task. Referring again to Figure 1 for emphasis, both languages are part of the Central Philippine subtree which opens the possibility of a cross-lingual application of linguistic features for future research.

This effectiveness of surface-based features is also seen for the optimized Logistic Regression model where using TRAD features obtained the best performance. In the case of the optimized Support Vector Machine model, the use of neural embeddings alone obtained better scores than the combination of traditional and syllable pattern features. This result affirms the observation in Imperial (2021) where the extracted neural embeddings can serve as substitute features and can relatively be at par with handcrafted features.

7 Discussion

7.1 Model Interpretation

To understand more about which specific linguistic feature is contributive during model training, we used two versions of model interpretation algorithms specifically used for Random Forest models: **permutation on full model** and **mean decrease in impurity (MDI)** as shown in Figures 3 and 2 respectively. Feature permutation recursively adds a predictor to a null model and evaluates the growth in accuracy while mean decrease impurity adds up all weighted impurity score reductions or homogeneity averaged for all tree estimators (Breiman, 2001). From both the feature importance results, the most important feature is the *v_density* or *singular vowel density*. This may indicate that the denser the vowels in a word, the more complex the text becomes. Likewise, both *cv_density* and *consonant clusters* emerged as second top predictors for both analysis which may suggest that in Cebuano, words with combined consonants with no intervening vowels are more apparent in complex sentences than from easier ones.

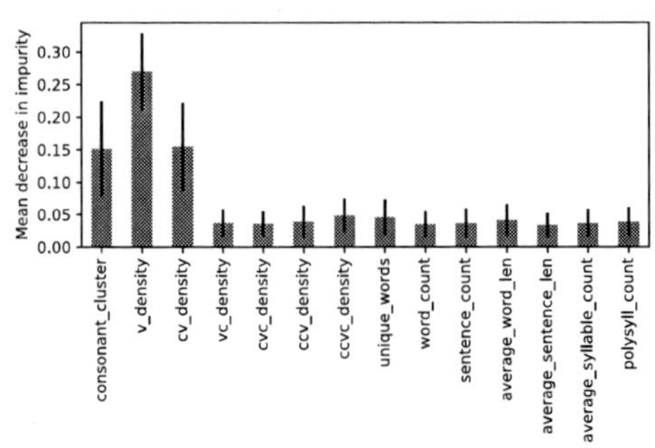

Figure 2: Feature importance by mean decrease impurity.

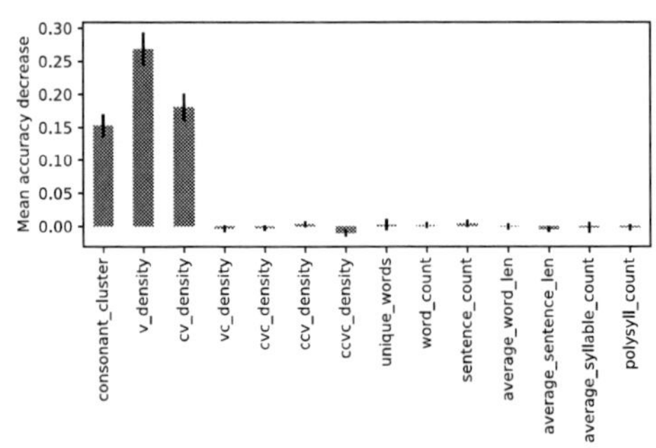

Figure 3: Feature importance by permutation on full model.

7.2 Feature Correlation

We also looked at model-independent feature analysis techniques through **Spearman correlation** with respect to readability levels. Table 5 shows the top ten highly correlated features. In support to the findings described in Sections 6 and 7.1, all correlated linguistic features belong to the TRAD and SYLL feature sets with *number of unique words* at the top. This may suggest that the density of unique words may increase relative to the readability level in a positive direction. In addition, *cv*, *cvc*, and *ccv* densities are the only syllable pattern features that placed top in both model-dependent and independent feature interpretation techniques. This may hint further potential as readability predictors for other text domains. To note, the *cv*-pattern in Cebuano is one of the most common consonant-vowel combinations (Zorc et al., 1976; Yap and Bunye, 2019).

Feature Set	Predictor	ρ
TRAD	unique_words	0.337
SYLL	cv_density	0.327
TRAD	word_count	0.298
	average_sentence_len	0.295
SYLL	cvc_density	0.293
TRAD	sentence_count	0.292
SYLL	consonant_cluster	0.293
	ccv_density	0.217
TRAD	polysyll_count	0.192
SYLL	vc_density	0.190

Table 5: Feature ranking using Spearman correlation.

8 Outlook

We developed the first ever baseline machine learning model for readability assessment in Cebuano. Among the three linguistic feature groups extracted to build the model, the combination of traditional or surface-based features (TRAD) with syllable pattern based features (SYLL) produced the highest performance using an optimized Random Forest model. One of the main challenges in the field is the limited amount of resource for tools and data especially for low-resource languages (Vajjala, 2021). To answer this call and encourage growth of research in this direction, we open-sourced the compiled dataset of annotated Cebuano reading materials and the code for model development.

Acknowledgements

The authors would like to thank the anonymous reviewers for their valuable feedback. This project is supported by the Google AI Tensorflow Faculty Grant awarded to Joseph Marvin Imperial.

References

Frank R Blake. 1904. Differences between tagalog and bisayan. *Journal of the American Oriental Society*, 25:162–169.

Leo Breiman. 2001. Random forests. *Machine learning*, 45(1):5–32.

Tovly Deutsch, Masoud Jasbi, and Stuart Shieber. 2020. Linguistic features for readability assessment. In *Proceedings of the Fifteenth Workshop on Innovative Use of NLP for Building Educational Applications*, pages 1–17, Seattle, WA, USA â†' Online. Association for Computational Linguistics.

Jacob Devlin, Ming-Wei Chang, Kenton Lee, and Kristina Toutanova. 2019. BERT: Pre-training of deep bidirectional transformers for language understanding. In *Proceedings of the 2019 Conference of the North American Chapter of the Association for Computational Linguistics: Human Language Technologies, Volume 1 (Long and Short Papers)*, pages 4171–4186, Minneapolis, Minnesota. Association for Computational Linguistics.

Rowena C Guevarra. 2011. Development of a filipino text readability index. In *UP College of Engineering Professorial Chair Colloquium*.

Joseph Marvin Imperial. 2021. BERT embeddings for automatic readability assessment. In *Proceedings of the International Conference on Recent Advances in Natural Language Processing (RANLP 2021)*, pages 611–618, Held Online. INCOMA Ltd.

Joseph Marvin Imperial and Ethel Ong. 2020. Exploring hybrid linguistic feature sets to measure filipino text readability. In *2020 International Conference on Asian Language Processing (IALP)*, pages 175–180. IEEE.

Joseph Marvin Imperial and Ethel Ong. 2021a. Application of lexical features towards improvement of filipino readability identification of children's literature. *arXiv preprint arXiv:2101.10537*.

Joseph Marvin Imperial and Ethel Ong. 2021b. Diverse linguistic features for assessing reading difficulty of educational filipino texts. *arXiv preprint arXiv:2108.00241*.

Heidi B Macahilig. 2014. A content-based readability formula for filipino texts. *The Normal Lights*, 8(1).

Constantino G Medilo Jr. 2016. The experience of mother tongue-based multilingual education teachers in southern leyte, philippines. In *International Forum Journal*, volume 19, pages 64–79.

Nathaniel Oco, Leif Romeritch Syliongka, Rachel Edita Roxas, and Joel Ilao. 2013. Dice's coefficient on trigram profiles as metric for language similarity. In *2013 International Conference Oriental COCOSDA held jointly with 2013 Conference on Asian Spoken Language Research and Evaluation (O-COCOSDA/CASLRE)*, pages 1–4. IEEE.

Voltaire Q Oyzon, Juven B Corrales, and Wilfredo M Estardo Jr. 2015. Validation study of waray text readability instrument. *International Journal of Evaluation and Research in Education*, 4(2):45–53.

Janice Redish. 2000. Readability formulas have even more limitations than klare discusses. *ACM Journal of Computer Documentation (JCD)*, 24(3):132–137.

Anna Rogers, Olga Kovaleva, and Anna Rumshisky. 2020. A primer in BERTology: What we know about how BERT works. *Transactions of the Association for Computational Linguistics*, 8:842–866.

Sowmya Vajjala. 2021. Trends, limitations and open challenges in automatic readability assessment research. *arXiv preprint arXiv:2105.00973*.

Aracelli M Villamin and ES de Guzman. 1979. Pilipino readability formula: The derivation of a readability formula and a pilipino word list. *Language Study Center: Philippine Normal University*.

Elsa P Yap and Maria VR Bunye. 2019. *Cebuano grammar notes*. University of Hawaii Press.

R Zorc et al. 1976. *The Bisayan dialects of the Philippines: Subgrouping and reconstruction*. Pacific Linguistics, Research School of Pacific and Asian Studies.

Generation of Synthetic Error Data of Verb Order Errors for Swedish

Judit Casademont Moner
University of Gothenburg / Sweden
guscasaju@student.gu.se

Elena Volodina
University of Gothenburg / Sweden
elena.volodina@svenska.gu.se

Abstract

We report on our work-in-progress to generate a synthetic error dataset for Swedish by replicating errors observed in the authentic error-annotated dataset. We analyze a small subset of authentic errors, capture regular patterns based on parts of speech, and design a set of rules to corrupt new data. We explore the approach and identify its capabilities, advantages and limitations as a way to enrich the existing collection of error-annotated data. This work focuses on word order errors, specifically those involving the placement of finite verbs in a sentence.

1 Introduction

The lack of sufficient data to train algorithms capable of detecting, labeling and correcting grammatical errors calls for the need to generate synthetic (i.e. machine-made, not human-produced) error datasets to enrich the existing resources. As mentioned by Stahlberg and Kumar (2021), the need for synthetic datasets (aka corrupt or artificial datasets) exists not only for low-resource languages, but also for high-resource languages like English. This is due to the fact that data for error detection and correction is far more sparse than required for most tasks in NLP, as grammatical errors are found in different frequencies and distributed unevenly across written language. Moreover, the appearance of grammatical errors in student essays depend notably on the speaker's particularities, such as their proficiency level, native language(s) and age. The need is especially acute for languages that are on the low-resource end in this respect, as is the case for Swedish.

In this paper, we present a pilot study to generate artificial error data for Swedish by mimicking error patterns present in authentic error datasets, namely, in the SweLL learner corpus (Volodina et al., 2019) and its one-error-per-sentence DaLAJ derivative (Volodina et al., 2021). We create a corruption pipeline to insert artificial errors into the sentences from COCTAILL, a corpus of textbooks used for teaching Swedish (Volodina et al., 2014). We expect the artificially produced error data to be a valuable resource for such tasks as Grammatical Error Detection / Labeling (GED) and Grammatical Error Correction (GEC) for Swedish, which at the moment are dormant fields.

In this pilot, we focus on word order errors involving placement of finite verbs (tagged S-FinV). The final dataset comprises 31,788 corrupted sentences each containing one error of the syntactical error type "S-FinV", paired with their correct counterparts. The code and the generated data can be found on GitHub[1].

2 Related work

Recently much attention has been given to practical and theoretical aspects of artificial error data generation as a way to enhance performance of grammatical error correction systems, both with respect to methods of generation, source (aka seed) corpora used for corruption and the ways pseudo-data is used in system architectures (e.g. Flachs et al., 2021). Takahashi et al. (2020) give probably the most nuanced introduction to the problem.

Approaches to generation of synthetic error datasets can be roughly divided into rule-based and model-based ones, which further exhibit variation with regards to presence or absense of error labels. Advantages of *model-based approaches* (e.g. Stahlberg and Kumar, 2021) is that they capture the variety of error types present in the authentic data and the artificial data is fast to generate. However, training a model for replicating errors requires access to large amounts of such data, which often is a problem to start with. It has also been observed that models may show biases towards the data they have been trained on, with a consequence that they are

[1] https://github.com/juditcasademont/Generation-of-synthetic-error-data-LTR-project

Proceedings of the 17th Workshop on Innovative Use of NLP for Building Educational Applications (BEA 2022), pages 33 - 38
July 15, 2022

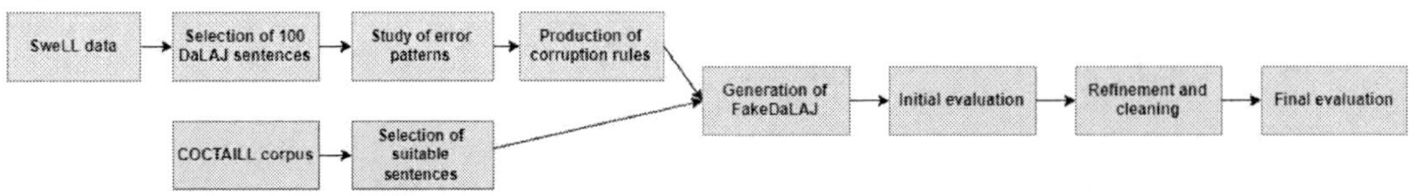

Figure 1: Overview of the pseudo-data generation process.

not general enough for unseen contexts or domains (e.g. Bryant et al., 2017).

Advantages of *rule-based approaches* (e.g. Grundkiewicz et al., 2019) are directly opposite, namely, that they can be created with zero or minimal access to gold data and can better generalize since they are kept on an abstract level. Some known rules include simple random operations, e.g. deletion of a word, randomly swapping neighbouring words, exchange of one inflected form with another or use of so-called confusion pairs, i.e. incorrect segment/token > corrected variant (e.g. Choe et al., 2019; Grundkiewicz et al., 2019).

A more linguistic approach to error rules, e.g. through abstracting to part of speech (POS) patterns or patterns including morpho-syntactic information, requires more time for designing corruption rules, but has one obvious advantage: using such rules allows control over the generated data and, importantly, it is possible to add error labels to corrupted sentences, which makes the pseudo-data applicable both to error correction and to error classification tasks. It also has an advantage of inserting realistic errors typical of learners, and has been shown to increase performance of GEC systems, compared to random error types (Takahashi et al., 2020) . Given the scarcity of the Swedish authentic data, we experiment with rule-based approaches using linguistic analysis to extract typical error patterns and to generate synthetic errors based on those.

3 Data and resources

The overview of the pseudo-data generation is shown in Figure 1. On the left, the top level shows steps for working with learner data, starting from the SweLL data, including preparation of one-error-per-sentence DaLAJ dataset, analysis of a 100 cleaned DaLAJ samples for identification of error patterns, and production of corruption rules. The bottom level on the left shows a parallel work involving selection of a seed corpus with correct language and preselection of sentences for corruption. On the right, the graph shows the process for corruption of the seed data and its subsequent cleaning and evaluation.

To perform the task at hand, thus, two main sources of textual data are needed: a corpus of tagged errors and a corpus of clean (i.e., error-free) texts. Additionally, a part of speech (POS) tagger to extract grammatical information is required.

3.1 Error-labeled learner data

In this project, we use SweLL-gold (Volodina et al., 2019), a collection consisting of 502 learner texts, manually corrected and tagged according to 6 top error categories which, in turn, have their own sub-categories (Rudebeck and Sundberg, 2021). The top error types are: **O**rthographic, **L**exical, **M**orphological, **P**unctuation, **S**yntactical and Other (the category Other contains comments and unitelligible strings). All texts are original and each sentence on average contains more than one error of more than one kind. The focus of this project is on **S**yntactical errors involving the position of **Fin**ite **V**erbs in a sentence, tagged in the SweLL corpus as "S-FinV". There are 701 instances of this tag in the corpus.

To better represent error types, we convert SweLL-gold to DaLAJ format (Volodina et al., 2021) where SweLL-gold data is represented as a set of sentence pairs (original-corrected) in a scrambled order. The most attractive feature of DaLAJ is that each sentence contains one error of one type only. This means that an original SweLL sentence has as many instances in the DaLAJ dataset as there are individual correction tags in its original form. This format supports easier detection and analysis of error patterns, for both humans and computers.

3.2 Seed data

The source of the error-free data, i.e. seed data to be corrupted with automatically generated errors, is the COCTAILL corpus (Volodina et al., 2014) containing 25,960 scrambled sentences from twelve course books of Swedish as a second language, labeled for levels of proficiency. They represent the following CEFR levels: Beginner (A1), Elementary (A2), Intermediate (B1), Upper Intermediate

(B2) and Advanced (C1). The Proficiency level (C2) is not represented. We assume that the lexical, grammatical and syntactical patterns in COCTAILL texts would be relatively close to the ones used in learner essays, thus fitting perfectly for our purposes. Out of the 25,960 sentences present in the COCTAILL corpus texts, 20,307 were deemed useful, as a filtering process was carried out to discard sentences not containing verbs as well as sentences shorter than two tokens.

3.3 POS tagging pipeline

Språkbanken Text's Sparv pipeline[2] (Borin et al., 2016) was used to extract grammatical information in the form of morphosyntactic tags. This pipeline was used in two distinct phases of the project: in the analysis of the error patterns and in the generation of corrupted data. The Sparv pipeline is a tool for text analysis that can be run from the command line or called programmatically through an API.

4 Methods

4.1 Error patterns

Swedish is a so-called "verb-second" language, which means that finite verbs, with a few exceptions, take the second position in a sentence (where positions are counted in phrases). Errors with placement of finite verbs are considered among the most typical ones for L2 learners of Swedish. Linguistic analysis of approx. 100 DaLAJ sentence pairs containing S-FinV errors has shown that three POS in specific positions in the sentence, have a tendency to be the cause of S-FinV errors, namely: pronouns (PN), nouns (NN) and adverbs (AB) (in the order of frequency). Additionally, there is a need to make a special case for proper names (PM).

Pronouns in the studied dataset are the most fruitful part of speech tag in the production of verb order errors, making two thirds of all S-FinV errors. The error production patterns involving pronouns can be grouped into two distinct groups: PN-VB →VB-PN and VB-PN →PN-VB (where the first part is correct →the second is erroneous).

To exemplify, in PN-VB →VB-PN*[3] errors, the error tends to happen right after a conjunction (KN), an interrogative or relative adverb (HA), or at the beginning of a sentence, like in the example below:

<ins>Jag</ins> **heter** Karin.[4] [5] →**Heter** <ins>jag</ins> Karin.*
Eng: My name is Karin.

The VB-PN →PN-VB* pattern, is decidedly the most frequent one in the "pronoun"-subtype, and appears in subordinate clauses, which requires the reversal of pronoun and verb positions. This phenomenon usually appears after interrogative or relative pronouns (HP) and adverbs (AB).

Errors involving the positions of verbs in relation to **adverbs** are also well-represented in our dataset, even though not as frequent as pronoun-related errors. Their typical error production patterns are: VB-AB →AB-VB* and AB-VB →VB-AB*.

In VB-AB →AB-VB* errors, the learner writes the adverb before the verb when its correct position is after the verb. It usually occurs in a sentence's main clause, probably because the writer wrongly applies the rule for subordinate clauses.

In contrast, errors of type AB-VB→VB-AB* appear in subordinate clauses where the verb and the adverb must switch positions in the sentence:

(...) om lillebror <ins>inte</ins> **ska** vara rädd för (...) →
(...) om lillebror **ska** <ins>inte</ins> vara rädd för (...)*
Eng: (...) if little brother must not be afraid of (...)

Error patterns involving **nouns** in close relation to verbs are slightly more varied than those having to do with pronouns and adverbs. The reason is that nouns can be modified by other parts of speech, such as determiners, possessives and adjectives. They can in addition be modified by adjective-like subordinate clauses.

Within this category, the primary error pattern is VB-NN →NN-VB* (or rather noun phrases), in which the verb needs to be placed before an unmodified noun. These errors are likely to occur when the initial position in a clause is taken by another word class, most frequently by an adverb:

Ibland **kommer** <ins>mormor</ins>. →
Ibland <ins>mormor</ins> **kommer**.*
Eng: Grandma comes sometimes.

Other subtypes involve pre-modifiers, e.g. determiners (DT), possessives (PS), adjectives (JJ):

(1) VB-DT-NN →DT-NN-VB;
(2) VB-PS-NN →PS-NN-VB, and
(3) VB-JJ-NN →JJ-NN-VB.

[2]spraakbanken.gu.se/sparv

[3]We use asterisk (*) to mark the incorrect pattern/example sentence

[4]In the examples, the first sentence is correct and the second one contains one error. The verbs are in bold, whereas the parts of speech that are being treated are underlined.

[5]All examples, unless stated otherwise, belong to the SweLL and DaLAJ datasets.

Corrupted sentence	Seed sentence	Error index corrupted	Error index seed	Confusion pairs	Error label	Split
Det ungefär finns 5 000 språk i världen .	Det finns ungefär 5 000 språk i världen .	['s1', 's2']	['t2', 't1']	['ungefär', 'finns', '-->', 'finns', 'ungefär']	S-FinV	Train
Far : Men nu jag är jättehungrig !	Far : Men nu är jag jättehungrig !	['s4', 's5']	['t5', 't4']	['jag', 'är', '-->', 'är', 'jag']	S-FinV	Train
Det snö är i luften .	Det är snö i luften .	['s1', 's2']	['t2', 't1']	['snö', 'är', '-->', 'är', 'snö']	S-FinV	Train

Figure 2: Corrupted data, selected columns.

The final pattern is based on **proper names**, exhibiting similar behaviour to noun-based error patterns. Due to pseudonymization, pseudonyms are used instead of the originally used proper names (as in the example below).

Han visste inte om Brad Pitt **vann** priset. →
Han visste inte om **vann** Brad Pitt priset.*
Eng: He didn't know if Brad Pitt won the prize.

The typical patterns are: (1) PM-VB →VB-PM and (2) PM-PM-VB →VB-PM-PM.

4.2 Corruption method

Using the identified error patterns, we reverse them to a set of rules for each error subtype (pronouns, adverbs, nouns and proper names) for shifting the position of words in COCTAILL sentences. We first extract POS tags from the correct sentences and store them. In the process, sentences shorter than two tokens and those not containing verbs are discarded. All of them share an initial filter to avoid changing the position of words before a colon, in case a verb is present, like in the example below. Capitalization is toggled if the initial capitalized word is involved in the corruption.
Stryka subjektet: Jag **är** mycket trött. →
Stryka subjektet: **Är** jag mycket trött.*
Eng: Cross out the subject: I am very tired.

We strictly keep to the rule of having one error per sentence. However, sentences may appear more than once in the synthetic dataset, as they can be corrupted several times, for example, if sentences contain more than one verb or fit into several error sub-patterns. In the end, a final scramble is performed to the order of the sentences before they are stored in a .csv file, with suggestions for data splits (80%-10%-10%) and confusion pairs (Figure 2).

5 Results

A total of 31,788 sentences were corrupted from the 20,307 usable sentences available. The distribution of error sub-types is shown in Table 1:

Error subtype	Produced errors
Pronoun-Verb	13,049
Adverb-Verb	9,922
Noun-Verb	8,041
Proper Name-Verb	776

Table 1: Error count of the final corrupted data.

Similarly to the frequency distribution in student essays, pronoun-dependent verb order errors are the most frequent ones in the corrupted data, with 41.05% of synthetic errors being of this type. The second most productive rules are the ones involving adverbs, with 31,21% of errors, followed by nouns at 25,3%. Finally, as expected, the corruption pipeline produced a considerably lesser quantity of errors involving proper names at 2,44%. The distribution in the corrupted data, thus, reflects the observed tendency in the authentic data.

To assess the quality of the corruption method, we carried out a small-scale evaluation. Two people have independently checked 100 randomly selected corrupted sentences in terms of how similar they are to hypothetical learner-made errors (i.e. to make sure they are high quality). Following Bryant et al. (2017), we used a three level scale of assessment: *Good*, *Acceptable* and *Bad*. For *Acceptable* and *Bad*, a reason could be indicated for further analysis.

The evaluation shows that 76% (67%) of sentences are *Good*, 14% (25%) are *Acceptable* and 10% (8%) are *Bad*. The numbers in brackets come from the second annotator. Some observed problems had to do with more complex phrase shifts that were missed. In others, the problem comes from the source data, incl. unfinished sentences with an uncertain sentence type (affirmative vs interrogative), which then sounds correct even if the verb and noun change places. It should be noted that the main purpose of this evaluation was to see whether humans think that the synthetic data will be useful for training algorithms, and the result where on average 90% sentences are either *Good* or *Acceptable* is very encouraging. It has been earlier claimed that even unrealistic errors are use-

Data type	Model type	Lexical	Morphological	Orthographic	Punctuation	Syntactical
Original learner data	BERT Bi-LSTM	0.54894179	0.60539215	0.57565789	0.46072507	0.64680232
Original learner data + 500 FakeDaLAJ	BERT Bi-LSTM	**0.60634328**	**0.63834422**	**0.61026936**	**0.56034482**	0.69732297
Original learner data + 1500 FakeDaLAJ	BERT Bi-LSTM	0.51798561	0.58823529	0.50641940	0.37499999	**0.71934945**

Table 2: F0.5 score results from some selected models on error classification task.

ful for pre-training GEC models (e.g. Flachs et al., 2021; Grundkiewicz et al., 2019). Given our results, therefore, we consider the produced dataset appropriate for the task.

We have run the first experiments exploring *effects of pseudo-data on the model performance* for the task of error detection and classification, where classification is limited to the top error categories (**O**rthographic, **L**exical, **M**orphological, **P**unctuation, **S**yntactical). Detailed description of that experiment is the topic of another publication, however, we can shortly name here that we have observed a tangible improvement of the classification results when 500 FakeDaLAJ sentences of S-FinV nature were added to the training data. When more sentences were added, the models seemed to learn to classify syntactical errors disadvantaging other error types. A sample of the results obtained, measured with the F0.5 score, are shown in Table 2.

6 Conclusions and future work

This paper introduces a process for generation of synthetic error datasets with corresponding error labels based on linguistic analysis of real-life learner errors in the context of limited error-annotated learner data. This process could be replicated for other error tags, or extended and adapted to other low-resource languages. Manually studying and designing corruption rules is time-consuming and can be inaccurate due to human error and language biases. Therefore, an alternative to optimize time and avoid human mistakes could be to rely on guided models as suggested by Stahlberg and Kumar (2021) or Sennrich et al. (2016). However, we have to adhere to rule-based approaches due to the lack of sufficient amount of gold data. Yet, we foresee considerable benefits of generating realistic errors.

The resulting fakeDaLAJ (S-FinV) dataset is released for public use.[6] Currently, we are testing this dataset in a task for error detection and classification. In the near future, we will also release a set of cleaned 100 DaLAJ sentences per each error tag in the SweLL-gold data, so that the community of interested researchers and developers can use them for generation of synthetic datasets for other error types.

[6] https://github.com/juditcasademont/Generation-of-synthetic-error-data-LTR-project

References

Lars Borin, Markus Forsberg, Martin Hammarstedt, Dan Rosén, Roland Schäfer, and Anne Schumacher. 2016. Sparv: Språkbanken's corpus annotation pipeline infrastructure. In *Proceedings of Swedish Language Technology Conference (SLTC)*. Umeå University.

Christopher Bryant, Mariano Felice, and Edward Briscoe. 2017. Automatic annotation and evaluation of error types for grammatical error correction. Association for Computational Linguistics.

Yo Joong Choe, Jiyeon Ham, Kyubyong Park, and Yeoil Yoon. 2019. A neural grammatical error correction system built on better pre-training and sequential transfer learning. *arXiv preprint arXiv:1907.01256*.

Simon Flachs, Felix Stahlberg, and Shankar Kumar. 2021. Data strategies for low-resource grammatical error correction. In *Proceedings of the 16th Workshop on Innovative Use of NLP for Building Educational Applications*, pages 117–122.

Roman Grundkiewicz, Marcin Junczys-Dowmunt, and Kenneth Heafield. 2019. Neural grammatical error correction systems with unsupervised pre-training on synthetic data. In *Proceedings of the Fourteenth Workshop on Innovative Use of NLP for Building Educational Applications*, pages 252–263.

Lisa Rudebeck and Gunlög Sundberg. 2021. SweLL correcrion annotation guidelines. Technical report, GU-ISS Research report series, Department of Swedish, University of Gothenburg. http://hdl.handle.net/2077/69434.

Rico Sennrich, Barry Haddow, and Alexandra Birch. 2016. Improving neural machine translation models with monolingual data. *Proceedings of the 54th Annual Meeting of the Association for Computational Linguistics (Volume 1: Long Papers), pages 86–96.*

Felix Stahlberg and Shankar Kumar. 2021. Synthetic data generation for grammatical error correction with tagged corruption models. *CoRR*, abs/2105.13318.

Yujin Takahashi, Satoru Katsumata, and Mamoru Komachi. 2020. Grammatical error correction using pseudo learner corpus considering learner's error tendency. In *Proceedings of the 58th Annual Meeting of the Association for Computational Linguistics: Student Research Workshop*, pages 27–32.

Elena Volodina, Lena Granstedt, Arild Matsson, Beáta Megyesi, Ildikó Pilán, Julia Prentice, Dan Rosén, Lisa Rudebeck, Carl-Johan Schenström, Gunlög Sundberg, and Mats Wirén. 2019. The SweLL Language Learner Corpus: From Design to Annotation. *Northern European Journal of Language Technology.*

Elena Volodina, Yousuf Ali Mohammed, and Julia Klezl. 2021. DaLAJ - a dataset for linguistic acceptability judgments for Swedish: Format, baseline, sharing. *Proceedings of the 10th Workshop on Natural Language Processing for Computer Assisted Language Learning (NLP4CALL 2021). Linköping Electronic Conference Proceedings 177:3, s. 28-37.*

Elena Volodina, Ildikó Pilán, Stian Rødven Eide, and Hannes Heidarsson. 2014. You get what you annotate: a pedagogically annotated corpus of coursebooks for Swedish as a Second Language. *Proceedings of the third workshop on NLP for computer-assisted language learning.*

A Dependency Treebank of Spoken Second Language English

Kristopher Kyle, Masaki Eguchi, Aaron Miller and Theodore Sither
Learner Corpus Research and Applied Data Science Lab
https://lcr-ads-lab.github.io/LCR-ADS-Home/
Linguistics Department, University of Oregon
https://linguistics.uoregon.edu/

Abstract

In this paper, we introduce a dependency treebank of spoken second language (L2) English that is annotated with part of speech (Penn POS) tags and syntactic dependencies (Universal Dependencies). We then evaluate the degree to which the use of this treebank as training data affects POS and UD annotation accuracy for L1 web texts, L2 written texts, and L2 spoken texts as compared to models trained on L1 texts only.

1 Introduction

In the field of applied linguistics, natural language processing tools such as part of speech (POS) taggers and syntactic parsers have been and continue to be used to investigate characteristics of second language (L2) use at scale (e.g., Biber et al., 2014; Kyle & Crossley, 2017; Lu, 2010; Paquot, 2018). Although taggers and parsers are increasingly accurate (achieving F1 scores of around .98 for POS taggers and .95 for dependency annotation) when evaluated on in-domain texts (i.e., texts with similar linguistic characteristics as the training data), accuracy can drop precipitously for out of domain texts (e.g., McClosky et al., 2006). A pressing issue, then, is the availability of appropriate annotated corpora to test and train tagging and parsing models on the types of data applied linguists often use (Kyle, 2021; Meurers & Dickinson, 2017). Although a treebank of written second language (L2) English is available (Berzak et al., 2016), to our knowledge no treebanks of spoken L2 speech are publicly and freely available. In this paper, we report on the development of an annotated corpus of spoken L2 English and evaluate the accuracy of a POS tagger and dependency parser when trained on L1 texts and a combination of L1 and L2 texts.

2 Applied linguistics research and NLP

The use of NLP tools such as taggers and parsers to examine characteristics of language use has a long history in the field of applied linguistics. Early studies (e.g., Biber, 1988) focused on the analysis of lexical and lexicogrammatical variation across registers (e.g., different spoken and written language use domains). As the subfield of learner corpus research has grown, taggers and parsers have also been used to investigate how second language learners' linguistic patterns change over time (e.g., Crossley & McNamara, 2014; Kyle et al., 2021) and/or differ across proficiency levels (e.g., Biber et al., 2014; Grant & Ginther, 2000; Kyle et al., 2018; Paquot, 2018).

2.1 Application of taggers and parsers in L2 research

POS taggers and syntactic parsers have been used in L2 research for a variety of purposes, ranging from relatively simple homograph disambiguation (e.g., Jarvis & Hashimoto, 2021) to the analysis of complex linguistic phenomena such as verb argument constructions (e.g., Kyle and Crossley, 2017). An abbreviated overview of this research is outlined below.

Grammatical error correction: A number of studies have used (and developed) tagging and parsing systems for identifying and correcting grammatical errors in L2 texts (e.g., Choshen & Abend, 2010; Nagata & Sakaguchi, 2016; Sakaguchi et al., 2017.)

Homograph disambiguation: One use of POS taggers in L2 research is homograph disambiguation. Homograph disambiguation can be particularly important in the measurement of lexical diversity, where the variety of words used by L2 learners can be an indicator of proficiency (e.g., Jarvis & Hashimoto, 2021; McCarthy & Jarvis, 2010).

Proceedings of the 17th Workshop on Innovative Use of NLP for Building Educational Applications (BEA 2022), pages 39 - 45
July 15, 2022

Lexical bigrams: The characteristics of lexical combinations that are used in L2 productions can be an important predictor of development and/or proficiency level. Research has shown that more proficient L2 writers and speakers tend to use more frequent and more strongly associated lexical bigrams than less proficient L2 users (e.g., Granger & Bestgen, 2014; Garner et al., 2019; Kyle et al. 2018). For more precise insights into linguistic development, some studies have constrained the lexical combinations that are used (e.g., adjective + noun or noun + noun combinations).

Even more recently, researchers have begun to use dependency parses to analyze lexical items in particular grammatical relationships (e.g., verb + object; Kyle & Eguchi, 2021; Paquot, 2018, 2019; Rubin, 2021).

Lexicogrammatical features: A number of studies have investigated the relationship between L2 proficiency and the use of lexicogrammatical features that are common in academic writing such as various types of noun phrase elaboration (e.g., Biber et al., 2014; Grant & Ginther, 2000; Picoral et al., 2021). A related line of research has explored the relationship between characteristics of verb argument construction use and L2 writing proficiency (e.g., Kyle & Crossley, 2017; Kyle et al., 2021).

Syntactic complexity: A particularly common use of NLP tools in second language research is the calculation of classic syntactic complexity indices such as mean length of clause and dependent clauses per clause (e.g., Lu, 2010, 2011) or more fine-grained indices such as the number of dependents per nominal (e.g., Kyle & Crossley, 2018; Díez-Bedmar & Pérez-Paredes, 2020). NLP tools have allowed research to examine relationships between syntactic complexity and language proficiency and/or development at a scale that would be infeasible for most researchers if manual analyses were used.

2.2 Evaluations of system performance on L2 data

The literature indicates that L2 researchers are fully aware of potential issues with tagger and parser performance (e.g., Meurers & Dickinson, 2017). However, most accuracy analyses have been small in scale and have not resulted in publicly available treebanks that can be used to improve future models (c.f., Berzak et al., 2016). Lu (2010), for example, which introduced the second language syntactic complexity analyzer (L2SCA), evaluated the accuracy of the tool using a 30-essay subset of texts used in a validation study. Polio and Yoon (2018) independently evaluated the accuracy of L2SCA using a different sample of texts. Kyle et al. (2021) evaluated the accuracy of verb argument construction identification using a sample of 100 sentences from a corpus of L2 essays. Similar procedures have been used in a number of other studies (e.g., Díez-Bedmar & Pérez-Paredes, 2020; Paquot, 2019; Rubin, 2021). While small-scale accuracy analyses are important for establishing the effectiveness of particular linguistic analysis tools for a particular data set, these datasets are rarely made publicly available and do not necessarily follow the annotation guidelines or formatting conventions of well-known treebanks. One exception to this pattern is the Treebank of Learner English (Berzak et al., 2016) which includes written L2 English sentences annotated for Penn POS tags and Universal Dependencies. While this is an important resource, no treebanks of spoken L2 English are currently available.

2.3 Contributions of this study

In this study, we introduce a freely and publicly available treebank of Spoken L2 English that includes gold standard annotations for Penn POS tags and Universal Dependencies. We then evaluate the performance of tagger and parser models on both L1 and L2 data when the training set includes only L1 data and when the training set includes both L1 and L2 data.

3 Method

3.1 Dependency Treebank of Spoken L2 English (SL2E)

The Dependency Treebank of Spoken L2 English (SL2E) consists of a random sample of sentences from the National Institute of Information and Communications Technology Japanese Learner English (NICT JLE) corpus (Izumi et al., 2004). NICT JLE includes transcripts of oral proficiency interviews (OPI). Prior to sampling, all interviewer language was removed, leaving only utterances produced by second language speakers. The corpus includes a range of L2 English proficiency levels (mid-beginner to lower advanced). In total, the annotated portion of the corpus includes 7,412 sentences (70,016 tokens) annotated for Penn POS tags (Santorini et al., 1990), of which 2,320 sentences (21,312 tokens) are also annotated for Universal Dependencies (Nivre et al, 2020).

POS Annotation: The annotation was conducted in multiple stages. Undergraduate Linguistics majors who had taken upper-level courses related to linguistic structure were recruited to work on the project. POS annotation training sessions were conducted with annotators, followed by the annotation of sample sentences. Feedback was provided based on performance on the sample sentences. After training, sentences were annotated independently by at least two annotators using the browser-based application WebAnno (Eckart de Castilho et al., 2016). Any disagreements between annotators were checked by a third annotator. In rare cases where the third annotator disagreed with both of the first annotators, adjudication between annotators was conducted. During the annotation period, annotators had access to the original Penn POS tagging guidelines, the Berzak et al. (2016) tagging guidelines, and gold standard corpora (which were accessed using AntConc; Anthony, 2019). We also had weekly meetings to discuss difficult cases, a Discord server to report and discuss difficult cases asynchronously, and an extended tagging guidelines manual that was created based on these discussions. Initial annotation agreement for POS tags (prior to third ratings and adjudication) was 95.1%.

Dependency Annotation: After sentences were annotated for POS tags, annotators were trained for dependency annotation using procedure outlined above. Annotators had access to the Universal dependencies guidelines (Version 2; Nivre, 2020), gold standard corpora (accessed via Tündra; Martens, 2013), weekly meetings, a Discord server, and updated guidelines. After POS and dependency annotation was complete, POS tags and dependency annotations were checked again for consistency, resulting in some minor corrections. Initial annotation agreement (prior to third ratings and adjudication) was 86.5% (labeled attachment agreement).

3.2 Other corpora used

In this study, we decided to use data that was publicly and freely available. Accordingly, we used selected annotated corpora from the UD project, each of which are outlined briefly below.

Treebank of Learner English (TLE): TLE (Berzak et al., 2016) consists of data from the CLC FCE Dataset (Yannakoudakis et al., 2011), which includes writing samples from the Cambridge ESOL First Certificate in English (FCE) exam. The FCE includes written responses across 5 registers (letter, report, article, composition, and short story) that prototypically range from 200-400 words. The TLE sample includes sentences from upper-intermediate learners of English across 10 first language (L1) backgrounds. TLE includes 97,681 tokens annotated for POS tags and universal dependencies.

Data Splits Used			
Data	**Train**	**Dev**	**Test**
EWT	204,579	25,149	25,097
GUM	103,400	16,270	16,216
PUD	21,176	n/a	n/a
UDEP	1,705	n/a	n/a
TLE	78,541	9,549	9,591
SL2E POS	55,873	6,815	7,328
SL2E UD	16,879	2,167	2,266
Training Data Summary			
Data	**L1**	**L1+L2**	**L1+L2e**
POS	432,826	567,240	435,624
UD	432,826	528,246	434,951

Table 1: Number of tokens in each split

English Web Treebank (EWT): The Universal Dependency (UD) version (Silveira, et al., 2014) of the EWT (Bies, et al., 2012) consists of annotated data divided roughly evenly across five web genres (weblogs, newsgroups, emails, reviews, and Yahoo! answers). The UD version includes 254,825 tokens annotated for Penn POS tags and Universal dependencies.

Georgetown University Multilayer Treebank (GUM): GUM (Zeldes, 2017) consists of annotated data from various online sources, including interviews, news stories, and forum discussions (among many others). In this study, we use the versions of GUM included in the UD 2.9, which also includes sentences from Reddit (Behzad & Zeldes, 2020). In total, the version of GUM used in this study includes 135,886 tokens annotated for POS tags and universal dependencies.

Parallel Universal Dependencies Treebank (PUD): PUD (Zeman et al., 2017) includes sentences from the news section of Wikipedia and comprises 21,312 tokens annotated for POS tags and universal dependencies. In this project, PUD was used as training data only.

UD-English Pronouns (UDEP): UDEP (Monarch, 2021) includes sentences designed to mitigate biases (e.g., gender biases) that exist in extant treebanks by including sentences with pronouns that are rare in other treebanks (e.g., *hers*). UDEP includes 1,705 tokens. In this project, UDEP is used as training data only.

3.3 Splits used

In this study, we used 80/10/10 splits for the Spoken L2 Treebank, and the extant splits in all treebanks available in UD release 2.9. Because more data was annotated for POS tags than for dependency relations, we created training/dev/test sets separately for POS annotation and dependency annotation. For each, we tested three versions of training data. The first (L1) included only L1 data (EWT, GUM, PUD, and UDEP). The second (L1+L2) included the L1 data plus the L2 data (TLE + SL2E). Given the relatively small datasets (and the positive relationship between the amount of training data and model accuracy), we also included a third version of the training data (L1+L2e) in which the number of tokens in the L1+L2 training data was made roughly equal to that of the L1 training data by excluding a random sample of L1 sentences. See Table 1 for the splits used in POS annotation and dependency annotation.

3.4 NLP pipeline

For this study, we used Spacy version 3.2 (Honnibal et al., 2020) to train transformer-based POS and dependency annotation models (L1, L1+L2, and L1+L2e models for each task). Spacy is freely available, easy to use, and has achieved state-of-the-art performance for both POS and dependency annotation (Honnibal et al., 2020). The models used pre-trained weights from RoBERTa-base (Liu, 2019). The POS and dependency layers listen to the transformer embedding, and they were optimized using Adam optimizer. The same hyperparameter settings were used for training all models. Training scripts, models generated during training, and evaluation scripts are available at (https://github.com/LCR-ADS-Lab/l2-nlp-training-spacy). POS annotation accuracy was measured using sentences with gold standard splits and tokenization. Dependency annotation accuracy was measured using gold standard splits and tokenization, and model-based POS tags (using the best-performing POS model).

POS Models			
Data	**L1**	**L1+L2**	**L1+L2e**
EWT	0.958	0.965	0.964
GUM	0.973	0.975	0.977
SL2E	0.936	0.970	0.966
TLE	0.953	0.969	0.966
Dependency Models			
Data	**L1**	**L1+L2**	**L1+L2e**
EWT	0.884	0.895	0.895
GUM	0.884	0.897	0.895
SL2E	0.876	0.935	0.938
TLE	0.886	0.920	0.918

Table 2: F1 scores for lexical tags

4 Results

4.1 POS annotation results

Despite the relatively small amount of training data used, all three models resulted in relatively high tagging accuracy for the L1 corpora (EWT and GUM), ranging from F1 scores of 0.958 to 0.977 on the test set (see Table 2). Somewhat surprisingly, the highest F1 scores for the L1 corpora were achieved when L2 data was added during the training (even when the number of tokens in the training data was held constant in L1+L2e), and these gains were modest (see Table 2). The lowest tagging accuracy was observed when the L1-trained model was applied to the L2 spoken test set (F1 = 0.936). However, when L2 data was included in the training set, the F1 scores for the L2 spoken test set (F1 = 0.970) were similar to those for L1 corpora.

4.2 Dependency annotation results

Labeled attachment scores (LAS) for test set data ranged from F1 scores of 0.876 (Spoken L2 data, L1 model) to F1 scores of 0.938 (Spoken L2 data, L1+L2e model). Accuracy for all models increased with the inclusion of L2 data in the training set (even when the total amount of training data was held constant). However, the most dramatic increases were for both written and spoken L2 data.

5 Discussion and conclusion

5.1 Summary of findings

The results of this study suggest that substantial improvements in POS tagging and dependency parsing performance on L2 texts can be made through the use of training sets that include L2 data, even when the total amount of training data is held constant. Following previous research (e.g., Berzak et al., 2016), these improvements were observed for written L2 data. However, the improvements were particularly marked for the spoken L2 data introduced in this study. It should also be clearly noted that the highest dependency annotation accuracy was observed with L2 spoken data (followed by L2 written data).

5.2 Limitations and future directions

While this study demonstrated accuracy gains in L2 tagging and parsing through the use of L2 training data, there are still a few limitations that should be addressed in future studies. First, although this study added to the amount of annotated data available for training, the total amount of publicly available gold standard data annotated for universal dependencies remains rather small. Future research should focus on providing more gold standard data across a variety of English domains (including L2 domains). Second, in this study we did not fully account for strength and weaknesses of each model with regard to particular lexical items or annotations. While overall F1 scores are a helpful gauge, many L2 researchers are interested in particular grammatical features (e.g., main verb + direct object pairs), and more precise accuracy figures should be considered in future research.

5.3 Conclusion

This study introduced a new gold standard treebank of spoken L2 English annotated with Penn part of speech tags and universal dependencies. Furthermore, this study has demonstrated that the addition of a relatively small amount of in-domain data can substantively improve tagging and parsing accuracy in L2 texts. The SL2E Treebank is publicly available for non-commercial purposes (https://github.com/LCR-ADS-Lab/SL2E-Dependency-Treebank).

Acknowledgments

This project was supported by a *Language Learning* Early Career Research Grant.

References

Anthony, L. (2019). *AntConc* (3.5.8) [Computer software]. Waseda University.

Behzad, S., & Zeldes, A. (2020). A cross-genre ensemble approach to robust Reddit part of speech tagging. *ArXiv Preprint ArXiv:2004.14312*.

Berzak, Y., Kenney, J., Spadine, C., Wang, J. X., Lam, L., Mori, K. S., Garza, S., & Katz, B. (2016). Universal dependencies for learner English. *Proceedings of the 54th Annual Meeting of the Association for Computational Linguistics*, 737–746.

Biber, D. (1988). *Variation across speech and writing*. Cambridge University Press.

Biber, D., Gray, B., & Staples, S. (2014). Predicting Patterns of Grammatical Complexity Across Language Exam Task Types and Proficiency Levels. *Applied Linguistics*, *37*(5), 639–668. https://doi.org/10.1093/applin/amu059

Bies, A., Mott, J., Warner, C., & Kulick, S. (2012). English web treebank. *Linguistic Data Consortium, Philadelphia, PA*.

Choshen, L. & Abend O. (2018). Reference-less Measure of Faithfulness for Grammatical Error Correction. In *Proceedings of the 2018 Conference of the North American Chapter of the Association for Computational Linguistics: Human Language Technologies, Volume 2 (Short Papers)*, pages 124–129, New Orleans, Louisiana. Association for Computational Linguistics.

Crossley, S. A., & McNamara, D. S. (2014). Does writing development equal writing quality? A computational investigation of syntactic complexity in L2 learners. *Journal of Second Language Writing*, *26*, 66–79. https://doi.org/10.1016/j.jslw.2014.09.006

Díez-Bedmar, M. B., & Pérez-Paredes, P. (2020). Noun phrase complexity in young Spanish EFL learners' writing: Complementing syntactic complexity indices with corpus-driven analyses. *International Journal of Corpus Linguistics*, *25*(1), 4–35.

Eckart de Castilho, R., Mújdricza-Maydt, É., Yimam, S. M., Hartmann, S., Gurevych, I., Frank, A., & Biemann, C. (2016). A Web-based Tool for the Integrated Annotation of Semantic and Syntactic Structures. *Proceedings of the Workshop on Language Technology Resources and Tools for Digital Humanities (LT4DH)*, 76–84. https://www.aclweb.org/anthology/W16-4011

Garner, J., Crossley, S., & Kyle, K. (2019). N-gram measures and L2 writing proficiency. *System*, *80*, 176–187. https://doi.org/10.1016/j.system.2018.12.001

Granger, S., & Bestgen, Y. (2014). The use of collocations by intermediate vs. Advanced non-native writers: A bigram-based study. *International*

Review of Applied Linguistics in Language Teaching, *52*(3), 229–252.

Grant, L., & Ginther, A. (2000). Using computer-tagged linguistic features to describe L2 writing differences. *Journal of Second Language Writing*, *9*(2), 123–145.

Honnibal, M., Montani, I., Van Landeghem, S., & Boyd, A. (2020). *spaCy: Industrial-strength Natural Language Processing in Python* [Python]. https://doi.org/10.5281/zenodo.1212303 (Original work published 2014)

Izumi, E., Uchimoto, K., & Isahara, H. (2004). The NICT JLE Corpus: Exploiting the language learners' speech database for research and education. *International Journal of The Computer, the Internet and Management*, *12*(2), 119–125.

Jarvis, S., & Hashimoto, B. J. (2021). How operationalizations of word types affect measures of lexical diversity. *International Journal of Learner Corpus Research*, *7*(1), 163–194.

Kyle, K. (2021). Natural language processing for learner corpus research. *International Journal of Learner Corpus Research*, *7*(1), 1–16.

Kyle, K., & Crossley, S. A. (2017). Assessing syntactic sophistication in L2 writing: A usage-based approach. *Language Testing*, *34*(4), 513–535.

Kyle, K., & Crossley, S. A. (2018). Measuring Syntactic Complexity in L2 Writing Using Fine-Grained Clausal and Phrasal Indices. *The Modern Language Journal*, *102*(2), 333–349. https://doi.org/10.1111/modl.12468

Kyle, K., Crossley, S. A., & Berger, C. M. (2018). The tool for the automatic analysis of lexical sophistication (TAALES): Version 2.0. *Behavior Research Methods*, *50*(3), 1030–1046. https://doi.org/10.3758/s13428-017-0924-4

Kyle, K., Crossley, S., & Verspoor, M. (2021). Measuring longitudinal writing development using indices of syntactic complexity and sophistication. *Studies in Second Language Acquisition*, *43*(4), 781–812.

Kyle, K., & Eguchi, M. (2021). Automatically assessing lexical sophistication using word, bigram, and dependency indices. In *Perspectives on the L2 Phrasicon: The View from Learner Corpora* (pp. 126–151). Multilingual Matters.

Liu, Y., Ott, M., Goyal, N., Du, J., Joshi, M., Chen, D., Levy, O., Lewis, M., Zettlemoyer, L., & Stoyanov, V. (2019). *RoBERTa: A Robustly Optimized BERT Pretraining Approach* (arXiv:1907.11692). arXiv. http://arxiv.org/abs/1907.11692

Lu, X. (2010). Automatic analysis of syntactic complexity in second language writing. *International Journal of Corpus Linguistics*, *15*(4), 474–496. https://doi.org/10.1075/ijcl.15.4.02lu

Lu, X. (2011). A corpus-based evaluation of syntactic complexity measures as indices of college-level ESL writers' language development. *TESOL Quarterly*, *45*(1), 36–62.

Martens, S. (2013). *TüNDRA: A web application for treebank search and visualization*. *133*.

McCarthy, P. M., & Jarvis, S. (2010). MTLD, vocd-D, and HD-D: A validation study of sophisticated approaches to lexical diversity assessment. *Behavior Research Methods*, *42*(2), 381–392. https://doi.org/10.3758/BRM.42.2.381

McClosky, D., Charniak, E., & Johnson, M. (2006). *Reranking and self-training for parser adaptation*. 337–344.

Meurers, D., & Dickinson, M. (2017). Evidence and interpretation in language learning research: Opportunities for collaboration with computational linguistics. *Language Learning*, *67*(S1), 66–95.

Monarch, R. M. (2021). *Human-in-the-Loop Machine Learning: Active learning and annotation for human-centered AI*. Simon and Schuster.

Nagata, R. & Sakaguchi, K. (2016). Phrase Structure Annotation and Parsing for Learner English. In *Proceedings of the 54th Annual Meeting of the Association for Computational Linguistics (Volume 1: Long Papers)*, pages 1837–1847, Berlin, Germany. Association for Computational Linguistics.

Nivre, J., Marneffe, M.-C. de, Ginter, F., Hajic, J., Manning, C. D., Pyysalo, S., Schuster, S., Tyers, F., & Zeman, D. (2020). *Universal Dependencies v2: An Evergrowing Multilingual Treebank Collection*. 4034–4043. https://aclanthology.org/2020.lrec-1.497

Paquot, M. (2018). Phraseological Competence: A Missing Component in University Entrance Language Tests? Insights From a Study of EFL Learners' Use of Statistical Collocations. *Language Assessment Quarterly*, *15*(1), 29–43.

Paquot, M. (2019). The phraseological dimension in interlanguage complexity research. *Second Language Research*, *35*(1), 121–145.

Polio, C., & Yoon, H. (2018). The reliability and validity of automated tools for examining variation in syntactic complexity across genres. *International Journal of Applied Linguistics*, *28*(1), 165–188.

Rubin, R. (2021). Assessing the impact of automatic dependency annotation on the measurement of phraseological complexity in L2 Dutch. *International Journal of Learner Corpus Research*, *7*(1), 131–162.

Sakaguchi, K., Post, M., and Van Durme, B. (2017). Error-repair Dependency Parsing for Ungrammatical Texts. In *Proceedings of the 55th Annual Meeting of the Association for Computational Linguistics (Volume 2: Short Papers)*, pages 189–195, Vancouver, Canada. Association for Computational Linguistics.

Santorini, B. (1990). Part-of-speech tagging guidelines for the Penn Treebank project (3rd revision, 2nd printing). *Ms., Department of Linguistics, UPenn. Philadelphia, PA.*

Silveira, N., Dozat, T., De Marneffe, M.-C., Bowman, S., Connor, M., Bauer, J., & Manning, C. (2014). A Gold Standard Dependency Corpus for English. *Proceedings of the Ninth International Conference on Language Resources and Evaluation (LREC'14)*, 2897–2904.

Yannakoudakis, H., Briscoe, T., & Medlock, B. (2011). *A new dataset and method for automatically grading ESOL texts*. 180–189.

Zeldes, A. (2017). The GUM corpus: Creating multilayer resources in the classroom. *Language Resources and Evaluation*, *51*(3), 581–612.

Zeman, D., Popel, M., Straka, M., Hajic, J., Nivre, J., Ginter, F., Luotolahti, J., Pyysalo, S., Petrov, S., & Potthast, M. (2017). *CoNLL 2017 shared task: Multilingual parsing from raw text to universal dependencies*. 1–19.

Starting from "Zero": An Incremental Zero-shot Learning Approach for Assessing Peer Feedback Comments

Qinjin Jia[1], **Yupeng Cao**[2], and **Edward F. Gehringer**[1]

[1]Department of Computer Science, North Carolina State University, Raleigh, NC, USA
{qjia3,efg}@ncsu.edu
[2]Department of Electrical & Computer Eng., Stevens Institute of Tech., Hoboken, NJ, USA
{ycao33}@stevens.edu

Abstract

Peer assessment is an effective and efficient pedagogical strategy for delivering feedback to learners. Asking students to provide quality feedback, which contains suggestions and mentions problems, can promote metacognition by reviewers and better assist reviewees in revising their work. Thus, various supervised machine learning algorithms have been proposed to detect quality feedback. However, all these powerful algorithms have the same Achilles' heel: the reliance on sufficient historical data. In other words, collecting adequate peer feedback for training a supervised algorithm can take several semesters before the model can be deployed to a new class. In this paper, we present a new paradigm, called incremental zero-shot learning (IZSL), to tackle the problem of lacking sufficient historical data. Our results show that the method can achieve acceptable "cold-start" performance without needing any domain data, and it outperforms BERT when trained on the same data collected incrementally.

1 Introduction

Peer assessment is a process whereby students assess other students' assignments by writing review comments against a set of assessment criteria provided by the instructor. This pedagogical strategy has been extensively applied across various academic fields and has demonstrated its effectiveness over the past decades (Double et al., 2020). Furthermore, peer assessment serves as a crucial tool for delivering necessary feedback in massive open online courses (MOOCs), as this assessment strategy allows MOOCs to scale up the feedback process while minimizing ongoing support costs.

Nevertheless, the benefits of peer assessment can only be achieved with quality peer feedback (Ashton and Davies, 2015; Van Zundert et al., 2010). Course staff can manually review the credibility of each submitted feedback, but this is very inefficient. Hence, there has been a surge of interest in automating the assessment of feedback quality by machine-learning algorithms. These algorithms typically assess quality by determining whether the feedback comprises certain features (e.g., contains "suggestion" and "problem" statements) (Nelson and Schunn, 2009). If those characteristics are not present in the submitted reviews, the peer-assessment system could suggest that the reviewer revise the feedback to add the missing features.

Although these machine-learning algorithms for assessing feedback quality are very effective, they all have the same Achilles' heel: dependence on enough domain-specific peer-feedback data. That is, for each new discipline, it takes several school terms to collect sufficient data before the model can be applied. Thus, a desideratum of peer-assessment platforms is an effective quality-assessment model that does not require domain-specific historical data in *"cold-start"* condition (i.e., no domain data is available for training). Additionally, this model should be capable of using incrementally collected data to progressively improve its performance.

In this paper, we present an approach, named *Incremental Zero-shot Learning* (IZSL), for addressing lack of historical data in automated feedback-quality evaluation. The core idea of the method is to treat the problem of detecting quality feedback as a natural language inference (NLI) task and utilize the pre-trained BART-based NLI model (Yin et al., 2019) to assess feedback quality. Our results show that IZSL can achieve acceptable performance in the "cold-start" condition on different datasets, and IZSL can substantially outperform BERT (Devlin et al., 2018) after training on the same incrementally collected data.

The rest of the paper is organized as follows: Section 2 presents related work. Section 3 describes datasets. Section 4 elaborates on our IZSL method for assessing feedback quality. Section 5 presents experimental results. Section 6 concludes the paper and provides some discussion about future work.

Proceedings of the 17th Workshop on Innovative Use of NLP for Building Educational Applications (BEA 2022), pages 46 - 50
July 15, 2022

Peer-Feedback Comments	Sugg.	Prob.
No model tests have been added. Basic controller tests generated by scaffold and devise are available.	0	1
The design is written great. It will be better to explain more about the pattern used.	1	0
A little short. Make the conclusion more powerful and mention how you would address it as a teacher.	1	1

Table 1: Sample data. The first two samples are from *CS-Peer-Feedback*. The last sample is from *Ed-Peer-Feedback*. "Sugg." and "Prob." indicate whether the comment provides suggestions and mentions problems, respectively.

2 Related Work

2.1 Automated Peer-Feedback Assessment

Automated peer-feedback assessment is defined as a task of automatically analyzing peer-feedback comments written by students and highlighting low-quality comments that need to be revised. The goal of the task is to improve the overall quality of peer feedback and consequently improve students' learning. As the first step towards building an effective automated peer-feedback assessment system, Cho (2008) pioneered various machine-learning methods to classify peer-feedback units.

Subsequent work typically focused on designing more sophisticated features or using deep-learning algorithms to improve the performance. For example, Xiong and Litman (2011) designed features to represent feedback by combining generic linguistic features and specialized features. Ramachandran et al. (2017) utilized word-order graphs to represent review texts to assess the quality of feedback. Xiao et al. (2020b) leveraged various deep-learning approaches to detect whether the peer-feedback comments contain problem statements.

After that, researchers have noticed and tried to address the problem of lacking training data for new curricula. For instance, Xiao et al. (2020a) attempted to reduce the need for domain-specific data by applying transfer-learning and active-learning techniques. Jia et al. (2021) proposed to leverage multi-task learning to alleviate the problem. Despite the fact that these techniques can considerably reduce the need for historical data, none of them can help when we do not have any domain data.

2.2 Zero-shot Learning

Traditionally, zero-shot learning most often refers to the task of training a classifier on one set of labels and then evaluating it on a different set of labels that the classifier has never seen before (Wang et al., 2019). With the emergence of the pre-training and fine-tuning paradigm, "zero-shot learning" has been generalized to refer to the situation where a pre-trained language model is used to predict for a downsteam task that it was not even fine-tuned on.

Yin et al. (2019) proposed to use a pre-trained NLI model as an out-of-the-box zero-shot text classifier and achieved promising results. A major advantage of this method over other zero-shot learning methods (e.g., Schick and Schütze, 2020) is that NLI-based zero-shot learning does not need access to task-specific hand-crafted prompt sentences.

3 Dataset

We captured data from Expertiza. In this system, learners can submit their work and write feedback comments on peers' submissions based on a set of rubric prompts. For example, each reviewer might be asked to provide a comment for the criterion, "Does the design incorporate all of the functionality required?" In this paper, the terms "feedback comments," "review comments," and "peer feedback" are used interchangeably to mean the textual responses to criterion in the rubric.

We obtained two datasets from the aforementioned peer-review platform for this study. The first dataset, *CS-Peer-Feedback*, is derived from a graduate-level object-oriented development course. This dataset consists of 12,053 data points and is mildly imbalanced. The second dataset, *Ed-Peer-Feedback*, comes from a graduate-level education course. The dataset contains 172 data points and is also mildly skewed. Some sample peer-feedback comments are displayed in Table 1.

All feedback comments have been manually annotated by a fluent English speaker who is familiar with the course context. To measure the reliability of the labels, we randomly sampled 100 comments from each dataset and asked a second annotator to annotate them. We measured the inter-annotator agreement on each set of 100 randomly selected samples using Cohen's κ coefficient. The average κ scores for the CS-Peer-Feedback dataset and the Ed-Peer-Feedback data were 0.88 and 0.85, respectively. These scores suggest that the annotations are reliable (Cohen's $\kappa > 0.81$ (McHugh, 2012)).

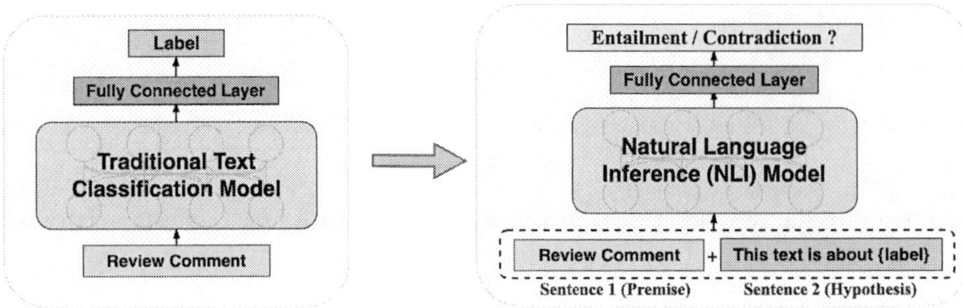

Figure 1: The key idea of IZSL is to convert the problem of evaluating peer-feedback comments into an NLI problem. The left part shows the traditional text classification setting for assessing feedback comments. The right part shows the NLI setting that treats the peer feedback as the premise and uses the label to formulate the hypothesis.

4 Methodology

4.1 Problem Formulation

We formulate the task of evaluating peer-feedback comments as follows: suppose that during the t-th semester of a class, we could collect a dataset $D^t = (X^t, Y^t)$ consisting of N^t data samples, where $X^t = \{x_1^t, x_2^t, \ldots, x_{N^t}^t\}$ denotes a set of N^t feedback comments collected in the t-th semester, and Y^t denotes corresponding labels indicating whether the feedback provides suggestions and/or mentions problems. In practice, these annotations can be obtained by, e.g., asking reviewees to determine if the received feedback contains the features. Additionally, it is worth noting that the labels Y^t can only be used for training after they are collected, i.e., after the t-th semester. **In the "cold-start" condition** (i.e., without any historical data, in the 0-th semester), the task of IZSL is to craft a classifier $\mathcal{F}_{IZSL}$ that can effectively make predictions for feedback comments X^0 without using any domain data to train the model. **In the incremental learning phase** (i.e., $t > 0$), we would have historical data $D^{<t}$, where $D^{<t}$ means $(D^0, D^1, ..., D^{t-1})$ (the data we collected in the first $(t-1)$ semesters). The task of IZSL in this phase is to update the classifier $\mathcal{F}_{IZSL}$ using all historical data $D^{<t}$ and to predict more accurately the labels for peer-feedback comments X^t.

4.2 Incremental Zero-shot Learning

We now describe our IZSL approach for classifying feedback comments. As shown in Figure 1, the overall idea of IZSL is to convert a text classification problem into a natural language inference (NLI) problem. NLI is the task of determining whether, given a premise, a hypothesis is true (entailment) or false (contradiction). We typically treat the text to be classified (i.e., feedback comments) as the premise, and construct the hypothesis from the class name of the label, "This text is about {label}," where "{label}" can be "suggestions" or "problems". If the NLI model tells us that the premise is likely to entail the hypothesis, we can conclude that the label is associated with the input feedback comment and vice versa.

We use BART (Lewis et al., 2019) to craft the NLI model and initialize all parameters with the "bart-large-mnli" checkpoint[1] (Yin et al., 2019), which is pretrained on the multi-genre NLI (MNLI) dataset. **In the "cold-start" condition**, using the pretrained weights makes us have an out-of-the-box NLI model for assessing feedback quality for any curriculum without needing historical data. This is not possible for traditional text classification models, since they need domain data to tune the output fully-connected layer. Then, **in the incremental learning phase**, we use incrementally collected data to further fine-tune the NLI model.

4.3 Baseline Classification Method

Although traditional text classification models cannot be applied in the "cold-start" condition, a BERT-based classifier is implemented to compare the performance of IZSL in the incremental learning phase. We build the classifier by stacking a dense layer on top of BERT. The parameters of BERT are initialized using a pretained checkpoint,[2] and the weights of the dense layer are randomly initialized using the uniform distribution. Then, we fine-tune the model utilizing the same incremental acquisition data as when fine-tuning IZSL.

[1] https://huggingface.co/facebook/bart-large-mnli
[2] https://huggingface.co/bert-base-uncased

Data	Model	Suggestions F_1	Suggestions P	Suggestions R	Suggestions AUC	Problems F_1	Problems P	Problems R	Problems AUC
0	IZSL	**61.2**±2.4	**70.1**±2.8	**59.6**±1.7	**73.5**±3.2	**60.9**±2.4	**63.1**±2.5	**61.2**±2.2	**70.3**±2.3
50	BERT	63.0±16.0	64.8±8.7	68.7±22.2	82.6±10.6	63.4±5.7	69.9±3.2	66.2±2.5	79.9±3.6
	IZSL	**91.5**±1.3	**90.0**±2.3	**94.5**±2.7	**97.5**±1.1	**84.8**±2.0	**85.4**±1.5	**85.0**±2.2	**93.4**±1.0
100	BERT	65.4±14.1	63.6±15.7	69.6±14.1	85.7±2.3	69.5±9.9	73.7±9.0	71.2±8.4	81.0±10.1
	IZSL	**92.3**±1.5	**92.5**±2.5	**92.2**±2.7	**97.1**±1.3	**87.0**±2.8	**87.7**±2.6	**87.0**±2.8	**94.1**±1.4
250	BERT	77.9±7.4	76.2±7.0	82.2±7.6	90.9±4.8	83.1±7.1	83.1±7.0	83.6±7.0	90.0±6.1
	IZSL	**93.5**±1.5	**92.8**±2.9	**94.4**±0.9	**97.9**±0.6	**87.9**±0.8	**87.8**±0.9	**88.4**±1.0	**94.4**±0.7
500	BERT	81.1±7.2	79.2±8.2	84.6±4.4	93.0±4.1	87.3±1.2	87.4±1.2	87.3±1.4	93.5±0.9
	IZSL	**93.5**±0.8	**92.8**±1.3	**94.2**±1.2	**98.2**±1.0	**89.1**±1.0	**89.1**±1.1	**89.1**±1.0	**94.9**±0.8
750	BERT	90.7±0.5	90.4±1.5	91.0±1.2	97.6±0.4	87.2±5.9	86.6±7.8	88.2±3.2	94.3±1.4
	IZSL	**93.7**±1.9	**92.7**±3.2	**94.9**±0.6	**98.2**±0.5	**90.2**±0.4	**90.2**±0.6	**90.3**±0.4	**95.6**±0.2
1000	BERT	91.7±1.0	90.5±1.1	93.2±2.0	98.1±0.9	88.8±1.0	88.8±0.9	88.9±1.1	94.6±0.6
	IZSL	**93.8**±0.9	**92.7**±1.4	**94.9**±0.9	**98.2**±0.4	**90.4**±1.3	**90.2**±1.2	**90.7**±1.6	**95.9**±1.3

Table 2: Performance evaluation of BERT (baseline) and IZSL on *CS-Peer-Feedback*. The first column is the number of training samples used. The best results in each setting are marked in bold. Confidence interval = 95% .

Data	Model	Suggestions F_1	Suggestions P	Suggestions R	Suggestions AUC	Problems F_1	Problems P	Problems R	Problems AUC
0	IZSL	**60.5**±2.0	**67.1**±3.2	**59.6**±1.6	**68.8**±0.7	**57.2**±2.3	**57.5**±2.2	**59.6**±3.0	**64.4**±2.3
50	BERT	52.1±14.7	51.3±18.0	56.7±10.9	69.6±9.0	56.3±11.7	59.8±20.4	56.9±7.6	67.4±7.6
	IZSL	**78.1**±3.3	**76.9**±2.7	**82.0**±6.8	**87.8**±1.4	**81.7**±2.7	**84.2**±3.4	**80.4**±4.7	**94.2**±1.0
100	BERT	68.7±14.8	77.6±11.7	68.5±15.6	80.3±9.2	62.0±14.6	66.3±21.8	64.3±10.5	75.8±15.0
	IZSL	**82.2**±1.8	**80.7**±1.8	**86.1**±4.2	**90.8**±1.3	**84.3**±3.8	**87.5**±3.6	**82.5**±5.0	**93.4**±2.2

Table 3: Performance evaluation of BERT (baseline) and IZSL on *Ed-Peer-Feedback* with 95% confidence interval.

5 Evaluation

5.1 Experimental Setup

Training and Optimization Details. We train our models on eight NVIDIA RTX6000 GPUs (24GB each) with a total batch size of 8, a learning rate of 2e-5/3e-5/5e-5, epochs of 2/3, and the Adam optimizer (Kingma and Ba, 2014).

Handling the Imbalanced Datasets. To alleviate the problem of class imbalance, we employ a cost-sensitive approach. Specifically, we weight the cross-entropy loss function based on the frequency of each class in the training set.

5.2 Results and Discussion

The evaluation results are shown in Tables 2 and 3. The first row (i.e., for "Data" = 0) of each table shows the performance of IZSL when we do not have any historical data. Then, the following rows of each table compare the results of IZSL and BERT when trained with incrementally collected data. **In the "cold-start" phase**, the F_1 scores for the labels "Suggestions" and "Problems" on the CS-Peer-Feedback dataset are 61.2 and 60.9, respectively. On the Ed-Peer-Feedback dataset, the F_1 scores for these two labels are 60.5 and 57.2, respectively. The results suggest that IZSL can achieve acceptable "cold-start" performance on data from different disciplines, considering that it does not use any domain data. However, it is worth noting that the performance of the IZSL model varies on datasets from different domains. It is still unclear how we can estimate the "cold-start" performance of IZSL on a particular dataset. We leave this research question to future studies. **In the incremental learning phase**, we surprisingly find that the F_1 scores of IZSL quickly jump to over 91.5 and 84.8 on the CS-Peer-Feedback dataset after training with only dozens of training samples, and we make a similar finding on the Ed-Peer-Feedback dataset. Our hypothesis for IZSL to perform better than BERT in "low-data" settings is that NLI-based classification models have better generalization ability than traditional classification methods. However, this hypothesis needs to be further tested by extensive experiments. By examining the following rows of the tables, the results clearly show that IZSL can consistently outperform BERT on all metrics across all settings, and the confidence intervals suggest that the performance of IZSL is more stable. **To summarize**, IZSL can achieve acceptable "cold-start" performance and consistently outperform the BERT model in the incremental learning phase, especially when we only have dozens of incrementally collected data points.

6 Conclusion and Future Work

The quality of peer feedback plays a vital role in peer assessment. However, lacking historical data for new curricula is a persistent problem. Our work proposes a novel method for assessing feedback quality by converting it into an NLI problem. The approach can potentially be generalized to other pedagogical tasks. Future plans include investigating how to improve "cold-start" performance.

References

Scott Ashton and Randall S Davies. 2015. Using scaffolded rubrics to improve peer assessment in a mooc writing course. *Distance education*, 36(3):312–334.

Kwangsu Cho. 2008. Machine classification of peer comments in physics. In *Educational Data Mining 2008*.

Jacob Devlin, Ming-Wei Chang, Kenton Lee, and Kristina Toutanova. 2018. Bert: Pre-training of deep bidirectional transformers for language understanding. *arXiv preprint arXiv:1810.04805*.

Kit S Double, Joshua A McGrane, and Therese N Hopfenbeck. 2020. The impact of peer assessment on academic performance: A meta-analysis of control group studies.

Qinjin Jia, Jialin Cui, Yunkai Xiao, Chengyuan Liu, Parvez Rashid, and Edward F Gehringer. 2021. All-in-one: Multi-task learning bert models for evaluating peer assessments. *arXiv preprint arXiv:2110.03895*.

Diederik P Kingma and Jimmy Ba. 2014. Adam: A method for stochastic optimization. *arXiv preprint arXiv:1412.6980*.

Mike Lewis, Yinhan Liu, Naman Goyal, Marjan Ghazvininejad, Abdelrahman Mohamed, Omer Levy, Ves Stoyanov, and Luke Zettlemoyer. 2019. Bart: Denoising sequence-to-sequence pre-training for natural language generation, translation, and comprehension. *arXiv preprint arXiv:1910.13461*.

Mary L McHugh. 2012. Interrater reliability: the kappa statistic. *Biochemia medica*, 22(3):276–282.

Melissa M Nelson and Christian D Schunn. 2009. The nature of feedback: How different types of peer feedback affect writing performance. *Instructional Science*, 37(4):375–401.

Lakshmi Ramachandran, Edward F Gehringer, and Ravi K Yadav. 2017. Automated assessment of the quality of peer reviews using natural language processing techniques. *International Journal of Artificial Intelligence in Education*, 27(3):534–581.

Timo Schick and Hinrich Schütze. 2020. Exploiting cloze questions for few shot text classification and natural language inference. *arXiv preprint arXiv:2001.07676*.

Marjo Van Zundert, Dominique Sluijsmans, and Jeroen Van Merriënboer. 2010. Effective peer assessment processes: Research findings and future directions. *Learning and instruction*, 20(4):270–279.

Wei Wang, Vincent W Zheng, Han Yu, and Chunyan Miao. 2019. A survey of zero-shot learning: Settings, methods, and applications. *ACM Transactions on Intelligent Systems and Technology (TIST)*, 10(2):1–37.

Yunkai Xiao, Gabriel Zingle, Qinjin Jia, Shoaib Akbar, Yang Song, Muyao Dong, Li Qi, and Edward Gehringer. 2020a. Problem detection in peer assessments between subjects by effective transfer learning and active learning. *International Educational Data Mining Society*.

Yunkai Xiao, Gabriel Zingle, Qinjin Jia, Harsh R Shah, Yi Zhang, Tianyi Li, Mohsin Karovaliya, Weixiang Zhao, Yang Song, Jie Ji, et al. 2020b. Detecting problem statements in peer assessments. *arXiv preprint arXiv:2006.04532*.

Wenting Xiong and Diane Litman. 2011. Automatically predicting peer-review helpfulness. In *Proceedings of the 49th Annual Meeting of the Association for Computational Linguistics: Human Language Technologies*, pages 502–507.

Wenpeng Yin, Jamaal Hay, and Dan Roth. 2019. Benchmarking zero-shot text classification: Datasets, evaluation and entailment approach. *arXiv preprint arXiv:1909.00161*.

On Assessing and Developing
Spoken 'Grammatical Error Correction' Systems

Yiting Lu, Mark Gales
ALTA Institute / Engineering Department, University of Cambridge, UK
{ytl28,mjfg100}@cam.ac.uk

Stefano Bannò
Fondazione Bruno Kessler / Department of Cognitive Science, University of Trento, Italy
sbanno@fbk.eu

Abstract

Spoken 'grammatical error correction' (SGEC) is an important process to provide feedback for second language learning. Due to a lack of end-to-end training data, SGEC is often implemented as a cascaded, modular system, consisting of speech recognition, disfluency removal, and grammatical error correction (GEC). This cascaded structure enables efficient use of training data for each module. It is, however, difficult to compare and evaluate the performance of individual modules as preceeding modules may introduce errors. For example the GEC module input depends on the output of non-native speech recognition and disfluency detection, both challenging tasks for learner data. This paper focuses on the assessment and development of SGEC systems. We first discuss metrics for evaluating SGEC, both individual modules and the overall system. The system-level metrics enable tuning for optimal system performance. A known issue in cascaded systems is error propagation between modules. To mitigate this problem semi-supervised approaches and self-distillation are investigated. Lastly, when SGEC system gets deployed it is important to give accurate feedback to users. Thus, we apply filtering to remove edits with low-confidence, aiming to improve overall feedback precision. The performance metrics are examined on a Linguaskill multi-level data set, which includes the original non-native speech, manual transcriptions and reference grammatical error corrections, to enable system analysis and development.

1 Introduction

Grammatical construction is one of the key elements in second language acquisition, and text-based grammatical error correction (GEC) has been widely studied over the past decade (Dale and Kilgarriff, 2011; Ng et al., 2014; Bryant et al., 2017). With speaking skills playing a big part in language learning, it has become increasingly important to analyse spoken grammars. Previous works have investigated grammatical error detection (GED) on spoken language transcriptions (Caines et al., 2020), and tighter integration of disfluency removal and grammar correction on spontaneous learner speech (Lu et al., 2020). This paper focuses on the spoken grammatical error correction (SGEC) task. There are several challenges facing SGEC: running automatic speech recognition (ASR) on learner English is harder than native speech due to potential pronunciation and grammatical errors; spoken language often comes with disfluent speech events such as repetitions and false starts, which are disruptive to downstream tasks; there is very little end-to-end speech to correction data that can be used for training. In this paper, SGEC adopts a cascaded structure: an ASR module produces transcriptions; a disfluency detection (DD) (Zayats et al., 2016) module recovers a fluent text flow; and a conventional machine translation style GEC (Yuan and Briscoe, 2016) module produces error corrections.

Several metrics have been developed to assess text-based GEC. GLEU (Napoles et al., 2015) score adopts BLEU (Papineni et al., 2002) based n-gram precision over the reference. It rewards word-level corrections, as well as correctly preserved source text. MaxMatch M^2 (Dahlmeier and Ng, 2012) captures phrase-level edits, and calculates $F_{0.5}$ scores accordingly. It assesses performance in terms of edits, which suits well with feedback oriented applications. For Spoken GEC assessment, however, it is not straight forward to apply those standard metrics. A common problem facing cascaded style spoken language applications is that it is difficult to compare across models when upstream modules (e.g. ASR) are different. For example, input text to GEC module varies when upstream ASR and DD models are changed. If standard GLEU and M^2 $F_{0.5}$ are to be applied, these metrics mean differently every time ASR transcriptions change, and thus results are incomparable

Proceedings of the 17th Workshop on Innovative Use of NLP for Building Educational Applications (BEA 2022), pages 51 - 60
July 15, 2022

across systems. Not only for cascaded systems, evaluation metrics is not clearly defined for end-to-end trained spoken systems. It is difficult to migrate text-based metrics to spoken tasks, since end-to-end models do not provide any intermediate variables for assessment.

This paper first discusses metrics to assess cascaded SGEC systems. When evaluating individual modules, standard metrics can be used. However, these metrics are not suitable for system-level assessment, since they sometimes take into account module inputs. When downstream module inputs change with its upstream modules, results can become incomparable across systems. To make systems comparable, we use edit distance based metrics instead and focus on the output quality. A common issue in cascaded systems is error propagation, since individual modules are trained separately. To mitigate this issue, semi-supervised fine-tuning is conducted. It aims to tune DD and GEC modules for optimal system performance with non-native ASR transcriptions. Self-distillation is also investigated, which learns from a rich distribution of semi-supervised references. Both fine-tuning experiments are conducted on learner English without readily available annotations. For system development purposes, we focus on optimising output quality; and for assisting language learning, we shift the emphasis to give high quality feedback. We first remove ambiguous corrections, and further filter out low-confidence edits to improve feedback precision as well as the overall quality.

2 Evaluation metrics

Cascaded spoken grammatical error correction (SGEC) consists of three modules, namely speech recognition (ASR), disfluency detection (DD) and grammatical error correction (GEC). It converts disfluent, grammatically incorrect audio sequences into fluent, grammatically correct text. Variables are notated as such: $\boldsymbol{x}$ for input audio, $\boldsymbol{w}$ for speech transcriptions, $\boldsymbol{t}$ for disfluency tags, $\boldsymbol{w}^f$ for transcriptions with disfluencies removed, and $\boldsymbol{y}$ for grammatically correct outputs. N.B.: bold letters are used to represent sequences, with subscripts omitted, e.g. $\boldsymbol{x}$ short for $x_{1:T}$.

$$x_{1:T} \xrightarrow{\text{ASR}} w_{1:N} \xrightarrow{\text{DD}} t_{1:N}, w^f_{1:M} \xrightarrow{\text{GEC}} y_{1:L} \quad (1)$$

When evaluating individual modules, standard metrics can be used. Word error rate (WER) is used for ASR to compute word-level edit distance. DD is modeled as a sequence tagging task, and F_1 score is used to indicate the mean of precision and recall (use hat, e.g. $\hat{a}$, to indicate hypothesises):

$$S_{\text{ASR}} = \text{WER}(\hat{\boldsymbol{w}}, \boldsymbol{w}) \quad (2)$$

$$S_{\text{DD}} = F_1(\hat{\boldsymbol{t}}, \boldsymbol{t}) \quad (3)$$

For GEC module, a standard evaluation is to compare reference and hypothesised edits, and use $F_{0.5}$ score to reflect a weighted precision and recall:

$$E = M^2(\boldsymbol{w}^f, \boldsymbol{y}) \quad (4)$$

$$\hat{E} = M^2(\boldsymbol{w}^f, \hat{\boldsymbol{y}}) \quad (5)$$

$$S_{\text{GEC}} = F_{0.5}(\hat{E}, E) \quad (6)$$

where reference and hypothesised edits E, $\hat{E}$ are extracted using MaxMatch (M^2) (Dahlmeier and Ng, 2012) alignment between inputs and outputs. Each edit is defined by a triplet `[st, ed, cor]` (`st`: start location of the error, `ed`: end location, `cor`: correction).

For cascaded systems, it is also important to look at system-level evaluation, which assesses a combination of modules. When evaluating ASR and DD combined, the standard DD metric F_1 score no longer apply. The reference tags $\boldsymbol{t}$ have a one-to-one correspondence with input word tokens $\boldsymbol{w}$, and we need a different set of reference $\boldsymbol{t}$ for different ASR transcriptions. It is therefore not feasible to compare across systems that have different ASR transcriptions if F_1 is used. Thus, we use WER instead, to directly analyse the output quality from disfluency removal:

$$S_{\text{ASR+DD}} = \text{WER}(\hat{\boldsymbol{w}}^f, \boldsymbol{w}^f) \quad (7)$$

When evaluating ASR, DD and GEC modules combined i.e. the SGEC system, standard GEC metric M^2 $F_{0.5}$ cannot be used, since it does not allow comparison across systems. It requires input sequences w_f to be given for edit extraction, and changes in upstream ASR and DD modules will lead to a different set of reference edits E. Therefore the focus is laid on the quality of outputs. We adopt sentence error rate (SER) to analyse sentence-level matches between references and hypotheses. To achieve greater granularity, we also adopt translation edit rate (TER) (Snover et al., 2006) to assess word-level distance from references.

$$S_{\text{ASR+DD+GEC}} = \text{SER/TER}(\hat{\boldsymbol{y}}, \boldsymbol{y}) \quad (8)$$

Individual module evaluation S_{ASR}, S_{DD} and S_{GEC} helps develop each module separately. System-level metrics $S_{\text{ASR+DD}}$ and $S_{\text{ASR+DD+GEC}}$ both emphasise output quality, which enables comparison across systems even when upstream modules change. They also help guide further tuning and development of the SGEC system as a whole.

3 Module error mitigation

Each module in the cascaded SGEC system is trained individually. DD is trained on a native spoken corpus, and GEC is trained on written text that is processed to be like speech transcripts (details in 5). Individual training allows efficient use of data on one hand, yet on the other hand, it suffers from error propagation due to mismatches between training and evaluation. For example, DD and GEC modules have not seen any ASR transcriptions during training, and thus any ASR error at evaluation time would potentially disrupt their performance. Ideally, fine-tuning on a non-native spoken corpus would most effectively mitigate error propagation, but similar to many other speech to text tasks, there is no readily available data for training. Therefore in this section, we adopt semi-supervised approaches to fine-tune the SGEC system on a spoken learner corpus without manual annotations. Here we use the ASR training corpus, which is comparatively abundant and less costly to obtain, compared to end-to-end SGEC annotation. It consists of audio sequences $\boldsymbol{x}$ and manual transcriptions $\boldsymbol{w}$.

3.1 Semi-supervised fine-tuning

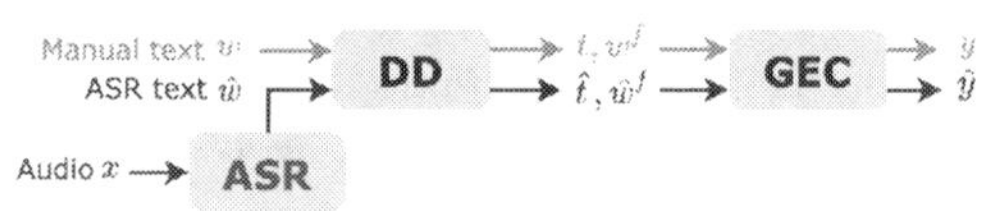

Figure 1: Semi-supervised fine-tuning pipeline. Orange denotes reference generation, blue denotes hypotheses. The greyed (ASR) block is frozen during fine-tuning; DD and GEC modules are separately tuned.

Fine-tuning aims to train the system to be more robust against error propagation. The ASR training set provides non-native audio sequences and their corresponding manual transcriptions, yet lacking references for grammatical error corrections. We generate pseudo references by feeding manual transcriptions through the baseline system, and hypotheses by feeding through audio sequences. The pseudo references are not impacted by ASR errors, and therefore minimising distance between references and hypotheses should help mitigate ASR error propagation. Figure 1 shows the fine-tuning pipeline. When fine-tuning the DD module, references and hypotheses are generated as such:

$$\boldsymbol{t}, \boldsymbol{w}^f = \text{DD}(\boldsymbol{w}) \tag{9}$$

$$\hat{\boldsymbol{t}}, \hat{\boldsymbol{w}}^f = \text{DD}(\text{ASR}(\boldsymbol{x})) \tag{10}$$

Reference tags and fluent text are produced by feeding manual transcriptions through DD module, and hypotheses are generated by feeding audio sequences through ASR and DD modules. For sequence tagging tasks, reference tags change with input word tokens, and thus reference tags $\boldsymbol{t}$ of manual transcriptions cannot be directly applied to ASR transcriptions during fine-tuning. Recalling that WER is used to assess output $\boldsymbol{w}^f$ when evaluating ASR and DD combined, we can apply the same idea and directly compare fluent text $\boldsymbol{w}^f$ and $\hat{\boldsymbol{w}}^f$ after disfluency removal. Reference tags $\boldsymbol{t}'$ can be derived by aligning $\boldsymbol{w}^f$ and $\hat{\boldsymbol{w}}^f$: all insertions in $\hat{\boldsymbol{w}}^f$ are treated as disfluencies, substitutions and matches are tagged as fluent words, whereas deletions are ignored (Table 1):

$\boldsymbol{w}^f$	a	cat	si-	sit	on		the	mat
$\hat{\boldsymbol{w}}^f$	a	cat		sat	on	um	the	mat
Aln	M	M	D	S	M	I	M	M
$\boldsymbol{t}'$	O	O	-	O	O	E	O	O

Table 1: An example of converting $\boldsymbol{w}^f$ and $\hat{\boldsymbol{w}}^f$ to $\boldsymbol{t}'$
M:match, D:deletion, S:substitution, I:insertion
E:disfluent, O:fluent, '-': no label for deleted words

Following this tagging scheme, applying binary cross entropy loss between $\hat{\boldsymbol{t}}$ and $\boldsymbol{t}'$ is equivalent to optimising for lower WER ($S_{\text{ASR+DD}}$). For GEC module fine-tuning, both ASR and DD modules are frozen. To obtain references $\boldsymbol{y}$, manual transcriptions are fed through DD and GEC modules; and for hypotheses $\hat{\boldsymbol{y}}$, audio sequences are fed through ASR, DD and GEC modules:

$$\boldsymbol{y} = \text{GEC}(\text{DD}(\boldsymbol{w})) \tag{11}$$

$$\hat{\boldsymbol{y}} = \text{GEC}(\text{DD}(\text{ASR}(\boldsymbol{x}))) \tag{12}$$

To optimise for a lower SER ($S_{\text{ASR+DD+GEC}}$), a standard cross entropy loss can be used with teacher forcing training:

$$L = \log P(\boldsymbol{y}|\hat{\boldsymbol{w}}^f) = \textstyle\sum_l \log P(y_l|\hat{\boldsymbol{w}}^f, y_{1:l-1}) \tag{13}$$

Minimising cross entropy loss is equivalent to maximising sentence-level probabilities, and therefore should directly help improve SER.

3.2 Self-distillation

Semi-supervised fine-tuning relies on pseudo references generated from manual transcriptions, the quality of which largely depends on the performance of the baseline SGEC system. DD and GEC are trained on native spoken and non-native written corpora respectively, both of which have not encountered any in-domain non-native spoken data. Therefore, it is likely that the pseudo references generated on the non-native spoken corpus are erroneous. To alleviate the potential degradation caused by this, we further apply self-distillation. Self-distillation is originated from knowledge distillation (Hinton et al., 2015), which often trains a student model to learn from predictions made by a teacher model. The teacher is usually superior to the student, e.g. larger in size than the student, or an ensemble teacher for a single model student. Self-distillation (Zhang et al., 2019) is originally proposed in the computer vision community. It extends the idea of knowledge distillation by proposing to use the same model for both teacher and student. It has been shown to be effective for improving both image (Zhang et al., 2019) and text-based tasks (Xu et al., 2020).

Here we adopt the same self-distillation idea, but use a semi-supervised corpus for training. The teacher model is always frozen, and the student model will be trained. The training objective is to minimise the Kullback–Leibler (KL) divergence of the per word posterior distribution between teacher and student:

$$L_{\text{KL}} = \sum_l \text{KL}[P_t(y_l|\hat{\boldsymbol{w}}^f, y_{1:l-1}), P_s(y_l|\hat{\boldsymbol{w}}^f, y_{1:l-1})] \quad (14)$$

where P_t, P_s are teacher and student distributions. Another common practice is to interpolate the KL divergence with cross-entropy loss in Eqn. 13:

$$L_{\text{dist}} = \alpha L_{\text{KL}} + (1 - \alpha)L \quad (15)$$

Despite the empirical success of self-distillation, the intuition behind adopting self-distillation on semi-supervised data here is to guide the student model with richer probability distributions, rather than relying solely on one-best predictions.

4 Feedback and confidence filtering

Section 2, 3 mainly focus on evaluating and optimising output quality. Another important aspect for language learning applications is feedback to learners, since feedback quality directly impacts learner's progression in language learning. This section first describes how feedback is extracted and assessed for SGEC systems, then introduces confidence-based filtering that aims to improve feedback precision.

For GEC tasks, feedback usually suggests where the error is and how to correct it. In written GEC, feedback edits are extracted using Eqn. 5 by comparing input and output sequences. Its quality is analysed using $F_{0.5}$ (Eqn. 6) by comparing hypotheses against reference edits. This is not applicable to spoken GEC, since reference edits change with upstream ASR transcriptions, are consequently $F_{0.5}$ scores are not comparable across systems. Here we modify the definition of reference and hypothesised edits as such:

$$E = M^2(\boldsymbol{w}^f, \boldsymbol{y}) \quad (16)$$

$$\hat{E} = M^2(\hat{\boldsymbol{w}}^f, \hat{\boldsymbol{y}}) \quad (17)$$

$F_{0.5}$ can be calculated as before. Reference edits E are generated using manual fluent transcripts $\boldsymbol{w}^f$ as source sequences. With reference E defined independent from ASR or DD module, feedback $F_{0.5}$ can be compared across systems. Hypothesised edits $\hat{E}$ use hypothesised fluent transcriptions $\hat{\boldsymbol{w}}^f$ as source sequences. Therefore $\hat{E}$ account for errors from all three modules, and reflects the true feedback given to users when the system is deployed. Note that such mismatched source sequences in E and $\hat{E}$ put extra penalty on $F_{0.5}$. To given an example: when system output $\hat{\boldsymbol{y}}$ matches with reference $\boldsymbol{y}$ i.e. the system output is perfectly correct, differences in $\boldsymbol{w}^f$ and $\hat{\boldsymbol{w}}^f$ will still result in differences in $\hat{E}$ from E, leading to degraded $F_{0.5}$ score.

SGEC is a very challenging task due to potential errors coming from transcriptions, disfluencies as well as the correction process. To avoid giving erroneous feedback to language learners, we do not want to give feedback on edits that our models have little confidence in, assuming lower confidence indicates lower accuracy. To conduct confidence filtering, we need to define a confidence measure. In the cascaded SGEC pipeline (Eqn. 1), each module produces a token-level confidence score associated with its prediction. We first define sentence-level confidence for each module as the lowest token probability over the entire sentence. Sentence-level filtering can be conducted by rejecting sentences with low confidence. We also explore the option of using edit-level confidence, i.e. confidences are calculated over each edit instead of sentence. Note that for ASR module, we always use the lowest over sentence, to mitigate a known issue of ASR error propagation. The overall confidence is calculated using a weighted sum of all thee modules:

$$\log P = \alpha \log P_{\text{ASR}} + \beta \log P_{\text{DD}} + \gamma \log P_{\text{GEC}} \tag{18}$$

where P_{ASR}, P_{DD} and P_{GEC} are sentence/edit-level confidence of each module.

5 Experimental results

5.1 Corpora and models

Corpus	Spoken	Use	#Sent	#Word	%Dsf
ASRtrn	✓	ASR Train	62K	2.5M*	-
SWBD	✓	DD Train	154K	940K	11.1
CLC	✗	GEC Train	1.9M	25.2M	0.0
BEA	✗	GEC Train	1M	11.5M	0.0
FCEtst	✗	Eval	2,681	37K	0.0
LIN	✓	Eval	3,361	38K	5.0

Table 2: Corpora statistics. Spoken: whether it is derived from speech; Audio: whether it provides audio sequences; %Dsf: percentage disfluencies contained in the corpus. (*: approximated value, no manual transcriptions available)

ASRtrn is used for ASR training, as well as module error mitigation in Section 3. It consists of 334 hours of an online English speaking test data, which mainly covers 28 L1s and the 5 CEFR (Council of Europe, 2001) grades ranging from A1 to C2. Different from usual ASR training corpus, it only provides crowd source transcriptions, the quality of which is far worse than manual transcriptions. A remedy for this is to use multi-stage teacher-student training: bootstrap the system with crowd source data, and use an ensemble teacher to generate higher quality transcriptions to guide a single student model (Wang et al., 2018). For experiments described in Section 3, by manual transcriptions we always refer to this higher quality transcriptions generated using the teacher ensemble. **Switchboard (SWBD)** (Meteer et al., 1995) consists of 260 hours of telephone conversations of native American English speakers. The Treebank-3 annotation (Taylor et al., 2003) provides manual transcripts and disfluency annotations on the Switchboard corpus. **Cambridge Learner Corpus (CLC)** (Nicholls, 2003) is a collection of written exams of candidates from 86 L1s at different proficiency levels. The corpus is annotated with grammatical errors. **BEA** (Bryant et al., 2019) is a collection of text-based grammatical error correction corpora, including Write & Improve, LOCNESS, Lang-8 and NUCLE (FCE train split excluded, since it overlaps with CLC). **FCEtst** (Yannakoudakis et al., 2011) is a hold out subset of the CLC for test. Punctuation and capitalisation are removed from all corpora derived from written text, to make them look more like speech transcriptions. **Linguaskill (LIN)** is derived from an English speaking test. It consists of 833 learners from over 15 L1s, evenly distributed across CEFR grades. Manual transcriptions are segmented at phrase level, with incomplete or ambiguous phrases rejected. The remaining set is annotated with disfluencies and grammatical errors. Relevant corpora statistics are summarised in Table 2.

Cascaded SGEC consists of three modules: ASR, DD and GEC. **ASR** uses a hybrid deep learning-HMM graphemic system. It is a teacher-student trained TDNN-F model (Povey et al., 2018; Wang et al., 2018) with trigram lattice generation. Succeeding word RNNLM (Chen et al., 2017) is used for rescoring. It has a WER of 19.97% on LIN. Confidence scores are returned by the ASR engines, followed by piece-wise linear mapping (Evermann et al., 2005). **DD** is a binary classification model which consists of a BERT layer (Devlin et al., 2019) in the version provided by the HuggingFace Transformer Library (Wolf et al., 2019) (*bert-base-uncased*), a first dense layer of 768 nodes, a second dense layer of 128 nodes, and finally the output layer of size 2. The model is trained on SWBD and uses an Adam optimiser (Kingma and Ba, 2014) with batch size 64, learning rate 1e-06 and dropout 0.1. **GEC** adopts a transformer-based sequence to sequence model. It is initialised from Gramformer[1], which is a T5 model (Raffel et al., 2020) trained on WikiEdits processed with synthetic error generation techniques (Lichtarge et al., 2019). It is further fine-tuned on CLC and BEA. Training uses Adam optimiser with a batch size of 256, and learning rate of 5e-4 with warm up. Maximum sentence length is set at 64, and the final model parameters are calculated using checkpoint averaging (Izmailov et al., 2018), which takes the average over the 5 best checkpoints. N.B.: all results are reported without standard deviations, since we initialise both DD and GEC modules with large pre-trained models and deviations due to random dropout are relatively small.

[1] `https://github.com/PrithivirajDamodaran/Gramformer`

5.2 Metrics and tuning

Modules	Metric	In-domain eval Data	Score	LIN-MAN eval Input	Score
ASR	WER ↓	-	-	x	19.97
DD	F_1 ↑	SWBD	89.66	w	79.52
GEC	M^2 ↑	FCEtst	56.60	w^f	53.57

Table 3: Individual module evaluation at their respective operating point. ASR uses LM scale=11, DD uses threshold=0.5.

Table 3 lists performance of each individual module in the SGEC system, comparing out-of-domain evaluation on manual transcriptions of LIN against in-domain test sets. ASR training is conducted in a semi-supervised fashion, therefore we only report WER on LIN-MAN. We always use manual transcriptions for individual module evaluation. For DD, going from native to non-native spoken English, a 10 percent loss is seen in F_1 score. For GEC, going from written to fluent spoken style data loses 3 points on M^2 $F_{0.5}$. Compared to domain mismatch, much larger degradation is induced by ASR errors. Table 4 evaluates combination of multiple modules for LIN, focusing on the overall output quality. It shows significant impact of ASR transcriptions, with the overall SER and TER increasing by 33.50 and 19.62 points respectively.

Modules	Metric	MAN	ASR
ASR+DD	WER ↓	1.96	21.20
ASR+DD+GEC	SER ↓	43.26	76.76
	TER ↓	8.27	27.89

Table 4: Evaluating combination of modules on LIN corpus. MAN and ASR columns show performance on manual and ASR transcriptions at their respective operating points.

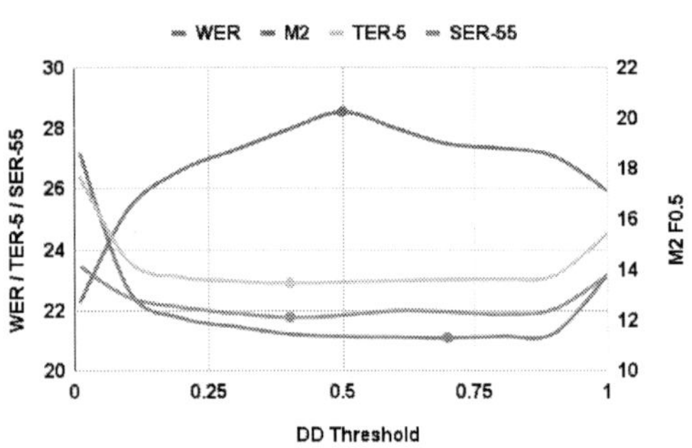

Figure 2: System tuning using SER/TER/M^2. Plot shows a sweep over DD thresholds at the chosen LM scale = 11.

Having defined system level metrics, we can jointly tune the modules in cascaded SGEC for better overall output quality. Here we focus on two variables: ASR language model (LM) scale factor, and DD disfluency removal threshold. A two-dimensional grid search is conducted over a range of LM factors (6-13) and DD threshold (0.0-1.0). Fig. 2 shows a sweep over disfluency removal thresholds at the chosen LM scale factor. It can be seen that all edit distance based metrics are relatively insensitive to the sweep, whereas feedback $F_{0.5}$ shows a stronger preference (more feedback analysis in Section 5.4). The best WER for the intermediate output w^f is at 0.7, and the best SER/TER for the overall output y sits at 0.4. Although differences are insignificant, this shows that an intermediate optima can be different from the overall optima, and confirms the necessity of overall performance metrics. The operating point is chosen according to SER/TER, at a LM scale of 11 and a disfluency threshold of 0.4.

5.3 Module error mitigation

As shown in Table 4, ASR errors result in large degradation, partly because DD and GEC modules have not encounter any non-native spoken data during training. Fine-tuning on a non-native spoken corpus is the most efficient way to mitigate ASR error propagation, yet limited by data availability, we conduct semi-supervised fine-tuning instead. As explained in Section 3.1, we use the SGEC pipeline to generate pseudo reference. Its performance on LIN-MAN (in Table 4) gives an approximation of how much we fall behind supervised fine-tuning. Table 5 lists the impact of tuning DD and GEC modules respectively.

Models	ASR+DD WER↓	ASR+DD+GEC SER↓	TER↓
Base	21.20	76.76	27.89
TuneDD	21.06	76.79	27.83
TuneGEC	-	76.35	27.47

Table 5: Impact of fine-tuning DD and GEC modules. Note: combination of the two doesn't yield better performance, thus using TuneGEC for future development.

Tuning DD module gives 0.14 decrease on WER of DD output w^f, yet fails to improve SER/TER of GEC output y. When generating reference tags t' as described in table 1, we minimise the edit distance between $\hat{w}^f$ and w^f, which directly optimises for lower WER. However, optimising for the intermediate output does not always help improve the overall output, and thus changes in WER of DD don't seem to have significant impact on downstream GEC. Tuning GEC module improves both SER and TER. The fine-tuning process maximises sentence-level probabilities, which helps to achieve lower SER/TER.

Semi-supervised fine-tuning of GEC module improves SER/TER, yet it is still not as effective as supervised fine-tuning. Aiming to further improve the output $\boldsymbol{y}$, we adopt semi-supervised self-distillation, which trains the model to learn a probability distribution at each time step, rather than predicting the correct word. The rationale is that probability distribution potentially offers richer information than a single prediction, especially when the reference $\boldsymbol{y}$ is synthetically generated.

Model	Init	KL coeff.	SER↓	TER↓
Teacher	-	-	76.35	27.47
Student	Base	0.5	76.58	27.49
		1.0	76.44	27.46
	Teacher	0.5	76.41	27.46
		1.0	76.35	27.51

Table 6: Self-distillation results. Base and teacher models are Base and TuneGEC from Table 5. Init: initialisation point of the student model. KL coeff.: coefficient of loss interpolation (α in Eqn. 15). Softmax temperature is set at 0.8 for all.

Table 6 contrasts the impact of student initialisation and coefficient of KL loss. The standard approach is to initialise from the teacher, which tends to lead the student to land on a local optima close to the teacher. An alternative is to initialise from Base, which allows the student to explore a larger space, potentially landing on a local minimum further away from the teacher. Larger KL coefficient forces the student to mimic the teacher predicted distribution rather than one-best prediction. However, both SER and TER are quite insensitive to self-distillation, although feedback $F_{0.5}$ shows some improvement (in Section 5.4).

5.4 Feedback and confidence filtering

Previous experiments focus on system analysis and development, this section shift the focus to analyse feedback quality. For optimal feedback, we adopt a slightly different operating point from before according to Fig. 2 (LM scale 11, DD threshold 0.5). Table 7 tabulates the results of system tuning evaluated using system TER and feedback $F_{0.5}$. Compared to system TER, feedback $F_{0.5}$ proves to be much more sensitive to system tuning. Semi-supervised fine-tuning and self-distillation improves feedback by 1.66 and 0.65 points respectively. We use the optimal $F_{0.5}$ (22.57) as our baseline for confidence filtering.

Feedback from SGEC, also called edits, suggests the error location, type and correction. To give

Models	Base	+Tune	+Distill
TER↓	27.89	27.47	27.46
Fdbk $F_{0.5}$↑	20.26	21.92	22.57

Table 7: Impact of semi-supervised fine-tuning and self-distillation on TER & feedback M^2 $F_{0.5}$. +Distill: self-distillation model initialises from Base, and uses KL coeff.=1.

high quality feedback to learners, it is important to pass on a clear and accurate message in terms of corrections as well as error types. Feedback edits are automatically typed using a rule-based framework ERRANT (Bryant et al., 2017). Some examples of error types: `M:PREP` (missing preposition), `U:DET` (unnecessary determiner). It sometimes predict error type as `OTHER` when edits do not fall into any other category. A large part of `OTHER` are paraphrases, which can be ambiguous to learners. Therefore we exclude edits typed as `OTHER`.

Table 8 shows that excluding `OTHER` removes approximately 10-15% edits from reference and hypothesis. Note that removing `OTHER` edits in reference reduces the total number of edits, and makes it much easier for models to achieve higher $F_{0.5}$ since most rejected edits are ambiguous and difficult to predict. Both precision and recall get boosted, thus improving the baseline $F_{0.5}$. `OTHERs` are excluded from scoring for confidence filtering experiments below.

	$F_{0.5}$↑		%Edits Exc.	
Eval	Inc.	Exc.	REF	HYP
FCEtst	56.60	59.73	13.87	9.65
LIN	22.57	24.30	14.21	12.54

Table 8: Feedback $F_{0.5}$ inc./exc. `OTHER`, and %edits being removed from reference and hypothesis by excluding `OTHER`.

To improve feedback precision, sentence-level and edit-level confidence filtering are applied to reject ill-conditioned edits. When conducting filtering, we expect both true positives (TP: correctly predicted edits) and false positives (FP: incorrectly predicted edits) to reduce. Under the hypothesis that there are more FPs than TPs in the low confidence region, we expect precision to improve, and consequently help $F_{0.5}$.

Fig. 3 shows change in feedback $F_{0.5}$ score as we filter out an increasing number of edits by setting higher confidence thresholds. Both sentence-level and edit-level filtering peak midway, and drop back as we continue to filter out more edits. Filtering operating at sentence-level tends to work better than edit-level. This can be explained by the na-

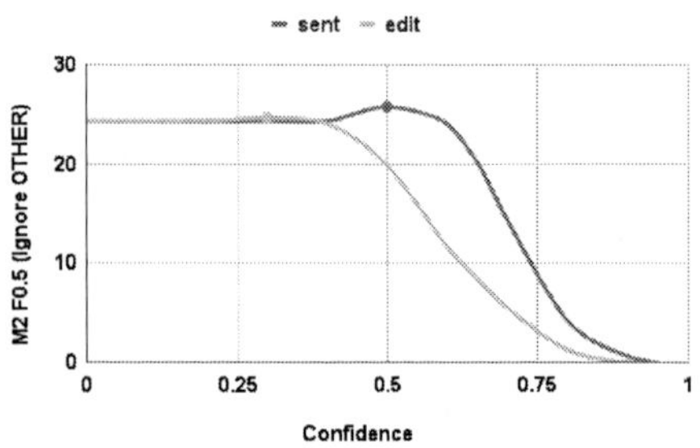

Figure 3: Comparing sentence-level and edit-level confidence filtering. Moving from left to right, confidence threshold increases, and more edits get filtered out.

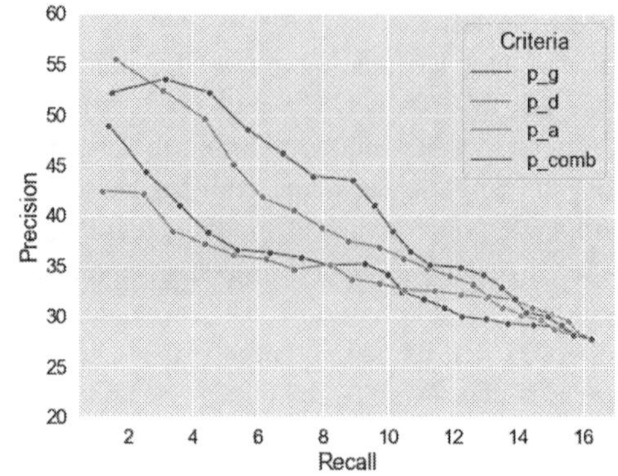

Figure 4: Precision and recall curves: filtering using sentence-level confidences of individual modules. P_{comb}: combined confidence, P_{a}: ASR, P_{d}: DD, P_{g}: GEC. From right to left, filtering out an increasing number of edits. The final α, β, γ coefficients are selected using the optimal $M^2 F_{0.5}$ score, which gives $\alpha = 0.3, \beta = 0.4, \gamma = 0.3$.

ture of grammatical corrections being intertwined within one sentence, i.e. removing one edit from a sentence could potentially result in inconsistencies with other corrections made to sentence. Table 9 shows the operating points of confidence filtering. Removing 33.8% of the edits using sentence filtering gives significant gains in both precision and $F_{0.5}$; whereas edit filtering gives mild improvement when 3.7% of edits are filtered out. When deploying SGEC systems, we can always change the confidence threshold to strike a balance between percentage removal and precision improvement.

Filter	P	R	$F_{0.5}$	%Rm
None	27.75	16.24	24.30	0
Sent	33.96	13.15	25.80	33.8
Edit	28.53	16.05	24.69	3.7

Table 9: Operating points of confidence filtering. P: precision, R: recall, %Rm percentage edits being removed

As explained in Eqn. 18, system confidence combines probabilities from all three modules. Fig. 4 analyses the impact of individual modules by contrasting filtering using sentence-level confidence of each module. As an increasing number of edits get filtered out, precision-recall curves move from bottom right to top left corner (precision increases, and recall decreases). Larger area under the curve indicates higher $F_{0.5}$ scores throughout the sweep. Filtering with P_{a} outperforms both P_{d} and P_{g}, suggesting that ASR confidence is quite indicative of feedback quality. Another implication from this observation is that quality of ASR transcriptions largely impacts downstream performances.

We also take a closer look at the impact of sentence-level filtering on different edit types. Table 10 shows the change in precision, recall and $F_{0.5}$ scores before and after filtering. Confidence filtering improves feedback $F_{0.5}$ on most edit types, among which most significant ones are `R:PREP`, `U:DET`, `M:PREP`[2]. The two degraded edit types are `R:VERB:TENSE`, `R:VERB:FORM`, both of which often have more than one feasible corrections. Confidence-based filtering tends to remove edits with diverse solutions, due to the high entropy, thus low confidence in the hypotheses. Such rejection pattern leads to significant drop in recall, and consequently reduces $F_{0.5}$ of edits with diverse corrections. On the other hand, for edits like `R:PREP`, `U:DET`, `M:PREP`, there usually exists a single, definite fix. Baseline $F_{0.5}$ scores on those edits are in general quite high, and confidence filtering helps to further improve the performance. Such observation suggests that confidence filtering helps to reduce feedback on ambiguous edits, and in the meantime, boosts precision on more deterministic corrections.

	NoFilter			Sent		
Edit Type	P	R	$F_{0.5}$	P	R	$F_{0.5}$
M:DET	30.18	27.39	29.57	35.86	22.61	**32.10**
R:PREP	37.86	18.47	31.29	46.88	15.68	**33.53**
R:NOUN:NUM	37.88	20.66	32.47	44.68	17.36	**33.98**
R:VERB:TENSE	35.63	13.60	**26.91**	35.00	9.21	22.44
U:DET	23.20	16.20	21.36	29.49	12.85	**23.42**
R:VERB	27.27	11.69	21.53	33.33	10.39	**23.12**
R:NOUN	11.77	4.29	8.72	18.52	3.57	**10.08**
M:PREP	23.29	13.39	20.29	35.56	12.60	**26.06**
R:VERB:FORM	31.17	20.00	**28.04**	38.10	13.33	27.78
R:VERB:SVA	31.92	27.78	30.99	37.31	23.15	**33.25**

Table 10: Comparing $P, R, F_{0.5}$ before and after sentence-level confidence filtering, breakdown by edit types.

[2]There are three prefixes - R: replacement, U: unnecessary, M: missing. The error types are defined using part-of-speech (POS) tags. E.g. `R:PREP` means replacement of preposition. More details on edit types see Bryant et al. 2017.

6 Conclusions

This paper focuses on assessing and developing cascaded SGEC systems. We discuss standard metrics for individual module assessment, as well as edit distance based metrics for system output evaluation. To mitigate module error propagation in cascaded systems, we experimented with semi-supervised fine-tuning and self-distillation approaches, aiming to improve system output quality. Lastly, confidence-based filtering is investigated, and it proves to be effective in improving feedback precision as well as the overall quality.

For future work, we plan to experiment with the state-of-the-art end-to-end ASR systems, which potentially gives lower WER and further improves the SGEC performances. Another research direction is to investigate tighter integration of modular SGEC systems, which allows a richer information flow cross module connections.

Acknowledgements

Thanks to Dr. Linlin Wang for building the ASR system and Dr. Kate Knill for helping generate the ASR confidence scores. This paper reports on research supported by Cambridge Assessment, University of Cambridge. Thanks to Cambridge English Language Assessment for support and access to the Linguaskill data, and Diane Nicholls and her team of ELiT Humannotators for annotating the data set. Work was done while Stefano Bannò was an exchange student at Cambridge.

References

Christopher Bryant, Mariano Felice, Øistein E. Andersen, and Ted Briscoe. 2019. The BEA-2019 shared task on grammatical error correction. In *Proceedings of the Fourteenth Workshop on Innovative Use of NLP for Building Educational Applications*, pages 52–75, Florence, Italy. Association for Computational Linguistics.

Christopher Bryant, Mariano Felice, and Ted Briscoe. 2017. Automatic annotation and evaluation of error types for grammatical error correction. In *Proceedings of the 55th Annual Meeting of the Association for Computational Linguistics (Volume 1: Long Papers)*, pages 793–805, Vancouver, Canada. Association for Computational Linguistics.

Andrew Caines, Christian Bentz, Kate Knill, Marek Rei, and Paula Buttery. 2020. Grammatical error detection in transcriptions of spoken english. In *Proceedings of the 28th International Conference on Computational Linguistics*, pages 2144–2162.

X. Chen, X. Liu, A. Ragni, Y. Wang, and M. J. F. Gales. 2017. Future word contexts in neural network language models. In *Proc. ASRU*, pages 97–103. IEEE.

Council of Europe. 2001. *Common European framework of reference for languages: Learning, teaching, assessment.* Cambridge University Press.

Daniel Dahlmeier and Hwee Tou Ng. 2012. Better evaluation for grammatical error correction. In *Proceedings of the 2012 Conference of the North American Chapter of the Association for Computational Linguistics: Human Language Technologies*, pages 568–572, Montréal, Canada. Association for Computational Linguistics.

Robert Dale and Adam Kilgarriff. 2011. Helping our own: The HOO 2011 pilot shared task. In *Proceedings of the 13th European Workshop on Natural Language Generation*, pages 242–249, Nancy, France. Association for Computational Linguistics.

Jacob Devlin, Ming-Wei Chang, Kenton Lee, and Kristina Toutanova. 2019. BERT: Pre-training of deep bidirectional transformers for language understanding. In *Proceedings of the 2019 Conference of the North American Chapter of the Association for Computational Linguistics: Human Language Technologies, Volume 1 (Long and Short Papers)*, pages 4171–4186, Minneapolis, Minnesota. Association for Computational Linguistics.

Gunnar Evermann, Ho Yin Chan, Mark JF Gales, Bin Jia, David Mrva, Philip C Woodland, and Kai Yu. 2005. Training LVCSR systems on thousands of hours of data. In *Proceedings.(ICASSP'05). IEEE International Conference on Acoustics, Speech, and Signal Processing, 2005.*, volume 1, pages I–209. IEEE.

Geoffrey Hinton, Oriol Vinyals, Jeff Dean, et al. 2015. Distilling the knowledge in a neural network. *arXiv preprint arXiv:1503.02531*, 2(7).

P Izmailov, AG Wilson, D Podoprikhin, D Vetrov, and T Garipov. 2018. Averaging weights leads to wider optima and better generalization. In *34th Conference on Uncertainty in Artificial Intelligence 2018, UAI 2018*, pages 876–885.

Diederik P Kingma and Jimmy Ba. 2014. Adam: A method for stochastic optimization. *arXiv preprint arXiv:1412.6980*.

Jared Lichtarge, Chris Alberti, Shankar Kumar, Noam Shazeer, Niki Parmar, and Simon Tong. 2019. Corpora generation for grammatical error correction. pages 3291–3301.

Y Lu, MJF Gales, and Y Wang. 2020. Spoken language'grammatical error correction'. In *Proceedings of the Annual Conference of the International Speech Communication Association, INTERSPEECH*, volume 2020, pages 3840–3844.

M. Meteer, A. Taylor, R. MacIntyre, and R. Iyer. 1995. Dysfluency Annotation Stylebook for the Switchboard Corpus. Technical report, Linguistic Data Consortium. Updated June 1995 by Ann Taylor.

Courtney Napoles, Keisuke Sakaguchi, Matt Post, and Joel Tetreault. 2015. Ground truth for grammatical error correction metrics. In *Proceedings of the 53rd Annual Meeting of the Association for Computational Linguistics and the 7th International Joint Conference on Natural Language Processing (Volume 2: Short Papers)*, pages 588–593, Beijing, China. Association for Computational Linguistics.

Hwee Tou Ng, Siew Mei Wu, Ted Briscoe, Christian Hadiwinoto, Raymond Hendy Susanto, and Christopher Bryant. 2014. The CoNLL-2014 shared task on grammatical error correction. In *Proceedings of the Eighteenth Conference on Computational Natural Language Learning: Shared Task*, pages 1–14, Baltimore, Maryland. Association for Computational Linguistics.

Diane Nicholls. 2003. The Cambridge Learner Corpus: Error coding and analysis for lexicography and ELT. In *Proc. of the Corpus Linguistics 2003 conference; UCREL technical paper number 16.*

Kishore Papineni, Salim Roukos, Todd Ward, and Wei-Jing Zhu. 2002. BLEU: a method for automatic evaluation of machine translation. In *Proceedings of the 40th Annual Meeting of the Association for Computational Linguistics*, pages 311–318, Philadelphia, Pennsylvania, USA. Association for Computational Linguistics.

Daniel Povey, Gaofeng Cheng, Yiming Wang, Ke Li, Hainan Xu, Mahsa Yarmohamadi, and Sanjeev Khudanpur. 2018. Semi-orthogonal low-rank matrix factorization for deep neural networks. In *INTERSPEECH*, pages 3743–3747.

Colin Raffel, Noam Shazeer, Adam Roberts, Katherine Lee, Sharan Narang, Michael Matena, Yanqi Zhou, Wei Li, and Peter J. Liu. 2020. Exploring the limits of transfer learning with a unified text-to-text transformer. *Journal of Machine Learning Research*, 21(140):1–67.

Matthew Snover, Bonnie Dorr, Richard Schwartz, Linnea Micciulla, and John Makhoul. 2006. A study of translation edit rate with targeted human annotation. In *Proceedings of the 7th Conference of the Association for Machine Translation in the Americas: Technical Papers*, pages 223–231.

Ann Taylor, Mitchell Marcus, and Beatrice Santorini. 2003. The Penn treebank: an overview. *Treebanks*, pages 5–22.

Y. Wang, J. H. M. Wong, M. J. F. Gales, K. M. Knill, and A. Ragni. 2018. Sequence teacher-student training of acoustic models for automatic free speaking language assessment. *Proc. IEEE Spoken Language Technology Workshop (SLT)*, pages 994–1000.

Thomas Wolf, Lysandre Debut, Victor Sanh, Julien Chaumond, Clement Delangue, Anthony Moi, Pierric Cistac, Tim Rault, Rémi Louf, Morgan Funtowicz, Joe Davison, Sam Shleifer, Patrick von Platen, Clara Ma, Yacine Jernite, Julien Plu, Canwen Xu, Teven Le Scao, Sylvain Gugger, Mariama Drame, Quentin Lhoest, and Alexander M. Rush. 2019. Huggingface's transformers: State-of-the-art natural language processing.

Yige Xu, Xipeng Qiu, Ligao Zhou, and Xuanjing Huang. 2020. Improving BERT fine-tuning via self-ensemble and self-distillation. *Journal of Computer Science and Technology*, 33:1–18.

Helen Yannakoudakis, Ted Briscoe, and Ben Medlock. 2011. A new dataset and method for automatically grading ESOL texts. In *Proceedings of the 49th Annual Meeting of the Association for Computational Linguistics: Human Language Technologies*, pages 180–189, Portland, Oregon, USA. Association for Computational Linguistics.

Zheng Yuan and Ted Briscoe. 2016. Grammatical error correction using neural machine translation. In *Proceedings of the 2016 Conference of the North American Chapter of the Association for Computational Linguistics: Human Language Technologies*, pages 380–386, San Diego, California. Association for Computational Linguistics.

Vicky Zayats, Mari Ostendorf, and Hannaneh Hajishirzi. 2016. Disfluency detection using a bidirectional LSTM. *arXiv preprint arXiv:1604.03209*.

Linfeng Zhang, Jiebo Song, Anni Gao, Jingwei Chen, Chenglong Bao, and Kaisheng Ma. 2019. Be your own teacher: Improve the performance of convolutional neural networks via self distillation. In *Proceedings of the IEEE/CVF International Conference on Computer Vision*, pages 3713–3722.

Automatic True/False Question Generation for Educational Purpose

Bowei Zou[1]*, **Pengfei Li**[2]*, **Liangming Pan**[3], **Ai Ti Aw**[1]
[1]Institute for Infocomm Research, A*STAR, Singapore
[2]Nanyang Technological University, Singapore
[3]National University of Singapore, Singapore
{zou_bowei,aaiti}@i2r.a-star.edu.sg
pengfei.li@ntu.edu.sg
liangmingpan@u.nus.edu

Abstract

In field of teaching, true/false questioning is an important educational method for assessing students' general understanding of learning materials. Manually creating such questions requires extensive human effort and expert knowledge. Question Generation (QG) technique offers the possibility to automatically generate a large number of questions. However, there is limited work on automatic true/false question generation due to the lack of training data and difficulty finding question-worthy content. In this paper, we propose an unsupervised True/False Question Generation approach (TF-QG) that automatically generates true/false questions from a given passage for reading comprehension test. TF-QG consists of a template-based framework that aims to test the specific knowledge in the passage by leveraging various NLP techniques, and a generative framework to generate more flexible and complicated questions by using a novel masking-and-infilling strategy. Human evaluation shows that our approach can generate high-quality and valuable true/false questions. In addition, simulated testing on the generated questions challenges the state-of-the-art inference models from NLI, QA, and fact verification tasks.

1 Introduction

For educational purposes, questioning not only assesses the acquisition of knowledge, but also reinforces the engagement and critical thinking of learners during effective teaching, which in turn enables learners to clearly guide their learning efforts and enhance their skills (Prince, 2004). With the ever-growing educational content on the internet and the increasing popularity of online tutoring applications during the COVID-19 pandemic, an automatic question creation process becomes a key technique to reduce the efforts in manually constructing questions and facilitate adaptive learning.

Text-based question generation for education aims to produce legible and pedagogically-salient questions from a given textual content to provide meaningful learning experiences, where the answer to the question can be found or derived from the content. Earlier QG models generate simple questions based on manually constructed rules (Rus et al., 2012; Lindberg et al., 2013; Lee, 2016). However, such questions often lack linguistic diversity and contain much ungrammatical or nonsensical content (Kurdi et al., 2020). Recently, with the development of deep learning and question answering (QA) techniques, the studies of QG have shifted towards neural question generation (NQG) which utilizes deep neural networks to generate more fluent and diverse questions (Pan et al., 2019). Depending on the QA datasets used for training, various types of questions can be generated such as span-based questions (Du et al., 2017; Gao et al., 2019), multiple-choice questions (Chung et al., 2020), and multi-hop questions (Pan et al., 2020; Su et al., 2020). However, due to the limitation of the current QA corpus, most of the generated questions focus on finding the information presented in the passage. Moreover, the majority of NQG models are used for improving QA or dialogue systems instead of for educational purposes (Duan et al., 2017; Sachan and Xing, 2018; Pan et al., 2021).

Among various types of educational-purposed questions, true/false (T/F) questions can yield valid assessments directly, simply, and efficiently (Ebel, 1970), which is useful to evaluate if the learners hold any misconceptions about the given material. In this paper, we take the approach of defining the T/F question as a declarative sentence (statement)[1], rather than an interrogative sentence like that in BoolQ (Clark et al., 2019). So far, automatically generating such type of questions is relatively less explored. Lee (2016) developed a system where the original sentences in passage are

* Equal contribution

[1]See more examples in Section 3.4.

Proceedings of the 17th Workshop on Innovative Use of NLP for Building Educational Applications (BEA 2022), pages 61 - 70
July 15, 2022 ©2022 Association for Computational Linguistics

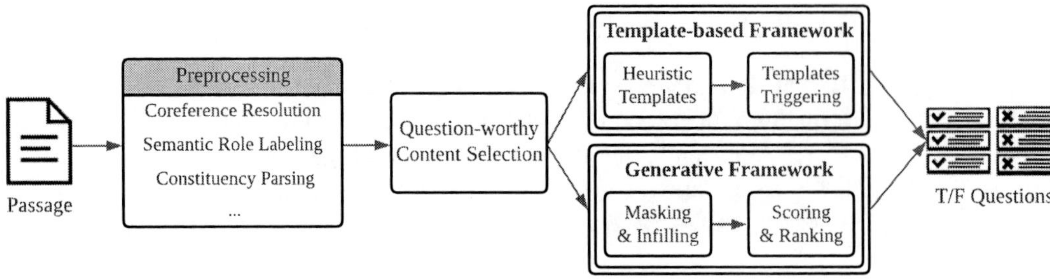

Figure 1: Overall architecture of TF-QG.

used as true questions and the false questions are generated by replacing the keywords with their antonyms or adding a negative keyword. Killawala et al. (2018)'s method was also based on simple syntactic templates. However, the quality of the generated questions is not good enough for assessment due to 1) the lack of training data and difficulty of finding good testing points from a given passage, and 2) the high occurrence of grammatical and semantic errors (Zhang and Bansal, 2019).

In this paper, we propose an unsupervised True/False Question Generation approach (TF-QG) for assessing the reading comprehension ability of English learners. TF-QG leverages both a traditional template-based method and a recently developed generative language model to generate high-quality T/F questions from a given passage. In the *template-based framework*, various NLP techniques are used for creating heuristic templates to test certain knowledge such as lexical, syntactic, and coreference understanding. In the *generative framework*, we propose a novel masking-and-infilling strategy to generate more flexible and complicated questions such as inferential questions that require deeper understandings of the passage. Specifically, to yield questions with valid testing points, we design several templates and mask selection protocols to select question-worthy contents from the passage. Then, the pretrained language model with text infilling objective is used to generate new statements based on both the prior knowledge and the context of the passage. Finally, we design a novel scoring mechanism to score and rank the generated questions based on their conciseness and relevance to the passage.

Extensive human evaluation shows that TF-QG is able to generate high-quality T/F questions containing both factoid and inferential content. In addition, simulated experiments on the generated T/F questions challenge the state-of-the-art NLI, QA, and fact verification systems, which indicates that these questions are difficult to some extent.

To summarize, our main contributions are:

- We propose an unsupervised system for T/F question generation with the educational purpose of testing students' reading comprehension ability. The question-worthy contents are selected by our designed templates and mask selection protocols targeting various testing points. Such templates and protocols can be customized by educators based on test points, making it easier to incorporate into TF-QG without modifying or retraining the model.
- We propose a masking-and-infilling question generation strategy that enables the system to generate more linguistically diverse and semantically complicated T/F questions.
- TF-QG provides a domain-independent solution for constructing a large-scale T/F reading comprehension dataset. Both human evaluation and simulated tests on reasoning tasks show the reasonableness and difficulty of the generated T/F questions.

2 TF-QG Model

Given a passage as reading material, TF-QG aims to generate T/F questions to test learners' understanding of the passage. The overall architecture is shown in Figure 1. The passage is first preprocessed to obtain the basic syntactic and semantic information (Section 2.1). Then, two unsupervised frameworks including the template-based framework (Section 2.2) and the generative framework (Section 2.3) are applied to generate T/F questions targeting the question-worthy contents in the passage. The question-worthy contents are selected according to our designed templates/protocols in the two frameworks which will be described in the respective sections.

2.1 Passage Pre-processing

We first conduct coreference resolution to resolve pronouns to their corresponding antecedents and gather antecedents representing the same concept into a *coreference set*. Then we implement semantic role labeling (SRL) and put the semantic roles of the same subject (Arg0) into respective *SRL sets*. The constituency parsing tree for each sentence is obtained by a syntactic parser. Finally, we extract *numeral sets* from the passage, each set contains instances of "number + quantifier" (e.g., "200 meters") with the same quantifier. Our implementations are based on the AllenNLP library (Gardner et al., 2017).[2]

2.2 Template-based Framework

To assess learners, intuitively, the generated T/F questions should be sufficiently similar to some fragments about the passage, but different from the passage at a pedagogically meaningful point. Although there be various definitions of what one might consider valuable test points, this paper focuses on the areas that we thought were most likely to be relevant to language learning and understanding. To this end, we design the following heuristic templates to generate T/F questions by selecting and modifying the question-worthy content in the given passage.

- **Coreference substitution template (Coref)** If a pronoun is more than one sentence away from its antecedent, we replace the pronoun with its antecedent to generate a true question. Besides, the pronoun is replaced with an irrelevant antecedent in the coreference set to generate a false question.
- **Coordination modification template (Coord)** From the constituency parsing tree, we find noun coordination structures in the form of "NP_1 CC NP_2" or "NP_1, NP_2, ..., CC NP_k".[3] Then we randomly select a NP_i ($i \in 1, ..., k$) node and use the templates "... only NP_i ..." and "... no NP_i ..." to generate false questions.
- **SRL modification template (SRL)** If there are same semantic role types in an SRL set, we exchange the two semantic roles into each other's sentences to generate two false questions.
- **Synonym/Antonym substitution template (Synonym/Antonym)** When we find an adjective or an adverb in a short sentence (<15 words), the word is replaced with its synonym or antonym from WordNet[4] to generate a true question or a false question, respectively.
- **Negation modification template (Negation)** If a sentence contains a verbal negation or a word from the negative cue list extracted from Bioscope (Vincze et al., 2008), we remove the negative word and take the rest of the sentence as a false question.
- **Number modification template (Num)** If there is more than one element in a numeral set, we randomly exchange two of them into each other's original sentences, to generate two false questions.
- **Definition modification template (Def)** If an appositive clause fits the pattern "... NP_1 <comma> NP_2 ...", we generate a corresponding true question as "NP_1 <copula> NP_2.".
- **Simplification rule** To make the question more concise and focus on the key information, we remove 1) the constituency structures "SBAR" and "IN+S", 2) the contents between two commas (parenthesis), and 3) the constituency structures "PP" and "ADVP" at the beginning of the question.

Each of the above heuristic templates is activated independently and repeatedly if its conditions are met. These templates aim to test the learners' understanding of the passage from different aspects: Coref, Num, and Def templates focus on the understanding of context meaning, number, and definition, respectively; Synonym/Antonym templates test learners' lexical understanding while Coord, SRL, and Negation template tests syntactic or semantic understanding.

Note that the above templates are customizable, i.e. educators could easily add new heuristic templates to TF-QG for specific teaching or testing purposes with. In addition, an advantage of the template-based framework is that it can generate T/F questions while determining whether their answers are true or false. On the other hand, the limitation of this template-based framework is that it requires educators to 1) know which types of language capabilities of the learners they would like to test and specify the test points (this is related to the educational process and difficult to be replaced by models), and 2) know the formulation of the fundamental NLP tasks, to smoothly convert the language test points to the templates with extra effort only once.

[2] `https://allennlp.org`

[3] NP: noun phrase; CC: coordinating conjunction.

[4] `https://wordnet.princeton.edu`

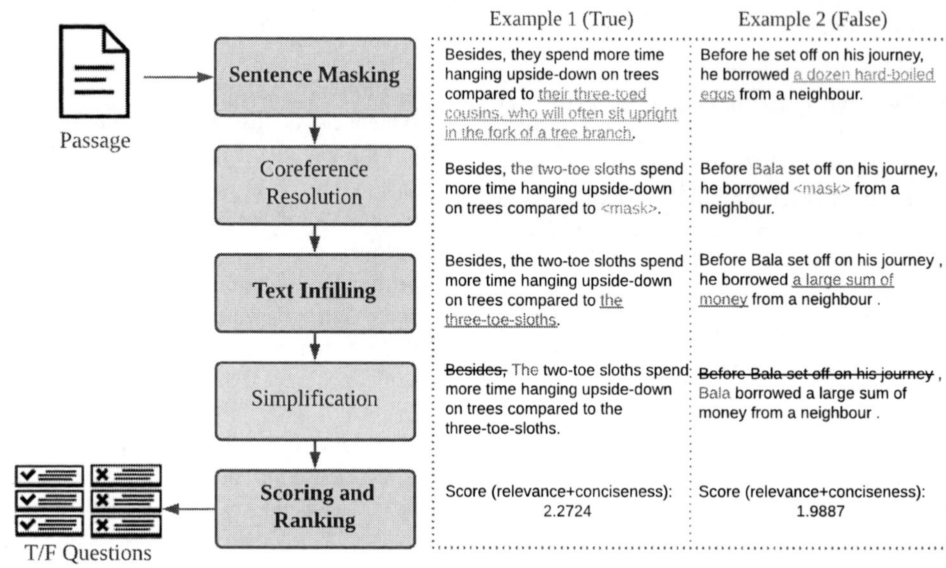

Figure 2: Generative framework of TF-QG. The processes and data-flow are shown on the left; two examples with step-by-step transformations are shown on the right.

2.3 Generative Framework

Generative framework aims to generate more flexible and complicated T/F questions. As shown on the left of Figure 2, the highlighted masking-and-infilling and scoring-and-ranking are the main components of our model. Two examples with step-by-step transformations are shown on the right. Example 1 is a true question generated from an expository passage, whereas Example 2 is a false question generated from a narrative passage. In the following, we describe each process in detail.

2.3.1 Sentence Masking

To pick question-worthy content from the passage and facilitate the generation of T/F questions, we design the following mask selection protocols.

- **Semantic role masking**. Mask the arguments of a predicate in the sentence based on the SRL results.
- **Subordinate clause masking**. Mask the part in a subordinate clause that follows a subordinating conjunction such as "that", "when", "since", etc.
- **Prepositional phrase masking**. Mask the part in a prepositional phrase that follows a preposition. We only consider the phrase with more than two words.
- **Adversative clause masking**. Mask the adversative clause in the sentence. The adversative relation is identified by the keywords such as "although", "but", etc. We also convert the keywords into coordinating conjunctions ("so"/"and") in order to generate false statements.
- **Declarative clause masking**. Mask the simple declarative clause after a preposition or subordinating conjunction (i.e. "IN+S").
- **Number masking**. Mask numbers. "one" is excluded since it is often used for other purposes.

These protocols identify the key information in the passage. Such information is replaced with a special <mask> token that represents a missing span in the sentence. More examples of the T/F questions generated from the above-mentioned mask selection protocols are provided in the case study in Section 3.4.

Coreference Resolution To improve clarity, the first-appeared pronouns in the sentence are replaced with their corresponding antecedents.

2.3.2 Text Infilling

To generate T/F questions from the masked sentences, we perform a text infilling task aiming to predict the missing span of text which are consistent with the preceding and subsequent text. We utilize a pretrained language model BART (Lewis et al., 2020) to perform text infilling, which is a Transformer-based denoising autoencoder pretrained on large text corpus with text infilling as a training objective. Hence, it has good capabilities of reconstructing a corrupted text by fitting the most suitable text to the missing span.

Criteria	Rating	Score	Description
Fluency (grammatical correctness)	bad	1	Not readable due to grammatical errors.
	fair	2	Contain few grammatical errors but not affect the readability too much.
	good	3	Free from grammatical errors.
Semantic (clarity and logical correctness)	bad	1	Have obvious logical/common-sense problem or indecipherable.
	fair	2	Have some semantic ambiguities.
	good	3	Semantically clear.
Relevance (to the passage)	bad	1	Totally irrelevant.
	fair	2	Part of the question is irrelevant.
	good	3	Relevant.
Answerability	bad	1	Not answerable.
	fair	2	Not sure about the correct answer.
	good	3	Can be answered by the right answer.
Difficulty	factoid	1	Can be inferred from a single sentence in the passage.
	inferential	2	Requires deeper understanding of the passage or longer context.

Table 1: Human evaluation metrics with description.

To make the generated text more relevant to the passage, we provide two sentences before and after the masked sentence as context to BART model. The model predicts the missing span based on both the context of the passage and the prior knowledge learned during language modeling. We also perform beam search with beam width 5 to obtain the top-5 outputs with the highest probabilities.

Simplification To make the question more concise, we perform the same simplification process as in the template-based framework by removing the auxiliary components of the sentence.

2.3.3 Scoring and Ranking

We propose a scoring mechanism to automatically evaluate and rank the generated questions based on their conciseness and relevance.

$$S = \frac{1}{1 + e^{-0.3(l_t - l_g)}} + \frac{R_l + R_c + R_s}{|g|}$$

The first term is the conciseness score where l_t and l_g are the lengths of the original and generated sentence, respectively. The second term is the relevance score where R_l is lexical relevance score measuring the number of overlapping words between the generated texts and the passage; R_c and R_s are conceptual and semantic relevance scores measuring the number of generated words that are conceptually and semantically relevant to the masked words. We use ConceptNet (Speer et al., 2017) to obtain the concept-relevant terms of the masked words, and FrameNet (Ruppenhofer et al., 2006) to obtain the semantic frames of both generated words and masked words. $|g|$ is a normalization term that counts the number of generated words.

Finally, we choose the question with the highest score from the beam search results. Then we rank all the questions generated from the passage and select the top-scoring questions as the final T/F questions.

3 Experimentation

3.1 Settings and Evaluation Metrics

Since there is no standard dataset available for automatic evaluation, we conduct human evaluation on the generated T/F questions. We randomly select 20 well-edited English passages from the quiz materials at a level of elementary education as our test set, which contains both expository writings (e.g., descriptive articles) and narrative writings (e.g., stories and diaries) on topics of general interest. For each passage, we collect all questions generated by the template-based framework and up to 20 questions generated by the generative framework. Finally, from the selected 20 passages, we obtain 401 questions in total, an average of 20 questions per passage.

Due to the educational nature of our purpose, we recruit three annotators with educational backgrounds to rate the produced questions. The annotators were first asked to read the passage, and then give judgments for fluency, semantic, relevance, answerability, and difficulty, as shown in Table 1. From the ratings given by the three annotators, we take the majority vote as the final ratings. In case of a tie, we choose the average rating (i.e. "fair"). In addition, for the results from the generative frame-

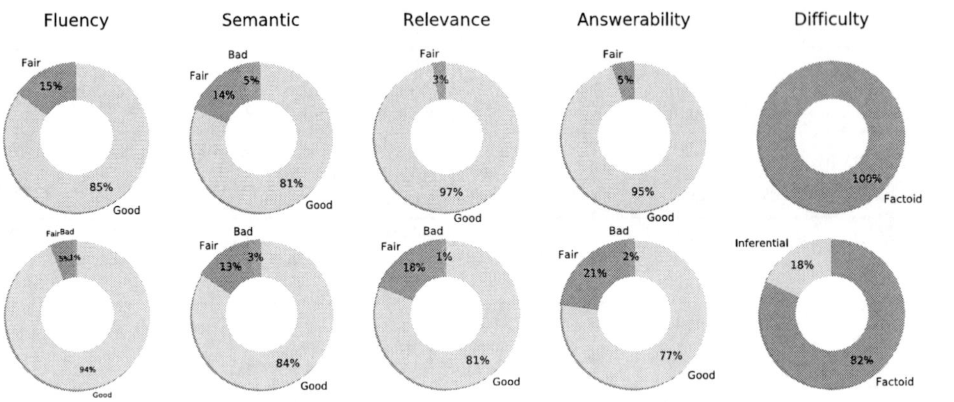

Figure 3: Human evaluation results of the T/F questions generated by TF-QG. Top row and bottom row show the results from template-based framework and generative framework, respectively.

Criteria	Template-based	Generative
Fluency	0.772	0.870
Semantic	0.723	0.710
Relevance	0.861	0.630
Answerability	0.812	0.620
Difficulty	0.881	0.813
Answer	/	0.725

Table 2: Annotator agreement. Scores denotes Randolph's kappa (Randolph, 2005) that measures the agreement from multiple annotators.

work, we also ask the annotators to label the answer (T/F) of the questions. Table 2 shows the inter-rater agreement, which indicates that all the annotations have substantial ($0.6 < \kappa \leq 0.8$) or almost perfect ($\kappa > 0.8$) agreement.

3.2 Experimental Results

The human evaluation results are presented in Figure 3. It is observed that the majority (>80%) of the questions generated by TF-QG have good fluency, semantic, relevance, and answerability. Hence, the questions are promising to be directly used for the educational purpose of assessing language learners' reading comprehension ability. However, we also observe that the generated questions have lower scores on the difficulty rating. All of the questions generated by the template-based framework are factoid, and only 18% of the questions from the generative framework are inferential. Finding such answers does not require too complicated reasoning efforts. Hence, we argue that the current method is still a long way from generating more complex questions, and this paper has played a role in exploring this direction.

For the template-based framework, templates offer the ability to produce questions lightly coupled with the exact wording of the original text. The results show that our TF-QG model can generate much more relevant questions with good answerability than the generative framework (relevance rating) since all generated questions are closely related to the passage, which makes the templates easy to leverage human linguistic expertise to produce questions tailored to specific educational content. In addition, the template-based framework also has the advantage that the answers are given explicitly since templates are designed for different types (true/false) of answers. However, the rigid transformations by templates may cause more grammatical (fluency rating) and logical (semantic rating) problems.

For the generative framework, the fluency and semantic of the questions are improved due to the benefits of language modeling. The two properties are crucial since if the generated questions do not satisfy such requirements, learners may easily be misled and frustrated, which reduces questions' pedagogical value. Besides, the syntactic and content of the questions are more flexible, enabling our model to generate more complicated questions. The human evaluation shows that our generative framework is able to produce inferential questions (18%) to test student's comprehensive understanding of the passage. However, due to the flexibility of generated content, the question may be irrelevant to the passage and hence their answerability may be affected.

Tasks	Dev	full	1sent	3sent	5sent
NLI	86.1	55.9	**66.2**	61.6	59.0
BoolQ	80.4	48.5	57.2	55.4	53.9
$BoolQ_d$	77.0	47.7	54.6	53.1	51.0
FEVER	95.3	50.3	52.8	51.0	52.6

Table 3: True/false reading comprehension accuracy (%). $BoolQ_d$: the questions are converted to declarative sentences. Dev: the performance on the development set of the fine-tuning tasks.

3.3 True/False Reading Comprehension

To further evaluate the difficulty of the questions generated by our model, we create a simulated task of true/false reading comprehension, which aims to test the capability of NLP models to answer T/F questions. To this end, we first construct a test set (TFQA) using the questions generated from the generative framework of TF-QG. Then, we ask the annotators to label the answers (True/False) of the questions. After removing the questions with bad answerability, the TFQA test set contains 210 false questions and 178 true questions. Finally, we test the performance of the state-of-the-art natural language inference (NLI), QA, and fact verification models on TFQA in a zero-shot transfer learning way. Specifically, we fine-tune a pretrained BERT (Devlin et al., 2019) model on various related tasks/datasets, including the NLI task with SNLI (Bowman et al., 2015) and MultiNLI (Williams et al., 2018), the bool QA task with BoolQ (Clark et al., 2019), and the fact verification task with FEVER (Thorne et al., 2018).

For BoolQ, we use two strategies to make the task similar to ours: 1) convert our questions to interrogative sentences during inference; 2) convert BoolQ questions to declarative sentences during fine-tuning. Besides using the full passage ("full") as input, we also test the performance using the question-related sentence ("1sent") and the sentence with contexts including one sentence ("3sent") and two sentences ("5sent") before and after the sentence.

Experimental results are shown in Table 3. Although the model can achieve near state-of-the-art performances on the fine-tuning tasks ("Dev"), the best accuracy on the TFQA test set is only 66.2%. This demonstrates that the questions generated by our model are challenging. To obtain better performance, more sophisticated models and training data are required under supervised settings. Although the point is outside the scope of this paper, our approach does offer the NLP community a possibility to construct a T/F question answering dataset.

3.4 Case Study

We present a case study on a passage about "Yellowstone National Park". The questions generated by our TF-QG model are shown in Table 4. We show only one question for each template/protocol due to the space limitation.

Generally, the questions generated from the templates meet our goal of testing certain knowledge such as coreference, lexical, and definition understanding. However, since the template does not refer to the contextual information when substituting synonyms, Question 1 is not fluent due to the wrong wording. Question 3 shows the advantages of the template-based framework on the testing target that aims to distinguish concepts. In the original passage, Old Faithful is described as a "geyser", while in the question, it is stated as another approximate concept "hot spring". Question 4 also fulfills the test goal of concept understanding, which distinguishes concepts between "Celsius" and "Fahrenheit", although the generated question merely swaps the numbers. Regarding other test points, Question 2 provides a simple verbal negative case. Question 5 tests both pronoun understanding and vocabulary comprehension.

The questions generated by the generative framework are more flexible and challenging. Many questions require inferring from longer context and they are useful to test learners' comprehensive understanding of the passage, such as Question 6-9. In particular, the generative model supplements Question 9 with the information that "boiling water comes from geyser", which can only be obtained from the above description. Such questions can well examine the learner's understanding of contextual consistency and cohesion. However, some questions are hard to answer due to bad coreference resolution or irrelevant content generated as shown in Question 10.

In general, we observe that the generated T/F questions can be effectively targeted to test many teaching inspection points. Currently, although these generated questions are relatively simple, they are sufficient for usage in some scenarios, such as reading comprehension tests for primary school

Yellowstone National Park is in the United States of America. It became the first National Park in 1872. [1]There are geysers and hot springs at Yellowstone. There are also many animals like elk, bison, sheep, grizzly bears, black bears, moose, coyotes, and more at Yellowstone. More than 3 million people visit Yellowstone each year. [2]During the winter, visitors can ski, go snowmobiling or join tours there. [6]Visitors can see steam and water from the geysers. During other seasons, visitors can go horse-riding, boating, fishing or take nature trails and tours. [3,7]Most visitors want to see Old Faithful, a very predictable geyser at Yellowstone. Visitors can check a schedule to see the precise time that Old Faithful is going to erupt. There are many other geysers and bubbling springs in the area. [8]Great Fountain Geyser erupts every 11 hours up to a height of 67 metres. Excelsior Geyser produces 4,000 gallons of boiling water each minute! [4,9]Boiling water is 100 degrees Celsius, or 212 degrees Fahrenheit – that's very hot! People also like to see the Grand Prismatic Spring. It is the largest hot spring in the park. [5]It has many beautiful colors, which are caused by bacteria in the water. [10]These are forms of life that have only one cell. Different bacteria live in different water temperatures. Visiting Yellowstone National Park can be a week–long vacation or more. It is beautiful, and there are activities for everyone.

No.	Framework	Template/Protocol	True/False Question
1	Template	Synonym	There are geysers and spicy springs at Yellowstone. (F)
2	Template	Coord+Negation	During the winter, visitors cannot ski. (F)
3	Template	Def+Coord	Old Faithful is a very predictable hot spring at Yellowstone. (F)
4	Template	Num	Boiling water is 212 degrees Celsius. (F)
5	Template	Coref+Antonym	The Grand Prismatic Spring has many ugly colors, which are caused by bacteria in the water. (F)
6	Generative	Preposition	Visitors can see steam and water from Yellowstone's geysers and hot springs. (F)
7	Generative	Semantic Role Arg1	Most visitors want to see Old Faithful when it is erupting. (T)
8	Generative	Semantic Role Arg0	Yellowstone National Park is home to the world's largest geyser,Yellowstone Geyser,which erupts every 11 hours up to a height of 67 metres.(F)
9	Generative	Number	The temperature of the geyser water is about 100 degrees Celsius, or 212 degrees Fahrenheit - that's very hot! (T)
10	Generative	Subordinate	These are forms of life that live on the surface of water. (?)

Table 4: Questions generated from a passage describing "Yellowstone National Park". The text where each question is generated from is highlighted in the passage with the corresponding number. The masked text in the generative framework is indicated using underline. "(?)" means unanswerable.

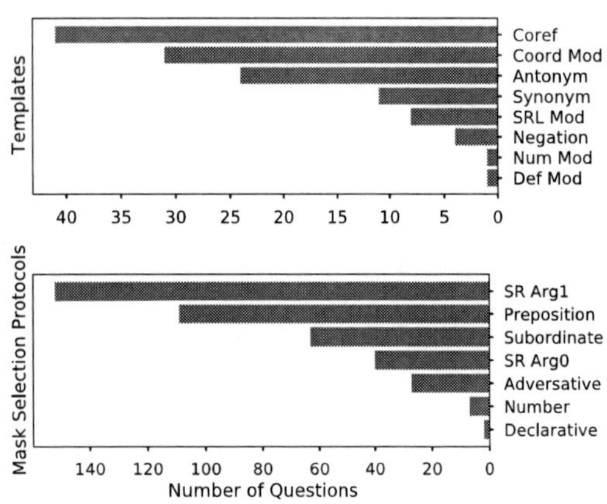

Figure 4: Number of questions generated from different templates (top) and mask selection protocols (bottom). "SR Arg0" and "SR Arg1" denote the semantic role masking protocol with the subject and object of the predicate being masked, respectively.

students or second language learners, or language education-oriented speech dialogue test systems.

3.5 Statistics of Templates and Protocols

We also study the frequency of different templates and mask selection protocols triggered by our TF-QG model. Figure 4 shows the number of questions generated from different templates/mask selection protocols based on the 20 testing passages. We can see that coreference, coordination, and antonym are the most frequently triggered templates for the template-based framework. For the generative framework, semantic role masking and prepositional phrase masking are the most frequently triggered mask selection protocols. The different numbers of the template- or protocol-triggered samples describe the distribution of the corresponding test points in the selected passages. Although we carefully selected different types of passages (including expository articles, stories, and diaries), more passages from different domains and genres still need to be explored to further verify the robustness of our proposed model on T/F question generation.

Besides, it is observed that the generative framework can the generate more questions than template-based framework in total. In fact, the masking-and-infilling approach allows the generative framework to produce an infinite number of questions, but the question quality still has to be considered. We currently pick questions by the generative confidence of the model. In future work, a more pedagogical question selection approach should be taken into account, such as which protocols should be selected in terms of practical quiz objectives, and which protocols are more suitable for generating inferential or challenging questions for different genres.

4 Conclusion

In this paper, we propose an automatic true/false question generation approach, which provides a feasible scheme for large-scale generation of educational content. Two unsupervised frameworks including template-based framework and generative framework are proposed to select question-worthy contents from the passage and generate high-quality questions. The novel masking-and-infilling strategy enables our model to generate more flexible and complicated true/false questions.

In future work, we will focus on how to design templates and mask selection protocols to match with pedagogically valuable test points proposed by domain experts. In addition, we will perform controlled lab or online studies to measure students' learning gains after studying the content generated by TF-QG. Furthermore, we expect to deploy the proposed approach on real educational platforms, including an interactive language learning and assessment system (for students), and a question generation assistance system (for teachers), to measure how much the approach could reduce the workload of educators in practical application scenarios.

Acknowledgements

The research has been supported by Institute of Infocomm Research of A*STAR (CR-2021-001). We thank the anonymous reviewers for their valuable and constructive feedback.

References

Samuel Bowman, Gabor Angeli, Christopher Potts, and Christopher D Manning. 2015. A large annotated corpus for learning natural language inference. In *Conference on Empirical Methods in Natural Language Processing, EMNLP 2015*, pages 632–642. Association for Computational Linguistics (ACL).

Ho-Lam Chung, Ying-Hong Chan, and Yao-Chung Fan. 2020. A bert-based distractor generation scheme with multi-tasking and negative answer training strategies. In *Proceedings of the 2020 Conference on Empirical Methods in Natural Language Processing: Findings*, pages 4390–4400.

Christopher Clark, Kenton Lee, Ming-Wei Chang, Tom Kwiatkowski, Michael Collins, and Kristina Toutanova. 2019. Boolq: Exploring the surprising difficulty of natural yes/no questions. In *Proceedings of the 2019 Conference of the North American Chapter of the Association for Computational Linguistics: Human Language Technologies, Volume 1 (Long and Short Papers)*, pages 2924–2936.

Jacob Devlin, Ming-Wei Chang, Kenton Lee, and Kristina Toutanova. 2019. Bert: Pre-training of deep bidirectional transformers for language understanding. In *Proceedings of the 2019 Conference of the North American Chapter of the Association for Computational Linguistics: Human Language Technologies, Volume 1 (Long and Short Papers)*, pages 4171–4186.

Xinya Du, Junru Shao, and Claire Cardie. 2017. Learning to ask: Neural question generation for reading comprehension. In *Proceedings of the 55th Annual Meeting of the Association for Computational Linguistics (Volume 1: Long Papers)*, pages 1342–1352.

Nan Duan, Duyu Tang, Peng Chen, and Ming Zhou. 2017. Question generation for question answering. In *Proceedings of the 2017 Conference on Empirical Methods in Natural Language Processing*, pages 866–874.

Robert L Ebel. 1970. The case for true-false test items. *The School Review*, 78(3):373–389.

Yifan Gao, Lidong Bing, Wang Chen, Michael R Lyu, and Irwin King. 2019. Difficulty controllable generation of reading comprehension questions. In *Proceedings of the 28th International Joint Conference on Artificial Intelligence*, pages 4968–4974. AAAI Press.

Matt Gardner, Joel Grus, Mark Neumann, Oyvind Tafjord, Pradeep Dasigi, Nelson F. Liu, Matthew Peters, Michael Schmitz, and Luke S. Zettlemoyer. 2017. Allennlp: A deep semantic natural language processing platform. *arXiv preprint arXiv:1803.07640*.

Akhil Killawala, Igor Khokhlov, and Leon Reznik. 2018. Computational intelligence framework for automatic quiz question generation. In *2018 IEEE International Conference on Fuzzy Systems (FUZZ-IEEE)*, pages 1–8. IEEE.

Ghader Kurdi, Jared Leo, Bijan Parsia, Uli Sattler, and Salam Al-Emari. 2020. A systematic review of automatic question generation for educational purposes. *International Journal of Artificial Intelligence in Education*, 30(1):121–204.

Jae-Young Lee. 2016. Dynamic relocation of true-false questions using ready-made arrays with random numbers. *International Journal of Software Engineering and Its Applications*, 10(8):91–100.

Mike Lewis, Yinhan Liu, Naman Goyal, Marjan Ghazvininejad, Abdelrahman Mohamed, Omer Levy, Veselin Stoyanov, and Luke Zettlemoyer. 2020. BART: Denoising sequence-to-sequence pre-training for natural language generation, translation, and comprehension. In *Proceedings of the 58th Annual Meeting of the Association for Computational Linguistics*, pages 7871–7880.

David Lindberg, Fred Popowich, John Nesbit, and Phil Winne. 2013. Generating natural language questions to support learning on-line. In *Proceedings of the 14th European Workshop on Natural Language Generation*, pages 105–114.

Liangming Pan, Wenhu Chen, Wenhan Xiong, Min-Yen Kan, and William Yang Wang. 2021. Unsupervised multi-hop question answering by question generation. In *Proceedings of the 2021 Conference of the North American Chapter of the Association for Computational Linguistics: Human Language Technologies*, pages 5866–5880, Online. Association for Computational Linguistics.

Liangming Pan, Wenqiang Lei, Tat-Seng Chua, and Min-Yen Kan. 2019. Recent advances in neural question generation. *arXiv preprint arXiv:1905.08949*.

Liangming Pan, Yuxi Xie, Yansong Feng, Tat-Seng Chua, and Min-Yen Kan. 2020. Semantic graphs for generating deep questions. In *Proceedings of the 58th Annual Meeting of the Association for Computational Linguistics*, pages 1463–1475.

Michael Prince. 2004. Does active learning work? a review of the research. *Journal of engineering education*, 93(3):223–231.

Justus J Randolph. 2005. Free-marginal multirater kappa (multirater κfree): An alternative to fleiss' fixed-marginal multirater kappa. In *Presented at the Joensuu Learning and Instruction Symposium*, volume 2005.

Josef Ruppenhofer, Michael Ellsworth, Miriam RL Petruck, Christopher R Johnson, and Jan Scheffczyk. 2006. Framenet ii: Extended theory and practice. berkeley. *CA: International Computer Science Institute*.

Vasile Rus, Brendan Wyse, Paul Piwek, Mihai Lintean, Svetlana Stoyanchev, and Cristian Moldovan. 2012. A detailed account of the first question generation shared task evaluation challenge. *Dialogue & Discourse*, 3(2):177–204.

Mrinmaya Sachan and Eric Xing. 2018. Self-training for jointly learning to ask and answer questions. In *Proceedings of the 2018 Conference of the North American Chapter of the Association for Computational Linguistics: Human Language Technologies, Volume 1 (Long Papers)*, pages 629–640.

Robyn Speer, Joshua Chin, and Catherine Havasi. 2017. Conceptnet 5.5: An open multilingual graph of general knowledge. In *Proceedings of the AAAI Conference on Artificial Intelligence*, volume 31.

Dan Su, Yan Xu, Wenliang Dai, Ziwei Ji, Tiezheng Yu, and Pascale Fung. 2020. Multi-hop question generation with graph convolutional network. In *Proceedings of the 2020 Conference on Empirical Methods in Natural Language Processing: Findings*, pages 4636–4647.

James Thorne, Andreas Vlachos, Christos Christodoulopoulos, and Arpit Mittal. 2018. Fever: a large-scale dataset for fact extraction and verification. In *Proceedings of the 2018 Conference of the North American Chapter of the Association for Computational Linguistics: Human Language Technologies, Volume 1 (Long Papers)*, pages 809–819.

Veronika Vincze, György Szarvas, Richárd Farkas, György Móra, and János Csirik. 2008. The bioscope corpus: biomedical texts annotated for uncertainty, negation and their scopes. *BMC bioinformatics*, 9(11):1–9.

Adina Williams, Nikita Nangia, and Samuel R Bowman. 2018. A broad-coverage challenge corpus for sentence understanding through inference. In *Proceedings of NAACL-HLT*, pages 1112–1122.

Shiyue Zhang and Mohit Bansal. 2019. Addressing semantic drift in question generation for semi-supervised question answering. In *Proceedings of the 2019 Conference on Empirical Methods in Natural Language Processing and the 9th International Joint Conference on Natural Language Processing (EMNLP-IJCNLP)*, pages 2495–2509.

Fine-tuning Transformers with Additional Context to Classify Discursive Moves in Mathematics Classrooms

Abhijit Suresh[1,2], **Jennifer Jacobs**[2], **Margaret Perkoff**[1],
James H. Martin[1,2], **Tamara Sumner**[1,2]
[1]Department of Computer Science, [2]Institute of Cognitive Science
University of Colorado Boulder
FirstName.LastName@colorado.edu

Abstract

"Talk moves" are specific discursive strategies used by teachers and students to facilitate conversations in which students share their thinking, and actively consider the ideas of others, and engage in rich discussions. Experts in instructional practices often rely on cues to identify and document these strategies, for example by annotating classroom transcripts. Prior efforts to develop automated systems to classify teacher talk moves using transformers achieved a performance of 76.32% F1. In this paper, we investigate the feasibility of using enriched contextual cues to improve model performance. We applied state-of-the-art deep learning approaches for Natural Language Processing (NLP), including Robustly optimized bidirectional encoder representations from transformers (Roberta) with a special input representation that supports previous and subsequent utterances as context for talk moves classification. We worked with the publically available TalkMoves dataset, which contains utterances sourced from real-world classroom sessions (human- transcribed and annotated). Through a series of experimentations, we found that a combination of previous and subsequent utterances improved the transformers' ability to differentiate talk moves (by 2.6% F1). These results constitute a new state of the art over previously published results and provide actionable insights to those in the broader NLP community who are working to develop similar transformer-based classification models.

1 Introduction

There is a strong theoretical and empirical basis for encouraging students' active participation in inquiry-based and socially constructed classroom environments (Vygotsky, 1978; Webb et al., 2008). Numerous efforts exist to support teachers to become more purposeful and effective in their efforts to facilitate such environments (Herbel-Eisenmann, 2017; Chen et al., 2020). Most approaches to providing teachers with detailed feedback about their discourse strategies require highly trained human observers (Correnti et al., 2015; Wolf et al., 2005). However, recent research has shown that the development and training of deep learning models to automate and scale certain discourse analyses from instructional episodes is feasible (Song et al., 2021), effective (Demszky et al., 2021), and reliable (Donnelly et al., 2017; Jensen et al., 2020; Suresh et al., 2019).

Accountable talk theory offers well-defined, research-based practices for teachers to engage in high-quality instruction, including the use of specific talk moves that promote students' equitable participation in a rigorous learning environment (O'Connor et al., 2015; Resnick et al., 2018). By using talk moves, teachers place the "intellectual heavy lifting" and balance of talk toward students and help ensure that the discussions will be purposeful, coherent, and productive (Michaels et al., 2010). Talk moves support classroom discourse to move beyond the traditional Initiate, Response, Evaluate linguistic sequence (Mehan, 1979); namely, by replacing the act of evaluating with practices that support a collective understanding that builds on and extends mathematical ideas (Michaels and O'Connor, 2015).In this way, talk moves enable dialogue shifts from teacher directed recitation to true discussions in which knowledge is informally shared and constructed rather than transmitted.

This paper draws inspiration from speech recognition systems for spoken dialog systems to investigate the feasibility of applying a novel input representation that utilizes tokens from previous and subsequent utterances to classify teacher talk moves (Schukat-Talamazzini et al., 1994). We explore three different context setups: previous-only utterances, subsequent-only utterances, and both previous and subsequent utterances (equal numbers of each) with different window sizes. In addition to the longer dialog window experiments, we re-

Proceedings of the 17th Workshop on Innovative Use of NLP for Building Educational Applications (BEA 2022), pages 71 - 81

port findings from fine-tuning transformers such as BigBird (Zaheer et al., 2020) and Longformer (Beltagy et al., 2020) which are architected to support longer sequences. Similarly, we report findings from fine-tuning MathBERT, a transformer architecture that was trained to establish semantic correspondence between mathematical formulas and their corresponding context (Peng et al., 2021). For training and evaluation, we use the TalkMoves dataset comprising 567 lesson transcripts derived from video recordings of K-12 mathematics classrooms (Suresh et al., 2022). The main contributions of this work are summarized as follows:

- We provide evidence for improved performance when fine-tuning transfomers with longer dialog windows.
- We observed that transformer architectures designed to handle longer contexts such as Longformer do not provide any additional benefit in differentiating instructional strategies.
- We observed that math-based models pretrained on mathematical formula understanding do not provide any improvement over the generic models.

2 Related Work

This section briefly describes the accountable talk theory framework, followed by a literature review on deep learning models for Natural Language Processing (NLP) focused on adding additional contexts and learning long-term dependencies.

2.1 Accountable talk theory framework

Accountable talk theory identifies and defines an explicit set of discourse moves intended to elicit a response within a classroom lesson (O'Connor and Michaels, 2019). These well-defined discursive techniques have been incorporated into various instructional practices and frameworks e.g., (Boston, 2012; Candela et al., 2020; Michaels et al., 2010). Their specificity makes talk moves well-suited for supervised multi-label sentence-pair classification. A number of research teams have made considerable progress in developing automated "intelligent agents" that are trained to emulate the role of the teacher. These agents prompt students to use designated aspects of accountable talk, such as revoicing and asking students to agree/disagree with another student. They typically act as facilitators or tutors during small group, text-based, online settings, taking part in and helping to focus the discussion at opportune moments e.g. (Adamson et al., 2013; Hmelo-Silver et al., 2013; Tegos et al., 2015). (Jacobs et al., 2022) and team developed an online application that provides personalized feedback to teachers on their classroom discourse practices, including the prevalence of talk moves. The system is fully automated and requires no human processing beyond the initial uploading of classroom recordings. Such education-focused NLP applications are in high demand to provide reliable feedback to teachers based on the accountable talk theory.

2.2 Transformers for additional context and long-term dependencies

The introduction of transformers has revolutionized the field of natural language processing. Unlike Recurrent Neural Networks (RNNs) and Long Short Term Memory networks (LSTMs), where training is performed sequentially, the design of transformer architecture enables parallel processing and allows for the creation of rich latent embeddings (Vaswani et al., 2017). Latent contextual representation of utterances through the self-attention mechanism makes transformers a powerful tool for various downstream applications such as question answering and text summarization (Devlin et al., 2018).

Research efforts to learn long-term dependencies with transformers were first introduced in Transformer-XL (Dai et al., 2019). Transformer-XL is a novel architecture that focuses on learning dependencies beyond the fixed length of vanilla transformers without disrupting the temporal coherence. This is achieved by saving the hidden state sequence of the previous segment to be used as context for the current segments, also known as the segment-level recurrence mechanism. In addition, to better encode the relationship between words, Transformer-XL uses relative positional embeddings. Results show that Transformer-XL can learn dependencies across the text with a window size of 900 words. Following Transformer- XL, (Yang et al., 2019) proposed XL-Net, which is a generalized autoregressive pretraining method that leverages the capabilities of Transformer-XL to solve the pre-train-finetune discrepancy commonly identified in early architectures such as BERT. XL-Net introduced two new developments. As an extension to the standard Causal Language Modeling (CLM), XL-Net uses permutation language modeling, which considers all possible permutations of the words within a sentence during the training phase. Also, XL-Net uses a secondary attention stream that focuses on the positional information of the predicted token. This additional attention stream led XL-Net to outperform many contemporary transformer architectures in downstream tasks, such as text classification. Similarly, to address the problem of processing long sequences with transformers, (Beltagy et al., 2020) introduced Longformer, which extends vanilla transformers with a modified self-attention mechanism to process long documents. The classic self-attention mechanism in BERT is computationally expensive, which explains the restriction of the maximum sequence length of 512 tokens. Instead, Longformer combines dilated sliding windows with global attention to achieve similar performance. As a result of reducing the computational complexity, Longformer can process long input sequences beyond the previously defined segment length of 512 tokens. Like Longfomers, Big-Bird (Zaheer et al., 2020) uses a sparse attention mechanism that includes a random attention component.

Over the past few years, we have seen an increasing trend in other approaches to supporting transformers to learn long-term dependencies, such as modifying pre-training methods and the classic attention mechanism. For example, to learn dependencies across documents, (Xie et al., 2020) adopted a simple approach to truncate the document used for classification. Similarly, (Joshi et al., 2019)) used a chunking approach where documents were broken down into multiple chunks, and the activations were then combined to perform the tasks. Another recent example is the BERT-Seq model for classifying Collaborative Problem Solving (Pugh et al., 2021). The BERT-Seq model uses a special input representation that combines embeddings from adjacent utterances as contextual cues for the model. Building on the prior work, we explored new ways to enrich transformers with additional contextual cues.

3 Current Work and Novelty

Currently, generating information about teachers' discourse strategies requires highly trained instructional experts to hand-code transcripts from classroom sessions (Correnti et al., 2015; Wolf et al., 2005), an approach that is expensive and not readily scalable. Encouragingly, a small number of researchers have recently trained computer models to automate and scale discourse analyses from instructional episodes, detecting educationally important discursive features such as instructional talk, authentic teacher questions, elaborated evaluation, and uptake (Dale et al., 2022; Demszky et al., 2021; Jensen et al., 2020). In prior work, (Suresh et al., 2021b,a) fine-tuned Roberta (Liu et al., 2019) to classify talk moves for each teacher utterance from a given classroom transcript. The input to Roberta was student-teacher sentence pairs, where the student sentence appeared immediately prior to the teacher's utterance. This paper builds upon the previous work to add contextual cues to transformers in various ways and evaluate their performance using the TalkMoves dataset. We experiment with modifying the input representation by combining multiple previous and subsequent utterances as context to classify teacher talk moves. This work serves as an example of how we can find new ways to use advances in natural language processing with classic ideas from speech recognition systems for spoken dialog system to capture the rich conversations between teachers and students in order to improve performance in applied domains such as education.

4 Method

This section discusses the different approaches we took to enrich contextual cues in the TalkMoves model in an effort to enhance performance.

4.1 Data

The TalkMoves dataset used in this study comprises 567 transcripts, including 174,186 teacher and 59,874 student utterances (Suresh et al., 2022). All the transcripts were human-generated from classroom audio and video recordings from K-12 mathematics classrooms. They were annotated for six teacher talk moves by two experts who established high inter-rater reliability (Suresh et al., 2021b, 2022). The talk moves in the dataset follow an uneven distribution, with certain moves being much more frequent than others (Figure 1). "Keeping everyone together" and "pressing for accuracy" are the most frequently used, whereas "getting students to relate" and "pressing for reasoning" are the least common. For training and testing split, we used the same split specified by (Suresh et al., 2022) in the TalkMoves dataset. Each teacher utterance in the TalkMoves dataset is annotated with one of six different teacher talk moves and "None". These talk moves are broadly classified into three categories based on their instructional purpose (Resnick et al., 2018): (1) accountability to the learning community, (2) accountability to content knowledge, and (3) accountability to rigorous thinking. See Table 1 for a brief description of each talk move, along with examples.

4.2 Research Motivation

In this study, we began working with transformers to classify talk moves. Prior attempts using non-transformers architecture achieved lower performance (65% F1 compared to 76.32% F1 with transformers) (Suresh et al., 2019, 2021b). The fine-tuned Roberta model proposed in (Suresh et al., 2022) employed a input representation of student-teacher sentence pairs to combine any given teacher utterance with the immediately prior student utterance (Suresh et al., 2021b). In order to understand the gaps in this model's performance, (Suresh et al., 2022) conducted an error analysis using a confusion matrix to consider examples where the Talk-Moves models were underperforming and often generated misclassifications. An initial analysis of those examples revealed several instances where the actual real-world context for the misclassified teacher utterance extended beyond the current representation of the previous student utterance. For example, consider the following dialogue "Student: Yes; Teacher: What do you think?". With limited context, it seems unclear if the teacher was relating to what a student said earlier or trying to prompt them to think. This challenge of limited context from prior work motivated us to find new ways to add contextual information to the existing models in order to improve performance.

4.3 Context-addition experiments

Constraints on the number of sequences in vanilla transformers, such as BERT and Roberta, prevents the direct application of transformers where there is a reliance on long-term dependencies. For example, consider a classroom session where a teacher encourages student X to think based on what student Y said earlier in the session. Without the expanded dialogue context, it can be challenging for transformers (and even humans) to classify the utterances. If we could expand the representation of available information such that it included the entire classroom session, the transformers may be more likely to learn to establish the long-term dependencies across the focal utterances or tokens. Given the importance of local context (Kovaleva et al., 2019), our input representation was modified from student-teacher sentence pairs to a fixed-size window surrounding each teacher utterance. This adjusted representation is atypical compared to the recommended input for fine-tuning, where a unique token separates two sequences (i.e., [SEP] in Bert and </s> in Roberta) (Devlin et al., 2018; Liu et al., 2019). There is a general notion that fine-tuning multiple utterances with multiple separator tokens, while theoretically possible, is not likely to work well. This notion was motivated by vanilla transformers, which were originally pre-trained on individual sentences or sentence pairs. We challenge this assumption by including additional past and future utterances in our adjusted input representation (Figure 2).

To establish a baseline performance level and generate information regarding the impact of context in classifying talk moves, we began with a simple input representation that includes only the target teacher utterance without any additional context. The output layer was a softmax over seven classes i.e., the six talk moves and "none" (no talk move). We also reproduced results from prior work on Roberta-base (Suresh et al., 2022). Following that, we experimented with three context setups: previous-only utterances, subsequent-only utterances, and both previous and subsequent utterances (equal numbers of each). In each setup, we evaluated several different window sizes. For example, the previous-only condition with a window size of three would have the immediately previous three utterances (with student(s) and/or the teacher as the speakers) serving as context cues for classifying the target utterance. If there was no prior utterance (such as at the start of a classroom session), we prepended empty strings. Similarly, given the previous and subsequent utterances condition with a window size of two, the target utterance would have two previous utterances prepended to the left and two subsequent utterances appended to the right. Separator tokens differentiated all of the utterances. As an additional preprocessing step, all utterances were truncated to 30 tokens long. The choice of truncation length was decided based on the distribution of sequence length (number of tokens) for all utterances in the dataset (see Figure 3). A token size of 30 accounted for more than 95% of the utterances in the dataset (two standard deviations from

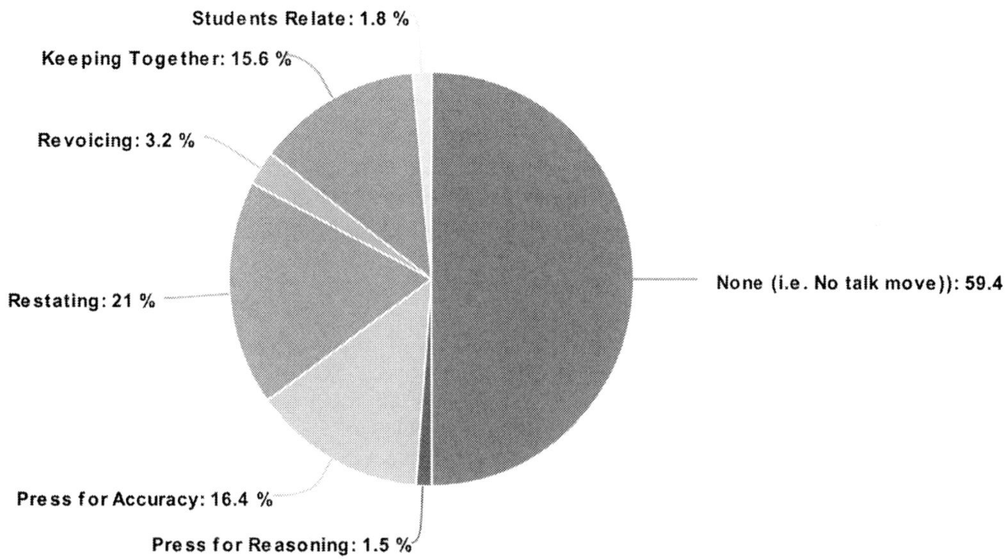

Figure 1: Distribution of teacher talk moves in the TalkMoves dataset

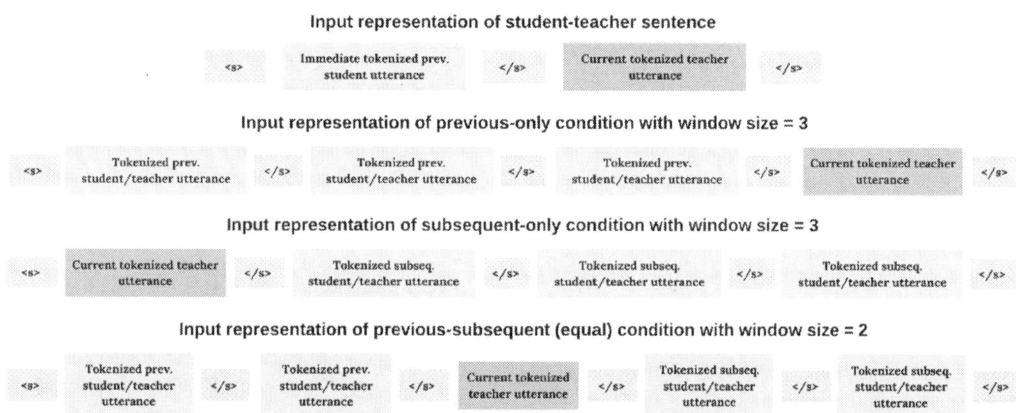

Figure 2: Modifying the input representation to support additional previous and subsequent utterances

the mean of the sequence length of seven tokens). We then fine-tuned transformers on the TalkMoves training set with different parameters using Amazon EC2 instances. We followed the recommended parameters from (Suresh et al., 2019, 2022) including learning rate (2e-5, 3e-5, 4e-5, 5e-5), number of epochs (3-6), batch size (4,8,16,32), warmup steps (0,100,1000) and maximum sequence length (512 for Roberta-like models) and (512,1024 for Longformer and BigBird). The performance on the testing set after fine-tuning is reported based on F1 measures and MCC (Suresh et al., 2021a). These measures work well for skewed datasets like TalkMoves (Chicco and Jurman, 2020; Suresh et al., 2021b). The code was implemented in Python 3.8

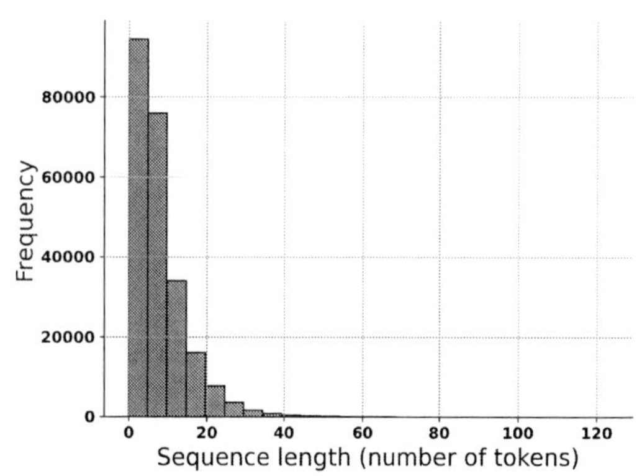

Figure 3: Number of utterances (frequency) vs sequence length (number of tokens) in TalkMoves dataset

Table 1: Teacher talk moves from TalkMoves dataset (Suresh et al., 2022)

Category	Talk move	Description	Example
		Teacher Talk Moves	
Learning Community	Keeping everyone together	Prompting students to be active listeners and orienting students to each other	"What did Eliza just say her equation was?"
Learning Community	Getting students to relate to another's ideas	Prompting students to react to what a classmate said	"Do you agree with Juan that the answer is 7/10?"
Learning Community	Restating	Repeating all or part of what a student said word for word	"Add two here."
Content Knowledge	Pressing for accuracy	Prompting students to make a mathematical contribution or use mathematical language	"Can you give an example of an ordered pair?"
Rigorous Thinking	Revoicing	Repeating what a student said but adding on or changing the wording	"Julia told us she would add two here."
Rigorous Thinking	Pressing for reasoning	Prompting students to explain, provide evidence, share their thinking behind a decision, or connect ideas or representations	"Why could I argue that the slope should be increasing?"

with Pytorch and HuggingFace library (Wolf et al., 2019). In addition to the context-addition experiments with Roberta-base, we fine-tuned similar transformers architectures. XLNet, Longformer and BigBird are transformer architectures which support longer sequences. Since the TalkMoves dataset is composed of utterances from K-12 mathematics classrooms, we fine-tuned MathBERT, a pretrained architecture with focus on mathematical formula understanding.

5 Results

In this section, we present the results from our experiments that involved providing additional context to transformers to support the process of learning long-term dependencies. The experiments were repeated with ten random seeds, and the average score is reported (Table 2, 3). For brevity, we report performance only on Roberta-base (the best performing model from (Suresh et al., 2021b) as indicated in the first column of (Table 2) and transformers such as Longformer and Bigbird (Table 3). All the models are Base models (Large models are beyond the scope of this work). In the second column, we describe the context that was provided to the target teacher utterance for classification. For example, Previous 1 should be interpreted as a single previous utterance prepended to the target teacher's utterance. Similarly, Subsequent 1 should be interpreted as a single subsequent utterance appended to the target utterance. The third and final column describes the performance of the testing set.

For imbalanced datasets like TalkMoves, the Matthew Correlation Coefficient (MCC) and F1 measure are good indicators of model performance. An MCC score of +1 indicates a perfect correlation while 0 indicates a random correlation and -1 indicates a negative correlation. Similarly, the F1 score ranges from 0-100% where 100% indicates perfect performance. We begin with the No-Context condition which achieved a performance of 71.93% F1. On prepending the immediately prior or subsequent student utterance, the model achieved a performance of 76.32% F1 (Suresh et al., 2022). Next we turn to results from various context conditions with different window sizes followed by results from Longformer, BigBird, and other models. The maximum sequence length in most of these models was 512 with the exception of Longformer and Bigbird which had a sequence length upto 1024. The results presented in this work are comprehensive but not exhaustive since training and testing for all possible models and parameters is infeasible.

The results table clearly illustrates the importance of context in enhancing performance. Starting with Roberta-Base, the performance on the previous-only condition gradually increased with an increase in window-size and saturated for larger window-sizes. Similarly, we observed an improvement in performance for the subsequent-only condition. However, we did not see any significant improvement for larger window-sizes in this condition, possibly due to the negative impact in performance on "Revoicing" and "Restating" which rely on immediately prior student sentences. Moreover, the combination of previous and subsequent utterances resulted in the best performing model. The performance gradually increased proportionally with a window size up to 7 before saturating. Likewise, the performance on Longformer, XLNet and BigBird were comparable with similar input representation. The most surprising result was the performance on MathBert which was signficantly lower than other models. In summary, Roberta-Base with equal previous-subsequent condition ($size$ =7) outperformed rest of the models and constitutes the state-of-the-art results.

The primary motivation of the error analysis using a confusion matrix was to improve the performance on the under-performing talk move categories and identify patterns among the misclassfied utterances to be leveraged as features for the models. When comparing the confusion matrix from prior work (Suresh et al., 2022) (see Table 4), the current study shows a significant improvement in performance across all the teacher talk moves labels except "Restating" (see Table 5). With "Restating", we hypothesize that the decrease in performance was a result of supplementing additional context. Further analysis has to be performed in order to validate this claim.

6 Discussion

Based on the results from our experiments to improve the performance of a talk moves classifier using transformers, it is evident that longer dialog windows play an important role in differentiating talk moves. We successfully validated that the local discursive context is an important feature in classifying teacher talk moves. We generated a 4% F1 increase in performance when including a single additional utterance (either previous or subsequent) as compared to the no-context condition. Also, we observed that previous utterances are more impactful than future utterances for classifying talk moves. This finding is not surprising given that several talk moves, such as the teacher "restating" and "revoicing" what a student has already said, depend entirely on previous utterances as context. We also observed that context windows with a combination of previous and future utterances outperform either condition alone. Finally, we found that a window size of seven previous and subsequent utterances achieves the best performance. Beyond the identified size of seven, the performance decreases. It is possible that much earlier or much later utterances provide confusing or conflicting contextual information, which hinders model performance. It is equally likely that longer dialog windows could lead to overfitting.

Prior efforts to address the imbalanced nature of TalkMoves dataset through weighted loss resulted in reduced performance (Suresh et al., 2019). As an alternative, we attempted to generate synthetic samples of tokenized utterances through SMOTE (Synthetic Minority Oversampling Data) (Chawla et al., 2002). With SMOTE, it was challenging to retain the syntactic information of the generated examples. It was also difficult to generate the supporting contextual student and teacher utterances. Preliminary efforts did not yield any improvement in performance.

To further improve the performance, we have identified two future directions that appear worthwhile to consider: (1) experimenting with punctuation and other linguistic markers in the existing TalkMoves dataset and (2) collecting more training data. In the TalkMoves dataset, all the punctuation and other non-alphanumeric characters from the teacher and student utterances were removed. These text processing steps are typical for most text-based NLP applications to produce text that closely aligns with the output of Automated Speech Recognition (ASR) systems. However, we hypothesize that punctuation could play a significant role in differentiating one talk move from another. For example, "Agreed?" with a question mark can be considered an instance of "Keeping everyone together" whereas "Agreed" as a statement would be an instance of "None." It remains to be determined the extent to which including punctuation markers might impact the performance of the models. Similarly, we can try incorporating speaker turns to indicate a student or teacher turn in previous and subsequent utterances as additional features to the model.

Table 2: Robert-Base performance with different window sizes

Model	Context	MCC	F1 (%)
Roberta-Base	No Context	0.7003	71.93
Roberta-Base	Immediate Student (Suresh et al., 2022)	0.7513	76.32
Roberta-Base	Previous 1	0.7460	76.01
Roberta-Base	Previous 5	0.7579	76.79
Roberta-Base	Previous 10	0.7615	77.08
Roberta-Base	Previous 15	0.7688	77.63
Roberta-Base	Previous 17	0.7657	77.35
Roberta-Base	Subsequent 1	0.7232	74.16
Roberta-Base	Previous 1 - Subsequent 1	0.7687	78.18
Roberta-Base	Previous 2 - Subsequent 2	0.7742	78.49
Roberta-Base	Previous 3 - Subsequent 3	0.7764	78.66
Roberta-Base	Previous 5 - Subsequent 5	0.7739	78.36
Roberta-Base	**Previous 7 - Subsequent 7**	**0.7805**	**78.92**
Roberta-Base	Previous 8 - Subsequent 8	0.7802	78.86

Table 3: Performance on classification of teacher talk moves on other models

Model	Context	MCC	F1 (%)
Roberta-Base	**Previous 7 - Subsequent 7**	**0.7805**	**78.92**
MathBERT	Previous 7 - Subsequent 7	0.6890	70.18
XLNet	Previous 7 - Subsequent 7	0.7709	78.06
Longformer	Previous 7 - Subsequent 7	0.7752	78.47
BigBird	Previous 7 - Subsequent 7	0.7694	77.89
BigBird	Previous 10 - Subsequent 10	0.7603	77.11

Another option that warrants consideration is supplementing data for the purpose of model pretraining. TalkMoves dataset (github.com/SumnerLab/TalkMoves) is a relatively small dataset for pretraining transformers when compared to Roberta which was pretrained on millions of data points. At the same time, we recognize the challenge in the collecting and annotating thousands of classroom transcripts. Moreover, there are important privacy concerns and other ethical considerations, given that these data involve minors, use proper names (which can be critical information for talk moves classification), and can be challenging to access in large quantities. We could potentially explore active learning to achieve greater accuracy with limited samples (Settles, 2009). Active learning is often sought as an option in machine learning applications where unlabeled instances are abundantly available (Schröder et al., 2021).

7 Conclusion

Documenting consequential elements of classroom instruction and providing teachers with feedback on their practices are critical endeavors in the education field. Taking into consideration the strong need to provide reliable feedback to teachers on productive classroom discourse, we need robust models to automatically classify teacher talk moves with high reliability. In this paper, we report on a number of experiments that involved providing longer dialog windows to the transformers in an effort to improve model performance. Based on these experiments, we generated a state-of-the-art 2.6% F1 improvement in performance (78.92% F1) over the previous models, primarily by adding a set number of previous and subsequent utterances to the input representation. Clearly, there are both challenges and opportunities for the development of innovative uses of AI techniques, particularly as they can be incorporated into tools that support teacher and student learning. The findings from this research open new avenues for exploration that can benefit both the education and NLP communi-

Table 4: Confusion matrix from Roberta-Base with Immediate student utterance as context

Roberta-Base (Immediate Student)		Actual							Precision	Recall	F1
0 - None	Predicted	42786	1779	67	54	232	1091	74	0.93	0.93	0.934
1 - Keeping Everyone together		1599	6549	106	139	99	518	30	0.73	0.72	0.73
2 - Getting students to relate		171	177	715	0	2	120	33	0.71	0.59	0.64
3 - Restating		112	18	3	932	21	12	0	0.79	0.85	0.82
4 - Revoicing		562	72	2	47	1063	44	0	0.72	0.59	0.62
5 - Pressing for accuracy		762	367	105	9	51	8289	669	0.82	0.86	0.84
6 - Pressing for reasoning		56	6	315	1	1	86	753	0.79	0.82	0.80

Table 5: Confusion matrix from Roberta-Base with Previous-7 and Subsequent-7 utterances as context. Compared to Table 4, we see an improvement in F1 score for almost all of the talk moves except Restating.

Roberta-Base (Previous 7 - Subsequent 7)		Actual							Precision	Recall	F1
0 - None	Predicted	14594	522	42	40	122	312	16	0.94	0.93	0.94
1 - Keeping Everyone together		512	2321	53	26	26	130	4	0.77	0.76	0.76
2 - Getting students to relate		31	23	206	0	0	37	9	0.64	0.67	0.65
3 - Restating		25	8	1	263	7	2	0	0.73	0.86	0.79
4 - Revoicing		179	24	0	25	326	7	1	0.66	0.58	0.62
5 - Pressing for accuracy		207	112	21	5	12	2678	41	0.84	0.87	0.85
6 - Pressing for reasoning		8	2	1	0	0	27	242	0.77	0.86	0.82

ties who might adopt our methods in applications where the local context may prove critical to improving performance.

Acknowledgements

The research team would like to thank Eddie Dombower and his team at Curve 10 for their contributions to the design and implementation of the TalkBack application. This material is based upon work supported by the National Science Foundation under Grant Numbers 1600325 and 1837986. This research was supported by the NSF National AI Institute for Student-AI Teaming (iSAT) under grant DRL 2019805. The opinions expressed are those of the authors and do not represent views of the NSF.

References

David Adamson, Colin Ashe, Hyeju Jang, David Yaron, and Carolyn Penstein Rosé. 2013. Intensification of group knowledge exchange with academically productive talk agents. In *CSCL (1)*, pages 10–17.

Iz Beltagy, Matthew E Peters, and Arman Cohan. 2020. Longformer: The long-document transformer. *arXiv preprint arXiv:2004.05150*.

Melissa Boston. 2012. Assessing instructional quality in mathematics. *The Elementary School Journal*, 113(1):76–104.

Amber G Candela, Melissa D Boston, and Juli K Dixon. 2020. Discourse actions to promote student access. *Mathematics Teacher: Learning and Teaching PK-12*, 113(4):266–277.

Nitesh V Chawla, Kevin W Bowyer, Lawrence O Hall, and W Philip Kegelmeyer. 2002. Smote: synthetic minority over-sampling technique. *Journal of artificial intelligence research*, 16:321–357.

Gaowei Chen, Carol KK Chan, Kennedy KH Chan, Sherice N Clarke, and Lauren B Resnick. 2020. Efficacy of video-based teacher professional development for increasing classroom discourse and student learning. *Journal of the Learning Sciences*, 29(4-5):642–680.

Davide Chicco and Giuseppe Jurman. 2020. The advantages of the matthews correlation coefficient (mcc) over f1 score and accuracy in binary classification evaluation. *BMC genomics*, 21(1):1–13.

Richard Correnti, Mary Kay Stein, Margaret S Smith, James Scherrer, Margaret McKeown, James Greeno, and Kevin Ashley. 2015. Improving teaching at scale: Design for the scientific measurement and learning of discourse practice. *Socializing Intelligence Through Academic Talk and Dialogue. AERA*, 284.

Zihang Dai, Zhilin Yang, Yiming Yang, Jaime Carbonell, Quoc V Le, and Ruslan Salakhutdinov. 2019. Transformer-xl: Attentive language models beyond a fixed-length context. *arXiv preprint arXiv:1901.02860*.

Meghan E Dale, Amanda J Godley, Sarah A Capello, Patrick J Donnelly, Sidney K D'Mello, and Sean P Kelly. 2022. Toward the automated analysis of teacher talk in secondary ela classrooms. *Teaching and Teacher Education*, 110:103584.

Dorottya Demszky, Jing Liu, Heather C Hill, Dan Jurafsky, and Chris Piech. 2021. Can automated feedback improve teachers' uptake of student ideas? evidence from a randomized controlled trial in a large-scale online course.

Jacob Devlin, Ming-Wei Chang, Kenton Lee, and Kristina Toutanova. 2018. Bert: Pre-training of deep bidirectional transformers for language understanding. *arXiv preprint arXiv:1810.04805*.

Patrick J Donnelly, Nathaniel Blanchard, Andrew M Olney, Sean Kelly, Martin Nystrand, and Sidney K D'Mello. 2017. Words matter: automatic detection of teacher questions in live classroom discourse using linguistics, acoustics, and context. In *Proceedings of the Seventh International Learning Analytics & Knowledge Conference*, pages 218–227. ACM.

Beth A Herbel-Eisenmann. 2017. *Mathematics Discourse in Secondary Classrooms: A Practice-based Resource for Professional Learning: Facilitator Guide*. Math Solutions.

Cindy E Hmelo-Silver, Clark A Chinn, Angela M O'Donnell, and Carol Chan. 2013. The international handbook of collaborative learning.

Jennifer Jacobs, Karla Scornavacco, Charis Harty, Abhijit Suresh, Vivian Lai, and Tamara Sumner. 2022. Promoting rich discussions in mathematics classrooms: Using personalized, automated feedback to support reflection and instructional change. *Teaching and Teacher Education*.

Emily Jensen, Meghan Dale, Patrick J Donnelly, Cathlyn Stone, Sean Kelly, Amanda Godley, and Sidney K D'Mello. 2020. Toward automated feedback on teacher discourse to enhance teacher learning. In *Proceedings of the 2020 CHI Conference on Human Factors in Computing Systems*, pages 1–13.

Mandar Joshi, Omer Levy, Daniel S Weld, and Luke Zettlemoyer. 2019. Bert for coreference resolution: Baselines and analysis. *arXiv preprint arXiv:1908.09091*.

Olga Kovaleva, Alexey Romanov, Anna Rogers, and Anna Rumshisky. 2019. Revealing the dark secrets of bert. *arXiv preprint arXiv:1908.08593*.

Yinhan Liu, Myle Ott, Naman Goyal, Jingfei Du, Mandar Joshi, Danqi Chen, Omer Levy, Mike Lewis, Luke Zettlemoyer, and Veselin Stoyanov. 2019. Roberta: A robustly optimized bert pretraining approach. *arXiv preprint arXiv:1907.11692*.

Hugh Mehan. 1979. *Learning lessons*. Harvard University Press Cambridge, MA.

Sarah Michaels and Catherine O'Connor. 2015. Conceptualizing talk moves as tools: Professional development approaches for academically productive discussion. *Socializing intelligence through talk and dialogue*, pages 347–362.

Sarah Michaels, Mary Catherine O'Connor, Megan Williams Hall, and Lauren B Resnick. 2010. Accountable talk® sourcebook. *Pittsburg, PA: Institute for Learning University of Pittsburgh. Murphy, PK, Wilkinson, IAG, Soter, AO, Hennessey, MN, & Alexander, JF*.

Catherine O'Connor and Sarah Michaels. 2019. Supporting teachers in taking up productive talk moves: The long road to professional learning at scale. *International Journal of Educational Research*, 97:166–175.

Catherine O'Connor, Sarah Michaels, and Suzanne Chapin. 2015. Scaling down" to explore the role of talk in learning: From district intervention to controlled classroom study. *Socializing intelligence through academic talk and dialogue*, pages 111–126.

Shuai Peng, Ke Yuan, Liangcai Gao, and Zhi Tang. 2021. Mathbert: A pre-trained model for mathematical formula understanding. *arXiv preprint arXiv:2105.00377*.

Samuel L Pugh, Shree Krishna Subburaj, Arjun Ramesh Rao, Angela EB Stewart, Jessica Andrews-Todd, and Sidney K D'Mello. 2021. Say what? automatic modeling of collaborative problem solving skills from student speech in the wild. *International Educational Data Mining Society*.

Lauren B Resnick, Christa SC Asterhan, and Sherice N Clarke. 2018. Accountable talk: Instructional dialogue that builds the mind. *Geneva, Switzerland: The International Academy of Education (IAE) and the International Bureau of Education (IBE) of the United Nations Educational, Scientific and Cultural Organization (UNESCO)*.

Christopher Schröder, Andreas Niekler, and Martin Potthast. 2021. Uncertainty-based query strategies for active learning with transformers. *arXiv preprint arXiv:2107.05687*.

E Schukat-Talamazzini, T Kuhn, and H Niemann. 1994. Speech recognition for spoken dialogue systems. In *Progress and Prospects of Speech Research and Technology: Proc. of the CRIM/FORWISS Workshop, PAI*, volume 1, pages 110–120.

Burr Settles. 2009. Active learning literature survey.

Yu Song, Shunwei Lei, Tianyong Hao, Zixin Lan, and Ying Ding. 2021. Automatic classification of semantic content of classroom dialogue. *Journal of Educational Computing Research*, 59(3):496–521.

Abhijit Suresh, Jennifer Jacobs, Charis Clevenger, Vivian Lai, Chenhao Tan, James H Martin, and Tamara Sumner. 2021a. Using ai to promote equitable classroom discussions: The talkmoves application. In *International Conference on Artificial Intelligence in Education*, pages 344–348. Springer.

Abhijit Suresh, Jennifer Jacobs, Charis Harty, Margaret Perkoff, James H Martin, and Tamara Sumner. 2022. The talkmoves dataset: K-12 mathematics lesson transcripts annotated for teacher and student discursive moves. *13th International Conference on Language Resources and Evaluation (LREC 2022).*

Abhijit Suresh, Jennifer Jacobs, Vivian Lai, Chenhao Tan, Wayne Ward, James H Martin, and Tamara Sumner. 2021b. Using transformers to provide teachers with personalized feedback on their classroom discourse: The talkmoves application. *AAAI 2021 Spring Symposium on Artificial Intelligence for K-12 Education.*

Abhijit Suresh, Tamara Sumner, Jennifer Jacobs, Bill Foland, and Wayne Ward. 2019. Automating analysis and feedback to improve mathematics teachers' classroom discourse. In *Proceedings of the AAAI conference on artificial intelligence*, volume 33, pages 9721–9728.

Stergios Tegos, Stavros Demetriadis, and Anastasios Karakostas. 2015. Promoting academically productive talk with conversational agent interventions in collaborative learning settings. *Computers & Education*, 87:309–325.

Ashish Vaswani, Noam Shazeer, Niki Parmar, Jakob Uszkoreit, Llion Jones, Aidan N Gomez, Łukasz Kaiser, and Illia Polosukhin. 2017. Attention is all you need. *Advances in neural information processing systems*, 30.

Lev Vygotsky. 1978. Interaction between learning and development. *Readings on the development of children*, 23(3):34–41.

Noreen M Webb, Megan L Franke, Marsha Ing, Angela Chan, Tondra De, Deanna Freund, and Dan Battey. 2008. The role of teacher instructional practices in student collaboration. *Contemporary educational psychology*, 33(3):360–381.

Mikyung Kim Wolf, Amy C Crosson, and Lauren B Resnick. 2005. Classroom talk for rigorous reading comprehension instruction. *Reading Psychology*, 26(1):27–53.

Thomas Wolf, Lysandre Debut, Victor Sanh, Julien Chaumond, Clement Delangue, Anthony Moi, Pierric Cistac, Tim Rault, Rémi Louf, Morgan Funtowicz, et al. 2019. Huggingface's transformers: State-of-the-art natural language processing. *arXiv preprint arXiv:1910.03771.*

Qizhe Xie, Zihang Dai, Eduard Hovy, Thang Luong, and Quoc Le. 2020. Unsupervised data augmentation for consistency training. *Advances in Neural Information Processing Systems*, 33:6256–6268.

Zhilin Yang, Zihang Dai, Yiming Yang, Jaime Carbonell, Russ R Salakhutdinov, and Quoc V Le. 2019. Xlnet: Generalized autoregressive pretraining for language understanding. *Advances in neural information processing systems*, 32.

Manzil Zaheer, Guru Guruganesh, Kumar Avinava Dubey, Joshua Ainslie, Chris Alberti, Santiago Ontanon, Philip Pham, Anirudh Ravula, Qifan Wang, Li Yang, et al. 2020. Big bird: Transformers for longer sequences. *Advances in Neural Information Processing Systems*, 33:17283–17297.

Cross-corpora experiments of automatic proficiency assessment and error detection for spoken English

Stefano Bannò
Fondazione Bruno Kessler, Italy
Department of Cognitive Science,
University of Trento, Italy
sbanno@fbk.eu

Marco Matassoni
Fondazione Bruno Kessler, Italy
matasso@fbk.eu

Abstract

The growing demand for learning English as a second language has led to an increasing interest in automatic approaches for assessing spoken language proficiency. One of the most significant challenges in this field is the lack of publicly available annotated spoken data. Another common issue is the lack of consistency and coherence in human assessment. To tackle both problems, in this paper we address the task of automatically predicting the scores of spoken test responses of English-as-a-second-language learners by training neural models on written data and using the presence of grammatical errors as a feature, as they can be considered consistent indicators of proficiency through their distribution and frequency. Specifically, we train a feature extractor on EF-CAMDAT, a large written corpus containing error annotations and proficiency levels assigned by human experts, in order to extract information related to grammatical errors and, in turn, we use the resulting model for inference on the CLC-FCE corpus, on the ICNALE corpus, and on the spoken section of the TLT-school corpus, a collection of proficiency tests taken by Italian students. The work investigates the impact of the feature extractor on spoken proficiency assessment as well as the written-to-spoken approach. We find that our error-based approach can be beneficial for assessing spoken proficiency. The results obtained on the considered datasets are discussed and evaluated with appropriate metrics.

1 Introduction

Automatic scoring of language proficiency is becoming a point of growing interest and importance in the field of second language (L2) assessment because the number of English-as-a-second-language (ESL) learners has been steadily increasing worldwide (Howson, 2013).

A common issue in this field is the lack of publicly available data specifically designed and annotated for automatic assessment, especially as regards spoken data. Another typical problem is the lack of consistency and coherence in human assessment, as it frequently relies on proficiency indicators that often have biases and are not clearly generalizable, therefore not easily transferable into automatic scoring systems (Zhang, 2013). Although L2 proficiency cannot be assessed on the mere basis of the presence of errors in learners' written and spoken productions, this aspect is highly consistent and plays a major role in language assessment by human experts (James, 2013). Nevertheless, to the best of our knowledge, the impact of errors on automatic spoken language assessment has not been thoroughly investigated yet, whereas other types of feature-based assessment have been more widely studied and explored (Crossley et al., 2015).

In this paper, we address the task of automatically predicting the scores of spoken responses of ESL learners leveraging written data and exploiting the presence of grammatical errors, thus tackling both the aforementioned problems: the issue related to the scarce availability of spoken data and the problem of inconsistency in human assessment.

In order to do so, we design a ranking of grammatical error gravity based on the frequency of each human-annotated error in the EF-Cambridge Open Language Database (EFCAMDAT), modelling it across 15 proficiency levels aligned with the CEFR (Common European Framework of Reference) levels ranging from A1 to C1 (Council of Europe, 2001); as our purpose is scoring spoken language proficiency, we discard spelling, punctuation and orthographic errors and we group errors into 5 categories.

Subsequently, we train a feature extraction model feeding the learners' texts of the EFCAMDAT as inputs and setting the 5 classes of errors as targets for our predictions and we use this model as an error feature extractor (EFEX) for inference on the Cambridge Learner Corpus - First Certificate

Proceedings of the 17th Workshop on Innovative Use of NLP for Building Educational Applications (BEA 2022), pages 82 - 91

in English (CLC-FCE) and on the International Corpus Network of Asian Learners of English (ICNALE), thus generating 5 labels corresponding to the aforementioned 5 classes of errors; then, we train a scoring model on the CLC-FCE injecting the 5 error labels generated by EFEX and we test it on the spoken annotated section of ICNALE.

Likewise, we use EFEX for inference on the TLT-school corpus. Subsequently, we train a scoring model on the written section of the corpus injecting the 5 error labels generated by EFEX and we test it on the spoken section. Figure 1 shows the proposed pipeline. Finally, we fine-tune our model on a small spoken subset.

The structure of the paper is as follows: in the next paragraphs, we briefly illustrate the theoretical framework and literature related to automatic scoring and assessment; in Section 2, we describe the data used in our experiments and our ranking of grammatical error gravity; in Section 3, we show the model architectures; in Section 4, we show the results of our experiments on the models; finally, in Section 5, we illustrate the conclusions of the study and reflect upon next steps.

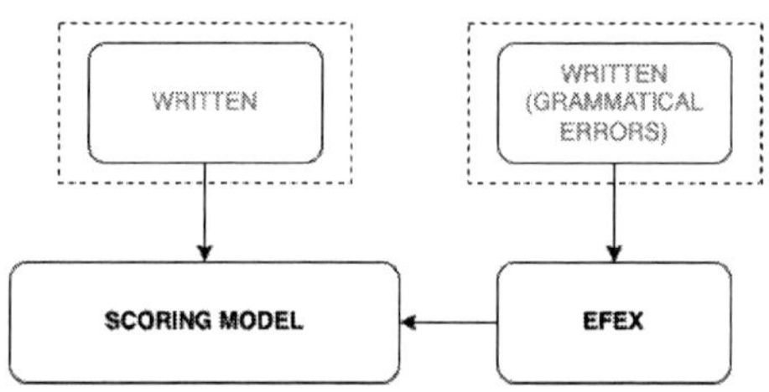

Figure 1: Diagram of the proposed training pipeline based on textual input (i.e the written train set). The scoring model is then used to predict proficiency scores on manual and ASR transcriptions (i.e. the spoken test set).

1.1 Theoretical framework

The origins of the field of L2 assessment date back to the influential work of Lado (1961), who believed that the problems of learning a new language could be predicted comparing the learners' native language and their target language, consistently with his structuralist perspective of language and contrastive linguistics. Language was taught - and thus assessed - as a set of distinct elements, starting from a contrastive analysis of sounds, grammar and vocabulary. As a result, errors play an important role in this construct. In response to and in continuation of contrastive analysis, at the end of the 1960s the work of Corder (1967) set the foundation for error analysis and considered the concept of error from a developmental perspective.

In the 1970s, the subsequent fundamental step in language testing and assessment was inspired by the forward-looking work on communicative competence by Hymes (1972), later refined and framed in the so-called communicative approach by Canale and Swain (1980). According to this approach, language is used to communicate meaning, which encompasses: grammatical knowledge, sociolinguistic competence, and strategic competence.

Around the 1990s, an approach theoretically rooted in the communicative approach, started to be developed and was later fixed in the Common European Framework of Reference (CEFR) (Council of Europe, 2001). Although it might seem that this approach privileges communication at the expense of formal correctness, errors still play a major role in assessing language proficiency (Pfingsthorn, 2013). Furthermore, Thewissen (2013) has shown that learner errors can be connected to CEFR proficiency levels and they can be considered as criterial features for each level, together with other linguistic features, as illustrated in Hawkins and Buttery (2010).

1.2 Reference to prior work

Deep learning techniques have brought significant improvements in the field of automatic scoring, for assessing both writing and speaking, such that end-to-end neural based approaches outperformed ETS's SpeechRater (Chen et al., 2018), one of the best known oral proficiency test engines (Xi et al., 2008). Specifically, transformer-based models have led to a remarkable improvement in tasks of predicting linguistic proficiency (Raina et al., 2020; Wang et al., 2021).

While grammatical error detection for speech assessment has been the focus of relatively few studies (Knill et al., 2019; Caines et al., 2020), grammatical errors have received more attention in the field of automatic essay scoring and are one of the features employed in Yannakoudakis et al. (2011) along with lexical, part-of-speech (POS) and syntactic features for automatically assessing ESL examination scripts, and they were found to be significant for enhancing the overall correlation between true scores and predicted ones. Gamon et al. (2013) uses Leacock and Chodorow (2003)'s findings on the influence of grammatical errors on

TOEFL (Test of English as a Foreign Language) scores for automatic essay scoring and feedback. Similarly, errors are a feature investigated in the work of Vajjala (2018), in which spelling and grammar errors are extracted by LanguageTool[1]. In this case, the error rate feature considered individually was found to have little impact on the classification performance. Similar experiments were conducted again by Vajjala and Rama (2018) with German, Czech and Italian, including errors as a feature. This work was reproduced by Caines and Buttery (2020), who applied such experiments also to English and Spanish corpora. Another research conducted on the CLC-FCE found that grammatical error detection highly influences essay scores (Cummins and Rei, 2018).

Recently, the work described by Ballier et al. (2019) has investigated the possibility of predicting CEFR proficiency levels based on manually annotated errors in the French and Spanish section of the EFCAMDAT corpus, but their study did not employ deep learning techniques. However, they identified that certain types of errors, such as punctuation, spelling and verb tense errors, are characteristic of specific CEFR proficiency levels. For our study, we reversed the process and we started from a ranking of error gravity across the CEFR proficiency levels.

Finally, some recent studies on automatic assessment of L2 proficiency have employed state-of-the-art models, combining associated auxiliary tasks (Craighead et al., 2020), none of which related to errors.

2 Datasets and setup

2.1 EFCAMDAT

Firstly, we use the EFCAMDAT corpus (Geertzen et al., 2014) that comprises L2 learners' scripts annotated with their respective score on a scale from 0 to 100, their proficiency level from 1 to 16 (mapped to CEFR levels from A1 to C2) and partially error-tagged by human experts. As our work investigates the efficacy of errors as features, we only use the error-tagged section of the EFCAMDAT Cleaned Subcorpus (Shatz, 2020), consisting of 498,208 scripts ranging from proficiency level 1 to 15 (i.e. from A1 to C1), which we divided into training and test set. The error tagset of the corpus consists of 24 types of errors, of which we discarded 7 related to spelling, punctuation and orthographic errors, as they would be of no use for

Code	Meaning	Code	Meaning
XC	change from x to y	NSW	no such word
AG	agreement	PH	phraseology
AR	article	PL	plural
D	delete	PO	possessive
PS	part of speech	PR	prepositions
EX	expression of idiom	SI	singular
IS	insert	VT	verb tense
MW	missing word	WC	word choice
WO	word order		

Table 1: EFCAMDAT error tagset without codes related to spelling, punctuation and orthographic errors.

assessing speech (see Table 1). As a preliminary analysis, we computed the KL-Divergence between the distribution of the 17 error labels counts across CEFR proficiency levels in EFCAMDAT. The labels were converted into a smoothed distribution, by applying add-one smoothing. The symmetric KL-Divergence was then calculated. Therefore, for error type t_i for proficiency level L_k:

$$\mathrm{P}(t_\mathrm{i}|L_\mathrm{k}) = \frac{\mathrm{cnt}(t_\mathrm{i}, L_\mathrm{k}) + 1}{\sum_{j=1}^{N}(\mathrm{cnt}(t_\mathrm{i}, L_\mathrm{k}) + 1)}$$

where $\mathrm{cnt}(t_\mathrm{i}, L_\mathrm{k})$ is the number of occurrences for a given label in a given grade.

The symmetric KL Divergence was subsequently calculated across proficiency levels:

$$\mathrm{KL}(L_\mathrm{k}|L_\mathrm{l}) = \left(\sum_{i=1}^{N} \mathrm{P}(t_\mathrm{i}|L_\mathrm{k})\log\left(\frac{\mathrm{P}(t_\mathrm{i}|L_\mathrm{k})}{\mathrm{P}(t_\mathrm{i}|L_\mathrm{l})}\right)\right) + \left(\sum_{i=1}^{N} \mathrm{P}(t_\mathrm{i}|L_\mathrm{l})\log\left(\frac{\mathrm{P}(t_\mathrm{i}|L_\mathrm{l})}{\mathrm{P}(t_\mathrm{i}|L_\mathrm{k})}\right)\right)$$

Table 2 reports the symmetric KL-Divergence between distributions of counts from all the 17 error labels across CEFR proficiency levels. It appears that we can consider errors as criterial features of linguistic proficiency, as there are differences in the distributions of grammatical errors across proficiency levels, to which we can correlate differences in their frequency.

[1] https://languagetool.org/

	A1	A2	B1	B2	C1
A1	0.0	0.055	0.065	0.085	0.066
A2	0.055	0.0	0.013	0.029	0.028
B1	0.065	0.013	0.0	0.005	0.009
B2	0.085	0.029	0.005	0.0	0.010
C1	0.066	0.028	0.009	0.010	0.0

Table 2: Symmetric KL Divergence between distributions of counts from all 17 error labels in EFCAMDAT.

2.2 Ranking of error gravity

In light of this, we analyzed the frequency of each type of error across the 15 proficiency levels of the corpus. We calculated it dividing the sum of all the occurrences of a given type of error in a given proficiency level by the number of texts assigned to a given proficiency level. We then decided to design a ranking of error gravity for each type of error in relation to each proficiency level, by introducing a negative bias in the error count when this amounts to 0:

$$b_t = \begin{cases} -1 & 0.1 \leq F_{t,L} < 0.2 \\ -2 & 0.2 \leq F_{t,L} < 0.3 \\ \dots & \\ -9 & 0.9 \leq F_{t,L} < 1.0 \end{cases}$$

where $F_{t,L}$ is the normalized frequency of error type t at proficiency level L; e.g. if $F_{AR,1}$ is 0.2, all the occurrences of error AR at level 1 reporting 0 errors are replaced by -2. The rationale behind this idea is to "award" learners who have not made a frequent error in their proficiency level. Subsequently, in order to avoid having a too sparse representation, we grouped the 17 types of errors into 5 classes of errors: verb tense (VT), lexis and use of words (LUW), prepositions, articles, possessives and part of speech (PAP), agreement (AG) and generic errors (GE), as shown in Table 3. We divided each of the 5 error counts by the word count, in order to weigh also the text length. Finally, the error count in each level is normalized on a scale from 0 to 1.

Before applying our ranking of error gravity and introducing the negative bias, we also calculated the averaged error rates (i.e. the number of errors divided by the number of words times 100) of each of the 5 classes and of their sum for each proficiency level (see Table 4). In the VT class, the increase of the error rate at A2 can be explained by the fact that A1 learners generally use a smaller variety of tenses. As a result, they tend to make fewer verb tense errors.

Errors	Class
VT	VT
NSW + PH + EX + MW + WC + WO	LUW
AR + PO + PR + PS	PAP
AG + PL + SI	AG
D + IS + XC	GE

Table 3: The 5 error classes we used for our study.

Furthermore, we performed ANOVA on each of the 5 classes and we always obtained significant p-values ($<$0.05), thus finding that there are significant differences between proficiency levels in terms of errors.

	mean (%)				
	A1	**A2**	**B1**	**B2**	**C1**
LUW	3.67	3.10	2.69	1.96	1.58
PAP	1.63	1.42	1.20	0.99	0.70
AG	0.99	0.49	0.47	0.36	0.31
GE	2.00	1.67	1.29	0.95	0.80
VT	0.31	0.43	0.41	0.36	0.19
total	8.62	7.13	6.08	4.63	3.59

Table 4: Averaged error rate of each error class and their sum across proficiency levels.

2.3 ICNALE

In order to test our approach, we consider ICNALE (Ishikawa), a publicly available dataset [2] comprising written and spoken responses of ESL learners ranging from A2 to B2 and partially of native speakers. The CEFR levels were assigned prior to collecting the data, as the ICNALE team required all the learners to take an L2 vocabulary size test and to present their scores in English proficiency tests such as TOEFL, TOEIC, IELTS, etc. On the basis of these two scores, the learners were classified into proficiency levels. Only a small section of dialogues and essays has been scored by human experts so far and has been included in the ICNALE Global Rating Archives (Ishikawa, 2020): it currently includes the assessments and scores (on a scale from 0 to 100) of 140 dialogues and 140 essays by 40 human raters. Since not all the dialogues and essays were previously assigned a proficiency level, for our experiments we selected only the ones classified into CEFR levels and scored by human experts, and we also considered the scored texts

[2] http://language.sakura.ne.jp/icnale/download.html

and speeches of native speakers, therefore reducing the written section to 121 essays and the spoken section to 116 dialogues, of which we considered only the learners' utterances. Out of the 40 raters involved in the project, we only selected the native speakers with more than 5 years of experience in ESL teaching and assessment, i.e. 4 raters for the written section and 3 raters for the spoken section. We set the average of these scores as targets. Details about average and standard deviation of the raters' scores can be found in Ishikawa (2020).

2.4 CLC-FCE

Due to the limited amount of annotated data in the ICNALE corpus, we train our models on the CLC-FCE corpus, a publicly available dataset [3], containing the scripts of an English language exam aimed at around B2 level of the CEFR, which is also the highest level of the ICNALE corpus. Its 1244 exam scripts include responses to two different prompts asking the test-takers to write a short answer (e.g. a letter, an article, a report, a short story) and range from 200 to 400 words on average. Each answer has been error-tagged and annotated by human experts with a mark. Note that we eliminated the answers that did not report a score. More information about the dataset can be found in Yannakoudakis et al. (2011).

2.5 TLT-school

In Trentino, an autonomous region in northern Italy, the linguistic competence of Italian students have been assessed over years through proficiency tests in both English and German (Gretter et al., 2020), involving about 3000 students ranging from 9 to 16 years old, belonging to four different school grade levels (5th, 8th, 10th, 11th) and three proficiency levels (A1, A2, B1). Since our experiments are conducted only on the B1 section of the English written and spoken parts of the corpus, we will not describe the section concerning the texts and utterances of the German section, as their analysis goes beyond the scope of this paper.

The written section consists of 895 answers to 2 question prompts. Test-takers are asked two questions: the first one requires them to write a blog entry in which they have to describe what happened during the day and to talk about their plans for the rest of the week, while the second one asks them to write an email to a friend who broke an object borrowed from them. The spoken section is composed of 442 responses to 7 small talk questions about everyday life situations. It is worth mentioning that some answers are characterized by a number of issues (e.g. presence of words belonging to multiple languages or presence of off-topic answers). We decided not to eliminate these answers from the data used in the experiments, but we removed the empty responses.

As regards the speech transcriptions, we eliminated the annotations related to spontaneous speech phenomena such as hesitations and fragments of words etc. Detailed information about the manual transcriptions and other aspects of the corpus can be found in Gretter et al. (2020).

As for the automatic speech recognition (ASR) output text, its word error rate is 35.9% on the whole spoken test data, whereas it amounts to 41.13% for the B1 subset we used in our experiments; acoustic and language models are described in Gretter et al. (2019).

The total score ranges from 0 to 8 in the written section and from 0 to 12 in the spoken section and consists of the sum of the subscores assigned by human experts for each specific proficiency indicator assigned by the human raters (i.e. fulfillment, formal correctness and lexical complexity, cohesion, and narrative and descriptive competences for writing; and relevance, formal correctness, lexical complexity, pronunciation, fluency, and communicative competence for speaking). For each indicator human raters could choose 0, 1 or 2 points. Since every utterance was scored by only one expert, it was not possible to evaluate any kind of agreement among experts. Note that the CEFR levels were assigned before the tests and should be considered as expected proficiency levels, whereas the test scores are effectively representing each learner's performance in the exam. Table 6 shows the number of answers and word counts of the TLT-school spoken test set across test scores.

3 Model architectures

We build our models using a BERT architecture (Devlin et al., 2018) in the version provided by the HuggingFace Transformer Library (Wolf et al., 2019) (*bert-base-uncased*). In both the feature extractor and the scoring models BERT layers are frozen.

[3] https://ilexir.co.uk/datasets/index.html

	ICNALE		CLC	TLT	
	Wr	Sp		Wr	Sp
Train	-	-	2122	594	345
Dev	-	-	160	-	-
Test	121	116	194	301	97
Avg. len	225	186	192	103	28
Max. len	302	455	462	279	221
Min. len	179	23	72	1	1
Score	0-100	0-100	1-40	0-8	0-12

Table 5: Statistics (number of answers and word counts) for the three test sets: ICNALE (Written and Spoken), CLC-FCE, TLT-school (Written and Spoken).

Score	Samples	Min. len	Max. len	Avg. len
0-3	27	1	100	11.18
3-6	23	9	85	22.00
6-9	14	11	51	27.07
9-12	33	20	196	55.57

Table 6: Statistics (number of answers and word counts) for the TLT-school spoken test set across test scores.

3.1 Feature extractor

Specifically, EFEX takes a sequence of token embeddings i.e. of the answers provided by the learners $[x_1, ..., x_n]$, as inputs and predicts the 'biased' estimate (see formula in section 2.1) of error rate of each class of error, i.e. VT, LUW, PAP, AG and GE. Each rate is calculated by a final dense layer and the model uses mean squared error (MSE) as the loss function. For the GE and LUW outputs we add one and two extra dense layers respectively. We used Adam optimizer (Kingma and Ba, 2014) with learning rate of 8e-6, batch size set at 16, validation split at 0.1, and we trained our models for 60 epochs. Figure 2 shows the architecture of EFEX.

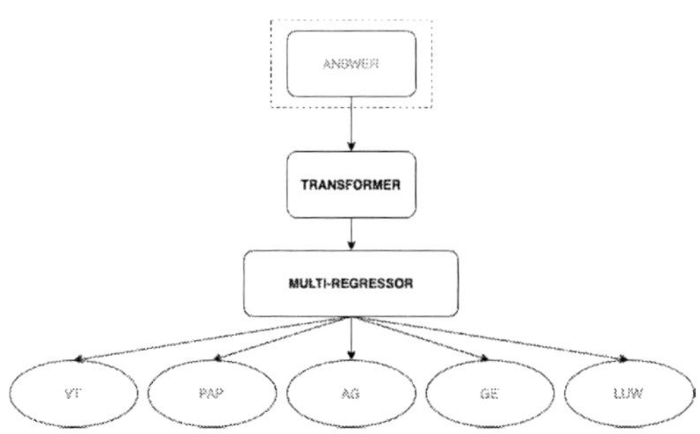

Figure 2: EFEX model architecture.

3.2 Scoring models

Before testing the impact of the labels generated by EFEX, we run several experiments on the selected datasets using our simple baseline scoring models, which take only a sequence of token embeddings, i.e. of the answers provided by the test-takers $[x_1, ..., x_n]$, as inputs and predict the total score of each answer normalized on a scale from -1 to 1. The EFEX-enriched models take the answers as inputs combined with a 5-dimensional vector, i.e. the number of classes of errors generated by EFEX, and have the same outputs as the baselines, as shown in Figure 3.

In both the baseline models and the EFEX-enriched models, the scores are calculated by a final dense layer and the model employs MSE as the loss function. The structure and hyper-parameters of the models are shown in Table 7. For the evaluation we consider two metrics: MSE and Pearson's correlation coefficient (PCC) between the true scores and the predicted ones.

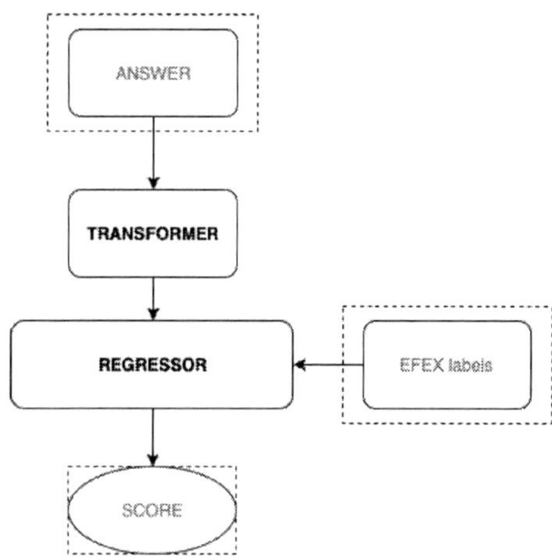

Figure 3: Scoring model architecture.

4 Experiments and results

4.1 CLC-FCE to ICNALE

We run a series of experiments starting from training EFEX on the EFCAMDAT dataset, setting VT, PAP, AG, GE and LUW as our prediction targets, feeding only the input text. We tested EFEX on the EFCAMDAT test set and we obtained significant results when comparing the true labels with the predicted ones in terms of PCC (see Table 8).

Secondly, we run the scorer on ICNALE (see Table 9); since we do not have enough ICNALE data for a proper training, we train our models on

	TLT	CLC/ICNALE
Max. seq. len.	256	512
Learning rate	9e-6	2e-6
Epochs	60 (120)	60 (150)
Batch size	32	16
1st Dense layer	768 - relu	768 - relu
Dropout	0.2	0.2
2nd Dense layer	128 - relu	64 - relu
Dropout	0.2	0.2
Output layer	1	1

Table 7: Model architectures and hyperparameters. The number of epochs in brackets refers to the EFEX-enriched model.

	PCC
LUW	0.796
PAP	0.862
AG	0.868
GE	0.831
VT	0.876

Table 8: EFEX performance in terms of PCC on EF-CAMDAT.

the CLC-FCE. Considering that we test our models trained on the CLC-FCE directly on out-of-domain data without fine-tuning, we achieve overall interesting results. In this case, the performance of the EFEX-enriched model is slightly lower than the baseline when tested on the scores of the ICNALE written set, but still better in terms of PCC when used for predicting the scores of the spoken set.

ICNALE	Written		Spoken	
Model	MSE	PCC	MSE	PCC
CLC baseline	0.201	0.719	0.121	0.614
+ EFEX labels	0.254	0.709	0.134	**0.625**

Table 9: Results on the ICNALE test dataset (MSE and PCC).

4.2 TLT-school - Written to spoken

Finally, we run our experiments on the TLT-school, training our baseline on the written training set and testing it on the spoken test set. We follow the same steps with our EFEX-enriched model and we gain

	TLT - Spoken			
	Man. transcr.		ASR	
	MSE	PCC	MSE	PCC
Baseline	0.555	0.734	0.793	0.605
+ fine-tuning	0.488	0.741	0.715	0.609
+ EFEX labels	0.468	0.759	0.688	0.638
+ fine-tuning	**0.400**	**0.764**	**0.606**	**0.642**

Table 10: Results on the TLT test dataset (MSE and PCC): baseline; baseline + fine-tuning; baseline + EFEX labels; baseline + EFEX labels + fine-tuning.

a higher performance when predicting the spoken scores both using the manual transcriptions and the ASR output text, as shown in Table 10. Additionally, we fine-tune our model on the spoken training set for 2 epochs reducing the learning rate to 2e-6 and we obtain our best performance, reaching a PCC of 0.764 on the manual transcriptions.

Also the results on the ASR output appear to be enhanced by fine-tuning, as we obtain a PCC of 0.642. Fine-tuning the baseline without additional features reaches a PCC of 0.741 on the manual transcriptions and of 0.609 on the ASR. We find that the EFEX-enriched model achieves higher results across both metrics.

Furthermore, we continue our analysis comparing the performance of the baseline and the EFEX-enriched model across test scores. Figure 4 shows the MSE variation across 4 ranges of scores, i.e. 0-3, 3-6, 6-9, 9-12. It can be observed that the MSE is always lower for the EFEX-enriched model except in the range of scores between 0 and 3 on both the manual transcriptions and ASR output text, for which the EFEX-enriched model shows a minute increase of the MSE. Such difference is probably due to the fact that, in this specific range of scores, learners' answers, in addition to having lower quality, are also shorter on average (about 11 words), as shown in Table 6. As the score increases, the word average rises to 56 for scores between 9 and 12. Fewer words also means fewer and less variety of errors. Therefore, EFEX might be introducing some information that is not needed for answers with lower scores.

Specifically, the error distribution for the lowest range might be less informative, as can be inferred from the Frobenius norm values of the EFEX vectors for each score range shown in Table 11.

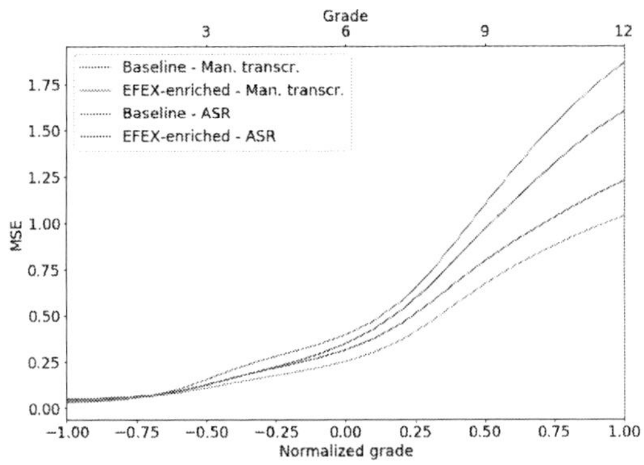

Figure 4: MSE variation across scores on manual transcriptions and ASR output text.

	Norm	
Score range	**Man. transcr.**	**ASR**
0-3	1.786	1.780
3-6	2.386	2.540
6-9	2.022	2.090
9-12	4.011	3.986

Table 11: Frobenius norm values of EFEX vectors across score ranges.

5 Conclusions and future work

In this work we presented a promising approach to automatic proficiency assessment of spoken responses based on the presence of errors across proficiency levels, extracted with an error feature extractor that we developed using a BERT-based architecture. Furthermore, we proposed to use models previously trained on written data in order to tackle the problem related to limited availability of spoken data. First, we tried our error-based approach on some publicly available datasets, training our models on the CLC-FCE and testing them on the ICNALE. In this case, our EFEX-enriched model managed to modestly improve the prediction of the dialogues scores in terms of PCC. Specifically for this experiment, one also has to consider the difference in domain and scoring metrics between the two corpora, albeit they are approximately around the same proficiency levels.

Subsequently, we discovered that the use of EFEX labels shows a more interesting improvement in scoring the spoken section of TLT-school after training our models on written data, suggesting that these additional features can mitigate the impact of ASR errors and some typical phenomena of the spoken modality. An example drawn from the data could be the following: *"in fact when a person does a lot of movement and moves a lot and goes out in the in the nature then his his body is in more healthy"*. The repetitions 'in the' and 'his' as well as what appears to be a wrongly inserted preposition 'in' would be considered actual errors if they occurred in written productions, but not necessarily so in spoken texts.

Our assumption is that BERT models, as they are trained on large written corpora, already possess written grammatical knowledge and are sensitive to grammatical violations to a certain extent. Therefore, when evaluating written proficiency, they do not need to be warned with explicit indications with regard to errors, but error-related features can be beneficial to understand and decode the typical phenomena of oral language and learn spoken and conversational grammar. Considering that in spoken responses the scoring module could take advantage of a distinction of errors made by the speaker or introduced by ASR (Knill et al., 2019), we assume that there is still room for improvement in the approaches that detect errors as additional features.

Further work should be undertaken starting from the first step of our pipeline, i.e. the error feature extractor, since, despite the good results shown in Table 8, we can still improve it and analyse its effectiveness in various ways, e.g. by rearranging the error classes and remapping the ranking of error gravity.

Considering that we removed spontaneous speech phenomena such as hesitations and fragments of words from the data for our experiments, we envisage a combination of the approach presented in this paper and the use of error-related features derived from audio recordings, such as phonological errors as well as repetitions and other types of disfluency.

Moreover, we plan to investigate the impact of models trained on written data and tested on spoken data also for other CEFR levels. Finally, we acknowledge that the presence of errors cannot be the only feature to be taken into account when assessing L2 proficiency at higher levels, but, if properly weighted and balanced with other proficiency indicators, it might improve consistency and objectivity in assessment.

References

N. Ballier, T. Gaillat, A. Simpkin, B. Stearns, M. Bouyé, and M. Zarrouk. 2019. A supervised learning model for the automatic assessment of language levels based on learner errors. In *EC-TEL 2019 14th European Conference on Technology Enhanced Learning*, pages 1–13.

A. Caines, C. Bentz, K. Knill, M. Rei, and P. Buttery. 2020. Grammatical error detection in transcriptions of spoken English. In *Proceedings of the 28th International Conference on Computational Linguistics*, pages 2144–2162.

A. Caines and P. Buttery. 2020. REPROLANG 2020: Automatic proficiency scoring of Czech, English, German, Italian, and Spanish learner essays. In *Proceedings of the 12th Conference on Language Resources and Evaluation*, pages 5614–5623.

M. Canale and M. Swain. 1980. Theoretical bases for communicative approaches to second language teaching and testing. *Applied Linguistics*, 1(1):1–47.

L. Chen, J. Tao, S. Ghaffarzadegan, and Y. Qian. 2018. End-to-end neural network based automated speech scoring. In *IEEE International Conference on Acoustics Speech and Signal Processing*.

S. P. Corder. 1967. The significance of learner's errors. *International Review of Applied Linguistics in Language Teaching*, V(1):161–170.

Council of Europe. 2001. *Common European Framework of Reference for Languages: Learning, Teaching, Assessment.* Cambridge University Press.

H. Craighead, A. Caines, P. Buttery, and H. Yannakoudakis. 2020. Investigating the effect of auxiliary objectives for the automated grading of learner english speech transcriptions. In *Proceedings of the 58th Annual Meeting of the Association for Computational Linguistics*, pages 2258–2269.

S.A. Crossley, K. Kyle, and D.S. McNamara. 2015. To aggregate or not? Linguistic features in automatic essay scoring and feedback systems. *The Journal of Writing Assessment*, 9(1):1–19.

R. Cummins and M. Rei. 2018. Neural multi-task learning in automated assessment. page arXiv:1801.06830.

J. Devlin, M. Chang, L. Kenton, and K. Toutanova. 2018. BERT: Pre-training of Deep Bidirectional Transformers for Language Understanding. *arXiv e-prints*, page arXiv:1810.04805.

M. Gamon, M. Chodorow, C. Leacock, and J. Tetreault. 2013. Grammatical error detection in automatic essay scoring and feedback. In M.D. Shermis and J.C. Burstein, editors, *Handbook of Automated Essay Evaluation*, chapter 15, pages 251–266. Routledge, New York.

J. Geertzen, T. Alexopolou, and A. Korhonen. 2014. Automatic linguistic annotation of large scale L2 databases: The EF-Cambridge Open Language Database (EFCamDat). In *Proceedings of the 2012 Second Language Research Forum*, pages 240–254.

R. Gretter, M. Matassoni, K. Allgaier, S. Tchistiakova, and D. Falavigna. 2019. Automatic assessment of spoken language proficiency of non-native children. In *IEEE International Conference on Acoustics, Speech and Signal Processing*.

R. Gretter, M. Matassoni, S. Bannò, and D. Falavigna. 2020. TLT-school: a corpus of non native children speech. In *Proceedings of the 12th Language Resources and Evaluation Conference*, Marseille, France. European Language Resources Association.

J.A. Hawkins and P. Buttery. 2010. Criterial features in learner corpora: Theories and illustrations. *English Profile Journal*, 1(1):1–23.

P. Howson. 2013. *The English effect.* British Council, London.

D. Hymes. 1972. On communicative competence. In J. Pride J. Holmes, editor, *Sociolinguistics: Selected Readings*, pages 269–293. Penguin, Harmondsworth.

S. Ishikawa. A new horizon in learner corpus studies: The aim of the ICNALE project. In *Corpora and language technologies in teaching, learning and research.* University of Strathclyde Press.

S. Ishikawa. 2020. Aim of the ICNALE GRA project: Global collaboration to collect ratings of asian learners' l2 english essays and speeches from an ELF perspective. *Learner Corpus Studies in Asia and the World*, 5:121–144.

C. James. 2013. *Errors in language learning and use: Exploring error analysis.* Routledge.

D.P. Kingma and J. Ba. 2014. Adam: a method for stochastic optimization. In *International Conference on Learning Representations.*

K. Knill, M. Gales, P. Manakul, and A. Caines. 2019. Automatic grammatical error detection of non-native spoken learner English. In *IEEE International Conference on Acoustics Speech and Signal Processing*, pages 8127–8131.

R. Lado. 1961. *Language testing: the construction and use of foreign language tests.* Longman, London.

C. Leacock and M. Chodorow. 2003. Automated grammatical error detection. In M.D. Shermis and J.C. Burstein, editors, *Automated essay scoring: a cross-disciplinary perspective*, pages 195–207. Lawrence Erlbaum Associates, Mahwah, NJ.

J. Pfingsthorn. 2013. *Variability in learner errors as a reflection of the CLT paradigm shift.* Frankfurt am Main.

V. Raina, M.J.F. Gales, and K.M. Knill. 2020. Universal adversarial attacks on spoken language assessment systems. In *Interspeech 2020*, pages 3855–3859.

I. Shatz. 2020. Refining and modifying the EFCAMDAT. *International Journal of Learner Corpus Research*, 6(2):220–223.

J. Thewissen. 2013. Capturing l2 accuracy developmental patterns: Insights from an error-tagged efl learner corpus. *The Modern Language Journal*, 97(1):77–101.

S. Vajjala. 2018. Automated assessment of non-native learner essays: Investigating the role of linguistic features. *International Journal of Artificial Intelligence in Education*, 28:79–105.

S. Vajjala and T. Rama. 2018. Experiments with universal cefr classification. In *Proceedings of 13th Workshop on Innovative Use of NLP for Building Educational Applications*, pages 147–153.

X. Wang, K. Evanini, Y. Qian, and M. Mulholland. 2021. Automated scoring of spontaneous speech from young learners of english using transformers. In *2021 IEEE Spoken Language Technology Workshop (SLT)*, pages 705–712.

T. Wolf et al. 2019. Huggingface's transformers: State-of-the-art natural language processing. page arXiv:1910.03771.

X. Xi, D. Higgins, K. Zechner, and D.M. Williamson. 2008. Automated scoring of spontaneous speech using SpeechRater SM v1.0.

H. Yannakoudakis, T. Briscoe, and B. Medlock. 2011. A new dataset and method for automatically grading ESOL texts. In *Proceedings of the 49th Annual Meeting of the Association for Computational Linguistics: Human Language Technologies*, volume 1, pages 180–189.

M. Zhang. 2013. Contrasting automated and human scoring of essays. *R&D Connections*, (21):1–11.

Activity focused Speech Recognition of Preschool Children in Early Childhood Classrooms

Satwik Dutta and **John H.L. Hansen**
Center for Robust Speech Systems
The University of Texas at Dallas, Richardson, Texas, USA
satwik.dutta@utdallas.edu, john.hansen@utdallas.edu

Dwight Irvin and **Jay Buzhardt**
Juniper Gardens Children's Project
The University of Kansas, Kansas City, Kansas, USA
dwirvin@ku.edu, jaybuz@ku.edu

Abstract

A supportive environment is vital for overall cognitive development in children. Challenges with direct observation and limitations of access to data driven approaches often hinder teachers or practitioners in early childhood research to modify or enhance classroom structures. Deploying sensor based tools in naturalistic preschool classrooms will thereby help teachers/practitioners to make informed decisions and better support student learning needs. In this study, two elements of eco-behavioral assessment: conversational speech and real-time location are fused together. While various challenges remain in developing Automatic Speech Recognition systems for spontaneous preschool children speech, efforts are made to develop a hybrid ASR engine reporting an effective Word-Error-Rate of 40%. The ASR engine further supports recognition of spoken words, WH-words, and verbs in various activity learning zones in a naturalistic preschool classroom scenario. Activity areas represent various locations within the physical ecology of an early childhood setting, each of which is suited for knowledge and skill enhancement in young children. Capturing children's communication engagement in such areas could help teachers/practitioners fine-tune their daily activities, without the need for direct observation. This investigation provides evidence of the use of speech technology in educational settings to better support such early childhood intervention.

1 Introduction

The preschool classroom is a viable space for capturing young children's interactions with teachers and peers. The quality and number of interactions children experience is a key factor in child language development (Hart and Risley, 1995). However, for supporting teachers working with young children with or without developmental delays, the use of direct observations or manual video recording and coding is not a scalable endeavor (Tapp et al., 1995). Sensor-based monitoring tools in classrooms can assist teachers in creating and maintaining a rich learning environment for all children. Feedback from these tools could allow teachers to better identify children who could benefit from further support. Rich and frequently available data can not only help in creating better classroom structure, but also create opportunities to maximize children's communication and interaction (Diamond et al., 2013).

Eco-behavioral observational assessment has often been used to measure moment-to-moment effects with multiple environmental events on specific behaviors and interactions that occur in an early childhood inclusive classroom (Greenwood et al., 1994; Watson et al., 2011). These assessment samples are centered around teacher and child behavior, and overall classroom learning context (e.g., the interactions between them) by adding situational or contextual factors. Specifically for inclusive classrooms, a child's daily interaction can influence their development and by using an eco-behavioral assessment, conclusions can be drawn between environmental contexts and the interactions that occur within them (Brown et al., 1999). These findings can inform practitioners how to arrange their inclusive environments to best support language development of all children. The variety of spontaneous language in an inclusive preschool classroom comes from a variety of speakers and includes both adults and children. Although the Language Environment Analysis (LENA) framework is used extensively by the early childhood research community for a digital measurement system that is automatic (Soderstrom and Wittebolle, 2013; Dykstra et al., 2013; Burgess et al., 2013;

Proceedings of the 17th Workshop on Innovative Use of NLP for Building Educational Applications (BEA 2022), pages 92 - 100
July 15, 2022

Irvin et al., 2017; Greenwood et al., 2018), LENA does not possess an Automatic Speech Recognition (ASR) engine to convert the child speech-to-text, nor does it capture location in the classroom. Apart from conversational speech, children's coordinated movement and location within classrooms also act as an acquisition context driver for critically important skills including language, cognition, and social communication (Eliot, 2000; Council et al., 2000; Piek et al., 2008). Therefore, automatic location tracking within the classroom can provide the ability to monitor interventions while maximizing learning opportunities (Irvin et al., 2018).

Our multi-disciplinary educational research project focuses on quantifying "learning" based on social engagement for use in classroom settings by teachers - and thus we are building a tool that captures the granularity of eco-behavioral observational assessment. It is based on spontaneous interactions between multiple teachers and preschool children (3 to 5 years) with and without developmental delays within naturalistic noisy preschool classroom environments. In this study, we present a translational framework to automatically track conversational speech of preschool children in various activity areas supported by speech technology based on ASR which is fine-tuned specifically for preschool children taking into account their developing nature and developmental delays.

2 Speech and language development in young children

Right from their first babbles, children start developing various speech sounds (Shriberg, 1993) until mid-elementary school. Typically-developing children are expected to progressively acquire various speech sounds throughout early childhood (birth to 8 years). These development occurs primarily in three stages: (i) 'Early' stage from 1 to 3 years, (ii) 'Middle' stage from 3 to $6\frac{1}{2}$, and (iii) 'Late' stage from 5 to $7\frac{1}{2}$. In the 'Early' stage, speech sounds like M (nasal; "mama"), B (stop; "baby"), Y (semivowel; "you"), N (nasal; "no"), W (semivowel; "we"), D (stop; "Daddy"), P (stop; "Pop"), HH (aspirate; "hi") are expected to be developed. While sounds like T (stop; "two"), NG (nasal; "running"), K (stop; "cup"), G (stop; "go"), F (fricative; "fish"), V (fricative, "van"), CH (affricate, "chew"), and JH (affricate, "jump") are expected to be acquired in the 'Middle' stage. Finally, in the 'late' stage, children develop slightly harder sounds like SH (fricative; "sheep"), S (fricative; "see"), TH (fricative; "think,that", R (liquid; "red"), Z (fricative; "zoo"), L (liquid; "like") and ZH (fricative; "measure"). Children may omit, substitute or have inconsistency in production of speech sounds while they are learning. Apart from speech, language planning is also evolving, so word selection and grammar may have issues. Not all children acquire these skills at a similar pace, especially those with developmental delays.

3 Challenges of developing Automatic Speech Recognition systems for young children

Various developmental factors like articulation/pronunciation, motor skills, vocabulary, etc., makes the task of developing ASR systems for children challenging than that for adults (Gerosa et al., 2007). Also, children in early childhood (birth to 8 years) have significantly different speech and language skills as compared to their older peers. Prior research from the Speech Technology community on Children ASR (Stemmer et al., 2003; Shivakumar et al., 2014; Tong et al., 2017; Wu et al., 2019; Shivakumar and Georgiou, 2020; Yeung et al., 2021; Rumberg et al., 2021; Gretter et al., 2021) is captivating. But these focused on: (i) older children, including kindergarten (6-15 yrs), (ii) data collected using head-mounted microphones or close-proximity handheld smartphones in clean/controlled settings under adult supervision, and (iii) with just one speaker using prompts or read stimuli, and limited spontaneous (not scripted) speech. Limited focus and data is available for processing of adult-child interactions in naturalistic preschool settings (3-5 yrs) while they are involved in various activities throughout the day. There is lack of publicly available young child speech corpora (primarily due to privacy/regulations). However, a recent study (Yeung and Alwan, 2018) described various challenges in developing ASR systems for single-word utterances read aloud by kindergarten (5-6 yrs) children achieving a Word Error Rate (WER) of 25%. Therefore, all these factors make the task of developing ASR systems for spontaneous preschool children speech in naturalistic educational settings extremely challenging.

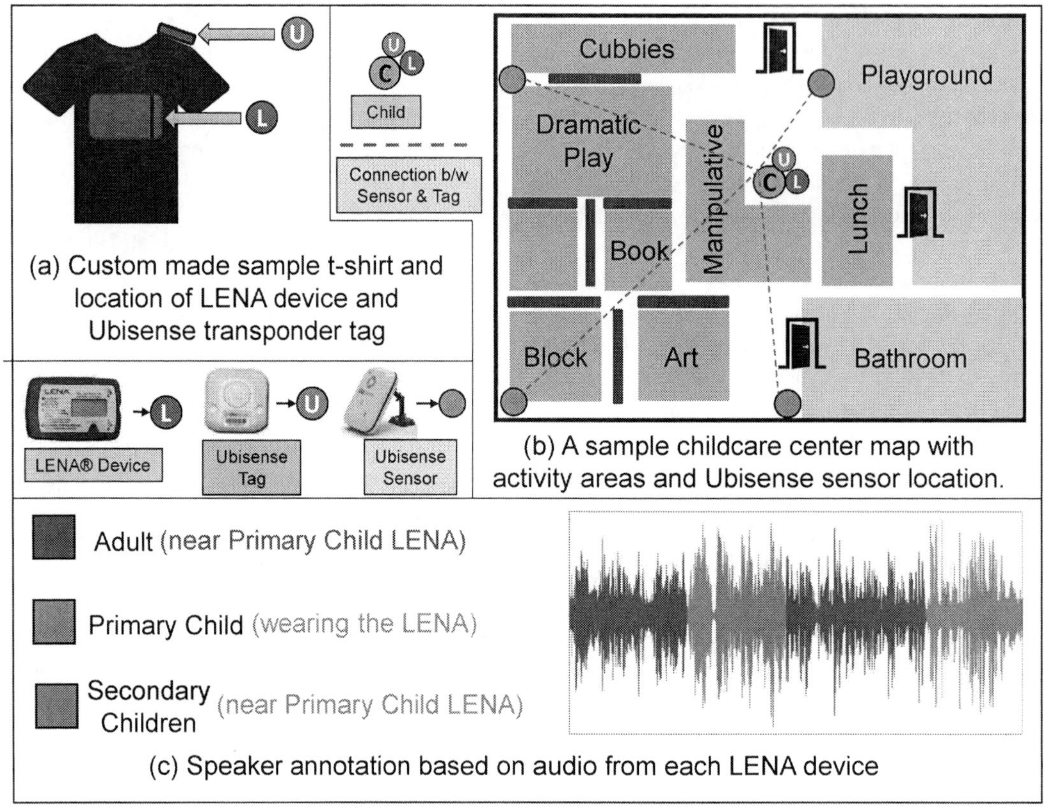

Figure 1: Speech and location data collection in preschool.

4 Data and Collection

4.1 Participants & Procedure

A total of 33 children aged 3 to 5 years with and without developmental delays, and 8 adults teachers participated in this study. The data was collected in preschool classrooms (refer Fig.1(b)) in a large urban community in a Southern state in US, and in multiple sessions over several days in different classrooms with different groups of participants. Data from each participant was linked to an anonymous id for privacy. All participants consented to the use of de-identified data for analysis. This study was approved by the Institutional Review Board of both KU and UTD for analysis.

4.2 Conversational Speech

Conversational speech was collected using a light weight compact digital audio recorder (LENA[1]) attached to participants (refer Fig.1(a)). The LENA Language ENvironmental Analysis system consists of an audio recorder and audio processing software (Ford et al., 2008). The recorder uses an omnidirectional microphone and the final audio is obtained by a computer or laptop running the software to which the recorder is plugged in. The final audio has a sampling frequency of 16 kHz, with a recording unit having a capacity of 16 hours. Although LENA provides adult word counts, conversational turns, and child and peer vocalizations; it does not provide the speech-to-text output. The LENA unit data can be considered as individual audio stream and was tagged into three speaker (Fig.1(c)) categories: Primary child (speech initiated by child wearing that LENA unit), Secondary child (speech originated by any other children within close proximity of primary child), and Adult (speech originated by any adult in close proximity). It is noted that for each LENA audio stream, there is only 1 Primary child and multiple Secondary Children and Adults (e.g., each LENA stream is associated with anonymous child id).

[1] https://www.lena.org/

4.3 Real-time Location

Ubisense [2], a Real-Time Location Tracking System (RTLS) based on Ultra-Wideband (UWB), is deployed in this study. Ubisense is capable of providing 3D location for every second simultaneously for up to 100 individuals both indoors and outdoors. The RTLS data can also provide information on movement patterns and direction apart from location. This system is established by the combination of receiver sensors and wearable light-weight transponder tags (refer Fig.1(a,b)), both of which broadcast live location co-ordinates to a laptop or computer in network running the Ubisense Location Engine software. With proper calibration, the accuracy of Ubisense is $\pm$15 cm under ideal measurement conditions, and $\pm$30 cm in challenging measurement conditions. Ubisense has been previously deployed in various clinical research studies for individuals at risk for dementia (Kearns et al., 2008; Vuong et al., 2014). Sensors are placed in four corners of the space to ensure maximum coverage and connected to a laptop computer via cords. Then the dimensions of the classroom are established based on the Ubisense measurements, followed by calibrating the real-time location system sensors to their 3-D (x, y, z) locations. Measures to minimize electronic interference caused by other devices (i.e., Wi-Fi routers) was considered. Real-time location was not recorded when the children went outside of the classroom dimension set by Ubisense sensors (like playground).

4.4 Mapping activity area with real-time location information and speech

Activity areas represent information about the location (permanent or temporary) of the child within the physical ecology of an early childhood setting. For this study, various individual literacy areas in the classroom were outlined in consultation with the preschool teachers. These areas are outlined in Table 1. This is followed by setting up boundaries around the individual literacy areas in the classroom using the Geometry feature of Ubisense. This subsequently helped to identify when children wearing a transponder tag were in these areas (refer Fig.1(b)). Ubisense scanning rate was set to 1 Hz. Human-transcriptions of conversational speech, the actual start time of the Ubisense location tracking system, and the actual recording start time of every individual LENA unit (worn by different children) were used for the mapping between the activity areas and spoken text.

[2]https://ubisense.com/

Table 1: *Activity Area Codes and their significance.*

Area Code	Significance
Art	Area for painting, drawing, coloring, writing, or sculpting
Snack	Area for snack/food breaks
Block	Areas with large building or construction materials, on floor
Cozy/Book	Areas with books for reading alone or in groups
Computer	Areas for computer activity
Dramatic play	Areas for dress up clothes, kitchen utensils, dollhouse, etc. or that support activities with other children that contain make-believe roles or themes like fireperson, doctor, etc.
Manipulative	Areas for small motor movements of the hand, fingers, wrists, and hand-eye coordination
Story	Areas for reading, listening and telling stories

5 Developing Preschool Children Automatic Speech Recognition System

5.1 Acoustic and Language Modelling

Acoustic model training and decoding experiments were performed using Kaldi (Povey et al., 2011), N-gram language models were trained using SRILM toolkit (Stolcke, 2002) and the RNN-based using PyTorch. Care was taken to avoid overlap of the same group of children between train/test. Ground-truth was based on human transcriptions and only the segments spoken by both primary and secondary children were considered for ASR assessment. The GMM-HMM systems were trained to provide frame-to-phone alignments for the DNN based systems. For the GMM-HMM systems, Mel-frequency cepstral coefficients (MFCCs) (Young, 1996) were extracted for every 25 ms window and 10 ms overlap. 13 MFCCs along with their Δ and $\Delta\Delta$ features were used as front-end features. The input features to the DNN-HMM models included a 40-D high resolution MFCCs of current and neighbouring frames and a 100-D i-vector(Hansen and Hasan, 2015) of the current frame. The i-vectors were calculated by generating speed-perturbed training data with 3 (0.9,1.0,1.1) speed factors. In

Table 2: *Child ASR Performance.*

#	Features ♣	Acoustic Model Training Data♠	Acoustic Model	Language Model Training Data♠	Language Model	WER (%) of Preschool Test
1	MΔ	PS	GMM-Tri3	LibriSpeech	3-gram	90.28
2	MΔ + I3	PS	TDNN-F(11)	LibriSpeech	3-gram	63.66
3	MΔ + I3	PS	TDNN-F(11)	PS	3-gram	49.02
4	E + I3	PS	TDNN-F(17)	PS	3-gram	47.02
5	E_S + I3	PS	CNN(6) + TDNN-F(9)	PS	3-gram	43.03
6	E_S + I3	PS	CNN(6) + TDNN-F(9) + Attn(1)	PS	3-gram	42.00
7	E_S + I3	PS	CNN(6) + TDNN-F(9) + Attn(1)	PS	LSTM	**40.67**
8	E_S + I3	PS + CMU + OGI	CNN(6) + TDNN-F(9) + Attn(1)	PS + CMU + OGI	3-gram	43.57

♣ MΔ → MFCC & Δ & ΔΔ, E/E_S → Filter-Bank Energy (/with SpecAugment), I3 → 3* Speed pert. i-vector
♠ PS → Preschool, CMU → CMU Kids Corpora, OS → OGI Kids Corpora

addition, these high-resolution MFCCs were also replaced with 40-dimensional Mel-frequency Filter Banks Energies (MFBE) (Paliwal, 1999) by Inverse Discrete Cosine Transform. Factorized time-delay neural networks (TDNN-F)(Povey et al., 2018a), originally proposed as a data-efficient alternative to TDNN for enhancing ASR performance of low-resource languages with less than 100 hours of data, were primarily used as hidden layers for the hybrid DNN-HMM acoustic models. Apart from TDNN-F layers, CNN layers were deployed. A time-restricted self-attention (Vaswani et al., 2017; Povey et al., 2018b) mechanism (with multiple heads) was also deployed. Another data augmentation approach called SpecAugment(Park et al., 2019) was applied directly to MFBEs. For the RNN-based LMs, we used 2-layer LSTMs of 650 embedding size and 650 hidden dimension. Dropout was considered to overcome overfitting. Lattice rescoring(Li et al., 2021) was used to decode the RNN-based LM. CMU Pronouncing Dictionary[3] was used. Various non-linguistic markers included: laugh, cough, scream, gasp, breath, babble, cry, loud music, crowd and play noise, and other noise. Data-augmentation using publicly available corpora like OGI Kids corpus (Shobaki et al., 2000) (≈ 60 hours; Kindergarten to Grade 10) and CMU Kids corpus (Eskenazi et al., 1997) (≈ 9 hours; Grade 3 to 5) was also considered.

5.2 ASR Model Performance & Discussions

Child ASR performance results are summarized in Table 2. A triphone GMM-HMM Acoustic model trained on Preschool speech generate a very high WER of 90.28% (#1) for pre-trained 3-gram LibriSpeech LM. As shown in #2, using an 11-layer TDNN-F based Acoustic model, 40 MFCC features and speed-perturbed i-vector (of factor 3), a much lower WER of 63.66% was achieved using the same language model. Now in #3, we notice a significant drop of WER to 49.02% by training the language model using our Preschool data. Using a language model trained on in-domain shows much benefit in our study than using pre-trained LibriSpeech language model, as compared to previous studies (Wu et al., 2019; Yeung et al., 2021) for older children speech where Librispeech just worked fine. This signifies that young children do not follow the same language patterns in spoken English or that of adults. In #4, #5, and #6, shows various acoustic model enhancements based on TDNN-F, CNN, and Attention layers with #6 reporting a WER of 42.00%. Finally, in #7 by replacing the 3-gram language model with an RNN-based one, with LSTM layers (see Section 5.1) we reach a WER of 40.67%. As shown in #8, data augmentation does not enhance the performance of the ASR model.

6 Activity-area based Child Speech Recognition and Discussions

All experiment results for this section are summarized in Table 3. The results here are shown for 3 preschool children who were typically developing (without delays) and were present in the same classroom. From a child ASR perspective, these 3 children belong to the test split of the Preschool data and were tagged as primary children (speakers wearing the LENA units). The ASR model used here is the best model as reported in Section 5.2. The results are primarily subdivided into three categories: (i) all words spoken, (ii) WH-words (who, what, where, etc.), and (iii) Verbs; followed by the child IDs: Primary Child #1, #2 and #3. Average WER (irrespective of activity areas) for Primary Child #1, #2 and #3 are 28.49%, 36.13%, and 47.59% respectively. Number of words in sen-

[3]http://svn.code.sf.net/p/cmusphinx/code/trunk/cmudict/

Table 3: *Activity-area based child Speech Recognition results.*

Table 3(A)									
	Primary Child #1			**Primary Child #2**			**Primary Child #3**		
Activity Area	Time (min)	WER (%)	Words spoken	Time (min)	WER (%)	Words spoken	Time (min)	WER (%)	Words spoken
Art/Snack	18.6	17.39	307	32.3	53.11	270	21.8	56.03	112
Block	<1	13.79	29	1.8	36.36	44	14.7	46.39	217
Computer	4.3	37.5	83	3.3	38.18	55	3.7	23.33	30
Cozy/Book	2.1	NA	0	4	47.61	20	1.9	NA	0
Dramatic Play	4.1	27.1	96	12.4	24.93	384	25.2	43.03	851
Manipulative	<1	12.5	7	9.8	26.62	342	2.1	32.25	31
Story	<1	25	13	1	58.33	12	<1	50	6

Table 3(B)									
	Primary Child #1			**Primary Child #2**			**Primary Child #3**		
Activity Area	Time (min)	WH-words (%)	Verbs (%)	Time (min)	WH-words (%)	Verbs (%)	Time (min)	WH-words (%)	Verbs (%)
Art/Snack	18.6	83.33	83.33	32.3	66.67	72.72	21.8	50	50
Block	<1	100	100	1.8	NA	100	14.7	50	71.48
Computer	4.3	100	57.14	3.3	100	60	3.7	NA	50
Cozy/Book	2.1	NA	NA	4	NA	50	1.9	NA	NA
Dramatic Play	4.1	100	66.67	12.4	83.33	84.61	25.2	66.67	68.22
Manipulative	<1	NA	100	9.8	100	82.22	2.1	0	100
Story	<1	100	50	1	NA	66.67	<1	NA	NA

Time (min) = Total time spent by each child in that specific activity area
WER (%) = Word error rate of the ASR model for all words spoken in that specific activity area
Words spoken = Total number of words spoken by each child in that specific activity area
WH-words (%) = Total % of WH-words correctly predicted by the ASR model spoken in that specific activity area
Verbs (%) = Total % of Verbs correctly predicted by the ASR model spoken in that specific activity area
NA = Not applicable; primarily due to no words spoken

tences, WH-words and verbs are a few of the prominent language learning milestones established by the American Speech–Language–Hearing Association [4], outlined by the American Academy of Pediatrics (Gerber et al., 2010; Zubler et al., 2022), and adopted as CDC's (Centers for Disease Control and Prevention) Developmental Milestones[5] program *"Learn the Signs. Act Early."* Table 3(A) shows the time spent by each child in an activity area, followed by WER and all words count spoken in that area. Table 3(B) shows the time spent by each child in an activity area, followed by % of total WH-words and verbs spoken those were predicted correctly in that area by the ASR engine. The "Time Spent" factor is important to better normalize the results across multiple subjects. Primary Child #1 spends the most quality time in 'Art/Snack' area (WER: 17.39%), followed by close to 5 mins in 'Computer'(WER: 37.5%) and 'Dramatic Play'(WER: 27.1%) areas. The amount of spoken words is relatively much higher in 'Art/Snack' area. Child #1 spends less than a minute in 'Block', 'Manipulative', and 'Story' areas, which is also reflected in the word spoken count. Overall across all activity areas, Primary Child #1 spends much less time and spoke less as compared to Child #2 and #3. Primary Child #2 and #3 spent more time in the classroom boundary, and therefore word counts spoken were much higher. Primary Child #2 spends quality time in 'Art/Snack' (WER: 53.11%), 'Dramatic play' (24.93%), 'Manipulative' (26.62%), and close to 4 mins in 'Computer'(WER: 38.18%) and 'Cozy/Book'(WER: 47.61) areas. Primary Child #3 spends quality time in 'Art/Snack' (WER: 56.03%), 'Block' (46.39%), 'Dramatic Play' (43.03%), and close to 4 mins in 'Computer'(WER: 23.33%) areas. Irrespective of the child, performance of the ASR engine in detecting WH-words and verbs across all activity areas is quite good, given the naturalistic noisy dynamic learning environment. While areas like 'Cozy/Book' are more personal learning spaces. Areas like 'Dramatic Play', 'Manipulative', 'Block', 'Art/Snack' alternatively encourage group activity. 'Computer' and 'Story' areas are more focused on listening or seeing. Some observations here can be: (i) Primary Child #1 did not engage much in areas of group activity - signifying difficulty to engage in groups, (ii) Primary Child #1 and #3 produced higher WH-word

[4] https://www.asha.org/public/speech/development/chart
[5] https://www.cdc.gov/ncbddd/actearly/milestones

counts (not shown in the Table) in 'Computer' and 'Dramatic Play' areas - signifying more curiosity. Longitudinal data of the same group of children over a significant time period should help in better informed decisions. However, amendments to classroom structure and plan will be at the discretion of teachers. Performance of the ASR engine can help to monitor/track such elements in a naturalistic preschool classrooms.

7 Towards Data-Based Inclusion Planning in Classrooms

Non-segregated or inclusive educational settings possess a design best suited to prepare young children with disabilities for kindergarten (US Dept. Health, 2015; Barton and Smith, 2015). Careful considerations regarding environmental factors are imperative for meaningful interactions between children in inclusive classrooms (Ganz, 2007). High-quality inclusive classrooms can also foster and support friendship development between children with and without disabilities (Buysse et al., 2008). Through communication skills and social interactions, individuals can begin to form meaningful social relationships and friendships, which could promote positive psychological states (e.g., happiness and self-efficacy; Umberson and Karas Montez, 2010). Teachers and peers as communicators can play important roles for inclusive classrooms to support communication skills of children with disabilities and facilitating social interactions between one another. The quantity and quality of interactions significantly influence the language environment and communication opportunities for young children with disabilities (W Vernon et al., 2018). Also, it may be more important for a child with Autism Spectrum Disorder (ASD) to spend quality time in activity areas that promote language and social engagament because of the social-communication and play limitations that accompany ASD. Using audio recorded by LENA and real-time location using Ubisense supported by advanced speech processing algorithms could provide teachers with information about "what" and "where" child interactions are taking place so that they may be better able to discern when to provide additional support.

8 Conclusion

This study has provided evidence and lays the foundation of deploying sensor-based monitoring tools to acquire and interpret eco-behavioral data (speech and location) in naturalistic early childhood settings to better support teachers and child learning. This work tends to address a major challenge faced by early childhood educators in supporting children (with and without developmental delays) due to a lack of real-time data to inform daily practices and that lead to longer-term school readiness outcomes. Another component in this study has addressed the development of ASR systems for preschool children, which is a very low-resource scenario. Both collection and transcription of such data is a major challenge, especially due to both noisy data and speech intelligibility of young children. Future work will focus on analyzing more children with and without developmental delays, and also collection of such naturalistic data. Future work will also consider speaker group classification (adult vs. child) using speaker-group diarization as compared to human transcriptions.

Acknowledgements

This study was supported by the National Science Foundation Grant #1918032 award to Hansen. The authors would like to thank all the families for participating in this study and the reviewers for their fruitful comments and suggestions.

References

Erin E Barton and Barbara J Smith. 2015. Advancing high-quality preschool inclusion: A discussion and recommendations for the field. *Topics in Early Childhood Special Education*, 35(2):69–78.

William H Brown, Samuel L Odom, Shouming Li, and Craig Zercher. 1999. Ecobehavioral assessment in early childhood programs: A portrait of preschool inclusion. *The Journal of Special Education*, 33(3):138–153.

Sloane Burgess, Lisa Audet, and Sanna Harjusola-Webb. 2013. Quantitative and qualitative characteristics of the school and home language environments of preschool-aged children with asd. *Journal of Communication Disorders*, 46(5-6):428–439.

Virginia Buysse, Barbara Davis Goldman, Tracey West, and Heidi Hollingsworth. 2008. Friendships in early childhood: Implications for early education and intervention.

National Research Council et al. 2000. From neurons to neighborhoods: The science of early childhood development.

Karen E Diamond, Laura M Justice, Robert S Siegler, and Patricia A Snyder. 2013. Synthesis of ies research on early intervention and early childhood education. ncser 2013-3001. *National Center for Special Education Research.*

Jessica R Dykstra, Maura G Sabatos-DeVito, Dwight W Irvin, Brian A Boyd, Kara A Hume, and Sam L Odom. 2013. Using the language environment analysis (lena) system in preschool classrooms with children with autism spectrum disorders. *Autism*, 17(5):582–594.

Lise Eliot. 2000. *What's going on in there?: how the brain and mind develop in the first five years of life.* Bantam.

M Eskenazi, J Mostow, and D Graff. 1997. The cmu kids corpus ldc97s63. *Linguistic Data Consortium database.*

Michael Ford, Charles T Baer, Dongxin Xu, Umit Yapanel, and Sharmi Gray. 2008. The lenatm language environment analysis system.

Jennifer B Ganz. 2007. Classroom structuring methods and strategies for children and youth with autism spectrum disorders. *Exceptionality*, 15(4):249–260.

R Jason Gerber, Timothy Wilks, and Christine Erdie-Lalena. 2010. Developmental milestones: motor development. *Pediatrics in review*, 31(7):267–277.

Matteo Gerosa, Diego Giuliani, and Fabio Brugnara. 2007. Acoustic variability and automatic recognition of children's speech. *Speech Communication*, 49(10-11):847–860.

Charles R Greenwood, Carmen Arreaga-Mayer, and Judith J Carta. 1994. Identification and translation of effective teacher-developed instructional procedures for general practice. *Remedial and Special Education*, 15(3):140–151.

Charles R Greenwood, Alana G Schnitz, Dwight Irvin, Shu Fe Tsai, and Judith J Carta. 2018. Automated language environment analysis: A research synthesis. *American Journal of Speech-Language Pathology*, 27(2):853–867.

R. Gretter, Marco Matassoni, D. Falavigna, A. Misra, C.W. Leong, K. Knill, and L. Wang. 2021. ETLT 2021: Shared Task on Automatic Speech Recognition for Non-Native Children's Speech. In *Proc. Interspeech 2021*, pages 3845–3849.

John HL Hansen and Taufiq Hasan. 2015. Speaker recognition by machines and humans: A tutorial review. *IEEE Signal processing magazine*, 32(6):74–99.

Betty Hart and Todd R Risley. 1995. *Meaningful differences in the everyday experience of young American children.* Paul H Brookes Publishing.

Dwight W Irvin, Stephen A Crutchfield, Charles R Greenwood, William D Kearns, and Jay Buzhardt. 2018. An automated approach to measuring child movement and location in the early childhood classroom. *Behavior research methods*, 50(3):890–901.

Dwight W Irvin, Stephen A Crutchfield, Charles R Greenwood, Richard L Simpson, Abhijeet Sangwan, and John HL Hansen. 2017. Exploring classroom behavioral imaging: Moving closer to effective and data-based early childhood inclusion planning. *Advances in Neurodevelopmental Disorders*, 1(2):95–104.

William D Kearns, Donna Algase, D Helen Moore, and Sadia Ahmed. 2008. Ultra wideband radio: A novel method for measuring wandering in persons with dementia. *Gerontechnology*, 7(1):48.

Ke Li, Daniel Povey, and Sanjeev Khudanpur. 2021. A parallelizable lattice rescoring strategy with neural language models. In *ICASSP 2021-2021 IEEE International Conference on Acoustics, Speech and Signal Processing (ICASSP)*, pages 6518–6522. IEEE.

Kuldip K Paliwal. 1999. On the use of filter-bank energies as features for robust speech recognition. In *ISSPA'99. Proceedings of the Fifth International Symposium on Signal Processing and its Applications (IEEE Cat. No. 99EX359)*, volume 2, pages 641–644. IEEE.

Daniel S. Park, William Chan, Yu Zhang, Chung-Cheng Chiu, Barret Zoph, Ekin D. Cubuk, and Quoc V. Le. 2019. SpecAugment: A Simple Data Augmentation Method for Automatic Speech Recognition. In *Proc. Interspeech 2019*, pages 2613–2617.

Jan P Piek, Lisa Dawson, Leigh M Smith, and Natalie Gasson. 2008. The role of early fine and gross motor development on later motor and cognitive ability. *Human movement science*, 27(5):668–681.

Daniel Povey, Gaofeng Cheng, Yiming Wang, Ke Li, Hainan Xu, Mahsa Yarmohammadi, and Sanjeev Khudanpur. 2018a. Semi-orthogonal low-rank matrix factorization for deep neural networks. In *Proc. Interspeech 2018*, pages 3743–3747.

Daniel Povey, Arnab Ghoshal, Gilles Boulianne, Lukas Burget, Ondrej Glembek, Nagendra Goel, Mirko Hannemann, Petr Motlicek, Yanmin Qian, Petr Schwarz, et al. 2011. The kaldi speech recognition toolkit. In *IEEE 2011 workshop on automatic speech recognition and understanding*, CONF. IEEE Signal Processing Society.

Daniel Povey, Hossein Hadian, Pegah Ghahremani, Ke Li, and Sanjeev Khudanpur. 2018b. A time-restricted self-attention layer for asr. In *2018 IEEE International Conference on Acoustics, Speech and Signal Processing (ICASSP)*, pages 5874–5878. IEEE.

Lars Rumberg, Hanna Ehlert, Ulrike Lüdtke, and Jörn Ostermann. 2021. Age-invariant training for end-to-end child speech recognition using adversarial multi-task learning. *Proc. Interspeech 2021*, pages 3850–3854.

Prashanth Gurunath Shivakumar and Panayiotis Georgiou. 2020. Transfer learning from adult to children for speech recognition: Evaluation, analysis and recommendations. *Computer speech & language*, 63:101077.

Prashanth Gurunath Shivakumar, Alexandros Potamianos, Sungbok Lee, and Shrikanth S Narayanan. 2014. Improving speech recognition for children using acoustic adaptation and pronunciation modeling. In *WOCCI*, pages 15–19.

Khaldoun Shobaki, John-Paul Hosom, and Ronald Cole. 2000. The ogi kids' speech corpus and recognizers. In *Proc. of ICSLP*, pages 564–567.

Lawrence D Shriberg. 1993. Four new speech and prosody-voice measures for genetics research and other studies in developmental phonological disorders. *Journal of Speech, Language, and Hearing Research*, 36(1):105–140.

Melanie Soderstrom and Kelsey Wittebolle. 2013. When do caregivers talk? the influences of activity and time of day on caregiver speech and child vocalizations in two childcare environments. *PloS one*, 8(11):e80646.

Georg Stemmer, Christian Hacker, Stefan Steidl, and Elmar Nöth. 2003. Acoustic normalization of children's speech. In *Eighth European Conference on Speech Communication and Technology*. Citeseer.

Andreas Stolcke. 2002. Srilm-an extensible language modeling toolkit. In *Seventh international conference on spoken language processing*.

Jon Tapp, Joseph Wehby, and David Ellis. 1995. A multiple option observation system for experimental studies: Mooses. *Behavior Research Methods, Instruments, & Computers*, 27(1):25–31.

Rong Tong, Lei Wang, and Bin Ma. 2017. Transfer learning for children's speech recognition. In *2017 International Conference on Asian Language Processing (IALP)*, pages 36–39. IEEE.

Debra Umberson and Jennifer Karas Montez. 2010. Social relationships and health: A flashpoint for health policy. *Journal of health and social behavior*, 51(1_suppl):S54–S66.

Education US Dept. Health, Human Services. 2015. Policy statement on inclusion of children with disabilities in early childhood programs. *Infants & Young Children*, 29(1):3–24.

Ashish Vaswani, Noam Shazeer, Niki Parmar, Jakob Uszkoreit, Llion Jones, Aidan N Gomez, Łukasz Kaiser, and Illia Polosukhin. 2017. Attention is all you need. *Advances in neural information processing systems*, 30.

Nhu Khue Vuong, Syin Chan, and Chiew Tong Lau. 2014. Automated detection of wandering patterns in people with dementia. *Gerontechnology*, 12(3):127–147.

Ty W Vernon, Amber R Miller, Jordan A Ko, Amy C Barrett, and Elizabeth S McGarry. 2018. A randomized controlled trial of the social tools and rules for teens (start) program: an immersive socialization intervention for adolescents with autism spectrum disorder. *Journal of Autism and Developmental Disorders*, 48(3):892–904.

Silvana MR Watson, Robert A Gable, and Charles R Greenwood. 2011. Combining ecobehavioral assessment, functional assessment, and response to intervention to promote more effective classroom instruction. *Remedial and Special Education*, 32(4):334–344.

Fei Wu, Leibny Paola García-Perera, Daniel Povey, and Sanjeev Khudanpur. 2019. Advances in automatic speech recognition for child speech using factored time delay neural network. In *Interspeech*, pages 1–5.

Gary Yeung and Abeer Alwan. 2018. On the difficulties of automatic speech recognition for kindergarten-aged children. *Interspeech 2018*.

Gary Yeung, Ruchao Fan, and Abeer Alwan. 2021. Fundamental frequency feature normalization and data augmentation for child speech recognition. In *ICASSP 2021-2021 IEEE International Conference on Acoustics, Speech and Signal Processing (ICASSP)*, pages 6993–6997. IEEE.

Steve Young. 1996. A review of large-vocabulary continuous-speech. *IEEE signal processing magazine*, 13(5):45.

Jennifer M Zubler, Lisa D Wiggins, Michelle M Macias, Toni M Whitaker, Judith S Shaw, Jane K Squires, Julie A Pajek, Rebecca B Wolf, Karnesha S Slaughter, Amber S Broughton, et al. 2022. Evidence-informed milestones for developmental surveillance tools. *Pediatrics*, 149(3).

Structural information in mathematical formulas for exercise difficulty prediction: a comparison of NLP representations

Ekaterina Loginova
Ghent University
ekaterina.loginova@ugent.be

Dries F. Benoit
Ghent University
dries.benoit@ugent.be

Abstract

To tailor a learning system to the student's level and needs, we must consider the characteristics of the learning content, such as its difficulty. While natural language processing allows us to represent text efficiently, the meaningful representation of mathematical formulas in an educational context is still understudied. This paper adopts structural embeddings as a possible way to bridge this gap. Our experiments validate the approach using publicly available datasets to show that incorporating syntactic information can improve performance in predicting the exercise difficulty.

1 Introduction

Online learning platforms aim to provide personalised tutoring at scale using data-driven personalisation (Romero and Ventura, 2010). A key component of a personalised system is a recommendation algorithm that suggests the next learning activity. To ensure that the recommendation is tailored to the student's level and learning needs, not only should the student's ability level model be considered, but also the learning content characteristics, such as its difficulty. Learning content can contain multiple media types (images, text, formulas), each of which must be converted to a numeric format compatible with machine learning models. While natural language processing (NLP) and computer vision allow us to efficiently represent texts and images, the meaningful representation of formulas in an educational context is still understudied. This paper proposes a method for representing mathematical expressions (considered as a form of text) based on an structural embeddings and investigates its effectiveness in predicting exercise difficulty.

2 Related work

Research directions in mathematics can be broadly categorised into three branches: generation, assessment and solving. In each task, we need to represent a mathematical exercise that may include a text description, a formula, and a picture. The majority of works in this area focuses on word problems that can be represented as bag-of-words (John et al., 2015) (optionally with binary indicators of whether the word is a mathematical term). Such a representation allows the use of rich semantic taggers that provide additional information about lexical units, such as their degree of concreteness or associated emotions (Slater et al., 2016). However, semantic taggers are usually developed for general language use rather than for a specialised domain such as mathematics with its large variety of special characters. Previous work accommodated this by manually introducing additional mathematical symbols to be parsed (Slater et al., 2016) or by considering entire mathematical expressions as tokens, an approach called bag-of-expressions (Lan et al., 2015). However, such an approach ignores the order of mathematical symbols. A possible extension is to use n-grams to represent chunks of symbols, thus preserving partial information about their order (Jurafsky and Martin, 2009). Its downside is that it is limited by the chosen length of the n-gram and thus cannot fully account for deeply nested expressions. In short, these approaches to representing content tend to be simplistic and do not allow syntactic or semantic information to be fully exploited. Therefore, previous research suggests that hierarchical representations should be used to capture deep features and generate higher quality content features (Li et al., 2013), an observation that motivates our study.

In natural language processing, the next level of representation after n-grams is a parse tree of a sentence. It captures syntactic information by representing words as nodes connected by syntactic dependencies: for example, an adjective used as a modifier of a noun. Similar to a natural lan-

Proceedings of the 17th Workshop on Innovative Use of NLP for Building Educational Applications (BEA 2022), pages 101 - 106
July 15, 2022

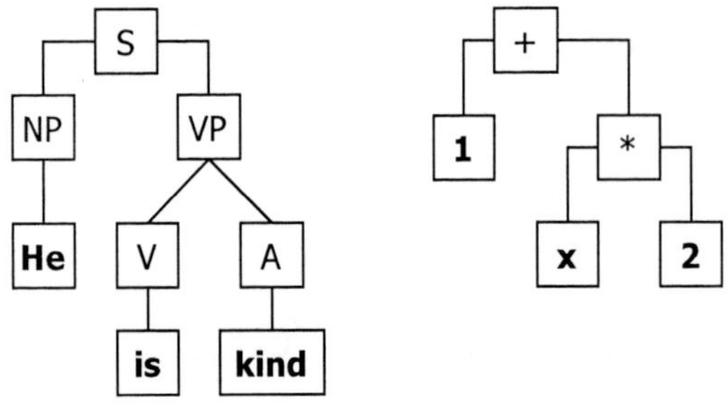

Figure 1: Left: a parse (constituency) tree for the sentence "He is kind" (simplified). Right: a parse tree for the mathematical expression `1 + 2*x`. Leaf nodes are in bold.

guage utterance, a mathematical formula can be represented by such a parse tree (Li et al., 2012). Algebraic trees have been successfully used to automatically solve algebra problems with template approaches (Roy and Roth, 2017; Huang et˜al., 2017). More recent approaches aim at generalisable solutions, for example, by using knowledge graphs (Zhao et al., 2019). Hierarchic representations have rarely been used for the task of predicting exercise difficulty. The approach closest to ours is using AST parse trees to analyse Python programs (Paaßen et al., 2021). However, mathematical formulas present their own unique challenges: for example, different formats for writing formulas, which can vary across datasets, even when the same typesetting system (e.g., LaTeX) is used. In addition, formulas use domain-specific alphabet and are much shorter than typical coding exercises.

This paper compares possible ways to encode syntactic information in mathematical exercises and adopts the structural embeddings approach to represent mathematical formulas (Liu et al., 2017). Each sentence is represented as a constituency parse tree. In such a tree for a natural language utterance, the non-terminal nodes correspond to grammatical relations (for example, `NP` stands for "noun phrase"), while the leaf nodes contain words. Each word is then represented as a sequence of nodes in a parse tree from its leaf to the root of the sentence. For example, if we want to represent the word "kind" in the sentence "He is kind", we construct the parse tree (Figure 1) and obtain the corresponding syntactic sequence `[S, VP, A]`. A representation obtained this way captures hierarchical information while facilitating the use of standard neural network models, e.g., an LSTM (Long-Short Term Memory) (Hochreiter and Schmidhuber, 1997). We refer the reader to the original paper for architectural details and intuition behind them. Generally speaking, it encodes a variable-length syntactic sequence into a fixed-length vector representation — the syntactic-semantic embeddings — and the final hidden state serves as input to a decision-making model.

3 Data

The experiments are conducted on two datasets: a recently released MATH (Hendrycks et al., 2021)[1] and a synthethic DeepMind Mathematics(Saxton et al., 2019)[2], one of the largest publicly available datasets for mathematics in educational data mining.

The DeepMind dataset consists of question and answer pairs, and each pair has a label corresponding to the difficult level, easy or hard. An advantage of this dataset is its clear and unified formatting: exercise often have a consistent phrasing that mostly differs on a formula step, which allows us to have a clearer comparison of how effective different formula representations are. For our experiments, we used a subset of 37 244 problems, covering a broad range of topics: algebra, arithmetic, calculus, comparison, numbers, polynomials. 18 608 problems are of high level and 18 636 are of low. Word descriptions are in English and formulas are not specifically separated but can be extracted using regex-based approach due to limited variability of the rest of the sequence.

The MATH dataset contains 12 498 problems from mathematics competitions in the US. Problems are labelled with five levels of difficulty (1001, 2242, 2723, 2904 and 3628 problems, respectively) and cover the following topics: Algebra, Counting & Probability, Geometry, Intermediate Algebra, Number Theory, Prealgebra, Precalculus. Word descriptions are in English and formulas are written in LaTeX and defined by $ operators.

4 Methodology

4.1 Data representation

As mentioned above, each exercise contains a textual description and a formula. For example, it can be the following task: `Calculate sqrt(121) - sqrt(36)`. In our case, a parse tree can be extracted with open-source libraries, such as AST

[1] https://github.com/hendrycks/math
[2] https://github.com/deepmind/mathematics_dataset

and SymPy[3]. A notable challenge at this step is the wide variety of notation conventions that renders converting a formula without errors a non-trivial problem. For example, differentiation can be written using `f\^{\prime}(x)` or `$f'(x)$`. Quite often, multiplication symbols are omitted or individual symbols are encoded; there might be several pieces of formula expressions per exercise. As a result, running a popular converter latex2sympy[4] on the MATH dataset results in only 1673 correctly parsed formulas out of 12500 (13% success rate). While natural language processing tasks such as tokenisation are well-explored and a plethora of high-quality public solutions exist, there appears to be no robust package. Thus we have developed processing scripts for mathematics.

A formula is pre-processed so that all numbers are replaced with a special `NUM` token (alternative per digit replacement did not seem to alter the results). It is important to consider differences in input types, as it prompts adjustments to the tokenisation procedure: for example, for AST parses and formulas, we need to consider a broader range of special symbols as separators (e.g., `(=)*/+-.\'^{}`) to avoid contaminating the vocabulary with too complex tokens that are actually sub-pieces of large expressions. `log` and `power` are transformed using regular expressions to act as functions accepting multiple arguments: `(a-1)\^\{3\}` becomes `power(a-1, 3)`. Decorative commands like `mathbb` are removed. Operators are also converted into their programming language equivalent (e.g., `\\neq` is replaced with `!=`) and a rule-based processing script unifies the notation by for example transforming different fraction encodings such as LaTeX's `\\frac{}{}` into `()/()`. Some tasks also include systems of formulas — while it is possible to try and represent them with special joining operators, in this study, we opted to use the longest correctly parsed formula. As a result, we obtain a more programmatic representation of a formula that drastically improves parsing correctness (7298 correct out of 12 498, 58%). We then construct a parse tree of mathematical expression and represent leaf nodes with their syntactic sequences (paths to the root). Parsing is done by either 1) using AST parser and NodeVisitor; or 2) using topological sorting on networkx[5] graph — and subsequently finding the shortest path with built-in library functions. As an example output, `x` from an algebraic expression `1 + 2*x` would be represented as `[*, +]`.

In resulting nested sequences, each formula term is represented as a syntactic sequence of nodes to the root of the syntax parse tree, and an entire formula then comprises a sequence of terms: `[[Add, Integer], [Add, Integer]]`. It is possible to simplify this representation by flattening sequences and concatenating them into a single string with an arbitrary separator as follows: `Add Integer . Add Integer`. A flattened sequence is a simplified representation of syntax information for which we can use more traditional methods, such as bag-of-words or vanilla LSTM.

In the end, we work with four types of exercise content: textual description (`Calculate`), raw formula text (`sqrt(121) - sqrt(36)`), and formula syntactic sequences (nested or flattened). They can be used independently as the only input to the classification model or combined. More details are provided in the following subsection.

4.2 Prediction models

We investigate the effectiveness of the proposed content representation by using them to estimate the difficulty of exercises. For the DeepMind dataset, it is a binary classification problem since the model must predict whether the exercise comes from an easy or hard level. For MATH, it is a multiclass classification problem with five classes (a range of levels from 1 to 5).

Our first model type is a vanilla LSTM that uses only one input source at a time, e.g., only the textual description. If we want to add syntax information to this model, it must be a string and can then be concatenated with the rest directly with an arbitrary separator (a space in our case). The second type is a multi-input modification that processes two different input types in a more nuanced manner similar to an idea of Siamese architectures in automated question answering domain: it passes them to individual submodels, and concatenates the output representations to feed into a feed-forward layer with softmax output for the final classification decision. This is motivated by different alphabet and structure of the sources: we hypothesise that it might be easier for the network

[3] https://www.sympy.org/en/

[4] https://github.com/augustt198/latex2sympy

[5] https://networkx.org/

Model 1: single input	DeepMind	MATH
Description	0.66	0.71
Description + Formula	0.69	0.73
Formula	0.58	0.68
AST parse	0.56	0.67
AST rootpaths (flat)	0.58	0.66
Sympy rootpaths (flat)	0.64	0.66
Description + AST rootpaths (flat)	0.72	0.72
Description + Sympy rootpaths (flat)	0.71	0.72
Description + AST pars	0.7	0.72

Model 2: multiple input	DeepMind	MATH
Formula & Description	0.66	0.72
AST parse & Description	0.66	0.72
AST rootpaths (flat) & Description	0.66	0.72
Sympy rootpaths (flat) & Description	0.66	0.72
Model 3: single input with structural embeddings	**DeepMind**	**MATH**
AST rootpaths	0.58	0.65
Sympy rootpaths	0.6	0.65
Model 4: multiple input with structural embeddings	**DeepMind**	**MATH**
AST rootpaths & Description	0.72	0.73
Sympy rootpaths & Descriptions	0.73	0.73

Table 1: 10-fold cross-validated ROC AUC. + corresponds to concatenating the input strings, & to adding a separate input layer to the network. Best results are highlighted in bold. We can see that adding syntax sequences improves the performance on DeepMind dataset.

to learn if mathematical expressions and the natural language representation are disentangled. While the described models operate on 2-dimensional data, the third type of model works with nested root path sequences as described above to obtain syntactic formula embeddings and therefore uses 3-dimensional input. It includes time-distributed wrappers to apply identical embedding and feature engineering layers to each term. Again, we can add another input that can work with conventional flat sequences and concatenate the resulting embeddings to make a classification decision, leading to the fourth and final model type.

5 Experiments

Neural networks were implemented in Tensorflow with Keras (Chollet et al., 2015) and trained on Google Colab Pro GPUs. We used early stopping, monitoring validation loss with the patience of 3 epochs.

5.1 Results

We compare data representations to investigate whether adding syntactic sequences improves classification performance. Performance was evaluated using 10-fold stratified cross-validation ROC AUC and is shown in Table 1. Regarding the baselines, majority and random baselines produce ROC AUC of 0.5 on a single run, and the best results of logistic regression models trained on the length of input sequences are 0.57 for MATH (on descriptions) and 0.66 for DeepMind (on formula), respectively.

Regarding other possible neural approaches to feature engineering, using word2vec algorithm (Mikolov et al., 2013) to produce pre-trained embeddings, contrary to our expectations, did not improve our results. We have also experimented with the graph embedding method node2vec (Grover and Leskovec, 2016), but the individual formulas prove to be too shallow for the approach to produce a meaningful representation. A promising direction is to use graph neural networks. Preliminary experiments with Graph Convolutional Networks (Kipf and Welling, 2017) using Spektral[6] on DeepMind dataset led to an improvement from 0.79 to 0.81 of a single-run accuracy score, but in this study for the rest of this section we continue to focus on structural embeddings extracted with LSTMs. Considering individual inputs, the parse tree representation alone, whether flat or nested, could not outperform the other models because the word description dominates it. Interestingly, the AST root paths are on par with the raw formula, and the SymPy root paths outperform it on the DeepMind dataset. Using nested syntactic sequences

[6]https://graphneural.network/

Exercise topic	D	F	SRP-F	D + F	D + SRP-F
numbers__is_factor_composed	0.64	0.53	*0.54*	0.63	*0.68*
algebra__linear_1d_composed	0.77	0.50	*0.52*	0.82	0.81
numbers__is_prime_composed	0.59	0.54	*0.56*	0.65	0.63
numbers__list_prime_factors_composed	0.68	0.53	*0.57*	0.66	*0.73*
arithmetic__add_sub_multiple	0.46	0.77	0.69	0.77	0.75
polynomials__simplify_power	0.51	0.86	0.78	0.86	0.84
polynomials__collect	0.50	0.56	*0.64*	0.59	*0.69*
numbers__round_number_composed	0.53	0.53	*0.59*	0.52	*0.53*
numbers__place_value_composed	0.80	0.56	*0.58*	0.76	*0.81*
calculus__differentiate	0.83	0.54	0.52	0.86	0.86
comparison__pair_composed	0.77	0.58	*0.61*	0.73	*0.78*
polynomials__coefficient_named	0.48	0.56	*0.57*	0.53	*0.57*
algebra__linear_2d	0.49	0.59	0.56	0.62	*0.63*
comparison__sort_composed	0.75	0.54	*0.55*	0.71	0.70
polynomials__expand	0.50	0.50	*0.53*	0.49	*0.52*
comparison__closest_composed	0.74	0.46	*0.60*	0.63	*0.74*
arithmetic__simplify_surd	0.47	0.94	0.84	0.94	0.87
algebra__linear_2d_composed	0.83	0.53	*0.55*	0.79	*0.81*
algebra__linear_1d	0.52	0.71	0.71	0.73	*0.78*
arithmetic__mixed	0.49	0.75	0.59	0.75	0.63
comparison__kth_biggest_composed	0.73	0.54	*0.56*	0.66	*0.71*
Average	0.62	0.60	0.60	0.70	0.72

Table 2: Per-topic single-run accuracy results on DeepMind dataset (test subset). D = description, F = formula, SRP-F = Sympy root paths, flat (were chosen for this comparison because of better individual results). Cases when using only root paths outperforms using only formula are highlighted in italic; similarly when description is added. We can see that the largest improvement is on `numbers__list_prime_factors_composed`, `polynomials__collect` and `comparison__closest_composed` exercise topics.

instead of flat sequences leads to comparable or slightly worse results. Nevertheless, adding syntactic sequences to descriptions noticeably increases performance on the DeepMind dataset, from 0.69 to 0.73 ROC AUC. Per topic accuracy scores for a single run are given in Table 2. Thus, we argue that structural embeddings have the potential to inform predictive models, especially when formula is an essential differentiating part of a task.

6 Conclusion & Future work

We proposed an adaptation of an NLP technique (Liu et al., 2017) from the field of machine comprehension to the area of mathematical educational data mining. We enrich the content representation by parsing mathematical formulas into syntax trees and embedding them with neural networks. Our experiments validate the approach using publicly available datasets and show that incorporating syntactic information can improve performance in predicting the difficulty of an exercise. These results suggest that the method may be of interest for personalised learning solutions. We hypothesise that the advantage of structural embeddings will be more evident for more advanced tasks. Therefore, as a next step, we plan to apply our approach to more complex state exams. Data have been collected and OCR-processed for initial experiments, and we intend to make the dataset publicly available. Our future research will also focus on predicting the similarity of mathematical formulas by comparing their syntax trees.

References

François Chollet et al. 2015. Keras. https://keras.io.

Aditya Grover and Jure Leskovec. 2016. node2vec: Scalable feature learning for networks. In *Proceedings of the 22nd ACM SIGKDD International Conference on Knowledge Discovery and Data Mining,*

San Francisco, CA, USA, August 13-17, 2016, pages 855–864. ACM.

Dan Hendrycks, Collin Burns, Saurav Kadavath, Akul Arora, Steven Basart, Eric Tang, Dawn Song, and Jacob Steinhardt. 2021. Measuring mathematical problem solving with the MATH dataset. *CoRR*, abs/2103.03874.

Sepp Hochreiter and Jürgen Schmidhuber. 1997. Long short-term memory. *Neural Comput.*, 9(8):1735–1780.

Danqing Huang, Shuming Shi, Chin-Yew Lin, and Jian Yin. 2017. Learning fine-grained expressions to solve math word problems. In *Proceedings of the 2017 Conference on Empirical Methods in Natural Language Processing, EMNLP 2017, Copenhagen, Denmark, September 9-11, 2017*, pages 805–814. Association for Computational Linguistics.

Rogers Jeffrey Leo John, Thomas S. McTavish, and Rebecca J. Passonneau. 2015. Semantic graphs for mathematics word problems based on mathematics terminology. In *Workshops Proceedings of EDM 2015 8th International Conference on Educational Data Mining, EDM 2015, Madrid, Spain, June 26-29, 2015*, volume 1446 of *CEUR Workshop Proceedings*. CEUR-WS.org.

Dan Jurafsky and James H. Martin. 2009. *Speech and language processing: an introduction to natural language processing, computational linguistics, and speech recognition, 2nd Edition*. Prentice Hall series in artificial intelligence. Prentice Hall, Pearson Education International.

Thomas N. Kipf and Max Welling. 2017. Semi-supervised classification with graph convolutional networks. In *5th International Conference on Learning Representations, ICLR 2017, Toulon, France, April 24-26, 2017, Conference Track Proceedings*. OpenReview.net.

Andrew S. Lan, Divyanshu Vats, Andrew E. Waters, and Richard G. Baraniuk. 2015. Mathematical language processing: Automatic grading and feedback for open response mathematical questions. In *Proceedings of the Second ACM Conference on Learning @ Scale, L@S 2015, Vancouver, BC, Canada, March 14 - 18, 2015*, pages 167–176. ACM.

Nan Li, William W. Cohen, and Kenneth R. Koedinger. 2012. Efficient cross-domain learning of complex skills. In *Intelligent Tutoring Systems - 11th International Conference, ITS 2012, Chania, Crete, Greece, June 14-18, 2012. Proceedings*, volume 7315 of *Lecture Notes in Computer Science*, pages 493–498. Springer.

Nan Li, William W. Cohen, and Kenneth R. Koedinger. 2013. Discovering student models with a clustering algorithm using problem content. In *Proceedings of the 6th International Conference on Educational Data Mining, Memphis, Tennessee, USA, July 6-9, 2013*, pages 98–105. International Educational Data Mining Society.

Rui Liu, Junjie Hu, Wei Wei, Zi Yang, and Eric Nyberg. 2017. Structural embedding of syntactic trees for machine comprehension. pages 815–824.

Tomas Mikolov, Ilya Sutskever, Kai Chen, Gregory S. Corrado, and Jeffrey Dean. 2013. Distributed representations of words and phrases and their compositionality. In *Advances in Neural Information Processing Systems 26: 27th Annual Conference on Neural Information Processing Systems 2013. Proceedings of a meeting held December 5-8, 2013, Lake Tahoe, Nevada, United States*, pages 3111–3119.

Benjamin Paaßen, Jessica McBroom, Bryn Jeffries, Irena Koprinska, and Kalina Yacef. 2021. ast2vec: Utilizing recursive neural encodings of python programs. In *Proceedings of the 14th International Conference on Educational Data Mining, EDM 2021, virtual, June 29 - July 2, 2021*. International Educational Data Mining Society.

Cristóbal Romero and Sebastián Ventura. 2010. Educational data mining: A review of the state of the art. *IEEE Trans. Systems, Man, and Cybernetics, Part C*, 40(6):601–618.

Subhro Roy and Dan Roth. 2017. Unit dependency graph and its application to arithmetic word problem solving. In *Proceedings of the Thirty-First AAAI Conference on Artificial Intelligence, February 4-9, 2017, San Francisco, California, USA*, pages 3082–3088. AAAI Press.

David Saxton, Edward Grefenstette, Felix Hill, and Pushmeet Kohli. 2019. Analysing mathematical reasoning abilities of neural models. In *7th International Conference on Learning Representations, ICLR 2019, New Orleans, LA, USA, May 6-9, 2019*. OpenReview.net.

Stefan Slater, Jaclyn Ocumpaugh, Ryan S. Baker, Peter Scupelli, Paul Salvador Inventado, and Neil T. Heffernan. 2016. Semantic features of math problems: Relationships to student learning and engagement. pages 223–230.

Tianyu Zhao, Chengliang Chai, Yuyu Luo, Jianhua Feng, Yan Huang, Songfan Yang, Haitao Yuan, Haoda Li, Kaiyu Li, Fu Zhu, and Kang Pan. 2019. Towards automatic mathematical exercise solving. *Data Science and Engineering*, 4(3):179–192.

The Specificity and Helpfulness of Peer-to-Peer Feedback in Higher Education

Roman Rietsche[1], Andrew Caines[2], Cornelius Schramm[1], Dominik Pfütze[1], Paula Buttery[2]
[1] Institute of Information Management, University of St Gallen, Switzerland
[2] ALTA Institute & Computer Laboratory, University of Cambridge, United Kingdom
roman.rietsche@unisg.ch, cornelius.l.schramm@gmail.com
{andrew.caines,paula.buttery}@cl.cam.ac.uk

Abstract

With the growth of online learning through MOOCs and other educational applications, it has become increasingly difficult for course providers to offer personalized feedback to students. Therefore asking students to provide feedback to each other has become one way to support learning. This peer-to-peer feedback has become increasingly important whether in MOOCs to provide feedback to thousands of students or in large-scale classes at universities. One of the challenges when allowing peer-to-peer feedback is that the feedback should be perceived as helpful, and an import factor determining helpfulness is how specific the feedback is. However, in classes including thousands of students, instructors do not have the resources to check the specificity of every piece of feedback between students. Therefore, we present an automatic classification model to measure sentence specificity in written feedback. The model was trained and tested on student feedback texts written in German where sentences have been labelled as general or specific. We find that we can automatically classify the sentences with an accuracy of 76.7% using a conventional feature-based approach, whereas transfer learning with BERT for German gives a classification accuracy of 81.1%. However, the feature-based approach comes with lower computational costs and preserves human interpretability of the coefficients. In addition we show that specificity of sentences in feedback texts has a weak positive correlation with perceptions of helpfulness. This indicates that specificity is one of the ingredients of good feedback, and invites further investigation.

1 Introduction

With thousands of students in MOOCs and hundreds of students in university classes, instructors increasingly apply the approach of peer-to-peer feedback (or, 'peer feedback'), where students provide feedback to their peers (van Popta et al., 2017; Lipnevich and Smith, 2018). Peer-feedback enables instructors to provide individual feedback on every piece of coursework by leveraging the potential of students to provide feedback to each other (Piech et al., 2013). Nevertheless, since students are often not experts in providing feedback, the instructors need to ensure that the feedback is helpful (Strijbos et al., 2010). Research has shown that one factor determining feedback helpfulness is whether the feedback points are generic or specific (Lipnevich and Smith, 2018; Shute, 2008; Hattie and Timperley, 2007). Generic feedback such as "improve your submission" are less helpful than detailed, targeted advice such as "add a timeline" or "change the caption in Figure 1".

However, the challenge is that instructors who do not have time for providing feedback themselves also do not have time for checking the specificity level of peer feedback (Mulryan-Kyne, 2010). One approach is to develop a model which automatically analyses feedback specificity using natural language processing. Recent work has been carried out into automatic classification of sentence specificity in newspaper articles; for instance by Li and Nenkova (2015), Louis and Nenkova (2011) and Ko et al. (2019).

Our work builds on this previous research and at the same time provides distinct contributions. Firstly, we apply the approach in the novel domain of education and peer-feedback, which is inherently different in its purpose and nature compared to the news domain which features in previous work. News articles are written for a general audience with the purpose to inform, whereas peer-feedback texts are written to reveal the strengths and weaknesses of written work and provide suggested improvements. Furthermore, in the peer-feedback scenario, each student has put effort into their assignments: thus they have a certain expectation as to the quality of feedback they ought to receive.

Secondly, we have developed a unique dataset

Proceedings of the 17th Workshop on Innovative Use of NLP for Building Educational Applications (BEA 2022), pages 107 - 117
July 15, 2022

of peer-feedback containing more than 1000 sentences labelled for specificity. Thirdly, the data we work with are in the German language: to the best of our knowledge, all previous related work has been on English. Fourthly, we find that there is a correlation, albeit weak, between sentence specificity and the perceived helpfulness of peer-feedback.

We train and evaluate four classifiers based on a feature set which is determined by methods described in previous work and our own observations of specificity in peer-feedback texts. We also explore the relationship between sentence specificity and perceived helpfulness of peer-feedback, finding a weak positive correlation, which suggests that specific sentences are helpful but also that further work is needed to uncover the other ingredients of good feedback.

We contribute our collected corpus of sentences from peer-feedback texts in German for further analysis and hope to provide researchers and practitioners with a detailed analysis and discussion of sentence specificity. The code and annotated corpus can be accessed via github[1].

2 Theoretical Background

2.1 Characteristics of Sentence Specificity

In general, definitions of sentence specificity are often related to the "quality of belonging or relating uniquely to a particular subject" (Lugini and Litman, 2017) as well as the amount of detail contained within a sentence. The example sentences (s) from newspapers and product reviews below include *S1* and *S2*, which are more specific than *S3* and *S4*.

S1 "90% of women wear Mascara making it the most commonly worn cosmetic, and women will spend an average of $4,000 on it in their lifetimes" (Ko et al., 2019, p. 1).

S2 "While American PC sales have averaged roughly 25% annual growth since 1984 and West European sales a whopping 40%, Japanese sales were flat for most of that time" (Louis and Nenkova, 2011, p. 1818).

S3 "This cosmetic is very popular and many people use it regularly" (Ko et al., 2019, p. 1).

S4 "Now, the personal-computer revolution is finally reaching Japan" (Louis and Nenkova, 2011, p. 1818).

General sentences are broad statements about a topic, while specific sentences contain details and can be used to support or explain the general sentences further (Louis and Nenkova, 2012). General sentences create expectations in the reader's mind of further evidence or examples from the author. Specific sentences can stand by themselves, since they provide detailed information (Li and Nenkova, 2015). This difference in the level of detail contained in general and specific sentences is often a matter of degree, rather than an entirely straightforward distinction. Therefore the linguistic realisation of sentence specificity and its automatic detection is a rather complex matter.

In the domain of online education platforms featuring peer-feedback systems, sentence specificity refers to the level of detail in the feedback text (Shute, 2008). The analysis of online forum dialogues has shown that argument quality is highly correlated with specificity of claims in the context of argument mining (Swanson et al., 2015). Specific feedback guides students directly to changes in their assignment by helping them to identify those parts of the text that the reviewer considers more or less conducive to successful performance (Goodman and Wood, 2004). A large body of evidence suggests that increasing the specificity of feedback has a positive relationship with immediate or short-term performance (Kluger and DeNisi, 1996; Ilgen et al., 1979).

2.2 Related Work on Sentence Specificity

Previous work on sentence level specificity prediction has mostly been focused on English texts and on domains starkly different from academic feedback texts such as news articles (Louis and Nenkova, 2011) or tweets (Ko et al., 2019). Sentence specificity prediction as a task is proposed by Louis and Nenkova (2011), who re-purposed discourse relation annotations from *Wall Street Journal* articles (Prasad et al., 2008) for sentence specificity training. Li and Nenkova (2015) incorporated more news sentences as unlabeled data and developed Speciteller, a tool for predicting the specificity score of sentences. They improved classification accuracy by using a semi-supervised co-training method on over 30K sentences from the Associated Press, *The New York Times*, and the *Wall Street*

[1] `https://github.com/RomanRietsche/feedbackspecificity`

	German (Original)	English
S1	Auf Seite 4 beim Modul 2 solltest du besser 'würde' statt 'könnte' geschrieben.	On page 4 in module 2, you should write 'would' instead of 'could'.
S2	Den ersten Schritt des Service Blueprints würde ich "Registrierung auf der Hotel Match Plattform" nennen → klar machen, dass es sich um eine Website/ ein online tool handelt.	I would call the first step of the service blueprint "Registration on the Hotel Match platform" → make it clear that this is a website/online tool.
G1	Deine Lösung gefällt mir insgesamt sehr gut.	Overall, I like your solution a lot.
G2	Der Service Blueprint ist extrem gut gemacht und strukturiert dargestellt.	The visualization of the service blueprint is extremely good and structured.

Table 1: Examples of specific (S) and general (G) feedback sentences from our dataset, originally in German with English translation.

Journal.

Li et al. (2016) developed the annotation scheme used in Louis and Nenkova (2011) and Li and Nenkova (2015) by considering contextual information, and by using a scale from 0 to 6 rather than binary specificity annotations. Lugini and Litman (2017) produced a system to predict sentence specificity for classroom discussions, though the dataset they use is not publicly available. All the above systems are classifiers trained with categorical data (2 or 3 classes). Ko et al. (2019) presented an unsupervised domain adaptation system for sentence specificity prediction, designed to output real-valued estimates from binary training labels to generalize predictions to domains where no labeled data are available.

3 Data

Our dataset consists of peer-feedback texts written by students on a Masters Course on Business Innovation at a German-speaking University, collected over the past five years. Students followed a peer-feedback process which is similar to the scientific paper review process in academia (Ziman, 1974). Students submitted their assignment to a learning management system. Each assignment was afterwards anonymously distributed to three reviewers who each wrote their feedback before then being sent back to the assignment author. There were no rules on how to write the feedback, students only received three guiding questions: *what was good, what was not so good and what possible improvements could be made?* Each feedback text is on average 250 words long.

Table 1 provides examples from our dataset taken from both ends of the specificity spectrum. Specific feedback gives the recipient a more direct indication of strengths, weaknesses, and suggested changes (e.g. [S1] and [S2]). General sentences such as [G1] and [G2], on the other hand, often refer to entire sections or the whole work and require further clarification-questions or interpretation by the feedback recipient. Note that peer-feedback has unique characteristics which differ from other domains. It is possible for sentences to contain generalized statements which would normally be classified as such, yet in the context of peer review feedback they are in fact specific suggestions. For instance the sentence, "young people are much less obsessed with their car's internal specs than older people", contains a rather generalized statement. Yet in the context of a reviewer critiquing the reviewee's business personas, it may appear to be more specific: "I do not think the persona of Anna would be interested in your service, because young people are much less obsessed with their car's internal specs than older people.". This more complex sentence becomes a more specific criticism than simply stating, "I don't think that the persona of Anna is realistic".

For the annotation process we randomly sampled 1000 feedback texts from our corpus and adopted two strategies for annotation. First, relying on many annotators who rated only a limited amount of sentences, whereby each sentence is annotated by 5 annotators and second, relying on two students who in several workshops receive training on how to annotate specificity and an expert in NLP as arbitrator for the two annotations. In both strategies the annotators rated the specificity on a scale of 1 (very general) to 5 (very specific) developed by Li et al. (2016) and Ko et al. (2019).

We chose the two strategies because, both have their advantages and disadvantages. For example, the first approach reduces systemic bias of one individual annotator on the whole dataset, since annotators only labelled a limited number of sentences. A downside of this strategy is that, there is no opportunity for annotators to learn over time and therefore reaching agreement on the level of specificity for one sentence is more difficult. The second strategy has the benefit of learning effects but the possible downside of systemic biases by two annotators labelling many sentences.

For the first strategy, we used Survey Circle[2]. The dataset was formed from a random sample of 1000 sentences from the 1000 feedback texts. We made the annotation job available to Survey Circle users based in Germany, Austria, Switzerland, specifying that they should be German speakers. The users on Survey Circle are typically students from a variety of disciplines. Overall, 1000 sentences where annotated by 200 users who each annotated 25 sentences. Each sentence was reviewed five times by five different annotators. For quality control, we removed ratings by users who chose the same label for every one of their sentences, and who did not complete at least 15 annotations. Since our focus was on high quality data we only chose sentences with an inter-annotator agreement (IAA) higher than 60% to further proceed with in our classification algorithm, leaving us with 331 sentences with an average IAA of 0.804. To create a final dataset, we took the mean of 5 annotations, which resulted in the final specificity score. The fact that we had to filter out so many sentences at this stage, due to low IAA, prompted us to try a different approach to annotation.

In the second strategy, we randomly selected 75 of the 1000 feedback texts and removed all sentences having a character length lower than 40 (since usually those sentences solely included bullet points, enumerations, or wrong sentence segmentations). This pre-processing resulted in a final dataset of 800 sentences. Two native German speakers annotated the sentences independently from each other in the same manner as done previously on Survey Circle, but this time using the decision tree shown in Figure 1. A team workshop and several calibration training sessions were performed to reach a common understanding of the annotation. 800 feedback texts were annotated by

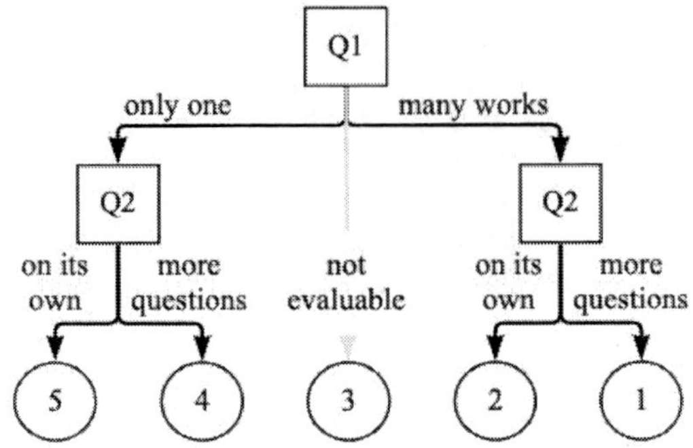

Figure 1: Specificity Annotator Prompt. Q1: "Is this feedback sentence only applicable to this individual work (eg. it references specific paragraphs, objects or people from the source text) or could it be written generically about many different works?" Q2: "Can this feedback sentence stand on its own, or does it require concretising questions or interpretation by the feedback recipient, in order to be implemented or understood?"

the two annotators – in case of disagreement an expert arbitrator was consulted in order to discuss the specific cases in detail and to reach an agreement between the two. The annotations resulted in an IAA of 0.746. To create a single version of the gold standard, the arbitrator took the final decision in cases where the two annotators still disagreed. Finally, we merged both datasets to give a total of 1131 sentences.

For our machine learning experiments we additionally obtained a binary label for each sentence, therefore we aggregated the ratings 4 and 5 to be specific (meaning a label of 1) whereas ratings 1 and 2 were deemed to be general (i.e. a label of 0). We chose to remove from the dataset the 170 sentences that received a rating of 3 "unrateable". This gave us an almost balanced dataset containing 48% general sentences and 52% specific sentences.

4 Classification Experiments

Using the data described in the previous section we undertake experiments to automatically classify sentences as specific or general. Being able to do so accurately will allow us to identify when a reviewer's text contains no specific feedback, and potentially encourage them to be more specific in downstream applications. We compare 'classic' feature-based classifiers with a BERT-based model (Devlin et al., 2019) fine-tuned on our dataset.

[2]https://www.surveycircle.com

4.1 Feature-based classification

We use the features described below for binary classification of sentence specificity based on those used in previous work and based on an intuition of what it means for a sentence to be specific or general in the context of peer feedback. We sample from the set of commonly used classifiers and train support vector machine (RBF kernel), logistic regression, and random forest models using the following features.

Sentence length: General sentences are expected to be shorter than specific ones (Louis and Nenkova, 2011). There are three features to capture this observation: the number of words in the sentence, the number of nouns, and the number of noun chunks as identified by spaCy[3]. Noun chunks are 'base noun phrases' – phrases with a noun as their head.

Word length: We compute the average length of words in each sentence, in characters, expecting long words to be indicative of more complex vocabulary and therefore more specific feedback (Ko et al., 2019).

Qualitative words: General sentences feature the frequent usage of qualitative words such as adjectives and adverbs (Louis and Nenkova, 2011). To capture this word-class based information we take counts of adjectives and adverbs in the texts.

Word specificity: We use three sets of features to capture specificity of words in the sentence. The first of these is based on GermaNet (Henrich and Hinrichs, 2010; Hamp and Feldweg, 1997), the German language adaptation of WordNet (Miller, 1995). We compute a specificity measure using the hypernym relations in GermaNet. For each noun and verb in our example sentences, we record the length of the path from the word to the root of the GermaNet hierarchy through the hypernym relations (Louis and Nenkova, 2011). The longer this path, the more specific we expect the word to be. The average, minimum and maximum values of these distances are taken for nouns and verbs found in GermaNet.

IDF: Another set of features is based on the inverse document frequency (IDF) of a word w (Sparck Jones, 1972), defined as $log\frac{N}{n}$, where N is the number of documents in a corpus, and n is the number of documents that contain the word w. We used 3 million German sentences taken from newspaper texts in 2015[4] from the Leipzig Corpus Collection (Goldhahn et al., 2012) to compute the idf (excluding punctuation and stop words). The features for a sentence are the average, minimum and maximum IDF scores for words in the sentence (Louis and Nenkova, 2011) – the intuition being that words in general sentences are more common whereas specific sentences contain words seen less often.

Sentiment: We noticed that general sentences were regularly found in positive feedback – often praising a section or even the entire work (recall examples [G1] and [G2] in Table 1). Therefore, we record the number of positive, negative, neutral and polar (not neutral) words per sentence using two lexicons – SentiWS, a publicly available German-language resource for sentiment analysis (Remus et al., 2010) and TextblobDE[5]. We add another set of features where each of these counts is normalized by the sentence length (Louis and Nenkova, 2011). In addition we obtain a count of **polar words** (non-neutral words) and a normalized **sentiment score** per sentence.

Discourse connectives: A count of the most common discourse connectives – "because", "furthermore", "either or", "on the other hand", *etc* – as these were often indicative of a point argued in greater detail which usually entailed a more specific sentence. Furthermore, we noticed that certain phrases were characteristic of general sentences ("in general", "overall", "all in all", *etc*) and count the occurrence of such words and phrases.

Non-alphanumeric characters: Another feature is the normalized count of non-alphanumeric or special characters (such as }%"§-'→) (Li and Nenkova, 2015). Due to the digital and conversational nature of the peer feedback we collected, symbols such as → were frequently used as substitutes for discourse connectives. Quotation marks, percentage or section signs were also often indicative of references to specific sections of the business plan.

URLs: Specific suggestions were sometimes accompanied with reference material in the form of internet links which is why we also count the number of URLs per sentence.

Named entities: These are generally regarded to be suggestive of specific sentences (Louis and Nenkova, 2011). In addition to counting all named entities using spaCy, we additionally count all mentions of *personas*, as they often appeared in contexts of the reviewer critiquing the recipient's pro-

[3]https://spacy.io

[4]https://www.kaggle.com/rtatman/3-million-german-sentences

[5]https://textblob-de.readthedocs.io

Model	Accuracy	Precision	Recall	F-measure
support vector	75.0	76.1	75.0	75.1
random forests	76.7	76.8	76.7	76.8
logistic regression	74.7	75.6	74.7	74.8
BERT_BASE cased	**81.1**	**81.5**	**81.1**	**81.0**

Table 2: Performance of sentence specificity classifiers on German sentences – accuracy, precision, recall, F-measure; mean of 10-fold cross-validation.

posed business personas.

Numbers: This is the count of numeric tokens or number words, since they are often associated with references to specific pages or other specifics of the student assignments.

Currency: In the context of business plans, currencies and currency symbols were often found in sentences criticising specific monetization or revenue schemes and therefore we count their occurrence in each text.

Morpho-syntactic labels: We use the spaCy dependency parser for German to extract a number of morpho-syntactic features from each sentence. We obtain counts of dependency relations, part-of-speech tags, and a concatenation of these for each token in a sentence. For instance, the sentence *Ich mag deine Arbeit* ('I like your work') would produce the following concatenated labels combining part-of-speech tags and dependency relations: PRON_sb, VERB_ROOT, DET_nk, NOUN_oa (subject, root, noun kernel element, accusative object in the TIGER treebank scheme (Rehbein and van Genabith, 2007)).

Word counts: We count the frequency of all non stop-words, as well as the sum of stop words both raw and normalized by sentence length.

Word vectors: We compute the average of the word vectors obtained from spaCy's `de_core_news_lg` model for German for each sentence, with L2 normalisation (Horn and Johnson, 2013). We also compute the vector average without the vectors of stop words.

4.2 BERT-based classification

It has become a common and successful practice in empirical NLP work in recent years to make use of large transformer language models for text classification in *transfer learning* scenarios (Rogers et al., 2020). Accordingly, we use the Hugging Face Transformers library to fine-tune the BERT_BASE cased model for German which was pre-trained and made available by deepset[6] (Wolf et al., 2020). We fine-tune to the training set in each of ten folds in our dataset in a cross-validation set-up.

4.3 Evaluation

Following Li and Nenkova (2015) we report four performance metrics for our experiments, where the *specific* label is viewed as the 'positive' one: *accuracy*, the proportion of correctly predicted sentence specificity labels; *precision*, the proportion of positive predictions which are correct; *recall*, the proportion of positive labels in the test set which are correctly identified; and the *F-measure*, the harmonic mean of precision and recall.

5 Results

In Table 2 we show performance metrics for the classification of sentence specificity in our German peer-feedback dataset. We report mean scores from ten-fold cross-validation, and we compare three feature-based classifiers with a fine-tuned BERT-based model.

To summarise, we find that the BERT-based fine-tuned classifier performs best. Not unexpectedly, the superior performance of BERT comes at a computational cost, as the fine-tuning of the transformer takes significantly longer than fitting the other models (>5mins as opposed to a few seconds), and requires GPU. Furthermore, BERT offers little in the way of interpretability. In this regard, algorithms such as logistic regression and random forests are advantageous due to their human understandable coefficients. We would therefore opt for a feature-based classifier if putting a sentence specificity detection system into production: the efficiency gains and advantage with respect to explainability in our view outweigh the performance boost provided by a BERT-based model.

We analysed which of our features were the best predictors of sentence specificity. To that end we

[6]`https://deepset.ai`

Feature	Ratio
numbers	1.98
noun chunks	1.59
non-alphanumeric characters	1.53
SentiWS negative words	1.42
named entities	1.42
discourse connectives	1.08
adjectives	1.05
discourse chunks	1.02
currency	1.00
SentiWS positive words	0.99
adverbs	0.91
TextblobDE negative words	0.90
minimum GermaNet hypernym path	0.86
TextblobDE sentiment score	0.84
TextblobDE polar words	0.80

Table 3: Top 15 features from the logistic regression model ranked by coefficient representing odds ratios.

rank the features from the logistic regression classifier by coefficient. The coefficients represent log odds that an observation is in the target class ('specific'), and thus we take the exponent of the coefficients to obtain odds ratios. Table 3 shows the top 15 features ranked by coefficient, where the latter indicate that for every one unit increase in the value of the feature the odds that the sentence is specific are n times greater than the odds that the sentence is not specific, with all other features held constant.

We find that features relating to *numbers and currency*, *non-alphanumeric characters*, and *named entities* are the most likely to occur in specific feedback. This reflects the fact that the subject domain is business but also that such features are associated with specific references to locations in the text, and the *non-alphanumeric characters* featuring in specific feedback formatting such as bullet points, section markers and parentheses, or punctuation used as connectives (e.g. right arrows and dashes). We find that other highly weighted features are representative of specific feedback texts in general, such as a high number of *noun chunks*, *named entities*, *words with clear polarity*, *adjectives* and *discourse connectives*. Finally, we note that a longer minimum *hypernym path* in GermaNet for words in a sentence is associated with more specific feedback, as we hypothesised (section 4.1).

6 Feedback Specificity and Helpfulness

We examined the interplay between feedback specificity and helpfulness to evaluate the hypothesis that more specific feedback is more helpful (Strijbos et al., 2010). We sampled 500 feedback texts from the business masters course previously referred to, presented them to Survey Circle annotators (students and PhDs), and asked them to score the strength of their agreement with the following four statements on a scale of 1 to 10 for each text: *"The feedback from the reviewer was helpful","The reviewer was able to provide constructive suggestions on their stated critical aspects", "The reviewer was able to identify critical aspects in the assignment"*, or *"The feedback from the reviewer was of high helpfulness"*. The mean of these Likert scores was taken from 5 annotators per text and across all 4 statements to give an overall feedback helpfulness score for each text between 1 and 10.

To derive a specificity score for a feedback text, we made per-sentence specificity predictions using the BERT-based model trained on the annotated peer-feedback set of 1000 sentences described above. The score per text was then the average sentence specificity prediction, a value between 0 and 1. The correlation between text specificity scores and helpfulness ratings showed a correlation of 0.21 with a statistically significant p-value <.001. This finding helps to corroborate the hypothesized relationship between specificity and feedback helpfulness, while reminding us that the relationship is not straightforwardly linear. A strongly helpful feedback text should not contain entirely general sentences or entirely specific ones, but some combination of the two. In Figure 2 we show a scatter plot of the feedback specificity per text (per cent of sentences in a text classified as specific by the model) against the feedback helpfulness score per text calculated in the way described above, and both the weak correlation and variation in the relationship are apparent.

7 Discussion

We show that sentence specificity can be classified successfully in German peer-feedback texts. This can be a useful first step for various education technology applications. For instance we can provide students with automated advice on how to improve their written peer-feedback. It can potentially help with feedback to students on their written assignments as well, in cases where students have not

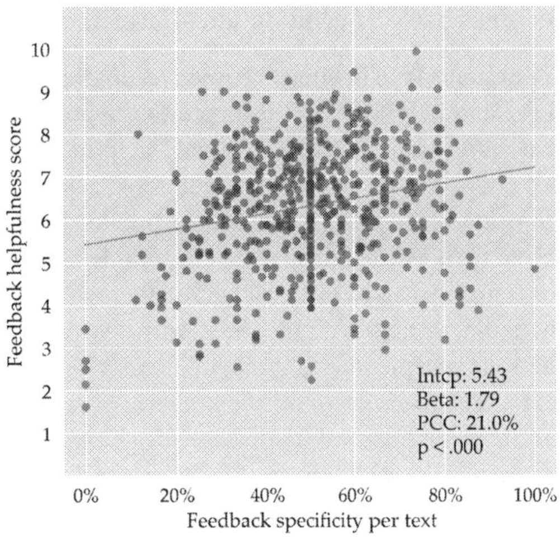

Figure 2: Correlation between text specificity (% specific sentences per text) and feedback helpfulness score (average human ratings of 4 criteria) for 500 peer feedback texts.

made sufficiently specific statements. For this reason, explainability and low computational cost are important factors in weighing up the performance of our feature-based and BERT-based specificity classification models.

One limitation of the current sentence level approach is that it fails to deal with dependent sentences where a feedback point is argued for over multiple sentences. To accurately rate the specificity in such cases, it can be crucial to take into account the context in which a sentence appears. Consider, for instance, the following example:

> **[1]** *Regarding your business processes on page 10 - does it really need a chatbot that asks for targets here?* **[2]** *One input line would be enough for that.* **[3]** *Chatbots only make sense when customers actually interact with them.*

Sentence **[3]**, taken on its own, contains a rather general statement and the logistic regression model assigns a probability of around 0.06 that it is specific (less than 0.5, thus 'general'). When taking its context into account, it becomes clear that the entire section is referencing a specific element of the business plan and calling into question a specific piece of the business process with a concrete argument. Consider a reformulation of the three previous sentences like so:

> **[4]** *I consider the chatbot that asks for destinations (page 10) to be superfluous,* as chatbots only make sense when customers interact with them — *one input line would be enough for that.*

Now the model assigns a probability of around 0.73 that the sentence is specific, thereby classifying it as 'specific'. Naturally, sentence **[4]** is more likely to have features associated with specificity since it is longer than sentence **[3]**, but the change in regression scores does illustrate how specificity of feedback can develop in context. Since we model specificity only at the sentence level in this work, the application of our model to feedback texts is determined by the author's punctuation choices and the sentence tokenization that results.

To address this issue in future work, we can attempt to segment texts into 'argumentation chunks' rather than sentences. Such an approach requires a combination of information density extraction, argumentation mining and specificity prediction. This observation is congruent with previous work which concluded that context information should be considered in the annotation procedure to mitigate the effect of anaphoric and topical references that may otherwise be inadequately dealt with (Louis and Nenkova, 2012; Li et al., 2016). In addition, it is apparent that any downstream application should be tuned so that recommendations on feedback specificity at a per-sentence level take the whole text into account, so that the student is encouraged to write a well structured mix of general and specific feedback.

Finally, we note that specificity could be just one of multiple components that determine the helpfulness of feedback. In truth, feedback helpfulness is difficult to measure objectively since in large part it is driven by how helpful a student *perceives* it to be. O'Donovan et al. (2019) state that, "what a student considers good assessment and feedback is shaped by the assumptions they hold as to the nature and certainty of knowledge (Baxter Magolda, 1992), their prior learning experiences (O'Donovan, 2017) as well as the timing of their consideration (Carless and Boud, 2018)". Just getting technical factors right will not ensure student satisfaction with feedback (p. 8)". In the long run, the sole focus on the feedback itself and its language is too narrow as it is only part of the complexity of providing good feedback (Evans, 2013). To make a holistic improvement to feedback procedures at large as well as enhance student engagement and satisfaction, peer assessment process design, pre-feedback conditions, and predictability need to be considered as well (O'Donovan et al., 2019). It is likely that perceptions of feedback helpfulness are influenced by a number of contributing factors, some of which are in the text – e.g. lexical content, pragmatic implication and argumentation – while others are external and concern the wider educational context of the assignment. For instance, the feedback should be relevant to the task, on topic, and consistent with the curriculum. We expect that specific sentences should also be used with more generic 'big picture' and bridging sentences, and that feedback providers could be prompted to provide a mixture of both. There is also the pedagogical question of timing: when more specific feedback is beneficial for the student and when it is not. These issues represent opportunities for future investigation.

8 Conclusion

We have presented experiments in automatic classification of the specificity of German sentences in peer feedback written by students in an online assignment reviewing system. We derived features based on previous work and the qualitative analysis of our dataset, and performed multiple experiments using machine learning models compared to a transfer learning approach with BERT (Devlin et al., 2019). We found that our classifiers were able to successfully predict sentence specificity with an accuracy of at least 70% for all models. The BERT model mostly outperforms the feature-based classifiers, but it has the highest computational cost and does not have human interpretable coefficients. SVM performs best on the peer-feedback texts for feature-based models, is computationally more efficient and provides per-feature coefficients which enable downstream explainability for any user-facing system.

In addition, in the analysis of our logistic regression model we report which features are most likely to indicate feedback specificity, and find that *numbers*, *noun chunks* and *non-alphanumeric characters* are at the top of the list. We found a weak correlation between crowdsourced assessments of feedback helpfulness and feedback specificity, underlining that texts containing relatively high proportions of specific sentences are more likely to represent good quality feedback.

Acknowledgements

The second and fifth authors are supported by Cambridge University Press & Assessment, University of Cambridge.

References

Marcia B. Baxter Magolda. 1992. *Knowing and reasoning in college: Gender-related patterns in students' intellectual development*, 1st ed. edition. The Jossey-Bass social and behavioral science series. Jossey-Bass, San Francisco.

David Carless and David Boud. 2018. The development of student feedback literacy: enabling uptake of feedback. *Assessment & Evaluation in Higher Education*, 43(8):1315–1325.

Jacob Devlin, Ming-Wei Chang, Kenton Lee, and Kristina Toutanova. 2019. BERT: Pre-training of Deep Bidirectional Transformers for Language Understanding. In *Proceedings of the 2019 Conference of the North American Chapter of the Association for Computational Linguistics: Human Language Technologies*, pages 4171–4186, Stroudsburg, PA, USA. Association for Computational Linguistics.

C. Evans. 2013. Making Sense of Assessment Feedback in Higher Education. *Review of Educational Research*, 83(1):70–120.

Dirk Goldhahn, Thomas Eckart, and Uwe Quasthoff. 2012. Building Large Monolingual Dictionaries at the Leipzig Corpora Collection: From 100 to 200 Languages. In *LREC*, volume 29, pages 31–43.

Jodi S. Goodman and Robert E. Wood. 2004. Feedback Specificity, Learning Opportunities, and Learning. *Journal of Applied Psychology*, 89(5):809–821.

Birgit Hamp and Helmut Feldweg. 1997. Germanet-a lexical-semantic net for german. In *ACL workshop on Automatic information extraction and building of lexical semantic resources for NLP applications*.

John Hattie and Helen Timperley. 2007. The power of feedback. *Review of Educational Research*, 77(1):81–112.

Verena Henrich and Erhard Hinrichs. 2010. GernEdiT-the GermaNet editing tool. In *Proceedings of the ACL 2010 System Demonstrations*, pages 19–24.

Roger A. Horn and Charles R. Johnson. 2013. *Matrix analysis*, second edition edition. Cambridge University Press, New York, NY.

Daniel R. Ilgen, Cynthia D. Fisher, and M. Susan Taylor. 1979. Consequences of individual feedback on behavior in organizations. *Journal of Applied Psychology*, 64(4):349–371.

Avraham N. Kluger and Angelo DeNisi. 1996. The effects of feedback interventions on performance: a historical review, a meta-analysis, and a preliminary feedback intervention theory. *Psychological Bulletin*, 119(2):254–284.

Wei-Jen Ko, Greg Durrett, and Junyi Jessy Li. 2019. Domain agnostic real-valued specificity prediction. In *Proceedings of the AAAI Conference on Artificial Intelligence*, volume 33, pages 6610–6617.

Junyi Jessy Li and Ani Nenkova. 2015. Fast and accurate prediction of sentence specificity. In *Twenty-Ninth AAAI Conference on Artificial Intelligence*, pages 2281–2287.

Junyi Jessy Li, Bridget O'Daniel, Yi Wu, Wenli Zhao, and Ani Nenkova. 2016. Improving the Annotation of Sentence Specificity. In *Proceedings of the Tenth International Conference on Language Resources and Evaluation (LREC'16)*, pages 3921–3927, Portorož, Slovenia. European Language Resources Association (ELRA).

Anastasiya A. Lipnevich and Jeffrey K. Smith, editors. 2018. *The Cambridge handbook of instructional feedback*. Cambridge University Press, Cambridge, United Kingdom.

Annie Louis and Ani Nenkova. 2011. General versus specific sentences: automatic identification and application to analysis of news summaries. *Technical Reports (CIS)*.

Annie Louis and Ani Nenkova. 2012. A corpus of general and specific sentences from news. In *The International Conference on Language Resources and Evaluation (LREC)*, pages 1818–1821.

Luca Lugini and Diane Litman. 2017. Predicting Specificity in Classroom Discussion. In *Proceedings of the 12th Workshop on Innovative Use of NLP for Building Educational Applications*, pages 52–61, Stroudsburg, PA, USA. Association for Computational Linguistics.

George A. Miller. 1995. WordNet: a lexical database for English. *Communications of the ACM*, 38(11):39–41.

Catherine Mulryan-Kyne. 2010. Teaching large classes at college and university level: Challenges and opportunities. *Teaching in Higher Education*, 15(2):175–185.

Berry O'Donovan. 2017. How student beliefs about knowledge and knowing influence their satisfaction with assessment and feedback. *Higher Education*, 74(4):617–633.

Berry M. O'Donovan, Birgit den Outer, Margaret Price, and Andy Lloyd. 2019. What makes good feedback good? Studies in Higher Education, 1-12. *Studies in Higher Education*, pages 1–12.

Chris Piech, Jonathan Huang, Zhenghao Chen, Chuong Do, Andrew Ng, and Daphne Koller. 2013. Tuned models of peer assessment in MOOCs. *arXiv*.

Rashmi Prasad, Nikhil Dinesh, Alan Lee, Eleni Miltsakaki, Livio Robaldo, Aravind Joshi, and Bonnie Webber. 2008. The Penn Discourse TreeBank 2.0. In *Proceedings of the Sixth International Conference on Language Resources and Evaluation (LREC'08)*, Marrakech, Morocco. European Language Resources Association (ELRA).

Ines Rehbein and Josef van Genabith. 2007. Treebank Annotation Schemes and Parser Evaluation for German. In *Proceedings of the 2007 Joint Conference on Empirical Methods in Natural Language Processing and Computational Natural Language Learning (EMNLP-CoNLL)*.

Robert Remus, Uwe Quasthoff, and Gerhard Heyer. 2010. SentiWS - A Publicly Available German-language Resource for Sentiment Analysis. In *Proceedings of the Seventh International Conference on Language Resources and Evaluation (LREC'10)*, Valletta, Malta. European Language Resources Association (ELRA).

Anna Rogers, Olga Kovaleva, and Anna Rumshisky. 2020. A Primer in BERTology: What We Know About How BERT Works. *Transactions of the Association for Computational Linguistics*, 8:842–866.

Valerie J. Shute. 2008. Focus on formative feedback. *Review of Educational Research*, 78(1):153–189.

Karen Sparck Jones. 1972. A Statistical Interpretation of Term Specificity and its Application in Retrieval: Journal of Documentation, 28(1), 11-21. *Journal of Documentation*, 28(1):11–21.

Jan-Willem Strijbos, Susanne Narciss, and Katrin Dünnebier. 2010. Peer feedback content and sender's competence level in academic writing revision tasks: Are they critical for feedback perceptions and efficiency? *Learning and Instruction*, 20(4):291–303.

Reid Swanson, Brian Ecker, and Marilyn Walker. 2015. Argument Mining: Extracting Arguments from Online Dialogue. In *Proceedings of the 16th Annual Meeting of the Special Interest Group on Discourse and Dialogue*, pages 217–226, Stroudsburg, PA, USA. Association for Computational Linguistics.

Esther van Popta, Marijke Kral, Gino Camp, Rob L. Martens, and P. Robert-Jan Simons. 2017. Exploring the value of peer feedback in online learning for the provider. *Educational Research Review*, 20:24–34.

Thomas Wolf, Lysandre Debut, Victor Sanh, Julien Chaumond, Clement Delangue, Anthony Moi, Pierric Cistac, Tim Rault, Remi Louf, Morgan Funtowicz, Joe Davison, Sam Shleifer, Patrick von Platen, Clara Ma, Yacine Jernite, Julien Plu, Canwen Xu, Teven Le Scao, Sylvain Gugger, Mariama Drame,

Quentin Lhoest, and Alexander Rush. 2020. Transformers: State-of-the-Art Natural Language Processing. In *Proceedings of the 2020 Conference on Empirical Methods in Natural Language Processing: System Demonstrations*.

John Michael Ziman. 1974. *Public knowledge: An essay concerning the social dimension of science*. Cambridge University Press, London.

Similarity-Based Content Scoring - How to Make S-BERT Keep Up With BERT

Marie Bexte and **Andrea Horbach** and **Torsten Zesch**
Research Cluster D^2L^2 - Digitalization, Diversity
and Lifelong Learning. Consequences for Higher Education.
FernUniversität in Hagen, Germany

Abstract

The dominating paradigm for content scoring is to learn an instance-based model, i.e. to use lexical features derived from the learner answers themselves. An alternative approach that receives much less attention is however to learn a similarity-based model. We introduce an architecture that efficiently learns a similarity model and find that results on the standard ASAP dataset are on par with a BERT-based classification approach.

1 Introduction

Most work on automatic content scoring follows an *instance-based* approach, where the input is a single student answer and the output is its score (Horbach and Zesch, 2019). In contrast, *similarity-based* approaches compare a student answer with a - or a set of - reference answers. The two approaches have rarely been compared directly, see Sakaguchi et al. (2015) as the rare exception, who found that instance-based methods outperform similarity-based ones. However, what many situations for which similarity-based methods are proposed have in common is that very little or no training data is available for an individual prompt.

In the following discussion of previous work, we restrict ourselves to those similarity-based approaches. An early example of using reference answers and a similarity function is c-rater (Leacock and Chodorow, 2003). Other examples of pre-neural similarity-based approaches use Wordnet-based and dependency graph alignment measures (Mohler and Mihalcea, 2009; Mohler et al., 2011). Similar approaches have been used for reading comprehension questions (Bailey and Meurers, 2008; Meurers et al., 2011) or scoring history exams (Rodrigues and Oliveira, 2014). The SemEval2013 Student Response Analysis Task (Dzikovska et al., 2013) links content scoring with recognizing textual entailment. Due to the task setup (large number of individual questions with relatively few individual training data per prompt), some participants of the task used similarity-based methods for scoring (Heilman and Madnani, 2013), including methods for recognizing (partial) textual entailment (Levy et al., 2013a,b).

In recent years, neural similarity-based scoring models have been developed. Gomaa and Fahmy (2019) use pretrained skip-thought vectors and learn a logistic classifier over the component-wise product and absolute difference vectors. Schneider et al. (2022) report promising results on a not-publicly-available dataset by learning embeddings for question-answer-pairs and utilize cosine similarity as distance metric.

While the work by Sakaguchi et al. (2015) seems to indicate that similarity-based approaches cannot compete with instance-based ones, such a comparison has so far to our knowledge not been made using powerful neural architectures.

We thus propose a method, where a pretrained Sentence-BERT (S-BERT) model is fine-tuned on answer pairs and then used in a knn-fashion to assign a score to a new learner answer based on the similarity to the already labeled ones.

We present this approach in the next section. Our code is publicly available here: https://github.com/mariebexte/s-bert-similarity-based-content-scoring.

2 Similarity-based Approach

In our similarity-based approach, we learn and apply a similarity function between reference answers and learner answers (see Figure 1). In the simplest case, we use the *all-MiniLM-L6-v2* pre-trained sentence-BERT model (Reimers and Gurevych, 2019) as is to encode answers (**S-BERT-orig**). Alternatively, we finetune the model using answer pairs from our dataset as input (**S-BERT-finetune**). For doing this, we use a CosineSimilarityLoss and a BinaryClassificationEvaluator. We consider answer pairs with the same human score as positive instances (i.e. highly similar) while we consider

Proceedings of the 17th Workshop on Innovative Use of NLP for Building Educational Applications (BEA 2022), pages 118 - 123
July 15, 2022

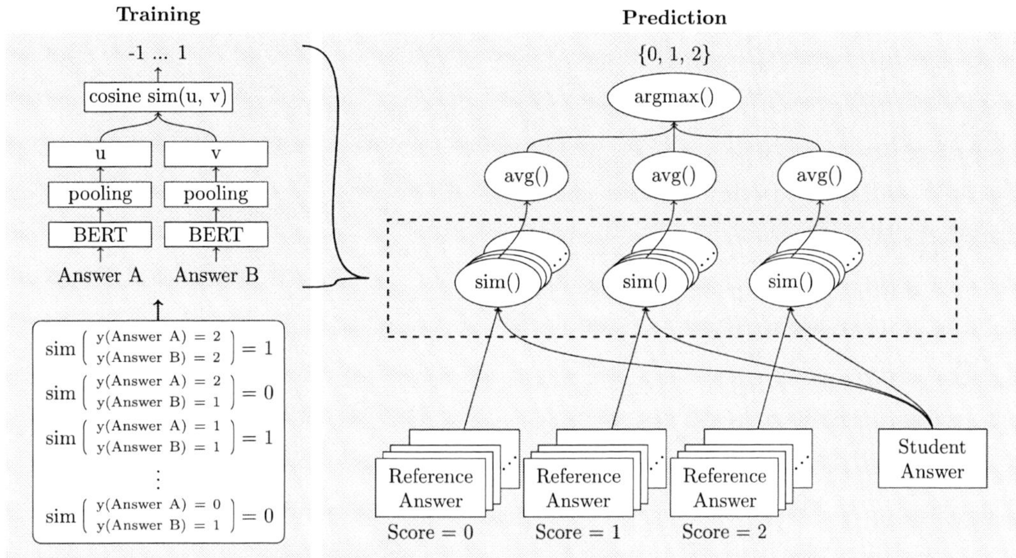

Figure 1: Visual description of our similarity-based approach when using the AVG-strategy to determine predictions.

pairs with different scores as dissimilar. To reflect this (dis-)similarity, we assign positive instances a similarity score of 1 and negative instances a score of 0. We thus refrain from encoding the distance between the number of points with different levels of similarity (ASAP prompts are scored on a range from 0 to 2 or 0 to 3 points), i.e. both pairing an answer that received 0 points with one that received 1 or one that received 2 points gives the same similarity label of 0. This is beneficial when models trained on one prompt are used to score answers to another prompt that has a different number of outcomes.

In the prediction step, we apply the S-BERT model to encode each answer as a single dense vector. We compute the cosine similarity between an answer and each available reference answer. Adopting a knn-inspired approach, we then take either the label of the closest reference answer (MAX) or the label of the group of answers with the same score that has the highest average similarity (AVG). In both cases, the number of necessary comparisons is determined by the number of reference answers. Therefore, scoring more answers will always just require comparing them to this fixed amount of reference answers, whose embeddings can be precomputed.

Note that in our experiments the same data was used to both fine-tune the similarity metric and for comparison in the prediction step. However, if runtime at test time is an issue, one could of course use fewer instances for the comparison than those used for fine-tuning. In our experiments, we observed that using a subset of just 60 of the over 1000 reference answers during inference lead to only a minor drop of QWK .01 in performance.

Do also note that, while we learn similarities between reference answers during training and use the same reference answers when later scoring answers, this does not reflect an inappropriate data leak between training and testing, as we are still scoring previously unseen answers.

3 Experimental Setup

We use the following setup to compare our approach against instance-based state-of-the-art systems. All results are averaged over five runs.

Instance-based Baselines To establish a baseline for instance-based classification, we train one supervised classifier per prompt. We use a Logistic Regression (LR) classifier in standard configuration (class_weight='balanced', max_iter=1000) with token uni- to trigram features provided through Scikit-learn as an instance of an explainable shallow learning classifier. As an instance for a neural classifier, we use a BERT model based on the Huggingface implementation.[1] We train for 6 epochs with batch size 16, CrossEntropyLoss, and Adam

[1] https://huggingface.co/bert-base-uncased

optimizer.

Dataset We use the ASAP-SAS dataset from the Kaggle short answer competition[2] containing 10 prompts with around 2,000 answers per prompt. The average answer length of the prompts ranges from 26.5 to 66.2 tokens per answer. Broad prompt topics fall into three categories: *Sciences* (prompts 1, 2 and 10), *English Language Arts* (*ELA*; prompts 3, 4, 7, 8 and 9) and *Biology* (prompts 5 and 6). We use this topic information later to check whether training on a different prompt from the same topic is beneficial. The dataset contains scoring rubrics but no specific set of reference answers for the individual scores. Whenever we talk about reference answers, we mean answers drawn from the pool of training data.

Data Split and Evaluation Method We randomly chose 10% of the answers for each prompt as testing data and report results as quadratically weighted kappa (QWK). As the amount of human-scored data needed to train a classifier is a crucial factor determining the costs of automatic scoring approaches, we compare two setups. *Limited data* contains 60 learner answers sampled from the full training data set in a way that all scores are equally represented. Mimicking a strategy where clear reference answers are provided to human annotators, we only select answers where both human annotators agreed on the score. *Full data* in contrast consists of the whole training set.

For our similarity-based approach we in the *limited data* setting use 48 of the 60 answers for training and the remaining 12 for validation. Within both of these sets, we build all possible pairs of answers, meaning that we end up with 2,256 training and 132 validation examples. As described in the previous section and visualized in Figure 1, these pairs are assigned a similarity score of 1 or 0, depending on whether they received the same or a different number of points.

For the *full data* setting, we randomly select 100 answers for validation and leave the rest for training. We pair every training (validation) answer with 10 other answers per score to create training pairs. Depending on the number of different possible scores of a prompt, this gives around 3,000 validation and between 40,000 and 60,000 training examples.

[2]https://www.kaggle.com/c/asap-sas

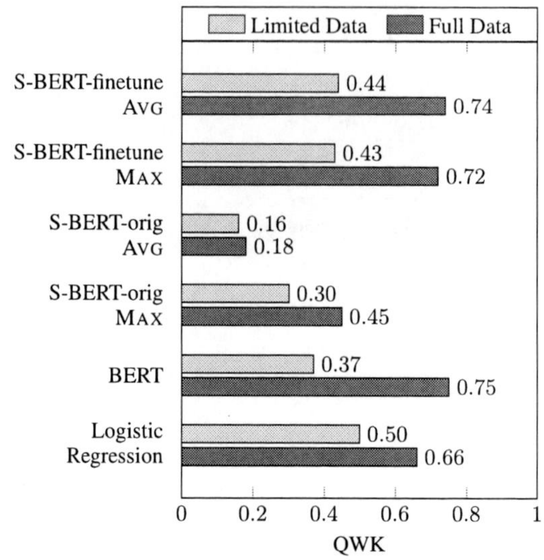

Figure 2: QWK averaged over all prompts (after Fisher-Z transformation), either using just 60 instances (limited data) or 90% of the ASAP data (full data).

4 Results

Figure 2 shows the comparison between the instance-based baseline and the similarity-based approach on both limited and full data. Note that the different amounts of training data also mean that there are different amounts of reference answers.

Comparing S-BERT-orig and S-BERT-finetune reveals that finetuning is highly beneficial. MAX performs much better than AVG with the pretrained model, perhaps due to just one similar enough answer sufficing for the MAX strategy to arrive at the correct classification outcome. For the finetuned models the performance difference between the two is much smaller, with AVG even giving slightly better results than MAX.

In the *limited data* setting, BERT is not able to learn a sufficiently good model from the few training instances. LR performs best in this setting, beating our S-BERT-finetune by QWK .06. In the *full* train setting, S-BERT-finetune is on par with BERT when using AVG to determine predictions, with both models outperforming LR.

Variance between Prompts Table 1 breaks results down to individual prompts. We see that performance is largely prompt-dependent and that there is no one-best model across all prompts. While LR gives the overall best performance when using limited data, there are prompts where S-

Topic	Prompt	Limited Train				Full Train			
		LR	BERT	S-BERT-finetune		LR	BERT	S-BERT-finetune	
				MAX	AVG			MAX	AVG
Science	1	.58	.26	.50	.54	.82	.89	.84	.88
	2	.52	.18	.34	.12	.67	.77	.79	.78
	10	.45	.53	.37	.47	.66	.70	.67	.74
ELA	3	.42	.44	.36	.38	.70	.67	.67	.72
	4	.54	.44	.49	.54	.70	.73	.67	.69
	7	.19	.15	.41	.29	.51	.72	.72	.74
	8	.49	.40	.35	.36	.43	.66	.58	.58
	9	.61	.53	.48	.53	.64	.71	.68	.69
Biology	5	.47	.35	.49	.48	.73	.77	.77	.77
	6	.66	.36	.52	.61	.66	.79	.72	.72

Table 1: QWK per prompt, either using 3-4% (60 instances, limited train) or 90% of the ASAP data (full train).

BERT-finetune performs better than LR, indicating that there are some prompts for which using a similarity-based approach is more suitable than for others. For prompts 2, 5 and 7, BERT gives rather low QWK on limited data, which is outperformed by S-BERT-finetune. While BERT gives much better performance on these prompts in the full data setting, it is again outperformed by or on par with S-BERT-finetune.

Cross-prompt Evaluation One of the assumed benefits of similarity-based scoring approaches is that they generalize better between prompts and are thus often used for prompt-independent scoring (Meurers et al., 2011; Mohler et al., 2011; Mohler and Mihalcea, 2009; Dzikovska et al., 2013). We hypothesize that using a model from the same topic (Science, Biology, ELA) will work better than using a model from a different topic. Table 2 reports results for models trained on a different prompt than the test data. In doing this, we use the larger number of training pairs from the full data setting to train a model and evaluate it with the smaller number of reference answers from the limited data setting.

We average across all prompts from the same topic, i.e. the cell *train/science - test/science* contains averaged results, where a model has been trained on one science prompt and tested on another science prompt. Results show that only for Biology prompts training on the same prompt is clearly beneficial as compared to training on other prompts. However, it still is much worse than fine-tuning directly on a single prompt. For example, the average QWK on the two Biology prompts is over 0.70 for the fine-tuned results, while it is only half of that in the cross-prompt setting. For the other topic areas (Science, ELA) the cross-prompt results are even worse.

Train	Test					
	Science		Bio		ELA	
	MAX	AVG	MAX	AVG	MAX	AVG
Science	.30	.29	.18	.09	.23	.16
Bio	.31	.18	.35	.40	.27	.17
ELA	.28	.16	.26	.19	.22	.16
S-BERT-orig	.34	.23	.24	.13	.30	.13

Table 2: Average QWK (after Fisher-Z transformation) for training S-BERT on a prompt from one topic group and testing on another prompt from the same/a different group.

Another cross-prompt setting would be to use the pretrained S-BERT-orig model as a zero-shot classifier (cf. the last line in Table 2). Results are in a similar ballpark as for the within-topic setting, which means that fine-tuning on one prompt and transferring to a similar one does not work better than not fine-tuning at all. Thus, it is necessary to learn a prompt-specific similarity function to arrive at reasonable performance levels. Contrary to our hypothesis, a similarity function learned on a different prompt from the same dataset and topic did not work better than using one that was trained on an entirely different dataset and topic.

5 Conclusion

In contrast to earlier work where instance-based methods outperformed similarity-based ones, the study in this paper finds that both paradigms are on par when a neural similarity model has been sufficiently fine-tuned. This seems to indicate that as soon as a similarity metric is complex enough, it incorporates the same capabilities as normally a classifier would. For the practitioner it might make little difference whether to use labeled instances to train an instance-based classifier or to fine-tune a similarity metric if both are applied in a prompt-specific way. Therefore, the next step in our line of research has to go into the direction of fully comparing the two paradigms, especially with respect to varying the amount of training data as well as exploring other datasets to allow for a better estimation which paradigm is preferable under which conditions.

One step that we already took in this direction was to use the architecture described here for our participation in the NAEP-AS challenge[3], where our generic scoring model won a grand prize. In contrast to the successful application there, our cross-prompt experiments reported here showed results varying tremendously between prompts, hinting that sensible training data selection plays a crucial role. We will explore this further in future work. To foster more work in this area, we make our experimental code publicly available.

6 Acknowledgments

This work was conducted in the framework of the Research Cluster D^2L^2 "Digitalization, Diversity and Lifelong Learning – Consequences for Higher Education" of the FernUniversität in Hagen, Germany (https://e.feu.de/english-d2l2). The work was partially conducted within the KI-Starter project "Explaining AI Predictions of Semantic Relationships" funded by the Ministry of Culture and Science Nordrhein-Westfalen, Germany.

References

Stacey Bailey and Detmar Meurers. 2008. Diagnosing meaning errors in short answers to reading comprehension questions. In *Proceedings of the third workshop on innovative use of NLP for building educational applications*, pages 107–115.

Myroslava O Dzikovska, Rodney D Nielsen, Chris Brew, Claudia Leacock, Danilo Giampiccolo, Luisa Bentivogli, Peter Clark, Ido Dagan, and Hoa T Dang. 2013. Semeval-2013 task 7: The joint student response analysis and 8th recognizing textual entailment challenge. Technical report, NORTH TEXAS STATE UNIV DENTON.

Wael Hassan Gomaa and Aly Aly Fahmy. 2019. Ans2vec: A scoring system for short answers. In *International Conference on Advanced Machine Learning Technologies and Applications*, pages 586–595. Springer.

[3]https://github.com/NAEP-AS-Challenge/info

Michael Heilman and Nitin Madnani. 2013. ETS: Domain adaptation and stacking for short answer scoring. In *Second Joint Conference on Lexical and Computational Semantics (* SEM), Volume 2: Proceedings of the Seventh International Workshop on Semantic Evaluation (SemEval 2013)*, pages 275–279.

Andrea Horbach and Torsten Zesch. 2019. The influence of variance in learner answers on automatic content scoring. In *Frontiers in Education*, volume 4, page 28. Frontiers.

Claudia Leacock and Martin Chodorow. 2003. C-rater: Automated scoring of short-answer questions. *Computers and the Humanities*, 37(4):389–405.

Omer Levy, Torsten Zesch, Ido Dagan, and Iryna Gurevych. 2013a. Recognizing partial textual entailment. In *Proceedings of the 51st Annual Meeting of the Association for Computational Linguistics (Volume 2: Short Papers)*, pages 451–455.

Omer Levy, Torsten Zesch, Ido Dagan, and Iryna Gurevych. 2013b. UKP-BIU: Similarity and entailment metrics for student response analysis. In *Second Joint Conference on Lexical and Computational Semantics (* SEM), Volume 2: Proceedings of the Seventh International Workshop on Semantic Evaluation (SemEval 2013)*, pages 285–289.

Detmar Meurers, Ramon Ziai, Niels Ott, and Janina Kopp. 2011. Evaluating answers to reading comprehension questions in context: Results for German and the role of information structure. In *Proceedings of the TextInfer 2011 Workshop on Textual Entailment*, pages 1–9.

Michael Mohler, Razvan Bunescu, and Rada Mihalcea. 2011. Learning to grade short answer questions using semantic similarity measures and dependency graph alignments. In *Proceedings of the 49th annual meeting of the association for computational linguistics: Human language technologies*, pages 752–762.

Michael Mohler and Rada Mihalcea. 2009. Text-to-text semantic similarity for automatic short answer grading. In *Proceedings of the 12th Conference of the European Chapter of the ACL (EACL 2009)*, pages 567–575.

Nils Reimers and Iryna Gurevych. 2019. Sentence-BERT: Sentence Embeddings using Siamese BERT-Networks. In *Proceedings of the 2019 Conference on Empirical Methods in Natural Language Processing*. Association for Computational Linguistics.

Fátima Rodrigues and Paulo Oliveira. 2014. A system for formative assessment and monitoring of students' progress. *Computers & Education*, 76:30–41.

Keisuke Sakaguchi, Michael Heilman, and Nitin Madnani. 2015. Effective feature integration for automated short answer scoring. In *Proceedings of the 2015 conference of the North American Chapter of the association for computational linguistics: Human language technologies*, pages 1049–1054.

Johannes Schneider, Robin Richner, and Micha Riser. 2022. Towards trustworthy autograding of short, multi-lingual, multi-type answers. *arXiv preprint arXiv:2201.03425*.

Don't Drop the Topic - The Role of the Prompt in Argument Identification in Student Writing

Yuning Ding and **Marie Bexte** and **Andrea Horbach**
Research Cluster D^2L^2 - Digitalization, Diversity
and Lifelong Learning. Consequences for Higher Education.
FernUniversität in Hagen, Germany

Abstract

In this paper, we explore the role of topic information in student essays from an argument mining perspective. We cluster a recently released corpus through topic modeling into prompts and train argument identification models on various data settings. Results show that, given the same amount of training data, prompt-specific training performs better than cross-prompt training. However, the advantage can be overcome by introducing large amounts of cross-prompt training data.

1 Introduction

Argumentative essays are among the most common essay types students are assigned to write in higher education contexts (Wingate, 2012). In such an essay, students have to state and justify their opinion on a certain topic elicited by a specific writing prompt. In order to score argumentative essays and give formative feedback automatically, the automatic identification and classification of components in the argumentative structure is important (Scheuer et al., 2010). While their holistic scoring can be seen as one variant of **automatic essay scoring**, identifying the argumentative structure within an essay is a Natural Language Processing (NLP) task known as **argument mining**.

Argument mining is the automatic identification and extraction of the structure of inference and reasoning expressed as arguments presented in natural language (Lawrence and Reed, 2020). The recent Kaggle competition "Feedback Prize - Evaluating Student Writing"[1] can be seen as an argument mining task in an educational scenario, which called on participants to identify argumentative elements in English essays written by U.S. students. Figure 1 shows an example from the dataset for an essay where students have been asked to express their attitude towards driverless cars. Individual argumentative elements such as *Position*, *Evidence* or *Concluding Statement* are highlighted in the text.

The argument mining task is not restricted to a certain domain or topic. For example, previous work considered legal (Mochales and Ieven, 2009), political (Walker et al., 2012) or educational (Stab and Gurevych, 2017) data. However, it is an open question to what extent argument mining algorithms pick up on topical words indicative not for, e.g., a conclusion in general, but for a conclusion within a specific topic. The Feedback Prize data mentioned above with its large amount of annotated student essays on various topics offers an ideal opportunity for first steps towards closing this gap.

In the data, we notice that very similar sentences can receive different argumentative labels depending on the topic and the context of an essay. For example, the sentence *"exercise is really good for your health"* was annotated as a **claim** in an essay on the topic *"Limiting Car Usage"* while the sentence *"(...) running is good for your body"* was marked as **evidence** for the topic *"No Sports at Grade C"*. Such examples highlight the relevance of topic and context information for the argument mining task and give rise to research questions like:

- In how far is the task of argument mining prompt-dependent, i.e., how does prompt-specific vs. cross-prompt training affect classification performance?
- What kind of information is learned by an automatic argument classifier? Are algorithms more susceptible to prompt-specific words, or do they learn the general structure of an essay?

To address these questions, we present in this paper experimental studies to investigate the influence of the prompt in an educational argument identifying task using the example of the newly released Kaggle Feedback Prize dataset.

[1] https://www.kaggle.com/c/feedback-prize-2021

Proceedings of the 17th Workshop on Innovative Use of NLP for Building Educational Applications (BEA 2022), pages 124 - 133
July 15, 2022 ©2022 Association for Computational Linguistics

4EC4E3EFD09A.txt

Lead Position Claim Counterclaim Rebuttal Evidence Concluding Statement

Driverless cars have been a big topic lately. In some ways driverless cars sound cool but they also seem a little scary. I think that diverless cars shouldn't be allowed on public roads because they are not safe.

Some think being able to have your car drive itself sounds nice. You could just sit in your car and listen to music while you wait to arive to your desination. Driverless cars would allow you to sit in your seat, hands on the wheel, but not acually driving. This idea does sound nice but as all other technology such as computers and phones, technology is not always reliable.

A driverless car could cause a marjor or even fatal crash. While most driverless cars require you to have hands on the wheel this does not mean you will be paying attention if somthing is about to happen. All it would take is for somthing in the car to mess up and people could be very seriously hurt.

I think that people driverless cars are not safe and they should not be allowed on public roads.

Figure 1: An example essay with different argumentative elements from the Kaggle competition "Feedback Prize - Evaluating Student Writing".

We find that argument mining benefits from within-prompt training data, but the same performance can be reached by using larger amounts of cross-prompt data. The argumentative elements *lead* and *conclusion* can be best identified because of their relatively fixed position within the essay. In an analysis of our models trained and tested with either topic or structure words masked, we find a tendency that within-prompt training benefits more from topic information while cross-prompt training rather picks up on structure words. We have made our experimental code, together with the automatic clustering results, publicly available at `https://github.com/yuningDING/BEA-NAACL-2022-38`.

2 Related Work

In the following, we discuss related work performing argument mining in the educational domain and work addressing the relevance of topic information.

Early work treated sentence boundaries as the natural separator of components in an essay. In such a scenario, the identification of argumentative elements boils down to a **sentence classification** task. For example, Burstein et al. (2003) classified sentences as *introductory material, position, main/supporting idea, conclusion, title* and *irrelevant* automatically, using features derived from Rhetorical Structure Theory trees and the occurrence of discourse markers. Ong et al. (2014) developed a rule-based algorithm to label each sentence in a student essay into one out of four types (*current study, hypothesis, claim, citation*).

We experimented with sentence classification approaches on the Kaggle dataset mentioned above, but found them unsuitable as they do not reflect the gold standard units well. As shown in Figure 2, one sentence can contain multiple argumentative elements, while one argumentative element can span sentences like the *lead*, *counterclaim* and *evidence* annotations in Figure 1. Our sentence classification experiments using a support vector machine reached an F1-Score of only 0.2. We thus did not further proceed with sentence classification on this dataset.

However, driverless cars should be looked at as useful and a positive alternative to everyday cars as they are aware and self-sufficient for their owner's benefit.

Figure 2: An example sentence with multiple argumentative elements from essay 03EA9F90F814 in the Kaggle dataset.

Based on a modification of the Toulmin argument model (Toulmin, 1958), Stab and Gurevych (2014b) proposed a model of argument components in scientific articles and persuasive essays at the **clause**-level using four label types - *major claim, claim, premise* and *non-argumentative*. Their annotation guidelines yielded substantial agreement in an annotation study on 90 persuasive essays in English (Stab and Gurevych, 2014a). Following this schema, the International Corpus of Learner English (Granger et al., 2009) was annotated by Persing and Ng (2015). They trained classification models to identify argument components and used them as features to predict argumentative scores in essays (Persing and Ng, 2016).

In recent research, the granularity of argumentative components was further increased to the **token** level. In this case, the identification of argumentative elements corresponds to assigning an argument label to each word. In this paradigm, sequence labeling techniques like Conditional Random Fields or pretrained BERT models started contributing to argument mining (Trautmann et al., 2020). The Kaggle competition "Feedback Prize - Evaluating Student Writing" can also be seen as a token labeling task as suggested by the organizers[2].

Most studies on argument mining mentioned above do not take the topic of the essay into consideration, assuming that arguments can be classified independently of a topic. However, as shown in studies like Daxenberger et al. (2017), argument mining models did not generalize well on cross-domain data. Subsequently, the importance of topic information has drawn more and more attention in the general argument mining task recently: Stab et al. (2018) found that a topic-general model could achieve comparable performance to a topic-specific model by adding limited amounts of topic-specific data. Fromm et al. (2019) proved that topic information connected with large pretrained language models like BERT provides a significant performance boost in argument mining.

However, the effect of topic information has not been fully examined in educational argument mining. The data released by the Kaggle competition gives us a chance to investigate this research gap, because it not only contains large amounts of student essays with gold standard annotation of different argumentative elements, but also covers essays from a variety of different writing prompts which, while not being annotated in the dataset, can be automatically inferred.

3 Data

As mentioned before, we use the dataset provided as part of the Kaggle competition "Feedback Prize - Evaluating Student Writing". The dataset consists of 15,594 argumentative students essays written by U.S. students from grades 6 to 12. Essays contain annotations for the following argumentative labels:[3]

- Lead: an introduction that begins with a statistic, a quotation, a description, or some other device to grab the reader's attention and point toward the thesis.
- Position: an opinion or conclusion on the main question.
- Claim: a claim that supports the position.
- Counterclaim: a claim that refutes another claim or gives an opposing reason to the position.
- Rebuttal: a claim that refutes a counterclaim.
- Evidence: ideas or examples that support claims, counterclaims, or rebuttals.
- Concluding Statement: a concluding statement that restates the claims.

Argumentative units have been annotated with an overall inter-rater reliability of .73. The lowest reliability was reported for counterclaims and rebuttals (which were often labeled as claims). The highest reliability was found for concluding statements. All disagreements were adjudicated by an expert rater.[4]

Figure 3 shows the frequency and average number of tokens per span for each label in the dataset. We notice that the argumentative components are very unevenly distributed. *Claim* and *evidence* occur substantially more frequently than the other labels, with *counterclaims* and *rebuttals* being particularly rare.

In terms of the length of the underlying span for a label, instances of the types *evidence*, *concluding statement* and *lead* correspond to the longest spans. The average length of all essays is 429 words, while the average length of *evidence* is 77 words, which means that, given the frequency of the label, *evidence* is the majority class on the token level. In contrast, *position* and *claim* have the shortest average length.

3.1 Clustering the Data into Underlying Prompts

The dataset is not annotated with prompt information. To obtain the individual prompts, we first use a topic modeling approach (Angelov, 2020), which resulted in a total of 11 clusters of essays. Manual inspection of a random sample of 25 essays per cluster finds two clusters to be a mixture of either 2 or 4 different prompts. We used a k-means clustering approach on tf-idf vectors per essay to

[2] https://www.kaggle.com/competitions/feedback-prize-2021/discussion/296010

[3] Explanations for the labels are directly taken from the competition webpage: https://www.kaggle.com/competitions/feedback-prize-2021/data

[4] https://www.kaggle.com/c/feedback-prize-2021/discussion/297688

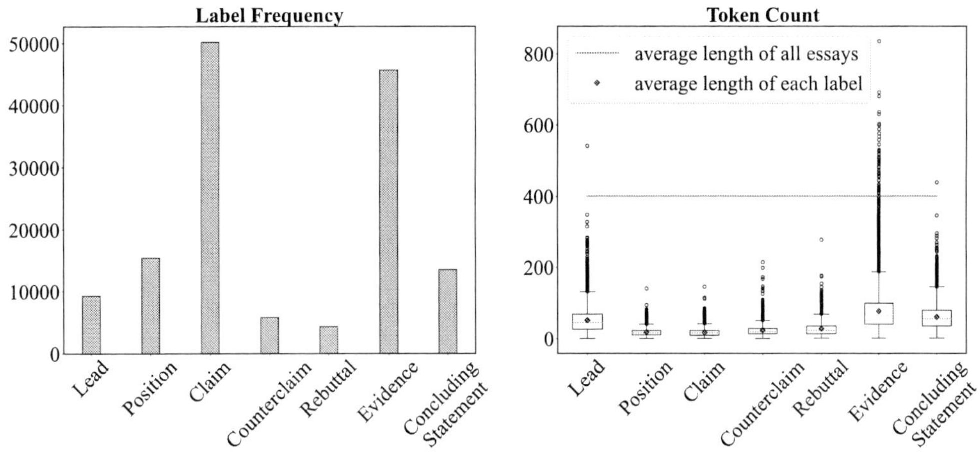

Figure 3: Frequency and token count of labels in the Kaggle Feedback Prize dataset.

further split those clusters into 2 and 4 sub-clusters respectively. The resulting 15 clusters each contain between 689 and 1826 individual essays.

To check the quality of the clusters, we manually annotated 100 instances per cluster and found cluster purity (Manning et al., 2010) to be between 0.78 and 1. Table 1 shows the detected topics and cluster evaluation numbers.

We consider this clustering to be good enough to be used for a topic-based modeling approach without time-intensive manual adjudication of clusters. However, it should be noted that especially for the *"Extracurricular Activities"* cluster with an outlier purity of .78 only, artifacts introduced by impure clustering might occur.

prompt	#essays	purity
Exploring Venus	930	1.00
Face on Mars	817	1.00
Electoral College	1826	1.00
Phones and Driving	705	.90
Driverless Car	1390	.99
Getting Advice	1414	.99
Phones in School	841	.96
Seagoing Cowboys	689	.97
Summer Projects	860	.98
Facial Action Coding	1055	.99
Community Center	712	1.00
Limiting Car Usage	991	.96
Extracurricular Activities	1146	.78
Online Classes	1457	1.00
No Sports at Grade C	761	1.00

Table 1: Topics detected in the dataset, number of essays per topic and purity of the detected cluster.

4 Experimental Study 1 - The Influence of Prompt Information

In this study, we train argument mining models with different combinations of prompt-specific and cross-prompt data and compare their performance on the same test datasets, in order to investigate our first research question: in how far is argument mining prompt-dependent? Furthermore, we analyze the performance difference among argument labels.

4.1 Experimental Setup

As our base model, we adopt a neural architecture developed for the structurally similar sequence labelling task of Named Entity Recognition (Grishman and Sundheim, 1996). As almost one third of all essays contains more than 512 tokens, we exchange the pretrained BERT token classification model (Devlin et al., 2018) for a pretrained Longformer model (Beltagy et al., 2020) where the attention mechanism scales linearly instead of quadratically with input length. The experiment pipeline is shown in Figure 4. We pre-process the annotated training data into tokens with Inside-Outside-Beginning (IOB) tags and use them as the input to the pretrained Longformer model for token classification (longformer-large-4096). After 10 epochs of training with a maximal length of 1536 tokens, the IOB-Tags of tokens are transformed into predictions for different argumentative elements in the post-processing.

We compare several configurations for the training data: In the **all prompts** condition, we train on the complete dataset with all 15 prompts. In the

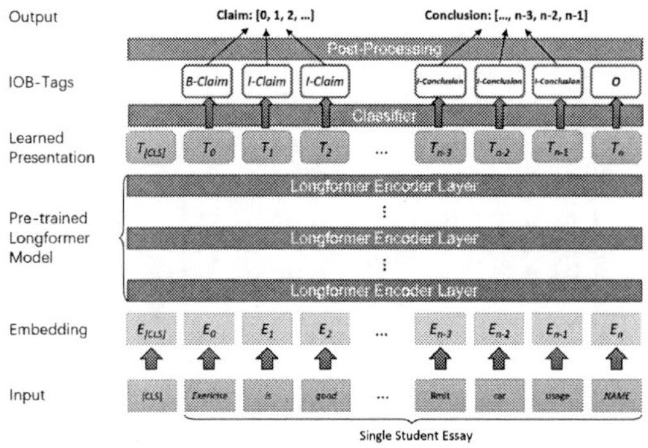

Figure 4: Training pipeline of baseline model.

same prompt condition, we only train on essays from the same prompt as the test data. To create a more controlled setting not influenced by the fraction of essays from the same prompt, we exclude them explicitly in the **other prompts** condition, using 12 of the 14 other prompts for training and 2 for validation. Some prompts in the dataset are closer to each other, as can be seen by the fact that they were confused by our topic clustering approach. To see whether using a **related prompt** is beneficial, we evaluate each of the three prompts *"Driverless Car"*, *"Phones and Driving"* and *"Limiting Car Usage"* under a model trained for either one of the other two prompts.

We split each prompt into 80% training data, 10% evaluation data and 10% test data. To make results across settings comparable, we make sure that we always test on the test data portion only (even for the setting **other prompts** where the whole dataset in a prompt would be available for testing). In order to get comparable models trained on similar amounts of data, we produce another version of the **all prompts** and **other prompts** conditions, where we sample down to the same average amount of training data as used in the **same prompt** condition, called **all prompts – small** and **other prompts – small**.

Following the evaluation scheme proposed by Kaggle, we evaluate based on the overlap between predicted spans and gold standard spans. A prediction is considered a true positive (TP) if the overlap between the prediction and the gold standard is greater than 50% in both directions. Any unmatched ground truths are false negatives (FN), and any unmatched predictions are false positives (FP). The final score is arrived at by calculating TP/FP/FN for each class, then taking the macro F1 score across all classes. Predictions of non-argument text are excluded from the evaluation.

4.2 Experiment 1a - Comparison between Different Training Setups

In our first experiment, we compare the overall performances of the different training setups averaged across all prompts. We cannot use the **related prompt** condition here, as we cannot use all prompts in this condition (simply because not every prompt has a similar other prompt).

Training Data	Avg. Amount Training Data	F1
same prompt	833	.53
other prompts – small	833	.49
all prompts – small	833	.52
other prompts	9983	.52
all prompts	12481	.55

Table 2: Results for Experiment 1a, F1 score averaged over all prompts.

According to the results shown in Table 2, using data from the **same prompt** condition for training brings benefits compared to a setup with the same size of training data drawn from other prompts (**other prompts – small**). **Other prompts** and **all prompts**, in comparison, show the performance on more than 10 times the amount of training data. We observe that using more cross-prompt data (i.e. **other prompts**) provides no advantage compared to fewer data from within the same prompt. However, if some amount of within-prompt data is available, as in **all prompts**, the model benefits from more data. Note that **all prompts** contains all training items from the **same prompt** condition plus material from other prompts. This implies that a prompt-specific model can be slightly improved by adding extra generic data.

4.3 Experiment 1b - Training on Related Prompts

We have seen in Experiment 1a that, given a fixed amount of training data, within-prompt training data from the same prompt is beneficial. However, this can be impractical in a real-life setting, as it might be expensive to obtain new training material for every new essay prompt. Therefore, we investigate in the following experiment whether training on a topic-wise related prompt already helps.

We select three prompts centered around cars and driving: *"Driverless Cars"*, *"Phones and Driving"* and *"Limited Car Usage"*. The fact that these three prompts were often confused during topic clustering shows their relatedness on the lexical level.

Results in Table 3 show that models trained on topic-related data do not have quite the same performance as those trained on data from the same topic or trained on all prompts. The **other prompts – small**, **all prompts – small** and **same prompt** models are the same as in Experiment 1a (but of course only averages over 3 prompts are reported).

Training Data	Avg. Amount Training Data	F1
same prompt	823	.48
other prompts – small	833	.46
all prompts – small	833	.49
related prompt	823	.46

Table 3: Results for Experiment 1b, F1 score averaged over prompts *Driverless Car*, *Phones and Driving* and *Limiting Car Usage*.

4.4 Experiment 2 - Performance Analysis for Individual Argument Labels

As we have seen in Section 3, the dataset is very skewed in terms of the distribution of individual labels. Therefore, we expect the performance of labels with a low frequency a) to be worse than that of more frequent labels and b) to benefit more from larger amounts of training data than the frequent labels.

Results shown in Figure 5 only partially confirm these expectations. We see that performance varies a lot for individual label types, but does not directly reflect the label distribution. While the most infrequent *rebuttal* label also shows the worst classification performance, the labels with the best performance are *lead* and *concluding statement*. Contrary to what we expected, the much more frequent *claim* and *evidence* can be found less precisely, with especially the label *claim* exhibiting the second-lowest performance of all labels.

We speculate that several factors contribute to this behavior. The two argumentation labels with the highest performance are those who potentially benefit most from positional information that a classifier might learn. In the gold standard, 49% of all texts indeed start with a *lead* annotation. If a lead is present in an essay, in 82% of all instances it occurs right in the beginning. Similarly, 70% of all essays end with a *concluding statement* and among all concluding statements, 81% are right at the end of a text. Claims, although very frequent, do not appear at a specific position in the text and are often not clearly marked by discourse markers. We checked the occurrence of a list of about 200 common discourse connectives and discourse markers such as *because*, *although* or *additionally* (Sileo et al., 2019) and found that *counterclaims* and *rebuttals* were most strongly marked by such words - a possible reason why their performance, although these labels are infrequent, is not far below that of claims.

We checked common confusions between labels in our classification results. Table 4 shows that the majority of all confusions occurs between a label and no assigned span, indicating that the assignment of correct argumentation unit boundaries is a problem, which leads to numerous spans with no counterpart with a sufficient overlap. When comparing the number of unmatched gold standard labels (3521) with that of unmatched predicted labels (5781), we see our algorithm tends to assign a label rather than not assign anything. Among the actual confusions between two labels, we observe some confusions also reported for humans, such as counterclaims often being mislabelled as claims.

5 Experimental Study 2 - What do we actually Learn?

Aiming to answer our second research question of whether the algorithms are more susceptible to prompt-specific or general information, we now transform the original data into **topic-only** and **structure-only** versions.

5.1 Experimental Setup

Experimental Study 1 indicated that the identification of argumentative elements benefits from prompt-specific information. However, it remains unclear whether we actually learn to detect topic words constituting, e.g., a typical claim for a certain Topic X or structural elements of a claim in Topic X, which could also be found in other topics. To disentangle the two effects from each other, we perform an additional set of analyses, as detailed in the following.

We filter the vocabulary according to how often it appears within a specific prompt and in the overall dataset. Similar to a tf-idf approach (Ramos et al., 2003), we consider vocabulary prompt-specific if it appears often within the essays of one prompt, but infrequently within the essays of other

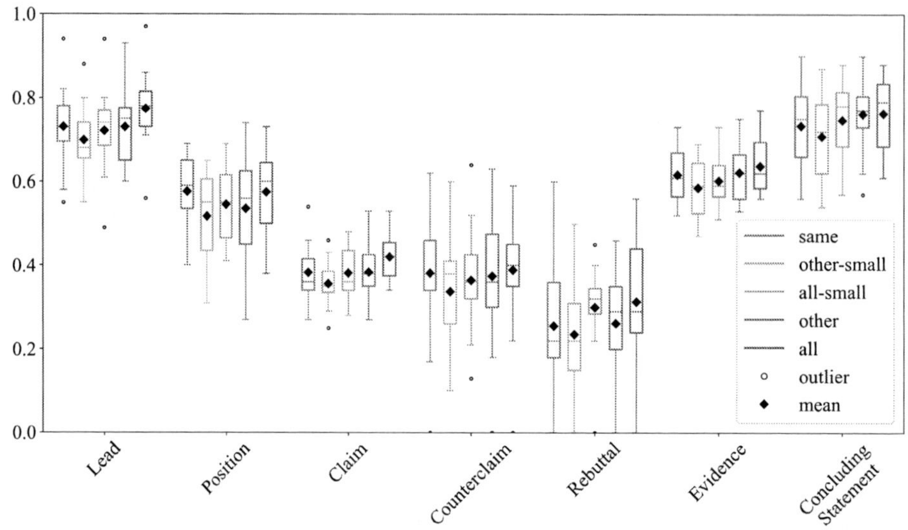

Figure 5: Results for Experiment 2, F1 scores of each label in different settings

	Lead	Position	Claim	Counter-claim	Rebuttal	Evidence	Conclu. Statem.	None
Lead	715	35	2	0	0	17	0	135
Position	38	765	12	6	2	11	2	578
Claim	8	75	1659	4	17	153	4	2912
Conterclaim	2	6	33	264	2	19	1	268
Rebuttal	0	4	19	4	149	23	2	234
Evidence	22	17	242	39	66	2934	29	1449
Conclu. Statem.	0	39	21	4	4	42	1098	205
None	147	245	1145	157	144	1388	302	N.A.

Table 4: Confusion matrix between gold standard (columns) and results in the *same prompt* setting (rows)

prompts. For example, the word *Mars* appears 7851 times in the *"Face on Mars"* prompt, but only 448 times in all other prompts. We rank word types in each prompt by their tf-idf value and consider the top 1000 types as the **topic words** of each prompt.

We then produce 4 versions of the data. In the **structure-only** versions, topic words in each prompt are replaced by the mask word *"dummy"* (**structure-only-dummy**) or their part-of-speech (POS) tags (**structure-only-pos**). The usage of POS tags is intended to keep the syntactic structure intact. In the complementary **topic-only** versions, every occurrence of any non-topical words as well as every function word is replaced by the dummy word (**topic-only-dummy**) or its POS tag (**topic-only-pos**). Table 5 shows an example for the resulting sentences.

We now perform scoring experiments comparable to those from Experimental Study 1 on the modified data. Similar to a feature ablation test, we want to examine how masking some part of the information present in an essay affects the classification outcome.

5.2 Experiment 3a - Modified Test Data

In this experiment, we use the method described above to modify only the test data (the same 10% test data used in Experiment 1). We compare the prediction of models from Experimental Study 1 trained in the settings **same prompt** and **other prompts – small** on the modified data in order to test what kind of information the models have learned. We hypothesize that the **same prompt** model learns both prompt-related and generic structural information, while **other prompts – small** - in the absence of prompt-specific information - learns only general structure as predictor for argumentative elements.

The results shown as orange bars in Figure 6 reveal that, unsurprisingly, the general performance of models is much lower than the performance on the original test data. Nevertheless, we see

Version	Sentence
Original	The Face on Mars is a natural landform
Structure-Only-Dummy	The dummy on dummy is a dummy dummy
Structure-Only-Pos	The [NNP] on [NNP] is a [JJ] [NN]
Topic-Only-Dummy	dummy Face dummy Mars dummy dummy natural landform
Topic-Only-Pos	[DT] Face [IN] Mars [VBZ] [DT] natural landform

Table 5: Four versions of one sentence generated according to our four individual conditions.

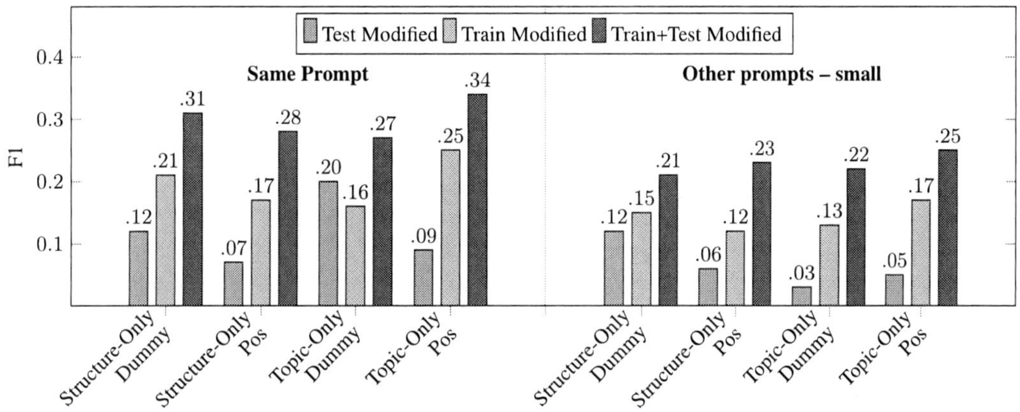

Figure 6: Performance of using the model trained on original data to evaluate modified testing data (test modified), training a model on modified data and testing it on the original testing data (train modified), or both training and testing on modified data.

that the models trained on the **same prompt** perform better on topic-only data than structure-only data. In the **other prompts – small** setting, in contrast, structure-only training data works better than topic-only data, indicating that those models indeed mainly learn structural information.

5.3 Experiment 3b - Modified Training Data

Similar to the **same prompt** and **other prompts – small** settings in Experimental Study 1, we train two models for each prompt on each of the four modified versions of the data. By applying these models to the original test data, we get the results shown as green bars in Figure 6.

Among all models, we expect models trained on topic-only data from **other prompts – small** to have the worst performance, since the predictors learned in these models are theoretically only content words related to other topics. However, the models trained on topic-only data have comparable performance to other models in the **other prompts – small** setting, a fact that needs further investigation and that might be due to either impure clusters or content word filtering (such that the training data still contains some usable lexical information), or to the fact that positional information is a strong predictor present in all our modified data variants.

In the **same prompt** setting, models trained on topic-only-pos data also have the best performance. But once the POS-tags are changed into *"dummy"* (i.e. topic-only-dummy), the models cannot beat those trained on structure-only data.

5.4 Experiment 3c - Modified Training and Test Data

Finally, we use the models trained in Experiment 3b on modified data and test on modified test data as well. Results are shown in Figure 6 as blue bars. Unsurprisingly, these models with train and test data modified in the same way yield better performance compared to those where only the train or the test data was modified and, similar to the results above, models trained on data from **same-prompt** perform better than those trained on data from **other prompts – small** in general. They still perform far below the level of the original experiments, indicating that in both conditions, models benefit from both structural and topical information. However, the loss is larger in the **other** conditions than for **same**.

Similar to the results in Experiment 3b, the models trained on topic-only-pos in the **same-prompt** setting have the best performance, because not only topic related information is kept in the training data, but also limited structural information is included by the POS-tags.

6 Conclusion

This work set out to investigate the importance of topic information in educational argument mining tasks. For this purpose, we first clustered a recently published dataset of student essays into underlying prompts. Secondly, we presented a study on the effect of prompt-specific and cross-prompt training material in the identification of argumentative elements. Results showed that within-prompt training data is beneficial when a fixed limited amount of training data is used. This advantage can be overcome by larger amounts of additional cross-prompt data. In the analysis of argumentative elements, we found that *lead* and *conclusion* can be best identified in all settings, presumably because of their relatively fixed position. Lastly, we separated topical from structural information in the essays. From experiments with this modified data, we found that argument mining benefits both from topic words and structure words, i.e. the information is not redundant, but that, unsurprisingly, topical information has a tendency to be more important in within-prompt classification while structure is more relevant across prompts.

These findings provide the following insights for future research: first, learning curve studies could investigate an optimal trade-off between topic-specific and generic training data. Second, the argumentative elements identified in student essays could be meaningful for the generation of formative feedback directed towards students, such as highlighting different argumentative elements. Another research direction is the evaluation of argument quality through analyzing discourse relations between these argument components in order to generate feedback towards coherence and cohesion aspects of student essays.

Acknowledgements

This work was conducted in the framework of the Research Cluster D^2L^2 "Digitalization, Diversity and Lifelong Learning – Consequences for Higher Education" of the FernUniversität in Hagen, Germany [5]. We thank our student assistants Finn Brodmann and Joey Pehlke (University of Duisburg-Essen) who contributed to data preparation and analysis.

References

Dimo Angelov. 2020. Top2Vec: Distributed Representations of Topics. *arXiv e-prints* pages arXiv–2008.

Iz Beltagy, Matthew E Peters, and Arman Cohan. 2020. Longformer: The Long-document Transformer. *arXiv preprint arXiv:2004.05150* .

Jill Burstein, Daniel Marcu, and Kevin Knight. 2003. Finding the WRITE Stuff: Automatic Identification of Discourse Structure in Student Essays. *IEEE Intelligent Systems* 18(1):32–39.

Johannes Daxenberger, Steffen Eger, Ivan Habernal, Christian Stab, and Iryna Gurevych. 2017. What is the Essence of a Claim? Cross-Domain Claim Identification. *arXiv preprint arXiv:1704.07203* .

Jacob Devlin, Ming-Wei Chang, Kenton Lee, and Kristina Toutanova. 2018. BERT: Pre-training of Deep Bidirectional Transformers for Language Understanding. *arXiv preprint arXiv:1810.04805* .

Michael Fromm, Evgeniy Faerman, and Thomas Seidl. 2019. TACAM: Topic And Context Aware Argument Mining. In *2019 IEEE/WIC/ACM International Conference on Web Intelligence (WI)*. IEEE, pages 99–106.

Sylviane Granger, Estelle Dagneaux, Fanny Meunier, Magali Paquot, et al. 2009. *International Corpus of Learner English*, volume 2. Presses universitaires de Louvain Louvain-la-Neuve.

Ralph Grishman and Beth M Sundheim. 1996. Message Understanding Conference-6: A Brief History. In *COLING 1996 Volume 1: The 16th International Conference on Computational Linguistics*.

John Lawrence and Chris Reed. 2020. Argument Mining: A Survey. *Computational Linguistics* 45(4):765–818.

Christopher Manning, Prabhakar Raghavan, and Hinrich Schütze. 2010. Introduction to Information Retrieval. *Natural Language Engineering* 16(1):100–103.

Raquel Mochales and Aagje Ieven. 2009. Creating an Argumentation Corpus: do Theories Apply to Real Arguments? A Case Study on the Legal Argumentation of the ECHR. In *Proceedings of the 12th international conference on artificial intelligence and law*. pages 21–30.

Nathan Ong, Diane Litman, and Alexandra Brusilovsky. 2014. Ontology-based Argument Mining and Automatic Essay Scoring. In *Proceedings of the First Workshop on Argumentation Mining*. pages 24–28.

[5] https://e.feu.de/english-d2l2

Isaac Persing and Vincent Ng. 2015. Modeling Argument Strength in Student Essays. In *Proceedings of the 53rd Annual Meeting of the Association for Computational Linguistics and the 7th International Joint Conference on Natural Language Processing (Volume 1: Long Papers)*. pages 543–552.

Isaac Persing and Vincent Ng. 2016. End-to-End Argumentation Mining in Student Essays. In *Proceedings of the 2016 Conference of the North American Chapter of the Association for Computational Linguistics: Human Language Technologies*. pages 1384–1394.

Juan Ramos et al. 2003. Using TF-IDF to Determine Word Relevance in Document Queries. In *Proceedings of the first instructional conference on machine learning*. Citeseer, volume 242, pages 29–48.

Oliver Scheuer, Frank Loll, Niels Pinkwart, and Bruce M McLaren. 2010. Computer-supported argumentation: A review of the state of the art. *International Journal of Computer-supported collaborative learning* 5(1):43–102.

Damien Sileo, Tim Van De Cruys, Camille Pradel, and Philippe Muller. 2019. Mining Discourse Markers for Unsupervised Sentence Representation Learning. In *Proceedings of the 2019 Conference of the North American Chapter of the Association for Computational Linguistics: Human Language Technologies, Volume 1 (Long and Short Papers)*. Association for Computational Linguistics, Minneapolis, Minnesota, pages 3477–3486.

Christian Stab and Iryna Gurevych. 2014a. Annotating Argument Components and Relations in Persuasive Essays. In *Proceedings of COLING 2014, the 25th international conference on computational linguistics: Technical papers*. pages 1501–1510.

Christian Stab and Iryna Gurevych. 2014b. Identifying Argumentative Discourse Structures in Persuasive Essays. In *Proceedings of the 2014 Conference on Empirical Methods in Natural Language Processing (EMNLP)*. pages 46–56.

Christian Stab and Iryna Gurevych. 2017. Parsing Argumentation Structures in Persuasive Essays. *Computational Linguistics* 43(3):619–659.

Christian Stab, Tristan Miller, and Iryna Gurevych. 2018. Cross-Topic Argument Mining from Heterogeneous Sources using Attention-based Neural Networks. *arXiv preprint arXiv:1802.05758* .

Stephen E Toulmin. 1958. The Uses of Argument .

Dietrich Trautmann, Johannes Daxenberger, Christian Stab, Hinrich Schütze, and Iryna Gurevych. 2020. Fine-Grained Argument Unit Recognition and Classification. In *Proceedings of the AAAI Conference on Artificial Intelligence*. volume 34, pages 9048–9056.

Marilyn Walker, Jean E Fox Tree, Pranav Anand, Rob Abbott, and Joseph King. 2012. A Corpus for Research on Deliberation and Debate. In *Proceedings of the Eighth International Conference on Language Resources and Evaluation (LREC'12)*. pages 812–817.

Ursula Wingate. 2012. 'Argument!' helping Students understand What Essay Writing is about. *Journal of English for academic purposes* 11(2):145–154.

ALEN App: Persuasive Writing Support To Foster English Language Learning

Thiemo Wambsganss[1], Andrew Caines[2], Paula Buttery[2]
[1] Machine Learning for Education Laboratory, EPFL, Switzerland
[2] ALTA Institute & Computer Laboratory, University of Cambridge, United Kingdom
thiemo.wambsganss@epfl.ch
{andrew.caines,paula.buttery}@cl.cam.ac.uk

Abstract

This paper introduces a novel tool to support and engage English language learners with feedback on the quality of their argument structures. We present an approach which automatically detects claim-premise structures and provides visual feedback to the learner to prompt them to repair any broken argumentation structures. To investigate, if our persuasive feedback on language learners' essay writing tasks engages and supports them in learning better English language, we designed the ALEN app (Argumentation for Learning English). We leverage an argumentation mining model trained on texts written by students and embed it in a writing support tool which provides students with feedback in their essay writing process. We evaluated our tool in two field-studies with a total of 28 students from a German high school to investigate the effects of adaptive argumentation feedback on their learning of English. The quantitative results suggest that using the ALEN app leads to a high self-efficacy, ease-of-use, intention to use and perceived usefulness for students in their English language learning process. Moreover, the qualitative answers indicate the potential benefits of combining grammar feedback with discourse level argumentation mining.

1 Introduction

Novel advances from Natural Language Processing (NLP) and Machine Learning (ML) are increasingly utilized and embedded in learner-centered writing support tools (e.g., Lauscher et al. (2019); Wang et al. (2020); Wambsganss et al. (2020a)). For example, researchers have successfully embedded novel argumentation mining models to identify persuasive components and their relations in order to provide students adaptive writing feedback (Lawrence and Reed, 2019; Wambsganss et al., 2020a). As Jonassen and Kim (2010) highlighted argumentation learning consists of at least two different dimensions: a) to train argumentation skills (*learning to argue*) and b) to use argumentation as a dialectical method to achieve other learning outcomes (*arguing to learn*), such as critical thinking, problem-solving or factual knowledge (Kuhn, 1992; Jonassen and Kim, 2010; Asterhan and Schwarz, 2016). While the former dimension of argumentation is steadily investigated in the context of NLP-based feedback with argumentation mining on students' learning processes (e.g., Lawrence and Reed (2019); Pardo et al. (2018)), the latter described learning context bears still promising potential for NLP-based argumentation feedback opportunities to foster other learning outcomes of students (Roz, 2004).

In this vein, Putra et al. (2021) has suggested that providing English language learners with feedback on their essays from a discourse perspective can enhance text coherence and comprehension. Nevertheless, little work exists which demonstrates the embedding of argumentation mining in writing support tools to investigate the effects of "arguing to learn", e.g., to engage and foster secondary language learning (Lawrence and Reed, 2019). In fact, different methods from NLP and ML have been used to provide students feedback on their grammatical errors or syntactical sentence structures to foster language learning (e.g., White and Rozovskaya (2020); Katinskaia and Yangarber (2021); Kerz et al. (2021)), but insights on the effects and concepts of discourse level feedback based on argumentation modelling on students learning process are few and far between.

Hence, in this paper, we demonstrate the ALEN app. The learning application provides English language learners with discourse level feedback in persuasive writing exercises. The underlying model is trained on a corpus of 1000 student-written texts to detect claims and premises as well as their relations (Wambsganss et al., 2020b). To investigate, if persuasive feedback on language learners' essay writing tasks engages and supports them in learning

Proceedings of the 17th Workshop on Innovative Use of NLP for Building Educational Applications (BEA 2022), pages 134 - 140

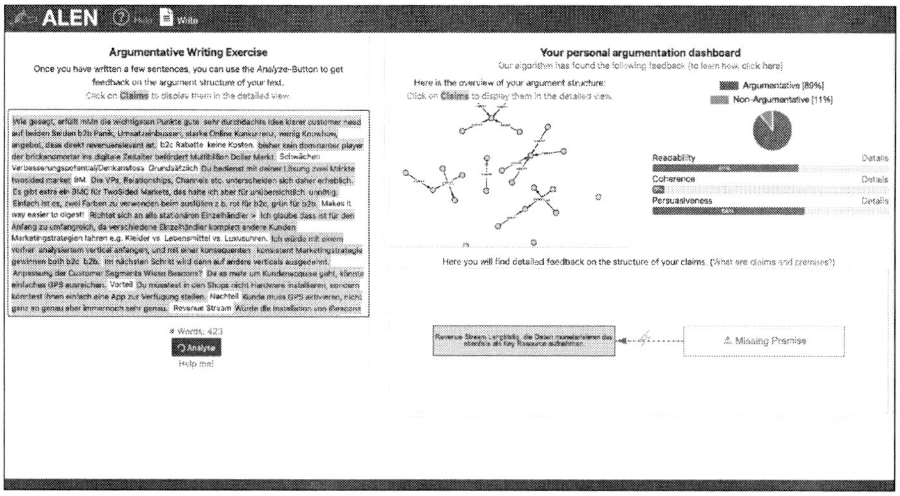

Figure 1: Screenshot of the ALEN interface based on the design of Wambsganss et al. (2020a). A English language learner is conducting a essay exercises and receives visual feedback to repair any broken argumentation structures.

better English language, we evaluated our tool in two field-studies with 28 students from a German high school. Our objective is to conduct a proof-of-concept study to explore the impact of prompting English language learners to repair any broken argumentation structure. Hence, we asked students to conduct an Cambridge English Assessment task for the language level B2 and use the ALEN app to write and evaluate their text's argumentation level and persuasiveness. Based on the literature stream of "arguing-to-learn" (e.g., (Jonassen and Kim, 2010)), our hypothesis is that adaptive argumentation feedback might engage students to evaluate their text, reflect about their discourse level writing and thus learn better English. The results from our small-scale evaluation provide first suggestions that adaptive argumentation feedback in English language learners essay writing task leads to a high self-efficacy, ease-of-use, intention to use and usefulness for students in their language learning process. Future work is needed to investigate the effects of adaptive argumentation support in large-scale field studies to measure the long-term learning success on students language learning outcomes.

2 Related Work

For the most part, NLP and ML have been used in education technology for language learners in ways which relate to word-level feedback and text scoring. Popular mobile applications such as Duolingo tend to focus on vocabulary and phrase learning, a writing assistant such as Grammarly gives feedback on spelling and grammar, as does the essay practice website Write & Improve whilst also providing essay scores pinned to the CEFR proficiency scale (Settles et al., 2020; Nadejde and Tetreault, 2019; Yannakoudakis et al., 2018). At the same time, there is now a growing interest in providing automated feedback at the discourse level, and efforts have been made to accumulate and analyse the training materials needed for feedback on argument quality – namely with the GAQCorpus (Ng et al., 2020; Lauscher et al., 2020).

Thus far only a few practical tools have been developed to provide learners with argumentation feedback. For instance, MARGOT is available as a web application and processes a text that is input in the corresponding editor field (Lippi and Torroni, 2016). The text is analyzed, claims are displayed in bold font, whereas premises are displayed in italic style. Or in TARGER a user can analyze the persuasive structure of an input text. Chernodub et al. (2019) trained multiple models on three different corpora along with three different pre-trained word embeddings. Thus, the user not only puts in a text to analyze, but different argumentation models may be selected. The results are then presented below the input, with claims being highlighted in red and premises being marked in green.

Neither MARGOT nor TARGER are easy-to-use in normal pedagogical scenarios, since the student has to select from several different models (the nuances of the choices may not be clear) and then

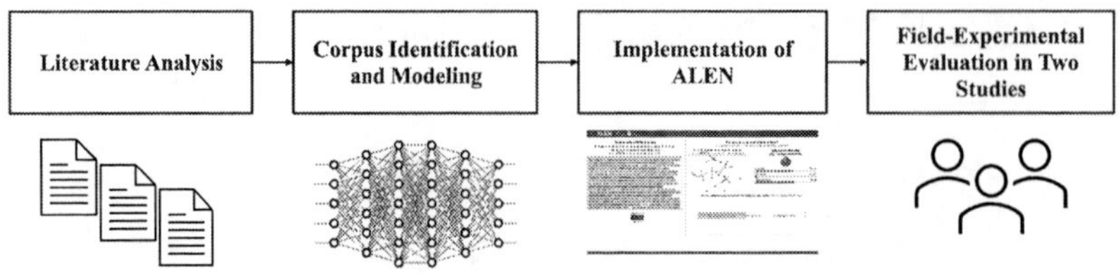

Figure 2: Overview of our methodology for building the ALEN app.

copy her text into the input field. This excludes students who are unsure about choosing from different models. Moreover, the models are not all trained on text extracted from the educational domain and therefore, might not be applicable to every pedagogical scenarios. Besides, argumentation mining was successfully embedded in AL (short for Argumentation Learning), a learner-centered tool which improved students persuasive writing skills with adaptive feedback (Wambsganss et al., 2020a). Moreover, Wambsganss et al. (2021) presented ArgueTutor, a dialogue-based argumentation learning tool, which tutors students with adaptive scaffolds and theory-explanation through a persuasive writing task. However, to the best of our knowledge literature on the embedding and demonstration of argumentation mining approach to foster language learning through engaging students in persuasive writing exercises are rather rare.

3 Design of ALEN

To build *ALEN*, we followed a three step methodology (see Figure 2). First, we analyzed the current state of argumentation learning and argumentation mining achievements in literature. Therefore, we reviewed multiple papers from the fields of *Educational Technology*, such as Pinkwart et al. (2009); Osborne et al. (2016); Scheuer et al. (2010); Wambsganss et al. (2020a); Wambsganss and Niklaus (2022); Weber et al. (2021) and *NLP*, such as Stab and Gurevych (2014, 2017); Wachsmuth et al. (2017); Lawrence and Reed (2019); Lippi and Torroni (2015); Landolt et al. (2021). Our goal was to gain a broad overview of current systems and approaches to support language learning with discourse-level feedback. With these insights, we guided our next research steps in building and designing ALEN.

Second, we investigated different corpora and trained models for argument detection and classification across multiple domains. We started by searching the literature for a corpus that fulfilled the following criteria: 1) the corpus contains annotated persuasive student essays, 2) it has a sufficient corpus size to be able to use the trained model in a real-world scenario, and 3) the annotations are based on a rigorous annotation guideline for guiding the annotators towards a moderate agreement. The business model peer review corpus published in Wambsganss et al. (2020b) fulfilled all these requirements. The corpus consists of 1000 business model peer feedback essays written by students extracted from a large-scale lecture scenario. We used the algorithm of Wambsganss et al. (2020b), to train a multi-class classifier on the sentence level to detect the argument components and their relations. For argument component classification, a Support Vector Machine (SVM) achieved the best results, with an accuracy of 65.4% on the test set. Regarding the persuasive relation classification, a binary classification task, an SVM again achieved the best results on the corpus, obtaining an accuracy of 72.1% on the test set. More information on the model and the replicated features we used can be found in (Wambsganss et al., 2020b,a).

Third, we designed and built an adaptive writing support system that provides students with individual feedback on their argumentation skill level during an English essay writing task based on our model. For the design of the tool, we followed the design principles of Wambsganss et al. (2020a). ALEN provides the user with a simple text input field with a word count in which they can write or copy a text (see Figure 1). Next to the text input, the user can ask for feedback on the argumentation structure of their text in a personal learning dashboard. The dashboard provides different granularity levels of feedback, which enables the user to control the amount of feedback information displayed (Scheiter and Gerjets, 2007). A visual graph-based representation of a text's argumentation structure and three summarizing scores provide a first assessment of the text's quality. To offer the user with a visual representation of argument structures in their essay, the identified claims are highlighted in green and the premises are highlighted in yellow in the written text. A visual graph-based representation of text-based augmentations has been found to be an effective element to guide learners argumentation (i.e., representational guidance theory (Suthers, 2003)). A more detailed perspective of the argument's discourse can be obtained by clicking on the highlighted text fields or the nodes in the graph. This displays whether a claim is well-supported or if it is missing a premise. Moreover, best practices and explanations about argumentation and argumentation theory are provided by clicking on the "*Explanation*" or "*Help*" button .

Three summarizing scores, calculated following Wambsganss et al. (2020a) – readability, coherence and persuasiveness – provide the student with an assessment of their text to provide automatic proficiency feedback. The methodology for computing the scores, as well as actual tips, action steps, and explanations on how the learner can improve her score level, can be found by clicking on the scores or on *details*.

4 Evaluating ALEN

Our objective was to empirically investigate the effect of our adaptive argumentation feedback on students' English language learning and their perception of usefulness in a real-world educational writing scenario. Therefore, we created a field experiment design in which language students were instructed to complete a persuasive writing exercise while receiving adaptive argumentation feedback from ALEN.[1] The study was conduct in cooperation with the English department of a German speaking high-school. We conduct two different studies based on a similar field-experimental design in two different English classes in the 12th grade. In both studies, we asked students to conduct a persuasive English language writing tasks. The only difference between study 1 and study 2 were the post-survey measurements (see following paragraph). The experiments were both conducted in the computer room of the high-school on desktop devices. In total, 28 students participated in both studies. The participants were on average 17.17 years old (SD = 0.5384); 11 were male, 11 were female, and 6 non-binary. The experiment design was two-fold (see Figure 3): 1) a persuasive writing task and 2) a post-survey.

1) Persuasive writing task: The students were given a link to a survey in the tool *unipark*[2]. We used unipark, since it is a standard tool for scientific experiments which allowed us to embed ALEN in scientific construct testing. Before receiving the actual writing tasks, the students were asked to watch an introduction video about the usage of ALEN to ensure that every participant is familiar with the interface and the functionalities of our app. Next, the students received one of three randomly assigned writing tasks retrieved from Cambridge English Assessment for the language level B2[3]. For example: "*Every country in the world has problems with pollution and damage to the environment. Do you think these problems can be solved? Evaluate the question within a 200-word text about the pros and cons.*" We asked the participants to use the ALEN app to write and evaluate their text's argumentation level and persuasiveness. During the task, students could click the analyze button where they received adaptive argumentation evaluation on their text.

2) Post-survey: In the post-survey of study 1 (ten participants), we measured the perceived ease-of-use, the intention to use, and the perceived usefulness for the participants following the technology acceptance model of Venkatesh and Bala (2008). Example items for the three constructs were: "*The use of the argumentation tool enables me to write better persuasive texts*", "*Imagining the tool would be available in my next course, would I use it?*", or "*I would find the tool to be flexible to interact with.*"

For study 2 (18 participants) our goal was to control for the self-efficacy of students for the task of English language learning based on seven items following Bandura (1991) to control for self-regulated learning. Exemplary items included, "*Compared to other students in this class, I expect to do well.*", or "*I am confident that I will be able to solve the problems and tasks set for me in this course.*". All constructs were measured on a Likert scale from 1 to 7 (1: totally disagree; 7: totally agree, with 4 being a neutral statement). Finally, we captured some demographic information and asked three qualitative questions: "*What did you particularly like about the use of the argumentation tool?*", "*What*

[1] The study design was approved by the institutional ethics board, the head of the high school we worked with and the legal representative of the participants.

[2] https://www.unipark.com/

[3] https://www.cambridgeenglish.org/exams-and-tests/first/

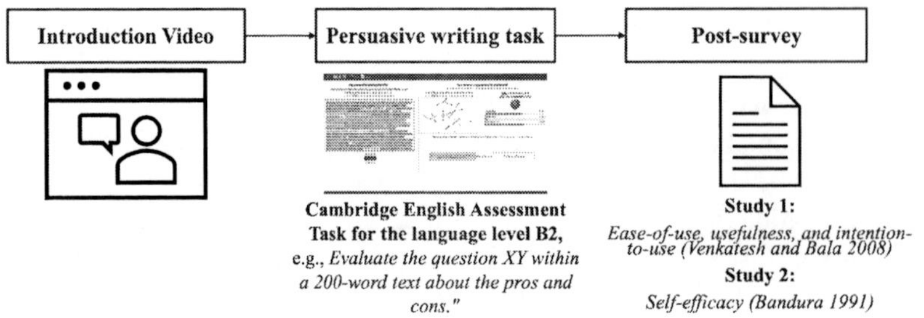

Figure 3: Overview of our evaluation of ALEN in two field-studies.

else could be improved?" and "*Do you have any other ideas?*".

Results

Study 1: The *perceived ease-of-use* of students using ALEN in experiment one for the English language task had a mean value of 5.77 (SD= 0.96, normalized 0.82). The *perceived usefulness* for ALEN was rated with a mean value of 5.60 (SD= 0.69, normalized 0.8) and the *intention to use* the tool as a English learning tool continuously was rated with 5.7 (SD= 0.79, normalized 0.81). All of the results are positive when compared to the mid-point scale of 4, indicating a positive technology acceptance of ALEN (Venkatesh and Bala, 2008).

Study 2: For the second study we received 18 valid answer from 4 males, 6 non-binary, an 8 females. Participants of the study 2 rated their *self-efficacy* for English language learning tasks with a mean value of 5.02 (SD= 1.24, normalized 0.71). This might indicate that ALEN could increase engagement and motivation when practising and learning persuasive English essay writing (Bandura, 1991). Finally, we analyzed the qualitative answers of both experiments and clustered similar responses into categories. In conclusion, the adaptive feedback based on in-text highlighting and the graph overview in combination with discourse level feedback was noted favorably multiple times. At the same time, students complained that the persuasive elements were sometimes wrongly highlighted. Moreover, many students asked for additional grammar feedback, since sometimes they were not sure if an argument was not persuasive or only the grammar structure was erroneous.

5 Discussion and Conclusion

We have presented *ALEN*, a novel writing support tool that provides students with persuasive feedback during an English language learning task. We embedded the SVM model of (Wambsganss et al., 2020b) to identify claim-premise structures in learners' texts and evaluated the proof-of-concept in two field-studies with 28 students. Based on the literature stream of "arguing-to-learn" (e.g., (Jonassen and Kim, 2010)), our hypothesis was that adaptive argumentation feedback might engage students to evaluate their text, reflect about their discourse level writing and thus learn better English. Our results suggest that the ALEN app leads to a high self-efficacy in the task of English essay writing and a high technology acceptance (intention to use, perceived usefulness and ease-of-use) for K12 language learners. Our study extends the current literature stream of NLP-based learning tools for argumentation (e.g., Wambsganss et al. (2020a); Afrin et al. (2021)) by adding a new perspective to leverage NLP-based argumentation feedback as a dialectical for other learning outcomes (i.e., Jonassen and Kim (2010)).

For future work, we suggest to combine discourse level argumentation feedback with grammar feedback for language learners to provide them with more nuanced guidance in their language learning process. Moreover, further studies are needed which investigated the human-computer interaction of discourse-level writing support tools for language learners. Finally, future research is needed to investigate the effects of adaptive argumentation support in large-scale field studies to measure the long-term learning success on students language learning outcomes.

Acknowledgements

The first author was supported by the Swiss National Science Foundation (grant 200207). The second and third authors are supported by Cambridge University Press & Assessment, University of Cambridge.

References

Tazin Afrin, Omid Kashefi, Christopher Olshefski, Diane Litman, Rebecca Hwa, and Amanda Godley. 2021. Effective Interfaces for Student-Driven Revision Sessions for Argumentative Writing. In *Proceedings of the 2021 CHI Conference on Human Factors in Computing Systems*, pages 1–13, New York, NY, USA. Acm.

Christa S.C. Asterhan and Baruch B. Schwarz. 2016. Argumentation for Learning: Well-Trodden Paths and Unexplored Territories. *Educational Psychologist*, 51(2):164–187.

Albert Bandura. 1991. Social cognitive theory of self-regulation. *Organizational Behavior and Human Decision Processes*, 50(2):248–287.

Artem Chernodub, Oleksiy Oliynyk, Philipp Heidenreich, Alexander Bondarenko, Matthias Hagen, Chris Biemann, and Alexander Panchenko. 2019. TARGER: Neural Argument Mining at Your Fingertips. pages 195–200.

David H. Jonassen and Bosung Kim. 2010. Arguing to learn and learning to argue: Design justifications and guidelines. *Educational Technology Research and Development*, 58(4):439–457.

Anisia Katinskaia and Roman Yangarber. 2021. Assessing grammatical correctness in language learning. In *Proceedings of the 16th Workshop on Innovative Use of NLP for Building Educational Applications*, pages 135–146, Online. Association for Computational Linguistics.

Elma Kerz, Daniel Wiechmann, Yu Qiao, Emma Tseng, and Marcus Ströbel. 2021. Automated classification of written proficiency levels on the CEFR-scale through complexity contours and RNNs. In *Proceedings of the 16th Workshop on Innovative Use of NLP for Building Educational Applications*, pages 199–209, Online. Association for Computational Linguistics.

Deanna Kuhn. 1992. Thinking as Argument. *Harvard Educational Review*, 62(2):155–179.

Severin Landolt, Thiemo Wambsganß, and Matthias Söllner. 2021. A taxonomy for deep learning in natural language processing. In *Proceedings of the Annual Hawaii International Conference on System Sciences*, pages 1–10, Hawaii, USA.

Anne Lauscher, Goran Glavaš, and Simone Paolo Ponzetto. 2019. An Argument-Annotated Corpus of Scientific Publications. pages 40–46.

Anne Lauscher, Lily Ng, Courtney Napoles, and Joel Tetreault. 2020. Rhetoric, logic, and dialectic: Advancing theory-based argument quality assessment in natural language processing. In *Proceedings of the 28th International Conference on Computational Linguistics*, Barcelona, Spain (Online). International Committee on Computational Linguistics.

John Lawrence and Chris Reed. 2019. Argument mining: A survey. *Computational Linguistics*, 45(4):765–818.

Marco Lippi and Paolo Torroni. 2015. Argument mining: A machine learning perspective. In *International Workshop on Theory and Applications of Formal Argumentation*, pages 163–176. Springer.

Marco Lippi and Paolo Torroni. 2016. MARGOT: A web server for argumentation mining. *Expert Systems with Applications*, 65:292–303.

Maria Nadejde and Joel Tetreault. 2019. Personalizing grammatical error correction: Adaptation to proficiency level and L1. In *Proceedings of the 5th Workshop on Noisy User-generated Text (W-NUT 2019)*, Hong Kong, China. Association for Computational Linguistics.

Lily Ng, Anne Lauscher, Joel Tetreault, and Courtney Napoles. 2020. Creating a domain-diverse corpus for theory-based argument quality assessment. In *Proceedings of the 7th Workshop on Argument Mining*, Online. Association for Computational Linguistics.

Jonathan F. Osborne, J. Bryan Henderson, Anna MacPherson, Evan Szu, Andrew Wild, and Shi Ying Yao. 2016. The development and validation of a learning progression for argumentation in science. *Journal of Research in Science Teaching*, 53(6):821–846.

Abelardo Pardo, Kathryn Bartimote, Simon Buckingham Shum, Shane Dawson, Jing Gao, Dragan Gašević, Steve Leichtweis, Danny Liu, Roberto Martínez-Maldonado, Negin Mirriahi, Adon Christian Michael Moskal, Jurgen Schulte, George Siemens, and Lorenzo Vigentini. 2018. OnTask: Delivering Data-Informed, Personalized Learning Support Actions. *Journal of Learning Analytics*, 5(3):235–249.

Niels Pinkwart, Kevin Ashley, Collin Lynch, and Vincent Aleven. 2009. Evaluating an Intelligent Tutoring System for Making Legal Arguments with Hypotheticals. *International Journal of Artificial Intelligence in Education*, 19:401–424.

Jan Wira Gotama Putra, Simone Teufel, and Takenobu Tokunaga. 2021. Parsing argumentative structure in English-as-foreign-language essays. In *Proceedings of the 16th Workshop on Innovative Use of NLP for Building Educational Applications*, pages 97–109, Online. Association for Computational Linguistics.

Ivanič Roz. 2004. Discourses of writing and learning to write. *Language and Education*, 18(3):220–245.

Katharina Scheiter and Peter Gerjets. 2007. Learner control in hypermedia environments. *Educational Psychology Review*, 19(3):285–307.

Oliver Scheuer, Frank Loll, Niels Pinkwart, and Bruce M. McLaren. 2010. Computer-supported argumentation: A review of the state of the art. *International Journal of Computer-Supported Collaborative Learning*, 5(1):43–102.

Burr Settles, Geoffrey T. LaFlair, and Masato Hagiwara. 2020. Machine learning–driven language assessment. *Transactions of the Association for Computational Linguistics*, 8.

Christian Stab and Iryna Gurevych. 2014. Annotating Argument Components and Relations in Persuasive Essays. In *Proceedings of COLING 2014, the 25th International Conference on Computational Linguistics: Technical Papers*, pages 1501–1510.

Christian Stab and Iryna Gurevych. 2017. Parsing Argumentation Structures in Persuasive Essays. *Computational Linguistics*, 43(3):619–659.

Daniel D. Suthers. 2003. Representational Guidance for Collaborative Inquiry. In *Arguing to Learn*, pages 27–46. Springer.

Viswanath Venkatesh and Hillol Bala. 2008. Technology acceptance model 3 and a research agenda on interventions. *Decision Sciences*, 39(2):273–315.

Henning Wachsmuth, Nona Naderi, Ivan Habernal, Yufang Hou, Graeme Hirst, Iryna Gurevych, and Benno Stein. 2017. Argumentation Quality Assessment: Theory vs. Practice. In *Proceedings of the 55th Annual Meeting of the Association for Computational Linguistics (Volume 2: Short Papers)*, pages 250–255, Vancouver, Canada. Association for Computational Linguistics.

Thiemo Wambsganss, Tobias Kueng, Matthias Söllner, and Jan Marco Leimeister. 2021. ArgueTutor: An Adaptive Dialog-Based Learning System for Argumentation Skills. In *Proceedings of the 2021 CHI Conference on Human Factors in Computing Systems*, pages 1–14. Association for Computing Machinery, New York, NY, USA.

Thiemo Wambsganss and Christina Niklaus. 2022. Modeling persuasive discourse to adaptively support students' argumentative writing. *60th Annual Meeting of the Association for Computational Linguistics, ACL 2012 - Proceedings of the Conference.*

Thiemo Wambsganss, Christina Niklaus, Matthias Cetto, Matthias Söllner, Jan Marco Leimeister, and Siegfried Handschuh. 2020a. AL: An Adaptive Learning Support System for Argumentation Skills. In *Proceedings of the 2020 CHI Conference on Human Factors in Computing Systems*, pages 1–14, New York, NY, USA. Association for Computing Machinery.

Thiemo Wambsganss, Christina Niklaus, Matthias Söllner, Siegfried Handschuh, and Jan Marco Leimeister. 2020b. A Corpus for Argumentative Writing Support in German. In *28th International Conference on Computational Linguistics (Coling)*, pages 1–14, Barcelona, Spain.

Wenting Wang, Deeksha Arya, Nicole Novielli, Jinghui Cheng, and Jin L.C. Guo. 2020. ArguLens: Anatomy of Community Opinions on Usability Issues Using Argumentation Models. In *ACM CHI Conference on Human Factors in Computing Systems*, New York, NY, USA. Association for Computing Machinery.

Florian Weber, Thiemo Wambsganss, Dominic Rüttimann, and Matthias Söllner. 2021. Pedagogical Agents for Interactive Lernaing: A Taxonomy of Conversational Agents in Education. In *Forty-Second International Conference on Information Systems*, pages 1–17, Austin, Texas, USA.

Max White and Alla Rozovskaya. 2020. A comparative study of synthetic data generation methods for grammatical error correction. In *Proceedings of the Fifteenth Workshop on Innovative Use of NLP for Building Educational Applications*, pages 198–208, Seattle, WA, USA → Online. Association for Computational Linguistics.

Helen Yannakoudakis, Øistein E. Andersen, Ardeshir Geranpayeh, Ted Briscoe, and Diane Nicholls. 2018. Developing an automated writing placement system for esl learners. *Applied Measurement in Education*, 31:251–267.

Assessing sentence readability for German language learners with broad linguistic modeling or readability formulas: When do linguistic insights make a difference?

Zarah Weiss
Department of linguistics
University of Tübingen
Germany
zweiss@sfs.uni-tuebingen.de

Detmar Meurers
Department of linguistics
University of Tübingen
Germany
dm@sfs.uni-tuebingen.de

Abstract

The paper presents a new state-of-the-art sentence-wise readability assessment model for German L2 readers. We build a linguistically broadly informed machine learning model and compare its performance against four commonly used readability formulas. To understand when the linguistic insights used to inform our model make a difference for readability assessment and when simple readability formulas suffice, we compare their performance based on two common automatic readability assessment tasks: predictive regression and sentence pair ranking. We find that leveraging linguistic insights yields top performances across tasks, but that for the identification of simplified sentences also readability formulas – which are easier to compute and more accessible – can be sufficiently precise. Linguistically informed modeling, however, is the only viable option for high quality outcomes in fine-grained prediction tasks.

We then explore the sentence-wise readability profile of leveled texts written for language learners at a beginning, intermediate, and advanced level of German. Our findings highlight that a texts' readability is driven by the maximum rather than the overall readability of sentences. This has direct implications for the adaptation of learning materials and showcases the importance of studying readability also below the document level.

1 Introduction

Comprehensible input is key to foster language learning (Swain, 1985), especially when it challenges learners by falling slightly above their individual level of language competence (Vygotsky, 1978; Krashen, 1985). Also in content-matter education, input comprehensibility has been linked to learning success (e.g., O'Reilly and McNamara, 2007). Thus, automatic readability assessment (ARA) is a crucial tool to support education. ARA seeks to align language input with readers' comprehension skills (Vajjala, 2021; Collins-Thompson, 2014). It can not only identify suitable reading materials, but can also ensure learner-input alignment in applications such as tutoring systems or educational conversational agents or as a validation tool for publishers of educational materials. Yet, most work on ARA focuses on English native speakers, leaving much potential for other languages and approaches specifically tailored to the needs of second or foreign language (L2) learners who experience language barriers differently than native speakers (Greenfield, 2004; Collins-Thompson, 2014).

Although most work on ARA has focused on estimating the readability of entire documents, there are many application scenarios in which sentence-level readability assessment is more suitable. Beyond the identification of text simplification targets (Vajjala and Meurers, 2014), they are also more suitable for very short text types including social media language (e.g., tweets and chats), questionnaire or test items used in assessment and empirical education research, or shorter text units in traditional learning materials (e.g., captions or tasks in schoolbooks). Furthermore, there has been little research on the link between sentence and document readability (but see Vajjala and Meurers, 2014) which is immediately relevant for the targeted design and adaptation of educational materials.

There is a startling gap between the methods proposed in ARA research and those used in practice. While for the last two decades, research on ARA has favored machine learning approaches over traditional readability formulas (Vajjala, 2021) due to their generally better performance (e.g., François and Miltsakaki, 2012), simple formulas continue to be used extensively in practice due to their ease of use and low computation demands (Benjamin, 2012). This discrepancy raises the practical question when simple approximations of readability through formulas suffice, and when the use of more

Proceedings of the 17th Workshop on Innovative Use of NLP for Building Educational Applications (BEA 2022), pages 141 - 153
July 15, 2022

elaborate systems is necessary.

This paper addresses these issues with four major contributions: First, we present a new state-of-the-art (SOTA) sentence-level readability model for L2 German readers which is based on broad linguistic complexity assessment. Its performance on a 7-point Likert scale is comparable to human raters when it comes to estimating the readability of sentences for German L2 readers. Second, we make this model accessible online to enhance the impact of our work outside academic discourse. Users can extract features from their texts using the publicly available web platform CTAP (Chen and Meurers, 2016; Weiss et al., 2021) and use the results as input for a pre-written R script that applies the model to users' input files in the format that is returned by CTAP.[1] Third, we compare our SOTA machine learning-based approach with commonly used readability formulas for the two common ARA tasks predictive regression and ranking to answer the question when using linguistic insights indeed makes a difference and for which tasks simple readability formulas suffice. Finally, we leverage our SOTA model to explore sentence profiles of leveled L2 articles to provide new insights into the role of sentence readability for document difficulty that can help inform input adaptation strategies for educational materials.

The remainder of this paper is structured as follows: after a brief literature review (Section 2), we introduce the data (Section 3) and linguistic features (Section 4) used for our studies. We then report on the model training and evaluation for predictive regression and sentence ranking (Section 5). Finally, we explore the readability profile of German L2 articles on a document level (Section 6) and discuss our overall findings (Section 7). We conclude with finals remarks on the impact of our findings and an outlook on future work (Section 8).

2 Related work

Early approaches to ARA date back to the last century when traditional readability formulas (e.g., Flesch, 1948; Dale and Chall, 1948) were developed, see DuBay (2004, 2006) for a comprehensive overview. Readability formulas estimate text readability solely based on surface level proxies of text characteristics (e.g., sentence and word length or word frequency). They have been heavily criticized for their lack of linguistic insight and robustness, and have been shown to yield inferior results to statistical approaches to ARA on authentic data (François and Miltsakaki, 2012; Collins-Thompson, 2014; Benjamin, 2012; Vajjala, 2021). Yet, they are still the most widely distributed form of ARA in practice due to their low computational demands, ease of use, and availability for a variety of languages (Benjamin, 2012). Common use cases include work on health literacy (Kiwanuka et al., 2017; Grootens-Wiegers et al., 2015; Esfahani et al., 2016) and as evaluation metrics in computational linguistic work on machine translation (Agrawal and Carpuat, 2019; Marchisio et al., 2019; Stymne et al., 2013) or conversational agents (Langevin et al., 2021; Gnewuch et al., 2018; Santhanam et al., 2020).

Since the early 2000s (cf. Vajjala, 2021), statistical approaches became dominant in research on ARA. This includes feature-based approaches leveraging rich linguistic information for their predictions as well as neural approaches without prior feature engineering. While either method has been shown to yield SOTA performances (e.g., Vajjala and Lučić, 2018; Weiss et al., 2021; Martinc et al., 2021; Bengoetxea et al., 2020) on the OneStopEnglish corpus by Vajjala and Lučić (2018), neural approaches have been argued to be more easily applicable for cross-linguistic readability assessment (Martinc et al., 2021; Madrazo Azpiazu and Pera, 2019), but see Weiss et al. (2021); De Clercq and Hoste (2016). Feature-based approaches, instead, are more appropriate when little data is available or when users need an explanation for the obtained readability score, as is commonly the case in education contexts and for publishers of leveled reading materials who might want to revise their texts after obtaining a readability score (Collins-Thompson, 2014). Established features measure aspects of syntax and lexicon (Collins-Thompson, 2014), morphology (Gonzalez-Dios et al., 2014; Hancke et al., 2012; Weiss et al., 2021), and discourse features. They intersect with common features from automatic writing quality assessment (Crossley, 2020) and Second Language Acquisition research (Vajjala and Meurers, 2012).

Only limited progress has been made on ARA for German, after early work on readability formulas (e.g., Amstad, 1978; Björnsson, 1983; Bamberger and Vanecek, 1984). The now unavailable

[1]Both, the complexity-based model and the R script can be accessed at `https://osf.io/jg6kc/?view_only=2d62778d592642a4a210eb4c7cc61f87`

DeLite system has been used to predict readability for German municipal texts (Vor der Brück and Hartrumpf, 2007; Vor der Brück et al., 2008a,b). Hancke et al. (2012) and Weiss and Meurers (2018) focused on the binary distinction of texts for adult versus young native speaking readers. However, binary ARA is of limited use in practice. Weiss et al. (2021) present to our knowledge the first and only multi-level classification approach for German documents after introducing the first multi-level readability corpus for German, which is part of a larger multi-lingual readability corpus for language learners. For sentence-wise readability assessment, Naderi et al. (2019a) compiled a German corpus of rated sentences and sentence simplification pairs. Naderi et al. (2019b) used this corpus to train a feature-based regression model yielding a root mean squared error (RMSE) of 0.847 which is to our knowledge the current SOTA on this data.

Little research has investigated the relationship between sentence and document readability, even though there has been some work testing the reliability of readability assessment for very short texts (Collins-Thompson and Callan, 2004) and sentences (Dell'Orletta et al., 2011; Vajjala and Meurers, 2014; Pilán et al., 2014). Vajjala and Meurers (2014) inspect readability differences between sentences from Wikipedia and Simple Wikipedia to investigate the poor performance of document-level ARA models for the identification of sentences from simple and regular texts. They find that sentences from Wikipedia are not systematically more complex than sentences from Simple Wikipedia. This raises several questions for further inquiry. The lack of observable differences might be caused by an insufficient sensitivity of the document-level model for sentence-level readability differences. Also, Simple Wikipedia has criticized as not systematically simpler than Wikipedia (e.g., Štajner et al., 2012; Xu et al., 2015; Yaneva et al., 2016). More research is needed to confirm or refute their finding that harder texts are not simply characterized by containing generally less readable sentences which would have direct implications for work on targeted document adaptation seeking to identify language barriers in educational materials.

3 Data

3.1 TextComplexityDE

The TextComplexityDE corpus (Naderi et al., 2019a) consists of 1,119 sentences. 1,019 sentences were extracted from 23 Wikipedia articles related to history, society, or science and 100 sentences from two articles in *Leichte Sprache* (engl. "simple language"). All were rated by 267 German L2 learners along three separate dimensions defined by Naderi et al. (2019a): readability, understandability, and lexical difficulty. For each dimension, sentences were rated by up to ten learners on a 7-point Likert scale. These ratings were aggregated into a single Mean Opinion Score (MOS). For this article, we focus on sentences' readability score (MOS-R).

	Mean	Std.	Min.	Max.
MOS-R	3.02	1.18	1.00	6.33
Words / sent.	20.08	10.62	4.00	63.00
Syll. / word	2.07	0.35	0.96	4.00

Table 1: Summary statistics for the TextComplexityDE sentences including number of words per sentence (sent.), number of syllables (syll.) per word, and the Mean Opinion Score for readability (MOS-R)

Table 1 contains summary statistics for the number of words per sentence sentence, the number of syllables per word, and MOS-R. It shows that MOS-R not quite uses the full range of the scale and that sentences are on average quite long (around 20 words) whereas words are relatively short (around two syllables). Sentence length has a strong Spearman rank correlation with MOS-R score ($r_s = 0.70; p < 0.01$). Word length only exhibits a weak correlation with MOS-R ($r_s = 0.26; p < 0.01$). The current SOTA performance for a ARA model lies at RMSE $= 0.847$ (Naderi et al., 2019b).

Sentence simplification pairs The corpus contains 250 sentence pairs of sentences with MOS-R > 4 sampled from all 23 Wikipedia articles and their simplifications. The texts were manually simplified by 75 native speakers and contain additional meta information on whether the simplification is only slightly or considerably simpler than the original. One sentence could not be successfully simplified and was excluded by us, resulting in 249 sentence pairs with valid simplifications.

3.2 Spotlight-DE

The Spotlight-DE corpus (Weiss et al., 2021) consists of 1.447 leveled articles by the Spotlight publisher. Articles' topics are connected to German politics, culture, and every-day life. The texts target L2 learners at a beginning ($N = 763$), medium ($N = 509$), or advanced ($N = 175$) level. The publisher aligns these three levels with the levels A2, B1/B2, and C1 of the Common European Framework of Reference (Council of Europe).

The reading levels in this corpus are assigned at the document level rather than at the sentence level. To obtain sentence-wise estimates, we split each article into individual sentences. Table 2 characterizes the resulting sentence-wise corpus. Compared

	Mean	Std.	Min.	Max.
Easy ($n = 16,694$)				
Words / sent.	11.00	5.09	1.00	73.00
Syll. / word	1.71	0.35	0.50	5.00
Medium ($n = 27,522$)				
Words / sent.	12.50	6.26	1.00	60.00
Syll. / word	1.73	0.35	0.33	6.00
Advanced ($n = 11,952$)				
Words / sent.	13.30	6.99	1.00	63.00
Syll. / word	1.78	0.37	0.50	5.50

Table 2: Summary statistics for the Spotlight-DE sentences across document reading levels (easy, medium, advanced) including number of number words per sentence (sent.), number of syllables (syll.) per word

to the TextComplexityDE corpus, sentences are much shorter. Also, there are no systematic differences in either sentence or work length across reading levels and no meaningful Spearman rank correlation between sentence length and article reading level ($r_s = 0.12; p < 0.001$) or word length and article reading level ($r_s = 0.06; p < 0.001$). Thus, unlike many other learner corpora, the SpotlightDE corpus does not rely on surface level simplifications to differentiate between proficiency levels.

4 Feature extraction and selection

We extracted 543 features of linguistic complexity from the linguistic domains of syntax, lexicon, and morphology as well as psycho-linguistic features of text cohesion, language use, and human language processing and surface level text features inspired by traditional readability formulas. All features have a long standing tradition in ARA research (Collins-Thompson, 2014) or in related work on automatic text scoring (Crossley, 2020) and Second Language Acquisition complexity research (Wolfe-Quintero et al., 1998; Housen et al., 2012).

For feature extraction, we used the CTAP system (Chen and Meurers, 2016, `http://ctapweb.com`) which has been extended to facilitate the analysis of German by Weiss et al. (2021). We chose this system, because it is to our knowledge the most extensive available analysis system for German. The underlying feature extraction engine for German has proven highly successful and robust in a variety of education-related tasks including readability assessment (Weiss and Meurers, 2018; Weiss et al., 2021; Kühberger et al., 2019) and work linked to writing quality assessment (Weiss and Meurers, 2019a,b; Weiss et al., 2019; Bertram et al., 2021; Riemenschneider et al., 2021). Also, using a publicly available web-based system increases the re-usability of any model using these features in practice.

4.1 Feature description

The German pipeline used in CTAP is described in detail in Weiss et al. (2021) and Weiss and Meurers (2021). The latter also contains a comprehensive definition of all complexity measures. We will limit ourselves here to summarize the types of features used to represent the individual linguistic domains.

Syntax The system measures 75 syntactic features which can be further distinguished into measures of clausal elaboration (e.g., *dependent clauses per clause* or *sentence coordination ratio*) and measures of phrasal elaboration (e.g., *prenominal modifiers per noun phrase* or *mean length of prepositional phrases*), as well as measures of syntactic variance (e.g., *edit distances between constituency parses* or *coverage of nominal modifier types*). This set also includes measures of specific grammatical patterns that have been associated with comprehension difficulties for non-native speakers of German (e.g., *the percentage of non-subject prefields* which Ballestracci (2010) identified as language barriers for Italian learners of German) and raw counts of syntactic patterns, such as the number of dependent clauses.

Lexicon There are 146 features of lexical complexity which can be further divided into measures of lexical richness (e.g., *MTLD* by McCarthy (2005) as well as different mathematical transformations of the type-token ratio), measures of lexical variation (e.g., *verb variation*), and lexical density (e.g., *noun type-token ratio* and other parts-of-speech specific type-token ratios). This group also contains also features measuring the overall occurrence of different parts-of-speech such as nouns, verbs, or puncuation marks.

Morphology CTAP measures 64 measures of morphological complexity for German. We extract features of nominal and verbal inflection (e.g., *genitive case per noun*), derivation (e.g., *derived nouns per noun*), and compounding (e.g., *average compound depth*). We also measure the variability of morphological exponents using different parametrizations of the Morphological Complexity Index (MCI; Brezina and Pallotti, 2019).

Cohesion We extract 46 measures of text cohesion and discourse for German. The features used here include explicit measures of cohesion (e.g., *causal connectives per sentence*) as well as implicit measures of cohesion linked to the use of pronouns and repetitions of subjects, objects, or nouns.

Language use The system offers 172 lexical language use features based on external German data bases. CTAP calculates average word frequencies and their standard deviations with and without log transformations and binned in log frequency bands for four frequency data bases that represent different types of language use: frequencies based on the Subtlex-DE data base consisting of movie and TV captions and Google Books 2000 (both Brysbaert et al., 2011), dlexDB frequencies (Heister et al., 2011) based on German newspaper articles, and frequencies and age of active use measures extracted from the Karlsruhe Children's Text corpus (Lavalley et al., 2015) consisting of essays written by German children in first to eighth grade.

Human sentence processing There are 21 measures of human processing that can be calculated for German. Weiss and Meurers (2018) and Weiss et al. (2021) have used features based on the Dependency Locality Theory (DLT; Gibson, 2000) for German readability classification using different weight configurations by Shain et al. (2016).

Surface length We extract 18 surface length features for German that solely rely on the identification of sentences, words, letters, and syllables. These features include the raw number of these constructs as well as means and standard deviations for sentence and word length based on these units, e.g., *mean sentence length in syllables*.

4.2 Feature selection

After extracting these features from the TextComplexityDE corpus, we removed all features with near-zero variance, i.e., all features for which at least 80% of the data exhibit the same value. This is the case for 31.3% of features ($N = 170$) due to near-exclusively zero values (i.e., not occurring in most data). This leaves 373 features for the analysis coming from all feature domains which were used for model training in Study 1 (Section 5).

This considerable reduction in the number of features is to be expected for data that is as short as the sentences in the TextComplexityDE corpus (e.g, Weiss and Meurers (2021) also report a reduction of 50% of complexity features for short texts). For example, only 7 of the 46 cohesion measures are sufficiently variable on this data, because most cohesion measures are calculated across sentence boundaries. Similarly, only 19 of 64 measures of morphological complexity are sufficiently variable, because there is not enough language material to produce a variety of inflectional properties. Conversely, nearly all language use and lexical features as well as most features of phrasal elaboration remain included in the reduced feature set.

5 Sentence-wise readability assessment

5.1 Set-up

We trained and compared several machine learning algorithms[2] using 10-folds cross-validation (10 CV) and the z-transformations of the 373 features selected in Section 4.2. We selected these algorithms based on their use in previous research or their robustness against large feature sets with multi-colinearity. The Bayesian Ridge Regression outperformed the other models and will be discussed in more detail in the following. To evaluate this complexity-based model's (henceforth: CBM) overall performance, we calculated its RMSE and Spearman rank correlation (r_s) during 10 CV (Section 5.2) and compared it against the current SOTA performance on the data (RMSE = 0.847, Naderi et al., 2019b). We also used the model to rank the pairs of regular and simplified sentences in TextComplexityDE (Section 5.3). We report the ranking accuracy in terms of the percentage of correctly ranked pairs for all i) pairs irrespec-

[2]Multiple linear regression with backward feature selection, linear support vector machine regression, random forests, Bayesian ridge regression (model averaged), Bayesian generalized linear model, quantile regression with LASSO penalty

tive of their degree of simplification ($N = 249$), ii) weakly simplified pairs ($N = 114$), and iii) strongly simplified pairs ($N = 135$).

In both evaluation steps, we compared the CBM's performance against five alternative models. We trained a Bayesian Ridge Regression model using only surface length measures as predictors as a baseline (henceforth: length-based model or LBM). We additionally use the following widely used readability formulas for both tasks:[3]

- the *Amstad Readability Index* (ARI; Amstad, 1978) which adapts the Flesch Reading Ease (Flesch, 1948) to German native speakers;
- the *Erste Wiener Sachtextformel* (WSF; Bamberger and Vanecek, 1984) designed for expository texts for German native speakers;
- The *LIX readability index* (Björnsson, 1983) which has been designed to align texts with adult native speakers' reading skills across a variety of languages including German; and
- the *Miyazaki EFL Readability Index* (MER; Greenfield, 1999, 2004) which was designed for English L2 readers.[4]

We calculated all formulas using a publicly available python-based readability calculator which we adjusted to use stanza (Qi et al., 2020) instead of NLTK (Bird and Loper, 2004) for segmentation.[5]

5.2 Results for regression with 10 CV

Table 3 shows the RMSE and Spearman rank correlation of the estimates with MOS-R in the TextComplexityDE data. Both, LBM and CBM outperform

	CBM	LBM	WSF	LIX	ARI	MER
RMSE	.685	.739	*n.a.*	*n.a.*	*n.a.*	*n.a.*
r_s	.806	.785	.681	.679	-.532	-.666

Table 3: RMSE and Spearman rank correlation between MOS-R and the predictions by CBM, LBM, and the readability formulas.

the current SOTA on the TextComplexityDE data ($RMSE = 0.847$; Naderi et al., 2019b). Our linguistically more informed CBM clearly outperforms the LBM in terms of both, RMSE and correlation. Due to the differences in the predicted scales, we cannot compute the RMSE for the four readability formulas, but the correlation shows that both, the CBM and LBM outperform the formulas.

	CBM	LBM	WSF	LIX	ARI	MER
Acc.	96.0	93.0	93.6	93.6	95.6	96.8
−	95.6	92.1	91.1	91.1	95.6	96.5
+	96.5	94.1	96.5	96.5	95.6	97.0

Table 4: Overall ranking accuracy (Acc.), ranking accuracy for weakly simplified pairs (−), and ranking accuracy for strongly simplified pairs (+)

The correlation of ARI with MOS-R is much lower than for the other formulas. This is unexpected, because all formulas use only sentence and word length features. However, ARI assigns a much larger weight to word length than the other formulas which in turn correlates only weakly with MOS-R in TextComplexity-DE (see Section 3.1).

CBM's prediction error lies at $\text{RMSE} = 0.685$ points on the Likert scale. This is comparable to the variance between raters in the TextComplexityDE data. Averaged across all rated sentences the across-rater standard deviation for MOS-R is at $1.03 \pm 0.51; IQR = [0.71; 1.41]$. This shows that the error of our CBM lies even below the acceptable range of disagreement exhibited by human raters.

5.3 Results for ranking of sentence pairs

Table 4 shows the results of the sentence ranking experiment. The ranking accuracy for all ARA models lies above 90%. With an overall accuracy of 96%, CBM again outperforms LBM and the readability formulas WSF and LIX. However, ARI and MER perform comparably to CBM despite their weak performance on the previous regression experiment. It seems that word length (which is weighted higher for these two formulas than for the rest) is more informative than sentence length for distinguishing simplified and regular sentences.

To also estimate if the models reflect the degrees of simplification in the data (weak vs. strong), we compare the difference in the predicted readability score between each sentence and its simplified counterpart. The difference should be systematically larger for strongly than for weakly simplified sentences. We test this assumption using significance testing[6] ($\alpha < 0.05$) and by estimating

[3] All formula equations are defined in Appendix A.

[4] We added this formula to include an estimate tailored to L2 readers despite the lack of German L2 readability formulas.

[5] `https://github.com/zweiss/RC_Readability_Calculator`

[6] We used a two-sided t-test or Wilcoxon Rank Sum and Signed Rank Tests depending on the normality of predictions determined with a Shapiro-Wilk Normality Test ($\alpha < .05$).

the effect size with Cohen's d.[7] We see a significant, small effect for CBM ($p = 0.02; d = 0.31$), LBM ($p = 0.04; d = 0.25$), MER ($p < 0.01; d = -0.36$), ARI ($p < 0.01; d = -0.30$), LIX ($p = 0.02; d = 0.35$), and WSF ($p = 0.01; d = 0.35$), see Appendix B for a visualization of the findings.

6 Exploring text profiles in leveled articles

6.1 Set-up

We used CBM to explore the text profiles of easy, medium, and advanced articles in the Spotlight-DE corpus, because it was the most precise model in Study 1. With CTAP, we extracted the 373 features from the sentence-split Spotlight-DE data that are used by the model and calculated their z-scores. We inspected the distribution of sentence readability scores across article levels from several perspectives. We first compared the overall differences in sentence complexity per article level and the differences in maximum sentence complexity using significance testing, effect size estimation (parallel to Study 1) and data visualization. We then evaluated the proportions of sentences within a 0.5 point sentence readability interval across article levels. Finally, we visualized the sentence readability of the first ten sentences in a sample of Spotlight-DE articles in three heatmaps, one for each article levels annotated in the Spotlight-DE corpus. This way, we obtain a non-aggregated estimate of the text profiles. To keep the heatmaps comparable, we used all 175 advanced articles as well as a random sample of 175 easy and 175 medium articles containing at least ten sentences.

6.2 Results

Figure 1 combines different perspectives on the sentence-wise article profiles split by article level. We see that the prediction ranges from 1 to 5, a reasonable coverage of the empirically observed MOS-R scale ($1 - 6.33$) in the TextComplexityDE data given the corpus characteristics discussed in Section 3. Figure 1a summarizes the overall sentence readability grouped by article levels with notches indicating the 95% confidence interval. There are small significant differences between easy and medium ($p < 0.001; d = -0.259$) and easy and advanced ($p < 0.001; d = -0.435$) articles, but only negligible albeit significant differences medium and advanced ($p < 0.001; d = -0.178$) articles. The boxplot shows considerable overlap for the 50% range of the data even between easy and advanced sentences. In Figure 1b, which considers only articles' maximum sentence readability scores, this overlap is considerably reduced. Here, we observe large significant differences between easy and advanced ($p < 0.001; d = -2.05$) and medium and advanced ($p < 0.001; d = -1.24$) articles, and moderate significant differences medium and advanced ($p < 0.001; d = -0.689$) articles. This indicates that the maximum sentence readability is more indicative for overall readability level of a text than considering the readability of all its sentences.

Figure 1c confirms this by comparing the percentage of sentences falling within a 0.5 point readability range across article levels. Sentences from articles at all levels are predominantly medium difficult (MOS-R= 3) and between 55.6% (advanced) to 64% (easy) of sentences fall in the range from $2.5 \leq$ MOS-R ≤ 3.5. Article levels differ mostly in the tails of the distribution. The difference is most pronounced for higher difficulty levels (MOS-R ≥ 4): 30% of sentences from advanced articles fall into this range, but only 23.1% of sentences from medium and 14.1% of sentences from easy articles. Even so, it is worth noting that the percentage of sentences with MOS-R ≤ 3 is systematically highest for easy articles and higher for medium than advanced articles. Inversely, the percentage of sentences with MOS-R > 3 is highest for advanced articles and higher for medium than easy articles.

Figure 1d visualizes the sentence readability scores of the first ten sentences of 175 articles per article level. The heatmap depicts the first ten sentences of each sampled article rather than summarizing across sentences and articles at the same article level to demonstrate the relative homogeneity of sentence reading scores for articles at the same article level and the systematic increase in the proportion of more demanding sentences across individual articles with higher article levels.

7 Discussion

Study 1 investigated the performance of linguistically informed readability models and readability formulas for sentence-wise readability assessment for two common ARA tasks: precise predictive regression (Section 5.2) and ranking to identify simplified sentences in sentence simplification pairs (Section 5.3). The results showcase the ver-

[7] We tested for unequal variance using an F test ($\alpha < .05$). In case of unequal variance, we used a Welch approximation for unequal variances to calculate Cohen's d.

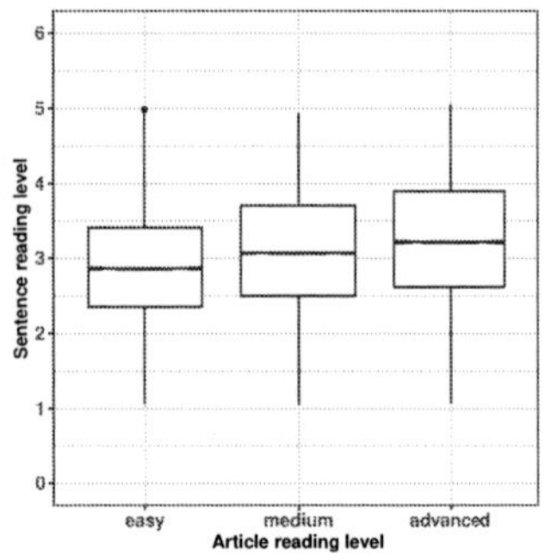

(a) Average sentence readability per article grouped by article level

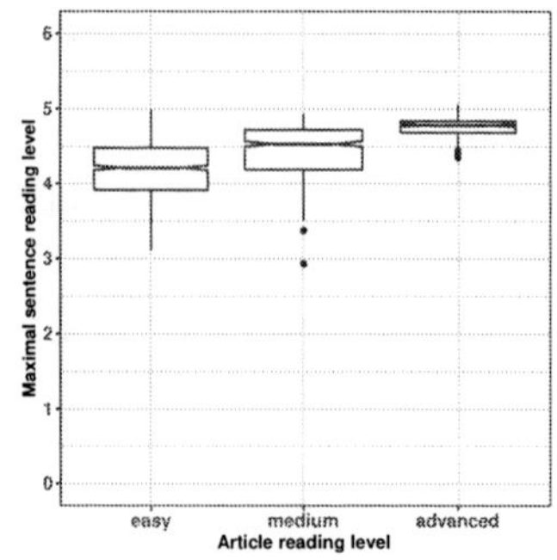

(b) Maximum sentence readability per article grouped by article level

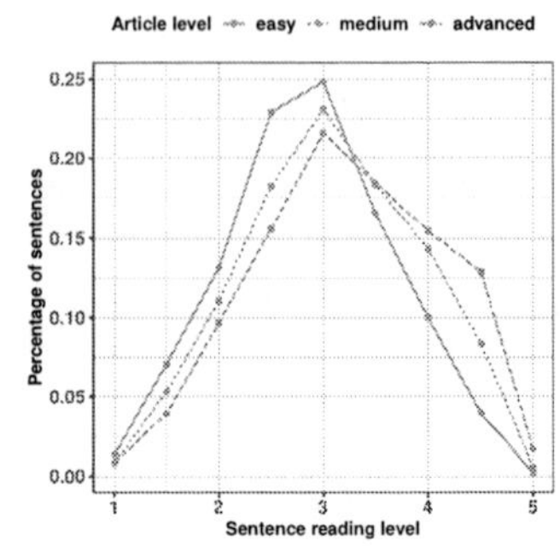

(c) Sentence-wise reading level distribution split by article levels

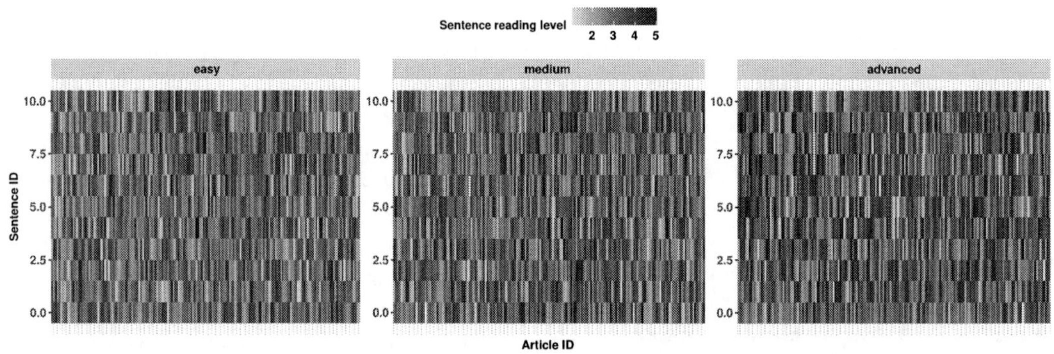

(d) Predicted sentence readability for the first ten sentences of 175 randomly sampled easy, medium, and advanced articles. Each sentence is represented by a cell. Its readability is encoded with the cell color. The cell's position on the x-axis encodes the article it belongs to and its position on the y-axis its position in that article, e.g., the third sentence in each article is located at $y = 3$.

Figure 1: Sentence readability profiles predicted by our complexity-based model on the Spotlight-DE corpus grouped by article levels (easy, medium, advanced) to showcase differences in sentence readability across documents at different difficulty levels.

satile performance of linguistically informed readability models: only our complexity-based model achieved top performance for both tasks. For the more difficult and authentic task of precise predictive regression, we showed that our linguistically informed complexity-based model clearly outperforms simplistic formulas and set a new SOTA performance (RMSE=0.685) on the data set. The better performance cannot be exclusively attributed to the statistically stronger method, because on both tasks, the complexity-based model clearly outperformed the length-based model. This shows that broad linguistic modeling adds valuable insights beyond the powerful statistical training method.

For ranking, all ARA models achieved an accuracy well above 90% and two readability formulas performed at par with our complexity-based model. This shows that even simple ARA approaches can successfully distinguish relative differences in readability between content-wise equivalent sentences that are being introduced by text simplification. Despite being a rather artificial task, this has some limited applications, e.g., when evaluating machine translation and text simplification systems.

In Study 2, we used our complexity-based model to inspect the sentence-wise readability profiles of leveled texts for L2 readers. Our findings clearly show that while there is a tendency for easier texts to contain more sentence with lower difficulty scores, also medium and advanced texts contain mostly accessible sentences. It is really the presence of difficult sentences within documents that dictates an articles' overall readability. This has clear implications for the design and simplification of educational materials: to efficiently adjust the overall readability level of a text, we need to identify specific sentences that form language barriers rather than simplifying the entire text.

8 Conclusion

We have presented a new SOTA sentence-wise ARA model for German L2 readers which is publicly available and accessible for users with minimal background in R. Leveraging broad linguistic insights, it predicts readability with a margin of error even below the acceptable disagreement range for humans raters. We showed that to flag simplified sentences also traditional readability formulas suffice, but that broad linguistic modeling is needed to obtain the precise predictive readability estimates that are often required in practice (e.g., to adapting learning and teaching materials).

We further explored leveled articles for German L2 readers to illustrate the practical benefits of sentence-level ARA and gain insights into text profiles of leveled documents. Our findings highlight that the readability of texts is driven by the maximum rather than the overall readability of sentences. This has direct implications for the adaptation of teaching materials, which should focus on identifying specific sentences posing language barriers rather than the simplification of all or any sentence in a text. To our knowledge, this is the first time detailed analysis of sentence profiles of leveled reading materials for German. Future work should further explore the implications of this for text simplification, for example using eye-tracking studies. Our work lays the foundation for further research on ARA for German and opens up numerous opportunities for educational applications, such as ARA for captions and task descriptions in school books or the analysis of social media and chat conversations with L2 learners.

References

Sweta Agrawal and Marine Carpuat. 2019. Controlling text complexity in neural machine translation. In *Proceedings of the 2019 Conference on Empirical Methods in Natural Language Processing and the 9th International Joint Conference on Natural Language Processing (EMNLP-IJCNLP)*, pages 1549–1564.

T. Amstad. 1978. *Wie verständlich sind unsere Zeitungen?* Ph.D. thesis, University of Zurich.

Sabrina Ballestracci. 2010. Der erwerb von verbzweitsätzen mit subjekt im mittelfeld bei italophonen dafstudierenden. erwerbsphasen, lernschwierigkeiten und didaktische implikationen. *Linguistik online*, 41(1).

Richard Bamberger and Erich Vanecek. 1984. *Lesen – Verstehen – Lernen – Schreiben. Die Schwierigkeitsstufen von Texten deutscher Sprache*. Jugend und Volk, Vienna.

Kepa Bengoetxea, Itziar González-Dios, and Amaia Aguirregoitia. 2020. AzterTest: Open source linguistic and stylistic analysis tool. *Procesamiento del Lenguaje Natural*, 64:61–68.

Rebekah George Benjamin. 2012. Reconstructing readability: Recent developments and recommendations in the analysis of text difficulty. *Educational Psychology Review*, 24:63–88.

Christiane Bertram, Zarah Weiss, Lisa Zachrich, and Ramon Ziai. 2021. Artificial intelligence in history education. linguistic content and complexity analyses of student writings in the cahist project (computational assessment of historical thinking). *Computers and Education: Artificial Intelligence*, page 100038.

Steven Bird and Edward Loper. 2004. Nltk: The natural language toolkit. In *Proceedings of the ACL demonstration session*, pages 214–217, Barcelona, Spain. Association for Computational Linguistics.

Carl-Hugo Björnsson. 1983. Readability of newspapers in 11 languages. *Reading Research Quarterly*, pages 480–497.

Vaclav Brezina and Gabriele Pallotti. 2019. Morphological complexity in written L2 texts. *Second language research*, 35(1):99–119.

Marc Brysbaert, Matthias Buchmeier, Markus Conrad, Arthur M. Jacobs, Jens Bölte, and Andrea Böhl. 2011. The word frequency effect: A review of recent developments and implications for the choice of frequency estimates in German. *Experimental Psychology*, 58:412–424.

Xiaobin Chen and Detmar Meurers. 2016. CTAP: A web-based tool supporting automatic complexity analysis. In *Proceedings of the Workshop on Computational Linguistics for Linguistic Complexity*, pages 113–119, Osaka, Japan. COLING.

Kevyn Collins-Thompson. 2014. Computational assessment of text readability: A survey of past, present, and future research. *International Journal of Applied Linguistics*, 165(2):97–135.

Kevyn Collins-Thompson and Jamie Callan. 2004. A language modeling approach to predicting reading difficulty. In *Proceedings of HLT/NAACL 2004*, Boston, USA.

Council of Europe. 2001. *Common European Framework of Reference for Languages: Learning, teaching, assessment*. Cambridge University Press, Cambridge.

Scott A. Crossley. 2020. Linguistic features in writing quality and development: An overview. *Journal of Writing Research*, 11(3):415–443.

Edgar Dale and Jeanne S. Chall. 1948. A formula for predicting readability. *Educational research bulletin; organ of the College of Education*, 27(1):11–28.

Orphée De Clercq and Véronique Hoste. 2016. All mixed up? Finding the optimal feature set for general readability prediction and its application to English and Dutch. *Computational Linguistics*, 42(3):457–490.

Felice Dell'Orletta, Simonetta Montemagni, and Giulia Venturi. 2011. Read-it: Assessing readability of Italian texts with a view to text simplification. In *Proceedings of the 2nd Workshop on Speech and Language Processing for Assistive Technologies*, pages 73–83.

William H. DuBay. 2004. *The Principles of Readability*. Impact Information, Costa Mesa, California.

William H. DuBay. 2006. *The Classic Readability Studies*. Impact Information, Costa Mesa, California.

B. Janghorban Esfahani, A. Faron, K. S. Roth, P. P. Grimminger, and J. C. Luers. 2016. Systematic readability analysis of medical texts on websites of German university clinics for general and abdominal surgery. *Zentralblatt fur Chirurgie*, 141(6):639–644.

Rudolf Franz Flesch. 1948. A new readability yardstick. *Journal of Applied Psychology*, 32(3):221–233.

Thomas François and Eleni Miltsakaki. 2012. Do nlp and machine learning improve traditional readability formulas? In *Proceedings of the First Workshop on Predicting and Improving Text Readability for target reader populations*, pages 49–57. Association for Computational Linguistics.

Edward Gibson. 2000. The dependency locality theory: A distance-based theory of linguistic complexity. In Alec Marantz, Yasushi Miyashita, and Wayne O'Neil, editors, *Image, language, brain: papers from the First Mind Articulation Project Symposium*, pages 95–126. MIT.

Ulrich Gnewuch, Stefan Morana, Carl Heckmann, and Alexander Maedche. 2018. Designing conversational agents for energy feedback. In *International Conference on Design Science Research in Information Systems and Technology*, pages 18–33. Springer.

Itziar Gonzalez-Dios, María Jesús Aranzabe, and Arantza Díaz de Ilarraza. 2014. Making biographical data in wikipedia readable: A pattern-based multilingual approach. In *Proceedings of the Workshop on Automatic Text Simplification - Methods and Applications in the Multilingual Society (ATS-MA 2014)*, pages 11–20, Dublin, Ireland. Association for Computational Linguistics and Dublin City University.

Jerry Greenfield. 1999. *Classic readability formulas in an EFL context: Are they valid for Japanese speakers?* Ph.D. thesis, Temple Univesity.

Jerry Greenfield. 2004. Readability formulas for efl. *JALT Journal*, 26(1):5–24.

Petronella Grootens-Wiegers, Martine C. De Vries, Tessa E. Vossen, and Jos M. Van den Broek. 2015. Readability and visuals in medical research information forms for children and adolescents. *Science Communication*, 37(1):89–117.

Julia Hancke, Sowmya Vajjala, and Detmar Meurers. 2012. Readability classification for German using lexical, syntactic, and morphological features. In *Proceedings of the 24th International Conference on Computational Linguistics (COLING)*, pages 1063–1080, Mumbai, India. http://aclweb.org/anthology-new/C/C12/C12-1065.pdf.

Julian Heister, Kay-Michael Würzner, Johannes Bubenzer, Edmund Pohl, Thomas Hanneforth, Alexander Geyken, and Reinhold Kliegl. 2011. dlexDB - eine lexikalische Datenbank für die psychologische und linguistische Forschung. *Psychologische Rundschau*, 62:10–20.

Alexis Housen, Folkert Kuiken, and Ineke Vedder. 2012. Complexity, accuracy and fluency: Definitions, measurement and research. In Alex Housen, Folkert Kuiken, and Ineke Vedder, editors, *Dimensions of L2 Performance and Proficiency*, Language Learning & Language Teaching, pages 1–20. John Benjamins.

Elizabeth Kiwanuka, Raman Mehrzad, Adnan Prsic, and Daniel Kwan. 2017. Online patient resources for gender affirmation surgery: an analysis of readability. *Annals of Plastic Surgery*, 79(4):329–333.

Stephen D Krashen. 1985. *The input hypothesis: Issues and implications*. Longman, New York.

Christoph Kühberger, Christoph Bramann, Zarah Weiss, and Detmar Meurers. 2019. Task complexity in history textbooks. a multidisciplinary case study on triangulation in history education research. *History Education International Research Journal (HEIRJ)*, 16(1). Special Issue on Mixed Methods and Triangulation in History Education Research.

Raina Langevin, Ross J Lordon, Thi Avrahami, Benjamin R Cowan, Tad Hirsch, and Gary Hsieh. 2021. Heuristic evaluation of conversational agents. In *Proceedings of the 2021 CHI Conference on Human Factors in Computing Systems*, pages 1–15.

Rémi Lavalley, Kay Berkling, and Sebastian Stüker. 2015. Preparing children's writing database for automated processing. In *LTLT@ SLaTE*, pages 9–15.

Ion Madrazo Azpiazu and Maria Soledad Pera. 2019. Multiattentive recurrent neural network architecture for multilingual readability assessment. *Transactions of the Association for Computational Linguistics*, 7:421–436.

Kelly Marchisio, Jialiang Guo, Cheng-I Lai, and Philipp Koehn. 2019. Controlling the reading level of machine translation output. In *Proceedings of Machine Translation Summit XVII: Research Track*, pages 193–203.

Matej Martinc, Senja Pollak, and Marko Robnik-Šikonja. 2021. Supervised and unsupervised neural approaches to text readability. *Computational Linguistics*, 47(1):141–179.

Philip M. McCarthy. 2005. *An assessment of the range and usefulness of lexical diversity measures and the potential of the measure of textual, lexical diversity (MTLD)*. Ph.D. thesis, University of Memphis.

Babak Naderi, Salar Mohtaj, Kaspar Ensikat, and Sebastian Möller. 2019a. Subjective assessment of text complexity: A dataset for german language. *arXiv preprint arXiv:1904.07733*.

Babak Naderi, Salar Mohtaj, Karan Karan, and Sebastian Möller. 2019b. Automated text readability assessment for german language: a quality of experience approach. In *2019 Eleventh International Conference on Quality of Multimedia Experience (QoMEX)*, pages 1–3. IEEE.

Tenaha O'Reilly and Danielle S McNamara. 2007. The impact of science knowledge, reading skill, and reading strategy knowledge on more traditional "high-stakes" measures of high school students' science achievement. *American educational research journal*, 44(1):161–196.

Ildikó Pilán, Elena Volodina, and Richard Johansson. 2014. Rule-based and machine learning approaches for second language sentence-level readability. In *Proceedings of the Ninth Workshop on Innovative Use of NLP for Building Educational Applications (BEA)*, pages 174–184, Baltimore, Maryland, USA. ACL.

Peng Qi, Yuhao Zhang, Yuhui Zhang, Jason Bolton, and Christopher D. Manning. 2020. Stanza: A Python natural language processing toolkit for many human languages. In *Proceedings of the 58th Annual Meeting of the Association for Computational Linguistics: System Demonstrations*.

Anja Riemenschneider, Zarah Weiss, Pauline Schröter, and Detmar Meurers. 2021. Linguistic complexity in teachers' assessment of german essays in high stakes testing. *Assessing Writing*, 50:100561.

Sashank Santhanam, Alireza Karduni, and Samira Shaikh. 2020. Studying the effects of cognitive biases in evaluation of conversational agents. In *Proceedings of the 2020 CHI Conference on Human Factors in Computing Systems*, pages 1–13.

Cory Shain, Marten van Schijndel, Richard Futrell, Edward Gibson, and William Schuler. 2016. Memory access during incremental sentence processing causes reading time latency. In *Proceedings of the Workshop on Computational Linguistics for Linguistic Complexity (CL4LC)*, pages 49–58, Osaka.

Sanja Štajner, Richard Evans, Constantin Orasan, and Ruslan Mitkov. 2012. What can readability measures really tell us about text complexity? In *In Proceedings of the First Workshop on Natural Language Processing for Improving Textual Accessibility*. European Language Resources Association (ELRA).

Sara Stymne, Jörg Tiedemann, Christian Hardmeier, and Joakim Nivre. 2013. Statistical machine translation with readability constraints. In *Proceedings of the 19th Nordic Conference of Computational Linguistics (NODALIDA 2013)*, pages 375–386.

Merrill Swain. 1985. Communicative competence: Some roles of comprehensible input and comprehensible output in its development. In Susan M. Gass and Carolyn G. Madden, editors, *Input in second language acquisition*, pages 235–253. Newbury House, Rowley, MA.

Sowmya Vajjala. 2021. Trends, limitations and open challenges in automatic readability assessment research. *arXiv preprint arXiv:2105.00973*.

Sowmya Vajjala and Ivana Lučić. 2018. OneStopEnglish corpus: A new corpus for automatic readability assessment and text simplification. In *Proceedings of the thirteenth workshop on innovative use of NLP for building educational applications*, pages 297–304.

Sowmya Vajjala and Detmar Meurers. 2012. On improving the accuracy of readability classification using insights from second language acquisition. In *Proceedings of the Seventh Workshop on Building Educational Applications Using NLP*, pages 163–173. `http://aclweb.org/anthology/W12-2019.pdf`.

Sowmya Vajjala and Detmar Meurers. 2014. Readability assessment for text simplification: From analyzing documents to identifying sentential simplifications. *International Journal of Applied Linguistics, Special Issue on Current Research in Readability and Text Simplification*, 165(2):142–222.

Tim Vor der Brück and Sven Hartrumpf. 2007. A semantically oriented readability checker for German. In *Proceedings of the 3rd Language & Technology Conference*, pages 270–274, Poznań, Poland. Wydawnictwo Poznańskie.

Tim Vor der Brück, Sven Hartrumpf, and Hermann Helbig. 2008a. A readability checker with supervised learning using deep syntactic and semantic indicators. *Informatica*, 32(4):429–435.

Tim Vor der Brück, Hermann Helbig, and Johannes Leveling. 2008b. The readability checker delite. Technical Report Technical Report 345-5/2008, Fakultät für Mathematik und Informatik, FernUniversität in Hagen.

Lev S. Vygotsky. 1978. *Mind in society: The development of higher psychological processes*. Harvard University Press, Cambridge, MA.

Zarah Weiss, Xiaobin Chen, and Detmar Meurers. 2021. Using broad linguistic complexity modeling for cross-lingual readability assessment. In *Proceedings of the Joint 10th Workshop on NLP for Computer Assisted Language Learning*, pages 38–54.

Zarah Weiss and Detmar Meurers. 2018. Modeling the readability of German targeting adults and children: An empirically broad analysis and its cross-corpus validation. In *Proceedings of the 27th International Conference on Computational Linguistics (COLING)*, Santa Fe, New Mexico, USA. https://www.aclweb.org/anthology/C18-1026.

Zarah Weiss and Detmar Meurers. 2019a. Analyzing linguistic complexity and accuracy in academic language development of German across elementary and secondary school. In *Proceedings of the 14th Workshop on Innovative Use of NLP for Building Educational Applications (BEA)*, Florence, Italy. Association for Computational Linguistics.

Zarah Weiss and Detmar Meurers. 2019b. Broad linguistic modeling is beneficial for German L2 proficiency assessment. In *Widening the Scope of Learner Corpus Research. Selected Papers from the Fourth Learner Corpus Research Conference*, Louvain-La-Neuve. Presses Universitaires de Louvain.

Zarah Weiss and Detmar Meurers. 2021. Analyzing the linguistic complexity of German learner language in a reading comprehension task: Using proficiency classification to investigate short answer data, cross-data generalizability, and the impact of linguistic analysis quality. *International Journal of Learner Corpus Research*, 7(1):84–131.

Zarah Weiss, Anja Riemenschneider, Pauline Schröter, and Detmar Meurers. 2019. Computationally modeling the impact of task-appropriate language complexity and accuracy on human grading of German essays. In *Proceedings of the 14th Workshop on Innovative Use of NLP for Building Educational Applications (BEA)*, Florence, Italy.

Kate Wolfe-Quintero, Shunji Inagaki, and Hae-Young Kim. 1998. *Second Language Development in Writing: Measures of Fluency, Accuracy & Complexity*. Second Language Teaching & Curriculum Center, University of Hawaii at Manoa, Honolulu.

Wei Xu, Chris Callison-Burch, and Courtney Napoles. 2015. Problems in current text simplification research: New data can help. *Transactions of the Association for Computational Linguistics*, 3:283–297.

Victoria Yaneva, Irina P. Temnikova, and Ruslan Mitkov. 2016. Evaluating the readability of text simplification output for readers with cognitive disabilities. In *Proceedings of the 10h International Conference on Language Resources and Evaluation (LREC)*, pages 293–299.

A Definition of readability formulas

Equation 1 shows the general form of all four readability formulas consisting of an intercept (β_0), a weighted sentence length estimate ($\beta_1 \times SL$), and a weighted word length estimate ($\beta_2 \times WL$).

$$y = \beta_0 + \beta_1 \times SL + \beta_2 \times WL \quad (1)$$

Table 5 shows the respective weights ($\beta_0, \beta_1, \beta_2$) and measurement units for sentence length (SL) and word length (WL). Equation 2 specifies the definition of the composite score for word length used in the *Erste Wiener Sachtextformel*.

y	β_0	β_1	β_2	SL	WL
LIX	0.0	1.0	1.0	words	syll.
ARI	180.0	−1.0	−58.6	words	syll.
MER	164.9	−1.9	−18.8	words	char.
WSF	0.0	0.2	1.0	words	Eq. 2

Table 5: Weights and measurement units across readability formulas (syll. = syllables, char. = characters)

$$WL_{WSF} = 0.19 \times 3SW + 0.13 \times 6CW \\ -0.03 \times 1SW - 0.88, \quad (2)$$

with $3SW$ being the percentage of three or more syllable words, $6CW$ being the percentage of six or more character words, and $1SW$ being the percentage of monosyllabic words. All weights in Table 5 and Equation 1 have been rounded to one decimal point for simplicity.

B Prediction differences between different degrees of simplification

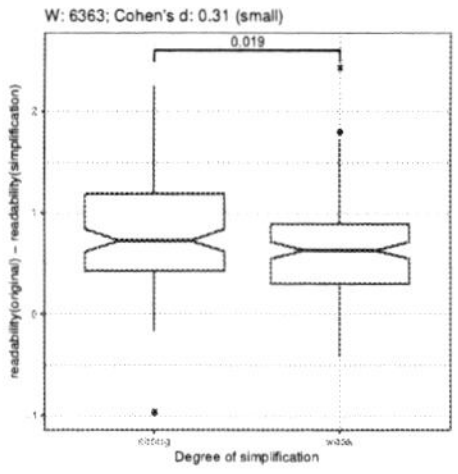

(a) CBM

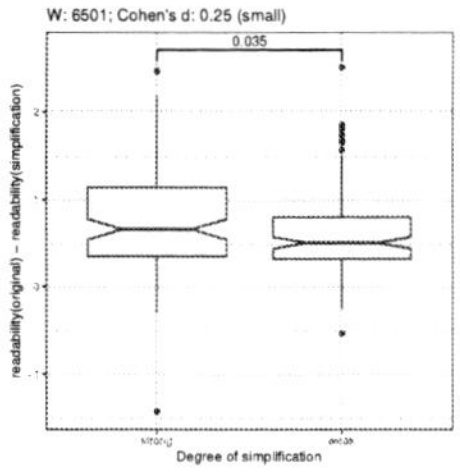

(b) LBM

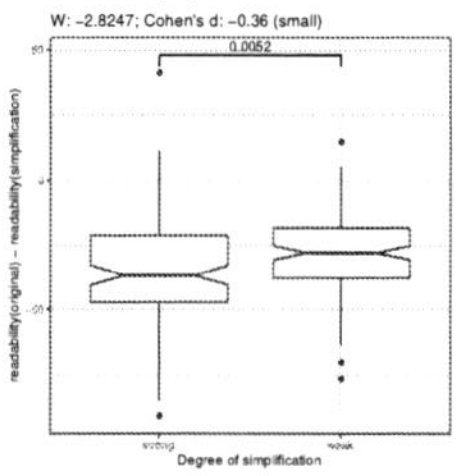

(c) MER

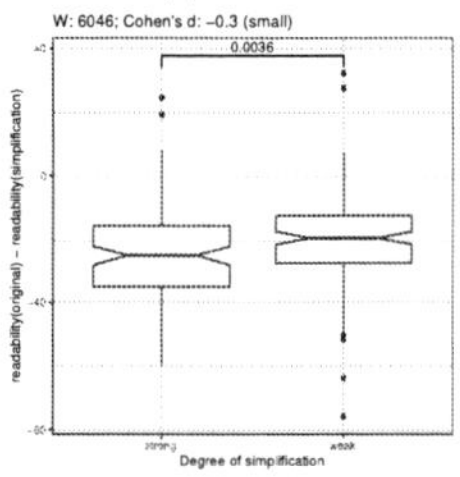

(d) ARI

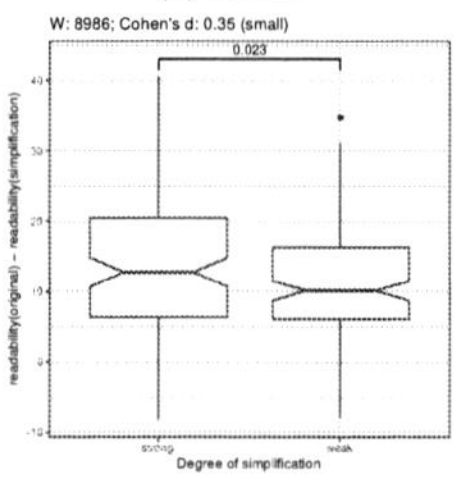

(e) LIX

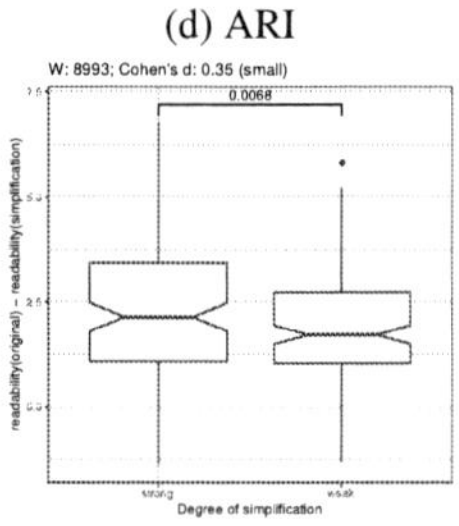

(f) EWS

Figure 2: Predicted readability difference between regular and simplified sentences by degree of simplification

Parametrizable exercise generation from authentic texts: Effectively targeting the language means on the curriculum

Tanja Heck
Universität Tübingen / Germany
`tanja.heck@uni-tuebingen.de`

Detmar Meurers
Universität Tübingen / Germany
`detmar.meurers@uni-tuebingen.de`

Abstract

We present a parametrizable approach to exercise generation from authentic texts that addresses the need for digital materials designed to practice the language means on the curriculum in a real-life school setting. The tool builds on a language-aware search engine that helps identify attractive texts rich in the language means to be practiced. Making use of state-of-the-art NLP, the relevant learning targets are identified and transformed into exercise items embedded in the original context.

While the language-aware search engine ensures that these contexts match the learner's interests based on the search term used, and the linguistic parametrization of the system then reranks the results to prioritize texts that richly represent the learning targets, for the exercise generation to proceed on this basis, an interactive configuration panel allows users to adjust exercise complexity through a range of parameters specifying both properties of the source sentences and of the exercises.

An evaluation of exercises generated from web documents for a representative sample of language means selected from the English curriculum of 7th grade in German secondary school showed that the combination of language-aware search and exercise generation successfully facilitates the process of generating exercises from authentic texts that support practice of the pedagogical targets.

1 Introduction

With digital learning contexts becoming increasingly common in Foreign Language Teaching and Learning, automatic exercise generation arguably will become a crucial tool for making individualized practice materials available that are adapted to the learner's individual needs and competencies (Liu et al., 2005). An ideal system for this purpose will generate exercises of parametrizable complexity for a given input text.

Form-focused exercises lend themselves especially well to automatic generation as their answer space is limited enough to support automatic evaluation (Sysoyev, 1999; Zanetti et al., 2021; Schwartz et al., 2004). Approaches in this domain can be subdivided into two categories: systems that generate simple exercise sentences using a rule-based approach, and tools that extract sentences which contain the targeted constructions from existing texts (Perez-Beltrachini et al., 2012). Working with authentic texts has been argued to have positive effects on learner motivation (Peacock, 1997), especially if as much context as possible is preserved (Romney, 2016). Since motivation is highest when the topic and contents of the text is of interest to the learner, allowing them to provide their own texts as input to exercise generation is advantageous (Zhuomin, 2010). Yet, authentic texts often do not include sufficient examples for the language means to be practiced (Chinkina et al., 2016). It is therefore important to assist learners in finding suitable documents that are of interest and richly represent the language means on the syllabus that are to be practiced, which has been referred to as input enrichment (Chinkina and Meurers, 2016).

More recently, an important need for automatically generated exercises is arising in the context of adaptive language tutoring systems (Pandarova et al., 2019). Adaptivity comprises elements both at the micro level and at the macro level (Rus et al., 2014). With respect to micro-adaptivity, scaffolding feedback is used to guide the learner towards the correct answer. Macro-adaptivity refers to the system capability to provide sequences of exercises at the right level for a given learner. Such systems thus need to either manipulate exercise difficulty in real-time (Beinborn, 2016) or to maintain large pools of exercises of varying complexity levels (Pandarova et al., 2019). Real-time manipulation is most feasible for aspects of the exercise, such as the number of distractors or hints, but not for linguistic

Proceedings of the 17th Workshop on Innovative Use of NLP for Building Educational Applications (BEA 2022), pages 154 - 166
July 15, 2022 ©2022 Association for Computational Linguistics

features of the seed sentence or the choice of the target item. This approach to macro-adaptivity in the language learning context has mainly been limited to C-tests (Beinborn, 2016; Lee et al., 2019).

Most educational institutions use some Learning Management System (LMS, Zabolotniaia et al., 2020). To be able to integrate generated exercises into regular classes, they should be compatible with the LMS system used. Exercises would thus be most beneficial to instructors when provided as globally usable web components or in a format that complies with standards such as xAPI[1] and cmi5[2]. In addition, it would be important to provide interfaces that make it possible to edit exercises that were generated to be able to correct or modify them to suit the instructor's needs and preferences.

Summing up the requirements mentioned above and in the wider literature, an exercise generation tool should provide input enrichment mechanisms for user-selected texts, be parametrizable and editable by the educators themselves, integrate feedback into the exercises, provide the exercises in a portable format, and support use of the exercises within the original context. To our knowledge, no tool has been developed so far which complies with all these features. Indeed, no fully automated exercise generation system for grammar exercises we know of even offers some of the features mentioned, such as an integrated input enrichment approach.

In this paper, we thus present an exercise generation extension of the language-aware search engine FLAIR[3] to address this gap. We start with section 2 introducing the research context on automatic generation of grammar exercises. Section 3 describes the implementation of the exercise generation extension of FLAIR and outlines its functionality and use. Section 4 evaluates the tool before section 5 summarizes and concludes with an outlook.

2 Related work

Our approach integrates automatic exercise generation into an educational document retrieval system. Therefore, we will first elaborate on previous work on educational information retrieval systems before discussing existing tools for form-based grammar exercise generation with respect to the outlined criteria we impose on such a system.

Similar to tutoring systems, educational **document rankings systems** often leverage information from a learner model to identify texts that match a learner's individual proficiency level. Two examples for such an approach are *REAP* and *TextFinder* (Bennöhr, 2005). The learner model is maintained within the system based on the learner's interaction with the tool. While *REAP* can work with texts from anywhere on the web, *TextFinder* operates on its own database of online news articles.

A less automated approach relies more on user interaction. Examples include the standalone tool *READ-X* (Miltsakaki and Troutt, 2008) and the web extension *LAWSE* (Ott and Meurers, 2011). Both tools calculate readability scores for web documents. While LAWSE merely displays them for the analyzed documents, READ-X matches the scores against a readability level which users need to specify, and filters the documents accordingly.

For narrowly defined use cases, tools may filter documents without either a learner model or user input. *SourceFinder* constitutes an example for such a system. It applies a binary filter to its corpus of online journals and identifies texts suitable in academic contexts (Sheehan et al., 2007).

Systems with the highest degree of flexibility allow users to filter documents according to contained grammatical constructions. This approach is for example realised in the authoring assistance tool *Sakumon* (Hoshino and Nakagawa, 2008) and the language-aware search engines FLAIR[4] (Chinkina et al., 2016) and KANSAS[5] (Dittrich et al., 2019). Sakumon maintains information on the article's reading level as well as on contained grammatical constructions in its database. FLAIR and KANSAS, the latter being based on FLAIR and specializing on low literacy in German, analyze web texts on demand. In addition to the filtering functionality, these two systems also allow users to rank all retrieved documents according to the occurrence of linguistic constructions. This kind of re-ranking of search results allows to identify documents containing certain linguistic constructions, such as those targeted by grammar exercises. Such a tool therefore lends itself well as basis into which we can integrate an exercise generation component.

Table 1 provides an overview of existing work on **automatic generation of grammar exercises** highlighting that while many of these systems incorporate some of the characteristics we consider rele-

[1] http://github.com/adlnet/xAPI-Spec

[2] http://aicc.github.io/CMI-5_Spec_Current

[3] The authors kindly made the source code available to us.

[4] http://flair.schule

[5] http://kansas-suche.de

	DR	CT	CS	AC	PO
Mgbeg					
GramEx			(•)		
KillerFiller			(•)		•
Task Generator		•	(•)	(•)	
MIRTO		•	•	(•)	(•)
GEG		•		(•)	
FAST			(•)		
ArikIturri		•			•
WebExperimenter			(•)	(•)	
Sakumon	•	(•)	•	(•)	
VIEW		•	(•)	•	•
ClozeFox		•	(•)	•	•
LEA		•	•	(•)	•
Lärka	(•)		(•)		
COLLIE		•		(•)	
Language Muse		•	(•)		

Table 1: Exercise generation system functionalities
Document ranking (DR), custom text input (CT), configurable settings (CS), authentic context (AC) and portable output (PO) marked by • if offered, by (•) if partially offered.

vant to automatically generated, form-based grammar exercises, none of them combines all features. Especially the selection of suitable documents is hardly targeted at all. Only *Sakumon*, which is also listed among the document ranking systems, offers full-fledged document filtering. Since it was developed as an assistant system, exercise generation has, however, not yet been fully automated.

Support for preserving the authentic context varies considerably from one system to the other. Rule-based systems do not rely on authentic texts at all. Examples include the *Mgbeg* exercise generator (Almeida et al., 2017) and *GramEx* (Perez-Beltrachini et al., 2012). Among the tools using authentic texts, a couple use only decontextualized, single sentences. This encompasses for example *Lärka*[6] (Volodina et al., 2014), *ArikIturri* (Aldabe et al., 2006) and *FAST* (Chen et al., 2006). A range of systems integrate the exercises into the base text, yet visual context such as markup elements and images are removed. This is, for instance, the case in the Tutor Assistant's *Task Generator* (Toole and Heift, 2001), *MIRTO* (Antoniadis et al., 2004), the *Grammar Exercise Generator (GEG)* (Melero and Font, 2001), the *Language Exercise App (LEA)* (Perez and Cuadros, 2017) and *COLLIE*[7] (Bodnar and Lyster, 2021). Visual context is only preserved in those exercise generation tools implemented as web plugins. Prominent examples include *VIEW*[8] (Meurers et al., 2010; Reynolds et al., 2014) and *ClozeFox*[9] (Colpaert and Sevinc, 2010).

Most of the exercise generation tools provide the generated exercises within the system and do not offer any export functionalities. Noticeable exceptions include *KillerFiller*, *ArikIturri* and the *LEA*. The web plugins *VIEW* and *ClozeFox* are also portable by nature.

The degree to which users can influence the exercises to be generated is generally rather low. Although in most systems, users can upload their own texts, they often have only rudimentary influence on the properties of the generated exercises. The most highly configurable applications include *MIRTO*, *Sakumon*, *Language Muse* (Madnani et al., 2016) and the *LEA*. Since *Sakumon* is an assistant system, instructors can and must select the target items and distractors manually from among the tool's suggestions. The *LEA* also allows to specify target constructions, bracket contents and distractors. *MIRTO* in addition lets users specify interactive supportive elements such as links to lookup pages. *Language Muse* generates a range of different activities for each text from which the user can choose the one which best suits their needs. These can be edited to allow further customization.

Our approach aims to combine the strengths of these systems into a single application.

3 System description

We integrate the exercise generation functionality into the language-aware search engine FLAIR. While the exercise generation is fully integrated into this application, we also considered the interface supporting integration of the generated exercises in the LMS serving as deployment platforms.

3.1 Implementation

FLAIR serves as base system to search the web for documents on user-specified topics. Just like ordinary web search engines, it supports restricting the search space to specific sites using operators. As illustrated in Figure 1, the system provides additional functionalities to filter and re-rank those documents based on the linguistic criteria selected by the user (left part).

[6] https://spraakbanken.gu.se/larkalabb/
[7] https://www.collietool.ca/
[8] http://purl.org/view
[9] https://wiki.mozilla.org/Education/Projects/JetpackForLearning/Profiles/ClozeFox

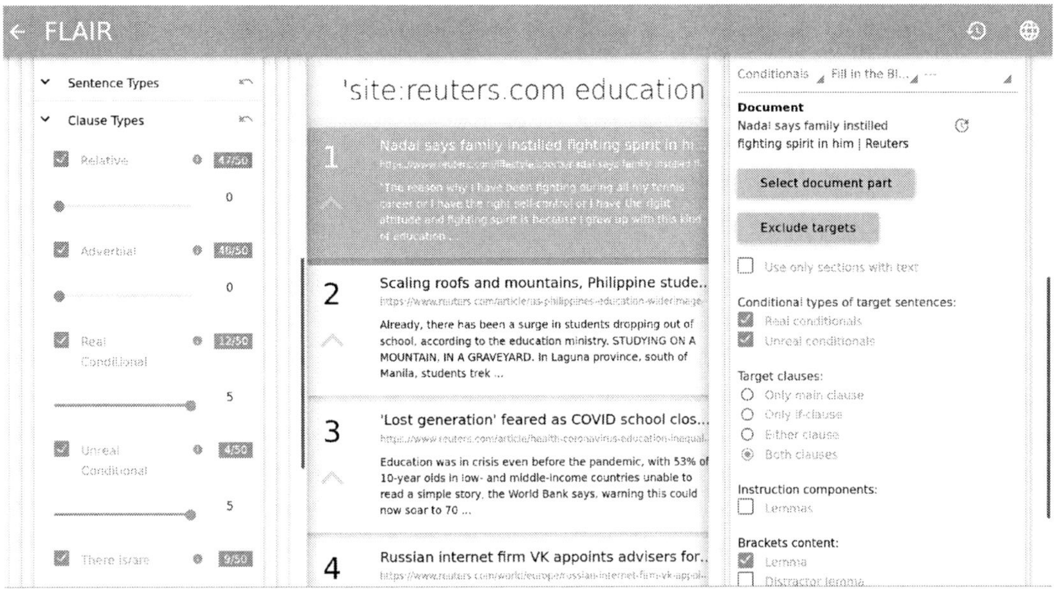

Figure 1: Exercise configuration in FLAIR

	FiB	SC	DD	MtW	M	JS
Simple present	•	•		•	•	•
Past tenses	•	•	•	•	•	•
Conditionals	•	•	•			•
Relatives	•	•	•	•		•
Comparatives	•	•	•	•	•	•
Passive	•		•			•

Table 2: Exercise types per topic
Fill-in-the-Blanks (FiB), Single Choice (SC), Drag and Drop (DD), Mark-the-Words (MtW), Memory (M), and Jumbled Sentences (JS) marked by • if offered.

Exercise generation comes into play after the documents have been retrieved and ranked. It offers the configuration panel displayed on the right of Figure 1. Supported language means for the exercises are based on the pedagogical goals of German 7th grade high schools (Ministerium für Kultus, 2016) and include Comparatives, Present and Past tenses, Passive, Conditionals and Relative pronouns. The available exercise types depend on the language means. Table 2 shows that while Fill-in-the-Blanks exercises are supported for all language means, other exercise types we generate, such as Single Choice, Mark the Words, Drag and Drop, Memory, and Jumbled Sentences exercises, are not universally applicable. Users are shown only those exercise settings that are applicable to the selected text. These settings, on the one hand, comprise a characterization of the exercises such as the exercise type or the number and features of distractors and, on the other hand, features to restrict the choice of seed sentences. For exercises on Passive, the parametrizable characteristics of seed sentences encompass the tense (past, present and future), the aspect (simple, perfect and progressive) and the voice (active and passive). Exercises targeting Tenses support parameters for the targeted tenses and the aspect, as well as for negated and interrogative contexts. For Simple present, additional parameters allow to exclude regular or irregular forms. Seed sentences for Comparatives can be selected to contain synthetic or analytic comparative or superlative forms of adjectives or adverbs, or both. Parameters for Conditionals include the conditional type. For exercises on Relative pronouns, sentences can be restricted to those containing specific relative pronouns. The parameters for seed sentences lead to a more fine-grained subdivision of each language means into target constructions. Some of the parameters serve to manipulate exercise complexity by including or excluding additional language means, such as questions or negation, from the exercises. Other parameters which are specific to the language means, such as active and passive voice, allow to put the focus of the exercise either on the acquisition of a specific form or on the distinction between multiple forms.

Figure 2 illustrates that even for the same lan-

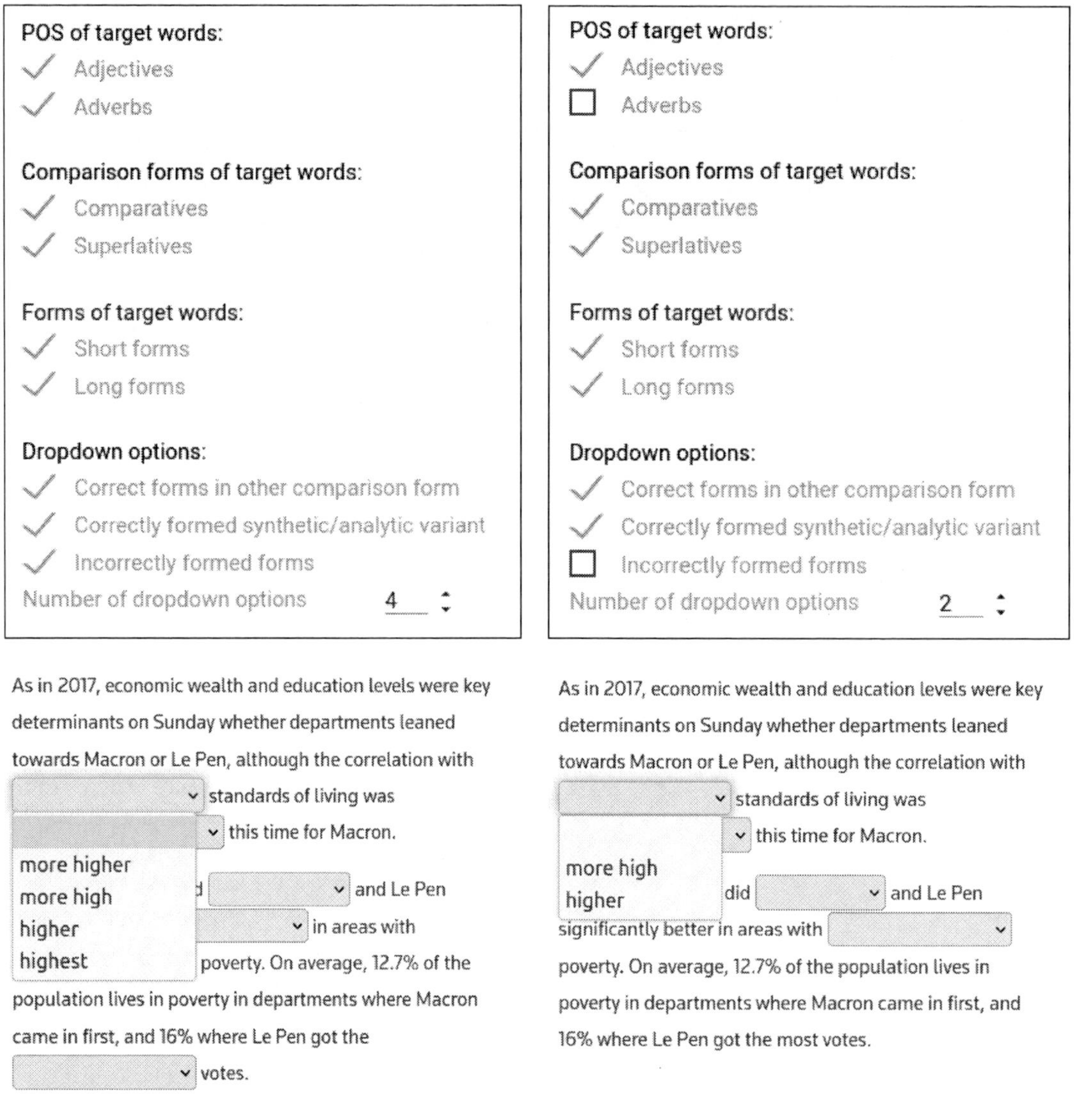

(a) Example 1: Parameters and generated exercise for default settings

(b) Example 2: Parameters and generated exercise for custom configuration

Figure 2: Comparison of generated exercises for different parametrizations

guage means and exercise type, in this case *Comparatives* and *Single Choice* respectively, the resulting exercises differ although they are based on the same document.[10] In Figure 2a where the default configuration is used, all comparative and superlative adjectives and adverbs are transformed into targets and the distractors also contain ill-formed forms. In Figure 2b, adverbs are excluded and the distractors contain only well-formed forms.

In order to generate an exercise from a document and an exercise specification, the algorithm automatically separates all of the markup elements in the web page from the plain text. It relies on the linguistic annotations used by the base system for document ranking and post-processes them in order to generate an abstract exercise definition. For most of the possible exercise configurations, the base system's distinction between linguistic constructions is not fine-grained enough to identify target items that comply with all activated settings options to

[10]The exercises were generated from Reuters article `https://www.reuters.com/world/europe/poverty-education-levels-draw-battle-lines-french-election-2022-04-12/` and uploaded into a Moodle instance.

select seed sentences. Target items thus correspond to elements which are assigned multiple annotations by FLAIR. As the scopes of the annotations relevant to the different parameters of an exercise target are not always congruent, the resulting scope of the exercise target is determined individually for each combination of settings parameters through a set of manually defined rules.

Apart from the target construction, the abstract exercise definition contains elements such as task descriptions, distractors and pre-compiled feedback. This feedback is obtained from the already established feedback generation algorithm of the FeedBook (Rudzewitz et al., 2018). The required exercise components differ slightly from one exercise type to another. While for Mark the Words and Drag and Drop exercises, no additional content is generated, Fill-in-the-Blanks exercises need hints which are displayed in parentheses, such as the lemma of the exercise item, and Single Choice exercises require distractors. For Memory tasks, the targeted language means determines what content has to be generated for the second card. Jumbled Sentences do not need supplementary content, yet they need further processing in order to determine the parts into which sentences containing a target construction are split. The particular characteristics of additional elements and processing depend on the settings defined by the user who may, for instance, select any or multiple of lemma, distractor lemma, tense or other options depending on the language means for hints in parentheses. Distractors are equally configurable, allowing users to include well-formed but context inappropriate options such as incorrect tenses or POS, as well as ill-formed options. While the generation of well-formed elements applies NLP technology including lemmatization and Natural Language Generation (NLG), ill-formed elements are generated based on manually defined transformation rules. Markup elements are also added to the exercise definition so that the authentic context of the document can be reconstructed.

This abstract representation is then used to generate the exercises in a portable format. Since most of the relevant standards are rather complex (Griffiths, 2020), we use the H5P[11] format which integrates multiple standards and offers a library of predefined, open source exercise types (López et al., 2021; Magro, 2021).

[11]https://h5p.org/

3.2 Usage

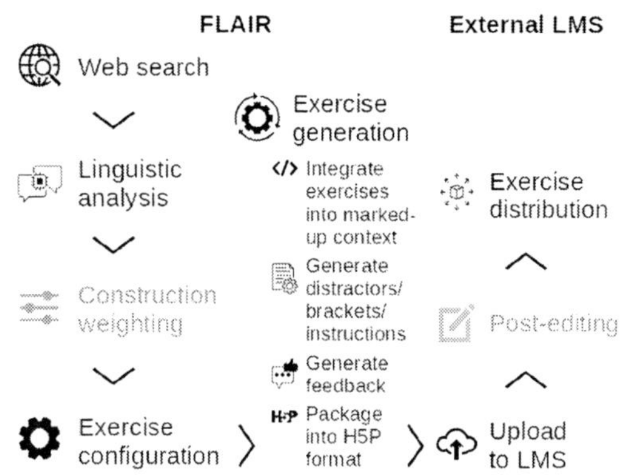

Figure 3: Exercise generation workflow

As outlined in Figure 3, the end user, typically a language instructor, will interact with FLAIR on the one hand in order to generate an exercise, and with the LMS on the other hand in order to provide the exercise to learners. The prototypical workflow starts in FLAIR where the instructor performs a web search which returns linguistically analyzed documents. Weighting linguistic constructions to re-rank the results is optional. After choosing a document from the results, the instructor configures one or multiple exercises. When exercise generation is triggered, a H5P exercise is generated, including the original mark-up, exercise components and pre-compiled feedback. The instructor then uploads the file to the LMS where he or she may edit the generated exercise and make it available to students as illustrated in Figure 4.[12] While working on the exercise, students will receive instant, dynamic feedback based on the pre-compiled feedback until they complete the task.

4 Evaluation

The quality of the exercise generation extension depends on its ability to identify documents which contain linguistic constructions that can successfully be transformed into exercise items. We conducted a three-step, pilot evaluation in order to determine the tool's performance in this respect. Due to time restrictions, the gold standard annotations and evaluations results were produced only by one of the authors.

[12]The exercise was generated from Reuters article https://www.reuters.com/lifestyle/sports/nadal-says-family-instilled-fighting-spirit-him-2022-03-13 and uploaded into a Moodle instance.

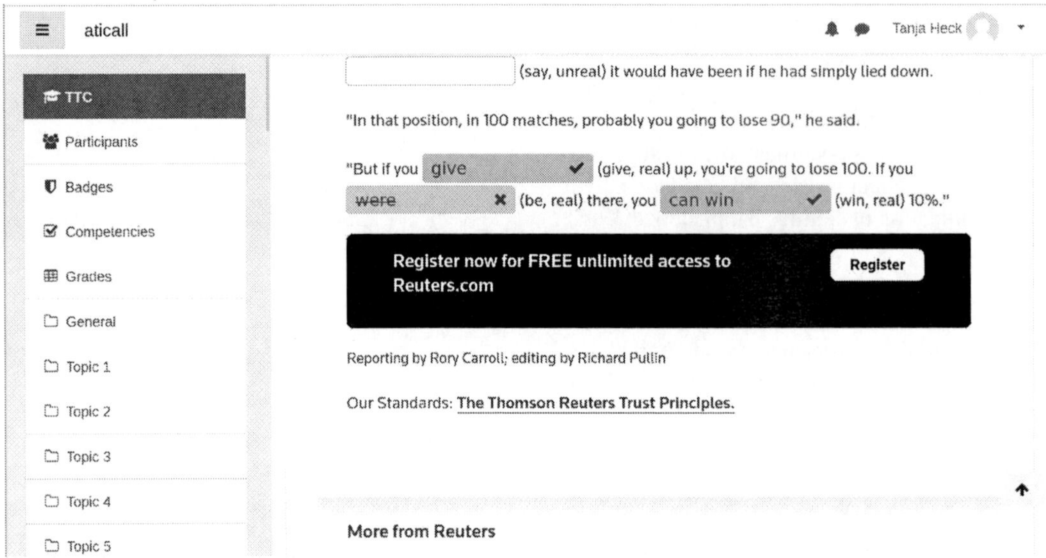

Figure 4: Excerpt of a generated H5P exercise in the LMS

4.1 Methodology

4.1.1 Suitable document selection

Suitable documents need to contain the targeted grammatical constructions relevant to the selected language means. The tool's performance in identifying them depends mostly on the reliability of the base system. We evaluated all supported language means, i.e., *Simple present*, *Past tenses*, *Comparatives*, *Conditionals*, *Relative pronouns* and *Passive sentences*. For each language means, we determined a binary score of whether the highest-ranked search result for the search term *education* contained constructions which could be transformed into exercise items. We used an additional flag to indicate whether this was possible with the default settings or only with the help of FLAIR's document ranking. When document ranking was applied, maximum weights were set for all constructions associated with the currently assessed language means.

Relevant construction identification Relevant constructions targeted by the language means can only be used for exercise generation if they are correctly annotated. Since the exercise generation extension uses a more fine-grained distinction between linguistic constructions than the base system, the performance of construction identification depends both on the base system's ability to correctly identify rather coarse-grained linguistic constructions and on the exercise generation tool's ability to correctly identify exercise targets from multiple, overlapping constructions. To this purpose, we sampled up to 10 occurrences for each type of exercise target from 100 arbitrarily selected web pages. Identical occurrences of target constructions were not considered and only web pages which contained at least one construction were taken into account. We report the precision for the identified constructions since the quality of most of our exercise types depends on the correctness of the used constructions, whereas recall is less important as long as sufficient exercise opportunities are found.

Target generation The target generation ratio is defined as the ratio of the number of actual exercise items in the generated exercises to the number of potential target constructions before post-processing. Although the identified constructions form the basis for exercise generation, some of them may be rejected during post-processing so that they cannot be transformed into exercise items. A perfect ratio of 1 indicates that all potential target constructions could be turned into an exercise target. Rejecting all constructions decreases the ratio to 0. In this evaluation which exclusively targets the performance of the exercise generation tool, we built on the search results obtained in the first evaluation step. The generation ratio was calculated for all supported language means-type combinations.

4.2 Results

4.2.1 Suitable document selection

The degree of difficulty in identifying **suitable documents** varied from one language means to another. For ***comparatives*** and ***simple present***, documents containing the targeted constructions were plentiful so that exercises could be generated on FLAIR's default settings. In order to find documents containing ***conditional***, ***passive*** or ***relative clause*** constructions, however, FLAIR's construction weighting needed to be applied. Setting high weights for conditional clauses, passive voice or relative pronouns respectively yielded high-ranked documents containing potential exercise items. ***Past tense*** exercises were also possible on documents identified with the standard settings, yet with little variety in the targeted tenses. When setting high weights for past tenses, the highest-ranked document contained past progressive constructions in addition to the previously included simple past and present perfect findings. Increasing the number of search results to 50 allowed to also target past perfect and present perfect progressive when setting construction weights. Only for past perfect progressive, none of the documents returned for the given search term contained any occurrences.

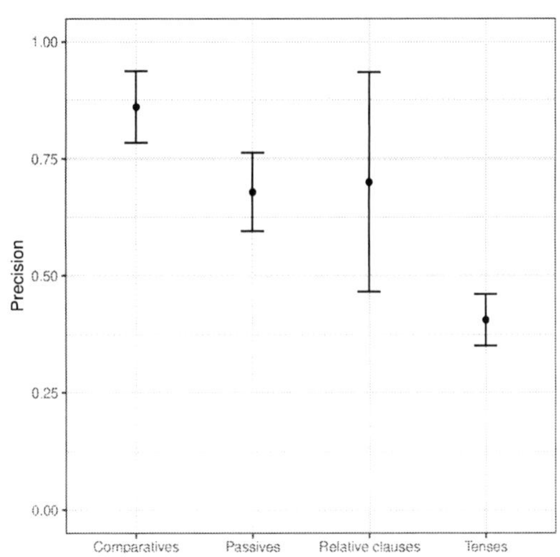

Figure 5: Precision of construction identification[13]

Relevant construction identification As illustrated by the plot in Figure 5 showing precision and standard error of pedagogical construction identification, the precision differs considerably between the language means as well as for the different instances of the language means. The full list of linguistic constructions subtypes relevant for each of these pedagogical language means is included in the Appendix. ***Comparative*** constructions all obtained fairly high precision values. Errors are mostly attributed to incorrectly assigned POS tags and thus already introduced in FLAIR's initial annotation. With respect to ***conditionals***, the performance for the two types differed considerably. While real conditionals were detected at high precision, most findings of unreal conditionals are in fact real conditionals. Performance with ***active and passive*** constructions was slightly lower on average. Tenses in simple aspect were rarely mislabelled for both active and passive voice. Constructions with progressive aspect, on the other hand, were often mislabelled, especially when combined with perfect aspect. Incorrect labels concern either aspect or voice. Precision values are only slightly better for active than for passive constructions. The performance for ***tenses*** was generally rather poor. Interrogative and negation annotations were not always correct, especially when the sentence constituted a question where the clause containing the construction was not in interrogative form. Past tenses in addition produced issues similar to those encountered with passive constructions that are not related to the active-passive distinction. The most prominent cause for incorrect labelling which was responsible for the overall poor performance in this category, with only 103 out of 232 occurrences labelled correctly, consists in the distinction between regular and irregular verbs. This generally resulted from the presence of an irregular auxiliary verb in the construction scope which incorrectly triggered the *irregular* label. Since simple present constructions do not distinguish between regular and irregular forms, performance for those was slightly better with 48 out of 80 occurrences labelled correctly. ***Relative pronouns*** performed very well for the most common pronouns *who*, *which* and *that* with 28 out of 30 occurrences labelled correctly. Only occurrences categorized as relative pronouns other than these three pronouns were incorrect, so the average precision is comparable to that of *Passives*.

Target generation Figure 6 depicts the target generation ratios for all language means. It shows that the results for the **target generation ratio** are generally reasonably high, although they vary from one language means to another. For ***past tense*** and ***relative pronoun*** exercises of all types, all predicted target constructions could be turned into

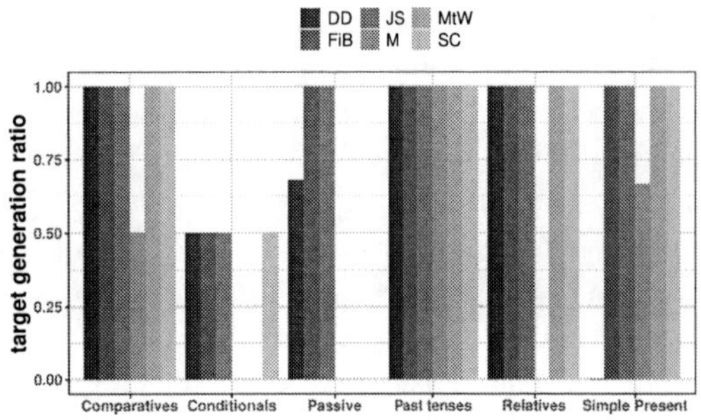

Figure 6: Target generation ratios

For each language means, the ratios are given for the following exercise types (left to right): Drag and Drop (DD), Fill-in-the-Blanks (FiB), Jumbled Sentences (JS), Memory (M), Mark-the-Words (MtW), and Single Choice (SC).

exercise targets. ***Comparative*** and ***simple present*** also exhibited good performance; only for Memory tasks did their resulting item number fall short of the prediction as some construction values were identical. Ratios for ***passive*** attained also maximum values except for Drag and Drop exercises where the NLP analysis in some cases failed to detect the relevant sentence parts targeted by this exercise. For ***conditional clause*** exercises, half of the constructions could be transformed into exercise targets. The other half deviated too much from standard tense and aspect constellations of conditional clauses so that they could not be analyzed by the NLP pipeline.

5 Conclusion

We presented a tool for automatic generation of English form-based grammar exercises from authentic web texts. It uses a language-aware search engine to address the challenge of identifying documents rich in the pedagogically targeted language means. While the integration of feedback aims at micro-adaptivity of the exercises, the tool also supports macro-adaptivity by allowing generation of parallel exercises at different levels of complexity. High parametrization of the exercise generation gives instructors control over the characterisitics of the generated exercises.

An evaluation of the current implementation yielded promising results. The tool robustly generates functional exercises that comply with the user configurations. While the evaluation considered the performance aspects in isolation, in the future we plan to perform an end-to-end evaluation in an authentic education context.

Limitations of our tool arise from building on an existing system for input enrichment before performing more detailed linguistic analyses to support exercise generation. As a result, some of the language material provided by the input enrichment system is rejected during the exercise generation phase. We are thus considering to enrich the initial linguistic analysis performed in the input enrichment component to the more fine-grained level that will make it possible to use it for both the document ranking component and the exercise generation.

Future work also will be important to determine the effect of the parameter settings on the exercise complexity as experienced by the learner and to determine which parameter constellations are appropriate for generating developmentally proximal exercises for a given target population. This will open the path for adaptive sequencing algorithms to offer exercises optimally adapted to the learner's current proficiency level and cognitive capabilities.

References

Itziar Aldabe, Maddalen Lopez de Lacalle, Montse Maritxalar, Edurne Martínez, and Larraitz Uria. 2006. Arikiturri: An automatic question generator based on corpora and nlp techniques. In *Proceedings of the 8th International Conference on Intelligent Tutoring Systems (ITS'06), Jhongli (Taiwan)*, pages 584–594. Springer-Verlag.

J. João Almeida, Eliana Grande, and Georgi Smirnov. 2017. Exercise generation on language specification. In *Recent Advances in Information Systems and Technologies*, pages 277–286, Cham. Springer International Publishing.

Georges Antoniadis, Sandra Echinard, Olivier Kraif, Thomas Lebarbé, Mathieu Loiseau, and Claude Ponton. 2004. Nlp-based scripting for call activities. In *Proceedings of the Workshop on eLearning for Computational Linguistics and Computational Linguistics for eLearning*, pages 18–25.

Lisa Beinborn. 2016. *Predicting and manipulating the difficulty of text completion exercises for language learning*. Ph.D. thesis, Department of Computer Science, Technische Universität Darmstadt.

Jasmine Bennöhr. 2005. *A web-based personalised textfinder for language learners*. Ph.D. thesis, Master's thesis, School of Informatics, University of Edinburgh.

Stephen Bodnar and Roy Lyster. 2021. Choose Your Own Content: a technology-based approach for automatically creating tailored grammar practice exercises from the web. 9th International Conference on Second Language Pedagogies.

Chia-Yin Chen, Hsien-Chin Liou, and Jason S. Chang. 2006. FAST – an automatic generation system for grammar tests. In *Proceedings of the COLING/ACL 2006 Interactive Presentation Sessions*, pages 1–4, Sydney, Australia. Association for Computational Linguistics.

Maria Chinkina, Madeeswaran Kannan, and Detmar Meurers. 2016. Online information retrieval for language learning. In *Proceedings of ACL-2016 System Demonstrations*, pages 7–12.

Maria Chinkina and Detmar Meurers. 2016. Linguistically-aware information retrieval: Providing input enrichment for second language learners. In *Proceedings of the 11th Workshop on Innovative Use of NLP for Building Educational Applications (BEA)*, pages 188–198, San Diego, CA. ACL.

Jozef Colpaert and Emre Sevinc. 2010. ClozeFox: Gap Exercise Generator with Scalable Intelligence for Mozilla Firefox. `https://github.com/emres/clozefox`. [Online; accessed 25-March-2022].

Sabrina Dittrich, Zarah Weiss, Hannes Schröter, and Detmar Meurers. 2019. Integrating large-scale web data and curated corpus data in a search engine supporting german literacy education. In *Proceedings of the 8th Workshop on Natural Language Processing for Computer Assisted Language Learning (NLP4CALL 2019), September 30, Turku Finland*, 164, pages 41–56. Linköping University Electronic Press.

Colleen Griffiths. 2020. All about the lms. *Learning Management Systems*.

Ayako Hoshino and Hiroshi Nakagawa. 2008. A cloze test authoring system and its automation. In *Advances in Web Based Learning – ICWL 2007*, pages 252–263, Berlin, Heidelberg. Springer Berlin Heidelberg.

Ji-Ung Lee, Erik Schwan, and Christian M Meyer. 2019. Manipulating the difficulty of c-tests. *arXiv preprint arXiv:1906.06905*.

Chao-Lin Liu, Chun-Hung Wang, Zhao-Ming Gao, and Shang-Ming Huang. 2005. Applications of lexical information for algorithmically composing multiple-choice cloze items. In *Proceedings of the Second Workshop on Building Educational Applications Using NLP*, pages 1–8, Ann Arbor, Michigan. Association for Computational Linguistics.

Sergio-Ramón Rossetti López, Ma Teresa García Ramírez, and Isaac-Shamir Rojas Rodríguez. 2021. Evaluation of the implementation of a learning object developed with h5p technology. *Vivat Academia*, 154:1–24.

Nitin Madnani, Jill Burstein, John Sabatini, Kietha Biggers, and Slava Andreyev. 2016. Language muse: Automated linguistic activity generation for english language learners. *Grantee Submission*.

Juliana Magro. 2021. H5p. *Journal of the Medical Library Association: JMLA*, 109(2):351.

Maite Melero and Ariadna Font. 2001. Construction of a Spanish Generation Module in the framework of a general-purpose, Multilingual Natural Language Processing System. *VII International Symposium on Social Communication*.

Detmar Meurers, Ramon Ziai, Luiz Amaral, Adriane Boyd, Aleksandar Dimitrov, Vanessa Metcalf, and Niels Ott. 2010. Enhancing authentic web pages for language learners. In *Proceedings of the 5th Workshop on Innovative Use of NLP for Building Educational Applications (BEA)*, pages 10–18, Los Angeles. ACL.

Eleni Miltsakaki and Audrey Troutt. 2008. Real time web text classification and analysis of reading difficulty. In *Proceedings of the Third Workshop on Innovative Use of NLP for Building Educational Applications (BEA-3) at ACL'08*, pages 89–97, Columbus, Ohio. Association for Computational Linguistics.

Jugend und Sport Ministerium für Kultus. 2016. Bildungsplan des Gymnasiums: Englisch als erste Fremdsprache [academic school track curriculum: English as first foreign language].

Niels Ott and Detmar Meurers. 2011. Information retrieval for education: Making search engines language aware. *Themes in Science and Technology Education*, 3(1-2):9–30.

Irina Pandarova, Torben Schmidt, Johannes Hartig, Ahcène Boubekki, Roger Dale Jones, and Ulf Brefeld. 2019. Predicting the difficulty of exercise items for dynamic difficulty adaptation in adaptive language tutoring. *International Journal of Artificial Intelligence in Education*, 29(3):342–367.

Matthew Peacock. 1997. The effect of authentic materials on the motivation of EFL learners. *ELT Journal*, 51(2):144–156.

Naiara Perez and Montse Cuadros. 2017. Multilingual CALL framework for automatic language exercise generation from free text. In *Proceedings of the Software Demonstrations of the 15th Conference of the European Chapter of the Association for Computational Linguistics*, pages 49–52, Valencia, Spain. Association for Computational Linguistics.

Laura Perez-Beltrachini, Claire Gardent, and German Kruszewski. 2012. Generating grammar exercises. In *Proceedings of the Seventh Workshop on Building Educational Applications Using NLP*, pages 147–156. Association for Computational Linguistics.

Robert Reynolds, Eduard Schaf, and Detmar Meurers. 2014. A view of Russian: Visual input enhancement and adaptive feedback. In *Proceedings of the third workshop on NLP for computer-assisted language learning*, NEALT Proceedings Series 22 / Linköping Electronic Conference Proceedings 107, pages 98–112, Uppsala. ACL.

Cameron Romney. 2016. Considerations for using images in teacher made materials. *The*, pages 280–289.

Björn Rudzewitz, Ramon Ziai, Kordula De Kuthy, Verena Möller, Florian Nuxoll, and Detmar Meurers. 2018. Generating feedback for English foreign language exercises. In *Proceedings of the Thirteenth Workshop on Innovative Use of NLP for Building Educational Applications*, pages 127–136, New Orleans, Louisiana. Association for Computational Linguistics.

Vasile Rus, Dan Stefanescu, William Baggett, Nobal Niraula, Don Franceschetti, and Arthur C Graesser. 2014. Macro-adaptation in conversational intelligent tutoring matters. In *International Conference on Intelligent Tutoring Systems*, pages 242–247. Springer.

Lee Schwartz, Takako Aikawa, and Michel Pahud. 2004. Dynamic language learning tools. *Proceedings of InSTIL/ICALL Symposium 2004.*

Kahtleen M. Sheehan, Irene W. Kostin, and Yoko Futagi. 2007. Sourcefinder: A construct-driven approach for locating appropriately targeted reading comprehension source texts. In *Proceedings of the 2007 Workshop of the International Speech Communication Association, Special Interest Group on Speech and Language Technology in Education.*

Pavel V Sysoyev. 1999. Integrative l2 grammar teaching: Exploration, explanation and expression. *The internet TESL journal*, 5(6):1–13.

Janine Toole and Trude Heift. 2001. Generating learning content for an intelligent language tutoring system. In *Proceedings of NLP-CALL Workshop at the 10th Int. Conf. on Artificial Intelligence in Education (AI-ED). San Antonio, Texas*, pages 1–8.

Elena Volodina, Ildikó Pilán, Lars Borin, and Therese Lindström Tiedemann. 2014. A flexible language learning platform based on language resources and web services. In *Proceedings of the Ninth International Conference on Language Resources and Evaluation (LREC'14)*, pages 3973–3978, Reykjavik, Iceland. European Language Resources Association (ELRA).

Mariia Zabolotniaia, Zhichao Cheng, Evgenij Dorozhkin, and Anton Lyzhin. 2020. Use of the lms moodle for an effective implementation of an innovative policy in higher educational institutions. *International Journal of Emerging Technologies in Learning (iJET)*, 15(13):172–189.

Arianna Zanetti, Elena Volodina, and Johannes Graën. 2021. Automatic generation of exercises for second language learning from parallel corpus data. *International Journal of TESOL Studies*, 3(2):55–71.

Sun Zhuomin. 2010. Language teaching materials and learner motivation. *Journal of Language Teaching and Research*, 1.

Appendix A: Detailed target identification results

Up to ten occurrences were randomly sampled for all target constructions. From these samples, the numbers of correctly and incorrectly labelled instances were determined and precision was calculated.

Grammatical construction	# correct	# incorrect	Precision
Conditional: real	9	1	0.9
Conditional: unreal	2	8	0.2
Passive: present simple	9	1	0.9
Passive: past simple	10	0	1.0
Passive: future simple	0	2	0.0
Passive: present perf.	10	0	1.0
Passive: past perf.	10	0	1.0
Passive: future perf.	1	7	0.125
Passive: present prog.	0	0	
Passive: past prog.	0	0	
Passive: future prog.	0	2	0.0
Passive: present perf. prog.	0	4	0.0
Passive: past perf. prog.	1	2	0.3333
Passive: future perf. prog.	0	0	
Active: present simple	6	4	0.6
Active: past simple	10	0	1.0
Active: future simple	10	0	1.0
Active: present perf.	10	0	1.0
Active: past perf.	10	0	1.0
Active: future perf.	6	4	0.6
Active: present prog.	10	0	1.0
Active: past prog.	10	0	1.0
Active: future prog.	10	0	1.0
Active: present perf. prog.	7	3	0.7
Active: past perf. prog.	5	5	0.5
Active: future perf. prog.	1	1	0.5
Past simple: stmt., affirm., reg.	9	1	0.9
Past simple: stmt., affirm., irreg.	10	0	1.0
Past simple: stmt., neg., reg.	1	9	0.1
Past simple: stmt., neg., irreg.	6	4	0.6
Past simple: quest., affirm., reg.	4	6	0.4
Past simple: quest., affirm., irreg.	4	6	0.4
Past simple: quest., neg., reg.	1	0	1.0
Past simple: quest., neg., irreg.	4	6	0.4
Present perf.: stmt., affirm., reg.	9	1	0.9
Present perf.: stmt., affirm., irreg.	10	0	1.0
Present perf.: stmt., neg., reg.	9	1	0.9
Present perf.: stmt., neg., irreg.	6	4	0.6
Present perf.: quest., affirm., reg.	4	6	0.4
Present perf.: quest., affirm., irreg.	3	7	0.3
Present perf.: quest., neg., reg.	3	1	0.75
Present perf.: quest., neg., irreg.	4	3	0.5714
Past perf.: stmt., affirm., reg.	0	0	
Past perf.: stmt., affirm., irreg.	4	6	0.4
Past perf.: stmt., neg., reg.	0	0	

Grammatical construction	# correct	# incorrect	Precision
Past perf.: stmt., neg., irreg.	5	5	0.5
Past perf.: quest., affirm., reg.	0	0	
Past perf.: quest., affirm., irreg.	0	9	0.0
Past perf.: quest., neg., reg.	0	0	
Past perf.: quest., neg., irreg.	0	1	0.0
Past prog.: stmt., affirm., reg.	0	3	0.0
Past prog.: stmt., affirm., irreg.	3	7	0.3
Past prog.: stmt., neg., reg.	0	0	
Past prog.: stmt., neg., irreg.	1	9	0.1
Past prog.: quest., affirm., reg.	0	0	
Past prog.: quest., affirm., irreg.	0	10	0.0
Past prog.: quest., neg., reg.	0	0	
Past prog.: quest., neg., irreg.	0	1	0.0
Present perf. prog.: stmt., affirm., reg.	0	7	0.0
Present perf. prog.: stmt., affirm., irreg.	3	7	0.3
Present perf. prog.: stmt., neg., reg.	0	1	0.0
Present perf. prog.: stmt., neg., irreg.	0	1	0.0
Present perf. prog.: quest., affirm., reg.	0	1	0.0
Present perf. prog.: quest., affirm., irreg.	0	4	0.0
Present perf. prog.: quest., neg., reg.	0	0	
Present perf. prog.: quest., neg., irreg.	0	0	
Past perf. prog.: stmt., neg., reg.	0	0	
Past perf. prog.: stmt., neg., irreg.	0	2	0.0
Past perf. prog.: quest., affirm., reg.	0	0	
Past perf. prog.: quest., affirm., irreg.	0	0	
Past perf. prog.: quest., neg., reg.	0	0	
Past perf. prog.: quest., neg., irreg.	0	0	
Present simple: stmt., affirm., 3rd pers.	7	3	0.7
Present simple: stmt., affirm., not 3rd pers.	8	2	0.8
Present simple: stmt., neg., 3rd pers.	9	1	0.9
Present simple: stmt., neg., not 3rd pers.	8	2	0.8
Present simple: quest., affirm., 3rd pers.	3	7	0.3
Present simple: quest., affirm., not 3rd pers.	4	6	0.4
Present simple: quest., neg., 3rd pers.	5	5	0.5
Present simple: quest., neg., not 3rd pers.	4	6	0.4
Relative pronouns: who	10	0	1.0
Relative pronouns: which	9	1	0.9
Relative pronouns: that	9	1	0.9
Relative pronouns: other relative pronoun	0	10	0.0
Adjective: comparative, synthetic	10	0	1.0
Adjective: superlative, synthetic	8	2	0.8
Adjective: comparative, analytic	9	1	0.9
Adjective: superlative, analytic	10	0	1.0
Adverb: comparative, synthetic	9	1	0.9
Adverb: superlative, synthetic	5	0	1.0
Adverb: comparative, analytic	10	0	1.0
Adverb: superlative, analytic	9	1	0.9

Selecting Context Clozes for Lightweight Reading Compliance

Greg A. Keim
Georgia Institute of Technology
greg.keim@gatech.edu

Michael L. Littman
Brown University
mlittman@brown.cs.edu

Abstract

We explore a novel approach to reading compliance, leveraging large language models to select inline challenges that discourage skipping during reading. This lightweight 'testing' is accomplished through automatically identified *context clozes* where the reader must supply a missing word that would be hard to guess if earlier material was skipped. Clozes are selected by scoring each word by the contrast between its likelihood with and without prior sentences as context, preferring to leave gaps where this contrast is high. We report results of an initial human-participant test that indicates this method can find clozes that have this property.

1 Introduction

Ideally, college students would complete assigned readings before class, allowing professors to lean on that shared knowledge, extending and deepening understanding rather than reteaching the textbook context during the class. However, there have been a number of studies showing that when student work is not directly checked in some way, reading compliance is low (Burchfield and Sappington, 2000; Clump et al., 2004; Connor-Greene, 2000).

An obvious approach to encouraging reading compliance is for the professor or publisher to create quizzes that confirm whether students have completed the associated reading. While such questions can aid learning, thoughtfully drawing connections between various parts of the text or encouraging deeper thinking, they also require time to create, complete and score and perhaps become less useful over time as the answers begin to circulate online.

Perusall is a social learning platform designed specifically to improve reading compliance (Johnson, 2019). The tool segments students into small groups, who can then annotate and discuss the readings online. The authors report impressive results, increasing reading compliance to as much as 90% in some cases. However, this method uses group learning and written responses, which may not be possible in all situations or desirable to all students.

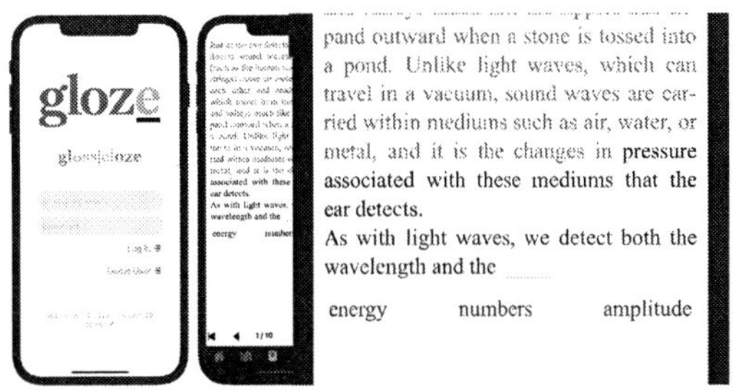

Figure 1: Gloze demonstration application, illustrating multiple choice context clozes for reading compliance.

We propose a new approach, demonstrated in a prototype application named **Gloze** (from gloss + cloze). A traditional *cloze* exercise requires a student to fill in words removed randomly or at fixed intervals from a passage. Such cloze exercises can be used to assess language proficiency, and have a long history in that literature (Alderson, 1979). In Gloze, we hope to leverage the cloze concept to increase reading compliance of long texts without time spent creating or grading external assessments. Shown in Figure 1, the method periodically requires the reader to choose the correct next word, using multiple choice with confusers to reduce the disruption of typing during reading. A key requirement of this approach is selecting challenges such that answering is easy if prior context has been read but difficult if not.

As an example of how context impacts a cloze exercise, consider the human-crafted sentence pair: *He caught the pass and scored another touchdown. There was nothing he enjoyed more than a good game of* _____ . (Federmeier and Kutas, 1999). Note that the answer (*football*) is clear with the context of the first sentence (assuming familiarity with the sport), but that with only the partial second sentence, the answer is ambiguous. We define this particular cloze formulation as a *context cloze*,

Proceedings of the 17th Workshop on Innovative Use of NLP for Building Educational Applications (BEA 2022), pages 167 - 172

where presence of prior context has an outsize (perhaps even opposite) impact relative to the immediate context. LAMBADA (Paperno et al., 2016) leverages a similar framing, though with human-computer roles reversed, to evaluate language understanding in large language models (LLMs). A test set is selected by having humans perform cloze exercises with and without broader context, selecting clozes that are easy with context and hard without.[1]

In this work, we focus on the issues of selecting context clozes with one contrasting confuser and validating that LLMs generally model the performance of human participants in this domain. Note that there are many more issues required for Gloze to be useful that are not addressed here, some of which are enumerated in the Future Work section.

All our examples and tests in this work use the text of the 685-page, freely available, anonymous college-level *Introduction to Psychology* ((Removed), 2015). However, the method could in theory be applied in any domain where confirmation that a long document has been read is important (e.g., legal agreements, safety manuals or human resources training documents).

2 Context Cloze Selection

A correlation between LLMs and human word predictions has already been demonstrated. Goldstein et al. (2020) conducted an experiment with human participants, asking them to predict each next word in a long narrative. They denoted the *predictability* of a word as the percentage of respondents that correctly generated it. Comparing human predictability scores to those from GPT-2 (Radford, 2020) on the same task, they found a strong correlation ($r = 0.79$ with a 100-word prior context). Therefore, it seems reasonable to leverage LLMs to approximate human predictability based on various contexts. In what follows, we use GPT-2 for our predictions.[2]

To choose the best context clozes with the LLM, we evaluate all words in the text, scoring each based on how the predictability changes with and without context. The reading application can use this complete weighted ordering of words to select the highest scoring cloze within some region of text.

[1]State of the art systems have achieved 89.7% on this metric (Chowdhery et al., 2022).

[2]In particular, we use the 117M parameter OpenAI "gpt2" model through HuggingFace (Wolf et al., 2020).

Note that this approach is not explicitly leveraging part of speech, text markup for key terms or measures of importance such as Term Frequency–Inverse Document Frequency (though our method may be implicitly finding similar "important" items, it isn't required).

After eliminating stop words, for each word in the text (a *target*), we compute this score by selecting the entire *prior* sentence and the *partial* sentence consisting of the words of the target's sentence up to the target.[3] If we define:

$t_0 = P(\textit{target}|\textit{partial})$

$t_1 = P(\textit{target}|\textit{prior}+\textit{partial})$

then we prefer targets that maximize $t_1 - t_0$ (i.e., targets with high likelihood with context and low likelihood without). Note that a high-scoring target does not necessarily need to be related to the content of the chapter but simply one with the right shift in predictability.

As we aim to present these targets as cloze exercises during reading as multiple choice selections, we also consider whether there is a candidate *confuser* that actually has the opposite predictability movement. As above, we define:

$c_0 = P(\textit{confuser}|\textit{partial})$

$c_1 = P(\textit{confuser}|\textit{prior}+\textit{partial})$

To select a confuser to contrast with the target from the same context, we examine the probabilities of the top 25 words in both contexts, selecting the confuser that maximizes $c_0 - c_1$ (i.e., the confuser that has the largest *decrease* in probability when context is included).

With these four next-word probabilities from GPT-2, we can define a target's score. For targets where $t_1 > t_0$ (target more likely with context), $c_0 > t_0$ (confuser more likely than target without context) and $t_1 > c_1$ (target more likely than confuser with context), we define a score $s = (c_0 - t_0) + (t_1 - c_1) + (t_1 - t_0)$. For the purposes of this work, all other words have $s = 0$.

However, we noted after initial examination of high-scoring targets that the score did not accurately capture the predictability of a student reading a textbook for a class. In particular, the student knows the subject area she is reading about, which shapes the predictability even in a partial context. To account for this observation, we added the first paragraph from Wikipedia's entry describing the field of Psychology as context in front of all prompts (Wikipedia contributors, 2021). With this

[3]First sentences in each chapter were ignored.

Prior	Partial	Target
There are also individual differences in need for sleep.	Some people do quite well with fewer than 6	hours
If a sound occurs on your left side, the left ear will receive the sound slightly sooner than the right ear, and the sound it receives will be more intense, allowing you to quickly determine the location of the sound.	Although the distance between our two	ears
When we are awake, our brain activity is characterized by the presence of very fast beta waves.	When we first begin to fall	asleep
The BART is a computer task in which the participant pumps up a series of simulated balloons by pressing on a computer key.	With each pump the balloon appears bigger on the	screen
When you touch a hot stove and immediately pull your hand back, or when you fumble your cell phone and instinctively reach to catch it before it falls, reflexes in your spinal cord order the appropriate responses before your brain even knows what is happening.	If the central	nervous

Table 1: High-scoring example sentences from the Psychology textbook.

Prior	Partial	Target
"Checkmate," Rosaline announced with glee.	She was getting to be really good at	chess
He wanted to make his wife breakfast, but he burned piece after piece.	I couldn't believe he was ruining even the	toast
Barb loved the feel of the waves on her feet, but she hated to walk barefoot.	As a compromise, she usually wore a pair of	sandals

Table 2: CPRAG20 example sentences.

context, clozes like "The scientific ____" no longer score well, as "method" is now likely given the expanded prompt. As it also felt more disruptive to have a gap early in a sentence, a small constant was added (when $s > 0$) to favor clozes that occurred after the first few words.[4]

This procedure produces a list of all words in the textbook ranked by score (a few high-scoring samples are shown in Table 1).

3 Human-Participant Comparison

The premise of the context cloze is that we can identify places in the text where the correct next word is *unlikely* given only local context (the sentence so far) but *likely* given the prior context (the past sentence). While the probability-based scoring used to rank context clozes guarantees this condition is true for the LLM, and we know that in general LLMs approximate human language models, how can we know that this scoring method provides a reasonable model of human responses to these cloze exercises? In this section, we describe an experiment we conducted to explore this question.[5]

3.1 Test Sets

Federmeier and Kutas (1999) measured electrical responses in the brain to understand the response to expected vs. unexpected next words in hand-built cloze exercises. They constructed 132 sentences specifically designed to have a highly likely next word response given an additional prior context sentence. More recently, this same dataset has been reused in work specifically aimed at understanding how LLMs respond to structured prompts (Ettinger, 2020), and we follow their convention in annotating the set as "CPRAG" after "Common Sense and Pragmatic Inference." In Table 2, several examples are shown to illustrate the contrast between reading both the prior context and partial sentence as opposed to just seeing the partial sentence.

While the original research involved differentiating between different types of next words (specifically, in/out of category), the measured human-participant predictability scores for these hand-built contexts can serve as a useful baseline for our own human-participant testing. Since this prior work required participants to generate the word (not choose it from a list), we use that method as well. In particular, we create two datasets with the same elements, (*prior*, *partial*, *target*), one from CPRAG and one from our context cloze method:

CPRAG20 We selected 20 examples to include in our experiment where we have average human predictability scores for both with and without context (see Table 2 for examples). The purpose of retesting this set is to validate our experimental design by replicating a prior data point.

PSYCH50 We selected 50 high-scoring context clozes from the introductory Psychology textbook (see Table 1 for examples). After programmatically scoring each word in the text, these examples

[4]Scores were increased by 0.5 if the partial context had at least 20 characters.

[5]This research was approved through Georgia Institute of Technology IRB, Protocol Number H21222.

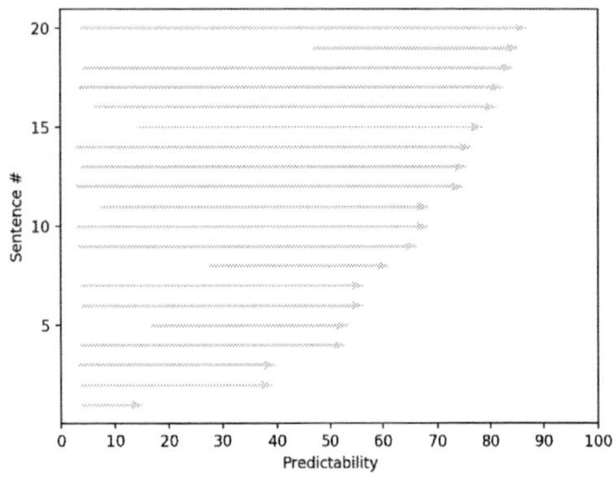

Figure 2: CPRAG20 sentences, sorted by the human predictability with context. Arrows indicate the gain in predictability from adding the prior sentence of context.

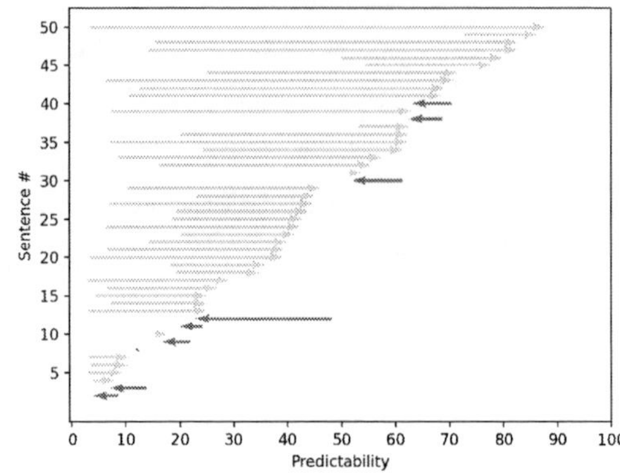

Figure 3: PSYCH50 sentences, sorted by the human predictability with context. Arrows indicate the gain or loss from adding a prior sentence context.

were selected by starting with the highest scores, skipping samples with repeated contexts, errors in sentence/word boundaries, or content that was judged might be offensive or disturbing given the absence of the full context of the chapter.[6]

3.2 Procedure

For each of the two prompt sets (CPRAG20 and PSYCH50), two sets (A and B) were created that randomly distributed with- and without-context versions of each of the prompts. Participants were randomly placed in either the A or B group of each prompt set, and then within that set they randomly responded to a subset of the prompts in a random order. In this way, no participant saw more than one form of the same prompt, everyone saw about the same number of with- and without-context prompts and any impacts from prompt order were minimized.

For each of the 70 items in CPRAG20 and PSYCH50, there were two conditions, with and without context, resulting in a total of 140 possible prompts. We tested 100 participants (online through Prolific and Qualtrics), each typing next words for 35 of these, totaling 3500 responses or about 25 answers per prompt across participants.

3.3 Results

For each target prompt attempted in the test, we calculated the predictability of the expected answer based on the percentage of respondents that typed that word. We did not correct spelling, but did remove punctuation, converted to lower case and only used the first word typed if a participant wrote the next several words.[7]

CPRAG20 Federmeier and Kutas (1999) found that human average predictability over the entire 132 sentences with context was around 74%. As selected a subset of 20 of these, we expected to get roughly the same predictability over our set. In Figure 2, predictability for both conditions of the 20 sentences are shown. Sentences are sorted by their "with context" scores, and are shown with an arrow from the without- to the with-context results. We found a 71.9% average predictability with context on our CPRAG20 subset (up from 5.7% average without), comparable to past work.

PSYCH50 As before, in Figure 3 we sort the 50 prompts by their "with context" predictability. Nine of the prompts actually decrease in predictability (shown with red leftward arrows) and some show only modest increases. However, as desired, the results do demonstrate that the method of scoring using LLMs is selecting clozes that on average show large increases in human predictability with context, from an average of 19.3% up to 47.4%, a mean absolute increase of 28.1% (with a standard deviation of 28.0).

In both the human-constructed and computer-selected cloze exercises, our testing method allowed us to confirm that some clozes have very

[6]Eighteen such examples were removed by researcher judgement.

[7]3.7% of all responses included more than one word.

low predictability (the without-context sentences on the left of the graphs). That there is this much variation (and separation) between possible cloze prompts helps justify our focus on smart selection, so as not to frustrate the reader with clozes that are too easy or too hard.

4 Future Work

As noted earlier, the initial test presented here only addresses one piece of what an actual system would require to be successful. In future work, we want to explore larger prior context windows as well as examine fine-tuning as a replacement for the field-description paragraph. It is also critical to characterize the frequency of adequate context clozes in textbooks relative to the frequency that would be required to ensure a particular level of reading attention. In addition, many aspects of confusers need to be explored: how they impact the choice of context clozes, how various selection strategies impact compliance metrics and how to ensure LLM-generated confusers, while not the right answer by design, aren't creating confusion or demonstrating bias by being presented in a particular context. We removed some high-scoring clozes from this human-participant test, for reasons that we believe would be alleviated when the system is run in context (isolated content concerns) or through additional improvements to text processing (tokenization and filtering)–however we would need to demonstrate this is true at scale. Finally, we hope to evaluate this approach in a few classes through a mobile reading application that uses our scoring method.

5 Conclusion

We described a method for selecting context clozes to encourage reading compliance, and ran this algorithm on an introductory college textbook. We took some of the best scoring clozes and conducted a human-participant test, which confirmed our hypothesis that LLMs are a reasonable proxy for human predictability for context cloze scoring and that these clozes on average demonstrate the desired shift in predictability with and without context.

References

J. Charles Alderson. 1979. The Cloze Procedure and Proficiency in English as a Foreign Language. *TESOL Quarterly*, 13(2):219.

Colin M Burchfield and John Sappington. 2000. Compliance with required reading assignments. *Teaching of Psychology*.

Aakanksha Chowdhery, Sharan Narang, Jacob Devlin, Maarten Bosma, Gaurav Mishra, Adam Roberts, Paul Barham, Hyung Won Chung, Charles Sutton, Sebastian Gehrmann, Parker Schuh, Kensen Shi, Sasha Tsvyashchenko, Joshua Maynez, Abhishek Rao, Parker Barnes, Yi Tay, Noam Shazeer, Vinodkumar Prabhakaran, Emily Reif, Nan Du, Ben Hutchinson, Reiner Pope, James Bradbury, Jacob Austin, Michael Isard, Guy Gur-Ari, Pengcheng Yin, Toju Duke, Anselm Levskaya, Sanjay Ghemawat, Sunipa Dev, Henryk Michalewski, Xavier Garcia, Vedant Misra, Kevin Robinson, Liam Fedus, Denny Zhou, Daphne Ippolito, David Luan, Hyeontaek Lim, Barret Zoph, Alexander Spiridonov, Ryan Sepassi, David Dohan, Shivani Agrawal, Mark Omernick, Andrew M. Dai, Thanumalayan Sankaranarayana Pillai, Marie Pellat, Aitor Lewkowycz, Erica Moreira, Rewon Child, Oleksandr Polozov, Katherine Lee, Zongwei Zhou, Xuezhi Wang, Brennan Saeta, Mark Diaz, Orhan Firat, Michele Catasta, Jason Wei, Kathy Meier-Hellstern, Douglas Eck, Jeff Dean, Slav Petrov, and Noah Fiedel. 2022. Palm: Scaling language modeling with pathways.

M.A. Clump, H. Bauer, and C. Bradley. 2004. The Extent to which Psychology Students Read Textbooks. *Journal of Instructional Psychology*, 31(3):227–232.

Patricia A. Connor-Greene. 2000. Assessing and Promoting Student Learning: Blurring the Line between Teaching and Testing. *Teaching of Psychology*, 27(2):84–88.

Allyson Ettinger. 2020. What BERT Is Not: Lessons from a New Suite of Psycholinguistic Diagnostics for Language Models. *Transactions of the Association for Computational Linguistics*, 8:34–48.

Kara D. Federmeier and Marta Kutas. 1999. A Rose by Any Other Name: Long-Term Memory Structure and Sentence Processing. *Journal of Memory and Language*, 41(4):469–495.

Ariel Goldstein, Zaid Zada, Eliav Buchnik, Mariano Schain, Amy Price, Bobbi Aubrey, Samuel A Nastase, Amir Feder, Dotan Emanuel, Alon Cohen, Aren Jansen, Harshvardhan Gazula, Gina Choe, Aditi Rao, Catherine Kim, Colton Casto, Fanda Lora, Adeen Flinker, Sasha Devore, Werner Doyle, Daniel Friedman, Patricia Dugan, Avinatan Hassidim, Michael Brenner, Yossi Matias, Kenneth A Norman, Orrin Devinsky, and Uri Hasson. 2020. Thinking ahead: Prediction in context as a keystone of language in humans and machines.

Steven Johnson. 2019. The Fall; and Rise, of Reading. *The Chronicle of Higher Education*, 65(31):A14–A14.

Denis Paperno, Germán Kruszewski, Angeliki Lazaridou, Ngoc Quan Pham, Raffaella Bernardi, Sandro

Pezzelle, Marco Baroni, Gemma Boleda, and Raquel Fernández. 2016. The LAMBADA dataset: Word prediction requiring a broad discourse context. In *Proceedings of the 54th Annual Meeting of the Association for Computational Linguistics (Volume 1: Long Papers)*, pages 1525–1534, Berlin, Germany. Association for Computational Linguistics.

Alec Radford. 2020. Language Models are Unsupervised Multitask Learners. *OpenAI Blog*, 1(May):1–7.

(Removed). 2015. *Introduction to Psychology*. University of Minnesota Libraries.

Wikipedia contributors. 2021. Psychology — Wikipedia, the free encyclopedia. `https://en.wikipedia.org/w/index.php?title=Psychology&oldid=1053798210`. [Online; accessed 13-November-2021].

Thomas Wolf, Lysandre Debut, Victor Sanh, Julien Chaumond, Clement Delangue, Anthony Moi, Pierric Cistac, Tim Rault, Remi Louf, Morgan Funtowicz, Joe Davison, Sam Shleifer, Patrick von Platen, Clara Ma, Yacine Jernite, Julien Plu, Canwen Xu, Teven Le Scao, Sylvain Gugger, Mariama Drame, Quentin Lhoest, and Alexander Rush. 2020. Transformers: State-of-the-Art Natural Language Processing. In *Proceedings of the 2020 Conference on Empirical Methods in Natural Language Processing: System Demonstrations*, pages 38–45, Stroudsburg, PA, USA. Association for Computational Linguistics.

'Meet me at the ribary' – Acceptability of spelling variants in free-text answers to listening comprehension prompts

Ronja Laarmann-Quante[1] and **Leska Schwarz**[2] and **Andrea Horbach**[1] and **Torsten Zesch**[1]
[1]Research Cluster D^2L^2 – Digitalization, Diversity and Lifelong Learning. Consequences for Higher Education.
FernUniversität in Hagen, Germany
[2]g.a.s.t./TestDaF-Institut, Bochum, Germany
{ronja.laarmann-quante|andrea.horbach|torsten.zesch}@fernuni-hagen.de
leska.schwarz@testdaf.de

Abstract

When listening comprehension is tested as a free-text production task, a challenge for scoring the answers is the resulting wide range of spelling variants. When judging whether a variant is acceptable or not, human raters perform a complex holistic decision. In this paper, we present a corpus study in which we analyze human acceptability decisions in a high stakes test for German. We show that for human experts, spelling variants are harder to score consistently than other answer variants. Furthermore, we examine how the decision can be operationalized using features that could be applied by an automatic scoring system. We show that simple measures like edit distance and phonetic similarity between a given answer and the target answer can model the human acceptability decisions with the same inter-annotator agreement as humans, and discuss implications of the remaining inconsistencies.

1 Introduction

Imagine a listening comprehension task where a student listens to two people scheduling a meeting at the library. The student is then supposed to answer the question 'Where do they want to meet?' and writes 'ribary' instead of 'library'. Is this answer acceptable or not?

The answer to this question is not an easy one. Human experts perform a complex holistic decision in such a case, primarily based on whether they assume that the learner understood the right answer (see Section 2). The aim of this paper is to get a deeper understanding on which factors influence the acceptability of a spelling variant and ultimately how to model this decision automatically. Thereby, we aim at a model that is transparent and uses features which allow to explain under which conditions the system accepts a variant and under which not. To this end, we conduct a corpus study based on real learner answers and human ratings in a high stakes test of German as a foreign language and explore different operationalizations of spelling variant acceptability. We show that our classifier does not yet reach an adjudicated gold standard, but the human decisions can be approximated up to the same level as human-human agreement. Finally, we discuss possible reasons and implications of the remaining inconsistencies.

The remainder of the paper is structured as follows: In Section 2, we give some background about listening comprehension tasks and the role of orthography. In Section 3, we introduce the data set and in Section 4, we analyze the distribution of spelling variants and the human acceptability decisions. Section 5 examines different features that could be used to operationalize the holistic human acceptability decisions.

2 Background

In many high stakes language tests, listening comprehension is tested with a free-text production task (e.g. DALF[1] for French, Goethe Certificate[2] and TestDaF[3] for German, Cambridge Certificate[4] for English). This means that the test takers have to listen to an audio prompt and formulate an answer in their own words. This gives rise to variance in the answers, e.g. synonyms or different syntactic or orthographic variants (Horbach and Zesch, 2019), which makes the automatic scoring of such answers a challenging NLP task.

While variance at the level of wording or syntax is a topic extensively covered both by short-answer-scoring in general (Ziai et al., 2012) as well as computational semantic similarity (Bär et al., 2012), the implications of orthographic variance are an understudied topic in automatic scoring. In e.g. reading comprehension tasks, where test takers can often copy material from the prompt, spelling errors are

[1]https://www.france-education-international.fr/en/delf-dalf
[2]https://www.goethe.de/de/spr/kup/prf/prf.html
[3]https://www.testdaf.de/
[4]https://www.cambridgeenglish.org/exams-and-tests/

Proceedings of the 17th Workshop on Innovative Use of NLP for Building Educational Applications (BEA 2022), pages 173 - 182
July 15, 2022

usually ignored (Horbach et al., 2017). In listening comprehension tasks, however, the assessment of orthographic variants (e.g. *ribary* or *librarie* for *library*), plays a much more central role, as we will briefly outline.

Receptive skills like listening comprehension can only be measured indirectly, i.e. by inferring comprehension from the performance in a derived task (Buck, 2001, p. 99), e.g. multiple-choice or true/false questions or free-text production tasks. All these tasks require skills that go beyond pure listening comprehension (Rost and Candlin, 2014, p. 183ff), e.g. reading comprehension for answering multiple-choice items and writing skills for free-text answers. Test designers have to carefully decide whether such a skill is considered to be relevant for the construct to be tested or not. In the context of academic listening, for example, note-taking is an important skill and therefore considered to be construct-relevant (Kecker, 2015). Orthography, in contrast, is considered a construct-irrelevant skill for the task and should thus be ignored for scoring. This means that if the test-taker had the right answer in mind without being able to express it in an orthographically correct way, the answer should be marked as correct (see e.g. Harding and Ryan (2009), Harding et al. (2011)). The crucial difficulty hereby is that the spelling of the word interferes with the assessment whether the test-taker had the right answer in mind. If the test-taker, for example, just produces some vague encoding of the relevant phonetic string, this likewise leads to a spelling variant of the correct answer but it should be marked as incorrect.

Hence, the acceptability of a spelling variant is based on a complex holistic decision that an automatic scoring system is not straightforwardly able to make in the same way. Nevertheless, an operationalization has to be found which leads to ratings that match the human ratings as closely as possible. Furthermore, in a high stakes test it is crucial that the decisions of the automatic scoring system are transparent and understandable to human experts.

3 Data Set

In this paper, we experiment with data from the digital TestDaF. It is a high stakes test designed for students planning to apply for studying at a German university. It assesses test-takers' language abilities at the TestDaF levels 3, 4 or 5, corresponding to the CEFR levels B2 to C1.

	FULL	SPELL
# prompts	17	17
# answers	3,777	310
# answer types	1,572	248
avg. # answ./prompt	222 ± 78	18 ± 15
avg. # types/prompt	92 ± 32	15 ± 9
avg. length (words)	1.6 ± 0.7	1.8 ± 0.7
avg. length (chars)	13.2 ± 6.1	16.3 ± 5.0
accepted answers	53.3 %	54.8 %
accepted answ. types	25.6 %	48.4 %

Table 1: Description of the full data sample (FULL) and the subsample consisting of spelling variants only (SPELL).

The listening comprehension section consists of seven different task types, including selected-response item formats like multiple-choice questions, as well as three constructed response tasks where test-takers are asked to write short answers, between single words and a few sentences in length. In this paper, we concentrate on the task that elicits very short answers of a maximum of five words per prompt. This task is particularly suitable to study the role of spelling variants because other sources of variation are limited compared to longer textual answers.

In this task, test-takers listen to a pre-recorded conversation between two or three native speakers in a situation typical for everyday student life, e.g. a conversation between a student and a professor. Test-takers are presented a table, form or chart related to the content of the listening text with five blanks that are to be filled while listening to the input text. See Figure 1 for an example. While test-takers can type in a maximum of five words per blank, all blanks can be answered correctly with one or two words.

For the analyses in this paper, we extracted all answers from 17 different prompts where each prompt corresponds to one blank in the task described above. Table 1, column FULL, shows some basic statistics of the extracted data.[5] Each answer had manually been rated by human experts for whether it was acceptable or not.

4 Human Ratings of Spelling Variants

In the following, we will focus on spelling variants in the data set.

[5]The data set cannot be made publicly available and not all target answers can be revealed in this paper. Some prompts are public, though, and the German examples used in this paper are all real answers to those prompts.

Figure 1: Example of a listening comprehension task in the digital TestDaF that elicits short free-text answers. Target answers are given in blue. We see a timetable for a job fair with the days as columns and morning and afternoon activities (*Was?*) and the corresponding locations (*Wo?*) as rows. The upper left gap, e.g., prompts the test-taker to complete the entry *Presentation about the topic "a career in ______"* with the target answer being *public service*.

4.1 Distribution of Spelling Variants

Two annotators labeled all answer types with a category that describes in which way the answer deviates from the target answer. For a subset of about 500 answer types, we compute the agreement of our two raters on the binary decision whether the answer is a spelling variant or some other variant. Other variants include for example grammatical deviations (e.g. singular/plural), synonyms (*Speicherstick* 'memory stick' for *USB-Stick*), or answers that are incomplete (*Raum* for *Raum 5*), unintelligible (*OS*) or referring to something different (*Kaffee* 'coffee' for *Workshops*). Inter-annotator agreement is Cohen's κ=.78, which shows that even for humans, distinguishing spelling variants from other variants, especially grammatical variants, is not trivial.

The two annotators then discussed those cases where they disagreed and decided on a final gold label. For the analyses in this paper, we extracted all answers gold-labeled as spelling variants, including real-word errors. Note that answers which differ from the target answer only with regard to capitalization, hyphenation or splitting a compound in two parts are not part of this set because they are always acceptable.

Table 1, column SPELL, shows some statistics of the spelling variant sample. In total, about 16% of the different answer variants are attributable to spelling, showing that they account for a non-negligible amount of variance in the data.

The distribution of spelling errors follows a Zipf distribution, i.e. most of the spelling variants in our data set occur only once while a few can be found several times. In other words, different test-takers make different kinds of errors, hence it is not possible to foresee all cases beforehand and include them in the rating guidelines or to hard-code them in an automatic scoring system.

The left panel of Figure 2 shows the number of different spelling variants per prompt. One can see that some prompts seem to be more prone to spelling errors than others, with some prompts triggering more than 30 different variants and others only triggering two. We found that there are more spelling variants in prompts with longer target answers than with shorter ones (Pearson correlation r =.58). As one can see in the right panel of Figure 2, the acceptance rate of spelling errors according to the human gold standard varies quite a lot. While for some prompts, most of the variants are accepted, for others, most are rejected. In total, 48% of the spelling variant types are accepted.

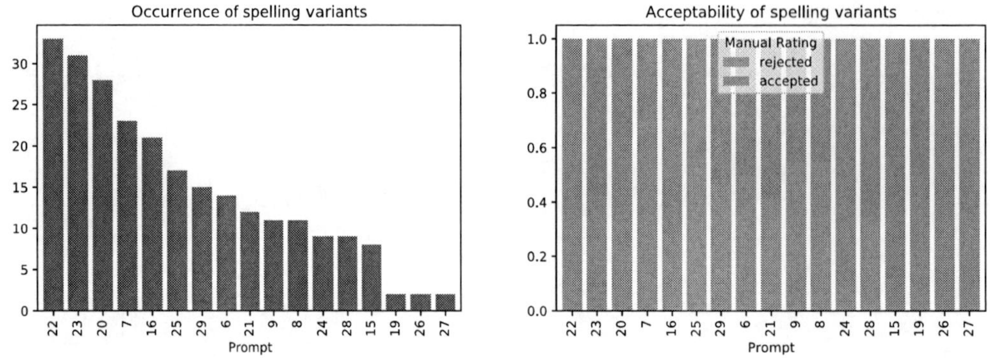

Figure 2: Occurrence (left panel) and acceptance rate (right panel) of spelling variant types per prompt.

4.2 Manual Acceptability Decisions

Test-takers' responses were rated by human experts in a dichotomous format as either *accepted* or *rejected*. Inconsistencies were adjudicated by an additional annotator. Some examples are shown in Table 2. Human raters also need clear criteria to ensure that they mark according to the same standard (Weir, 1993). To achieve this, they were provided with rating guidelines, rater training sessions and standardization meetings.

The rating guidelines consist of general parts, for example that common abbreviations are accepted in an answer, and item-specific parts that contain samples of correct and incorrect answers as well as what is in general expected of a correct response for this item. For example, the guidelines for the target answer *USB-Stick* include the following:

- *USB Stik* is an accepted spelling variant but *USB Tick* and *USP Stick* are not
- *Speicherstik* (*memory stick*) is an accepted synonym with an accepted spelling error (*stik* instead of *stick*)
- *USB Gerät* (*USB device*) is not accepted because it is too general
- *USB* alone similarly does not contain enough information

We compute the inter-annotator agreement of the human experts for the acceptability decision on the same subset as for the annotation if something is a spelling variant. We observe that spelling variants are substantially harder for humans to judge than other answer variants, with a κ value of .60 for spelling variants as opposed to .83 for all other items (see Table 3). Such scoring inconsistencies by human raters despite regular training, annotation guidelines and thorough pre-testing are in line with Buck (2001).

Answer	Accept
Text Entworf	yes
Textentwürf	yes
Testentworf	no
textentw	no
text entworft	no
textintforf	no
Text Einwurf	no

Table 2: Examples of spelling variants and acceptability decisions for the target word *Textentwurf* ('text draft').

	κ	% agreement
all answers	.80	.93
spelling variants	.60	.83
other variants	.83	.94

Table 3: Inter-annotator agreement (Cohen's Kappa) for rating answer variants as acceptable or not.

5 Operationalizing Acceptability Decisions

In the following, we will analyze criteria for the acceptability ratings of spelling variants which could be used by an automatic system. We base our analyses on the set of different spelling variant types. Thereby, we always use the adjudicated labels as the gold standard.

5.1 Surface Distance to Target

The manual scoring guidelines do not prescribe how many errors per word are allowed in order for the answer to count as correct. However, in our sample we can see that the Levenshtein distance

Dist.	SURFACE		STANDARDIZED		PHONEMES	
	#	% acc	#	% acc	#	% acc
0	-	-	1	1.00	20	.85
1	63	.70	147	.66	63	.59
2	72	.60	58	.29	66	.61
3	49	.47	22	.14	36	.31
4	32	.16	13	.15	33	.30
5	17	.24	2	.00	11	.27
≥ 6	15	.07	5	.00	19	.11

Table 4: Frequency and acceptance rate (% acc) of the human raters for all spelling variants with a particular Levenshtein distance (Dist.). The Levenshtein distance is measured on the character level (SURFACE), standardized character level (STANDARDIZED, i.e. ignoring capitalization, hyphens and whitespace) and on the phoneme level (PHONEMES).

between a given answer and the target answer is correlated with the acceptability of the answer. This is detailed in Table 4, column SURFACE. However, despite a trend that words with higher Levenshtein distances are less likely to be accepted, we do not see a threshold above which all answers are rejected or below which all are accepted.

Most frequently, we find a Levenshtein distance of 2 between the given and the target answer. Recall that answers which differ from the target answer only with regard to letter case, hyphenation or splitting a compound in two parts are not included in our spelling variant data set because these deviations by themselves are always acceptable. However, an inspection of the included spelling variants showed that many answers mix capitalization or word-splitting errors with other error types like letter substitutions, e.g. *text entworft* for *Textentwurf*. The Levenshtein distance currently does not take into account that e.g. a capitalization error itself is not as problematic as a different letter substitution. This may blur the actual influence of the Levenshtein distance. Therefore, we standardize the given answers and the target answers by lowercasing, removing hyphens and whitespace and then re-compute the Levenshtein distance.

We can see that a clear majority of standardized answers only has a Levenshtein distance of 1 to the target answer (see Table 4, column STANDARDIZED). Furthermore, there is a clearer trend that the majority of answers with a distance of 1 is accepted while most answers with a higher distance are rejected. Still, an automatic classifier that accepts all answers with a Levenshtein distance ≤ 1 and rejects all other answers would have an accuracy of only 71%. This is clearly above the majority-class baseline of 52% (achieved if all spelling variants are classified as rejected) but far from a sufficiently high accuracy for being used in practice.

5.2 Influence of Keyboard

There are spelling deviations which are intuitively recognized as typos, e.g. *Öffentlivchendienst* for *öffentlichen Dienst*. A typo implies that the test-taker actually knew the word so that it should be marked as correct. As a proxy for whether a spelling variant is actually a typo, we can look whether the substitution or insertion of an erroneous character pertains to a key adjacent to the target key.

Hence, our operationalization of what counts as a typo is as follows: if a standardized answer contains exactly one substitution or one insertion of a character which is adjacent to the target key on a keyboard with QWERTZ, QWERTY, or AZERTY layout, we consider this answer as 'probably only containing a typo'. Using this method, we identified 18 unique typos in the analyzed sample. In 13 of these answers, there are additional deviations in terms of capitalization or the use of whitespace. The human experts scored (only) 12 of the 18 answers as correct, which shows that a spelling variant that is likely a typo is not automatically accepted. The human experts reported that since they cannot know on which type of keyboard a test-taker wrote the answer, they do not explicitly treat (potential) typos differently from other types of errors.

5.3 Phonetic Similarity

In German orthography, most sounds can be represented in more than one way, using different characters or character combinations. For example, a long [aː] can be spelled as <a> (*Tal* 'valley'), <ah> (*Zahl* 'number') or <aa> (*Saal* 'hall'). This means that there can be answers which differ from the target answer in terms of spelling but which are nevertheless pronounced in the same or a very similar way. As with the similarity on the surface level, we can determine the similarity on the pronunciation level by computing the Levenshtein distance between a given answer and the target answer on the phoneme level. We obtained the phoneme representation of each answer from the web service *G2P* of the Bavarian Archive of Speech Signals

Answer		**Target Answer**		**Accept**
Wokshops	*wok shops*	Workshops	*workshops*	yes
Vortag	*previous day*	Vortrag	*presentation*	yes
öffentlichen**dings**	*public thingy*	öffentlichen Dienst	*public service*	no
litersuchen	*liter search*	Literatursuche	*literature search*	no
Testentworf	*test draft*	Textentwurf	*text draft*	no
Text **Einwurf**	*text insertion*	Textentwurf	*text draft*	no
Eigenen**testverwurf**	*own test rejection*	eigenen Textentwurf	*own text draft*	no

Table 5: Examples of real-word spelling variants. Those parts of the word that correspond to another existing word are printed in bold.

(BAS) (Reichel, 2012; Reichel and Kisler, 2014).[6] As one can see from the column PHONEMES in Table 4, most answers with the same pronunciation as the target answer are accepted (85%), but not all. On the other hand, most answers with quite a different pronunciation are rejected, but again there are exceptions. This shows that phonetic similarity alone is not a decisive factor either.

5.4 Similarity to Other Words

In our data sample, we manually identified a total of 34 spelling variants that resulted in other existing words (real-word errors). Most of them occurred only once, resulting in 27 unique variants. Hence, 11% of all spelling variant types are real-word errors. Not all prompts trigger real-word errors to the same degree. For 8 out of the 17 prompts, no real-word error could be found while one of the prompts triggered eight different real-word error types.

Most of the real-word errors are rejected by the human raters – but not all of them: 3 out of the 27 real-word error types were accepted. What is noteworthy is that all of the accepted real-word errors have a Levenshtein distance (on the character level) to the target word of 1. In contrast, the rejected real-word errors have a mean Levenshtein distance of 3.6. Hence, a factor influencing the acceptability of the real-word error seems to be the surface similarity. However, among the rejected answers, there are also four real-word errors with a Levenshtein distance of 1 to the target answer, which shows that there are more complex mechanisms at work. Human experts reported that one factor influencing their decision is whether the meaning of the real-word error would be somewhat plausible yet still incorrect in the context of the given task, and therefore would be confusing in a real-life setting. In contrast, if an answer is far-fetched or consists of a word that is very infrequent, human raters would assume that the error was indeed only an orthographic error and the learner actually meant to write the correct word.

To illustrate this, Table 5 shows some example answers and their acceptability. Most target answers are compound words and the real-word spelling errors mostly only pertain to one part of the word. As a consequence, the error results in a grammatically well-formed answer but often in a non-lexicalized word. In some cases, the meaning of the new compound is far off the meaning of the target answer, e.g. *Workshop* and *Wokshop* (in English, the corresponding words are *workshop* and *wok shop*, i.e. the compound that is a result of the spelling error would have to be written as two words, which is not the case in German). In other cases, the meanings are somewhat close and could lead to a misunderstanding in real communication, e.g. *Textentwurf* ('text draft') and *Testentworf* ('test draft'). It remains to be seen with a larger sample of accepted real-word errors how well this can be operationalized by an automatic scoring system.

5.5 Combination of Features

While all of the criteria presented above play a role for the acceptability decision, we could see that none of these factors alone suffices to differentiate between accepted and rejected answers. In the next step, we examine whether a combination of the features can be used to approximate the human acceptability decisions. We aim for a model that yields interpretable results so that one can identify under which conditions a spelling variant is accepted or rejected.

[6] https://clarin.phonetik.uni-muenchen.de/BASWebServices/interface/Grapheme2Phoneme

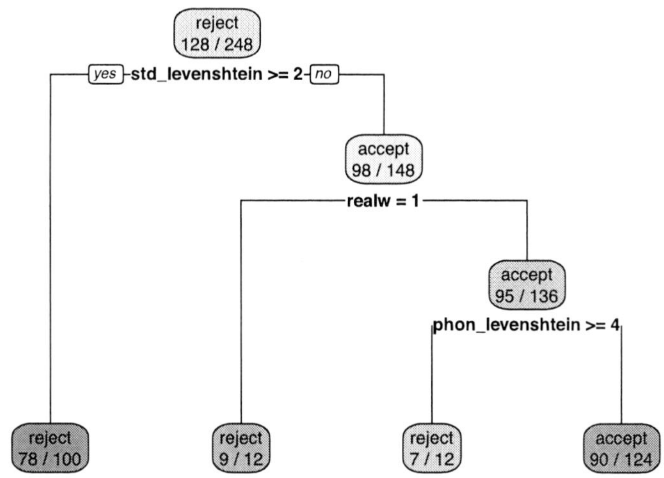

Figure 3: Simple decision tree (pruned) for the acceptability decision.

In order to do so, we train different decision trees on the whole set of spelling error types and the adjudicated gold labels using the R package *rpart* (Therneau and Atkinson, 2019). We then apply the trees to a test set of 127 spelling variant types from 5 new prompts, i.e. a new set of learner and target answers. We use classification accuracy as evaluation metric.

In addition, we apply the trees to the training data set itself in order to get an estimate how consistently the data can be modeled, i.e. whether the features suffice to tell accepted and rejected answers apart or whether there are answers with the same combination of features but different human judgments. The results are shown in Table 6.

Baselines If all instances are classified as rejected, this **majority-class** baseline reaches an accuracy of 52% on the training set. In the test set, the classes are evenly distributed, i.e. the baseline is 50%. Using **character edit-distance** alone as classification criterion, as discussed in Section 5.1, the accuracy rises to 71% on the training set and 73% on the test set.

Simple Trees First, we build a decision tree with default configuration using the features and their operationalizations that were described in the previous sections:

- edit distance on the character level between standardized given answer and standardized target answer, i.e. ignoring letter case, hyphens and whitespace (`std_levenshtein`, numeric)
- edit distance on the phoneme level (`phon_levenshtein`, numeric)
- whether the word is a real-word error (`realw`, binary)
- whether the word probably only contains a typo (`probably_typo`, binary)

This tree is grown with default parameters, which in particular means that it is automatically **pruned**, i.e. not grown to full depth. For a predictive model, this is necessary in order to prevent overfitting on the training data. The resulting tree is shown in Figure 3. In prose, the tree accepts a spelling variant if the edit distance on the character level is < 2, it is not a real-word error and the edit distance on the phoneme level is < 4. The nodes show how many data points fall into the respective class and how many of them are categorized correctly when applied to the training data. In total, the tree reaches an accuracy of 74.2% on the training set and 70.9% on the independent test set. For the test set, this is worse than using character edit-distance alone.

In order to find out whether the features do actually suffice in order to model the data that the tree was trained on, we next grow the tree to **full** depth. The resulting tree has a depth of 8 (compared to the depth of 3 in Figure 3) but still only reaches an accuracy of 76.2% on the training data. This means that there are answers with the same feature set but different acceptability decisions (see discussion in Section 5.6). As one would expect due to overfitting, the full-depth tree performs worse on the test set than the pruned tree.

Advanced Trees One potential limitation of the current feature set is that our version of edit distance is not sensitive to word length. Therefore, we normalize the character edit distance by the number of characters in the target word and also allow for transpositions of characters to count as one edit (`norm_std_damerau_lev`). The other three features remain the same. The default **pruned** tree based on this adapted feature set has a depth of 5 and an accuracy of 75.4% on the training set, which is very similar to the result of the simple tree. See Figure 4 for an illustration of the advanced tree.

However, on the test set, the tree produces much better results than the simple tree with an accuracy of 84.3%. That the result for this tree on the test set is even better than that on the training set indicates that the tree's rules for accepting an answer are indeed transferable to new data sets. In fact, some of the rules even fit the test data better than the training data. For example, 45.6% of the training data and 46.5% of the test data fall into the rightmost leaf node in Figure 4. The answers that fall into this node are predicted to be accepted. In the training data, this decision is correct in 73% of the cases, whereas in the test data, the decision is correct even for 85%.

If we grow the advanced tree to full depth (= depth of 14), the overall accuracy on the training set rises notably, but only to 85.1%. Hence, it still does not reach the adjudicated gold standard but the result is comparable to the human-human agreement of 83%. As we will discuss shortly, the fact that we do not reach 100% accuracy even with this full-grown tree shows that more or different features are needed to tell accepted and rejected answers apart. Since this tree overfits the data, its performance on the test set is much worse than that of the pruned tree, hence it is not suitable for predicting new data points.

5.6 Discussion

We observe that our features do not suffice to perfectly model the acceptability decisions of human raters according to an adjudicated gold standard. There are conflicting cases which cannot be resolved on the basis of the features we currently examine. Some examples are given in Table 7.

	Accuracy	
Method	**Training**	**Test**
majority baseline	.52	.50
char. edit distance	.71	.73
simple pruned tree	.74	.71
simple full tree	.76	.69
advanced pruned tree	.75	.84
advanced full tree	.85	.72
human agreement	.83	-

Table 6: Overview of classification results.

Answer	**Human Accept**
Öffenlichtendienst	yes
offentlischen Dienst	yes
kreatives schnieben	yes
höffentliche Dienst	no
oofentlichen DIENST	no
offentlichene Dienst	no
krätives schreiben	no

Table 7: Examples of answers (target answers = *öffentlichen Dienst*, *kreatives Schreiben*) that all fall within the same node of the advanced full tree but are rated differently by human raters.

Differences between the accepted and not-accepted cases are subtle and human experts often argue in terms of whether an answer looked "too far off" without being able to specify a general rule supporting their decision. Additional features might be able to distinguish between those cases. However, it may also mean that the human ratings are not fully consistent, which is in line with our observed inter-annotator agreement. In fact, the accuracy of the overfitted tree (85%) is very similar to the human-human agreement on the same data (83%), which we discussed in Section 4.2, hence, we may not expect a system to ever go significantly beyond this value. Therefore, basing the acceptability decision on objectively measurable features instead of individual holistic decisions of human raters could be a way to arrive at more consistent and more explainable results especially in a high stakes test.

6 Conclusion and Future Work

We presented an analysis of the rating of spelling variants in a listening comprehension task from the TestDaF test. We found that spelling variants are more challenging to score for human experts than other types of variants. Furthermore, we ex-

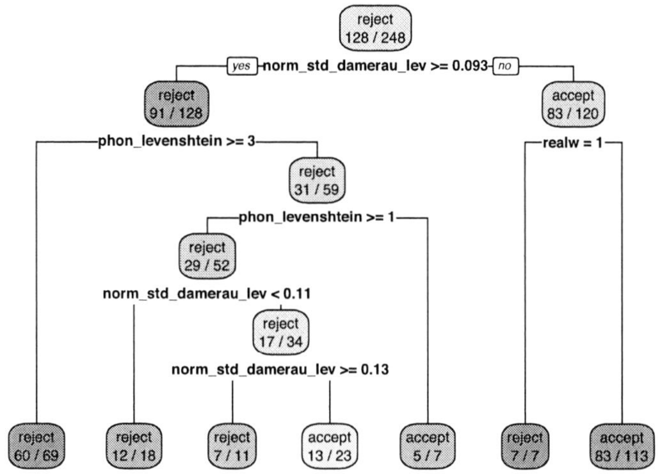

Figure 4: Advanced decision tree (pruned) for the acceptability decision.

plored how the acceptability decision can be operationalized with automatically extractable features such as edit distance and phonetic similarity as a first step towards an automatic scoring system for spelling variants. Their combination in a decision tree reaches a performance similar to human-human agreement, but not exceeding it. This can mean either that human decisions are not fully consistent or that further features are needed to differentiate between cases that currently end up in the same leaf node of the tree.

Options for such additional features include specific error categories as opposed to generic distance-based measures, such as the spelling error categories defined in the Litkey Corpus (Laarmann-Quante et al., 2019). These error categories can be divided into 'systematic' ones (like omitting an <e> that corresponds to an (almost) non-audible [ə]) and 'non-systematic' ones (such as omitting a full vowel). First explorations indicate that 'systematic' errors more likely lead to acceptable spelling variants than 'non-systematic' ones. As another option to obtain more consistent annotations, we plan to explore annotation studies where human raters have access to the automatically extracted features and/or the scoring suggestion learnt by the classifier as a basis for their scoring decision.

Acknowledgments

This research was partly funded by g.a.s.t. (Gesellschaft für Akademische Studienvorbereitung und Testentwicklung e. V./ *Society for Academic Study Preparation and Test Development*) and conducted in the framework of the Research Cluster D^2L^2 "Digitalization, Diversity and Lifelong Learning – Consequences for Higher Education" of the FernUniversität in Hagen, Germany (https://e.feu.de/english-d2l2). We would like to thank Frederik Wollatz and Lisa Prepens (students from the University of Duisburg-Essen) for their annotation work.

References

Daniel Bär, Chris Biemann, Iryna Gurevych, and Torsten Zesch. 2012. Ukp: Computing semantic textual similarity by combining multiple content similarity measures. In ** SEM 2012: The First Joint Conference on Lexical and Computational Semantics–Volume 1: Proceedings of the main conference and the shared task, and Volume 2: Proceedings of the Sixth International Workshop on Semantic Evaluation (SemEval 2012)*, pages 435–440.

Gary Buck. 2001. *Assessing Listening*. Cambridge Language Assessment. Cambridge University Press.

Luke Harding, John Pill, and Kerry Ryan. 2011. Assessor decision making while marking a note-taking listening test: The case of the OET. *Language Assessment Quarterly*, 8(2):108–126.

Luke Harding and Kerry Ryan. 2009. Decision making in marking open-ended listening test items: The case of the OET. *SPAAN FELLOW*, 1001:99.

Andrea Horbach, Yuning Ding, and Torsten Zesch. 2017. The Influence of Spelling Error on Content Scoring

Performance. In *Proceedings of the 4th Workshop on Natural Language Processing Techniques for Educational Applications*, pages 45–53, Taipei, Taiwan. AFNLP.

Andrea Horbach and Torsten Zesch. 2019. The influence of variance in learner answers on automatic content scoring. *Frontiers in Education*, 4:28.

Gabriele Kecker. 2015. "He listens well who takes notes" – Mit welchen Aufgabenformaten kann Hörverstehen in Vorlesungen an der Hochschule valide getestet werden?". In Jessica Böcker and Anette Stauch, editors, *Konzepte aus der Sprachlehrforschung – Impulse für die Praxis*, pages 511—-526. Peter Lang, Bern, Switzerland.

Ronja Laarmann-Quante, Anna Ehlert, Katrin Ortmann, Doreen Scholz, Carina Betken, Lukas Knichel, Simon Masloch, and Stefanie Dipper. 2019. The Litkey Spelling Error Annotation Scheme: Guidelines for the Annotation of Orthographic Errors in German Texts. *Bochumer Linguistische Arbeitsberichte (BLA)*.

Uwe D. Reichel. 2012. PermA and Balloon: Tools for string alignment and text processing. In *INTERSPEECH*, Portland, Oregon.

Uwe D. Reichel and Thomas Kisler. 2014. Language-independent grapheme-phoneme conversion and word stress assignment as a web service. In R. Hoffmann, editor, *Elektronische Sprachverarbeitung: Studientexte zur Sprachkommunikation 71*, pages 42–49. TUDpress.

Michael Rost and CN Candlin. 2014. *Listening in language learning*. Routledge.

Terry Therneau and Beth Atkinson. 2019. *rpart: Recursive Partitioning and Regression Trees*. R package version 4.1-15.

Cyril J Weir. 1993. *Understanding and developing language tests*. Prentice Hall New York.

Ramon Ziai, Niels Ott, and Detmar Meurers. 2012. Short answer assessment: Establishing links between research strands. In *Proceedings of the Seventh Workshop on Building Educational Applications Using NLP*, pages 190–200.

Educational Tools for Mapuzugun

Cristian Ahumada[1] **Claudio Gutierrez**[1] **Antonios Anastasopoulos**[2]
[1]Department of Computer Science, Universidad de Chile
[2]Computer Science Department, George Mason University
ahumada.860@gmail.com cgutierr@dcc.uchile.cl antonis@gmu.edu

Abstract

Mapuzugun is the language of the Mapuche people. Due to political and historical reasons, its number of speakers has decreased and the language has been excluded from the educational system in Chile and Argentina. For this reason, it is very important to support the revitalization of the Mapuzugun in all spaces and media of society. In this work we present a tool towards supporting educational activities of Mapuzugun, tailored to the characteristics of the language. The tool consists of three parts: design and development of an orthography detector and converter; a morphological analyzer; and an informal translator. We also present a case study with Mapuzugun students showing promising results.

Short abstract in Mapuzugun: Tüfachi küzaw pegelfi kiñe zugun küzawpeyüm kelluaetew pu mapuzugun chillkatufe kimal kizu tañi zugun.

1 Introduction

Recent years have seen unprecedented progress for Natural Language Processing (NLP) on almost every NLP subtask. Along with research progress, several tools have been developed and are currently aiding millions of users every day. However, most of this progress is limited on a handful of languages (Joshi et al., 2020). For example, learners of English can nowadays avail themselves to tools like Grammarly; English speakers can use Duolingo to start learning 38 languages, including Hawaiian, Navajo, as well as High Valyrian and Klingon.[1] The only option a Mapuzugun speaker would have in practice, though, would be to use language technologies in a language other than her own (likely Spanish).

Despite Duolingo's commendable inclusion of Hawaiian and Navajo for English speakers, and of Guaraní for Spanish speakers,[2] learning resources for Indigenous languages are hard to come by, let alone ones that incorporate language technologies in the educational setting in order to aid learners. In particular, it is undeniable that the development of NLP tools that reach the users lags further behind that NLP research itself (Blasi et al., 2021).

In this work, we develop a tool for educational use in an Indigenous language of south America, Mapuzugun. This tool was created by a speaker and instructor of the language and as such is tailored specifically to the instructional needs and linguistic characteristics of Mapuzugun.

Importantly, this work shows how linguistic research (grammars), minimal community resources (dictionaries), and NLP research (e.g. FST-based morphological analyzers) can be transformed into tools useful to Indigenous communities, in particular for efforts towards preservation and revitalization of endangered languages. Our tool is publicly available through an online interface (in Mapuzugun and Spanish) at `crahumadao.pythonanywhere.com`.[3]

2 The Mapuzugun Language

Mapuzugun (iso 639-3: `arn`) is an indigenous language of the Americas spoken natively in Chile and Argentina, with an estimated 100 to 200 thousand speakers in Chile and 27 to 60 thousand speakers in Argentina (Zúñiga, 2006, 41–3). It is an isolate language and is classified as threatened by Ethnologue, hence the critical importance of all documentary efforts. Although the morphology of nouns is relatively simple, Mapudungun verb morphology is highly agglutinative and complex. Some analyses provide as many as 36 verb suffix slots (Smeets, 1989). A typical complex verb form may consist of five or six morphemes. See example in Table 1.

[1]As of March 2022.

[2]Which are due to immense efforts by the Indigenous communities themselves.

[3]Username: `epu` and Password: `meli`

Proceedings of the 17th Workshop on Innovative Use of NLP for Building Educational Applications (BEA 2022), pages 183 - 196
July 15, 2022

Word	Kim mapuzuguyekümelleaiñ
Segmentation	Kim mapu-zugu-yekü-me-lle-a-iñ
English Transl.	We are indeed going to learn the Mapuche language.

Table 1: Segmentation of a Mapuzugun verb phrase.

Mapudungun has several interesting grammatical properties. It is a polysynthetic language in the sense of Baker (1996); see (Loncon Antileo, 2011) for explicit argumentation. As with other polysynthetic languages, Mapudungun has Noun Incorporation; however, it is unique insofar as the Noun appears to the right of the Verb, instead of to the left, as in most polysynthetic languages (Baker et al., 2005). One further distinction of Mapudungun is that, whereas other polysynthetic languages are characterized by a lack of infinitives, Mapudungun has infinitival verb forms; that is, while subordinate clauses in Mapudungun closely resemble possessed nominals and may occur with an analytic marker resembling possessor agreement, there is no agreement inflection on the verb itself. One further remarkable property of Mapudungun is its inverse voice system of agreement, whereby the highest agreement is with the argument highest in an animacy hierarchy regardless of thematic role (Arnold, 1996).

Beyond morphology and other interesting typological properties, an additional challenge in the computational processing of Mapuzugun is the lack of a single standardized orthography. In particular, the community uses three different alphabets, namely the "Unificado", "Ragileo", and "Azümchefe" alphabets.[4]

3 System Overview

The system is comprised of the following components, with the pipeline shown in Figure 1:

1. the orthography detector, which detects which of the three alphabets is used in the input;
2. the orthography transliterator, which can convert between orthographies if conversion is needed;
3. the morphological analyzer, which produces the possible segmentations of a word or phrase;
4. the mapping of the analyzed morphemes to user-friendly notation/phrases; and
5. the final presentation of the output.

[4]See Figure 5 in Appendix A.

The user can use these tools through an interface available both in Mapuzugun and in Spanish. A screenshot of the landing page of the interface is shown in Figure 2.

4 Orthography Detection and Transliteration

The differences between the three orthographies are showcased in Figure 3. where "Jampvzken" is written in Ragileo, "Llampüdken" in Unificado and "Llampüzken" in Azümchefe, all three referring to the same Mapudungun phonetics of the English word "butterfly". This example shows the relationship between the 'J' in Ragileo with the 'Ll' in Azümchefe and Unificado.

We identified and constructed the conversion tables between these orthographies. In total, for the Unified-Ragileo relationship, there are 10 differences that are shown in the Table 4, in the following case Unified-Azümchefe there are 8 differences (Table 5) and for the Ragileo-Azümchefe relationship there are 8 differences, outlined in Table 6.

Utilizing these conversion tables makes it straightforward to detect the orthography of any given input, by following a process of round-trip translation. For example, if we assume the input is in Ragileo, then if we convert to Azümchefe (or Unificado) and back to Ragileo and the final output is the same as the original input, then the input is declared to be Ragileo. If any of the intermediate translations fail it would have been exactly because our initial assumption of the input being in Ragileo was false. If no changes happen in the translation process, then all orthographies represent the input in a similar manner.

Orthography Converter Given the differences between the orthographies, special care must be taken in graphemes that have another grapheme as a substring. An example of this is the Unificado grapheme `Ng`, which also contains the grapheme `G`, which in turn is used in the same writing system for another phoneme. Or, cases in which three graphemes contain the same letter, such as the letter "`L`" in `L`, `Lh`, and `LL`. The only orthography that does not have this internal problem is Ragileo, because it uses unique letters for each Mapuzugun phoneme. This makes conversion from Ragileo to other orthographies straighforward, always taking care of the order of the transformations whose output can generate morpheme ambiguities during conversion.

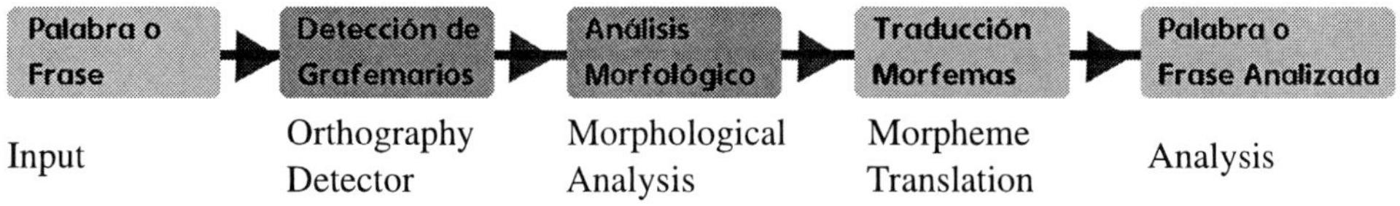

Figure 1: Pipeline of the full system.

Figure 2: Screenshot of the user interface.

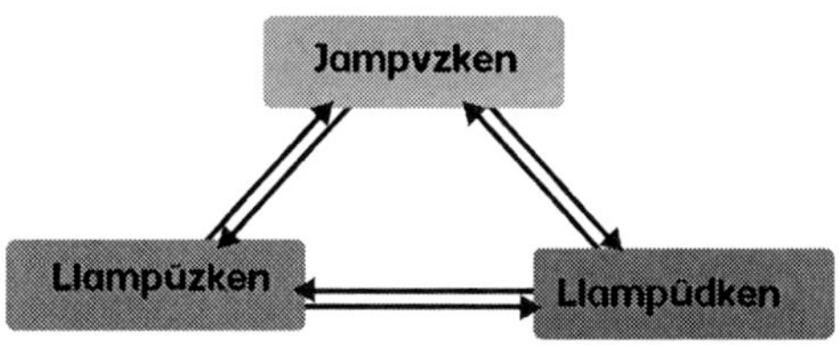

Figure 3: Conversions between orthographies for the Mapuzugun word for 'butterfly'. Top: Ragileo; bottom left: Azümchefe; bottom right: Unificado.

The order that must be taken into account because if a morpheme is contained by another, it must first be disambiguated and then continue with other changes. In the case of `Ng` and `g`, to go from Unificado to Ragileo or Azümchefe, as long as there is a `g` and there is no `N` preceding it, it can be changed to `Q`, therefore before making the transformations the `Ng` must be checked, saving the result `G`) in an auxiliary variable to be able to convert later all `G`s of the Unificado to `Q`. Once this last step is done, the auxiliary variable is removed and the `G` resulting from the change is put back.

5 Morphological Analyzer

The morphological analyzer is responsible for producing the possible segmentations: separating words into a composition of morphemes.

5.1 Design

The analyzer is implemented through series of regular expressions, based on established grammars of Mapuzugun (Smeets, 1989; Cañumil, 2011; Chiguailaf, 1972). As another source, the compilation that was made in `azümchefe.cl` of the grammar of the language (Chiguailaf, 1972) was taken.

We worked with hand-crafted sets of regular expressions that contain the morphemes of the language. These sets separate, by function: in verb root, noun/adverb/adjective, suffixes, and endings. In addition, the position plays an important role, because each of the morphemes has a particular slot (Smeets, 1989).

From these regular expressions, the chain of a word is traversed and possible derivations tree is generated. Only branches evaluated to be valid are passed on to the next "informal translator" step. The morphemes and their order must meet certain restrictions that have to do with the correct formulation of words in Mapuzugun, both in order, as mentioned before, but also in the compatibility of two morphemes being in the same word.

This module assumes input in the Ragileo orthography, therefore any word from another orthography must necessarily pass through the orthography converter. This decision has to do with Ragileo's advantage of 1-to-1 phoneme-to-grapheme mappings, making it easier to model morphemes.

5.2 Informal Analysis Translator

Once the segmentation is done, we implemented a module crucial for deploying the tool in educational revitalization settings: the "informal analysis translator". It assigns to each individual morphemes (or to combinations of them according to communicative role) a definition in plain Spanish. The rationale was to simplify the definition as much as possible leaving out technical linguistic features and jargon. For the case of substantives, verbs and adjectives, the definition was taken from the Mapuzugun-Spanish dictionary (Pérez, 2015).

As an example, we show the case of the word `txekayawkelai`. One of the possible segmentations

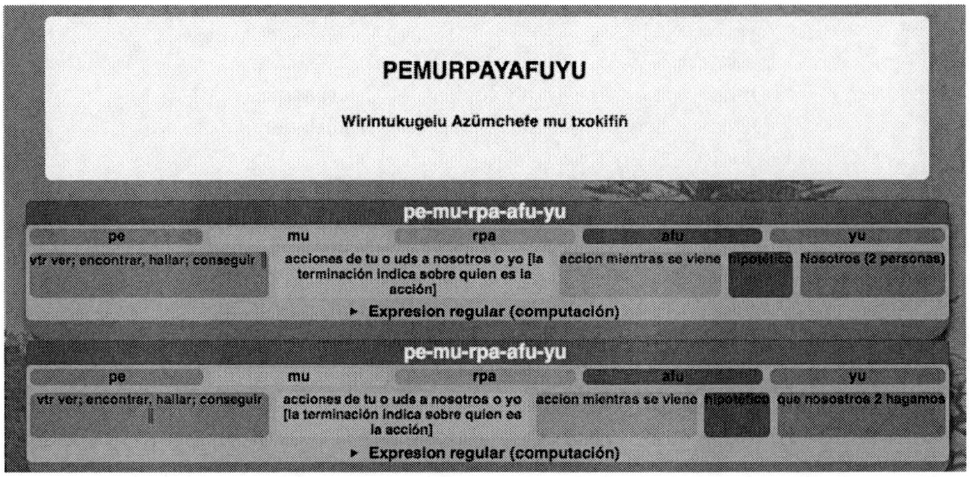

Figure 4: Segmentation of the word "pemurpayafuyu" as presented by the tool.

is **txeka-yaw-ke-la-i**, with each component of the word being:

txekan- : vi & vtr caminar, marchar, pasear || vtr medir con pasos *to walk, to take a walk*

-yaw- : andar *to go*

-ke- : habitualmente *usually*

-la- : negación a modo "normal" indicativo *negation*

-i : el / ella *he/she*

Given this,[5] the goal is that the learner deduces "el/ella no anda caminando habitualmente" *"he/she does not usually go for walks"*.

The challenges of this informal analyzer are many. Among them: how to give enough meaningful translations so that they can match the initial experience of learners, but as well, do not confuse them; how to deal with compositional morphemes (i.e. morphemes that have a different meaning when co-occurring than when occurring separately, for example transitions from second to first person); and how to include context to help the translation. We resolved these issues by relying on the expertise of an instructor of Mapuzugun.[6]

6 Usability Studies with Learners

The system (software) was tested on several groups of initial learners of Mapuzugun.

[5]"vi" and "vtr" correspond respectively to intransitive and transitive verb.

[6]One of the authors is a speaker and instructor of Mapuzugun.

Study Design The first phase of the study design was to get access to study participants. As in the case of most endangered languages, it was difficult to identify test groups for various reasons. First, most current Mapuzugun courses are informal, given different types of social organizations with a great variety of methodologies, contents, levels. Second, students of Mapuzugun differ widely according to interests, degree of systematization and materials used. Third, there is a strong distrust by the interested community of learners in institutions, like academia, that historically have "used" aboriginal speakers as mere sources of information.

In a first preliminary round, more than 200 people (known to have been in courses or being students of Mapuzugun in the last 5 years) were contacted. From them, 30 people engaged to answer the questionnaire and from them, only 9 answers were obtained (3 of advanced knowledge of Mapuzugun).

With their feedback, the tool was refined. A second round was done by a public call in social networks related to Mapuzugun, and 32 people registered for the study, which were then classified in 5 groups:

- Group 0. Beginners (6 people);
- Group 1. Basic studies; able to greet but do not understand conversations (8 people);
- Group 2. Studies: able to understand conversations (7 people);
- Group 3. Studies; able to perform conversations (8 people); and
- Group 4. Speakers from early infancy (3 people).

The experiment consisted of giving a small set

Word	Group 0	Group 1	Group 2	Group 3	Group 4	General
`elukelafimu`	2 / 2	2 / 1.6	2 / 1.86	2.75 / 2.86	2 / -	2.33 / 2.14
`pemurpayafuyu`	1 / 3	1 / 2	1.83 / 2.17	2.33 / 2.83	2 / -	1.94 / 2.44
`kujinerkeeiñmu`	0 / 1.33	0.67 / 1.4	1.75 / 2	2.43 / 2.86	3 / -	1.81 / 2.05
Phrase	1 / 3	2 / 2.25	2.57 / 2.71	3 / 3	2.67 / -	2.42 / 2.72

Table 2: Summary of the study with learners. showing the mean performance of each group for each task word. Scale goes from 0 (wrong translation) to 3 (perfect translation). The pairs A / B mean: without / with the tool.

	Group 0	Group 1	Group 2	Group 3	Group 4	General
Difficulty of use	2.67	2.71	1.86	1.86	3	2.33
Diff. of word transl.	3.17	2.86	3.0	2.43	3	2.87
Diff. of phrase transl.	3.33	3.71	2.71	3.14	1.67	3.0
Visual evaluation	3.83	3.29	4.14	3.86	2.33	3.63
General evaluation	3.17	4.0	4.71	4.29	3.33	4.0

Table 3: Summary of Usability Test. Scale goes from 1 (low) to 5 (top).

of Mapuzugun words (and one phrase[7]) to each participant. The task was to translate each word in Spanish, first without and then with the tool.

We additionally collected information on usability of the software tool: difficulty of use, difficulty to translate words, difficulty to translate phrases, evaluation of visual interface and finally, a general evaluation. Last, we requested open-ended general qualitative feedback.

Translation Results Table 2 summarizes quality of the produced translations, with and without the tool, for each user group.[8] For two words, `pemurpayafuyu` and `kujinerkeeiñmu`, using the tool improves the translation capabilities for all user groups. The word `elukelafimu` is a word that is typically accessible in basic levels of Mapuzugun, and hence, the segmentation plus the translation could have confused users (they realized that the word was more complex than they thought). Another encouraging sign is that the translation of the phrase also improved for the first three groups when using the tool. Last, we found that experienced learners (group 4), preferred not to use the tool because they felt secure in their knowledge.

Usability Results Table 3 summarizes the scores received by the users (in a Likert scale). User groups 2 and 3 seem to be the ones showing less difficulty to use the tool, and also those that can take more advantage of it. Beginners got stuck with instructions (many were in Mapuzugun; they will also be provided in Spanish in future iterations) and ability to compose particles. We suspect that experienced speakers (group 4) probably did not invest effort because they did not need the tool.

All groups except experienced speakers rated the phrase as more difficult to translate than single words. The visual aspects of the interface and the tool in general mostly received very positive scores.

As a summary, our small study shows that, at its current stage of development, our tool is appropriate *and* useful for intermediate learners.

Qualitative Feedback We summarize here the qualitative feedback we received from user groups.

In general, all groups were particularly positive about the tool's presentation of the segmentation of the words. All groups were also very positive towards our informal translator that provides the explanations of each word segment.

In general, comments in the beginners' group (group 0) mentioned the difficulty to produce the translations, even though each part of the segmentation could be understood, a note that highlights the utility and importance of our proposed "informal translation". What was liked the most was the possibility of "see" in a graphical form the composition of words. This group also struggled with certain labeling words like VTR, VI, that are not widely known.

Users in group 1 positively mentioned the possibility to see the different segmentation options. Some people signaled that there should be exam-

[7]The words are shown in Table 2. The phrase was: `Pichikalu iñche , amukefun chillkatuwe ruka mew , fewla chillkatuwekelan`.

[8]The translations were rated for accuracy by an instructor.

ples of the usage.[9]

Group 2 was the one that gave most comments. Some mentioned that a scenario when a morpheme occurs duplicated with different communicative functions was confusing. They also indicated that they would have wanted the ability to actually see the the correct translation, not just the segmentation and its explanation; unfortunately, the current state of MT for Mapuzugun does not allow this, but it provides a concrete avenue for future work.

They also liked the segmentation and its explanation, and suggest that give the possibility to practice conjugation. On the other hand, words without context can be used in different forms and this could confuse beginners.

Last, there were comments about the choice of colors of the interface, as well as a suggestion for turning the tool into a mobile app.

Group 3 suggested that beginners could get confused by the amount of options that are shown for certain words. Some of them mentioned that the program helped them to understand certain particles. They also mentioned the need of context for the words. Regarding negative issues, some persons mentioned the need to have a translation besides morphemes, although one person liked the idea that you must make efforts to compose instead of receiving the translation immediately. Group 4 did not made relevant comments.

It is worth noting, last, that many of the comments reflected the excitement that such a tool was even available for Mapuzugun.

7 Related Work

Computational Work on Mapuzugun Today there are various initiatives of computational linguistics on Mapuzugun. There is an orthographic normalizer and a morphological analyzer (Chandía, 2012), but its accuracy is low, since it is rule-based. Another aspect that could be improved is that, currently, there is no possibility of choosing the output alphabet, restricting it to only one form of writing. This is still inconvenient today, as there is still no agreement on orthography standardization. This implementation is based on a set of rules through regular expressions, with a finite state transducer, which have been released on the author's website.

The purpose of another project, called AVENUE, in which the Universidad de la Frontera, the Intercultural Bilingual Education Program and the Language Technologies Institute of Carnegie Mellon University (CMU) collaborated, was to generate simple and low-cost translations, in addition to helping to preserve the Indo-American languages. This project first developed an alphabet that was used to transcribe (but not fully revise) a 170-hour audio corpus along with Spanish translations (Duan et al., 2020), and last deployed prototype translation systems and base spell checkers that are available for OpenOffice.

In the educational field, there is software to learn Mapuzugun called MAPU from a project at the Pontificia Universidad Católica de Valparaíso that also includes voice recognition to control the application, which works correctly, but is not robust to pronunciation (Troncoso, 2012). This work also refers to another Mapuzugun-to-Spanish voice-text translation prototype, based on recordings, and to a chatbot from the Pandora project.

Last, we refer the reader to Appendix B for an additional discussion of further computational work on other south American Indigenous languages.

8 Conclusion and Future Work

We have presented a system comprised of set of NLP tools appropriate for educational purposes in Mapuzugun, an Indigenous south American language, and we have demonstrated its usefulness through a small user study. Our study also provided a guide for future improvements. As more data will hopefully become available in Mapuzugun, we plan to incorporate more recent statistical machine learning components, both for the orthography converted and the morphological analyzer. We will also hopefully be able to deploy full-fledged machine translation systems to provide free-form translations of words or phrases to learners. Many users would benefit by the incorporation of a text-to-speech component (as long as it is of high quality), that would also allow the teaching of Mapuzugun pronunciation.

Going further, the tool could be complemented with a system that permits annotation of words and/or phrases in order to collect data for future tasks, as more users adopt it – especially if language instructors use our tool in their courses. We are also hoping to create an offline version of the tool to make it accessible in areas with low connectivity. We will also attempt to incorporate any available corpora of Mapuzugun such as the those

[9] Examples are provided as part of the documentation, but they probably did not find them.

of Levin et al. (2000) and Duan et al. (2020) to use as educational examples.

We release our code[10] in the hopes that more Indigenous communities are able to use it to develop similar systems for their languages.

Ethical Considerations

Working with endangered/Indigenous languages and language data, there is always substantial risk of unwittingly perpetuation of colonial harms (Bird, 2020). This is obviously an extremely complex issue, but according to Bird (2020) and other working in the space of NLP for endangered/Indigenous languages, perhaps the most critical aspect in working with Indigenous language data is that researchers actively develop meaningful relationships with members of these respective language communities.

In our case, our work is lead by an instructor of Mapuzugun and member of the Chilean Mapuche community, who knows first-hand the oppression the Mapuche people have sufferred and the harms they have undergone by being forced to operate in Spanish. This work is also partially funded by a program dedicated to addressing the long-standing colonial harms in Chile, by specifically helping Indigenous students through their studies.

We do not anticipate any serious harms by the development of our system, and we believe that the positive reception by the Mapuche volunteers who participated in our case study will be mirrored by its reception by the wider Mapuche community. It is also important, though, to acknowledge its limitations and make it clear that our tool is meant to be a companion tool for learning and can by no means substitute instructors of the language.

No indigenous language data were collected or are released through this project. We re-used existing, publicly available tools and corpora. The tool is provided for free: it is currently behind a simple username and password setting to ensure that its traffic is not overwhelming, so that the tool remains available to the Mapuzugun instructors and learners that need it the most (and who already have access to it).

Acknowledgements

We are thankful to the Mapuzuguletuaiñ organization for their support and initial feedback, and to the volunteer Mapuzugun speakers who took part in our study. The first author was funded by the Programa de Pueblos Indígenas, FCFM, Universidad de Chile. Antonios Anastasopoulos is generously supported by the NSF through project BCS-2109578.

[10]https://github.com/crahumadao/kaxvkaam

References

Carlo Alva and Arturo Oncevay. 2017. Spell-checking based on syllabification and character-level graphs for a peruvian agglutinative language. In *Proceedings of the First Workshop on Subword and Character Level Models in NLP*, pages 109–116.

Marco Espinoza Alvarado. 2019. El 'nativohablantismo'en la investigación de las lenguas indígenas: el caso del mapudungun en chile. *Trabalhos em Linguística Aplicada*, 58:795–825.

Gabriel E Alvarado Pavez. 2020. Glotopolítica de la desigualdad: Ideologías del mapudungun y el español en chile (2009–2019).

Belén Villena Araya, María Teresa Cabré Castellví, and Sabela Fernández-Silva. 2019. Noun formation in mapudungun: Productivity, genuineness and language planning. *Revista Signos*, 52(100):615.

Jennifer Arnold. 1996. The inverse system in Mapudungun and other languages. *RLA: Revista de Lingüística teórica y aplicada*, 34:9–47.

Mark Aronoff and Janie Rees-Miller. 2020. *The handbook of linguistics*. John Wiley & Sons.

Antti Arppe, Jordan Lachler, Trond Trosterud, Lene Antonsen, and Sjur N Moshagen. 2016. Basic language resource kits for endangered languages: A case study of plains cree. In *Proceedings of the 2nd Workshop on Collaboration and Computing for Under-Resourced Languages Workshop (CCURL 2016), Portorož, Slovenia*, pages 1–8.

Alicia Alexandra Assini. 2013. Natural language processing and the mohawk language: creating a finite state morphological parser of mohawk formal nouns.

Mark C. Baker. 1996. *The Polysynthesis Parameter*. Oxford University Press, Oxford.

Mark C. Baker, Roberto Aranovich, and Lucía A. Golluscio. 2005. Two types of syntactic noun incorporation: Noun incorporation in Mapudungun and its typological implications. *Language*, 81(1):138–176.

Ximena Bertin. 2016. Encuesta cep: 67% de la población mapuche no habla ni entiende el mapuzugun.

Steven Bird. 2020. Decolonising speech and language technology. In *Proceedings of the 28th International Conference on Computational Linguistics*, pages 3504–3519, Barcelona, Spain (Online). International Committee on Computational Linguistics.

Damián Blasi, Antonios Anastasopoulos, and Graham Neubig. 2021. Systematic inequalities in language technology performance across the world's languages. arXiv:2110.06733.

María Catrileo. 2017. *Diccionario Lingüístico Etnográfico de la Lengua Mapuche: Mapudungun-Español-English*, volume 7. Ediciones Universidad Austral de Chile.

Tulio Fernando Cañumil. 2011. *Estudio del idioma mapuche, Mapucezugun ñi gvnezuam*. Florencio Varela: Editorial Xalkan.

Andrés Chandía. 2012. *Dungupeyem _alfa 2 _v0. 1: un prototipo de analizador morfológico para el mapudungun a través de transductores de estados finitos*. Ph.D. thesis, Tesis de Máster sin publicar, Universitat Pompeu Fabra, Barcelona.

Maria Rayen Catrileo Chiguailaf. 1972. *A tagmemic sketch of Mapuche grammar*. The University of Texas at El Paso.

Francesco Chiodi and Elisa Loncón. 1999. Crear nuevas palabras. *Editorial Pillan, Universidad de la Frontera, Corporación Nacional de Desarrollo Indígena, Temuco.*

Pascual Coña. 2019. *Kuyfi mapuche chumgechi ñi azmogekeel egün*. Editorial Genlol. In Mapuzugun.

Robert A Croese. 2014. Tiempo verbal en mapudungun. *Lenguas y Literaturas Indoamericanas*, (1).

Mingjun Duan, Carlos Fasola, Sai Krishna Rallabandi, Rodolfo Vega, Antonios Anastasopoulos, Lori Levin, and Alan W Black. 2020. A resource for computational experiments on mapudungun. In *Proceedings of The 12th Language Resources and Evaluation Conference*, pages 2872–2877, Marseille, France. European Language Resources Association.

Alexandra Espichán-Linares and Arturo Oncevay-Marcos. 2017. Language identification with scarce data: A case study from peru. In *Annual International Symposium on Information Management and Big Data*, pages 90–105. Springer.

Pratik Joshi, Sebastin Santy, Amar Budhiraja, Kalika Bali, and Monojit Choudhury. 2020. The state and fate of linguistic diversity and inclusion in the NLP world. In *Proceedings of the 58th Annual Meeting of the Association for Computational Linguistics*, pages 6282–6293, Online. Association for Computational Linguistics.

Katharina Kann, Jesus Manuel Mager Hois, Ivan Meza-Ruiz, and Hinrich Schütze. 2018. Fortification of neural morphological segmentation models for polysynthetic minimal-resource languages. In *Proceedings of the 2018 Conference of the North American Chapter of the Association for Computational Linguistics: Human Language Technologies, Volume 1 (Long Papers)*, pages 47–57.

Cristián Lagos. 2012. El mapudungun en santiago de chile: vitalidad y representaciones sociales en los mapuches urbanos. *RLA. Revista de lingüística teórica y aplicada*, 50(1):161–184.

Lorraine Levin, Rodolfo M Vega, Jaime G Carbonell, Ralf D Brown, Alon Lavie, Eliseo Cañulef, and Carolina Huenchullan. 2000. Data collection and language technologies for mapudungun.

Ariadna Font Llitjós. 2005. Developing a quechua-spanish machine translation system.

Elisa Loncon. 2010. Derechos educativos y lingüísticos de los pueblos indígenas de chile. *ISEES: Inclusión Social y Equidad en la Educación Superior*, (7):79–94.

Elisa Loncon Antileo. 2011. *Morfología y Aspectos del Mapudungun*. Universidad Autónoma Metropolitana, México, D.F.

Manuel Mager, Ximena Gutierrez-Vasques, Gerardo Sierra, and Ivan Meza-Ruiz. 2018. Challenges of language technologies for the indigenous languages of the americas. In *Proceedings of the 27th International Conference on Computational Linguistics*, pages 55–69.

Manuel Manquilef. 1911. Comentarios del pueblo araucano (la faz social). In *Anales de la Universidad de Chile*, pages ág–393.

Manuel Manquilef. 1914. Comentarios del pueblo araucano ii, la jimnasia nacional (juegos, ejercicios i bailes). In *Anales de la Universidad de Chile*, 72, pages ág–239.

José Millalén, Pablo Marimán, Rodrigo Levil, and Sergio Caniuqueo. 2006. Escucha winka. *Santiago de Chile: LOM Ediciones.*

Christopher Moseley. 2012. *The UNESCO atlas of the world's languages in danger: Context and process*. World Oral Literature Project.

Viktor Naqill Gomez. 2016. Lengua y emancipación nacional.

Aldo Olate Vinet, Paula Alonqueo Boudon, and Jaqueline Caniguan Caniguan. 2013. Interactividad lingüística castellano/mapudungun de una comunidad rural bilingüe. *Alpha (Osorno)*, (37):265–284.

John Ortega and Krishnan Pillaipakkamnatt. 2018. Using morphemes from agglutinative languages like quechua and finnish to aid in low-resource translation. In *Proceedings of the AMTA 2018 workshop on technologies for MT of low resource languages (LoResMT 2018)*, pages 1–11.

César Pérez. 2015. *Diccionario Mapuzugun-Castellano*.

Ricardo Rosasa, María Isabel Larab, Victoria Espinozaa, María Paz Ramíreza, Felipe Porflitta, and Catalina Benaventea. Mapudungun mew: Software para la enseñanza del mapudungun en la escuela1.

Alex Rudnick. 2011. Towards cross-language word sense disambiguation for quechua. In *Proceedings of the Second Student Research Workshop associated with RANLP 2011*, pages 133–138.

Scott Sadowsky, Héctor Painequeo, Gastón Salamanca, and Heriberto Avelino. 2013. Mapudungun. *Journal of the International Phonetic Association*, 43(1):87–96.

Felipe Hasler Sandoval, Aldo Olate Vinet, and Guillermo Soto Vergara. 2020. Origen y desarrollo del sistema evidencial del mapudungun. *CÍCULO de Linguística Aplicada a la Comunicación*, 81:9.

Catharina Johanna Smeets. 1989. *A Mapuche grammar*. Ph.D. thesis, Rijksuniversiteit Leiden.

Marco Antonio Alvarado Troncoso. 2012. *Sistema para el Aprendizaje del Mapudungun. Incluyendo características de reconocimiento de voz y bot conversacional.* Ph.D. thesis, Pontificia Universidad Católica de Valparaíso.

uatv.cl. 2020. Organizaciones mapuche convocan a novena marcha por el mapuzugun.

Fernando Wittig. 2009. Desplazamiento y vigencia del mapudungún en chile: un análisis desde el discurso reflexivo de los hablantes urbanos. *RLA. Revista de lingüistíca teoríca y aplicada*, 47(2):135–155.

Fernando Zúñiga. 2006. *Mapudungun: El Habla Mapuche.* Centro de Estudios Públicos, Santiago, Chile.

A Notes on Mapuzugun

In this section, to understand the context and the need for this work, it will be explained how Mapugugun went from being a language of a million speakers in the 16th century to becoming, according to UNESCO, an endangered language today.

History of Mapuzugun The Mapuche people have their origin in the territory known as Wallmapu (which can be considered as the Mapuche Country (Millalén et al., 2006)). This territory ranges from Coquimbo to Chiloé, also including areas on the "other side" of the mountain range, such as Neuquén, in a vast area demarcated by the Río Negro. Throughout this territory different denominations for this people can be found, shareing many cultural aspects (Millalén et al., 2006). This is the area in which the scope of the language known as Mapuzugun can be framed – also in accordance with what the Spaniards defined at the end of the 16th century.

Mapuzugun, at its height, at the arrival of the Spaniards, was spoken by around a million people (Millalén et al., 2006). One of the first published books on this language is entitled "Art and Grammar of the General Language that runs throughout the Kingdom of Chile, with a Vocabulary and Confessionary" published in 1606 by Luis de Valdivia (Alvarado Pavez, 2020). In addition, toponyms with a clear Mapuzugun origin are still preserved, such as Huente Lauquen in the north, Puchuncaví, Curacaví, Pudahuel, Vitacura, with examples even in Puel Mapu (or what we know today as Argentina), and Chiloé in the south.

During the interaction of Mapuche with Spaniards during the Colony, the place of the Mapuzugun in all spheres of society can be appreciated, from the family, to international political relations, as were the Koyagtun (or Parliaments) mainly with the Spanish Empire, the Chilean and Argentine States, but also with the French, Dutch, and English. In all of these, the figure of the *'lenguaraz'* stood out, who acted as a translator to try to faithfully reproduce the ideas that were held in Mapuzugun to foreign representatives.

It was during the construction of the Chilean and Argentine national states in the 19th century -which initially did not include Mapuche territory- with the so-called "Campaign of the Desert" and "Pacification of Araucanía", when these states politically subjected the Mapuche people. Along with this, as part of the construction of the identities of Chile and Argentina, space was taken away from Mapuzugun and the Mapuche culture through schools and the church, which, through evangelization and punishment, denied indigenous identity along with their language.

Then at the beginning of the 20th century, after that territorial dispossession, there was a strong Mapuche migration to the most important cities of Chile, in search of better living conditions. This translated into cultural loss, often due to racism and discrimination. However, some efforts were made by the Mapuche themselves to maintain the culture and language, as shown by publications such as those by Coña (2019) and Manquilef (1911, 1914), which were written in both Mapuzugun and Spanish.

During the dictatorship and since the 90's, the Mapuche people began to have a greater political position. With this, the Mapuche language was recovered hand in hand with a recovery of identity in various areas, in addition to maintaining territories in which Mapuzugun is spoken as the first language. Today, according to the 2017 census, the majority of the Mapuche population would be in Santiago, but most do not speak or understand their language.

Today, there are various organizations that offer courses or tools that contribute to the revitalization of Mapuzugun. These instances have a milestone in a march that is organized during February, within the framework of the commemoration of the "International Mother Language Day" (uatv.cl, 2020), having, as a movement, important demands such as the officialization of Mapuzugun (Naqill Gomez, 2016).

Various sources estimate the number of Mapuzugun speakers to be between 100,000 and 300,000 (Bertin, 2016).[11] They constitute about 5 to 10% of the Mapuche population (1,745,147), who make up 9.9% of the total population of Chile (17,574,003).

According to UNESCO, a language is in danger when it is no longer used, when it is used in fewer areas and when it is no longer transmitted. From this it is stated that "about 90% of all languages "could be replaced by the dominant ones by the end of the 21st century". All this, added to insufficient documentation, generates that there are extinct or endangered languages. , which are

[11] https://news.un.org/es/story/2019/04/1454571

unrecoverable (Aronoff and Rees-Miller, 2020).

There are six degrees to define the state of danger of these languages. Within this classification is the Mapuzugun, referred to as Huilliche and, both in Chile and Argentina, as Mapuche, as can be seen in the Unesco Atlas (Moseley, 2012). They are in grade 1 ("In a critical situation", Huilliche), 2 ("Seriously in danger or threatened", Mapuche, Argentina) and 3 ("Clearly in danger or threatened", Mapuche, Chile).

But not only through UNESCO, research has been carried out on the state of the Mapuzugun. There are also various studies from the area of sociolinguistics to understand certain current language processes and their incorporation into public policies (Naqill Gomez, 2016; Loncon, 2010; Catrileo, 2017; Wittig, 2009; Lagos, 2012; Olate Vinet et al., 2013) [46].

Typological Notes Linguistically, Mapuzugun is defined as an agglutinative and polysynthetic language, which means that its expressions have a main root to which defined and distinguishable suffixes are added to form phrases. For example the word Kim mapuzuguyekümelleaiñ, which is explained in Table 2.1. Examples such as English, Chinese or Spanish are not in this category, and therefore the processing techniques used in those languages differ from the techniques that could be used for Mapuzugun.

Before colonization, Mapuzugun is described as a purely oral language. Today, until recently it was not formally taught or used by public and educational institutions in Chile. This has meant that it does not have a standardization of its writing or spelling. Today there are different ways of writing it and also, territorial orthographic variations, because in different regions there are phonetic differences for certain sounds and that translates, in general, into different writings. Today there are three main graphemaries to write Mapuzugun: Ragileo, created by Anselmo Raguileo in 1985; Unified, created by María Catrileo in 1989; and Azümchefe, created by Necul Painemal for CONADI (National Corporation for Indigenous Development) in 2008.

Among these graphemaries certain visible differences can be noted in Table 2.2. In the case of Ragileo, this grapheme uses only one grapheme per phoneme, and on certain occasions, the sounds associated with these graphemes do not correspond to those of Spanish, so it is a little more difficult to learn than the others. The Unified has a script more similar to Castilian. Although, although most of the graphemes are the same, there are phonemes that can be considered similar, but are not the same between Castilian and Mapuzugun. Finally, the Azümchefe is a kind of intermediate point, but it also presents difficulties and differences between graphemes and phonemes in Spanish. It is used by public institutions such as CONADI.

This lack of standardization of Mapuzugun brings complications to people who are studying the language and who only master a grapheme. This also affects the processing of Mapuzugun, since there would be inconsistencies when taking data from different sources or even from the same source, especially in topics such as automatic translation or semantic analysis, where the same word could have various forms and affect learning. some model. This probably affects the current lack of basic tools in this language.

In this direction, there are currently various works related purely to Mapuzugun linguistics: descriptions (Zúñiga, 2006; Smeets, 1989; Chiguailaf, 1972), but also specific academic articles on technical aspects of the language (Chiodi and Loncón, 1999; Olate Vinet et al., 2013; Sadowsky et al., 2013; Croese, 2014; Araya et al., 2019; Alvarado, 2019; Sandoval et al., 2020) and dictionaries (Catrileo, 2017).

A.1 Computational Work on Mapuzugun

Today there are various initiatives of computational linguistics on Mapuzugun. There is an orthographic normalizer and a morphological analyzer (Chandía, 2012), but it still has some errors derived from the fact that it directly applies a series of rules without analyzing the input it receives. These are aspects that could be improved. Another aspect that could be improved is that, currently, there is no possibility of choosing the output grapheme, restricting it to only one form of writing. This is inconvenient today that there is still no agreement on the standardization of writing. This implementation was made from a set of rules through regular expressions, with a finite state transducer, which have been released on the author's website. This author is also working on a prototype morphological analyzer and spell checker, based on Xerox finite state tools. There are also corpus exploitation interfaces annotated with these same tools, created in an interuniversity master's degree in Barcelona, (coordinated by the University of Barcelona) and an automatic Mapuzugun translator is being targeted. As he is in the process of doctoral work, the results of these tools have not yet been published, but they can be reviewed in his thesis proposal.

On the other hand, there was a project called AVENUE, in which the Universidad de la Frontera, the Intercultural Bilingual Education Program and the Institute of Language Technologies of Carnegie Mellon University (CMU) collaborated. The purpose of this project was to generate simple and low-cost translators, in addition to helping to preserve the Indo-American languages. This project resulted in four products: 1. In the first place, a graphemebook for the purposes of processing and computer development of the Project. 2. A 170-hour corpus that has been transcribed, but not fully revised. 3. A translation prototype consisting of a trained example-based translator. In addition, one based on transfer rules was worked on in parallel (both with Spanish as a pair). This prototype also has a morphological analyzer. After the Avenue project, CMU also worked on the automatic improvement of translations. 4. A spell checker that is said to contain an estimated 6,000,000 words, for OpenOffice. And that consists of two dictionaries, one for roots and the other for suffixes, which within OpenOffice's MySpell, correct a text in the typical way that the user is used to. This continues to have the limitation of the grapheme, in addition to not having the security that when writing a word in another grapheme it will convert it to the one used by the system.

In the educational field, there is software to learn Mapuzugun called MAPU from a job at the Pontificia Universidad Católica de Valparaíso that also includes voice recognition to control the application, which works correctly, but is not robust to pronunciation (Troncoso, 2012). In this work, it also refers to another Mapuzugun-to-Spanish voice-text translation prototype, based on recordings, and to a chatbot from the Pandora project.

In addition, the CEDETI of the Pontificia Universidad Católica, which is dedicated to working on technologies for integration, has language learning software called Mapudungun mew (Rosasa et al.).

A.2 The three orthographies currently used

See Figure 5 for a comparison.

Unificado	Ragileo
CH	C
D	Z
G	Q
L	B
Ll	J
N	H
Ng	G
Tr	X
T	-
Ü	V

Table 4: Differences and conversion between the Unificado and Ragileo orthographies.

Unificado	Azümchefe
D	Z
G	Q
L	Lh
N	Nh
Ng	G
Tr	Tx
T	T'
S	Sh

Table 5: Differences and conversion between the Unificado and Azümchefe orthographies.

B Computational Work on South American Indigenous Languages

Mager et al. (2018) review the challenges for indigenous languages in America in terms of language technologies and NLP, which is also a review of the experiences that have been had for different languages throughout the continent. Beyond Mapuzugun, it also addresses languages such as Quechua, Nahuatl, Wixarika, Shipibo Konibo, Guaraní, among others. The challenges have to do mainly with the insufficient or not well developed corpora, translations, and morphological analyzers. In addition, experiences are named in the different common tasks for NLP.

Llitjós (2005) presents the most complete process of what would be the result of the AVENUE project, whose product was a Quechua - Spanish translator. This could not be completed for the Mapuzugun case, but there is a methodology with which it could continue. One can also see the use of Bayesian classifiers and K nearest neighbors (k-nearest neighbors, KNN) for disambiguation in

Unificado	Ragileo	Azümchefe
A a	A a	A a
Ch ch	C c	Ch ch
D d	Z z	Z z
E e	E e	E e
F f	F f	F f
G g	Q q	Q q
I i	I i	I i
K k	K k	K k
L l	L l	L l
Ll ll	J j	Ll ll
M m	M m	M m
N n	N n	N n
Ñ ñ	Ñ ñ	Ñ ñ
N n	H h	Nh nh
Ng ng	G g	G g
O o	O o	O o
P p	P p	P p
R r	R r	R r
S s	S s	S s * Sh sh
T t	T t	T t
Tr tr	X x	Tx tx
T t	T t	T' t'
U u	U u	U u
Ü ü	V v	Ü ü
W w	W w	W w
Y y	Y y	Y y

Figure 5: Comparison of the three alphabets used by the Mapuche.

Ragileo	Azümchefe
C	Ch
B	Lh
J	Ll
H	Nh
S	Sh
X	Tx
-	T'
V	Ü

Table 6: Differences and conversion between the Ragileo and Azümchefe orthographies.

Quechua translation (Rudnick, 2011).

Also in Quechua, the improvement of morpheme recognition from its comparison with Finnish, due to the fact that they have similar structures, especially in the agglutination part (Ortega and Pillaipakkamnatt, 2018).

The closeness in typology also happens with other languages that are in Peru and the rest of the continent, such as Mexicanero, Nahuatl, Wixarika and Yorem Nokki (Kann et al., 2018). Or the Mohawk and Plains Cree (Arppe et al., 2016), from further north.

At the University of Limerick a thesis was developed on a morphological analyzer for the Mohawk case. This is done through finite states and their training from the language data (Assini, 2013).

Espichán-Linares and Oncevay-Marcos (2017) present a study of low-resource Peruvian languages. This is done from the construction of a vector space model for languages, from bigrams and trigrams, and a matrix from "term frequency - inverse document frequency" or (TF-IDF, for its acronym, in English). It is classified by sentences and a performance of over 96% is achieved in classification with support vector machine. Although these are good results, there is no way to know if it is exactly the orthography used or if it is just the closest.

Alva and Oncevay (2017) propose a corrector based on syllabification and characters for an agglutinating Peruvian language. This is done with graphs of syllables and characters from models extracted from the corpus. This method proposes three closest corrections for a misspelled word with distance metrics per character, also saving the previous corrections. This method is complete and takes into account the syllables and characters, which would be important in the case of orthographies which have subtle differences, as if they were spelling errors. Although the error can be improved (76%), it could be a solution for the normalizer, if it is extended to multiple languages (or in this case orthographies).

An Evaluation of Binary Comparative Lexical Complexity Models

Kai North[1], **Marcos Zampieri**[1], **Matthew Shardlow**[2]
[1]Rochester Institute of Technology, Rochester, NY, USA
[2]Manchester Metropolitan University, Manchester, UK
kn1473@rit.edu

Abstract

Identifying complex words in texts is an important first step in text simplification (TS) systems. In this paper, we investigate the performance of binary comparative Lexical Complexity Prediction (LCP) models applied to a popular benchmark dataset — the CompLex 2.0 dataset used in SemEval-2021 Task 1. With the data from CompLex 2.0, we create a new dataset contain 1,940 sentences referred to as CompLex-BC. Using CompLex-BC, we train multiple models to differentiate which of two target words is more or less complex in the same sentence. A linear SVM model achieved the best performance in our experiments with an F1-score of 0.86.

1 Introduction

Children, second language learners, or individuals suffering from a reading disability, such as dyslexia or aphasia, can find certain words hard to read, interpret, or learn (Devlin and Tait, 1998; Carroll et al., 1998; Kajiwara et al., 2013; Rello et al., 2013; Malmasi et al., 2016). In readability and text simplification (TS) literature, these words are known as complex words.

Complex and non-complex words are distinguishable. Statistical, morphological, and psycholinguistic features are indicative of lexical complexity (Shardlow et al., 2022; Desai et al., 2021). Complex words are on average longer, morphologically more unique, and less frequent in general corpora, than non-complex words (Paetzold and Specia, 2016; Yimam et al., 2018; Shardlow et al., 2021).

With the growing popularity of distance learning platforms, the demand for new technologies that make texts more accessible for independent and remote learning has seen an exponential increase (Morris et al., 2020). Among these technologies, are TS systems that automatically simplify texts for various target populations. The first step in TS is generally referred to as lexical complexity prediction (LCP). LCP aims to identify which words in a text are complex and therefore are in need of simplification. It has been modeled as a binary classification task (Paetzold and Specia, 2016), as a regression task (Yimam et al., 2018), and more recently as a multi-class classification task (Shardlow et al., 2020).

In this paper, we explore binary comparative LCP where the goal is to determine when one target word is more or less complex than another. This new type of LCP is motivated by the need for comparative prediction methods that allow for the pairwise ranking of target words based on newly available data assigned with continuous complexity values (Shardlow et al., 2020). Binary comparative LCP aims to aid TS by improving the selection and ranking of substitute candidates for a particular complex word. It achieves this by allowing for more data to be generated from a finite dataset. For instance, a dataset consisting of 10,000 complex words assigned with complexity values can be converted into 100 million comparative instances, since every complex word can be compared to every other complex word. A binary comparative LCP classifier trained on this dataset can then make binary comparative judgements as part of a sorting algorithm. This lets a lexical simplification (LS) system effectively find the most appropriate simplification for any given complex word improving the efficiency of TS and other down-stream applications.

We aim to determine whether binary comparative LCP is possible when attempting to differentiate the complexities of two different target words in the same sentence (Table 3). We have accomplished this by adapting a recent baseline LCP dataset: CompLex 2.0 (Shardlow et al., 2020), and by asking the following research question: can LCP be modeled as a binary comparative classification task?

Proceedings of the 17th Workshop on Innovative Use of NLP for Building Educational Applications (BEA 2022), pages 197 - 203
July 15, 2022

The main contributions of this paper are:

1. CompLex-BC, the first binary comparative LCP dataset built from continuous data obtained through 5-point likert-scale annotation.

2. An evaluation of SVM, BERT, and BERT + MLP models for binary comparative LCP.

2 Related Work

Traditionally, LCP comes in two forms, it is either: a). a binary classification task, known as complex word identification (CWI) (Paetzold and Specia, 2016; Zampieri et al., 2017; Yimam et al., 2018), or b). a linear regression based task, simply referred to as LCP (Shardlow et al., 2021). Both CWI and LCP datasets contain target words labeled with a complexity value. This complexity value is used by a machine learning (ML) model to determine the complexity of a target word. CWI assigns a binary complexity value of either 1 (complex), or 0 (non-complex). LCP alternatively assigns a complexity value on a continuum, ranging from 0 to 1. This continuum contains multiple labels with differing complexity thresholds: very easy (0), easy (0.25), neutral (0.5), difficult (0.75), to very difficult (1) (Shardlow et al., 2020). An example is shown in Table 1.

	Folly	is	**set**	in	**great**	**dignity**
BC	1	is	0	in	0	0
CC	0.57	is	0.18	in	0.15	0.42

Table 1: Example of a sentence annotated with both binary complexity (BC) and continuous complexity (CC) values from CWI and LCP systems respectively. Target words are in bold.

Other approaches have attempted to model LCP as a multi-class classification task. Pintard and François (2020) assigned six readability levels, belonging to the Common European Framework of Reference for languages (CEFR), to target words as a means of rating their complexity for second language learners. Alfter (2021) trained a variety of models, including a convolutional neural network (CNN) and a recurrent convolutional neural network (RCNN), to predict the correct CEFR labels of target words taken from a multitude of CERF vocabulary lists.

LCP research has also included the ranking of complex words (Paetzold and Specia, 2017; Maddela and Xu, 2018). Neural regressors have been trained to identify which of two target words is more or less complex by predicting a continuous positive or negative value belonging to an inputted word pair. A positive value indicates that the first target word is more complex than the second, whereas a negative value dictates that the second target word is more complex than the first. The magnitude of the returned value also represents the degree of difference between the two target words. Positive and negative values closer to +1 or -1 respectively, show that the difference between the target words' complexities is more extreme compared to those values closer to 0 (Table 2).

Word Pair	CC Values	Label
{set, great}	{0.18, 0.15}	+0.03
{set, dignity}	{0.18, 0.42}	-0.24

Table 2: Example of two word pairs annotated with continuous comparative complexity labels. The first word pair have a similar level of complexity, whereas the second word pair have a greater disparity between their complexities.

Binary comparative LCP provides a binary complexity label that defines when the first target word is more complex (1) or less complex (0) than a second target word, be it either the same or a different target word in the same or a variety of contexts. Examples of two different target words in the same context, in this case sentence, are shown in Table 3.

Binary comparative LCP is now only recently possible due to the release of the Complex 2.0 dataset that provides a more fine-grained representation of target word complexity (Shardlow et al., 2020). This is since CompLex 2.0 is the first of its kind to contain continuous complexity values obtained through the use of a 5-point rather than a 6-point likert-scale annotation scheme that does not account for neutral labeling (Maddela and Xu, 2018), or through the use of binary annotation. Binary comparative LCP is thus a new form of complexity prediction that differs from the complexity ranking previously attempted by Paetzold and Specia (2017) and Maddela and Xu (2018), as it uses new and more fine-grained continuous complexity values to make binary comparative predictions.

Target Word 1	Target Word 2	Context	L
wood	**hyssop**	...he shall take it, and the cedar **wood**, and the scarlet, and the **hyssop**...	0
sequencing	**fly**	...the **sequencing** projects of human, mouse, rat, fruit **fly** and...	1
fish	**invertebrates**	...such as mammals, **fish**, and amphibians, but not in **invertebrates**...	0
Nehemiah	**district**	...**Nehemiah** the son of Azbuk, the ruler of half the **district** of Beth...	1
example	**avoidance**	...for **example**, a QTL for PROP **avoidance** has been suggested on...	0

Table 3: Example of the Complex-BC dataset. Target words are in bold. Only snapshots of context are shown. Label (L) 0 refers to when target word 1's complexity < target word 2's complexity, and label 1 refers to when target word 1's complexity > target word 2's complexity.

No.	Input Type	Encoding Strategies
a	Target Word only	<CLS>set<SEP>dignity<SEP>
b	Single Context	<CLS>Folly is <B>**set**<E> in great <B>**dignity**<E><SEP>
c	Two Contexts - TW	<CLS>Folly is in great dignity<SEP>Folly is set in great<SEP>

Table 4: Examples of input types and encoding strategies used.

3 Data

CompLex 2.0 The CompLex 2.0 dataset contains 9,000 instances of individual words in context. Each of its extracts were taken from the Bible (Christodouloupoulos and Steedman, 2015), biomedical articles (Koehn, 2005), and EuroParl (Bada et al., 2012). Its annotators were crowd-sourced from "the UK, USA, and Australia" (Shardlow et al., 2020).

CompLex-BC We created a new dataset containing binary comparative labels (Table 3). Complex-BC consists of 1,940 sentences that house two differing target words identified as being complex within the CompLex 2.0 dataset and that also belonged to the same sentence. Each entry comprises of a target word, a second target word, and a label. For example, given the sentence *"he shall take it, and the cedar wood, and the scarlet, and the hyssop"* from the CompLex 2.0 dataset, our new dataset adapts this sentence and provides "*wood*" as target word 1, "*hyssop*" as target word 2, and a new binary comparative label of "0" that indicates that in this sentence, target word 1: "*wood*", was rated as being less complex than target word 2: "*hyssop*" by the annotators of the CompLex 2.0 dataset (Table 3).

4 Models

We trained a SVM model given its high performance at binary CWI (Zampieri et al., 2016; Choubey and Pateria, 2016; Sanjay et al., 2016; Kuru, 2016), a BERT model (Devlin et al., 2019) per its competitive performance at LCP-2021 (Shardlow et al., 2021; Yaseen et al., 2021; Pan et al., 2021; Rao et al., 2021), and a BERT + multi-layer perceptron (MLP) model (Gu and Budhkar, 2021) to take full advantage of BERT inferred contextual features as well as the word-level features fed into our SVM model. Two naive baseline models were used to evaluate the performances of our SVM, BERT, and BERT + MLP models: a random classifier (RC) and a majority classifier (MC).

We used an integrated Intel UHD Graphics 620 GPU to train each model. Our SVM and BERT models were trained over 5 epochs. The train and test split of our dataset was set to 70:30% respectively. No target words were shared between the train and test sets.

SVM Our SVM model used a Radial Basis Function (RBF) kernel and was trained on a set of well established statistical and psycholinguistic features for LCP as these have been previously found to achieve the best results (Shardlow et al., 2022; Desai et al., 2021). These features were word length, word frequency, syllable count, average age of acquisition (AoA), and prevalence (familiarity). Word frequency being calculated in accordance to the target word's frequency in the British National Corpus (BNC) (Consortium, 2007), average AoA being calculated by averaging the AoAs within an updated version of the Living Word Vocabulary Dataset (Dale and O'Rourke, 1981; Brysbaert and Biemiller, 2017), and prevalence being calculated in accordance to the percentage of people who knew the target word as shown in the dataset provided by Brysbaert et al. (2019). These features were obtained in regards to the target word only and were not applied to any of the target word's neighbouring words.

BERT After experimenting with different hyperparameters, our BERT model (bert-base-uncased) was set to have a softmax activation layer, a batch size of 200, and a learning rate of 1e-5. Several inputs were also experimented with that took into consideration the target word along with varying degrees of contextual information. Encoding strategies adopted by the leading systems of LCP–2021 (Rao et al., 2021; Shardlow et al., 2021) and suggested by Hettiarachchi and Ranasinghe (2021), were then applied to these inputs and fed into our model.

We encoded each input into sub-word units, otherwise known as WordPiece tokens (Devlin et al., 2019). We then used the class identifier special token: <CLS>, the separator special token: <SEP>, and two custom special tokens: <B> and <E>, to distinguish between two differing target words. We referred to these as (a) the target word only, (b) single context, and (c) two contexts - TW encoding strategies respectively (Table 4). Encoding strategies (a) and (b) included the target word.

BERT + MLP As BERT assumes full sentences to encode the correct contextual information, we use a second BERT-based architecture for a fairer evaluation with the SVM model. We built a BERT + MLP model by feeding encoding strategies (a), (b), and (c) into our BERT model and then concatenate the outputted contextual features with those features used by our SVM model per Gu and Budhkar (2021). Our final BERT + MLP model then utilizes both set of contextual and word-level features for binary comparative LCP.

	Weighted Average			
Model	P	R	F1	A
SVM	**0.85**	**0.86**	**0.86**	**0.86**
BERT + MLP	0.74	0.88	0.80	0.81
BERT	0.49	0.48	0.44	0.48
MC	0.30	0.55	0.39	0.55
RC	0.50	0.50	0.50	0.50

Table 5: Best performances ranked in order of highest to least accuracy and split between test and baseline models.

5 Results

Table 5 shows the best performances of our SVM, BERT, and BERT + MLP models. Performances were measured in terms of weighted average precision (P), recall (R), and F1-score (F1). Our models' accuracies (A) were also reported.

Our SVM model achieved a F1-score of 0.86, whereas our BERT model attained a noticeably worst score of 0.44. Both models also produced drastically different accuracies of 0.86 for our SVM model and 0.48 for our BERT model with our BERT model attaining an accuracy on par with our naive MC and RC baseline classifiers. This suggests that there was not enough information for our BERT model to converge and therefore its final output labels were likely chosen at random. These performances were achieved by taking into consideration only the target words (a) and not any of their surrounding contexts (Table 4). Other encoding strategies (b) and (c) failed to surpass these performances for our BERT model.

Our BERT + MLP model achieved a greater performance compared to that attained by our standalone BERT model. It was found that by concatenating the contextual features outputted by our BERT model from single context input (b) with those features used for our SVM model, our BERT + MLP model achieved a precision, recall, f1-score, and accuracy of 0.74, 0.88, 0.80 and 0.81 respectively. Additional encoding strategies (a) and (c) attained lower performances, with an F1-score of 0.56 being returned by the former and 0.64 being achieved by the latter.

6 Analysis and Discussion

Comparing the complexities of two target words in the same sentence allowed us to fully utilize the CompLex 2.0 dataset that contained multiple instances of target words in the same context. It allowed us to generate binary comparative predictions that can be used to aid substitute selection and ranking (Sections 1 and 3).

Binary comparative LCP also allowed us to identify which words within a sentence contributed the most or the least to a context's overall complexity. Therefore, by comparing the complexities of two target words in the same sentence, we were able to identify which part of a sentence is in need of priority simplification. However, modeling binary comparative LCP in this way is not without its challenges. This is reflected in our models' performance.

Two factors are responsible for the superior performance of our SVM model in comparison to our standalone BERT model: 1). contextual similarity between the two target words, and 2). small dataset size.

One of the main advantages of transformer-based models, such as BERT, is their ability to infer bi-directional contextual relationships between a target word and its surrounding words and then use this contextual information to make accurate predictions (Devlin et al., 2019). However, since the two target words we are trying to compare are in the same sentence, BERT's inferred contextual features in relation to target word 1 were extremely similar to those inferred for target word 2, when given encoding strategy (c) (Table 4). This confused our BERT model, by making classes 0 (target word 1 is less complex) and 1 (target word 1 is more complex) hard to distinguish.

Our SVM model's word-level features of word length, word frequency, syllable count, average age of acquisition, and prevalence (familiarity) alternatively do not utilize contextual information. Instead, they rely purely on the characteristics of each target word and therefore resulted in feature representations that were more dissimilar. This had the effect of making classes 0 and 1 easier to differentiate for our SVM model and thus explaining its superior performance.

The superiority of word-level features is further demonstrated by the performance of our BERT + MLP model. Encoding strategy (b) returns from our BERT model contextual information related to the shared context (Table 4). Encoding strategy (c), however, attempts to encode contextual information belonging to each target word minus the target word.

Our BERT + MLP model performed poorly on encoding strategy (c) as it was presented from BERT two inferred contextual feature representations which were near identical. Encoding strategy (c) alternatively supplied only one inferred contextual feature representation from BERT, which allowed our BERT + MLP model to rely more heavily on its engineered word-level features. Nevertheless, encoding strategy (b) still failed to surpass our BERT + MLP model's performance beyond that of our SVM model. This indicates that the utilization of BERT's inferred contextual feature representation from encoding strategy (b), is still inferior to an SVM model using word-level features.

Another explanation for our models' performance is our dataset's size. The CompLex-BC dataset contains 1,940 instances with binary labels. Transformer-based models require large amounts of data to infer meaningful feature representations (Devlin et al., 2019), whereas an SVM model when trained on a set of relevant features requires less data and is also well suited for binary classification (Cortes and Vapnik, 1995).

7 Conclusion and Future Work

This paper sought to determine whether binary comparative LCP was possible when attempting to differentiate the complexities of two different target words in the same sentence. Only our SVM and BERT + MLP models were found to be successful having achieved F1-scores of 0.86 and 0.81 respectively. This led to the conclusion that our SVM and BERT + MLP models benefited from more varied word-level feature representations of target word only input than in comparison to less varied contextual input. We also believe that more data is required to conduct further experimentation and achieve greater performances, especially with transformer-based models. The CompLex-BC dataset will be made freely available to the research community after the publication of this manuscript.

We are currently working on exploring different variables that may impact the modeling of binary comparative LCP. This includes evaluating the performance of models on target words in different contexts as well as exploring a "neutral" class with words with similar complexity scores.

Finally, we are interested in investigating the feasibility of binary comparative LCP on languages other than English. At this point, the 5-point likert-scale annotation introduced by CompLex 2.0 is only available in English, however, we expect multilingual versions of CompLex 2.0 to become available soon enabling us to work on languages other than English.

Acknowledgements

We would like to thank the anonymous BEA reviewers for their insightful feedback and suggestions.

References

David Alfter. 2021. *Exploring natural language processing for single-word and multi-word lexical complexity from a second language learner perspective*. Ph.D. thesis, University of Gothenburg, Sweden.

Michael Bada, Miriam Eckert, Donald Evans, Kristin Garcia, Krista Shipley, Dmitry Sitnikov, William A Baumgartner, K Bretonnel Cohen, Karin Verspoor, Judith A Blake, et al. 2012. Concept annotation in the craft corpus. *BMC bioinformatics*, 13(1):161.

Marc Brysbaert and Andrew Biemiller. 2017. Test-based age-of-acquisition norms for 44 thousand english word meanings. *Behavioural Research*, 49:1520–1523.

Marc Brysbaert, Pawel Mandera, Samantha McCormick, and Emmanuel Keuleers. 2019. Word prevalence norms for 62,000 english lemmas. *Behavior Research Methods*, 51:467–479.

John Carroll, Guido Minnen, Yvonne Canning, Siobhan Devlin, and John Tait. 1998. Practical Simplification of English Newspaper Text to Assist Aphasic Readers. In *Proceedings of AAAI-98 Workshop*.

Prafulla Choubey and Shubham Pateria. 2016. Garuda & Bhasha at SemEval-2016 Task 11: Complex Word Identification Using Aggregated Learning Models. In *Proceedings of SemEval-2016*.

Christos Christodouloupoulos and Mark Steedman. 2015. A massively parallel corpus: the bible in 100 languages. *Language Resources and Evaluation*, 49(2):375–395.

BNC Consortium. 2007. British national corpus, XML edition. Oxford Text Archive.

Corinna Cortes and Vladimir Vapnik. 1995. Support-vector networks. *Machine Learning*, 20(1):273–297.

Edgar Dale and Joseph O'Rourke. 1981. *The living word vocabulary, the words we know: A national vocabulary inventory*. World Book.

Abhinandan Desai, Kai North, Marcos Zampieri, and Christopher Homan. 2021. LCP-RIT at SemEval-2021 Task 1: Exploring Linguistic Features for Lexical Complexity Prediction. In *Proceedings of SemEval-2021*.

Jacob Devlin, Ming-Wei Chang, Kenton Lee, and Kristina Toutanova. 2019. Bert: Pre-training of deep bidirectional transformers for language understanding. In *Proceedings of NAACL*.

Siobhan Devlin and John Tait. 1998. The use of a psycholinguistic database in the simplification of text for aphasic readers. *Linguistic Databases*, pages 161–173.

Ken Gu and Akshay Budhkar. 2021. A package for learning on tabular and text data with transformers. In *Proceedings of NAACL*.

Hansi Hettiarachchi and Tharindu Ranasinghe. 2021. Transwic at semeval-2021 task 2: Transformer-based multilingual and cross-lingual word-in-context disambiguation. In *Proceedings of SemEval-2021*.

Tomoyuki Kajiwara, Hiroshi Matsumoto, and Kazuhide Yamamoto. 2013. Selecting proper lexical paraphrase for children. In *Proceedings of ROCLING 2013*.

Philipp Koehn. 2005. Europarl: A parallel corpus for statistical machine translation. In *Proceedings of MT Summit*.

Onur Kuru. 2016. AI-KU at SemEval-2016 Task 11: Word Embeddings and Substring Features for Complex Word Identification. In *Proceedings of SemEval-2016*.

Mounica Maddela and Wei Xu. 2018. A word-complexity lexicon and a neural readability ranking model for lexical simplification. In *Proceedings of EMNLP*.

Shervin Malmasi, Mark Dras, and Marcos Zampieri. 2016. LTG at SemEval-2016 Task 11: Complex Word Identification with Classifier Ensembles. In *Proceedings of SemEval-2016*.

Neil P. Morris, Mariya Ivancheva, Taryn Coop, Rada Mogliacci, and Bronwen Swinnerton. 2020. Negotiating growth of online education in higher education. *International Journal of Educational Technology in Higher Education*, 17(48):1–16.

Gustavo Paetzold and Lucia Specia. 2016. SemEval 2016 Task 11: Complex Word Identification. In *Proceedings of SemEval-2016*.

Gustavo Paetzold and Lucia Specia. 2017. Lexical simplification with neural ranking. In *Proceedings of EACL*.

Chunguang Pan, Bingyan Song, Shengguang Wang, and Zhipeng Luo. 2021. DeepBlueAI at SemEval-2021 Task 1: Lexical Complexity Prediction with A Deep Ensemble Approach. In *Proceedings of SemEval-2021*.

Alice Pintard and Thomas François. 2020. Combining expert knowledge with frequency information to infer CEFR levels for words. In *Proceedings of READI*.

Gang Rao, Maochang Li, Xiaolong Hou, Lianxin Jiang, Yang Mo, and Jianping Shen. 2021. RG PA at SemEval-2021 Task 1: A Contextual Attention-based Model with RoBERTa for Lexical Complexity Prediction. In *Proceedings of SemEval-2021*.

Luz Rello, Ricardo Baeza-Yates, Laura Dempere-Marco, and Horacio Saggion. 2013. Frequent words improve readability and short words improve understandability for people with dyslexia. In *Proceedings of INTERACT*.

S.P Sanjay, Kumar M. Anand, and K.P Soman. 2016. AmritaCEN at SemEval-2016 Task 11: Complex Word Identification using Word Embedding. In *Proceedings of SemEval-2016*.

Matthew Shardlow, Michael Cooper, and Marcos Zampieri. 2020. CompLex — a new corpus for lexical complexity prediction from Likert Scale data. In *Proceedings of READI*.

Matthew Shardlow, Richard Evans, Gustavo Paetzold, and Marcos Zampieri. 2021. Semeval-2021 task 1: Lexical complexity prediction. In *Proceedings of SemEval-2021*.

Matthew Shardlow, Richard Evans, and Marcos Zampieri. 2022. Predicting lexical complexity in english texts: The complex 2.0 dataset. *Language Resources and Evaluation*.

Bani Yaseen, Qusai Ismail, Sarah Al-Omari, Eslam Al-Sobh, and Malak Abdullah. 2021. JUST-BLUE at SemEval-2021 Task 1: Predicting Lexical Complexity using BERT and RoBERTa Pre-trained Language Models. In *Proceedings of SemEval-2021*.

Seid Muhie Yimam, Chris Biemann, Shervin Malmasi, Gustavo Paetzold, Luci Specia, Sanja Štajner, Anaïs Tack, and Marcos Zampieri. 2018. A Report on the Complex Word Identification Shared Task 2018. In *Proceedings of BEA*.

Marcos Zampieri, Shervin Malmasi, Gustavo Paetzold, and Lucia Specia. 2017. Complex Word Identification: Challenges in Data Annotation and System Performance. In *Proceedings of NLPTEA*.

Marcos Zampieri, Liling Tan, and Josef van Genabith. 2016. MacSaar at SemEval-2016 Task 11: Zipfian and Character Features for ComplexWord Identification. In *Proceedings of SemEval-2016*.

Toward Automatic Discourse Parsing of Student Writing Motivated by Neural Interpretation

James Fiacco
Language Technologies Institute
Carnegie Mellon University
jfiacco@cs.cmu.edu

Shiyan Jiang
Language Technologies Institute
North Carolina State University
sjiang24@ncsu.edu

David Adamson
Turnitin
dadamson@turnitin.com

Carolyn P. Rosé
Language Technologies Institute
Carnegie Mellon University
cprose@cs.cmu.edu

Abstract

Providing effective automatic essay feedback is necessary for offering writing instruction at a massive scale. In particular, feedback for promoting coherent flow of ideas in essays is critical. In this paper we propose a state-of-the-art method for automated analysis of structure and flow of writing, referred to as Rhetorical Structure Theory (RST) parsing. In so doing, we lay a foundation for a generalizable approach to automated writing feedback related to structure and flow. We address challenges in automated rhetorical analysis when applied to student writing and evaluate our novel RST parser model on both a recent student writing dataset and a standard benchmark RST parsing dataset.

1 Introduction

Automatic writing feedback technologies (e.g., MI Write (Palermo and Wilson, 2020), Criterion (Burstein et al., 2003), Coh-Metrix (McNamara et al., 2010), Writing Pal (Roscoe and McNamara, 2013), and Revision Assistant (West-Smith et al., 2018)) show promises in helping students to develop writing skills at scale. One challenging area where these technologies meet is in providing feedback for improving coherence of student essays (Cotos, 2011; Fiacco et al., 2019b). Efforts have been made to address the challenge of providing structural level feedback via automatically extracting discourse structure from essays (Burstein et al., 2003). Extracting hierarchical discourse structure and organization from documents has been shown to be valuable for numerous applications including text categorization, authorship attribution, and automatic essay feedback (Feng and Hirst, 2014b; Jiang et al., 2019).

A popular approach to analysis of the structure of writing that leverages principles of the dependency-based hierarchical nature of text and is common across genres is the discourse analytic framework known as Rhetorical Structure Theory (RST, described in section 3.1) (Mann and Thompson, 1988). RST holds the promise of providing specific structural writing feedback for free-form essays (Burstein et al., 2001). However, RST parsing has remained a challenging task due to the dearth of annotated data and the challenges of decision making for discourse relations based on local context (Mabona et al., 2019). This paper builds on the same theoretical foundation using a Neural Network Based RST parser as a means for automation. Specifically, we propose a novel neural approach to automated RST analysis that improves over the best previously published approach from the field of Language Technologies. In particular, of existing neural architectures for RST parsing, neural transition based parsers have been making headway (Yu et al., 2018; Mabona et al., 2019), however, at their core, transition parsers make parsing decisions locally. While they use recurrent models to construct their stacks and buffers, in practice, recurrent models have been shown to primarily to use very near context (Khandelwal et al., 2018). This is a limitation for discourse parsing where knowledge about the document as a whole may provide essential context for judging relations.

We therefore propose and evaluate two improvements to the neural transition parser paradigm that provide better performance, both on standard RST parsing and on student writing by utilizing the limited data more efficiently:

1. By adding a co-task of predicting the most nuclear unit of the RST tree, we can increase the model's performance with the intuition that it may incentivize the model to maintain a broader document context that it can use for predicting individual tree spans and nuclear-

Proceedings of the 17th Workshop on Innovative Use of NLP for Building Educational Applications (BEA 2022), pages 204 - 215
July 15, 2022 ©2022 Association for Computational Linguistics

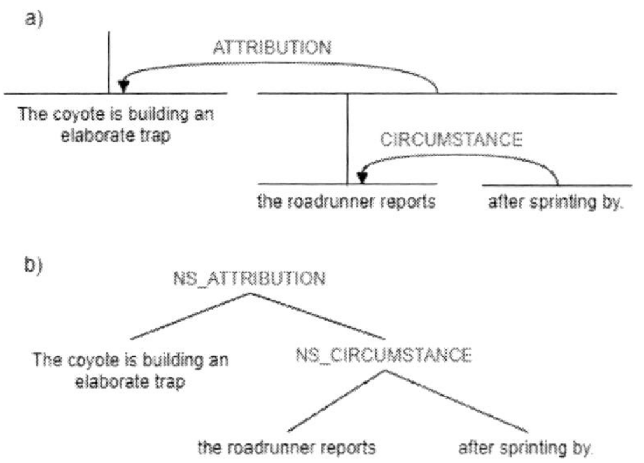

Figure 1: Example RST tree fragment with nuclearity and relations. a) The traditional depiction of an RST tree structure. b) The RST tree form corresponding to the labeled attachment decisions of (a).

ity.

2. By selectively introducing parser states from a previously trained parser into a new model during training, we can guide the training of the new model towards better performance on less structured writing.

The first improvement builds on the general concept of multitask learning in NLP (Bingel and Søgaard, 2017; Peng et al., 2017) and the intuition that a topic-like sentence, as a common key component in many writing assessments and rubrics (Aull, 2015), may provide important contextual information to aid local parser decision-making. The second improvement suggests a potential for a reflective form of neural network learning related neural component reuse that grows out of state-of-the-art work in neural network interpretation.

In the following sections, we evaluate our parsing model on both the standard English RST Discourse Treebank (RST-DT) (Carlson et al., 2003) and a more recent RST dataset of student writing (Jiang et al., 2019).

2 Rhetorical Structure Theory

Rhetorical Structure Theory decomposes a document into basic units of analysis called elementary discourse units (EDU) that can be combined through rhetorical relations between units into larger composite units (Mann and Thompson, 1988). Thus, the rhetorical relations combine to build a hierarchical tree structure that represents the overall structure of the document (Figure 1a). Each relation has one (mononuclear) or more (multinuclear) nuclei where a nucleus is an essential span which, if deleted, would leave the remaining text incoherent. Mononuclear relations have satellites that are related to the nucleus by means of a rhetorical relation. They play a supporting role, and are therefore not necessary for coherence of the document. Each node of the tree represents a relation tuple $\langle S, N, R \rangle$ where S is the span, N is the direction of nuclearity, and R is the relation label. This is more readily seen in Figure 1b which depicts an alternate representation of the RST tree structure.

RST has a long history (Mann and Thompson, 1988), and its original formulation continues to be treated as authoritative. However, for some types of writing, especially student writing, additional and combined relations have been proposed in order to bring the set of used relations in line with the writing practices that are applicable to the corpus (Jiang et al., 2019).

3 Related Work

This paper makes its fundamental contribution to work on automated feedback for student writing by expanding analysis capabilities that lay a foundation for a new form of support. Our technical contribution is grounded within the field of neural network modeling, contributing to work on neural approaches to Rhetorical structure analysis and leveraging approaches originating in the area of neural model interpretation.

An effective method for performing discourse parsing has been to utilize techniques from syntactic parsing and applying them at the document level. While RST parsing research has more frequently seen parsers influenced by another approach referred to as constituency parsing, it was shown that using techniques pioneered for dependency parsing could be as or more effective (Morey et al., 2018). As methods for RST parsing moved from those that rely on discourse markers and hand-coded rules (Marcu, 2000; LeThanh et al., 2004) to those that rely on deep learning (Li et al., 2014; Ji and Eisenstein, 2014; Braud et al., 2017), many of the improvements have been through techniques from syntactic parsing (Soricut and Marcu, 2003; Luong et al., 2013). In a similar way, our work builds on past RST parsers using neural transition parsing (Yu et al., 2018; Mabona et al., 2019). We extend this work by leveraging another area of neural network research, namely neural network interpretation, in order to yield a reflective form of learning that improves performance by leveraging lessons learned in an earlier stage of the training, as in a stage-based regression.

Neural pathways (Fiacco et al., 2019a) refer to a method for pinpointing sets of a model's neurons that function together in groups. These groups of neurons are referred to as pathways because they cut across architectural layers and allow representation of the flow of activation through a network, potentially from input all the way to output. For our application, we follow the original authors and use PCA (Hotelling, 1933) for this step as the resulting factor loadings (DeCoster, 1998) can then be used to determine which neurons belong to each pathway, and that forms the basis for our pruning approach. The remaining stages of this approach are not used in the work reported here but offer opportunities for promising follow up work.

In offering an abstraction over the details of a neural model, this approach offers the possibility of identifying portions of learned networks that can be dissected from the network as a whole and then reused as pre-packaged basic functionality within a more complex model learned at a later stage. Thus, we seek to harvest components pretrained on a simpler dataset to aid in learning a more robust model later on a more challenging dataset. While a deep dive into the differences between the learned functions of an RST parser trained on a relatively clean standard dataset and one trained solely on a noisier student writing dataset is beyond the scope of this paper, we will demonstrate that this work provides inspiration for development of what we will refer to as a neural pruning method that protects important simple generalizations while enabling accounting for complex special cases as well, and to represent an awareness of the difference between these in the final decision making.

4 A Corpus of Student Writing

In this section, we first offer more understanding about RST and then describe a corpus of student writing that has been annotated with RST.

4.1 Applying Rhetorical Structure Theory to Student Writing

Since we are using a neural approach, annotated data is necessary for training. The English RST Discourse Treebank is a common benchmark dataset for RST parsing. It includes 385 articles from the Wall Street Journal (Carlson et al., 2003), consti-

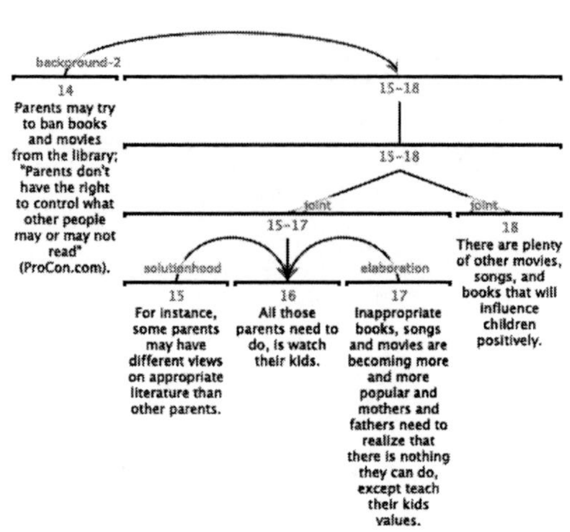

Figure 2: Example RST tree of a fragment of student writing.

tuting approximately 180,000 words of texts and covering a wide range of topics, such as finance and arts. These articles were created by professional writers, and are thus typically well-written, consistently structured, and copy-edited. (Palmer et al., 2010).

We also consider an RST corpus of less-polished student writing (Jiang et al., 2019). The corpus consists of 274 essays collected from Turnitin Revision Assistant (West-Smith et al., 2018), responding to standards-aligned formative writing tasks (Valencia and Wixson, 2001). These tasks cover a range of genres, including literary analysis, historical analysis, argumentative, and informative writing. For example, one writing task asks the student write an essay to the head of the school board, to argue whether competitive sports are more helpful or harmful to young people. These essays are drawn from a diverse set of secondary classrooms across the United States, representing a broad range of writing skills and student backgrounds. We hold out 25 documents as a development set, and 28 documents as a test set.

4.2 Comparison of Datasets

As we bridge between work on the original corpus and the student writing corpus, we must consider differences in properties. In addition to unconventional grammar and usage, many developing student essays lack clear cohesion or structure. These issues may make the modeling task more challenging than with the relatively clean RST-DT dataset. Common organizational issues in the corpus include (1) essays lacking transitional phrases (e.g., "However," or "In conclusion"), or transition words used inappropriately; (2) pronoun reference ambiguity; (3) paragraphs where the topic sentence is not clearly indicated, or where there are multiple main ideas (and sometimes contradictory ideas) in one paragraph; (4) sentences not presented in a logical progression. These areas of focus for developing writers are also highlighted in the literature (de Jong and Harper, 2005). Ambiguous and weakly structured essays may indicate an opportunity for automated feedback, but they also pose challenges for the parsing task.

The prevalence of the JOINT relation captures some of the difference between RST-DT and the Turnitin corpus. JOINT indicates a lack of rhetorical relations between nuclei. It indicates that there is no relation that could describe the connection between sentences (Jiang et al., 2019). In newspaper articles, this lack of connection is very rare. However, in student essays the lack of coherent rhetorical relations is common because of the wide range of experience among developing writers.

4.3 Designing Feedback from RST Relations

Three veteran secondary English teachers provided feedback and commentary on the structure and flow of 18 essays from the Turnitin dataset. Their comments reveal a handful of organizing principles and focal points for structure-driven feedback that provide guidance on how an RST style analysis could form the foundation for automated feedback.

In particular, almost all of the suggestions for improvement highlight a lack of connection or a break in flow between units of the essay. Some of these comments addressed breaks between consecutive sentences within a paragraph, for example "Strange jump in focus here... The rest of the intro does not lead to this statement naturally," and "Immediate departure from the initial question in sentence 1." Other comments, in contrast, deal specifically with the logical flow between whole paragraphs: "Transitions between paragraphs are relatively non-existent and make for pretty large jumps from one topic to another" and "To keep the organizational structure clear, this needs a more explicit connection to the introduction and thesis, including attention to the two distinct texts."

These comments, anchored to sentences or paragraphs in the student texts, roughly correspond to the locations of JOINT relations in the gold RST annotations. For example, Figure 2 is part of a gold RST annotation of student-generated essays. This essay has five paragraphs. The subtree (sentence 14-18) is a part of the third paragraph arguing that parents should guide children in evaluating "inappropriate" books, instead of pushing libraries to ban them. While sentence 18 is related to the overall argument in this paragraph, the connection between sentence 18 and other sentences is not clear. Potential automated feedback could be: "There may be ideas in this sentence that don't clearly relate to the paragraph's focus. Connect these ideas to the paragraph's main point by adding transition words, or consider whether this sentence should be revised or removed." This example shows that identifying the missing link (referring to the relation of JOINT) holds the promise of triggering meaningful revision actions. As our previous studies suggested that teachers viewed the structure of a developing essay as an archipelago of internally cohesive text islands[cite book chapter], we seek to validate RST's suitability to represent this segmentation. Using the locations of teacher comments as gold-truth segment boundaries using WindowDiff (Pevzner and Hearst, 2002) and Beeferman's P_k (Beeferman et al., 1999). Both WindowDiff and P_k range from 0 to 1 where a lower value indicates a lower probability that a given sentence is assigned to an incorrect segment, in practice a value of 0.2 to 0.4 is considered reasonable in state-of-the-art systems (Badjatiya et al., 2018). We observe a mean WindowDiff of 0.31 and P_k of 0.34 between these teacher-reviewed essays and the RST JOINT annotations. This suggests a plausible upper bound on an RST parser's ability to identify these critical boundaries.

5 Improving and Validating RST Parsing for Student Writing

In this section, we begin with and then improve on the best previously published approach in automating RST analysis for writing. Transition parsers are common among state-of-the-art models for discourse parsing with RST in the past several years. Their power lies in their ability to make strong local decisions about the next action the parser must take given an embedding that, because of recurrent neural models, has the capacity to contain features from the whole document. However, recurrent neural networks often do not in practice retain sufficient context for long range dependencies (Bahdanau et al., 2014; Khandelwal et al., 2018). We

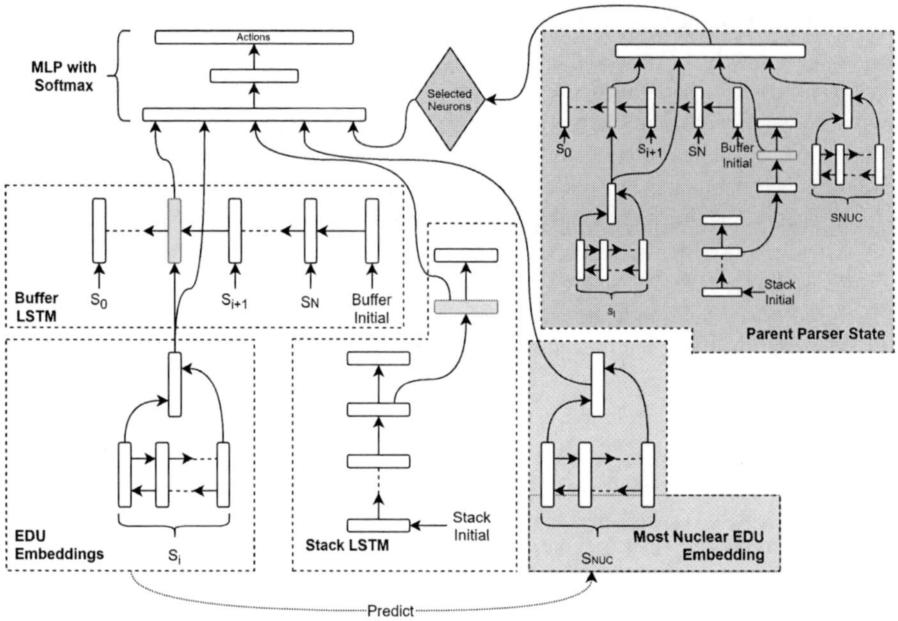

Figure 3: Diagram of neural transition parser model architecture for RST parsing augmented with our changes (shaded purple and green). The parent parser state (purple) has the same basic architecture as the rest of the diagram with the exception of having another parent parser state component. The dotted line from EDU Embedding to Most Nuclear EDU Embedding (green) indicates choice made by the model for which EDU to use.

address this by providing an additional embedding for the predicted most nuclear sentence of the document to provide a reference point for the parsing decisions. Furthermore, inspired by neural interpretation techniques, we further augment the model with a two stage parsing approach that allows the second stage of the model to learn from mistakes made by the first.

5.1 Neural Transition Parsing Model

The model presented in this work is based on a recurrent neural network based RST parser (Yu et al., 2018). For the benefit of the reader this subsection provides an overview of the base model, however, for a full mechanical description see their paper. Our augmentations of the model follow in the remaining subsections.

The model constructs a neural representation that is used to decide whether to make a SHIFT or REDUCE action analogous to those in a simple LR-parser (Knuth, 1965). Furthermore, the model maintains a neural analogue to a stack and buffer to track progress through the parse, which is illustrated in the unshaded regions of Figure 3.

EDU Embedding: Each sentence in the document is embedded using a BiLSTM over word embeddings for each word in the EDU. The final states of the forward and backward LSTMs are used as the EDU representation.

Dependency Parse Embedding: In addition to the embedding generated by the BiLSTM, an embedding of syntactic information was included (Braud et al., 2017; Mabona et al., 2019). The information was integrated via concatenating the produced arc embedding from the dependency parse obtained from a strong neural dependency parser (Dozat and Manning, 2017) with the output from the BiLSTM above.

Buffer: The buffer is an LSTM that inputs each EDU embedding from the end of the document to the beginning. Each state is stored in memory such that it can be accessed sequentially as items are removed from the buffer. Each state of the buffer is therefore an aggregate representation of all of the EDUs from the current EDU to the end of the document.

Stack: The stack is a Stack LSTM (Swayamdipta et al., 2016). The stack state is updated via the result of an MLP given the two stacks states popped off the stack during a REDUCE action procedure. If an item is popped off the stack, the stack state is updated to the output state of the LSTM of the previous cell.

Action and Relation Prediction: At each timestep the parser either predicts a SHIFT action or one of the many REDUCE actions. Each REDUCE action has an associated relation label and predicting the correct REDUCE action amounts to choosing the correct relation for the current subtree. The prediction is made by a multi-layer perceptron (MLP) that is provided a concatenation of the EDU embedding, the current neural state of the buffer, the current neural state of the stack, and additional neural representations that will be described in depth in the next sections. The input layer to the MLP will be referred to as the parser state at a given time. For each action, a deterministic procedure is executed in line with the transition parsing paradigm. In the case where there is only one possible action, the model is forced to use that action without choice.

5.2 Most Nuclear EDU Embedding

To provide the model a reference for making parsing decisions for a given document, we include in the parser state an EDU embedding of the predicted most nuclear EDU. Formally, we consider the most nuclear EDU the leaf node of the RST tree that is reached when, starting at the root node, one follows the direction of nuclearity at each branch. For multinuclear nodes, we arbitrarily take the left branch. In Figure 1, the most nuclear EDU would be "The coyote is building an elaborate trap."

The most nuclear EDU S_{NUC} is selected by the model by choosing the EDU with the maximum score computed by an MLP given the EDU embedding and choosing the highest scoring sentence. This can be formalized as:

$$S_{NUC} = \arg\max_{s \in S} W \cdot \mathbf{s}$$

Where S is a set of all of the sentence EDU computed by the neural transition parser.

The most nuclear EDU embedding is constructed via a BiLSTM in much the same manner as the EDU embeddings in the neural transition parser. This BiLSTM has its own set of learned parameters, though it uses shared word embeddings as those used for the EDU embeddings.

Because there is only one predicted most nuclear EDU for a document, the effective training samples for this embedding is equal to the number of documents in the training set rather than the number of EDUs. Because of this, it is necessary to restrict the size of the embedding to prevent overfitting. Furthermore, the error from the RST parsing task cannot backpropagate to W through the argmax so we include a separate error signal for predicting the correct most nuclear EDU. The most nuclear EDU of a document can be trivially obtained from the gold trees.

5.3 Parent Parser State

Recent work has shown there is evidence that neural models may be learning general heuristics and memorizing exceptions to those heuristics that increase performance on a given task (Fiacco et al., 2019a). Assuming this is the case, we attempt to exploit this behavior to offload some of the complexity of learning the RST discourse parsing task into multiple phases of training. A fully trained parent model, which includes all of the features in the previous sections, is executed concurrently to the child model and a subset of the parser state of the parent model is concatenated with the parser state of the child model.

The parser state for the parent model is updated along with the child model using the action chosen by the child model, though with its own stack and buffer representations. This ensures that even if the parent and child models diverge in their predicted actions, the parser states are consistent. Maintaining this consistency is important for the neural transition parser as the representation of the stack can contain a representation of a larger segment of the document than just a single EDU.

Neuron Selection via Pathways: For datasets with noisy data, we prune the parser state from the parent model to only use the dimensions of the state that correspond to the neurons that are part of the neural pathways that explain the most variance of the model. The intuition for this pruning is that the groups of neurons that explain the largest amount of variance in the model will regularize the model via eliminating overfitted parameters.

These neurons are obtained by extracting the parser state for each training instance and constructing an activation matrix with the dimensions of the parser state as columns and the training instances as rows. A PCA is performed over the matrix, and the subset of resulting factors that cumulatively explain more than a tunable threshold of the variance are chosen as the subset of pathways of interest. For each selected factor, the factor loadings of each neuron are computed and the N neurons with the highest loadings are added to the set of neurons to be transferred. The value of N can be tuned by optimizing performance on a validation set.

5.4 Training

There are three phases to the training of the model: parent model training, neuron selection, and child model training. The procedure for training the parent and child models are identical except for the usage of the parent neurons as features for the child model. The neuron selection phase is only applicable for the noisier Turnitin data and is described in the Parent Parser State section.

There are three objectives that are optimized using negative log likelihood loss during the model training. The first training objective (L_m) is predicting the most nuclear EDU at the document level. The second objective (L_n), at the action level, is to predict the nuclearity of each relation given the parser state. This objective affects how the model composes the embeddings when combining via a REDUCE action. The final training objective, (L_a), is to choose the correct action given the parser state. We do not fine tune the embedding from the dependency parser during training. The third phase of training follows the same procedure as the first phase with selected neurons from the parent parser state included. The final loss for a document is described as:

$$L = \alpha_m L_m + \alpha_n \sum_A L_n + \alpha_a \sum_A L_a$$

where A is the set of all actions required for the parse and each α is a scaling factor that can be tuned for each loss.

For noisy datasets, an additional step is required for the training procedure; the neurons that will be used by the child model must be selected. This is performed by computing the neural pathways of the parent model using the parser state via PCA. The pathways that explain the most variance are chosen and the heaviest loaded neurons on those pathways are selected. During training, no gradient is passed back to the parent model so the neuron selection process need not be continuous nor differentiable. Training the child model thereby uses the parser state of the parent model as though it were a fixed input.

6 Experiments

We provide three quantitative evaluations of our method: first, in order to compare our parser to previous RST parsers, we train and evaluate our parser on the English RST-DT corpus. Second, we provide an ablation study of the added components of our model along with the model we used as a base. The ablation study uses the same test set as the first experiment, so results are directly comparable. Lastly, we train another version of our model on the Turnitin dataset, which has a very different set of properties when compared to the RST-DT corpus. This last set of experiments is designed to test the ability of the model to handle unpolished, less structured text. The model is compared to the strongest baseline from the RST-DT corpus retrained on the Turnitin dataset.

6.1 Evaluation Metrics

The evaluations of this work follow the setup described by a recent metric enhancement for RST (Morey et al., 2017) and, for consistency, only compare to models that were included in that replication study or use the same evaluation method. The reason for this restriction is that it was found that RST Parseval, the previous standard evaluation metric, artificially raised scores and had been used inconsistently (Morey et al., 2017). Our models are therefore evaluated using micro-averaged F1 scores on labeled attachment decisions for the four standard metrics: span attachments (S), span attachments with nuclearity (N), span attachments with relations (R), and span attachments with both nuclearity and relation labels (F).

6.2 Implementation Details

The models were implemented using the DyNet neural network toolkit (Neubig et al., 2017). Training was performed on a NVIDIA GTX 1080. Early stopping was performed based on the F1 scores of the model without an oracle on the development set, with a patience of 3. The ADAM optimizer (Kingma and Ba, 2014) is used for training with a learning rate of 0.001. Dropout (Srivastava et al., 2014) is used for regularization and a dropout of 0.3 is applied to each hidden layer. All tunable α hyperparameters were left at 1.

For the RST parsing models, word embeddings for both the parent and child models were randomly initialized with 128 dimensional vectors. Each LSTM in the parent model had 256 dimensions while in the child model, each LSTM had 512 dimensions. For neuron selection, the 16 neurons with the highest factor loadings from the PCA were chosen for each pathway that explained more than

Model	F1 Scores *Span*	*Nuclearity*	*Relation*	*Full*
JI & EISENSTEIN (2014)(JI AND EISENSTEIN, 2014)*	64.1	54.2	**46.8**	**46.3**
FENG & HIRST (2014)(FENG AND HIRST, 2014A)*	68.6	55.9	45.8	44.6
LI ET AL. (2016) (LI ET AL., 2016)*	64.5	54.0	38.1	36.6
BRAUD ET AL. (2016) (BRAUD ET AL., 2016)*	59.5	47.2	34.7	34.3
BRAUD ET AL. (2017)(BRAUD ET AL., 2017)*	62.7	54.5	45.5	45.1
MABON ET AL. (2019) (MABONA ET AL., 2019)	67.1	57.4	45.5	45.0
ZHANG ET AL. (2020)(ZHANG ET AL., 2020)	67.2	55.5	45.3	44.3
OUR MODEL	**71.7**	**60.3**	44.5	44.3
-DEPENDENCY PARSE EMBEDDINGS	71.2	58.4	43.6	43.6
-PARENT PARSER STATE	70.2	57.2	43.0	42.9
-MOST NUCLEAR EDU EMBEDDINGS	68.4	57.2	42.7	42.4
TRANSITION PARSER ONLY	67.2	53.7	39.9	39.8

Table 1: RST-DT test set micro-averaged F1 scores for labeled attachment decisions for our model with varying components removed. Parsers from previous work are reported as they appear in their original publication, with the exception of those marked with an * where the reported results come from the replication study with the improved metric (Morey et al., 2017).

1% of the model variance. The number of dimensions for the PCA was tuned to explain 90% of the variance in neuron activations.

The dependency parser was pretrained on Universal Dependencies v1 (Nivre et al., 2016) derived from the Penn Treebank 3 (Marcus et al., 1999) using version 3.9.2 of the Stanford Universal Dependency Converter. Word embeddings and label MLP dimensions were set to 64 while the recurrent layers and the arc MLP layers were set to 128. Choice of optimizer, dropout, and early stopping criteria were the same for the dependency parser pretraining.

7 Evaluation

7.1 Parsing Results

Table 1 shows the performance across parsers on the labeled attachments metrics for the RST-DT test set. We include reported metrics for several models beyond the best baseline in order to provide a comprehensive view of recent work in the field, including other neural based models. The best version of our model gains a 4.5% increase in F1 score for the span metric (S) and a 7.9% increase in F1 score for combined span and nuclearity metric (N) in comparison with the Feng Hirst (Feng and Hirst, 2014a) model, the next best model for those metrics. The increase was gained with a competitive, albeit 2.8% lower span and relation metric (R).

Furthermore, we achieve these results with only the dependency parser as external data. Pretrained embeddings of any kind were not required for either the dependency parser nor the final RST parser and were found to not contribute empirically. Using pretrained GloVe embeddings (Pennington et al., 2014) do not significantly improve the performance over random initialization.

7.2 Ablation

We evaluated the model with key components removed to evaluate the effects of each of those components on the final performance of the model. The components ablated were the dependency parser embedding, the most nuclear EDU embedding, and the parent parser state. These results are presented in the lower section of Table 1.

From the results we see that the largest contributor to our model's performance was the inclusion of the most nuclear EDU co-task without which, the parser does not outperform the previous state-of-the-art on any metric. The parent model's parser state as a feature for action and relation prediction had the next largest effect with the span and nuclearity metric (N) falling to the same level as when the most nuclear EDU embedding was not used. Lastly, the syntactic information carried in the dependency parser embedding contributed the least, but still had a significant effect on all metrics.

We also present the performance of the base model, our implementation of the base neural transition parser (Yu et al., 2018) with the same settings

Model	F1 Scores Span	Nuclearity	Relation	Full
RST-DT				
JI & EISENSTEIN (2014)(JI AND EISENSTEIN, 2014)*	64.1	54.2	**46.8**	**46.3**
OUR MODEL	**71.7**	**60.3**	44.5	44.3
OUR MODEL (W/ NEURON SELECTION)	70.6	59.7	44.4	44.3
Turnitin Corpus				
JI & EISENSTEIN (2014)(JI AND EISENSTEIN, 2014)*	**56.1**	**33.4**	1.2	1.1
OUR MODEL	44.1	22.9	14.0	12.4
OUR MODEL (W/ NEURON SELECTION)	47.6	28.4	**18.0**	**17.0**

Table 2: Test set micro-averaged F1 scores for labeled attachment decisions for our model on the RST-DT corpus and the Turnitin dataset. The models were evaluated on each dataset both with and without pruning the parent parser state (W/ NEURON SELECTION).

as each of the other models from the ablation study. While it has competitive performance to prior work on the span only metric (S), all of the metrics are considerably lower than the final model. All ablation conditions were significantly different from the final model with $p < 0.05$.

7.3 Model Robustness with Neuron Selection

As our goal is to facilitate automatic essay feedback with RST, we evaluated our model, as well as the best performing model for predicting Relations, on the Turnitin dataset to test the ability of each model to handle the less consistently structured student writing data. Table 2 shows a comparison of the model performance on both the RST-DT corpus and the Turnitin dataset. For each dataset, we include versions of our model that use neuron selection as described in the Parent Parser State section and without. Each model was trained on the RST-DT dataset and fine-tuned on the Turnitin Corpus. All models saw significant degradation of performance on the student writing data as compared to the Wall Street Journal articles. Our model variations both has significantly ($p < 0.001$) less loss of performance for Relation prediction compared to the previous best performing model. Our model that used the neuron selection significantly ($p < 0.001$) increased performance on the Turnitin dataset compared to the model without.

Qualitatively, the JOINT relation was the most problematic for each parser as it was being considerably over-generated despite being only the 5th most common relation type. For variably structured writing such as student essays, understanding these conditions would likely go the furthest for improving RST parsing performance.

8 Conclusion

We presented two principal augmentations to neural transition parsers for RST that resulted in a 7.9% increase in span prediction and a 4.5% increase in nuclearity prediction. These improvements were made while remaining competitive on relation prediction, though no improvement was observed for that metric. Furthermore, we evaluated our model on an alternate, noisier dataset. We found that on this dataset our model had more accurate relation predictions than past approaches from the inclusion of a neuron selection step between the training of parent and child models in a boosting-like neural ensemble enhancement.

For future work, we want to empirically verify that the prediction of structural breaks (JOINT relations) in student writing align with teacher-identified organization feedback. This can enable automated essay feedback on the absence of structure, providing support where it's needed most. Furthermore, conveying the necessary information contained within RST trees to students and teachers provides an additional rich area of inquiry. It is worthwhile to further explore how prospective users respond to the technological instruction support to facilitate students' ability to locate places for revision and teachers' ability to integrate the automated feedback into their instruction.

Acknowledgements

This work was supported in part by NSF grant DRL 1949110 and funding from the Schmidt foundation.

References

Laura Aull. 2015. Connecting writing and language in assessment: Examining style, tone, and argument in the us common core standards and in exemplary student writing. *Assessing writing*, 24:59–73.

Pinkesh Badjatiya, Litton J Kurisinkel, Manish Gupta, and Vasudeva Varma. 2018. Attention-based neural text segmentation. In *European Conference on Information Retrieval*, pages 180–193. Springer.

Dzmitry Bahdanau, Kyunghyun Cho, and Yoshua Bengio. 2014. Neural machine translation by jointly learning to align and translate. *arXiv preprint arXiv:1409.0473*.

Doug Beeferman, Adam Berger, and John Lafferty. 1999. Statistical models for text segmentation. *Machine learning*, 34(1):177–210.

Joachim Bingel and Anders Søgaard. 2017. Identifying beneficial task relations for multi-task learning in deep neural networks. In *Proceedings of the 15th Conference of the European Chapter of the Association for Computational Linguistics: Volume 2, Short Papers*, pages 164–169.

Chloé Braud, Ophélie Lacroix, and Anders Søgaard. 2017. Cross-lingual and cross-domain discourse segmentation of entire documents. In *Proceedings of the 55th Annual Meeting of the Association for Computational Linguistics (Volume 2: Short Papers)*, pages 237–243, Vancouver, Canada. Association for Computational Linguistics.

Chloé Braud, Barbara Plank, and Anders Søgaard. 2016. Multi-view and multi-task training of rst discourse parsers. In *Proceedings of COLING 2016, the 26th International Conference on Computational Linguistics: Technical Papers*, pages 1903–1913.

Jill Burstein, Daniel Marcu, Slava Andreyev, and Martin Chodorow. 2001. Towards automatic classification of discourse elements in essays. In *Proceedings of the 39th annual meeting of the Association for Computational Linguistics*, pages 98–105.

Jill Burstein, Daniel Marcu, and Kevin Knight. 2003. Finding the write stuff: Automatic identification of discourse structure in student essays. *IEEE Intelligent Systems*, 18(1):32–39.

Lynn Carlson, Daniel Marcu, and Mary Ellen Okurowski. 2003. Building a discourse-tagged corpus in the framework of rhetorical structure theory. In *Current and new directions in discourse and dialogue*, pages 85–112. Springer.

Elena Cotos. 2011. Potential of automated writing evaluation feedback. *Calico Journal*, 28(2):420–459.

Ester J de Jong and Candace A Harper. 2005. Preparing mainstream teachers for english-language learners: Is being a good teacher good enough? *Teacher Education Quarterly*, 32(2):101–124.

Jamie DeCoster. 1998. Overview of factor analysis.

Timothy Dozat and Christopher D. Manning. 2017. Deep biaffine attention for neural dependency parsing. In *ICLR 2017*.

Vanessa Wei Feng and Graeme Hirst. 2014a. A linear-time bottom-up discourse parser with constraints and post-editing. In *Proceedings of the 52nd Annual Meeting of the Association for Computational Linguistics (Volume 1: Long Papers)*, pages 511–521, Baltimore, Maryland. Association for Computational Linguistics.

Vanessa Wei Feng and Graeme Hirst. 2014b. Patterns of local discourse coherence as a feature for authorship attribution. *Literary and Linguistic Computing*, 29(2):191–198.

James Fiacco, Samridhi Choudhary, and Carolyn Rose. 2019a. Deep neural model inspection and comparison via functional neuron pathways. In *Proceedings of the 57th Annual Meeting of the Association for Computational Linguistics*, pages 5754–5764.

James Fiacco, Elena Cotos, and Carolyn Rose. 2019b. Towards enabling feedback on rhetorical structure with neural sequence models. In *Proceedings of the 9th International Conference on Learning Analytics & Knowledge*, pages 310–319.

Harold Hotelling. 1933. Analysis of a complex of statistical variables into principal components. *Journal of educational psychology*, 24(6):417.

Yangfeng Ji and Jacob Eisenstein. 2014. Representation learning for text-level discourse parsing. In *Proceedings of the 52nd Annual Meeting of the Association for Computational Linguistics (Volume 1: Long Papers)*, pages 13–24, Baltimore, Maryland. Association for Computational Linguistics.

Shiyan Jiang, Kexin Yang, Chandrakumari Suvarna, Pooja Casula, Mingtong Zhang, and Carolyn Rose. 2019. Applying rhetorical structure theory to student essays for providing automated writing feedback. In *Proceedings of the Workshop on Discourse Relation Parsing and Treebanking 2019*, pages 163–168.

Urvashi Khandelwal, He He, Peng Qi, and Dan Jurafsky. 2018. Sharp nearby, fuzzy far away: How neural language models use context. In *Proceedings of the 56th Annual Meeting of the Association for Computational Linguistics (Volume 1: Long Papers)*, pages 284–294.

Diederik P Kingma and Jimmy Ba. 2014. Adam: A method for stochastic optimization. *arXiv preprint arXiv:1412.6980*.

Donald E Knuth. 1965. On the translation of languages from left to right. *Information and control*, 8(6):607–639.

Huong LeThanh, Geetha Abeysinghe, and Christian Huyck. 2004. Generating discourse structures for written texts. In *Proceedings of the 20th international conference on Computational Linguistics*, page 329. Association for Computational Linguistics.

Jiwei Li, Rumeng Li, and Eduard Hovy. 2014. Recursive deep models for discourse parsing. In *Proceedings of the 2014 Conference on Empirical Methods in Natural Language Processing (EMNLP)*, pages 2061–2069.

Qi Li, Tianshi Li, and Baobao Chang. 2016. Discourse parsing with attention-based hierarchical neural networks. In *Proceedings of the 2016 Conference on Empirical Methods in Natural Language Processing*, pages 362–371.

Minh-Thang Luong, Michael C Frank, and Mark Johnson. 2013. Parsing entire discourses as very long strings: Capturing topic continuity in grounded language learning. *Transactions of the Association for Computational Linguistics*, 1:315–326.

Amandla Mabona, Laura Rimell, Stephen Clark, and Andreas Vlachos. 2019. Neural generative rhetorical structure parsing. In *Proceedings of the 2019 Conference on Empirical Methods in Natural Language Processing and the 9th International Joint Conference on Natural Language Processing (EMNLP-IJCNLP)*, pages 2284–2295.

William C Mann and Sandra A Thompson. 1988. Rhetorical structure theory: Toward a functional theory of text organization. *Text-interdisciplinary Journal for the Study of Discourse*, 8(3):243–281.

Daniel Marcu. 2000. The rhetorical parsing of unrestricted texts: A surface-based approach. *Computational linguistics*, 26(3):395–448.

Mitchell P Marcus, Beatrice Santorini, Mary Ann Marcinkiewicz, and Ann Taylor. 1999. Penn treebank-3. *Linguistic Data Consortium, LDC99T42, University of Pennsylvania.*

Danielle S McNamara, Max M Louwerse, Philip M McCarthy, and Arthur C Graesser. 2010. Coh-metrix: Capturing linguistic features of cohesion. *Discourse Processes*, 47(4):292–330.

Mathieu Morey, Philippe Muller, and Nicholas Asher. 2017. How much progress have we made on RST discourse parsing? a replication study of recent results on the RST-DT. In *Proceedings of the 2017 Conference on Empirical Methods in Natural Language Processing*, pages 1319–1324, Copenhagen, Denmark. Association for Computational Linguistics.

Mathieu Morey, Philippe Muller, and Nicholas Asher. 2018. A dependency perspective on RST discourse parsing and evaluation. *Computational Linguistics*, 44(2):197–235.

Graham Neubig, Chris Dyer, Yoav Goldberg, Austin Matthews, Waleed Ammar, Antonios Anastasopoulos, Miguel Ballesteros, David Chiang, Daniel Clothiaux, Trevor Cohn, et al. 2017. Dynet: The dynamic neural network toolkit. *arXiv preprint arXiv:1701.03980.*

Joakim Nivre, Marie-Catherine De Marneffe, Filip Ginter, Yoav Goldberg, Jan Hajic, Christopher D Manning, Ryan McDonald, Slav Petrov, Sampo Pyysalo, Natalia Silveira, et al. 2016. Universal dependencies v1: A multilingual treebank collection. In *Proceedings of the Tenth International Conference on Language Resources and Evaluation (LREC'16)*, pages 1659–1666.

Corey Palermo and Joshua Wilson. 2020. Implementing automated writing evaluation in different instructional contexts: A mixed-methods study. *Journal of Writing Research*, 12(1).

Martha Palmer, Daniel Gildea, and Nianwen Xue. 2010. Semantic role labeling. *Synthesis Lectures on Human Language Technologies*, 3(1):1–103.

Hao Peng, Sam Thomson, and Noah A Smith. 2017. Deep multitask learning for semantic dependency parsing. In *Proceedings of the 55th Annual Meeting of the Association for Computational Linguistics (Volume 1: Long Papers)*, pages 2037–2048.

Jeffrey Pennington, Richard Socher, and Christopher D Manning. 2014. Glove: Global vectors for word representation. In *Proceedings of the 2014 conference on empirical methods in natural language processing (EMNLP)*, pages 1532–1543.

Lev Pevzner and Marti A Hearst. 2002. A critique and improvement of an evaluation metric for text segmentation. *Computational Linguistics*, 28(1):19–36.

Rod D Roscoe and Danielle S McNamara. 2013. Writing pal: Feasibility of an intelligent writing strategy tutor in the high school classroom. *Journal of Educational Psychology*, 105(4):1010.

Radu Soricut and Daniel Marcu. 2003. Sentence level discourse parsing using syntactic and lexical information. In *Proceedings of the 2003 Conference of the North American Chapter of the Association for Computational Linguistics on Human Language Technology-Volume 1*, pages 149–156. Association for Computational Linguistics.

Nitish Srivastava, Geoffrey Hinton, Alex Krizhevsky, Ilya Sutskever, and Ruslan Salakhutdinov. 2014. Dropout: a simple way to prevent neural networks from overfitting. *The journal of machine learning research*, 15(1):1929–1958.

Swabha Swayamdipta, Miguel Ballesteros, Chris Dyer, and Noah A Smith. 2016. Greedy, joint syntactic-semantic parsing with stack lstms. *arXiv preprint arXiv:1606.08954*.

Sheila W. Valencia and Karen K. Wixson. 2001. Commentary: Inside english/language arts standards: What's in a grade? *Reading Research Quarterly*, 36(2):202–217.

Patti West-Smith, Stephanie Butler, and Elijah Mayfield. 2018. Trustworthy automated essay scoring without explicit construct validity. In *AAAI Spring Symposia*.

Nan Yu, Meishan Zhang, and Guohong Fu. 2018. Transition-based neural rst parsing with implicit syntax features. In *Proceedings of the 27th International Conference on Computational Linguistics*, pages 559–570.

Longyin Zhang, Yuqing Xing, Fang Kong, Peifeng Li, and Guodong Zhou. 2020. A top-down neural architecture towards text-level parsing of discourse rhetorical structure. *arXiv preprint arXiv:2005.02680*.

Educational Multi-Question Generation for Reading Comprehension

Manav Rathod[1], Tony Tu[2], and Katherine Stasaski[1]
[1]UC Berkeley
[2]Georgia Institute of Technology
[1]{manav.rathod, katie_stasaski}@berkeley.edu
[2]ttu32@gatech.edu

Abstract

Automated question generation has made great advances with the help of large NLP generation models. However, typically only one question is generated for each intended answer. We propose a new task, Multi-Question Generation, aimed at generating multiple semantically similar but lexically diverse questions assessing the same concept. We develop an evaluation framework based on desirable qualities of the resulting questions. Results comparing multiple question generation approaches in the two-question generation condition show a trade-off between question answerability and lexical diversity between the two questions. We also report preliminary results from sampling multiple questions from our model, to explore generating more than two questions. Our task can be used to further explore the educational impact of showing multiple distinct question wordings to students.

1 Introduction

Automatic question generation (QG) is a well-established task in natural language processing. Large generation models have had success producing answer-informed factual comprehension questions, where the intended answer is a span located in a passage (Qi et al., 2020; Wang et al., 2018; Rajpurkar et al., 2016).

Automatically generating factual questions from a passage can benefit students in a reading comprehension environment (Kurdi et al., 2020). However, the majority of question generation work has focused on generating a single question with an intended answer. In a student practice environment, however, it is valuable to have multiple wordings for the same question. This allows students to practice a concept multiple times without encountering identical language. This additionally allows a wording of the question to be held out for assessment.

We propose a new question generation task, *multi-question generation*, which takes as input an intended answer and produces both (1) an initial question and (2) n reworded questions which maintain the semantic meaning of the original question while varying language used. Although multiple questions can be generated about different concepts pertaining to an intended answer, we specifically aim to generate questions which assess knowledge of the same concept, varying only the language used in the question.

Another issue with current generation systems is the large overlap in words between the reading passage and generated question. Table 1 shows an example of an undesired output from a current question generation system. Note the large overlap between the generated question and input passage, allowing students to scan for the answer in the paragraph. For our task, we additionally specify that the text of resulting questions should differ from the content passage.

We propose automatic metrics grounded in desirable properties of the generated set of questions. Because we intend the questions to have the same intended answer, we measure both (1) whether a *question answering* (QA) model is able to produce the correct answer for each question (Yuan et al., 2017) and (2) the semantic similarity between the generated questions, measured using SBERT (Reimers and Gurevych, 2019). Also, because we intend for the questions to have distinct wordings, we propose using a known n-gram overlap metric, Paraphrase In N-Gram Changes (PINC), between pairs of questions (Chen and Dolan, 2011). Finally, because each generated question is tied to a passage, we propose using PINC to compare overlap between each question and the input passage.

We report results using a variety of question generation conditions, including a paraphrase model, a QG model fine-tuned to generate two questions, and the use of decoding constraints to improve question wording diversity. Our publicly-released code and generated questions can be used to ex-

Proceedings of the 17th Workshop on Innovative Use of NLP for Building Educational Applications (BEA 2022), pages 216 - 223

Original Passage	The Sarah Jane Adventures, starring Elisabeth Sladen **who reprised her role as investigative journalist Sarah Jane Smith**, was developed by CBBC; a special aired on New Year's Day 2007 and a full series began on 24 September 2007. A second series followed in 2008, notable for (as noted above) featuring the return of Brigadier Lethbridge-Stewart. A third in 2009 featured a crossover appearance from the main show by David Tennant as the Tenth Doctor. In 2010, a further such appearance featured Matt Smith as the Eleventh Doctor alongside former companion actress Katy Manning reprising her role as Jo Grant. A final, three-story fifth series was transmitted in autumn 2011 uncompleted due to the death of Elisabeth Sladen in early 2011.
Answer	Elisabeth Sladen
Question	**who reprised her role as investigative journalist sarah jane smith**?

Table 1: Example passage taken from SQuAD dataset with corresponding question generated from ProphetNet (Qi et al., 2020). Bolded text shows overlap between the input passage and generated question, which is not desired.

plore the impact of integrating these questions into educational applications[1].

2 Related Work

2.1 Question Generation

Many question generation models are fine-tuned from large language models, achieving considerable success in producing factual reading comprehension questions (Grover et al., 2021; Chan and Fan, 2019; Sultan et al., 2020). Other work aims to generate questions given passages from educational textbooks (Wang et al., 2018; Stasaski et al., 2021). However, these QG models are trained to only produce a single question from a context paragraph and intended answer.

2.2 Educational Question Application

Anderson and Biddle (1975) find that asking factual questions during reading can aid in the ability to recall a story. Furthermore, providing students with multiple phrasings of the same question has the potential to ensure students have fully mastered a concept (Kurdi et al., 2020). Rephrasing a question when students answer incorrectly has been included in best practices for educational question asking (Tofade et al., 2013) as well as a component of Elaborative Feedback (Murphy, 2007). Additionally, past educational research has also found that providing a human-written paraphrased wording of the same question has been shown to improve reading comprehension of students who are less skilled compared to a baseline with only one question wording (Cerdán et al., 2019).

Following this past educational work, we propose leveraging neural systems to generate multiple diverse question wordings. Our new task allows future work to study this at scale.

3 Multi-Question Generation

Given the potential educational benefits that come from answering questions with different wordings, we propose *Multi-Question Generation*, with the goal of producing multiple semantically similar, lexically diverse questions with the same intended answer. An intended answer and a passage are the input to the task while the multiple diversely-worded questions are the output. Although an intended answer can have multiple concepts with which questions can be generated from, these multiple questions should assess the same concept. An example of this can be seen in Table 2.

3.1 Evaluation

We propose an evaluation framework to assess the quality of the generated questions. Because we do not have a gold human-collected dataset of rephrased questions, we propose heuristic evaluation metrics. We evaluate the generated questions using a combination of PINC, a QA model, and SBERT cosine similarity.

Because the set of questions should have limited lexical overlap, we use PINC to measure the n-gram overlap among pairs of questions (Chen and Dolan, 2011). Specifically, for two generated questions q_1 and q_2, the PINC score is calculated

[1]Code is available at `https://github.com/kstats/MultiQuestionGeneration`.

Original Passage	Victoria (abbreviated as Vic) is a state in the south-east of Australia. Victoria is Australia's most densely populated state and its second-most populous state overall. Most of its population is concentrated in the area surrounding Port Phillip Bay, which includes the metropolitan area of its capital and largest city, Melbourne, which is Australia's second-largest city. Geographically the smallest state on the Australian mainland, Victoria is bordered by Bass Strait and Tasmania to the south,[note 1] New South Wales to the north, the Tasman Sea to the east, and South Australia to the west.
Answer	second-largest
Question 1	where does melbourne rank in terms of the size of cities in australia?
Question 2	what is melbourne's population status?

Table 2: Selected *Two-Question Generation* output from the 2QG No Question Trigram model, presented in Section 4.

as:

$$PINC(q_1, q_2) = \frac{1}{N}\sum_{n=1}^{N} 1 - \frac{|\text{n-gram}_{q_1} \cap \text{n-gram}_{q_2}|}{|\text{n-gram}_{q_2}|}$$

where N is the maximum n-gram considered and n-gram_{q_1} and n-gram_{q_2} are the list of n-grams in the first and second questions, respectively.

However, since this metric is not symmetric and there is no reason to treat one question as the standard over another, we compute the score in both directions and average:

$$PINC_{sym}(q_1, q_2) = \frac{PINC(q_1, q_2) + PINC(q_2, q_1)}{2}$$

We use $PINC_{sym}$ to calculate distinction among the set of generated questions Q for a given example as: $\forall_{q_i,q_j \in Q\,:\,i \neq j} PINC_{sym}(q_i, q_j)$.

We additionally propose using PINC to calculate the distance from each question to the context paragraph C: $\forall_{q_i \in Q} PINC(C, q_i)$. Note that here we use the asymmetric PINC since we want to explicitly reward the question for introducing new n-grams not found in the context paragraph.

We calculate PINC up to trigrams, manually confirming this to balance allowing important phrases to be restated when appropriate without allowing for long copied phrases.

Next, we draw from past work which has used Question Answering models to evaluate the accuracy of Question Generation systems (Yuan et al., 2017). Following this, we use the performance of a Question Answering model[2] to ensure the generated questions are answerable. For measuring QA accuracy, we use a macro-averaged F1, treating the predicted answer and ground truth as bags of tokens, as done in the original SQuAD paper (Rajpurkar et al., 2016).

Lastly, we aim to measure the semantic similarity between generated questions to ensure that the questions assess the same content. To do this, we use a pre-trained SBERT model[3] (Reimers and Gurevych, 2019) to encode each question into an embedding and take the cosine similarity between each pair of embeddings.

4 Experimental Conditions

We begin with the task of generating two questions (results of generating more than two questions can be seen in Section 6). To approach this task, we leverage a high-quality neural question generation model, ProphetNet (Qi et al., 2020). In order to generate multiple questions, we explore (1) transforming ProphetNet's single question output into a paraphrased second question, (2) fine-tuning ProphetNet to output two questions sequentially, and (3) sampling multiple times from ProphetNet.

All models use beam search with a beam size of 10 unless otherwise stated. For sampled results, we use nucleus sampling (Holtzman et al., 2020) with $p = 0.95$. All results are reported on the SQuAD 1.1 development set (Rajpurkar et al., 2016).

[2]`https://huggingface.co/bert-large-uncased-whole-word-masking-finetuned-squad`

[3]`https://huggingface.co/sentence-transformers/all-mpnet-base-v2`

4.1 Question Paraphrasing

For our first approach (1QG+Para), we use the ProphetNet model to generate a single question given the context and answer. We then pass this generated question into a paraphrasing model. Ideally, paraphrasing the original input will preserve the meaning of the question while modifying the lexical content. We use a T5-based model (Raffel et al., 2020) that is trained on the Quora Question (Chen et al., 2018) pairs dataset[4].

4.2 Two-Question Generation

The previous approach (1QG+Para) is not ideal because the paraphrase model does not have access to the context or intended answer. Thus, we finetune ProphetNet to output two question for any given context and answer (2QG). We finetune ProphetNet on a dataset of paraphrased questions created from 1QG+Para's paraphrase model. We augment each training example in the SQuAD training dataset with an additional paraphrase and then finetune ProphetNet to predict a sequence of two questions separated by a separator token, "[X_SEP]."

We fine-tuned ProphetNet for 10 epochs using a learning rate of 1e-5 using the Adam Optimizer (Kingma and Ba, 2015) on the entire SQuAD training set. We initialized the model using the weights from Transformers (Wolf et al., 2020) [5]. We trained on an NVIDIA Titan RTX for 2 days.

4.2.1 Constrained Generation

While 2QG is able to output two well-formed questions, its ability to vary lexical diversity may be limited by the training data. To further encourage the model to output different questions, we add constraints to the 2QG model's generation process to force this property. We explore two constraints: 1) requiring the generated questions to not repeat any trigrams across both questions (2QG No Question Trigram) and 2) requiring the generated questions to not repeat any trigrams from the input passage (2QG No Context Trigram). We also explore a version of ProphetNet which has both of these constraints (2QG No Question-Context Trigram).

4.3 Sampling

Finally, we explore potential questions which can be uncovered by sampling from the QG model's learned distribution. For the 1QG case, we sample from ProphetNet twice to generate the two questions (1QG 2-Sample). For the 2QG model (2QG Sample), we sample once as the model output already contains two well-formed questions. In Section 6, we explore sampling from the 2QG model more than once.

[4]https://huggingface.co/ramsrigouthamg/t5_paraphraser

[5]https://huggingface.co/docs/transformers/model_doc/prophetnet

5 Two-Question Generation Results

Two-Question Generation Results can be found in Table 3. Appendix A contains randomly-sampled model output for one of the best-performing models, 2QG No Question Trigram.

We observe that restricting the repetition of trigrams in the question generation increases the PINC score, which is expected as generating repeating trigrams is constrained. However, this comes at the cost of having a lower QA score.

We also note higher QA scores for the first question compared to the second, meaning answerability might be less important when rephrasing the initial question. The drop in performance from QA1 to QA2 for 1QG+Para is anticipated as the paraphrase model does not have access to the answer or context passage. However, surprisingly, we observe similar performance drops with 2QG models (in particular 2QG No Question Trigram). The gap in quality is increased when the PINC score between the questions is higher, indicating a tradeoff between PINC score and QA score. We also observe that restricting the trigrams from the *context paragraph* (2QG No Context Trigram) increases the PINC score with respect to the context paragraph as expected, but does so at a smaller cost to the QA score.

Lastly, we note an inverse relationship between inter-question PINC score and SBERT similarity. This indicates that diversifying lexical content of questions may come at the cost of maintaining semantic similarity between the two questions.

6 Toward Multi-Question Generation

We next explore bridging the gap from Two-Question Generation to Multi-Question Generation. While the 2QG model was fine-tuned to produce two questions sequentially, we explore the extent to which sampling from this model can produce sets of more questions. We take the 2QG model and sample from it multiple times using nucleus sampling (p=0.95). We consider sets of 2, 4, 6, and 8 questions.

Model	Q1-Q2	C-Q1	C-Q2	QA1	QA2	SBERT
1QG 2-Sample	0.32	0.49	0.50	**0.83**	**0.82**	0.91
1QG+Para	0.33	0.49	0.58	**0.83**	0.63	**0.98**
2QG	0.11	0.57	0.59	0.82	0.80	**0.98**
2QG Sample	0.12	0.58	0.60	**0.83**	0.80	**0.98**
2QG No Context Trigram	0.12	**0.75**	0.75	0.79	0.77	**0.98**
2QG No Question Trigram	**0.77**	0.58	0.76	**0.83**	0.63	0.83
2QG No Question-Context Trigram	**0.77**	**0.75**	**0.80**	0.79	0.62	0.85

Table 3: Two-Question Generation results. Models explored are discussed in Section 4. The first three columns report the PINC score between the first question (Q1), the second question (Q2), and the context (C). The next two columns report the QA model's F1 score for the first (QA1) and second (QA2) generated question. The last column reports the SBERT cosine similarity between the generated questions. Higher values are better for all metrics.

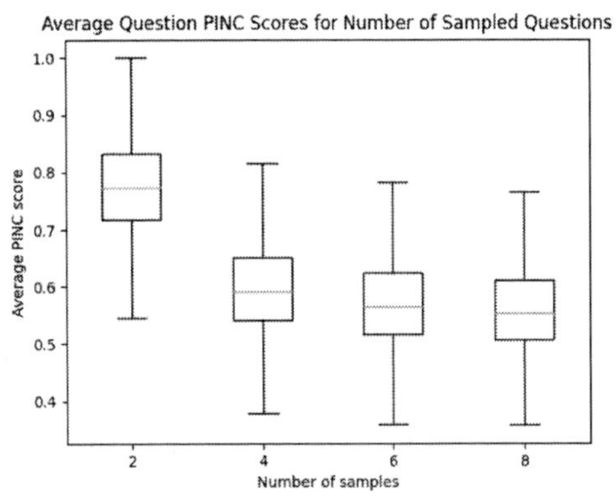

Figure 1: Average PINC between-question scores for increasing number of question samples.

We examine the average between-question PINC scores for the generated question sets, to explore whether sampling can uncover unique question wordings. Results can be seen in Figure 1. We find a sharp decline in PINC score for more than two questions. Future work should explore other ways of generating more than two questions.

7 Future Work and Conclusion

Although automated evaluation metrics can measure the desirable properties of our Two-Question Generation model outputs at scale, they are also limited. Future work could include human evaluation metrics to measure the semantic quality and lexical diversity more robustly.

Future work should also explore using desirable question metrics in a reinforcement learning objective to produce higher quality questions, similar to previous work in abstractive summarization (Laban et al., 2020) and text simplification (Laban et al., 2021).

Additionally, more advanced paraphrase systems, such as the syntax-aware system proposed in Kumar et al. (2020), could be leveraged for our task. This work can explore which syntactic exemplars can be leveraged to generate questions with varying syntactic structure.

Additionally, future work should also include teacher evaluation to collect education-specific feedback on sets of questions and our desirable question properties. This work can help better define what constitutes a good question and potentially uncover different automated metrics.

Future work can leverage our task to evaluate the educational impact of multiple diverse question wordings. Multi-Question Generation can be integrated into a reading comprehension environment to test student reactions to a reworded question. Generating multiple question wordings can fully test the students' reading comprehension and ability to apply information in new situations. Our publicly-released pipeline has the potential to generate multiple wordings of the same questions to enrich educational resources at scale.

Acknowledgements

This work was supported by an AWS Machine Learning Research Award and an NVIDIA Corporation GPU grant. We thank the three anonymous reviewers as well as Marti Hearst, Emily Xiao, Philippe Laban, and the Hearst Lab research group for their useful comments.

References

Richard Anderson and Barry Biddle. 1975. On asking people questions about what they are reading. *Psychology of Learning and Motivation*, 9.

R. Cerdán, A. Pérez, E. Vidal-Abarca, and J. F. Rouet. 2019. To answer questions from text, one has to understand what the question is asking: differential effects of question aids as a function of comprehension skill. *Reading and Writing*, 32(8):2111–2124.

Ying-Hong Chan and Yao-Chung Fan. 2019. A recurrent BERT-based model for question generation. In *Proceedings of the 2nd Workshop on Machine Reading for Question Answering*, pages 154–162, Hong Kong, China. Association for Computational Linguistics.

David Chen and William Dolan. 2011. Collecting highly parallel data for paraphrase evaluation. In *Proceedings of the 49th Annual Meeting of the Association for Computational Linguistics: Human Language Technologies*, pages 190–200, Portland, Oregon, USA. Association for Computational Linguistics.

Zihan Chen, Hongbo Zhang, Xiaoji Zhang, and Leqi Zhao. 2018. Quora question pairs. *URL https://www. kaggle. com/c/quora-question-pairs.*

Khushnuma Grover, Katinder Kaur, Kartikey Tiwari, Rupali, and Parteek Kumar. 2021. Deep learning based question generation using t5 transformer. In *Advanced Computing*, pages 243–255, Singapore. Springer Singapore.

Ari Holtzman, Jan Buys, Li Du, Maxwell Forbes, and Yejin Choi. 2020. The curious case of neural text degeneration. In *8th International Conference on Learning Representations, ICLR 2020, Addis Ababa, Ethiopia, April 26-30, 2020*. OpenReview.net.

Diederik P. Kingma and Jimmy Ba. 2015. Adam: A method for stochastic optimization. In *3rd International Conference on Learning Representations, ICLR 2015, San Diego, CA, USA, May 7-9, 2015, Conference Track Proceedings*.

Ashutosh Kumar, Kabir Ahuja, Raghuram Vadapalli, and Partha Talukdar. 2020. Syntax-guided controlled generation of paraphrases. *Transactions of the Association for Computational Linguistics*, 8:329–345.

Ghader Kurdi, Jared Leo, Bijan Parsia, Uli Sattler, and Salam Al-Emari. 2020. A systematic review of automatic question generation for educational purposes. *International Journal of Artificial Intelligence in Education*, 30(1):121–204.

Philippe Laban, Andrew Hsi, John Canny, and Marti A. Hearst. 2020. The summary loop: Learning to write abstractive summaries without examples. In *Proceedings of the 58th Annual Meeting of the Association for Computational Linguistics*, pages 5135–5150, Online. Association for Computational Linguistics.

Philippe Laban, Tobias Schnabel, Paul Bennett, and Marti A. Hearst. 2021. Keep it simple: Unsupervised simplification of multi-paragraph text. In *Proceedings of the 59th Annual Meeting of the Association for Computational Linguistics and the 11th International Joint Conference on Natural Language Processing (Volume 1: Long Papers)*, pages 6365–6378, Online. Association for Computational Linguistics.

Philip Murphy. 2007. Reading comprehension exercises online: The effects of feedback, proficiency and interaction. *Language Learning & Technology*, 11(3):107–129.

Weizhen Qi, Yu Yan, Yeyun Gong, Dayiheng Liu, Nan Duan, Jiusheng Chen, Ruofei Zhang, and Ming Zhou. 2020. ProphetNet: Predicting future n-gram for sequence-to-SequencePre-training. In *Findings of the Association for Computational Linguistics: EMNLP 2020*, pages 2401–2410, Online. Association for Computational Linguistics.

Colin Raffel, Noam Shazeer, Adam Roberts, Katherine Lee, Sharan Narang, Michael Matena, Yanqi Zhou, Wei Li, and Peter J. Liu. 2020. Exploring the limits of transfer learning with a unified text-to-text transformer. *Journal of Machine Learning Research*, 21(140):1–67.

Pranav Rajpurkar, Jian Zhang, Konstantin Lopyrev, and Percy Liang. 2016. SQuAD: 100,000+ questions for machine comprehension of text. In *Proceedings of the 2016 Conference on Empirical Methods in Natural Language Processing*, pages 2383–2392, Austin, Texas. Association for Computational Linguistics.

Nils Reimers and Iryna Gurevych. 2019. Sentence-BERT: Sentence embeddings using Siamese BERT-networks. In *Proceedings of the 2019 Conference on Empirical Methods in Natural Language Processing and the 9th International Joint Conference on Natural Language Processing (EMNLP-IJCNLP)*, pages 3982–3992, Hong Kong, China. Association for Computational Linguistics.

Katherine Stasaski, Manav Rathod, Tony Tu, Yunfang Xiao, and Marti A. Hearst. 2021. Automatically generating cause-and-effect questions from passages. In *Proceedings of the 16th Workshop on Innovative Use of NLP for Building Educational Applications*, pages 158–170, Online. Association for Computational Linguistics.

Md Arafat Sultan, Shubham Chandel, Ramón Fernandez Astudillo, and Vittorio Castelli. 2020. On the importance of diversity in question generation for QA. In *Proceedings of the 58th Annual Meeting of the Association for Computational Linguistics*, pages 5651–5656, Online. Association for Computational Linguistics.

Toyin Tofade, Jamie Elsner, and Stuart T. Haines. 2013. Best practice strategies for effective use of questions as a teaching tool. *American journal of pharmaceutical education*, 77(7):155–155. 24052658[pmid].

Zichao Wang, Andrew S. Lan, Weili Nie, Andrew E. Waters, Phillip J. Grimaldi, and Richard G. Baraniuk. 2018. Qg-net: A data-driven question generation model for educational content. In *Proceedings of the Fifth Annual ACM Conference on Learning at Scale*, L@S '18, New York, NY, USA. Association for Computing Machinery.

Thomas Wolf, Lysandre Debut, Victor Sanh, Julien Chaumond, Clement Delangue, Anthony Moi, Pierric Cistac, Tim Rault, Remi Louf, Morgan Funtowicz, Joe Davison, Sam Shleifer, Patrick von Platen, Clara Ma, Yacine Jernite, Julien Plu, Canwen Xu, Teven Le Scao, Sylvain Gugger, Mariama Drame, Quentin Lhoest, and Alexander Rush. 2020. Transformers: State-of-the-art natural language processing. In *Proceedings of the 2020 Conference on Empirical Methods in Natural Language Processing: System Demonstrations*, pages 38–45, Online. Association for Computational Linguistics.

Xingdi Yuan, Tong Wang, Caglar Gulcehre, Alessandro Sordoni, Philip Bachman, Saizheng Zhang, Sandeep Subramanian, and Adam Trischler. 2017. Machine comprehension by text-to-text neural question generation. In *Proceedings of the 2nd Workshop on Representation Learning for NLP*, pages 15–25, Vancouver, Canada. Association for Computational Linguistics.

A Generated Output

Context	Answer	Q1	Q2	Q1-Q2	C-Q1	C-Q2
The annual NFL Experience was held at the Moscone Center in San Francisco. In addition, "Super Bowl City" opened on January 30 at Justin Herman Plaza on The Embarcadero, featuring games and activities that will highlight the Bay Area's technology, culinary creations, and cultural diversity. More than 1 million people are expected to attend the festivities in San Francisco during Super Bowl Week. San Francisco mayor Ed Lee said of the highly visible homeless presence in this area "they are going to have to leave". San Francisco city supervisor Jane Kim unsuccessfully lobbied for the NFL to reimburse San Francisco for city services in the amount of $5 million.	$5 million	how much did kim ask the nfl to reimburse san francisco for city services during the super bowl?	what did lee ask for from the nfl in terms of financial assistance for san francisco during the superbowl?	0.79	0.42	0.75
Newcastle has three cathedrals, the Anglican St. Nicholas, with its elegant lantern tower of 1474, the Roman Catholic St. Mary's designed by Augustus Welby Pugin and the Coptic Cathedral located in Fenham. All three cathedrals began their lives as parish churches. St Mary's became a cathedral in 1850 and St Nicholas' in 1882. Another prominent church in the city centre is the Church of St Thomas the Martyr which is the only parish church in the Church of England without a parish and which is not a peculiar.	Coptic	what is the third cathedral in newcastle?	what are the three cathedrals of newcastle?	0.86	0.65	0.71
With Rivera having been a linebacker with the Chicago Bears in Super Bowl XX, and Kubiak replacing Elway at the end of the Broncos' defeats in Super Bowls XXI and XXIV, this will be the first Super Bowl in which both head coaches played in the game themselves.	Super Bowl XX	what was the first super bowl in which both head coaches played?	in what way did the first superbowl ever take place?	0.84	0.18	0.86
Cultural imperialism is when a country's influence is felt in social and cultural circles, i.e. its soft power, such that it changes the moral, cultural and societal worldview of another. This is more than just "foreign" music, television or film becoming popular with young people, but that popular culture changing their own expectations of life and their desire for their own country to become more like the foreign country depicted. For example, depictions of opulent American lifestyles in the soap opera Dallas during the Cold War changed the expectations of Romanians; a more recent example is the influence of smuggled South Korean drama series in North Korea. The importance of soft power is not lost on authoritarian regimes, fighting such influence with bans on foreign popular culture, control of the internet and unauthorised satellite dishes etc. Nor is such a usage of culture recent, as part of Roman imperialism local elites would be exposed to the benefits and luxuries of Roman culture and lifestyle, with the aim that they would then become willing participants.	Roman	what culture is an example of cultural imperialism?	what is cultural imperialism and what are some examples of this?	0.77	0.70	0.77
BSkyB's standard definition broadcasts are in DVB-compliant MPEG-2, with the Sky Movies and Sky Box Office channels including optional Dolby Digital soundtracks for recent films, although these are only accessible with a Sky+ box. Sky+ HD material is broadcast using MPEG-4 and most of the HD material uses the DVB-S2 standard. Interactive services and 7-day EPG use the proprietary OpenTV system, with set-top boxes including modems for a return path. Sky News, amongst other channels, provides a pseudo-video on demand interactive service by broadcasting looping video streams.	Dolby Digital	what kind of soundtracks are optional on sky movies and sky box office?	what kinds of soundtracks do sky sky box offices and sky movies use?	0.69	0.46	0.70

Table 4: Randomly-sampled model output from the 2QG No Question Trigram model.

Computationally Identifying Funneling and Focusing Questions in Classroom Discourse

Sterling Alic[1] Dorottya Demszky[1] Zid Mancenido[2] Jing Liu[3]
Heather Hill[2] Dan Jurafsky[1]

[1]Stanford University [2]Harvard University [3]University of Maryland

{salic, ddemszky}@stanford.edu

Abstract

Responsive teaching is a highly effective strategy that promotes student learning. In math classrooms, teachers might *funnel* students towards a normative answer or *focus* students to reflect on their own thinking, deepening their understanding of math concepts. When teachers focus, they treat students' contributions as resources for collective sensemaking, and thereby significantly improve students' achievement and confidence in mathematics. We propose the task of computationally detecting funneling and focusing questions in classroom discourse. We do so by creating and releasing an annotated dataset of 2,348 teacher utterances labeled for funneling and focusing questions, or neither. We introduce supervised and unsupervised approaches to differentiating these questions. Our best model, a supervised RoBERTa model fine-tuned on our dataset, has a strong linear correlation of .76 with human expert labels and with positive educational outcomes, including math instruction quality and student achievement, showing the model's potential for use in automated teacher feedback tools. Our unsupervised measures show significant but weaker correlations with human labels and outcomes, and they highlight interesting linguistic patterns of funneling and focusing questions. The high performance of the supervised measure indicates its promise for supporting teachers in their instruction.[1]

1 Introduction

Students are more engaged and learn more when teachers pose carefully chosen questions to draw out student thinking, and then attend closely to what students say (Blazar, 2015; Herbel-Eisenmann and Breyfogle, 2005). One way that teachers do this is by using focusing question patterns; i.e., "attending to what the students are thinking, pressing them to communicate their thoughts

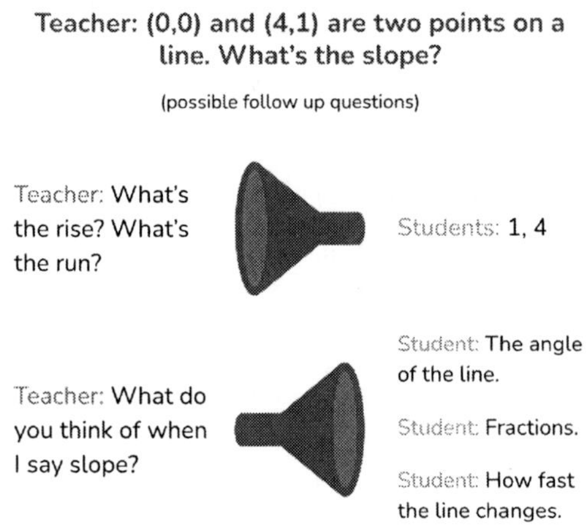

Figure 1: Example teacher utterance and possible student replies, illustrating the difference in funneling (top exchange) and focusing (bottom exchange). (Herbel-Eisenmann and Breyfogle, 2005)

clearly, and expecting them to reflect on their thoughts and those of their classmates" (National Council of Teachers of Mathematics, 2014, hereafter NCTM). Focusing is often contrasted to the less effective yet more common question pattern of funneling, where teachers pose "a set of questions to lead students to a desired procedure or conclusion, while giving limited attention to student responses that veer from the desired path" (NCTM, 2014). The use of focusing questioning patterns has been linked to better student learning outcomes and confidence in mathematics (Hagenah et al., 2018; Franke and Kazemi, 2001).

Supporting teachers to use more focusing question patterns requires first helping them to identify the extent to which they are focusing or funneling in their own classrooms. However, the current methods of measuring funneling and focusing are resource intensive, requiring manual classroom observation (e.g., Hagenah et al., 2018). Developing computational methods for identifying funneling

[1]Data and code are available at https://github.com/sterlingalic/funneling-focusing

Proceedings of the 17th Workshop on Innovative Use of NLP for Building Educational Applications (BEA 2022), pages 224 - 233
July 15, 2022

and focusing thus present an opportunity to provide automated feedback for questioning patterns at scale. Recent tools that provide automated feedback to teachers on discourse moves have been effective at improving their uptake of student contributions and student outcomes (Demszky et al., 2021b) and helped raise awareness about different instructional talk moves (Jacobs et al., 2022b). One promising application of an automated measure of questioning patterns is to build a similar tool that encourages teachers to engage with their students by asking more focusing questions.

We propose several approaches for computationally identifying funneling and focusing questions, including supervised and unsupervised modeling. In order to develop our approaches, we create a dataset of 2,348 student-teacher exchanges sampled from elementary math classroom transcripts, each annotated by three domain experts for teachers' use of funneling and focusing questions, or neither. Then, we fine-tune a supervised RoBERTa model (Liu et al., 2019) on the annotated data. This model has the highest correlation of .76 with human judgments, among our proposed models.

We also explore several unsupervised learning approaches, in order to encourage domain-transferability, to account for the lack of labeled data in most educational settings, and to analyze the linguistic patterns that drive funneling vs focusing questions. Our first unsupervised model hinges on the assumption that the range of possible student responses are narrower for funneling questions than for focusing ones. In Figure 1, we see that the teacher's funneling questions about the rise and run are quantitative in nature, so we can more confidently predict that the student response will be a number. Conversely, focusing utterances, which encourages students to reflect on their own thinking, tend to have a wider range of valid responses. The teacher's focusing question in Figure 1 shows that the students can think about the slope in many different ways, so we can less confidently predict what the student reply will be. Following this intuition, we adapt Zhang and Danescu-Niculescu-Mizil (2020)'s measure of *forwards-range*, an unsupervised measure that quantifies the strength of our expectation of a reply to a given utterance.

We also use other linguistic features informed by educational theory as measures to identify funneling and focusing. Since focusing examples probe student thinking and understanding, we use the count of *cognitive verbs* present in an utterance as one of the features. *Question words and phrases* also provide insight into classifying closed-ended and open-ended questions, so we include both the count of unigram and bigram question words as features. Table 2 shows the list of words we used for each feature. We find that while some of these features correlate significantly with human judgments (e.g. forwards-range and the use of "why"), these correlations are significantly weaker than those of the RoBERTa model.

To further validate our measures and to understand the link between funneling and focusing and educational outcomes, we correlate our measures with observation scores of instruction quality and student engagement and with value-added scores. Value-added scores are statistical estimates of a teacher's contribution to student test score growth, which serve important indicator of student learning and achievement. We find that our RoBERTa model correlates strongly with all of these outcomes, which is a significant finding in the context of educational measurement (Kraft, 2020), and it indicates the promise of this measure to support teachers and students.

2 Contributions

We make the following contributions in this paper.

1. We propose the task of identifying funneling and focusing questions in classroom discourse.

2. We create and release an annotated dataset of 2,348 teacher turns labeled for funneling or focusing questions or neither.

3. We propose supervised and unsupervised approaches to identify funneling and focusing questions. Our unsupervised approaches include counting lexical features (e.g. question words and cognitive verbs) and estimating the expected diversity of responses to a teacher utterance. Our best-performing approach, a RoBERTa model, has a correlation of .761 with human annotations.

4. We show that our estimates of funneling and focusing have a significant positive correlation with meaningful educational outcomes related to instruction quality and student achievement.

3 Related Work

Many researchers have measured the types of question patterns that teachers use in classrooms by hiring and training raters to manually code transcripts of teacher-student discourse (Boaler and Brodie, 2004; Kane et al., 2015; Gregory et al., 2017). While this measurement approach has been useful for identifying effective teaching practice in well-funded large-scale research studies, it is too costly to be scalable.

Computational methods for measuring question patterns in classrooms offer both the potential to undertake more research in this area, as well as the potential to support teachers to improve their classroom practice by automatically coding aspects of their classroom discourse for them to review.

Prior work in computationally analyzing classroom discourse has employed a variety of techniques to automatically detect teacher discourse variables. Recent advances in natural language processing has led to a larger presence of work applying neural methods with varying levels of success in detecting classroom discourse variables, such as semantic content, instructional talk, and elaborated evaluation (Jensen et al., 2021; Song et al., 2021). For unsupervised approaches, Demszky et al. (2021a), which is also most similar to our work in terms of approach and dataset, propose an unsupervised measure of teachers' uptake of students' contributions, and we use their sample in our annotation for funneling and focusing. Other computational work on questions in classroom discourse has focused on detecting questions in live classroom audio (Donnelly et al., 2017; Blanchard et al., 2016) and measuring the authenticity of questions in classroom discourse (Cook, 2018; Kelly et al., 2018). Our task closely relates to the task of detecting authentic questions but instead of using the CLASS framework used by prior work, we draw on the math education literature to develop our own coding instrument for funneling and focusing. In addition, while prior work in computationally analyzing questions uses feature-based classification, we also apply state-of-the-art neural machine learning models to solve this task.

Our proposed task of identifying funneling and focusing questions is situated among related dialogue tasks where the goal is to predict a label for a set of turns in dialogue. General approaches to this task have employed supervised classifiers in a variety of settings, such as to classify sarcasm in social media dialogue and participant roles in cyberbullying (Lukin and Walker, 2013; Jacobs et al., 2022a). Similar to our approach of identifying patterns that generalize beyond annotated data, others in this domain have also found meaningful patterns and features in labeled data that successfully generalized to unlabeled data (Oraby et al., 2015a,b).

Our work is also closely related to the computational study of conversations. We build on Zhang and Danescu-Niculescu-Mizil (2020)'s unsupervised measure of forwards-range, which was originally developed to analyze strategies in counseling conversations.

4 Dataset

We create a new open-source dataset labeled for funneling and focusing questions with the help of domain experts. We recruit former and current math teachers and educators trained in classroom observation to annotate 2,348 examples of teacher-student exchanges. We use the same sample of exchanges as Demszky et al. (2021a) — they are sampled from transcripts of 45-60 minute long 4th and 5th grade elementary math classroom observations collected by the National Center for Teacher Effectiveness (NCTE) between 2010-2013 (Kane et al., 2015).[2] The transcripts represent data from 317 teachers across 4 school districts in New England that serve largely low-income, historically marginalized students. Transcripts are fully anonymized: student and teacher names are replaced with terms like "Student", "Teacher" or "Mrs. H".[3]

4.1 Annotation

Our annotation framework for funneling vs focusing is designed by experts in math quality instruction, including our collaborators, math teachers and raters for the Mathematical Quality Instruction (MQI) coding instrument, used to assess math instruction (Teaching Project, 2011). We prepare a dataset of utterance pairs (S, T) for annotation,

[2]The only difference between our sample and that of Demszky et al. (2021a) is that we include an additional 102 examples that were rated by all 13 raters, instead of only the examples rated by 3 raters.

[3]Parents and teachers gave consent for the study (Harvard IRB #17768), and for de-identified data to be retained and used in future research. The transcripts were anonymized at the time they were created.

where S is a student utterance and T is a subsequent teacher utterance following the approach of Demszky et al. (2021a). In the annotation interface, raters can see the utterance pair (S, T), the lesson topic, which is manually labeled as part of the original dataset, and two utterances immediately preceding (S, T) for context.

A teacher utterance needs to meet three criteria in order to be categorized as funneling vs focusing: it needs to (i) relate to math, (ii) follow up on the previous student utterance, (iii) include a question. For example, a question such as "Can you sit down please?" cannot be classified as funneling or focusing because it does not relate to math. Similarly, if the teacher asks a question on a new topic, their question cannot be rated for funneling vs focusing, since it does not follow up on the previous student utterance. Therefore, annotators are first asked if a teacher utterance meets these three criteria. If so, raters are asked to indicate whether the utterance can be categorized as funneling or focusing. The coding protocol is included among the supplementary materials.

We recruited expert raters (with experience in teaching and classroom observation) whose demographics were representative of US K-12 teacher population. We followed standard practices in education for rater training and calibration. We conducted several pilot annotation rounds (5+ rounds with a subset of raters, 2 rounds involving all 13 raters), quizzes for raters, thorough documentation with examples, and meetings with all raters. After training raters, we randomly assign each example to three raters. Table 1 includes a sample of our annotated data, with majority rater judgments.

Post-processing. We create two datasets to separately measure our methods' ability to identify funneling and focusing questions in naturally occurring data — i.e. including data that does not meet the criteria above — and its ability to separate funneling questions from focusing ones. We create a dataset called UNFILTERED, where we replace raters' judgments for a teacher utterance not meeting the criteria above with 0, funneling with 1 and focusing with 2. We also create a dataset called FILTERED, where we replace raters' judgments for a teacher utterance not meeting the criteria above with NaN, funneling with 0 and focusing with 1. Then, we z-score each raters' judgments, and compute the average of z-scores across raters to obtain a single label for each example in each dataset. This

Example	Label
S: I disagree with Student A because if you skip count by 100 ten times, that will get you to 1,000. T: Let's try it. You ready? Let's start right here with Student F. S: A hundred.	focus
S: I first got 32 and then I got 48. T: And how did you find that? S: Because I did 16 times two is 32.	focus
S: We did 5 times 2 equals 10. T: No. We did 5 times 1 equals 5, darling. S: Oh, that's to solve the whole –	funnel
S: 4 minus 2 equals 2. T: Two and eight tenths. Does everybody understand? S: Yes.	funnel
S: Are we gonna out in the hallway? T: Yeah. S: Please.	N/A
S: I'm not going to [keep it]. T: Why? When you're ready to let me help you, please let me know. S: [Multiple conversations].	N/A

Table 1: Examples from our annotated data, showing the majority label for each example.

process yields 2348 unique examples for UNFILTERED and 1566 unique examples for FILTERED.

Rater agreement. We obtain an average interrater leave-out Spearman correlation of $\rho = .644$ for UNFILTERED (Fleiss $\kappa = .415^4$), and $\rho = .318$ for FILTERED (Fleiss $\kappa = .318$). Our interrater agreement values are considered high comparable to those obtained by Demszky et al. (2021a) for uptake, and those obtained in widely-used classroom observation protocols such as MQI and the Classroom Assessment Scoring System (CLASS) (Pianta et al., 2008). The lower agreement value for FILTERED indicates that distinguishing funneling vs focusing questions is more subjective than evaluating if a teacher utterance meets the criteria for a follow-up question. This is expected, since the criteria are relatively straightforward and do not require domain expertise.

4.2 Educational Outcomes

In order to understand the relationship between funneling and focusing and instruction quality and learning outcomes, we leverage variables associated with the original transcript dataset described

[4]We prefer to use correlations because kappa has undesirable properties (see Delgado and Tibau, 2019) and correlations are more interpretable and directly comparable to our models' results (see later sections).

above, from which we sampled our data. We use classroom observation scores from the MQI coding instrument (Hill et al., 2008) for the following items: (1) students provide explanations (scale: not present, low, mid, high), (2) overall student-participation and meaning making and reasoning (scale: not present, low, mid, high), (3) mathematical quality of instruction (5 point scale: low, low/mid, mid, mid/high, high). We chose these items as they relate most closely to questioning patterns and their effect on students discourse. We also use value-added scores, statistical estimates of a teacher's contribution to student test score growth. Value-added models make statistical adjustments to account for differences in student learning that might result from student background or school-wide factors outside the teacher's control. Numerous studies in education and economics have shown that value-added scores are an unbiased estimate of teacher impact on student achievement (e.g. Chetty et al., 2014). It has also been widely used in teacher evaluation systems around the country.

5 Proposed Methods

We use a variety of supervised and unsupervised methods to identify funneling and focusing questions.

RoBERTa. We fine-tune a RoBERTa-based regression model (Liu et al., 2019) on our annotated data. For our FILTERED and UNFILTERED subsets, we trained and evaluated separate models on their respective splits. We performed a small hyperparameter search over the number of epochs, which led to our best model trained over 10 epochs and with the default parameters from the Simple Transformers library (Rajapakse, 2019).

Forwards-range. The natural split in the diversity of responses to funneling and focusing utterances led us to adapt Zhang and Danescu-Niculescu-Mizil (2020)'s forwards-range measure for our task. The forwards-range is an unsupervised measure that quantifies the strength of our expectation of a reply to a given utterance. This measure was used in Zhang and Danescu-Niculescu-Mizil (2020)'s paper originally to analyze counseling conversations, and here we apply this measure to our dataset.

We use the implementation of the forwards-range from ConvoKit, an open-source toolkit for analyzing conversations (Chang et al., 2020). ConvoKit transforms each utterance into a vector representation using TF-IDF re-weighting. Then, to calculate the forwards-range for a given word or phrase, it calculates the weighted average of the vectors for all utterances containing the word/phrase, which Zhang and Danescu-Niculescu-Mizil (2020) calls the central point. The forwards-range of the word is then calculated as the average cosine distance between the observations containing the word and the central point.

Before we calculate the forwards-range, we also apply an original pre-processing pipeline to adapt the forwards-range measure to best work in the context of educational data. We apply the following pre-processing pipeline to reduce the vocabulary size and better capture teachers' rhetorical moves. We first delexicalize all nouns and numbers with "[NOUN]" and "[NUMBER]" tokens. Then, we keep either the last two sentences or the last twenty tokens, whichever one yields the most tokens, following the observation that teachers' questions tend to be at the end of their utterance. We then clean the text by removing punctuation and converting to lowercase. Finally, using the Phrases module of the open-source NLP library Gensim, we find the most common pairs of words in our UNFILTERED split of the NCTE dataset (Rehurek and Sojka, 2011). We use a threshold of 1.0 to the default Phrases scoring function and a minimum count of 500. The module then joins the individual words in the bigrams by an underscore character. For example, "okay and how did you do that" becomes "okay and how_did you do that". We then apply the ConvoKit framework to our dataset to generate forwards-range scores.

Length and lexical features. We also explore the effectiveness of other features in measuring funneling and focusing. We look at (1) length, (2) the count of cognitive verbs, and (3) the count of question words. We calculate length as the number of tokens in a teacher utterance without any pre-processing; this serves as a baseline lexical feature with which to compare performance. In selecting other features, we saw that focusing utterances tended to contain cognitive verbs, which makes sense intuitively since focusing asks students to reflect on their own and/or their classmates' thinking. For the count of cognitive verbs, we source our cognitive verbs from research in cognitive linguistics (Roque et al., 2018). We also include question words after exploratory data analysis, which revealed question words to be predictors of the di-

Features	
Cognitive verbs	understand, think, know, believe, figure out, find out, deduce, remember, imagine, realize, discover
Question Words - Unigrams	who, what, where, when, why, how, which
Question Phrases - Bigrams	how many, how do, what is, what else, etc.

Table 2: The list of of our lexical features. We count the appearances of all cognitive verbs and each question word/phrase in an utterance as features to predict funneling and focusing.

versity of responses (e.g., a high range of responses to "why_did" versus a smaller range of responses for "how_many"). For question words and phrases, we take the most frequent unigram and bigram question words and phrases present in the NCTE dataset. Table 2 includes these features.

6 Experiments and Results

We evaluate the ability of our models to identify funneling and focusing questions on both the UNFILTERED and the FILTERED datasets. We train separate models on each dataset, the idea being that the model trained on the UNFILTERED set can help identify funneling and focusing questions in "in the wild" – i.e. in any teacher utterance, while the model trained on the FILTERED set can help categorize a dataset of questions as funneling or focusing.

The results are shown in Table 3. We find that the RoBERTa models have a strong positive Spearman correlation with human expert labels both on the UNFILTERED ($\rho = .761$) and the FILTERED ($\rho = .443$) sets. Given that the model's score is in a similar range as human agreement[5], it is unclear if our model has hit a ceiling, or if there is room for improvement above these correlations.

Only few of the unsupervised measures show significant correlations with human judgments. The forwards-range has a significant negative correlation for the UNFILTERED set ($\rho = -.130$), but it changes to a significant positive correlation for the FILTERED set ($\rho = .159$). The positive correlation on the FILTERED set validates our assumption that focusing questions receive a greater variety of student responses. The negative correlation of the UNFILTERED suggests that replies to follow-up questions are less varied than other student utterances, which makes intuitive sense, since replies to follow-up questions may reuse words (e.g. "I think...", "Yes.") and they tend to stay within the same topic as the teachers' question.

The correlation pattern for length is the opposite as that of the forwards-range, showing a positive correlation with human judgments on the UNFILTERED set and a negative correlation on the FILTERED set. This suggests that overall, teacher utterances containing follow-up questions tend to be longer but that focusing questions tend to be shorter than funneling ones.

As for the other linguistic features, we see a significant positive correlation between the use of "why", "how do", and "what else" on the FILTERED set, confirming our hypotheses that indicators of open-ended questions are also indicators of focusing. In contrast, the use of "when" has a negative correlation with focusing on the FILTERED set, indicating that that teachers tend to use "when" when they expect a normative answer. Interestingly, other question words do not show a significant correlation on the FILTERED set, indicating that question words in themselves are not strong indicators of funneling and focusing. Question words and cognitive verbs tend to have a positive correlation with humans on the UNFILTERED set, which is unsurprising, as these features are all indicators of questions. Overall, the trend that we see throughout the unsupervised measures is that there is not enough signal for them to reliably identify funneling and focusing questions.

To measure the practical utility of our models in classroom settings, we also calculated the correlations of our model outputs with educational outcomes (see Section 4.2). Table 4 show the results of this analysis. The observation scores are annotated at the transcript level, so, similar to (Demszky et al., 2021a), we first mean-aggregate each model's outputs to yield a model score per transcript. We then use ordinary least squares re-

[5]Human agreement and model scores are not directly comparable. The human agreement values are averaged leave-out estimates across raters (skewed downward). The models' scores represent correlations with an averaged human score, which smooths over the interrater variance of 3 raters.

Model	UNFILTERED (N=2348)	FILTERED (N=1566)
Forwards-range	-0.130***	0.159***
Length	0.153***	-0.149***
Question Words		
Who	0.015	-0.026
What	0.276***	0.002
When	0.026	-0.065*
Where	0.027	-0.020
How	0.189	-0.036
Why	0.188***	0.128***
How Many	0.065**	-0.040
How Do	0.104***	0.080**
What's	0.051*	-0.035
What Else	0.116***	0.111***
Cognitive Verbs	0.193***	-0.027
RoBERTa UNFILTERED	**0.761*** **	0.329***
RoBERTa FILTERED	0.374***	**0.443*** **
Interrater correlation	0.619 [0.530, 0.694]	0.318 [0.220, 0.413]

Table 3: Spearman correlations of model outputs from the supervised RoBERTa model, unsupervised forwards-range model, and word phrase count features with the averages of human labels for question category. Asterisks indicate that the correlation is significant (p-value: *: <0.05, **<0.01, ***<0.001). The brackets for interrater correlation indicate the range of values for 13 raters, where each value represents leave-out correlation for a particular rater.

gression to compute the correlation of the models' outputs and the outcome scores, controlling for the number of student-teacher exchanges in each transcript. We find that there is a positive linear correlation of the RoBERTa model output scores with all three educational outcome scores for the NCTE dataset. We also find that there is a significant, but weaker correlation between the forwards-range measure and the educational outcomes.

We conduct a similar analysis with value-added scores. Since value-added scores are linked to teachers, we mean-aggregate each models' outputs at the teacher-level. Then, we compute the linear correlation between each feature and the outcome. The predictions from the RoBERTa model trained on the FILTERED dataset have a significant correlation with value-added scores, indicating that the measure of funneling and focusing teacher questions captures meaningful variance in students' academic outcomes.

7 Qualitative Analysis of Model Outputs

To better understand the performance of our models, we analyzed the predictions of our RoBERTa model fine-tuned on the FILTERED set and the forwards-range. Here, we choose to analyze performance on the FILTERED set to better understand the performance of our models in specifically distinguishing between funneling and focusing, rather than including the UNFILTERED set for the related but easier task of identifying if the teacher prompted the student. Some selected examples that we examined are shown in Table 5. For utterances without question phrases, the RoBERTa model and forwards-range model perform better than stand-alone question phrase features, as shown in the last example in Table 5. Many funneling teacher utterances do not actually include question words, but rather prompt the student to finish the teacher's sentence. The complexity of these classes of sentences, covering a wide range of topics with unique vocabulary tokens, motivates the use of our forwards-range and RoBERTa models, which are able to correctly classify these examples.

The RoBERTa model was also able to classify more complex examples that include several different question phrases. For instance, the first example in the table, includes the question phrase "how many", which correlates with funneling. But then the teacher also asks the student about their thinking, asking "what do you mean" by that, which makes the utterance an example of focusing. This suggests that the RoBERTa model is able to account for contextual factors and weigh the importance of different question phrases. On the other hand, the forwards-range predicted this example as "funneling", which shows one of its weaknesses as a bag-of-words model that lacks context.

One area of improvement across all the models we found through manual inspection is a class of focusing examples where the teacher calls on students to reflect on other students' contributions. For example, if a teacher asks a student Student B, "Is Student A correct?", this is a closed-ended question that could be interpreted as funneling, but it is focusing since the student is reflecting on the thinking of another student. The second entry in Table 5 also illustrates this, as the teacher asks a

	Mathematical Quality of Instruction (MQI5) (N=1657)	Overall Student Participation in Meaning-Making and Reasoning (N=1657)	Students Provide Explanations (N=1310)	Value-Added Scores (N=304)
Forwards-range	0.111***	0.209***	0.134***	0.031
Length	0.039	-0.085*	-0.111***	-0.096
Question Words				
Who	0.063***	0.008	0.009	-0.361
How	0.098***	0.001	0.003	-0.101†
What	0.029	-0.006	-0.009	-0.012
Where	0.020	-0.007	-0.013	-0.091
When	0.049*	-0.016**	-0.0185†	-0.045
Why	0.095***	0.050***	0.0420***	-0.03
How Many	0.054**	-0.008	-0.008	-0.117*
How Do	0.076***	0.023***	0.012	0.072
What's	0.001	-0.018**	-0.024**	0.027
What Else	-0.031†	0.007	0.013	0.005
Cognitive Verbs	0.105***	0.070*	0.081**	0.003
RoBERTa (unfiltered)	0.315***	0.270***	0.350***	0.098†
RoBERTa (filtered)	0.067**	0.388***	0.376***	**0.124***

Table 4: Standardized coefficients showing the correlation between each measure, including RoBERTa, forwards-range, length and our lexical features, and the outcomes from the NCTE dataset. Each co-efficient comes from its own linear model, with the number of student-teacher exchanges in each transcript as a control variable (p-value: †: <0.1, *: <0.05, **<0.01, ***<0.001).

follow up to one student after receiving an answer from a different student. The RoBERTa model predicts this as funneling, likely because the utterance ends with a short, closed-ended question. However, this is an example of focusing, as the teacher calls on Student K to reflect on the previous student's thinking. The forwards-range predicts this example as focusing, but we do not believe that, as a bag of words model, the forwards-range actually captures the nuance of this example. It instead might be unsure of the expected reply and default predicts focus since the majority of its scores are clustered around relatively high forwards-range scores.

8 Conclusion and Future Work

We propose several approaches for computationally measuring funneling and focusing, an important aspect of classroom discourse, and evaluate their strengths and weaknesses. Our supervised approach using the fine-tuned RoBERTa model has the strongest linear correlation of the models we tested with human expert ratings for funneling and focusing; it similarly had the strongest correlations of the models with educational outcomes. This shows the potential of the RoBERTa model to be used in future feedback and professional development tools for teachers.

Still, our unsupervised measures show significant correlations with the expert labels for funneling and focusing, as well as with educational outcomes. This provides a foundation for future work combining different unsupervised approaches to build a robust measure of funneling and focusing. Other paths for future NLP work include using probing and attention weights to better understand the predictions of the RoBERTa model, improving the supervised approaches via an extensive hyperparameter search and by exploring models beyond RoBERTa, and importantly, improving and testing the generalizability of this measure to other classrooms and domains.

In education, there is potential for future work in exploring how this measure can best support instruction and learning outcomes for students across different educational settings. One possible avenue for this is examining discipline-specific ways of identifying focusing or funneling to provide more

Example Exchange	Human label	Models	
		RoBERTa	Forwards-Range
Student: To see how many twirls. Teacher: How many – what do you mean? Student: How many [inaudible] there are.	Focusing	focusing	funneling
Student: H-U-N-D-E-R-E-T-H? Teacher: Sh. Don't steal his knowledge. And Student K? Student: Thousandths.		funneling	focusing
Student: I put about, about is that about? Teacher: It is close. Student: What's the about sign?	Funneling	funneling	funneling
Student: Three twelfths also equals one quarter. Teacher: Yes, it does, and we'll talk about that in another lesson, okay? Number 10. Cover Shape B with – Student: Hexagons.		funneling	funneling

Table 5: Example model predictions from the forwards-range and our RoBERTa model fine-tuned on the FILTERED set. Correct predictions are in green, and incorrect predictions are in red.

fine-grained feedback to teachers. Another is investigating the extent to which it is helpful that teachers know quantitatively in feedback they receive how much they are focusing versus funneling, or if there's a qualitative element about focusing and funneling that could similarly be helpful to teachers if provided in feedback.

Acknowledgments

We thank the anonymous reviewers for their helpful feedback. We are also grateful for the generous support of the Stanford CURIS program (to S. Alic) and the Melvin and Joan Lane Stanford Graduate Fellowship (to D. Demszky).

References

Nathaniel Blanchard, Patrick Donnelly, Andrew Olney, Borhan Samei, Brooke Ward, Xiaoyi Sun, Sean Kelly, Martin Nystrand, and Sidney K D'Mello. 2016. Identifying teacher questions using automatic speech recognition in classrooms. In *Proceedings of the 17th annual meeting of the special interest group on discourse and dialogue*, pages 191–201.

David Blazar. 2015. Effective teaching in elementary mathematics: Identifying classroom practices that support student achievement. *Economics of Education Review*, 48:16–29.

Jo Boaler and Karin Brodie. 2004. The importance, nature and impact of teacher questions. *North American Chapter of the International Group for the Psychology of Mathematics Education October 2004 Toronto, Ontario, Canada*, page 774.

Jonathan P. Chang, Caleb Chiam, Liye Fu, Andrew Z. Wang, Justine Zhang, and Cristian Danescu-Niculescu-Mizil. 2020. Convokit: A toolkit for the analysis of conversations.

Raj Chetty, John N Friedman, and Jonah E Rockoff. 2014. Measuring the impacts of teachers i: Evaluating bias in teacher value-added estimates. *American economic review*, 104(9):2593–2632.

Connor Cook. 2018. An open vocabulary approach for detecting authentic questions in classroom discourse. In . *Proceedings of the 11th International Conference on Educational Data Mining (EDM 2018)*.

Rosario Delgado and Xavier-Andoni Tibau. 2019. Why cohen's kappa should be avoided as performance measure in classification. *PloS one*, 14(9):e0222916.

D. Demszky, Jing Liu, Zid Mancenido, Julie Cohen, Heather Hill, Dan Jurafsky, and Tatsunori Hashimoto. 2021a. Measuring Conversational Uptake: A Case Study on Student-Teacher Interactions. In *Proceedings of the 59th Annual Meeting of the Association for Computational Linguistics (ACL)*.

Dorottya Demszky, Jing Liu, Heather C Hill, Dan Jurafsky, and Chris Piech. 2021b. Can automated feedback improve teachers' uptake of student ideas? evidence from a randomized controlled trial in a large-scale online course. *EdWorkingPapers*.

Patrick J. Donnelly, Nathaniel Blanchard, Andrew M. Olney, Sean Kelly, Martin Nystrand, and Sidney K. D'Mello. 2017. Words matter: Automatic detection of teacher questions in live classroom discourse using linguistics, acoustics, and context. In *Proceedings of the Seventh International Learning Analytics amp; Knowledge Conference*, LAK '17, page 218–227, New York, NY, USA. Association for Computing Machinery.

Megan Loef Franke and Elham Kazemi. 2001. Learning to teach mathematics: Focus on student thinking. *Theory into practice*, 40(2):102–109.

A Gregory, E Ruzek, CA Hafen, A Yee Mikami, JP Allen, and RC Pianta. 2017. My teaching partner-secondary: A video-based coaching model. *Theory into practice*, 56(1):38–45.

Sara Hagenah, Carolyn Colley, and Jessica Thompson. 2018. Funneling versus focusing: When talk, tasks, and tools work together to support students' collective sensemaking. *Science Education International*, 29(4):261–266.

Beth Herbel-Eisenmann and M. Breyfogle. 2005. Questioning our patterns of questioning. *Mathematics Teaching in the Middle School*, 10:484–489.

Heather C Hill, Merrie L Blunk, Charalambos Y Charalambous, Jennifer M Lewis, Geoffrey C Phelps, Laurie Sleep, and Deborah Loewenberg Ball. 2008. Mathematical knowledge for teaching and the mathematical quality of instruction: An exploratory study. *Cognition and instruction*, 26(4):430–511.

Gilles Jacobs, Cynthia Van Hee, and Véronique Hoste. 2022a. Automatic classification of participant roles in cyberbullying: Can we detect victims, bullies, and bystanders in social media text? *Natural Language Engineering*, 28(2):141–166.

Jennifer Jacobs, Karla Scornavacco, Charis Harty, Abhijit Suresh, Vivian Lai, and Tamara Sumner. 2022b. Promoting rich discussions in mathematics classrooms: Using personalized, automated feedback to support reflection and instructional change. *Teaching and Teacher Education*, 112:103631.

Emily Jensen, Samuel L. Pugh, and Sidney K. D'Mello. 2021. A deep transfer learning approach to modeling teacher discourse in the classroom. In *LAK21: 11th International Learning Analytics and Knowledge Conference*, LAK21, page 302–312, New York, NY, USA. Association for Computing Machinery.

T Kane, H Hill, and D Staiger. 2015. National center for teacher effectiveness main study. icpsr36095-v2.

Sean Kelly, Andrew M Olney, Patrick Donnelly, Martin Nystrand, and Sidney K D'Mello. 2018. Automatically measuring question authenticity in real-world classrooms. *Educational Researcher*, 47(7):451–464.

Matthew A Kraft. 2020. Interpreting effect sizes of education interventions. *Educational Researcher*, 49(4):241–253.

Yinhan Liu, Myle Ott, Naman Goyal, Jingfei Du, Mandar Joshi, Danqi Chen, Omer Levy, Mike Lewis, Luke Zettlemoyer, and Veselin Stoyanov. 2019. RoBERTa: A robustly optimized BERT pretraining approach. *arXiv preprint arXiv:1907.11692*.

Stephanie Lukin and Marilyn Walker. 2013. Really? well. apparently bootstrapping improves the performance of sarcasm and nastiness classifiers for online dialogue. In *Proceedings of the Workshop on Language Analysis in Social Media*, pages 30–40, Atlanta, Georgia. Association for Computational Linguistics.

National Council of Teachers of Mathematics. 2014. *Principles to actions: Ensuring mathematical success for all*, pages 35–41. The National Council of Teachers of Mathematics.

Shereen Oraby, Lena Reed, Ryan Compton, Ellen Riloff, Marilyn Walker, and Steve Whittaker. 2015a. And that's a fact: Distinguishing factual and emotional argumentation in online dialogue. In *Proceedings of the 2nd Workshop on Argumentation Mining*, pages 116–126, Denver, CO. Association for Computational Linguistics.

Shereen Oraby, Lena Reed, Ryan Compton, Ellen Riloff, Marilyn Walker, and Steve Whittaker. 2015b. And that's a fact: Distinguishing factual and emotional argumentation in online dialogue. In *Proceedings of the 2nd Workshop on Argumentation Mining*, pages 116–126, Denver, CO. Association for Computational Linguistics.

Robert C Pianta, Karen M La Paro, and Bridget K Hamre. 2008. *Classroom Assessment Scoring System: Manual K-3*. Paul H Brookes Publishing.

T. C. Rajapakse. 2019. Simple transformers. `https://github.com/ThilinaRajapakse/simpletransformers`.

Radim Rehurek and Petr Sojka. 2011. Gensim–python framework for vector space modelling. *NLP Centre, Faculty of Informatics, Masaryk University, Brno, Czech Republic*, 3(2).

Lila San Roque, Kobin H. Kendrick, Elisabeth Norcliffe, and Asifa Majid. 2018. Universal meaning extensions of perception verbs are grounded in interaction. *Cognitive Linguistics*, 29(3):371–406.

Yu Song, Shunwei Lei, Tianyong Hao, Zixin Lan, and Ying Ding. 2021. Automatic classification of semantic content of classroom dialogue. *Journal of Educational Computing Research*, 59(3):496–521.

Learning Mathematics for Teaching Project. 2011. Measuring the mathematical quality of instruction. *Journal of Mathematics Teacher Education*, 14:25–47.

Justine Zhang and Cristian Danescu-Niculescu-Mizil. 2020. Balancing objectives in counseling conversations: Advancing forwards or looking backwards. In *Proceedings of the 58th Annual Meeting of the Association for Computational Linguistics*, pages 5276–5289, Online. Association for Computational Linguistics.

Towards an open-domain chatbot for language practice

Gladys Tyen[1], Mark Brenchley[2], Andrew Caines[1], Paula Buttery[1]
[1] ALTA Institute & Computer Laboratory, University of Cambridge, United Kingdom
[2] Cambridge University Press & Assessment, University of Cambridge, United Kingdom
{gladys.tyen,andrew.caines,paula.buttery}@cl.cam.ac.uk
mark.brenchley@cambridge.org

Abstract

State-of-the-art chatbots for English are now able to hold conversations on virtually any topic (e.g. Adiwardana et al., 2020; Roller et al., 2021). However, existing dialogue systems in the language learning domain still use handcrafted rules and pattern matching, and are much more limited in scope. In this paper, we make an initial foray into adapting open-domain dialogue generation for second language learning. We propose and implement decoding strategies that can adjust the difficulty level of the chatbot according to the learner's needs, without requiring further training of the chatbot. These strategies are then evaluated using judgements from human examiners trained in language education. Our results show that re-ranking candidate outputs is a particularly effective strategy, and performance can be further improved by adding sub-token penalties and filtering.

1 Introduction

Studies in second language acquisition have shown that interaction is an important aspect of language learning (e.g. Loewen and Sato, 2018; Plonsky and Oswald, 2014; Mackey, 2013; Long, 1996). However, interaction typically involves one-on-one sessions with a teacher, which can be costly or may simply be unavailable to some learners. In addition, learners may experience language anxiety during interaction, which can be detrimental to learning (Horwitz, 2001).

Artificial dialogue systems provide an alternative way to learn through interaction. Learners can chat with the system in their target language at their own convenience, without needing a teacher.

Existing systems typically rely on handcrafted rules, and require learners to practise within a specified context (e.g. shopping at a supermarket) (cf. Bibauw et al., 2019). They are therefore quite limited in scope and require much manual work to anticipate possible responses.

In our work, we leverage existing chatbot technology that can generate responses in virtually any topic (Roller et al., 2021). As a first step towards integrating this technology into language education, we experiment with ways to **adjust the difficulty** of chatbot messages to a specified level (e.g. one that matches the learner's proficiency level).

Our contributions are as follows:

1. We propose two types of decoding-based strategies for adjusting the difficulty of generated text – **vocabulary restriction** and **re-ranking** – as well as ways to augment them.
2. In total, we implemented 5 different variants of these strategies, and we release the code and demo at `https://github.com/WHGTyen/ControllableComplexityChatbot/`.
3. For our evaluation process, we generated self-chats from the chatbot and determined their difficulty level and quality. We release the annotated data alongside the code and demo.

2 Related work

We provide an overview of four related topics: 1) dialogue systems; 2) decoding strategies for adding various desired attributes to text; 3) text simplification methods for transforming *existing* text (instead of *generating* text at a specified difficulty level); and 4) methods for predicting linguistic complexity.

2.1 Dialogue systems

Dialogue systems can be classified into goal-oriented systems, which are designed for a specific task, or non-goal-oriented systems, designed for general "chit-chat" (Chen et al., 2017). In this paper, we focus on open-domain text systems for chit-chat, which allow learners to practise chatting in any topic they choose.

Early open-domain systems relied on pattern matching and rules (e.g. Weizenbaum, 1966; Car-

Proceedings of the 17th Workshop on Innovative Use of NLP for Building Educational Applications (BEA 2022), pages 234 - 249
July 15, 2022

penter), but were somewhat limited in their conversational ability. More recent neural dialogue systems can produce a wider range of responses using generative models, retrieval-based models, or some combination of both (e.g. Papangelis et al., 2021; Adiwardana et al., 2020; Roller et al., 2021). Generative models produce entirely new sentences using beam search or similar decoding algorithms, while retrieval-based models select appropriate responses from an existing corpus.

Dialogue systems are also present in the Computer Assisted Language Learning (CALL) literature. Bibauw et al. (2019) present an investigation of dialogue-based CALL, where, notably, only 22 out of 96 systems allow completely free dialogue. Of those, most rely on handcrafted rules, and none make use of neural methods. To our knowledge, our work is the first attempt to use a neural generative chatbot for language learning purposes.

2.2 Decoding strategies

Neural models for text generation tasks typically maximise the likelihood of the generated output using beam search (e.g. Li et al., 2016; Rush et al., 2015; Sutskever et al., 2014). However, the most likely output may not be the most desirable one – e.g. in this paper, we would like to produce outputs of a particular difficulty level. One way to achieve desirable results is to further fine-tune the language model (e.g. Welleck et al., 2019; Roller et al., 2021), but this requires having (or being able to easily generate) data containing such desired traits.

Instead, it is possible to change the decoding strategy to produce desired outputs without further training of the language model. For example, to increase semantic and linguistic diversity, researchers have proposed changing the softmax temperature (Ackley et al., 1985; Caccia et al., 2020), or to use Stochastic Beam Search (Kool et al., 2019), top-k sampling (Fan et al., 2018), Nucleus Sampling (Holtzman et al., 2020), or conditional Poisson stochastic beam search (Meister et al., 2021). Decoding strategies have been also employed to control other linguistic attributes, such as output length (Kikuchi et al., 2016), style (Ghazvininejad et al., 2017), repetition, specificity, response-relatedness and question-asking (See et al., 2019). To our knowledge, our methods are the first to adjust the difficulty level during decoding.

2.3 Text simplification

Text simplification (TS) is the task of transforming complex text into simpler, more readable text that conveys the same meaning. Previous approaches are typically only designed to simplify where possible (e.g. Nisioi et al., 2017; Zhang and Lapata, 2017). More recently, methods have been proposed for controllable TS, where text can be simplified to a desired level of difficulty, such as Scarton and Specia (2018) and Nishihara et al. (2019), though both methods require training of a sequence-to-sequence model from scratch. Maddela et al. (2021) use a hybrid approach where the degree of simplification operations can be controlled, though not explicitly to a specified difficulty level.

Existing TS methods apply *transformative* operations to an existing piece of text. The main drawback is that some complex words may be impossible to simplify as there is no simpler alternative that conveys the same meaning (Shardlow, 2014). Our paper takes a different approach entirely, and instead adjusts difficulty of text when it is *generated*.

There is also research on specific operations within the TS pipeline. In particular, we discuss complex word identification (CWI) in subsection 2.4 below. Other operations such as sentence splitting (Narayan et al., 2017; Aharoni and Goldberg, 2018) and paraphrase generation (Gupta et al., 2018; Fu et al., 2019) are also transformative operations, where the outcome needs to convey the same meaning as the original input. Our generation methods do not have the same constraint.

2.4 Linguistic complexity

Lexical complexity Previous work on lexical complexity typically involves predicting the complexity of words within a context. There have been multiple shared tasks related to lexical complexity: the 2016 CWI shared task (Paetzold and Specia, 2016b) to identify complex words; the 2018 CWI shared task (Yimam et al., 2018) also to identify complex words, and to predict the probability that a word is complex; and the 2021 Lexical Complexity Prediction shared task (Shardlow et al., 2021) to predict the difficulty level of words, as determined by Likert-scale annotations. Submissions to the first two shared tasks were mostly dominated by feature-based approaches (e.g. Gooding and Kochmar, 2018; Kajiwara and Komachi, 2018). The 2021 shared task was won by Pan et al.

(2021) using an ensemble of pre-trained Transformers (Vaswani et al., 2017), but submissions with feature-based models also ranked highly (Mosquera, 2021; Rotaru, 2021).

Readability assessment Beyond the word level, research on linguistic complexity is typically done on long-form texts. Traditionally, researchers have derived formulae such as the Flesch-Kincaid score (Kincaid et al., 1975) and the Coleman-Liau index (Coleman and Liau, 1975) to estimate readability, but many such formulae do not account for semantic content or linguistic structure, or are outperformed by data-driven methods (Si and Callan, 2001). Later machine learning methods for readability assessment may rely on feature extraction (e.g. Meng et al., 2020; Deutsch et al., 2020; also see Martinc et al. (2021) for an analysis of different approaches).

3 Implementation

We propose 5 different decoding strategies to adjust the chatbot difficulty to one of 6 CEFR levels[1].

For our implementations, we used Facebook's Blender 2.7B (version 1[2], generator model) (Roller et al., 2021) as the basis, though our methods can be used or adapted to other language models that use beam search or sampling-based generation.

For comparability, all strategies use top-k sampling[3] (Fan et al., 2018) using $k = 40$ with a beam size of 20. We did not use the additional safety mechanisms (as described by Roller et al. (2021)) to ensure fair comparison of results.

Some of our methods use regression, either during generation or beforehand. For all regression tasks described below, we use a continuous scale from 0 to 5 to denote CEFR values, even though they are typically differentiated by qualitative properties (Council of Europe, 2020). This is because:

a) We have limited training data, and a scalar value provides more information to a regression model than a classification label; and
b) Due to the subjectivity of difficulty levels, there are often situations where examiners refer to values *between* CEFR levels, such as a "high B2/low C1". Using a continuous scale allows us to represent such in-between values.

3.1 Method 1: Vocabulary restriction with EVP

As a baseline strategy, we implemented a simple vocabulary filter based on a list of words manually labelled by CEFR[4]. The English Vocabulary Profile[5] (EVP) (Capel, 2015) maps 6,750 words and phrases to one or multiple CEFR levels according to their particular sense and usage. If the lowest[6] CEFR level of a word/phrase is higher than the target CEFR level, we prevent that word/phrase from being generated by setting the probability to 0[7][8]. For example, the word *absolutely* is labelled as B1, C1, or C2 depending on its usage. If the target CEFR level is B1 or above, the word is allowed and will retain its original probabilities; if the target CEFR level is A2 or below, the word will always have a probability of 0, and can never be generated.

As the EVP does not contain proper nouns, we also added a list of the most common first and last names (Social Security Administration; United States Census Bureau), and U.S. state names[9]. All

[1]Throughout this paper, we draw on the Common European Reference Framework (CEFR) (Council of Europe, 2020) to denote proficiency levels. An international standard for describing language ability, the CEFR organises ability into 6 levels, beginning with A1, continuing to A2, B1, B2, C1, and ending with C2, representing mastery of a second language.

[2]Version 2 had not been released at the time of our experiments.

[3]We use top-k sampling here because it was found to be equivalent to the default settings (in Roller et al., 2021) of beam size 10, with beam blocking of 3-grams and a minimum length of 20. Beam search, however, is deterministic, so top-k sampling allows us to generate multiple self-chats using the same settings.

[4]We chose to use a manually curated list to minimise errors, and because such vocabulary lists are often available as a language learning resource for widely-spoken languages. Alternatively, it is possible to produce similar word lists either in an unsupervised or semi-supervised manner (e.g. Jenny Ortiz-Zambrano, 2020).

[5]`https://www.englishprofile.org/wordlists/evp`

[6]We ignore the higher CEFR labels and collapse words with multiple meanings or usages into a single entry, because it is often impossible to determine the correct meaning during generation, when the rest of the sentence is missing.

[7]After modifications, the sum of all "probabilities" would no longer be 1, though we continue to refer to these as probabilities for the sake of exposition.

[8]Blender uses Byte-Level BPE tokenisation (Roller et al., 2021; Sennrich et al., 2016), so a word is not fully formed until the subsequent sub-token (beginning with a whitespace or punctuation denoting a word boundary) is chosen. To ensure that the 0 probabilities are assigned to the correct word, we also assign them to subsequent sub-tokens that begin with a word boundary.

[9]Since Blender is pre-trained on data from Reddit, where a large part of the user base comes from the U.S., we found that many of the dialogues contained names of U.S. states. We also noticed that when vocabulary is restricted and no proper names are allowed, the generated text sometimes contained approximations of locations in the U.S., such as "I live in wash in n" for *I live in Washington*. For this reason, we decided

added entries assume a CEFR level of A1, and so are always allowed regardless of the target CEFR level.

3.2 Method 2: Vocabulary restriction with extended EVP

Unfortunately, manually curated word lists typically have limited coverage. For example, the EVP only contains 6,750 words and phrases. For our 2nd method, we extended the list by training a regressor to predict the CEFR level of words outside of the EVP. We opted for a feature-based approach that is based purely on the surface word form rather than different word senses (as above), due to the lack of 1) training data and 2) available context while decoding[10]. Adapting the winning system (Gooding and Kochmar, 2018) of the 2018 CWI shared task, we selected a subset of features that are non-context-dependent[11]. The list of features used can be found in the appendix.

As in the original paper, we used the Random Forest implementation from *scikit-learn*[12] , but for regression instead of binary classification. CEFR levels in the training data were converted into integers from 0 to 5 (inclusive), and predicted values were rounded to the nearest CEFR level.

To evaluate this word complexity prediction model, we randomly selected one-fifth of the original EVP data as the test set, taking care to ensure that words from the same root cannot be found in both the training and test set. Results are shown in Table 1.

After evaluation, the model was re-trained on the whole dataset, then used to predict the CEFR levels of an additional 10,000 of the most common[13] English words that are not in the EVP. The prediction of CEFR levels is done beforehand to minimise computational costs at runtime.

Spearman's ρ	Pearson's r	MAE
0.694	0.712	0.826

Table 1: Spearman's and Pearson's correlation and mean absolute error (MAE) of predicted CEFR levels of words in the EVP. Both correlation statistics are significant ($p \leq 0.001$). MAE of 1 corresponds to a difference of 1 CEFR level.

3.3 Method 3: Re-ranking

One main drawback of vocabulary restriction is that text difficulty is not necessarily determined by vocabulary choice alone. We want to generate outputs that are of the appropriate difficulty level in terms of structure, content, as well as choice of words.

For our 3rd method, we propose a re-ranking method that considers multiple candidate messages, before selecting the most appropriate one. As described in section 3, our models use beam size = 20, which generates 20 candidate messages for every message sent to the user.

We first trained a regressor to predict the CEFR level of sentences. When the chatbot is in use, the regressor will predict the CEFR level of all candidate messages, allowing us to compute a score that combines the original ranking and the predicted CEFR. This score will then be used to re-rank the candidates, and the top candidate message will be sent to the user.

For the regressor, we used a RoBERTa model pre-trained on a dynamic masked language modelling (Liu et al., 2019), which is then distilled (Sanh et al., 2019), as implemented in Huggingface Transformers (Wolf et al., 2020). We fine-tuned this model to predict text difficulty on the Cambridge Exams (CE) dataset (Xia et al., 2016), which contains English texts from Cambridge Exams aimed at learners of different CEFR levels. However, instead of training our model on entire texts, we used spaCy (Montani et al., 2021) to detect sentence boundaries, and trained the model to predict the CEFR level from individual sentences, as they are more similar in length to the messages generated by Blender. Since the prediction of candidate messages must occur during live interactive use, the distilled version of the model was chosen to minimise computational overhead.

As with the previous word complexity prediction model, we randomly selected one-fifth of the CE sentences as a test set for the sentence complexity

to include in our vocabulary a list of U.S. states, along with popular first and last names from the U.S.

[10]As above, the CEFR level of a word is used to determine the probability of a sub-token at a given time step during decoding, where the rest of the sentence is still missing.

[11]Other features used in the original paper were context-dependent, and so were unsuitable for our use case.

[12]https://scikit-learn.org/

[13]Word frequency is estimated from the Exquisite Corpus, which combines frequencies from Wikipedia, subtitle corpora, news corpora, Google Books, and other resources. https://github.com/LuminosoInsight/exquisite-corpus

prediction model, taking care to ensure that sentences from the same text cannot be found in both the training set and the test set. After evaluation, we re-trained the model using all available data, to be used to generate text. Initial evaluation results from the test set are shown in Table 2.

Spearman's ρ	Pearson's r	MAE
0.701	0.734	0.634

Table 2: Spearman's and Pearson's correlation and mean absolute error (MAE) of predicted CEFR levels of sentences from the Cambridge Exams dataset. Both correlation statistics are significant ($p \leq 0.001$). MAE of 1 corresponds to a difference of 1 CEFR level.

Our proposed re-ranking procedure accounts for:

(1) $P(C_i)$ the original probability of each **C**andidate C_i according to the chatbot language model

(2) L_{C_i} the difficulty **L**evel of each **C**andidate

(3) L_t the **t**arget difficulty **L**evel

We compute the new rank R of each candidate C_i by taking the average of its original rank (based on $P(C_i)$) and its difficulty rank (based on distance away from the target difficulty level).

$$R = \frac{r(P(C_i)) + w \cdot r(|L_t - L_{C_i}|)}{2} \quad (1)$$

r denotes a function that returns the rank of the candidate out of all candidates. That is: $r(P(C_i))$ is the ranking of probabilities from the model (where higher probability = higher rank), and $r(|L_t - L_{C_i}|)$ is the ranking of distance to target difficulty (where smaller distance = higher rank). r essentially normalises the probability values and difficulty levels before the final rank is computed. w is an adjustable weight that controls the importance of distance to the target difficulty.

To select a value for w, we manually annotated ideal rankings for 10 sets of 20 candidate outputs, and found that the original rank and the difficulty rank contribute equally to the final rankings. Therefore, for methods 3, 4 and 5, we use $w = 1$.

3.4 Method 4: Re-ranking with sub-token penalties

With method 3, we sometimes found that all 20 generated candidates would be of a similar difficulty level, which may be some distance away form the learner's CEFR level. For example, we might have 20 candidate responses at C1 level, while the learner is a B1 speaker.

In order to increase the probability that a candidate message is at the target CEFR level, we implemented an additional penalty system, which penalises sub-tokens that are too difficult. Sub-tokens that are too easy are not penalised, as many are words serving grammatical functions or common words, which are also frequently used in difficult texts. Note that, as with vocabulary restriction, penalties must be assigned to sub-tokens rather than words, because words are not fully formed until a following sub-token with a word boundary is chosen.

The penalty for a given sub-token varies depending on how difficult it is. To determine the CEFR level of a sub-token, we tokenised the texts in the CE dataset to identify which sub-tokens appeared at which CEFR level. The lowest CEFR level is then chosen for each sub-token. For example, a sub-token that appears in a B1 exam but not in A1 or A2 exams will be classified as a B1 sub-token.

The penalty values scale according to the difference between the target CEFR level and sub-token's CEFR level. For example, an A2 chatbot will assign a smaller penalty (or a larger weight) to a B1 sub-token (e.g. *_absolutely, _opportun, initely*) than a B2 sub-token (e.g. *_humanity, _adop, iable*)[14]. The penalty values are taken from a Gaussian distribution, where μ is a CEFR level difference of 0, and σ is 2 CEFR levels[15].

The new probability of a given sub-token is therefore calculated as follows:

$$p' = \begin{cases} p \cdot \varphi(L_s - L_t) & \text{if } L_s > L_t \\ p & \text{otherwise} \end{cases} \quad (2)$$

where p and p' denote the original and new probability respectively, L_s is the CEFR level of the sub-token, and L_t is the target CEFR level. φ represents the Gaussian distribution described above.

[14] where _ represents a whitespace character.

[15] We settled on this value for σ for relatively lenient penalties, because:

a) The Cambridge Exams dataset only contains 331 texts (averaging at 531 words each), so a low frequency token of e.g. B1 level may only appear at B2 level or above. Having more lenient penalties can account for such potential discrepancies.

b) If the resulting candidate is too difficult, it is likely to be filtered out in the re-ranking process.

However, this value can be adjusted based on the language model or applicational needs.

3.5 Method 5: Re-ranking with sub-token penalties and filtering

With method 4, we noticed that occasional nonsense words are generated. This was typically due to how penalties are assigned to sub-tokens rather than words: for example, on one occasion, *backpacking* was generated as *backpicking*.

To combat this, we added a vocabulary filter[16] to look for words that are out-of-vocabulary, ignoring capitalised words and punctuation. If a candidate message contains such a word, it is removed from the pool of candidates.

	1	2	3	4	5	B
A1	50	50	50	50	50	0
A2	50	50	50	50	50	0
B1	50	50	50	50	50	0
B2	50	50	50	50	50	0
C1	50	50	50	50	50	0
C2	50	50	50	50	50	0
N/A	0	0	0	0	0	100
Total	300	300	300	300	300	100

Table 3: Number of self-chats generated for each method / CEFR combination. **B** refers to self-chats generated using the original **B**lender configurations with no modifications, which cannot be targeted at a given CEFR level.

4 Evaluation

For each of our 5 methods, we generated 300 self-chat dialogues using Blender, where the chatbot talks to itself (Li et al., 2016). Each self-chat was generated using the settings for a specific CEFR level: for example, method 1 at B1 level would only generate vocabulary at B1 level or below; method 3 at C1 level would re-rank outputs based on how close it is to C1 difficulty.

Then, to determine whether these methods are truly able to generate messages at the intended level, we recruited English language examiners to judge the *true* difficulty level of each self-chat.

We chose self-chats rather than human-model chats (i.e. chats between a human and the language model) for three reasons: firstly, because we did not want the examiner's judgement of the chatbot output to be biased by the proficiency level of the user; secondly, because it is cheaper and less time consuming to generate self-chats; and finally, because second language users may struggle to communicate with the chatbot. Additionally, previous work comparing self-chats to human-model chats found that they produced similar results (Li et al., 2019).

Each self-chat consists of 18 messages, all prompted by an initial message, "Hello!". An example of a generated self-chat can be found in the appendix. The 300 dialogues for each method are split evenly into 6 sets of 50, each set targeting a different CEFR level. An additional 100 dialogues were generated without any modifications for comparison, resulting in an overall total of 1600 dialogues (see Table 3).

We recruited 10 English language examiners from Cambridge University Press & Assessment. All 10 examiners were provided with a set of genre-specific descriptors adapted from the CEFR[17]. In addition, to assess the general quality of the produced text, each message in the dialogue was labelled according to whether it was sensible and whether it was specific (following Adiwardana et al., 2020), as well as whether it was grammatical. Examiners were given additional guidance on edge cases to support their application of these labels.

Each dialogue was annotated by at least 3 different examiners. For the final results, disagreements between examiners are resolved by taking the average of all annotations. The inter-annotator agreement for our CEFR annotations is 0.79, measured with weighted Fleiss' κ (Fleiss, 1971), and assuming equal distance between CEFR levels. For the grammatical, sensible, and specific labels, we used Gwet's AC_1 (Gwet, 2014)[18]. The agreement scores are 0.62 for grammaticality labels, 0.23 for sensibleness labels, and 0.67 for specific labels.

Agreement in sensibleness is noticeably lower than the others: feedback from annotators suggested that sensibleness of a particular message is often unclear when the previous context already contained messages that were not sensible. Experimental results from Adiwardana et al. (2020) suggest that agreement scores may be higher if annotators are only asked to label single responses within a pre-written, sensible context. However, they also note that "final results are always aggregated labels", so the overall proportion of sensible

[16]We use a list of words (containing only letters) from `https://github.com/dwyl/english-words`.

[17]Descriptors were adapted from 3 CEFR scales: Overall Reading Comprehension, Overall Oral Interaction, and Conversation. The descriptors we used in our experiments can be found in the appendix.

[18]rather than Krippendorff's α, because our data is very skewed (containing 87.0% grammatical, 75.7% sensible, and 91.6% specific responses), and AC_1 accounts for marginal probabilities.

Method	Spearman's ρ	Pearson's r	MAE	%gramm.	%sensible	%specific
Original	N/A	N/A	N/A	**90.2%**	**81.9%**	**94.1%**
Method 1	0.229	0.243	1.410	89.0%	76.5%	91.4%
Method 2	0.196	0.194	1.461	89.5%	77.3%	91.7%
Method 3	0.719†	0.707†	1.120	87.4%	77.0%	93.0%
Method 4	0.680†	0.681†	1.174	87.2%	76.1%	91.9%
Method 5	**0.755†**	**0.731†**	**1.090**	87.3%	76.4%	92.1%

Table 4: Table showing, for each method: Spearman's and Pearson's correlation between target CEFR and true CEFR; mean absolute error (MAE) of target CEFR compared to true CEFR, where MAE of 1 corresponds to a difference of 1 CEFR level; and percentage of grammatical, sensible, and specific responses. † indicates a significant correlation ($p \leq 0.001$). For all 5 methods, proportions of grammatical, sensible, and specific messages are found to be statistically equivalent (Wellek, 2010) to the original ($\epsilon = 0.001$, $p \leq 0.001$).

labels is still indicative of chatbot quality, despite relatively low agreement scores.

5 Results and discussion

Our results are in Table 4. To our knowledge, this is the first attempt at adjusting text difficulty during open-ended text generation – therefore, we were unable to find comparable results to be included here. Where possible, we include results for the original (unmodified) generation method, which cannot be targeted at any specific CEFR level.

For each of the methods, we compared the target CEFR to the CEFR determined by examiners – henceforth referred to as the *true* CEFR. Spearman's ρ and Pearson's r show the correlation between the two, and MAE is the mean absolute error, where an MAE of 1 refers to the difference of 1 CEFR level. %gramm., %sensible, and %specific refers to the percentage of grammatical, sensible, and specific responses out of all responses (excluding the original "Hello!" prompt).

From the correlation and MAE scores, we can see that the re-ranking methods work best, with method 5 – reranking with sub-token penalties and filtering – achieving the strongest correlation and lowest MAE between the target and true CEFR. Both vocabulary-based methods performed poorly, achieving almost no correlation and high MAE scores. This is somewhat surprising, as one might expect vocabulary to be a key factor in determining text difficulty. We suspect that this is because many of the easier words in the EVP also have more difficult word senses, but our method only considered the lowest CEFR level. Additionally, we looked at a set of 10 randomly sampled dialogues and counted 66 multi-word expressions (MWEs) in total, averaging at 0.36 MWEs per message. MWEs might often be more difficult than their constituent words individually: for example, the idiom *a cut above the rest* consists of words that are individually simple, but the phrase itself is relatively complex. Unfortunately, our vocabulary restriction methods are not able to account for this.

5.1 CEFR distribution

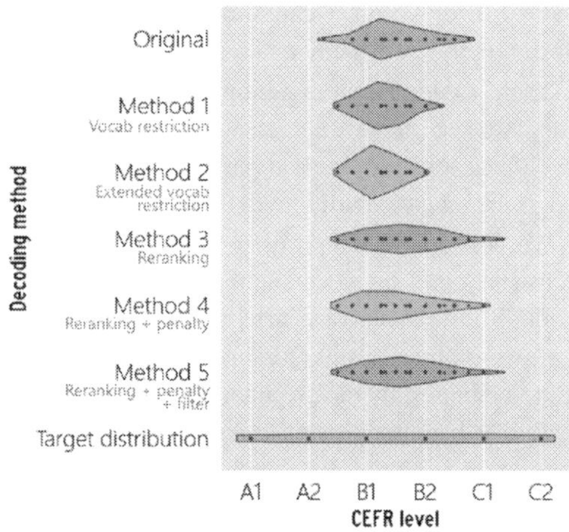

Figure 1: The first 6 violin plots shows distribution of CEFR levels for each method, along with the original version, all scaled for comparison. The last violin plot shows the target distribution for our 5 methods. It is spread evenly across all CEFR levels, as we had generated the same number of self-chats for each level (see Table 3).

Figure 1 contains violin plots showing the distribution of CEFR level for each method, including the original version with no modifications. The last violin plot is the ideal distribution for our 5 variants, which is evenly spread throughout all 6 levels. Out of the 5 variants, the 3 re-ranking variants have the most even distribution.

One surprising finding from this study is that

the CEFR level of dialogues that were generated *without* modifications to difficulty were mostly in the B1 to B2 range, rather than C1 and C2, which would be closer to a "native-like" difficulty, i.e. intended for users of native proficiency. Since the restriction-based methods served to reduce the difficulty level rather than increase it, the result is that none of the generated dialogues were labelled as C1 or C2, so the CEFR distribution clustered around the B1 level. On the other hand, the reranking based methods performed better because, when the target CEFR is C1 or C2, the reranking procedure would select texts that are more difficult than the most likely output. However, we suspect that the imbalance of CEFR levels in dialogues generated by the original model affects all 5 variants, and may adversely affect the MAE scores.

Another observation from our data is that none of our dialogues were labelled as A1, which is the lowest CEFR level. We suspect that this is because dialogic communication is inherently difficult for beginners, and there are simply too few topics and words that are suitable for all A1 learners. For example, the CEFR scale for written interaction simply states that A1 learners "can ask for or pass on personal details" (Council of Europe, 2020). However, we leave it to future work to explore other ways of generating dialogue data at A1 level.

5.2 Message quality

While our grammaticality, sensibleness, and specificity scores were found to be statistically equivalent ($\epsilon = 0.001$, $p \leq 0.001$), it may not be surprising to see a slight degradation of quality in Blender's messages when using our decoding methods. Our methods are designed to reject the most likely output if its difficulty level is not appropriate, and to select the next best output that falls within our constraints.

The focus of this paper is on the decoding methods rather than the original language model, which may be improved on or replaced by a different generative model. However, we acknowledge that the quality of messages may detract from the learning experience, particularly ones that are not grammatical or not sensible.

According to the inter-annotator agreement scores in section 4, there was relatively little agreement on what was considered sensible. In future work, it would be important to refine the criteria to better evaluate the quality of messages. Additionally, it may be possible to implement style classifiers or contradiction detection tools to mitigate this issue.

Sampling 100 messages from ones which were considered ungrammatical by at least one examiner, we identified three types of 'ungrammaticality':

- Around half (51) involved colloquialisms (e.g. "LOL", comma splicing, and other capitalisation or punctuation errors) that are ungrammatical in written English, but are more accepted in online messaging.
- More than a quarter (29) contained awkward phrasing depending on the context and/or was marked as not sensible. This becomes a grey area where it is difficult to determine whether the intended meaning was not sensible, or if the surface linguistic form was incorrect.
- Only a fifth (20) were clearly ungrammatical (e.g. "on your free time") or involved a spelling mistake (e.g. "clausterphobia").

Since Blender was pre-trained on large amounts of data from Reddit (Roller et al., 2021), it is unsurprising to see internet colloquialisms in the generated messages. While this may not be desirable for formal written work, learners are likely to come across similar forms of language in online or computer-mediated interaction. Alternatively, it may be possible to use grammatical error detection tools or style classifiers to filter out these messages. We leave to future work to investigate ways of filtering undesirable messages.

6 Conclusion and future work

This paper presents an initial foray into using open-domain chatbots for language practice. We propose and compare 5 variants of decoding strategies to adjust the difficulty level of generated text. We then evaluate these methods on dialogue generation, and find that our re-ranking strategies significantly outperform vocabulary-based methods. Our best variant achieved a Spearman's ρ of 0.755 and Pearson's r of 0.731.

Our current work only looks at self-chat difficulty from a teacher/examiner's perspective, which may not transfer well to interactive difficulty. It is also important to ensure that language learners would benefit from this endeavour. For our future work, we will directly engage with learners to investigate the utility and impact of chatbots on language learning.

However, there are also areas where the chatbot

needs to be significantly improved upon. For example, to cater for A1 learners, we need to be able to generate messages at A1 difficulty. This paper only looked at text complexity in terms of vocabulary, but it may also be possible to adjust the complexity by paraphrasing or altering the sentence structure.

We also need to ensure that generated messages are grammatical, sensible, specific, and appropriate. There is ongoing research on grammatical error detection (cf. Wang et al., 2021), toxic language detection (e.g. Dinan et al., 2019), and improving dialogue consistency (e.g. Li et al., 2020), which can be used to improve the chatbot.

Additionally, a language learning chatbot can be further augmented with other technologies to enhance the user experience, such as grammatical error correction tools, dictionary lookup, or personalisation mechanisms. However, it is not always clear what tools or mechanisms would best facilitate language learning: for example, immediate grammar correction could distract and cause communication breakdown (Lyster et al., 2013). We leave this investigation to future research.

7 Ethical concerns

By building a chatbot for language learning, we hope to make interactive, open-domain language practice more accessible to all learners. However, there are ethical risks that must be considered before providing learners with such a tool. In particular, we highlight three areas in which open-domain chatbots may have harmful effects, especially for younger learners.

1. **Toxic language**
   Open-domain chatbots are typically based on pre-trained large language models. These models, especially ones trained on internet data, are known to produce outputs that are toxic (e.g. Gehman et al., 2020) or that contain harmful biases (e.g. Nadeem et al., 2021; Sheng et al., 2019). There is existing and ongoing research on ways to mitigate these outputs (e.g. Xu et al., 2020; Dinan et al., 2019; Faal et al., 2022; Dinan et al., 2020), though Gonen and Goldberg (2019) argue that debiasing methods are insufficient and do not remove bias entirely. It remains an important ethical concern, especially for younger learners. For our experiments, we only recruit adult participants, who are warned about such messages beforehand.

2. **Inaccurate information**
   Large language models are also known to hallucinate knowledge during text generation (Roller et al., 2021; Maynez et al., 2020). While there is ongoing work to reduce this (Zhao et al., 2020; Komeili et al., 2020, e.g.), users should also be made aware that the information generated by a chatbot may not be accurate.

3. **Human likeness**
   Users should know that they are interacting with a machine rather than a human. Weizenbaum (1966) remarks, "In human conversation a speaker will make certain (perhaps generous) assumptions about his conversational partner." This is also known as the ELIZA effect (Hofstadter, 1995), which affects a user's perception of and emotional response to a chatbot.

In our experiments, evaluation was done through self-chats, and annotators did not interact with the chatbot directly. All annotators involved are adults and were asked to identify nonsensical or inaccurate statements (sensibility), and to flag any inappropriate language. In total, 6 of the 1600 (0.4%) self-chat dialogues we generated contained inappropriate language, or touched on inappropriate topics. We will make use of these in future work to address inappropriate chatbot turns.

Acknowledgements

We thank Helen Allen, Sian Gooding, David Strohmaier, and Andrew Rice for their advice and support. We also thank our anonymous reviewers for their valuable comments and suggestions. This paper reports on research supported by Cambridge University Press & Assessment. This work was performed using resources provided by the Cambridge Service for Data Driven Discovery (CSD3) operated by the University of Cambridge Research Computing Service (`www.csd3.cam.ac.uk`), provided by Dell EMC and Intel using Tier-2 funding from the Engineering and Physical Sciences Research Council (capital grant EP/P020259/1), and DiRAC funding from the Science and Technology Facilities Council (`www.dirac.ac.uk`).

References

David H. Ackley, Geoffrey E. Hinton, and Terrence J. Sejnowski. 1985. A learning algorithm for boltzmann machines. *Cognitive Science*, 9(1):147–169.

Daniel Adiwardana, Minh-Thang Luong, David R So, Jamie Hall, Noah Fiedel, Romal Thoppilan, Zi Yang, Apoorv Kulshreshtha, Gaurav Nemade, Yifeng Lu, et al. 2020. Towards a human-like open-domain chatbot.

Roee Aharoni and Yoav Goldberg. 2018. Split and rephrase: Better evaluation and stronger baselines. In *Proceedings of the 56th Annual Meeting of the Association for Computational Linguistics (Volume 2: Short Papers)*, pages 719–724, Melbourne, Australia. Association for Computational Linguistics.

Serge Bibauw, Thomas François, and Piet Desmet. 2019. Discussing with a computer to practice a foreign language: research synthesis and conceptual framework of dialogue-based call. *Computer Assisted Language Learning*, 32(8):827–877.

Massimo Caccia, Lucas Caccia, William Fedus, Hugo Larochelle, Joelle Pineau, and Laurent Charlin. 2020. Language gans falling short. In *8th International Conference on Learning Representations, ICLR 2020, Addis Ababa, Ethiopia, April 26-30, 2020*. OpenReview.net.

Annette Capel. 2015. The english vocabulary profile. In Julia Harrison and Fiona Barker, editors, *English Profile in Practice*, chapter 2, pages 9–27. UCLES/Cambridge University Press.

Rollo Carpenter. jabberwacky - live chat bot - ai artificial intelligence chatbot - jabber wacky - talking robot - chatbots - chatterbot - chatterbots - jabberwocky - take a turing test - loebner prize - chatterbox challenge - entertainment robots, robotics, marketing, games, digital pets - jabberwhacky. Available at `http://www.jabberwacky.com/` (2022/05/17).

Hongshen Chen, Xiaorui Liu, Dawei Yin, and Jiliang Tang. 2017. A survey on dialogue systems: Recent advances and new frontiers. *ACM SIGKDD Explorations Newsletter*, 19(2):25–35.

Meri Coleman and Ta Lin Liau. 1975. A computer readability formula designed for machine scoring. *Journal of Applied Psychology*, 60(2):283–284.

William Coster and David Kauchak. 2011. Simple English Wikipedia: A new text simplification task. In *Proceedings of the 49th Annual Meeting of the Association for Computational Linguistics: Human Language Technologies*, pages 665–669, Portland, Oregon, USA. Association for Computational Linguistics.

Council of Europe. 2020. *Common European Framework of Reference for Languages: Learning, Teaching Assessment*, 3rd edition. StrasBourg.

Tovly Deutsch, Masoud Jasbi, and Stuart Shieber. 2020. Linguistic features for readability assessment. In *Proceedings of the Fifteenth Workshop on Innovative Use of NLP for Building Educational Applications*, pages 1–17, Seattle, WA, USA → Online. Association for Computational Linguistics.

Emily Dinan, Angela Fan, Adina Williams, Jack Urbanek, Douwe Kiela, and Jason Weston. 2020. Queens are powerful too: Mitigating gender bias in dialogue generation. In *Proceedings of the 2020 Conference on Empirical Methods in Natural Language Processing (EMNLP)*, pages 8173–8188, Online. Association for Computational Linguistics.

Emily Dinan, Samuel Humeau, Bharath Chintagunta, and Jason Weston. 2019. Build it break it fix it for dialogue safety: Robustness from adversarial human attack. In *Proceedings of the 2019 Conference on Empirical Methods in Natural Language Processing and the 9th International Joint Conference on Natural Language Processing (EMNLP-IJCNLP)*, pages 4537–4546, Hong Kong, China. Association for Computational Linguistics.

Farshid Faal, Jia Yuan Yu, and Ketra Schmitt. 2022. Reward modeling for mitigating toxicity in transformer-based language models.

Angela Fan, Mike Lewis, and Yann Dauphin. 2018. Hierarchical neural story generation. In *Proceedings of the 56th Annual Meeting of the Association for Computational Linguistics (Volume 1: Long Papers)*, pages 889–898, Melbourne, Australia. Association for Computational Linguistics.

Joseph L. Fleiss. 1971. Measuring nominal scale agreement among many raters. *Psychological Bulletin*, 76(5):378–382.

Yao Fu, Yansong Feng, and John P Cunningham. 2019. Paraphrase generation with latent bag of words. In *Advances in Neural Information Processing Systems*, volume 32. Curran Associates, Inc.

Samuel Gehman, Suchin Gururangan, Maarten Sap, Yejin Choi, and Noah A. Smith. 2020. RealToxicityPrompts: Evaluating neural toxic degeneration in language models. In *Findings of the Association for Computational Linguistics: EMNLP 2020*, pages 3356–3369, Online. Association for Computational Linguistics.

Marjan Ghazvininejad, Xing Shi, Jay Priyadarshi, and Kevin Knight. 2017. Hafez: an interactive poetry generation system. In *Proceedings of ACL 2017, System Demonstrations*, pages 43–48, Vancouver, Canada. Association for Computational Linguistics.

Yoav Goldberg and Jon Orwant. 2013. A dataset of syntactic-ngrams over time from a very large corpus of English books. In *Second Joint Conference on Lexical and Computational Semantics (*SEM), Volume 1: Proceedings of the Main Conference and the Shared Task: Semantic Textual Similarity*, pages

241–247, Atlanta, Georgia, USA. Association for Computational Linguistics.

Hila Gonen and Yoav Goldberg. 2019. Lipstick on a pig: Debiasing methods cover up systematic gender biases in word embeddings but do not remove them. In *Proceedings of the 2019 Conference of the North American Chapter of the Association for Computational Linguistics: Human Language Technologies, Volume 1 (Long and Short Papers)*, pages 609–614, Minneapolis, Minnesota. Association for Computational Linguistics.

Sian Gooding and Ekaterina Kochmar. 2018. CAMB at CWI shared task 2018: Complex word identification with ensemble-based voting. In *Proceedings of the Thirteenth Workshop on Innovative Use of NLP for Building Educational Applications*, pages 184–194, New Orleans, Louisiana. Association for Computational Linguistics.

Ankush Gupta, Arvind Agarwal, Prawaan Singh, and Piyush Rai. 2018. A deep generative framework for paraphrase generation. *Proceedings of the AAAI Conference on Artificial Intelligence*, 32(1).

Kilem L Gwet. 2014. *Handbook of Inter-Rater Reliability*, 4th edition. Advanced Analytics, LLC, Gaithersburg, MD.

Douglas R Hofstadter. 1995. *The ineradicable Eliza effect and its dangers*, chapter Preface 4.

Ari Holtzman, Jan Buys, Li Du, Maxwell Forbes, and Yejin Choi. 2020. The curious case of neural text degeneration. In *8th International Conference on Learning Representations, ICLR 2020, Addis Ababa, Ethiopia, April 26-30, 2020*. OpenReview.net.

Elaine Horwitz. 2001. Language anxiety and achievement. *Annual Review of Applied Linguistics*, 21:112–126.

Arturo Montejo-Ráez Jenny Ortiz-Zambrano. 2020. Overview of alexs 2020: First workshop on lexical analysis at sepln. In *Proceedings of the Iberian Languages Evaluation Forum (IberLEF 2020)*, volume 2664, pages 1–6.

Tomoyuki Kajiwara and Mamoru Komachi. 2018. Complex word identification based on frequency in a learner corpus. In *Proceedings of the Thirteenth Workshop on Innovative Use of NLP for Building Educational Applications*, pages 195–199, New Orleans, Louisiana. Association for Computational Linguistics.

Yuta Kikuchi, Graham Neubig, Ryohei Sasano, Hiroya Takamura, and Manabu Okumura. 2016. Controlling output length in neural encoder-decoders. In *Proceedings of the 2016 Conference on Empirical Methods in Natural Language Processing*, pages 1328–1338, Austin, Texas. Association for Computational Linguistics.

J Peter Kincaid, Robert P Fishburne Jr, Richard L Rogers, and Brad S Chissom. 1975. Derivation Of New Readability Formulas (Automated Readability Index, Fog Count And Flesch Reading Ease Formula) For Navy Enlisted Personnel. Technical report, Naval Technical Training Command Millington TN Research Branch.

Mojtaba Komeili, Kurt Shuster, and Jason Weston. 2020. Internet-augmented dialogue generation.

Wouter Kool, Herke Van Hoof, and Max Welling. 2019. Stochastic beams and where to find them: The gumbel-top-k trick for sampling sequences without replacement. In *International Conference on Machine Learning*, pages 3499–3508.

Jiwei Li, Will Monroe, Alan Ritter, Dan Jurafsky, Michel Galley, and Jianfeng Gao. 2016. Deep reinforcement learning for dialogue generation. In *Proceedings of the 2016 Conference on Empirical Methods in Natural Language Processing*, pages 1192–1202, Austin, Texas. Association for Computational Linguistics.

Margaret Li, Stephen Roller, Ilia Kulikov, Sean Welleck, Y-Lan Boureau, Kyunghyun Cho, and Jason Weston. 2020. Don't say that! making inconsistent dialogue unlikely with unlikelihood training. In *Proceedings of the 58th Annual Meeting of the Association for Computational Linguistics*, pages 4715–4728, Online. Association for Computational Linguistics.

Margaret Li, Jason Weston, and Stephen Roller. 2019. Acute-eval: Improved dialogue evaluation with optimized questions and multi-turn comparisons. In *33rd Conference on Neural Information Processing Systems: Conversational AI Workshop*.

Yinhan Liu, Myle Ott, Naman Goyal, Jingfei Du, Mandar Joshi, Danqi Chen, Omer Levy, Mike Lewis, Luke Zettlemoyer, and Veselin Stoyanov. 2019. Roberta: A robustly optimized bert pretraining approach.

Shawn Loewen and Masatoshi Sato. 2018. Interaction and instructed second language acquisition. *Language Teaching*, 51(3):285–329.

Michael H Long. 1996. The role of the linguistic environment in second language acquisition. In William C. Ritchie and T.K. Bhatia, editors, *Handbook of Second Language Acquisition*, chapter 13, pages 413–454. Academic Press.

Roy Lyster, Kazuya Saito, and Masatoshi Sato. 2013. Oral corrective feedback in second language classrooms. *Language Teaching*, 46(1):1–40.

Alison Mackey. 2013. *Conversational Interaction in Second Language Acquisition*. Oxford Applied Linguistics. Oxford University Press.

Mounica Maddela, Fernando Alva-Manchego, and Wei Xu. 2021. Controllable text simplification with explicit paraphrasing. In *Proceedings of the 2021 Conference of the North American Chapter of the Association for Computational Linguistics: Human Language Technologies*, pages 3536–3553, Online. Association for Computational Linguistics.

Matej Martinc, Senja Pollak, and Marko Robnik-Šikonja. 2021. Supervised and unsupervised neural approaches to text readability. *Computational Linguistics*, 47(1):141–179.

Joshua Maynez, Shashi Narayan, Bernd Bohnet, and Ryan McDonald. 2020. On faithfulness and factuality in abstractive summarization. In *Proceedings of the 58th Annual Meeting of the Association for Computational Linguistics*, pages 1906–1919, Online. Association for Computational Linguistics.

Clara Meister, Afra Amini, Tim Vieira, and Ryan Cotterell. 2021. Conditional Poisson stochastic beams. In *Proceedings of the 2021 Conference on Empirical Methods in Natural Language Processing*, pages 664–681, Online and Punta Cana, Dominican Republic. Association for Computational Linguistics.

Changping Meng, Muhao Chen, Jie Mao, and Jennifer Neville. 2020. Readnet: A hierarchical transformer framework for web article readability analysis. In *Advances in Information Retrieval*, pages 33–49, Cham. Springer International Publishing.

Ines Montani, Matthew Honnibal, Matthew Honnibal, Sofie Van Landeghem, Adriane Boyd, Henning Peters, Paul O'Leary McCann, Maxim Samsonov, Jim Geovedi, Jim O'Regan, György Orosz, Duygu Altinok, Søren Lind Kristiansen, , Roman, Explosion Bot, Leander Fiedler, Grégory Howard, Wannaphong Phatthiyaphaibun, Yohei Tamura, Sam Bozek, , Murat, Mark Amery, Björn Böing, Pradeep Kumar Tippa, Leif Uwe Vogelsang, Bram Vanroy, Ramanan Balakrishnan, Vadim Mazaev, and GregDubbin. 2021. explosion/spacy: v3.2.0: Registered scoring functions, doc input, floret vectors and more.

Alejandro Mosquera. 2021. Alejandro mosquera at SemEval-2021 task 1: Exploring sentence and word features for lexical complexity prediction. In *Proceedings of the 15th International Workshop on Semantic Evaluation (SemEval-2021)*, pages 554–559, Online. Association for Computational Linguistics.

Moin Nadeem, Anna Bethke, and Siva Reddy. 2021. StereoSet: Measuring stereotypical bias in pretrained language models. In *Proceedings of the 59th Annual Meeting of the Association for Computational Linguistics and the 11th International Joint Conference on Natural Language Processing (Volume 1: Long Papers)*, pages 5356–5371, Online. Association for Computational Linguistics.

Shashi Narayan, Claire Gardent, Shay B. Cohen, and Anastasia Shimorina. 2017. Split and rephrase. In *Proceedings of the 2017 Conference on Empirical Methods in Natural Language Processing*, pages 606–616, Copenhagen, Denmark. Association for Computational Linguistics.

Daiki Nishihara, Tomoyuki Kajiwara, and Yuki Arase. 2019. Controllable text simplification with lexical constraint loss. In *Proceedings of the 57th Annual Meeting of the Association for Computational Linguistics: Student Research Workshop*, pages 260–266, Florence, Italy. Association for Computational Linguistics.

Sergiu Nisioi, Sanja Štajner, Simone Paolo Ponzetto, and Liviu P. Dinu. 2017. Exploring neural text simplification models. In *Proceedings of the 55th Annual Meeting of the Association for Computational Linguistics (Volume 2: Short Papers)*, pages 85–91, Vancouver, Canada. Association for Computational Linguistics.

Charles Kay Ogden. 1930. *Basic English: A general introduction with rules and grammar.* Paul Treber & Co., Ltd., London.

Gustavo Paetzold and Lucia Specia. 2016a. Collecting and exploring everyday language for predicting psycholinguistic properties of words. In *Proceedings of COLING 2016, the 26th International Conference on Computational Linguistics: Technical Papers*, pages 1669–1679, Osaka, Japan. The COLING 2016 Organizing Committee.

Gustavo Paetzold and Lucia Specia. 2016b. SemEval 2016 task 11: Complex word identification. In *Proceedings of the 10th International Workshop on Semantic Evaluation (SemEval-2016)*, pages 560–569, San Diego, California. Association for Computational Linguistics.

Chunguang Pan, Bingyan Song, Shengguang Wang, and Zhipeng Luo. 2021. DeepBlueAI at SemEval-2021 task 1: Lexical complexity prediction with a deep ensemble approach. In *Proceedings of the 15th International Workshop on Semantic Evaluation (SemEval-2021)*, pages 578–584, Online. Association for Computational Linguistics.

Alexandros Papangelis, Paweł Budzianowski, Bing Liu, Elnaz Nouri, Abhinav Rastogi, and Yun-Nung Chen, editors. 2021. *Proceedings of the 3rd Workshop on Natural Language Processing for Conversational AI*. Association for Computational Linguistics, Online.

Luke Plonsky and Frederick L. Oswald. 2014. How big is "big"? interpreting effect sizes in l2 research. *Language Learning*, 64(4):878–912.

Princeton University. 2010. About WordNet. `https://wordnet.princeton.edu/`.

Stephen Roller, Emily Dinan, Naman Goyal, Da Ju, Mary Williamson, Yinhan Liu, Jing Xu, Myle Ott, Eric Michael Smith, Y-Lan Boureau, and Jason Weston. 2021. Recipes for building an open-domain chatbot. In *Proceedings of the 16th Conference of the European Chapter of the Association for Computational Linguistics: Main Volume*, pages 300–325, Online. Association for Computational Linguistics.

Armand Rotaru. 2021. ANDI at SemEval-2021 task 1: Predicting complexity in context using distributional models, behavioural norms, and lexical resources. In *Proceedings of the 15th International Workshop on Semantic Evaluation (SemEval-2021)*, pages 655–660, Online. Association for Computational Linguistics.

Alexander M. Rush, Sumit Chopra, and Jason Weston. 2015. A neural attention model for abstractive sentence summarization. In *Proceedings of the 2015 Conference on Empirical Methods in Natural Language Processing*, pages 379–389, Lisbon, Portugal. Association for Computational Linguistics.

Victor Sanh, Lysandre Debut, Julien Chaumond, and Thomas Wolf. 2019. Distilbert, a distilled version of bert: smaller, faster, cheaper and lighter.

Carolina Scarton and Lucia Specia. 2018. Learning simplifications for specific target audiences. In *Proceedings of the 56th Annual Meeting of the Association for Computational Linguistics (Volume 2: Short Papers)*, pages 712–718, Melbourne, Australia. Association for Computational Linguistics.

Abigail See, Stephen Roller, Douwe Kiela, and Jason Weston. 2019. What makes a good conversation? how controllable attributes affect human judgments. In *Proceedings of the 2019 Conference of the North American Chapter of the Association for Computational Linguistics: Human Language Technologies, Volume 1 (Long and Short Papers)*, pages 1702–1723, Minneapolis, Minnesota. Association for Computational Linguistics.

Rico Sennrich, Barry Haddow, and Alexandra Birch. 2016. Neural machine translation of rare words with subword units. In *Proceedings of the 54th Annual Meeting of the Association for Computational Linguistics (Volume 1: Long Papers)*, pages 1715–1725, Berlin, Germany. Association for Computational Linguistics.

Matthew Shardlow. 2014. Out in the open: Finding and categorising errors in the lexical simplification pipeline. In *Proceedings of the Ninth International Conference on Language Resources and Evaluation (LREC'14)*, pages 1583–1590, Reykjavik, Iceland. European Language Resources Association (ELRA).

Matthew Shardlow, Richard Evans, Gustavo Henrique Paetzold, and Marcos Zampieri. 2021. SemEval-2021 task 1: Lexical complexity prediction. In *Proceedings of the 15th International Workshop on Semantic Evaluation (SemEval-2021)*, pages 1–16, Online. Association for Computational Linguistics.

Emily Sheng, Kai-Wei Chang, Premkumar Natarajan, and Nanyun Peng. 2019. The woman worked as a babysitter: On biases in language generation. In *Proceedings of the 2019 Conference on Empirical Methods in Natural Language Processing and the 9th International Joint Conference on Natural Language Processing (EMNLP-IJCNLP)*, pages 3407–3412, Hong Kong, China. Association for Computational Linguistics.

Luo Si and Jamie Callan. 2001. A statistical model for scientific readability. In *Proceedings of the 10th International Conference on Information and Knowledge Management*, pages 574–576. ACM Press.

Social Security Administration. Top names over the last 100 years.

Ilya Sutskever, Oriol Vinyals, and Quoc V Le. 2014. Sequence to sequence learning with neural networks. In *Advances in Neural Information Processing Systems*, volume 27. Curran Associates, Inc.

United States Census Bureau. Frequently occurring surnames from the 2010 census.

Ashish Vaswani, Noam Shazeer, Niki Parmar, Jakob Uszkoreit, Llion Jones, Aidan N Gomez, Ł ukasz Kaiser, and Illia Polosukhin. 2017. Attention is all you need. In *Advances in Neural Information Processing Systems*, volume 30. Curran Associates, Inc.

Yu Wang, Yuelin Wang, Kai Dang, Jie Liu, and Zhuo Liu. 2021. A comprehensive survey of grammatical error correction. *ACM Transactions on Intelligent Systems and Technology*, 12(5):1–51.

Joseph Weizenbaum. 1966. Eliza—a computer program for the study of natural language communication between man and machine. *Commun. ACM*, 9(1):36–45.

Sean Welleck, Ilia Kulikov, Stephen Roller, Emily Dinan, Kyunghyun Cho, and Jason Weston. 2019. Neural text generation with unlikelihood training.

Stefan Wellek. 2010. *Testing Statistical Hypotheses of Equivalence and Noninferiority*, 2nd edition, chapter 9.2. Chapman & Hall/CRC, Boca Raton, FL.

Michael Wilson. 1988. MRC psycholinguistic database: Machine-usable dictionary, version 2.00. *Behavior Research Methods, Instruments, & Computers*, 20(1):6–10.

Thomas Wolf, Lysandre Debut, Victor Sanh, Julien Chaumond, Clement Delangue, Anthony Moi, Pierric Cistac, Tim Rault, Remi Louf, Morgan Funtowicz, Joe Davison, Sam Shleifer, Patrick von Platen, Clara Ma, Yacine Jernite, Julien Plu, Canwen Xu, Teven Le Scao, Sylvain Gugger, Mariama Drame, Quentin Lhoest, and Alexander Rush. 2020. Transformers: State-of-the-art natural language processing. In *Proceedings of the 2020 Conference on Empirical Methods in Natural Language Processing: System Demonstrations*, pages 38–45, Online. Association for Computational Linguistics.

Menglin Xia, Ekaterina Kochmar, and Ted Briscoe. 2016. Text readability assessment for second language learners. In *Proceedings of the 11th Workshop on Innovative Use of NLP for Building Educational Applications*, pages 12–22, San Diego, CA. Association for Computational Linguistics.

Jing Xu, Da Ju, Margaret Li, Y-Lan Boureau, Jason Weston, and Emily Dinan. 2020. Recipes for safety in open-domain chatbots.

Seid Muhie Yimam, Chris Biemann, Shervin Malmasi, Gustavo Paetzold, Lucia Specia, Sanja Štajner, Anaïs Tack, and Marcos Zampieri. 2018. A report on the complex word identification shared task 2018. In *Proceedings of the Thirteenth Workshop on Innovative Use of NLP for Building Educational Applications*, pages 66–78, New Orleans, Louisiana. Association for Computational Linguistics.

Xingxing Zhang and Mirella Lapata. 2017. Sentence simplification with deep reinforcement learning. In *Proceedings of the 2017 Conference on Empirical Methods in Natural Language Processing*, pages 584–594, Copenhagen, Denmark. Association for Computational Linguistics.

Xueliang Zhao, Wei Wu, Can Xu, Chongyang Tao, Dongyan Zhao, and Rui Yan. 2020. Knowledge-grounded dialogue generation with pre-trained language models. In *Proceedings of the 2020 Conference on Empirical Methods in Natural Language Processing (EMNLP)*, pages 3377–3390, Online. Association for Computational Linguistics.

A Implementational details

A.1 Blender settings

We used the Blender 2.7B generative model released through ParlAI[19] (model file: `zoo:blender/blender_3B/model`) as the basis for our chatbot models. Table 5 lists the hyperparameters used for all chatbot models in our experiment.

During this project, we noticed that the generated dialogues sometimes contained sequences such as "+/u/dogetipbot", since Blender was pre-trained on large amounts of Reddit data (Roller et al., 2021). As this is beyond the scope of our project, and to prevent this from affecting our results, we decided to filter out sequences containing "u/" and "r/" for all dialogues, so that results are still comparable. This filtering step occurs just before a message is selected from the pool of candidates: if a candidate contains either "u/" or "r/", it is removed from the pool, and the next best candidate is selected and sent to the user.

[19] `https://parl.ai/`

Hyperparameter	Value
Beam size	20
Top-k	40
Temperature	1.0
Beam delay	30
Beam length penalty	0.65
Beam block n-gram	3
Beam context block n-gram	3
Number of encoder layers	2
Number of decoder layers	2
Embedding size	2560
Number of attention heads	32
Hidden layer dropout	0.1
Attention dropout	0.1
Activation function	GELU

Table 5: Hyperparameters and corresponding values used for our chatbot models.

A.2 Word difficulty prediction model

For our word difficulty prediction model used for method 2 (restriction with extended EVP), we used the `RandomForestRegressor` from the *scikit-learn* library[20]. We used the following features:

- Word length
- Number of syllables
- Number of WordNet synsets (Princeton University, 2010)
- Number of WordNet hypernyms
- Number of WordNet hyponyms
- Word frequency in subtitles from Movies and Series for Children in the SubIMBD corpus (Paetzold and Specia, 2016a)
- Word frequency in the SimpleWiki[21] (Coster and Kauchak, 2011)
- Word presence in Ogden's Basic English list (Ogden, 1930)
- Word frequency according to syntactic-ngrams compiled by Goldberg and Orwant (2013)
- Number of phonemes (from the MRC Psycholinguistic Database, Wilson, 1988)
- Kucera-Francis frequency norms (MRC)
- Thorndike-Lorge frequency (MRC)
- Familiarity (MRC)
- Concreteness (MRC)
- Imageability (MRC)
- Age of acquisition (MRC)

[20] `https://scikit-learn.org/`
[21] `https://simple.wikipedia.org/`

Hyperparameter	Value
Number of estimators	5000
Splitting criterion	MSE
Min. number of samples for splitting	2
Min. number of samples at leaf node	1
Min. impurity decrease	None
Sample weighting	None

Table 6: Hyperparameters and corresponding values used for our word difficulty prediction model.

Hyperparameter	Value
Learning rate	9.737×10^{-6}
Batch size	32
Number of epochs	3
Random seed	18
Number of encoder layers	6
Embedding size	768
Number of attention heads	12
Hidden layer dropout	0.1
Attention dropout	0.1
Activation function	GELU

Table 7: Hyperparameters and corresponding values used for our sentence difficulty prediction model.

CEFR levels in the training data were converted into integers from 0 to 5 (inclusive), and predicted values were rounded to the nearest CEFR level accordingly. Hyperparameters for this model are listed in Table 6.

A.3 Sentence difficulty prediction model

For the sentence difficulty prediction model in our reranking-based methods, we used the `distilroberta-base` implementation from Huggingface Transformers (Wolf et al., 2020), and added a regression head to output a value representing difficulty. We tuned the learning rate, batch size, number of epochs, and random seed for this model using Optuna[22]. The final hyperparameters for this model are listed in Table 7.

The training data is taken from the Cambridge Exams dataset (Xia et al., 2016), where the text is split up into sentences using SpaCy's (Montani et al., 2021) `en_core_web_sm` model. As above, CEFR levels in the training data were converted into integers from 0 to 5 (inclusive), and predicted values were rounded to the nearest CEFR level accordingly.

[22]https://optuna.org/

C2	Appropriate for a reader who can understand and interpret critically virtually all messages and dialogues including abstract, structurally complex, or highly colloquial text. Appropriate for a reader who can appreciate subtle distinctions of style and implicit as well as explicit meaning, including idiomatic expressions and colloquialisms.
C1	Appropriate for a reader who can understand in detail complex dialogues, whether or not they relate to their own area of speciality, provided he/she can reread difficult messages. Appropriate for a reader who can understand a wide range of demanding messages, and recognise implicit meaning, including emotional, allusive, and joking usage of language.
B2	Appropriate for a reader who can understand the main ideas of complex dialogues across a range of concrete and abstract topics, and has a broad active reading vocabulary, but may experience some difficulty with low-frequency idioms.
B1	Appropriate for a reader who can understand straightforward factual messages on subjects related to his/her field and interest with a satisfactory level of comprehension. Appropriate for a reader who can understand the main points of clear messages on familiar matters regularly encountered in work, school, leisure, etc.
A2	Appropriate for a reader who can understand short, simple messages on familiar matters of a concrete type which consist of high frequency everyday or job-related language (including simple everyday polite forms of greetings and farewells; introductions; invitations and apologies; giving thanks), or shared international vocabulary items. Appropriate for a reader who can understand sentences and frequently used expressions related to areas of most immediate relevance (e.g. very basic personal and family information, shopping, local geography, employment).
A1	Appropriate for a reader who can understand very short, simple messages a single phrase at a time, picking up familiar names, words and basic phrases and rereading as required. Appropriate for a reader who can understand familiar everyday expressions and very basic phrases aimed at the satisfaction of simple needs of a concrete type.

Table 8: CEFR descriptors provided to examiners to annotate difficulty levels.

Speaker 1:	Hello!
Speaker 2:	Hello there. Do you listen to music? I'm all about rock. Songs that have a melody are my favorite.
Speaker 1:	Yes, I love the melodies in rock music. I think that is the foundation of all music after all.
Speaker 2:	I agree. Music can have many meanings and have spiritual and religious elements too. How about you?
Speaker 1:	Yes, music can have a strong emotional impact too. It can enhance an experience or provoke a response.
Speaker 2:	Definitely! Music also can be interpreted through different cultural lenses as well. Have you ever thought about that?
Speaker 1:	Yes, that is true, since music can come in a wide variety of genres and structures.
Speaker 2:	Absolutely! Since it is so dynamic and changes from time to time, it has a tendency to change and evolve with the culture as well!
Speaker 1:	Yes, I think it is a good thing that music is dynamic though. Cultures have a way of shaping and defining what music is.
Speaker 2:	You're absolutely right! Humans have been using music for communication and for artistic inspiration for much of history so I wouldn't want it any other way!
Speaker 1:	Music can also influence the way we view our relationships, our ideas, and even our language as well.
Speaker 2:	Yes exactly! Music, art, language, entertainment, and science all play major roles in human society!
Speaker 1:	Sometimes I wonder if there is such thing as the soul, because it seems to come to people through their interpretation of music.
Speaker 2:	Yes there definitely is! The soul is definitely subjective and a big part of the human psyche so it makes sense that people interpret music in different ways!
Speaker 1:	I think we see it in art all the time. Artists often are influenced by their influences, such as their relationships.
Speaker 2:	In the past, many considered the relationship between the musician and audience to be one of the most important aspects of the medium!
Speaker 1:	Yes! I agree with that, as artists are affected by their art in a very personal way.
Speaker 2:	Yes and for a lot of artists the subject matter can be important to the storytelling and emotions of their music as well.
Speaker 1:	Indeed. And they often do not even realize how impactful their work is until after the fact.

Table 9: A cherry-picked example of a C1 self-chat dialogue generated using method 5 (reranking with sub-token penalties and filtering).

Response Construct Tagging: NLP-Aided Assessment for Engineering Education

Ananya Ganesh[◇] **Hugh Scribner**[◇] **Jasdeep Singh**[◇]
Katherine Goodman[♠] **Jean Hertzberg**[◇] **Katharina Kann**[◇]
[◇]University of Colorado Boulder [♠]University of Colorado Denver
{ananya.ganesh, katharina.kann}@colorado.edu

Abstract

Recent advances in natural language processing (NLP) have greatly helped educational applications, for both teachers and students. In higher education, there is great potential to use NLP tools for advancing pedagogical research. In this paper, we focus on how NLP can help understand student experiences in engineering, thus facilitating engineering educators to carry out large scale analysis that is helpful for redesigning the curriculum. Here, we introduce a new task we call *response construct tagging* (RCT), in which student responses to tailored survey questions are automatically tagged for six constructs measuring transformative experiences and engineering identity of students. We experiment with state-of-the-art classification models for this task and investigate the effects of different sources of additional information. Our best model achieves an F1 score of 48. We further investigate multi-task training on the related task of sentiment classification, which improves our model's performance to 55 F1. Finally, we provide a detailed qualitative analysis of model performance.

1 Introduction

Engineering Education Research (EER) investigates effective pedagogical practices in engineering through qualitative and quantitative methods. A major focus of this research is curriculum design, particularly, inculcating "engineering thinking" (Moore et al., 2014; Pugh, 2002) and identity (Stevens et al., 2008) along with technical skills. In order to develop and improve such curricula, one effective method is to evaluate student experiences in engineering courses in a subjective manner, assessing several attributes such as their perception towards engineering in daily life, and the impact of the curriculum on their self-identity as an engineer (Clifford and Montgomery, 2015).

A popular framework to carry out such assessments is to administer surveys before and after completing a course, where students provide responses to carefully designed questions that probe for identity or affect (Sheppard et al., 2010). Surveys typically include some open-ended questions, such as *"How relevant is design for your intended career?"* to which students provide *text responses.* These are then manually analyzed to see, for example, whether students experience affective gain towards engineering after taking the course. In this paper, we propose using natural language processing (NLP) to enable educators to carry out this analysis faster and at a larger scale by automatically tagging student responses for their affective state towards pre-defined constructs which are of interest to educators.

Construct	Description
Transformative Experience	
Expansion of Perception	The student sees everyday objects through the lens of course content
Motivated Use	The student applies ideas from course to everyday experiences
Affective Value	The student values course content for enriching everyday life
Engineering Identity	
Disciplinary Knowledge	The student displays grasp of technical concepts
Identification	The student sees themselves as an engineer
Navigation	The student sees their path towards becoming an engineer

Table 1: Descriptions of the constructs towards which affective state is classified.

We focus specifically on an industrial design course introduced in the mechanical engineering department of a large public university. Entry and exit surveys measure whether students undergo a *transformative experience* (Pugh, 2002) in the course, and assess the impact of the course on their

Proceedings of the 17th Workshop on Innovative Use of NLP for Building Educational Applications (BEA 2022), pages 250 - 261
July 15, 2022

engineering identity (Stevens et al., 2008). These aspects are characterized by six specific constructs, listed in Table 1. We introduce a new task, **response construct tagging (RCT)**, in which the goal is to identify student affect towards all six constructs from an open-ended response. For example, if a student response says *"I'm not sure what specific career I will pursue, but as long as it's engineering, I'm fine with it."*, then, they are displaying a positive affect towards the *Identification* construct since they see themselves as an engineer. Table 2 contains more examples of responses and human-annotated affect labels towards specific constructs.

Concretely, for each response, the RCT task is to classify affect corresponding to each of the six listed constructs. Our data consists of 232 student responses, annotated by a trained human annotator.[1] We investigate how NLP can be used to solve RCT, focusing on three research questions: 1) What is the most suitable NLP model for RCT? 2) What information relevant to the survey needs to be encoded? 3) Can other NLP tasks – specifically, sentiment classification – help with RCT through multi-task learning? We experiment with a classification model based on RoBERTa (Liu et al., 2019), a state-of-the-art language representation model, which achieves a score of 48 F1, and outperforms several baselines. We also find that multitask learning (Caruana, 1993) is highly effective, helping the classifier achieve an improvement of 6 points, from 48 F1 to 55 F1. Finally, we provide a detailed qualitative analysis of our model, looking at performance on individual survey questions, as well as errors made by the model.

2 RCT: Background and Task Description

2.1 Assessment in EER

Engineering Education Research (EER) is a field of inquiry (Jesiek et al., 2009; Froyd and Lohmann, 2014) that investigates and improves pedagogical practices in engineering disciplines, with the goals of increasing learning and student retention, including that of underrepresented groups (Prados, 1998). Research methodology in EER includes quantitative, qualitative and mixed-methods research (Borrego et al., 2009). Quantitative methods use statistics to study relationships between variables (such as class sizes) and outcomes (such as GPA). Qualitative research complements the above through analysis of data such as surveys and student interviews, which are frequently textual.

Several works discuss the value of qualitative studies for assessing educational practices (Borrego et al., 2009; Koro-Ljungberg and Douglas, 2008). Particularly, Olds et al. (2005) discuss the role of surveys, in which subjects self-report their experiences through open-ended or selected responses. Responses on surveys can be used to assess the effectiveness of various aspects of the engineering curriculum (Froyd et al., 2012), such as students' engagement. Educators are also interested in assessing whether the curriculum changes student perceptions of engineering as applied to their daily lives (Goodman, 2015), also known as undergoing a *transformative experience*. Another aspect of interest is the effect of the curriculum on the *engineering identity* of a student, i.e., whether the student sees themselves "becoming an engineer" (Stevens et al., 2008) in addition to acquiring technical skills. Entry and exit surveys before and after undertaking a course can indicate if the course resulted in affective gain towards such aspects. By analyzing student responses, educators can then redesign engineering curricula to promote such learning experiences, thereby increasing student motivation and retention (Baillie and Fitzgerald, 2000).

2.2 Industrial Design Course Survey

In this work, we look at an industrial design course at a large public university, which encourages students to use their engineering skills to create aesthetics-based design (Goodman et al., 2015). To assess the effect of the class on students, the instructors administer a 68-item survey (Sheppard et al., 2010) to students at the beginning and end of the course. Here, we describe only the open-response questions and the corresponding constructs they measure Example responses for each question, along with some of the constructs and corresponding affect, can be found in Table 2.

Open-response questions. The survey contains four open-ended questions, designed to elicit responses through which the specified constructs can be measured: **Q1)** *What motivates you when choosing an aesthetic while designing something?* This question helps us understand how students perceive the importance of design over pure functionality.

[1]Data, code and models can be found here `https://nala-cub.github.io/resources/`

Question	Response	Construct	Affect
What motivates you when choosing an aesthetic while designing something?	How will someone interact/ feel with this product. What emotion will it evoke.	Expansion of Perception	Positive
	I mostly focus on what will be the most functional aesthetic.	Motivated Use	Negative
How does making things on your own make you feel at the beginning of the process? Why does it make you feel that way?	I love the beginning of making things. Brainstorming and concept generation are some the most fun I have had in engineering.	Identification	Positive
	It makes me feel a little clueless, mostly because I always assume that there is a better or "perfect" way to carry out my design.	Disciplinary Knowledge	Negative
Are aesthetics important to the career you intend to pursue after graduation? Explain. Feel free to include what career you are interested in.	Very important, I am pursuing a career in human-centered design. My first job after college is as a Footwear Concept Engineer at Nike!	Navigation	Positive
	I am not sure what career I will be working in, but I know I enjoy design so aesthetics will be important to my career.	Affective Value	Positive
Are aesthetics important in your non-professional life? Explain.	No, I'm a pretty plain Jane. My walls are bare and I have no non-functional decorations.	Affective Value	Negative
	Personally, they aren't. However, I believe they would be if I had more disposable income.	Expansion of Perception	Neutral

Table 2: Examples from the industrial design course survey, with human-annotated affect labels.

Q2) *How does making things on your own make you feel at the beginning of the process? Why does it make you feel that way?* The purpose of this question is to gain insight into the ideation process. **Q3)** *Are aesthetics important to the career you intend to pursue after graduation? Explain. Feel free to include what career you are interested in.* Responses to this question shed light on whether students see themselves pursuing engineering careers. **Q4)** *Are aesthetics important in your non-professional life? Explain.* This question tells us whether students think of applying aesthetic design in their daily lives.

Constructs. We are interested in determining if students undergo a *transformative experience*, and whether the course has an impact on their *engineering identity*. Transformative experience can be characterized by three constructs: expansion of perception, motivated use and affective value.

- **Expansion of Perception:** the realization that how you view the world has changed due to the content you learned from the course. Students indicate this by observing learned concepts in their day-to-day lives.
- **Motivated Use:** the ability and desire to apply classroom learning to daily lives. Students indicate this by using ideas from courses without prompting in work or personal lives.
- **Affective Value:** the realization that learned concepts have some value in the real world. Students thus indicate a positive emotional state towards the course.

Engineering identity can be characterized by three constructs: disciplinary knowledge, identification, and navigation.

- **Disciplinary Knowledge:** the student indicates knowledge of concepts that engineers know. Additionally, the student thinks they can do what engineers do, and apply learning to the real world.
- **Identification:** the student indicates being identified as an engineer by themselves or others, which fosters a sense of belonging within the student towards engineering.
- **Navigation:** the student indicates their perception of how they are doing at becoming an engineer. This includes completing engineering-related coursework, and pursuing engineering internships or jobs.

Affect. Responses can indicate either `positive`, `negative`, or `neutral` affect towards a particular construct, as shown in Table 2. Responses that do not discuss a construct, or contain no affect information are annotated as `unavailable`.

2.3 Formal Definition of RCT

To automatically identify student affect towards constructs, we introduce the task of response construct tagging (RCT). We define this as a classification task, where, given a student response r together with a construct c, the goal is to predict the student's affect a towards c as expressed in r.

In this paper, $c \in$ {Expansion of Perception, Motivated Use, Affective Value, Disciplinary Knowledge, Identification, Navigation} and $a \in$ {Positive, Negative, Neutral, Unavailable}.

3 Datasets

3.1 Survey Data

Our data consists of 232 anonymized responses across all four questions from 29 students, both before and after completing the course. These responses were then annotated for affect by a trained human annotator for all six constructs.

We create training, development and test splits from 50%, 17%, and 33% of the data, containing, respectively, 114, 40 and 78 responses. Since each response is annotated for six constructs, we create six *training instances* from each response, where a training instance consists of the response and the construct name as input, and the affect label as the output. This finally gives us training, development and test sets of sizes 708, 240, and 468 respectively.

The distribution of labels in the training set is shown in Figure 1. We see that the labels are not evenly distributed – 480 responses, or 68% of the data, do not display any affective state, and are labeled as `unavailable`. Of the other labels, 174 responses, or 24%, are labeled as `positive`, 29 responses as `neutral`, and only 25 responses, or 3.5% of the data are labeled as `negative`. Further, Figure 1 also shows how the distribution of labels corresponds to the six constructs – we see that for several constructs, particularly those corresponding to *transformative experience*, no affect can be detected in the responses.

Table 3 shows the average statistics of responses in our training set, corresponding to the four affect labels. We see that responses annotated as `positive` are longer than others, containing more sentences and more tokens on average. We also compute the percentage of tokens that overlap between our responses and the Bing Liu sentiment lexicon (Hu and Liu, 2004), which contains word lists corresponding to positive and negative sentiment. Responses annotated as `positive` have a 5.82% overlap with the positive lexicon, however, `neutral` responses and those with no affect have more of an overlap, 6.25% and 6.22% respectively. With the responses that express `negative` affect, only 1.16% of tokens overlap with the negative lexicon. We compare this with a prototypical sentiment analysis dataset, also containing classroom survey responses (Welch and Mihalcea, 2016) in the last two rows of Table 3. Here, positive responses have a 9.67% overlap with the positive lexicon, while negative responses have a 4.59% overlap with the negative lexicon on average. This indicates that the affective states we are interested in are different from sentiment.

Feature	Pos.	Neg.	Neu.	NA
Num sentences	2.17	1.65	1.92	1.86
Num tokens	39.4	26.9	37.1	33.1
Pos. lexicon % overlap	5.82	4.90	6.25	6.22
Neg. lexicon % overlap	0.75	1.16	0.60	1.15
EECS				
Pos. lexicon % overlap	9.67	4.82	3.36	
Neg. lexicon % overlap	0.91	4.59	1.80	

Table 3: Average statistics of training set responses.

3.2 EECS data

Transfer learning via multitask learning (Caruana, 1993) has been shown to be successful in NLP (Collobert and Weston, 2008; Ruder, 2017). We therefore make use of the Michigan EECS Targeted Sentiment Analysis Dataset (Welch and Mihalcea, 2016) for training our model in an MTL setup. This dataset consists of student feedback from the Computer Engineering program posted on an online forum. Since responses may refer to either the course material or to the instructor, all responses include gold annotations for the entities mentioned in them. Responses are explicitly annotated for positive and negative sentiment, with the absence of annotations indicating neutral sentiment. The dataset contains a total of 1144 responses, from which we create training, development and test sets of sizes 645, 121, and 378 respectively.

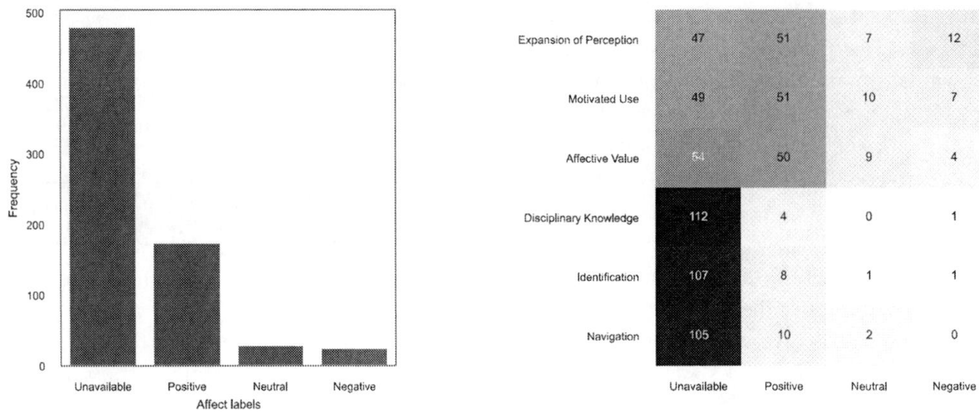

Figure 1: Distribution of affect labels in our training set.

4 Models

4.1 RoBERTa Classifier

Pretrained language representation models (Devlin et al., 2019; Liu et al., 2019) define the state-of-the-art on many language understanding tasks, including text classification (Wang et al., 2018). We thus finetune the RoBERTa model (Liu et al., 2019) for sequence classification, using the HuggingFace Transformers library (Wolf et al., 2020).

We train all models with a cross-entropy loss. We use the default hyperparameters of RoBERTa-base, with an embedding size of 512 and a hidden layer size of 768. We use a dropout probability of 0.1 on the attention layers and the hidden layers. We train for 50 epochs with early stopping on the development set, using the Adam optimizer (Kingma and Ba, 2014) and a learning rate of 1e-5. Training time was 10 minutes on a single nVidia V100 GPU.

4.2 Multitask Learning

Multitask learning (Caruana, 1993) enables models to learn from a similar task, and has been successfully used in NLP, particularly for tasks with a limited amount of data (Ruder, 2017; Benton et al., 2017; Mrini et al., 2021). We therefore perform multitask training on two tasks, namely RCT and sentiment classification on student course feedback. We use the Michigan EECS Targeted Sentiment Analysis Dataset (Welch and Mihalcea, 2016), as described in Section 3.2. This is done by jointly training a single model across both tasks, with a shared encoder and two separate classification heads.

5 Experiments

5.1 Baselines

Random The random baseline randomly selects one out of the four affect labels.

Majority The majority baseline predicts the label of the majority class, which is Unavailable.

Bag-of-Words + SVM Our final baseline represents each input response and construct as a bag-of-words. We vectorize the input using the Tf-idf vectorizer from scikit-learn (Buitinck et al., 2013). We then train an SVM classifier with a hinge loss, L2 regularization penalty of 1e-4, and a learning rate of 1e-5.

5.2 Additional input

We experiment with passing additional input available in our data – specifically, the question corresponding to a response, and the description of a construct as per the annotation guideline. As an example, for the construct *Navigation*, the description is “A response is tagged Positive for navigation if it discussed how the student felt that they were doing things that engineers do, such as accepting a position as a full-time engineer after graduation. Responses are marked as having negative navigation only if not feeling like an engineer was expressly mentioned”. The complete list of descriptions can be found in the appendix. The additional input signals are concatenated to the text response before passing it to the model.

5.3 Metrics

For all models, we report accuracy, precision, recall, and F1 score. We compute F1 for all

Model	Acc.	Prec.	Recall	F1	Positive F1	Negative F1	Neutral F1	Unavailable F1
Random	23.7	24.4	21.8	18.2	23.5	11.7	2.7	34.8
Majority	68.1	17.0	25.0	20.2	0.0	0.0	0.0	81.1
BoW–SVM	67.5	48.7	36.2	35.7	45.5	5.8	10.5	81.0
RoBERTa	74.3	45.7	45.9	45.8	61.7	29.5	5.8	86.3
RoBERTa–Questions	77.9	49.8	47.4	48.4	64.9	33.3	6.9	88.7
RoBERTa–Question–Description	73.7	46.3	44.4	44.2	58.4	14.6	18.1	85.8
RoBERTa-Upsample	78.6	50.5	45.8	46.4	**66.9**	15.3	14.2	88.9
RoBERTa-Class-Weights	74.1	42.4	42.4	42.2	60.4	15.6	5.7	87.2
RoBERTa-MTL	79.2	65.8	54.2	**55.1**	62.0	**49.2**	**20.0**	**89.4**

Table 4: Model performance on the test set of RCT. Bold values indicate the model with the highest macro-averaged F1 on a specific category.

four classes individually, and additionally calculate macro-averaged F1 as an overall score for our dataset.

5.4 Balancing Classes

To counteract the label imbalance in our dataset, we experiment with two strategies: class weighting, and upsampling. With class weighting, we calculate weights for each output class, inversely proportional to its frequency in the training data, and use these weights while computing the cross-entropy loss. With upsampling, we repeat instances of the less frequent classes multiple times in the training set, such that all output classes are evenly represented.

5.5 Results

Table 4 shows the performance on our test set. Looking at the baselines, we see that while the *Random* and *Majority* baseline are comparable, the *BoW-SVM* baseline outperforms them by 15 F1. However, looking at the performance of the RoBERTa model, we can see that better input representations from pretraining makes a dramatic difference: RoBERTa outperforms our strongest baseline by 10 F1. Looking at performance on individual labels, we see that the model predicts with a high accuracy the labels which are dominant in the training set, i.e., `unavailable` and `positive`. However, it is negatively impacted by class imbalance – on the rarest label, `neutral`, it scores 5.8 F1, and on `negative`, it scores 29.5 F1.

Next, we incrementally encode additional input signals with both models as described in Section 5.2. We observe that encoding the question is effective, and overall performance increases to 48.4 F1 with RoBERTa. Particularly, on the `negative` affect label, performance increases by 4 F1. However, we find that additionally including the description of the construct doesn't result in further overall improvement over encoding the question.

We investigate two strategies for counteracting class imbalance as described in Section 5.4, namely upsampling and class weighting. We observe that upsampling has a positive effect on the rarest label, `neutral`, where RoBERTa performance goes up from 6.9 F1 to 14.2 F1. However, on the other labels, there is either a drop in performance or no noticeable change. On the other hand, class weighting does not result in improvement on any of the rarer classes, or overall.

Finally, we observe that the multi-task learning model achieves the highest performance on RCT, with an F1 of 55.1. Comparing to the equivalent single-task model RoBERTa-Questions, the MTL model improves by 6.7 F1, from 48.4 F1 to 55.1 F1. We also see a steep improvement on the rarer classes – on `negative`, performance improves by 15.9 F1, from 33.3 F1 to 49.2 F1, and on `neutral`, performance improves by 14.2 F1, from 5.8 F1 to 20.0 F1. Our results thus indicate that jointly training on the related task of sentiment classification helps the model learn the affect labels in our data better.

6 Analysis

6.1 Question-Level Performance

Figure 2 breaks down the performance of our best model, RoBERTa-MTL, across the four questions

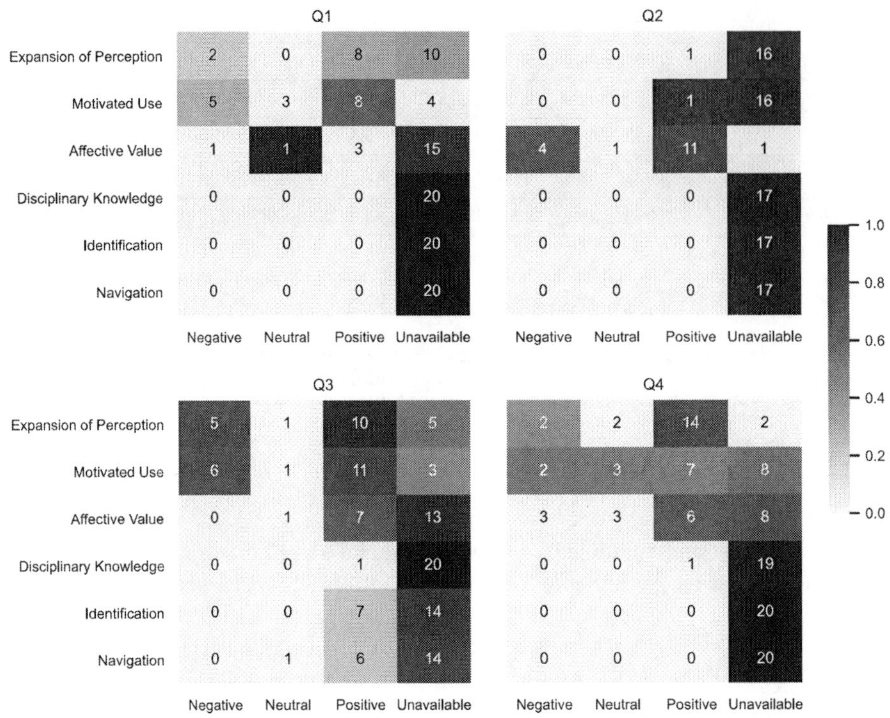

Figure 2: Performance of RoBERTa-MTL across questions for each construct and affect. Cell color intensity indicates F1, and cell values indicate label count.

on the survey as described in Section 2.2. The cell values show the count of each affect label corresponding to a construct on the test set, and the color intensity shows the model's F1 on a scale of 0–1. Overall, we see that the most frequent label is `unavailable`, on which the model's performance is also high across all constructs. This is particularly noticeable for the constructs of *Disciplinary Knowledge, Identification*, and *Navigation*, for which almost all annotations fall under `unavailable` except for Q3.

Next, we look at the plots for individual questions. We observe that for Q1, for the *Motivated Use* construct, the model does well on the `positive` and `negative` affect labels, but does not predict the other two classes correctly. For the *Affective Value* construct, the model predicts the `neutral` label correctly, but not `positive` or `negative`. For Q2, which asks students about their feelings towards starting a project, both `positive` and `negative` affect labels are frequent, and the model also performs well on these classes. On Q3, for both the constructs of *Expansion of Perception* and *Motivated Use*, F1 is high on both the `positive` and `negative` affect labels, but lower on the `unavailable` and `neutral` labels. Finally, for Q4, the model does well on the `positive` and `negative` labels for *Expansion of Perception*. On *Motivated Use*, the model achieves comparable performance on all labels, and on the *Affective Value* construct, the model does poorly at predicting `neutral` and `negative` labels.

6.2 Qualitative Analysis

We also look at specific errors made by the model on the test set, as shown by the confusion matrix in Figure 3. We observe that the major source of error is from confusing a true class of any label with the `positive` label. An example of a true `negative` response to Q1 being predicted as `positive` towards *Motivated Use* is: *"I generally just design to my own tastes and hope that its appealing to others"*. Here, the student indicates that they do not make use of learned concepts while designing which indicates negative affect towards *Motivated Use*. However, this could be perceived as positive, since the student indicates an interest in design, and potentially due to the use of the word "appealing", which typically

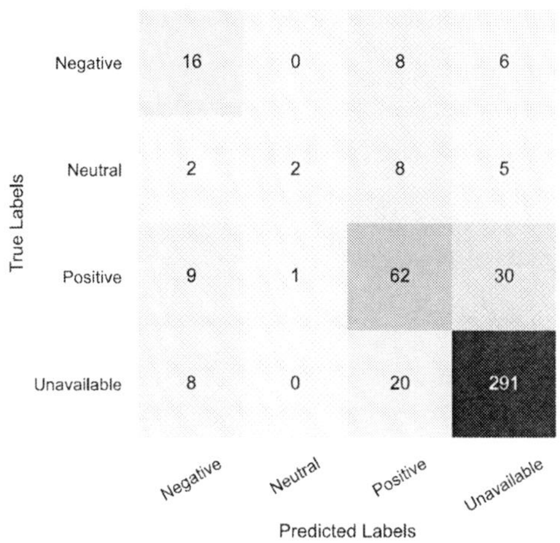

Figure 3: Confusion matrix of RoBERTa–MTL predictions.

co-occurs with positive text for sentiment classification. We also observe that when the true class is `positive`, the majority errors are due to predicting `unavailable` or `negative`. An example of a true `positive` response, predicted as `negative` is, in response to Q4: *"It is important sometimes, like when I'm trying to decorate my house or choosing an outfit to go out in."*

7 Related Work

Prior research has investigated how NLP can be used to analyze student feedback, with the goal of improving teaching and learning. Similar to our work is sentiment analysis for classifying student's affective states after completing a course (Dolianiti et al., 2018; Kastrati et al., 2021). More specifically, aspect-based sentiment analysis (Pontiki et al., 2016) is used to determine sentiment towards distinct entities such as instructors or course material (Ramesh et al., 2015; Welch and Mihalcea, 2016), as well as attributes such as teachers' helpfulness (Nikolić et al., 2020) or quality of examples used (Chathuranga et al., 2018). Several methods have been investigated for this problem, including sentiment lexicons (Welch and Mihalcea, 2016; Wen et al., 2014b), probabilistic models (Ramesh et al., 2015), convolutional neural networks (Kastrati et al., 2020), and LSTM models (Nguyen et al., 2018). However, our proposed task differs from aspect-based sentiment analysis since the constructs we are looking for are implicit, and are never explicitly mentioned in a student response.

Beyond sentiment classification, other applications have been studied for understanding student feedback: Luo and Litman (2015) automatically summarize student responses to open-ended reflection prompts, and Luo et al. (2016) summarize student feedback on courses. Wen et al. (2014a) analyze posts on MOOC forums to determine student motivation and engagement. In engineering education research, NLP has been used for determining "disciplinary discourse" in student resumés (Berdanier et al., 2018), and for measuring metacognitive development of students in engineering classrooms (Bhaduri, 2018).

In our experiments, we use pretrained models for classification through fine-tuning, which have proven to be highly effective for NLP tasks (Wang et al., 2018, 2019). Pretrained models have also been used successfully in educational applications (Alikaniotis and Raheja, 2019; Benedetto et al., 2021; Katinskaia and Yangarber, 2021). We also use multi-task learning (Caruana, 1993), which has been investigated for tasks such as text classification (Liu et al., 2017) and sequence labeling (Hu et al.; Bingel and Søgaard, 2017). Multi-task learning has proven to be particularly effective in low-resource settings (Benton et al., 2017; Schulz et al., 2018; Mrini et al., 2021), which is applicable for our task as well.

8 Conclusion

We introduce a new task, response construct tagging, to automatically tag student survey responses for the affective state of a student towards six predefined constructs. We present a classification model for this task based on the RoBERTa pretrained model, that outperforms multiple baselines. On investigating the different information sources this model can utilize, we find that the best performance of 48.4 F1 can be attained by encoding a response, construct, and the corresponding question. We also demonstrate the benefits of training our model in a multitask learning setting on the related task of sentiment classification, which achieves a score of 55.1 F1, a 6.7 F1 improvement. Our task, and corresponding model, enables educators to assess the effectiveness of their curriculum in influencing students' identity and perceptions of engineering, and thereby to design curricula that maximize positive influence.

Limitations and Future Work Our proposed model can detect certain constructs and affects with high accuracy, such as the positive labels. However, RCT is a challenging task – differences between affect labels are nuanced, and a single response can indicate different affective states towards different constructs. Moreover, the sparsity of labels in our dataset makes it difficult to learn the rarer combinations of affect and constructs, such as negative *Identification*. However, this is an inherent limitation with the classroom assessment framework, since students might be unwilling or unlikely to express feelings such as "not identifying as an engineer". One way to mitigate this problem might be to generate student responses artificially for constructs and affects that are not represented in the dataset. In future work, we will investigate how this can be done both manually, i.e., using human annotators, and automatically, such as conditionally generating responses that display a desired affect.

Acknowledgments

We would like to thank the reviewers for their feedback and suggestions. This research was supported by the NSF National AI Institute for Student-AI Teaming (iSAT) under grant DRL 2019805. The opinions expressed are those of the authors and do not represent views of the NSF. This research was also supported by the Interdisciplinary Research Themes initiative at the University of Colorado Boulder.

References

Dimitris Alikaniotis and Vipul Raheja. 2019. The unreasonable effectiveness of transformer language models in grammatical error correction. In *Proceedings of the Fourteenth Workshop on Innovative Use of NLP for Building Educational Applications*, pages 127–133, Florence, Italy. Association for Computational Linguistics.

Caroline Baillie and Geraldine Fitzgerald. 2000. Motivation and attrition in engineering students. *European Journal of Engineering Education*, 25(2):145–155.

Luca Benedetto, Giovanni Aradelli, Paolo Cremonesi, Andrea Cappelli, Andrea Giussani, and Roberto Turrin. 2021. On the application of transformers for estimating the difficulty of multiple-choice questions from text. In *Proceedings of the 16th Workshop on Innovative Use of NLP for Building Educational Applications*, pages 147–157, Online. Association for Computational Linguistics.

Adrian Benton, Margaret Mitchell, and Dirk Hovy. 2017. Multitask learning for mental health conditions with limited social media data. In *Proceedings of the 15th Conference of the European Chapter of the Association for Computational Linguistics: Volume 1, Long Papers*, pages 152–162, Valencia, Spain. Association for Computational Linguistics.

Catherine G.P. Berdanier, Eric Baker, Weiqin Wang, and Christopher McComb. 2018. Opportunities for natural language processing in qualitative engineering education research: Two examples. In *2018 IEEE Frontiers in Education Conference (FIE)*, pages 1–6.

Sreyoshi Bhaduri. 2018. *NLP in Engineering Education-Demonstrating the use of Natural Language Processing Techniques for Use in Engineering Education Classrooms and Research*. Ph.D. thesis, Virginia Tech.

Joachim Bingel and Anders Søgaard. 2017. Identifying beneficial task relations for multi-task learning in deep neural networks. In *Proceedings of the 15th Conference of the European Chapter of the Association for Computational Linguistics: Volume 2, Short Papers*, pages 164–169, Valencia, Spain. Association for Computational Linguistics.

Maura Borrego, Elliot P Douglas, and Catherine T Amelink. 2009. Quantitative, qualitative, and mixed research methods in engineering education. *Journal of Engineering education*, 98(1):53–66.

Lars Buitinck, Gilles Louppe, Mathieu Blondel, Fabian Pedregosa, Andreas Mueller, Olivier Grisel, Vlad Niculae, Peter Prettenhofer, Alexandre Gramfort, Jaques Grobler, Robert Layton, Jake VanderPlas, Arnaud Joly, Brian Holt, and Gaël Varoquaux. 2013. API design for machine learning software: experiences from the scikit-learn project. In *ECML PKDD Workshop: Languages for Data Mining and Machine Learning*, pages 108–122.

Richard Caruana. 1993. Multitask learning: A knowledge-based source of inductive bias. In *Proceedings of the Tenth International Conference on Machine Learning*, pages 41–48. Morgan Kaufmann.

Janaka Chathuranga, Shanika Ediriweera, Ravindu Hasantha, Pranidhith Munasinghe, and Surangika Ranathunga. 2018. Annotating opinions and opinion targets in student course feedback. In *Proceedings of the Eleventh International Conference on Language Resources and Evaluation (LREC 2018)*, Miyazaki, Japan. European Language Resources Association (ELRA).

Valerie Clifford and Catherine Montgomery. 2015. Transformative learning through internationalization of the curriculum in higher education. *Journal of Transformative Education*, 13(1):46–64.

Ronan Collobert and Jason Weston. 2008. A unified architecture for natural language processing: Deep neural networks with multitask learning. In *Proceedings of the 25th international conference on Machine learning*, pages 160–167.

Jacob Devlin, Ming-Wei Chang, Kenton Lee, and Kristina Toutanova. 2019. BERT: Pre-training of deep bidirectional transformers for language understanding. In *Proceedings of the 2019 Conference of the North American Chapter of the Association for Computational Linguistics: Human Language Technologies, Volume 1 (Long and Short Papers)*, pages 4171–4186, Minneapolis, Minnesota. Association for Computational Linguistics.

Foteini S Dolianiti, Dimitrios Iakovakis, Sofia B Dias, Sofia Hadjileontiadou, José A Diniz, and Leontios Hadjileontiadis. 2018. Sentiment analysis techniques and applications in education: A survey. In *International Conference on Technology and Innovation in Learning, Teaching and Education*, pages 412–427. Springer.

Jeffrey E. Froyd and Jack R. Lohmann. 2014. *Chronological and Ontological Development of Engineering Education as a Field of Scientific Inquiry*, page 3–26. Cambridge University Press.

Jeffrey E Froyd, Phillip C Wankat, and Karl A Smith. 2012. Five major shifts in 100 years of engineering education. *Proceedings of the IEEE*, 100(Special Centennial Issue):1344–1360.

Katherine Goodman, Hunter Porterfield Ewen, Jiffer W Harriman Jr, and Jean Hertzberg. 2015. Aesthetics of design: A case study of a course. In *2015 ASEE Annual Conference & Exposition*, 10.18260/p.23504, Seattle, Washington.

Katherine Ann Goodman. 2015. *The transformative experience in engineering education*. Ph.D. thesis, University of Colorado at Boulder.

Minqing Hu and Bing Liu. 2004. Mining and summarizing customer reviews. In *Proceedings of the tenth ACM SIGKDD international conference on Knowledge discovery and data mining*, pages 168–177.

Yun Hu, Mingxue Liao, Pin Lv, and Changwen Zheng. An empirical study of multi-domain and multi-task learning in chinese named entity recognition. In *Artificial Neural Networks and Machine Learning – ICANN 2019: Deep Learning*, page 743–754, Berlin, Heidelberg. Springer-Verlag.

Brent K. Jesiek, Lynita K. Newswander, and Maura Borrego. 2009. Engineering education research: Discipline, community, or field? *Journal of Engineering Education*, 98(1):39–52.

Zenun Kastrati, Blend Arifaj, Arianit Lubishtani, Fitim Gashi, and Engjëll Nishliu. 2020. Aspect-based opinion mining of students' reviews on online courses. In *Proceedings of the 2020 6th International Conference on Computing and Artificial Intelligence*, ICCAI '20, page 510–514, New York, NY, USA. Association for Computing Machinery.

Zenun Kastrati, Fisnik Dalipi, Ali Shariq Imran, Krenare Pireva Nuci, and Mudasir Ahmad Wani. 2021. Sentiment analysis of students' feedback with nlp and deep learning: A systematic mapping study. *Applied Sciences*, 11(9):3986.

Anisia Katinskaia and Roman Yangarber. 2021. Assessing grammatical correctness in language learning. In *Proceedings of the 16th Workshop on Innovative Use of NLP for Building Educational Applications*, pages 135–146, Online. Association for Computational Linguistics.

Diederik P Kingma and Jimmy Ba. 2014. Adam: A method for stochastic optimization. *arXiv preprint arXiv:1412.6980*.

Mirka Koro-Ljungberg and Elliot P Douglas. 2008. State of qualitative research in engineering education: Meta-analysis of jee articles, 2005–2006. *Journal of engineering education*, 97(2):163–175.

Pengfei Liu, Xipeng Qiu, and Xuanjing Huang. 2017. Adversarial multi-task learning for text classification. In *Proceedings of the 55th Annual Meeting of the Association for Computational Linguistics (Volume 1: Long Papers)*, pages 1–10, Vancouver, Canada. Association for Computational Linguistics.

Yinhan Liu, Myle Ott, Naman Goyal, Jingfei Du, Mandar Joshi, Danqi Chen, Omer Levy, Mike Lewis, Luke Zettlemoyer, and Veselin Stoyanov. 2019. Roberta: A robustly optimized bert pretraining approach. Cite arxiv:1907.11692.

Wencan Luo and Diane Litman. 2015. Summarizing student responses to reflection prompts. In *Proceedings of the 2015 Conference on Empirical Methods in Natural Language Processing*, pages 1955–1960, Lisbon, Portugal. Association for Computational Linguistics.

Wencan Luo, Fei Liu, Zitao Liu, and Diane Litman. 2016. Automatic summarization of student course feedback. In *Proceedings of the 2016 Conference of the North American Chapter of the Association for Computational Linguistics: Human Language Technologies*, pages 80–85, San Diego, California. Association for Computational Linguistics.

Tamara J Moore, Aran W Glancy, Kristina M Tank, Jennifer A Kersten, Karl A Smith, and Micah S Stohlmann. 2014. A framework for quality k-12 engineering education: Research and development. *Journal of pre-college engineering education research (J-PEER)*, 4(1):2.

Khalil Mrini, Franck Dernoncourt, Seunghyun Yoon, Trung Bui, Walter Chang, Emilia Farcas, and Ndapa Nakashole. 2021. A gradually soft multi-task and data-augmented approach to medical question understanding. In *Proceedings of the 59th Annual Meeting of the Association for Computational Linguistics and the 11th International Joint Conference on Natural Language Processing (Volume 1: Long Papers)*, pages 1505–1515, Online. Association for Computational Linguistics.

Vu Duc Nguyen, Kiet Van Nguyen, and Ngan Luu-Thuy Nguyen. 2018. Variants of long short-term memory for sentiment analysis on vietnamese students' feedback corpus. In *2018 10th international conference on knowledge and systems engineering (KSE)*, pages 306–311. IEEE.

Nikola Nikolić, Olivera Grljević, and Aleksandar Kovačević. 2020. Aspect-based sentiment analysis of reviews in the domain of higher education. *The Electronic Library*.

Barbara M Olds, Barbara M Moskal, and Ronald L Miller. 2005. Assessment in engineering education: Evolution, approaches and future collaborations. *Journal of Engineering Education*, 94(1):13–25.

Maria Pontiki, Dimitrios Galanis, Haris Papageorgiou, Ion Androutsopoulos, Suresh Manandhar, Mohammad Al-Smadi, Mahmoud Al-Ayyoub, Yanyan Zhao, Bing Qin, Orphée De Clercq, et al. 2016. Semeval-2016 task 5: Aspect based sentiment analysis. In *International workshop on semantic evaluation*, pages 19–30.

John W. Prados. 1998. Engineering education in the united states: Past, present, and future.

Kevin Pugh. 2002. Teaching for transformative experiences in science: An investigation of the effectiveness of two instructional elements. *Teachers College Record*, 104:1101–1137.

Arti Ramesh, Shachi H. Kumar, James Foulds, and Lise Getoor. 2015. Weakly supervised models of aspect-sentiment for online course discussion forums. In *Proceedings of the 53rd Annual Meeting of the Association for Computational Linguistics and the 7th International Joint Conference on Natural Language Processing (Volume 1: Long Papers)*, pages 74–83, Beijing, China. Association for Computational Linguistics.

Sebastian Ruder. 2017. An overview of multi-task learning in deep neural networks. *arXiv preprint arXiv:1706.05098*.

Claudia Schulz, Steffen Eger, Johannes Daxenberger, Tobias Kahse, and Iryna Gurevych. 2018. Multi-task learning for argumentation mining in low-resource settings. In *Proceedings of the 2018 Conference of the North American Chapter of the Association for Computational Linguistics: Human Language Technologies, Volume 2 (Short Papers)*, pages 35–41, New Orleans, Louisiana. Association for Computational Linguistics.

Sheri D. Sheppard, Shannon K. Gilmartin, Helen L. Chen, Krista Donaldson, Gary Lichtenstein, Ozgur Eris, Micah Lande, and George Toye. 2010. Exploring the engineering student experience: Findings from the academic pathways of people learning engineering survey (apples).

Reed Stevens, Kevin O'connor, Lari Garrison, Andrew Jocuns, and Daniel M Amos. 2008. Becoming an engineer: Toward a three dimensional view of engineering learning. *Journal of Engineering Education*, 97(3):355–368.

Alex Wang, Yada Pruksachatkun, Nikita Nangia, Amanpreet Singh, Julian Michael, Felix Hill, Omer Levy, and Samuel Bowman. 2019. Superglue: A stickier benchmark for general-purpose language understanding systems. In *Advances in Neural Information Processing Systems*, volume 32. Curran Associates, Inc.

Alex Wang, Amanpreet Singh, Julian Michael, Felix Hill, Omer Levy, and Samuel Bowman. 2018. GLUE: A multi-task benchmark and analysis platform for natural language understanding. In *Proceedings of the 2018 EMNLP Workshop BlackboxNLP: Analyzing and Interpreting Neural Networks for NLP*, pages 353–355, Brussels, Belgium. Association for Computational Linguistics.

Charles Welch and Rada Mihalcea. 2016. Targeted sentiment to understand student comments. In *Proceedings of COLING 2016, the 26th International Conference on Computational Linguistics: Technical Papers*, pages 2471–2481, Osaka, Japan. The COLING 2016 Organizing Committee.

Miaomiao Wen, Diyi Yang, and Carolyn Rosé. 2014a. Linguistic reflections of student engagement in massive open online courses. In *Proceedings of the International AAAI Conference on Web and Social Media*, volume 8, pages 525–534.

Miaomiao Wen, Diyi Yang, and Carolyn Rose. 2014b. Sentiment analysis in mooc discussion forums: What does it tell us? In *Educational data mining 2014*. Citeseer.

Thomas Wolf, Lysandre Debut, Victor Sanh, Julien Chaumond, Clement Delangue, Anthony Moi, Pierric Cistac, Tim Rault, Remi Louf, Morgan Funtowicz, Joe Davison, Sam Shleifer, Patrick von Platen, Clara Ma, Yacine Jernite, Julien Plu, Canwen Xu, Teven Le Scao, Sylvain Gugger, Mariama Drame, Quentin Lhoest, and Alexander Rush. 2020. Transformers: State-of-the-art natural language processing. In *Proceedings of the 2020 Conference on Empirical Methods in Natural Language Processing: System Demonstrations*, pages 38–45, Online. Association for Computational Linguistics.

A Appendix

A.1 Construct Descriptions

Here, we provide a description of each construct, including when a particular affect label is annotated for the construct.

- **Expansion of Perception:** A response was tagged as Expansion of Perception if the student expressed seeing aesthetics in their daily life. Students who expressed that aesthetics were generally unimportant were tagged as negative expansion of perception.

- **Motivated Use:** A response was coded as relating to motivated use if a student expressed a desire (or lack thereof) to use aesthetics and design in their work or daily lives. Additionally, if a student expressed that they felt that their learning could be applied, their response was tagged for motivated use.

- **Affective Value:** In order for a response to be tagged with a shift in affective value the student needed to provide an emotional response about a topic relating to those discussed in AesDes, this meant that student responses proving a positive feeling towards aesthetics or design would be flagged as experiencing a positive shift in affect.

- **Disciplinary Knowledge:** A response was tagged for Disciplinary Knowledge if the student discussed their perception of their learning. Very few students discussed Disciplinary Knowledge in their open responses, and no neutral Disciplinary Knowledge code was found.

- **Identification:** A response was tagged for identification if the student discussed either seeing themselves as an engineer, such as saying "I am an engineer" or if they mentioned someone else calling them anengineer. No students provided responses that were indicative of negative Identification.

- **Navigation:** A response was tagged for navigation if it discussed how the student felt that they were doing things that engineers do, such as accepting a position as a full-time engineer after graduation. Responses were marked as having negative navigation only if not feeling like an engineer was expressly mentioned.

Towards Automatic Short Answer Assessment for Finnish as a Paraphrase Retrieval Task

Li-Hsin Chang, Jenna Kanerva, and Filip Ginter
TurkuNLP Group
Department of Computing
Faculty of Technology
University of Turku, Finland
{lhchan, jmnybl, figint}@utu.fi

Abstract

Automatic grouping of textual answers has the potential of allowing batch grading, but is challenging because the answers, especially longer essays, have many claims. To explore the feasibility of grouping together answers based on their semantic meaning, this paper investigates the grouping of short textual answers, proxies of single claims. This is approached as a paraphrase identification task, where neural and non-neural sentence embeddings and a paraphrase identification model are tested. These methods are evaluated on a dataset consisting of over 4000 short textual answers from various disciplines. The results map out the suitable question types for the paraphrase identification model and those for the neural and non-neural methods.

1 Introduction

Computer-assisted assessment brings about the promise of alleviating the workload of teachers, allowing them to concentrate manual efforts towards more creative pedagogical tasks. Not all assessment types, however, have widely adopted fully automated or computer-assisted grading methods. Essays, for example, are a common way to evaluate student knowledge, but are resource-demanding to grade. An angle to automatic essay evaluation is to group together similar essays for batch grading, but this is complicated by the complex structure of essays. Short answers, on the other hand, often consist of only one or a few claims, and thus represent a desirable starting point for textual answer clustering. In addition to being a simplified target for studying textual answer clustering, short answers are also a common form of assessment; Very short answer questions have been shown to have desirable traits of reliable assessments, such as the scores showing a fair and balanced distribution (Puthiaparampil and Rahman, 2020).

Automated short answer assessment is used in this paper as an umbrella term to refer to computationally assisting the evaluation of short textual answers, while there is no unified definition for short textual answers (Roy et al., 2015). Whereas some impose only length restrictions on the textual answers (e.g. one phrase to one paragraph), others have additional criteria such as the answer being a natural language response, or the focus of the assessment being knowledge content instead of grammar (Burrows et al., 2015; Roy et al., 2015). In practice, the definition for short textual answers depends on the actual application, and the answers vary in terms of textual length, topic, assessment criteria, educational level of students, etc. These variations have fueled the long ongoing research on automated assessment of short textual answers. Roy et al. (2015) survey computer-assisted assessment techniques developed in the years 2000–2015 targeting short answers ranging from a sentence long to a maximum of 100 words. They suggest a matchmaking framework to guide the choice of appropriate techniques for practitioners and call for computer-assisted assessment methods that do not rely on model answers, as automated short answer grading (ASAG) systems usually do. One such alternative method is to group together semantically similar short textual answers for batch grading. This is a less explored research area but has been shown to effectively reduce the number of manual actions required for grading (Basu et al., 2013).

The essence of both ASAG and short answer grouping is how the texts are represented, and thus their research methods are influenced by the advances in semantic textual similarity (STS) and paraphrase research. Here, a typical ASAG system would measure the similarity between teacher-supplied model answer(s) and student answers, whereas short answer grouping measures and groups student answers among themselves. Apart from traditional string-based and corpus statistics-based methods, dense vector representation meth-

Proceedings of the 17th Workshop on Innovative Use of NLP for Building Educational Applications (BEA 2022), pages 262 - 271
July 15, 2022 ©2022 Association for Computational Linguistics

ods based on deep learning are naturally highly applicable to the task. A typical example of such methods are Sentence-Transformers (Reimers and Gurevych, 2019) that adapt the BERT model to sentence representation by explicitly optimizing the similarity of dense-vector representation for pairs of sentences known to carry the same meaning. Such models can be applied to answer grouping in a straightforward manner by comparing the dense representations of sentences across different answers. In a different line of work, Kanerva et al. (2021b) approach paraphrase detection as a form of semantic search by training a question-answering type of a model to detect a paraphrase of a query from a given context document. This methodology can be seen as highly relevant to examining answer grouping: given an answer, or a part of an answer constituting a single claim, such model can then identify answers containing the same claim or its paraphrase among other students' answers. Such an approach would, in theory, then allow the grading teacher to retrieve all such answers and carry out a common grading action. While not eliminating manual grading work, this approach could potentially significantly reduce the need, if paired with an appropriate interface and workflow.

In this paper, we pursue this direction, approaching answer grouping from an information retrieval (IR) perspective, i.e. given an answer, or a claim from one answer, the task is to identify other answers containing the same claim or its paraphrase, not relying on the availability of model answers. The objective here is to retrieve similar answers for a given query to support e.g. batch grading. While we do not want to limit our methods to short answer assessment only, full long essays are likely too long as retrieval candidates. Rather than retrieving on essay level, the natural unit for the retrieval would be to do it on the claim level, looking for similar claims inside the essays. However, for the time being we lack any manual annotation for individual claims posed in the essays, making the evaluation of such claim-level retrieval methods difficult. Therefore, we approach the problem by using short answers only, where the answer typically includes only one or a few claims. The overall score assigned for the answer can then be used as a proxy of claim similarity, as all answers with high scores can be assumed to contain similar claims, even if using different wordings. We therefore formulate the overall task setup as such: Given one claim as a query (in the form of a short answer), how well the experimented models are able to retrieve a similar claim among all candidates answering the same prompt (here "prompt" refers to the question posed by the teacher to which the students are answering) when judging the similarity based on the scores assigned to the answers. We use a dataset of over 4,000 teacher-graded short answers from actual university examinations of 24 distinct courses. We test non-neural and neural sentence embedding methods as well as the above-mentioned question answering -based paraphrase retrieval model, and map which types of questions are suitable for what types of answer grouping methods.

2 Related work

The most researched direction for automated evaluation of short textual answers is automatic short answer grading (ASAG). This research field has seen the application of rule-based, machine learning, and deep learning methods (Burrows et al., 2015; Roy et al., 2015; Bonthu et al., 2021). ASAG is typically modelled as a supervised learning task and seen as either a classification or a regression task, where a student answer is compared to a model answer, and the output label or score is based on their similarity. Consequently, model answers are usually required for these systems. Camus and Filighera (2020) test the performance of various Transformer-based (Vaswani et al., 2017) language models on the SemEval-2013 dataset (Dzikovska et al., 2013), one of the most common ASAG dataset. They find that a Robustly Optimized BERT Pretraining Approach (RoBERTa)-large model (Liu et al., 2019) fine-tuned on the Multi-Genre Natural Language Inference (MNLI) dataset (Williams et al., 2018) performs best.

Short answer grouping is a less explored research direction, where short textual answers are grouped together based on their similarity. Basu et al. (2013) use a feature-based similarity metric to group short textual answers into hierarchical clusters. Their features include i.a. difference in length, fraction of words with matching base forms, and cosine-similarity of TFIDF vectors. They show that such clustering can effectively reduce the number of actions required for grading. Hämäläinen et al. (2018) use the Hyperlink-Induced Topic Search (HITS) algorithm (Kleinberg, 1999) to cluster open-ended questionnaire answers from students. Applying this method to both English and Finnish datasets, they obtain satisfactory results on the English dataset but less ideal results on the Finnish dataset, potentially due to the Finnish answers being longer in length. Both the study of Basu et al. (2013) and Hämäläinen et al. (2018) predate the era of deep neural network-based methods of meaning representation.

3 Data

Our experiments are based on a large scale dataset of over 261K anonymized textual answers from different university-level examinations. However, for the purpose of this study, the dataset is heavily filtered in order to obtain a subset including only examples considered as short answers suitable for the study. We aim to find prompts looking for concise fact-based descriptions, which are likely to contain only a single claim and therefore have an increased likelihood that two answers with a high score are likely to be paraphrases of each other (although that naturally cannot be guaranteed without manual annotation). Such suitable prompts ask for example term definitions, listings of the components of certain concepts, explanation of the workings of a process or device, explanations why e.g. a German noun is of a certain gender, or basically anything targeting to a short semantic-focused answer. In addition to the proper answer content, we also need the prompts to fit to our retrieval task setting, meaning that for each unique prompt, we need to have several student answers as retrieval candidates. One such example prompt together with few graded student answers for it is given in Table 1.

The original dataset is a collection[1] of 261K student answers gathered across various disciplines in the University of Turku, Finland. Together with the textual answers, the data include the course identifier, question prompt, assigned score, and possible score range for each answer. The textual answers are written by mainly undergraduate students, and the most common languages are Finnish and English. Figure 1 illustrates the data filtering process. The filtering criteria for identifying a suitable short answer subset for this study are as follows: the prompt length must be under 10 tokens and the answer length under 30 tokens as determined based on the FinBERT model tokenizer[2], and the language of the answer must be Finnish. All answers with 0 as the highest possible score are excluded, as these are often dummy prompts related to course feedback, assignment submission, or attendance rather than being actual exam questions. Additionally, due to the retrieval task setup used, each prompt included in the subset must have at least 10 answers passing the above-mentioned filtering in order to have enough retrieval candidates in the experiments.

After the automatic filtering, some amount of manual cleaning is also used to remove answers and prompts unsuitable for the experiments. These mostly include prompts from language courses targeting to grammatical correctness rather than semantics (therefore including very little variation), prompts asking the students to name parts of a figure, or occasional dummy prompts that passed the zero score filter.

Statistics of the final filtered subset are summarized in Table 2, the final dataset including prompts from 24 different courses and 12 different disciplines. In total, there are 4,082 student answers. The disciplines of the courses are otherwise evenly distributed, except for life sciences, which has 9 courses with 93 prompts and 2523 answers, accounting for more than half of the obtained short answers. On average, each prompt has about 24 different answers. The maximum number of answers a prompt has is 75, while 22 prompts pass the filter with the minimum of 10 answers. Since the highest possible score varies across courses and prompts, the assigned scores of each answer are normalized to a range of 0–1 with respect to the highest possible score. For pass-fail questions, scores of passed answers are converted to 1 and the failed ones 0. The normalized score distribution of the short answers is shown in Table 3.

4 Experiments

The grouping of semantically similar answers is approached from an IR point of view. For each answer, the answer itself is considered the query and all the other answers to the same prompt are considered the documents. This is repeated for every answer of a prompt. Three methods are tested for retrieval: TFIDF, Sentence-Transformers, and the paraphrase span detection model (Kanerva et al., 2021a). The grade is used as a proxy allowing for method comparison: intuitively, a correct retrieval i.e. an answer which paraphrases the answer used

[1] The nature of student examination answer data unfortunately precludes its free distribution.

[2] `https://huggingface.co/TurkuNLP/bert-base-finnish-cased-v1`

Prompt: digital legacy

Score	Answer
1.0	A digital legacy is all the files and data about a person that remain on the internet or the digital world after the death of the person.
1.0	The trace that we leave behind digitally when we die (e.g. files, digital photos and usernames).
1.0	All the digital material that remains of a person after death. Digital legacies include for examples passwords, usernames and photos of the deceased person.
0.5	Traces left by the user of a computer or other technological device. What websites they have visited and what software they have on their device.
0.5	Any data a person leaves behind on the Internet or other computer systems.
0.0	All the things that were born in the digital form.
0.0	Digital legacy means electronic waste, often exported to the third world.
0.0	The evolutionary trajectory of digital devices.

Table 1: An illustrative example of one example prompt together with few student answers for it translated into English.

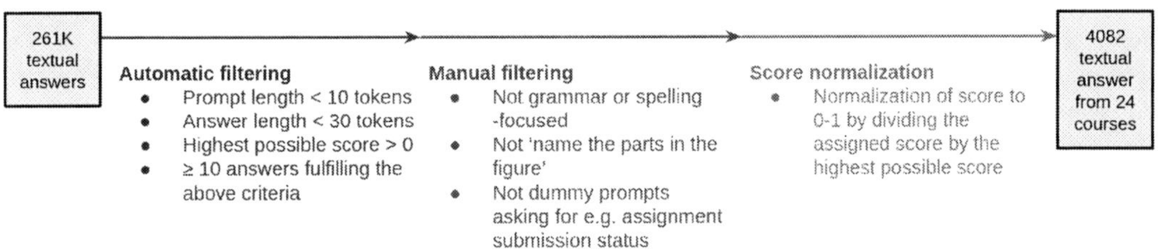

Figure 1: Illustrative diagram of the data filtering process.

	Courses	Prompts	Answers
Full dataset			
Total	1,745	—	261K
Filtered subset			
Communication	1	1	10
Computer sciences	1	14	393
Economics	1	3	37
Educational sciences	2	6	62
German	1	14	172
Information systems science	1	11	437
Life sciences	9	93	2523
Media research	1	1	10
Medicine	2	3	33
Philology	1	6	86
Philosophy	1	5	65
Psychology	3	14	254
Total	24	171	4,082

Table 2: Statistics of the filtered short answers dataset used in this study.

Normalized score	**Occurrence**
0.0	754
0.25	53
0.5	298
0.75	137
1.0	2792

Table 3: Occurrences of the normalized score of 4082 short answers. 15 values between the range of 0-1 are omitted in the table due to low (<10) occurrences.

as the query, should have the same grade. Consequently, a method which is better at the retrieval task should, on average, be more likely to retrieve answers with the same score as the query than a method which is worse at the retrieval task. As we are mostly interested in relative method performance, we measure and report the success of the retrieval by top-1 accuracy and R-precision. The relevance of the retrieval is binary, meaning that retrieval with matching grade to the query is counted as "correct", and otherwise "incorrect".

4.1 TFIDF

The term frequency–inverse document frequency (TFIDF) represents a commonly used family of IR metrics based on lexical overlap. TFIDF estimates the importance of a word in a document by the number of times it appears in the document, and the inverse of the number of documents the word appears in a document collection. It generates sparse high-dimensional vectors without inherent similarity between words.

For our experiments, TFIDF representation is generated for every short answer. The TFIDF representation of an answer is calculated from the entire collection of over 201K Finnish textual answers. The features used are the ngrams (n=2–5) of character within word boundaries. The short answers are used as-is, without stop word removal or lemmatization because these processing did not improve the results in our preliminary experiments.

4.2 Sentence-Transformers

Sentence-Transformers are trained from language models such as BERT or XLM-R (Conneau et al., 2020) using Siamese or triplet networks to induce sentence encoders whose representation can be compared using cosine similarity (Reimers and Gurevych, 2019). The resulting representations are dense, low-dimensional, and context-sensitive. For our experiments, two Sentence-Transformer models available on HuggingFace (Wolf et al., 2019) are tested: `sbert-cased-finnish-paraphrase` and `paraphrase-xlm-r-multilingual-v1` (thereafter SBERT-Finn and XLM-R←SBERT-para). The SBERT-Finn model is based on the FinBERT-base-cased model (Virtanen et al., 2019), fine-tuned for an epoch on the Finnish Paraphrase Corpus (Kanerva et al., 2021a), as well as 500K of positive and 5M of negative automatically collected paraphrase pair candidates[3], with mean pooling and a classification objective. The XLM-R←SBERT-para is fine-tuned from the XLM-RoBERTa-base model (Conneau et al., 2020) to mimic the embeddings of the English Sentence-BERT (Reimers and Gurevych, 2020). The fine-tuning uses a teacher–student framework and parallel data of over 50 languages. The resulting model was reported to outperform multiple competitive baselines on the multilingual semantic textual similarity 2017 dataset (Cer et al., 2017).

4.3 Span detection model

Treating paraphrase recognition as a span detection task, Kanerva et al. (2021b) train FinBERT models to paraphrase recognition taking inspiration from the question answering task, where given a query, a question answering model retrieves a span out of a given document as the answer to the query. Instead of retrieving answers, the paraphrase span detection model takes in a query and identifies a span from the given document that paraphrases the query. The models are trained on the Finnish Paraphrase Corpus, which includes not only the paraphrase pairs but also their context documents where each paraphrase statement originally occurred. They train two flavors of models, one with only positive examples always selecting a span from the given document, and the other being able to produce a null span, indicating that no paraphrase of the query can be detected from the given document.

For our experiments, an answer of a prompt is used as the query and all other answers from the same prompt are concatenated as the context document, as shown in Figure 2. The model produces candidate spans that it detects as paraphrases of the query, and the most likely prediction is selected as the final retrieval. The full model that also predicts null spans is used as there may not always be other answers that are semantically similar to an answer. The model produces several (start-of-span, end-of-span) candidates sorted based on an assigned probability score for each. The model is modified so that the probability is always calculated for a whole answer, instead of arbitrary spans. The retrieved spans can be considered as all the predictions ranked before the null span.

4.4 Evaluation metrics

Top 1 accuracy measures if the first retrieved document (an answer to the same prompt as a query) is correct, i.e. if it has the same grade/score as the query. Top 1 accuracy allows for quick understanding of how well the method roughly works, though it does not take into account the expected value of a random retrieval (e.g. if all the answers to the prompt score the same, the accuracy is high no matter what the model retrieves), nor how close numerically the score of the retrieval is to that of the query, if they are not equal. The course-wise top 1 accuracy is reported, which is calculated as the arithmetic average of the prompt-wise top 1 accuracy. The prompt-wise top 1 accuracy is in turn calculated from the arithmetic average of the top 1 accuracy of all the queries answering the same prompt. For the span detection model, a null prediction is ignored for the calculation of top 1 accuracy. That is, the first non-null prediction is taken if the first prediction is null.

Since the grades of all the answers are available,

[3]`https://turkunlp.org/paraphrase.html`

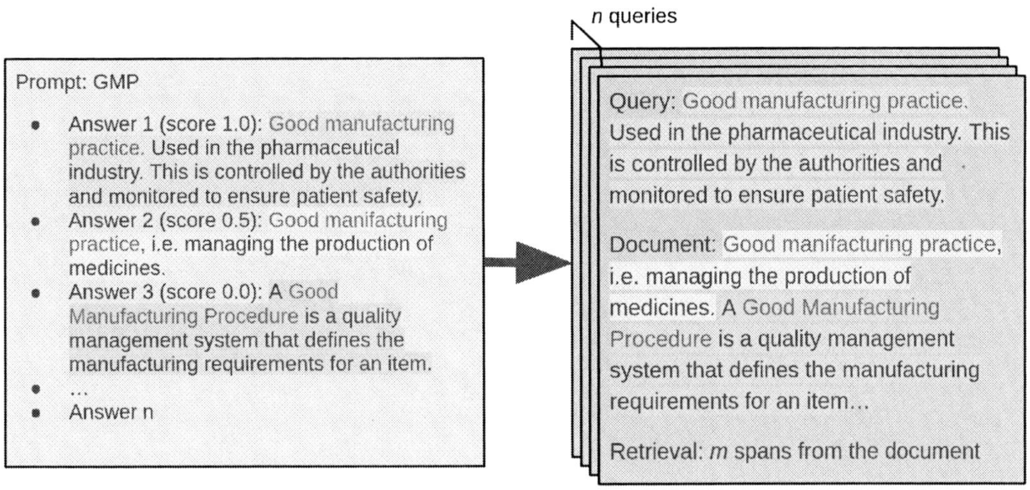

Figure 2: Illustration of the span detection setup. The blue text is in its original language while the black text has been translated from Finnish.

the total number of relevant documents is known. This allows for the calculation of R-precision, the number of relevant documents in the first R retrievals, where R is the total number of relevant documents for a query. R-precision is also equal to recall with R as cutoff. As with the top 1 accuracy, null spans are ignored for the calculation of R-precision in the case of the span detection model.

5 Results

The top 1 accuracy and R-precision of the methods across the 24 courses are shown in Tables 4 and 5 respectively. Courses numbers 8 and 17 have values of 1.0 on both metrics for all methods because both of them have 10 answers to a prompt where all students answer correctly. Excluding these two courses, the span detection model scores the best or equally the best with another method on 11 and 12 courses respectively on top 1 accuracy and R-precision, outperforming the other methods. SBERT-Finn performs well in terms of R-precision on the life sciences discipline, performing the best on 8 out of 9 courses. The numerical differences of the accuracy values among these four methods are oftentimes minimal, and we investigate the ones with bigger differences to establish whether certain kinds of prompts are particularly suitable for a given method. We observe that the neural representation is advantageous when the prompts are challenging, which leads to the students inventing plausible answers using the keywords. An example of a query from a prompt where the TFIDF method underperforms the neural method by a large margin (0.4 vs. 0.7) is shown in Table 6. This prompt is challenging not only because it requires the recollection of certain principles, but also that there are multiple key points the students have to make to obtain a full score.

Compared to the other methods, the span detection model performs well on retrieving relevant answers, but it also assigns relatively high probabilities to null spans. When using the position of the null span as cutoff instead of the number of relevant documents, we observe that the span detection model scores the best or equally the best on only 6 out of 24 courses, whereas TFIDF, SBERT-Finn and XLM-R←SBERT-para achieve 10, 14, and 7 respectively[4].

6 Discussion

In this paper, the span detection model is forced to only predict the probabilities of whole documents being paraphrases of the query. If this restriction is removed, the span detection model is capable of predicting arbitrary spans as the paraphrases of the query. This becomes relevant when obtaining the full score requires mentioning of multiple claims. For example, if a prompt asks students to explain abbreviations, a full scoring answer requires the student to provide the full form of an abbreviation and explain what it means. In our initial experi-

[4]This result is not shown, since the cutoff is only meaningful for the span detection model, and its application to the other methods is merely for comparison purposes

Course ID	Discipline	TFIDF	SBERT-Finn	XLM-R←SBERT-para	Span detection	No. prompts	No. queries
1	communication	**0.6**	**0.6**	0.3	**0.6**	10	1
2	computer sciences	0.619	0.622	**0.654**	0.649	393	3
3	economics	0.30	**0.39**	**0.39**	0.31	37	2
4	educational sciences	0.3	0.3	0.1	**0.4**	21	1
5	educational sciences	0.49	**0.56**	0.44	**0.56**	41	2
6	German	**0.84**	0.81	0.76	0.82	172	2
7	information systems science	0.471	0.474	0.458	**0.489**	437	3
8	life sciences	**1.0**	**1.0**	**1.0**	**1.0**	10	1
9	life sciences	**0.97**	**0.97**	0.91	0.91	32	2
10	life sciences	0.49	0.46	0.36	**0.54**	33	2
11	life sciences	0.855	**0.867**	0.859	0.864	748	3
12	life sciences	0.852	0.841	0.853	**0.864**	365	3
13	life sciences	0.89	0.88	0.88	**0.90**	198	2
14	life sciences	**0.83**	0.76	0.75	0.75	114	2
15	life sciences	0.788	0.794	0.779	**0.800**	990	3
16	life sciences	**0.74**	0.70	0.68	0.65	33	2
17	media research	**1.0**	**1.0**	**1.0**	**1.0**	10	1
18	medicine	0.6	**1.0**	0.8	**1.0**	12	1
19	medicine	0.5	**0.7**	0.6	0.5	21	1
20	philology	0.73	0.65	0.68	**0.76**	86	2
21	philosophy	0.44	**0.47**	0.45	0.45	65	2
22	psychology	**0.58**	0.44	0.52	0.50	94	2
23	psychology	0.66	0.68	**0.75**	**0.75**	68	2
24	psychology	0.54	**0.67**	0.55	0.66	92	2
	Number of best or equal best	8	11	5	**13**	—	—

Table 4: Top 1 accuracy by course. *No. prompts* refers to the number of prompts, or exam questions, in a course. *No. queries* refers to the total number of short answers in a course.

ments, we observe that the span detection model can retrieve a span out of the full answer which is semantically equivalent to a partial answer. The evaluation of such retrievals, however, is not possible given our current data without manual annotations because a full scoring answer has a different score than a partial answer, nor is there a way to attribute which sub-spans of the full answer contribute how much to the final score. The exploration of how the span detection model can be applied to answers consisting of multiple claims may pave the way to eventually automatically evaluating essays. A potential way is to combine the answers of related prompts as queries and documents. We leave this to future work.

A challenge for experimental design is the selection of suitable metrics. Top 1 accuracy has the advantage of being easily understandable and interpretable, but its calculation ignores the expected value of random retrievals. R-precision mitigates the randomness to some extend, since it takes into account the top R retrievals where R is the number of relevant documents. When all the documents are relevant, R-precision is always 1 and it is not immediately obvious if the model performs meaningful prediction, though this can arguable be regarded as unsuitable data for retrieval, or, from a practical point of view, the retrievals will always be relevant. The design of R-precision is not completely compatible with the nature of the span detection model, as the model predicts null, which has to be taken into account if it ranks among the top R. The null prediction can either be regarded as an irrelevant prediction, or ignored altogether as we have done so in this paper. The use of binary relevance means a retrieved document is either relevant if it has the same score as the query, or irrelevant if it does not. This does not take advantage of some of the scores being of higher granularity. For example, if the query scores 1 and model A retrieves a document scoring 0.7 and model B a document scoring 0.3, the retrieval of model A is likely better than that of model B. An ideal metric would thus take into account the numerical difference between the scores of the query and the retrieval, as well as the informativeness of the set of documents available for retrieval.

A class of metrics we have explored but did not eventually use is normalized discounted cumulative gain (NDCG). NDCG is a class of commonly used IR metrics, where the discounted cumulative gain, which sums the relevance of the query and retrieval (which can be graded instead of binary) discounted by the ranked position, is normalized by the ideal

Course ID	Discipline	TFIDF	SBERT-Finn	XLM-R← SBERT-para	Span detection	No. prompts	No. queries
1	communication	**0.5**	0.4	**0.5**	**0.5**	10	1
2	computer sciences	0.589	0.608	0.600	**0.615**	393	3
3	economics	0.29	0.38	0.35	**0.44**	37	2
4	educational sciences	0.4	0.4	0.3	**0.5**	21	1
5	educational sciences	0.42	0.48	0.42	**0.54**	41	2
6	German	**0.86**	0.82	0.78	0.80	172	2
7	information systems science	0.387	**0.403**	0.393	0.400	437	3
8	life sciences	**1.0**	**1.0**	**1.0**	**1.0**	10	1
9	life sciences	0.93	**0.96**	0.91	0.84	32	2
10	life sciences	0.59	**0.63**	0.59	0.62	33	2
11	life sciences	0.790	**0.802**	0.792	0.799	748	3
12	life sciences	0.809	**0.829**	0.817	0.822	365	3
13	life sciences	**0.89**	**0.89**	0.88	0.88	198	2
14	life sciences	0.76	0.74	0.76	**0.77**	114	2
15	life sciences	0.737	**0.741**	0.738	0.734	990	3
16	life sciences	0.60	**0.64**	0.59	0.54	33	2
17	media research	**1.0**	**1.0**	**1.0**	**1.0**	10	1
18	medicine	0.6	0.6	0.5	**0.7**	12	1
19	medicine	**0.6**	**0.6**	**0.6**	**0.6**	21	1
20	philology	0.58	0.58	0.56	**0.60**	86	2
21	philosophy	0.43	0.43	0.42	**0.44**	65	2
22	psychology	0.42	**0.45**	0.40	0.42	94	2
23	psychology	0.65	0.68	0.70	**0.71**	68	2
24	psychology	0.54	0.56	0.54	**0.59**	92	2
	Number of best or equal best	6	12	4	**14**	—	—

Table 5: R-precision by course. *No. prompts* refers to the number of prompts, or exam questions, in a course. *No. queries* refers to the total number of short answers in a course.

Query	0.5	The central principle of processing level theories is that the quality of information is thought to be more important than its duration.
Model	**Score**	**Top 1 retrieval**
TFIDF	0.0	In processing level theory, stimuli are processed in parts, at different levels.
SBERT-Finn	0.5	The theory is that the more information you process, the better it is remembered. The quality of processing is more important than the duration.
XLM-R← SBERT-para	0.5	The most important thing in information processing is quality, not duration.
Span detection	0.5	The most important thing in information processing is quality, not duration.

Table 6: Example retrievals of the four methods to a query answering the prompt "Key principles of the theory of processing levels". Example of a full-scoring answer is "The quality of a process means more than its duration. The processing of meanings improves memory retention."

discounted cumulative gain (Wang et al., 2013). It is not suitable for this task, however, as the task differs from typical IR scenarios in that we have a small number of answers where the retrieval of all relevant answers are important, whereas in e.g. web search the focus is on ranking the most relevant document as high as possible.

The multilingual sentence embedding model does not outperform the non-neural baseline. This is somewhat surprising, as some of the short answers contain code-switching, such as the examples in Figure 2. This shows that language-specific sentence embeddings and models are still more suitable for this task.

The task setup is only an approximation. The same grade does not imply the query and document being paraphrases, not for high grades nor for low grades, unless the grading criteria is semantically stringent, in the cases of e.g. translation studies. However, the hope is that the noise can be mitigated by using a large dataset and some signals can be seen as to whether the models are able to retrieve semantically documents. Our results show that they indeed can.

7 Conclusion

In this work, we explored several methods for grouping student answers to exam prompt. In addition to the standard setup whereby whole short answers are represented as either sparse (TFIDF) or dense (Transformer) vectors and compared to one another, we also tested a more retrieval-style approach, whereby we formed documents by concatenating a number of answers to the same prompt and testing to what extent the model is able to retrieve similar answers from such documents. This approach models the case of matching individual claims in longer answers.

Unsurprisingly, we find that the dense representations are more suitable to the task. Interestingly, we find that a span detection model trained on Finnish paraphrase data performs better than sentence-level embedding comparison methods. It might therefore be fruitful to pursue models which are not restricted to apriori given sentence boundaries, and which are capable of finding individual claims in collections of potentially longer essay-style answers.

While the study is based on real exam answers from a number of courses, the data lacks manual annotation of the semantic equivalence of answers, which is challenging to produce. Further, to be able to use the grades as a proxy to retrieval evaluation, we had to restrict ourselves to short, fact-checking questions, only using a small portion of the over 200,000 answers we have at our disposal. A natural further study would expand the use of the retrieval model to longer answers and employ teachers to evaluate the retrievals provided by the model and establish the overall benefit of such approach.

Acknowledgements

We warmly thank Totti Tuhkanen and Kaapo Seppälä for administrative support and data collection. Computational resources were provided by *CSC — the Finnish IT Center for Science*. This research was supported by the Academy of Finland and the DigiCampus consortium. We thank the anonymous reviewers for their useful comments.

References

Sumit Basu, Chuck Jacobs, and Lucy Vanderwende. 2013. Powergrading: a clustering approach to amplify human effort for short answer grading. *Transactions of the Association for Computational Linguistics*, 1:391–402.

Sridevi Bonthu, S. Rama Sree, and M. H. M. Krishna Prasad. 2021. Automated short answer grading using deep learning: A survey. In *Machine Learning and Knowledge Extraction*, pages 61–78.

Steven Burrows, Iryna Gurevych, and Benno Stein. 2015. The eras and trends of automatic short answer grading. *International Journal of Artificial Intelligence in Education*, 25:60–117.

Leon Camus and Anna Filighera. 2020. Investigating transformers for automatic short answer grading. In *Artificial Intelligence in Education*, pages 43–48, Cham. Springer International Publishing.

Daniel Cer, Mona Diab, Eneko Agirre, Iñigo Lopez-Gazpio, and Lucia Specia. 2017. SemEval-2017 task 1: Semantic textual similarity multilingual and crosslingual focused evaluation. In *Proceedings of the 11th International Workshop on Semantic Evaluation (SemEval-2017)*, pages 1–14, Vancouver, Canada. Association for Computational Linguistics.

Alexis Conneau, Kartikay Khandelwal, Naman Goyal, Vishrav Chaudhary, Guillaume Wenzek, Francisco Guzmán, Edouard Grave, Myle Ott, Luke Zettlemoyer, and Veselin Stoyanov. 2020. Unsupervised cross-lingual representation learning at scale. In *Proceedings of the 58th Annual Meeting of the Association for Computational Linguistics*, pages 8440–8451, Online. Association for Computational Linguistics.

Myroslava Dzikovska, Rodney Nielsen, Chris Brew, Claudia Leacock, Danilo Giampiccolo, Luisa Bentivogli, Peter Clark, Ido Dagan, and Hoa Trang Dang. 2013. SemEval-2013 task 7: The joint student response analysis and 8th recognizing textual entailment challenge. In *Second Joint Conference on Lexical and Computational Semantics (*SEM), Volume 2: Proceedings of the Seventh International Workshop on Semantic Evaluation (SemEval 2013)*, pages 263–274, Atlanta, Georgia, USA. Association for Computational Linguistics.

Wilhelmiina Hämäläinen, Mike Joy, Florian Berger, and Sami Huttunen. 2018. Clustering students' open-ended questionnaire answers. *CoRR*, abs/1809.07306.

Jenna Kanerva, Filip Ginter, Li-Hsin Chang, Iiro Rastas, Valtteri Skantsi, Hanna-Mari Kupari, Jemina Kilpeläinen, Jenna Saarni, Maija Sevón, and Otto Tarkka. 2021a. Finnish paraphrase corpus. In *Proceedings of the 23rd Nordic Conference on Computational Linguistics (NoDaLiDa 2021)*.

Jenna Kanerva, Hanna Kitti, Li-Hsin Chang, Teemu Vahtola, Mathias Creutz, and Filip Ginter. 2021b. Semantic search as extractive paraphrase span detection. arXiv:2112.04886.

Jon M Kleinberg. 1999. Hubs, authorities, and communities. *ACM computing surveys (CSUR)*, 31(4es):5–es.

Yinhan Liu, Myle Ott, Naman Goyal, Jingfei Du, Mandar Joshi, Danqi Chen, Omer Levy, Mike Lewis, Luke Zettlemoyer, and Veselin Stoyanov. 2019. RoBERTa: A robustly optimized BERT pretraining approach. arXiv:1907.11692.

Thomas Puthiaparampil and Md Mizanur Rahman. 2020. Very short answer questions: a viable alternative to multiple choice questions. *BMC Medical Education*, 20.

Nils Reimers and Iryna Gurevych. 2019. Sentence-BERT: Sentence embeddings using Siamese BERT-networks. In *Proceedings of the 2019 Conference on Empirical Methods in Natural Language Processing and the 9th International Joint Conference on Natural Language Processing (EMNLP-IJCNLP)*, pages 3982–3992, Hong Kong, China. Association for Computational Linguistics.

Nils Reimers and Iryna Gurevych. 2020. Making monolingual sentence embeddings multilingual using knowledge distillation. In *Proceedings of the 2020 Conference on Empirical Methods in Natural Language Processing (EMNLP)*, pages 4512–4525, Online. Association for Computational Linguistics.

Shourya Roy, Yadati Narahari, and Om Deshmukh. 2015. A perspective on computer assisted assessment techniques for short free-text answers. pages 96–109.

Ashish Vaswani, Noam Shazeer, Niki Parmar, Jakob Uszkoreit, Llion Jones, Aidan N Gomez, Łukasz Kaiser, and Illia Polosukhin. 2017. Attention is all you need. In *Advances in Neural Information Processing Systems*, volume 30. Curran Associates, Inc.

Antti Virtanen, Jenna Kanerva, Rami Ilo, Jouni Luoma, Juhani Luotolahti, Tapio Salakoski, Filip Ginter, and Sampo Pyysalo. 2019. Multilingual is not enough: BERT for Finnish. arXiv:1912.07076.

Yining Wang, Liwei Wang, Yuanzhi Li, Di He, Wei Chen, and Tie-Yan Liu. 2013. A theoretical analysis of NDCG ranking measures. In *Proceedings of the 26th annual conference on learning theory (COLT 2013)*, volume 8, page 6. Citeseer.

Adina Williams, Nikita Nangia, and Samuel Bowman. 2018. A broad-coverage challenge corpus for sentence understanding through inference. In *Proceedings of the 2018 Conference of the North American Chapter of the Association for Computational Linguistics: Human Language Technologies, Volume 1 (Long Papers)*, pages 1112–1122, New Orleans, Louisiana. Association for Computational Linguistics.

Thomas Wolf, Lysandre Debut, Victor Sanh, Julien Chaumond, Clement Delangue, Anthony Moi, Pierric Cistac, Tim Rault, Rémi Louf, Morgan Funtowicz, Joe Davison, Sam Shleifer, Patrick von Platen, Clara Ma, Yacine Jernite, Julien Plu, Canwen Xu, Teven Le Scao, Sylvain Gugger, Mariama Drame, Quentin Lhoest, and Alexander M. Rush. 2019. HuggingFace's Transformers: State-of-the-art natural language processing. arXiv:1910.03771.

Incremental Disfluency Detection for Spoken Learner English

Lucy Skidmore and **Roger K. Moore**
Speech and Hearing Research Group
Department of Computer Science
University of Sheffield, UK
{lskidmore1,r.k.moore}@shef.ac.uk

Abstract

Incremental disfluency detection provides a framework for computing communicative meaning from hesitations, repetitions and false starts commonly found in speech. One application of this area of research is in dialogue-based computer-assisted language learning (CALL), where detecting learners' production issues word-by-word can facilitate timely and pedagogically driven responses from an automated system. Existing research on disfluency detection in learner speech focuses on disfluency removal for subsequent downstream tasks, processing whole utterances non-incrementally. This paper instead explores the application of laughter as a feature for incremental disfluency detection and shows that when combined with silence, these features reduce the impact of learner errors on model precision as well as lead to an overall improvement of model performance. This work adds to the growing body of research incorporating laughter as a feature for dialogue processing tasks and provides further support for the application of multimodality in dialogue-based CALL systems.

1 Introduction

Speech disfluencies such as hesitations, repetitions and false starts are an inherent artefact of spoken language. Systematic in their structure, disfluencies comprise of a reparandum phrase, optional interregnum phrase and repair phrase (Levelt, 1983).

$$\text{I'd like a } \Big[\underbrace{\text{coffee}}_{\text{reparandum}} + \underbrace{\{\text{uh}\}}_{\text{interregnum}} \underbrace{\text{tea}}_{\text{repair}}\Big] \text{ please}$$

Following the notation scheme described by Shriberg (1994), the example above shows the components of a disfluency. The speaker changes their drink order by replacing "*coffee*" with the intended word "*tea*". The + represents the 'interruption point', often marked prosodically with features such as silence or reparandum word cutoff. The following, optional interregnum phrase can contain filled pauses such as "*uh*" like in the example, edit terms such as "*I mean*" and finally discourse markers such as "*you know*".

Detecting such disfluencies is of particular interest in the context of dialogue-based CALL, where learners interact with an automated system in order to practice conversation in the language that they are learning. In the task-based scenario where a learner is practicing ordering a drink at a café, having a system that can identify and appropriately respond to learners' disfluencies in real-time is highly desirable and not something that is available in existing approaches thanks to the lack of incremental processing (Bibauw et al., 2019).

With the above in mind, this work builds on incremental disfluency detection research and applies it to a language learning setting. The nature of disfluencies in learner speech are explored and learner errors are identified as an area of difficulty in existing approaches. Subsequently, the non-lexical features of laughter and silence are suggested as possible solutions to this issue and their impact is tested and compared to a baseline model. Findings are reported and considerations for future work in this area are discussed.

2 Related Work

Disfluency detection is a widely studied area of research, with the most successful approaches leveraging BERT transformer models to achieve high accuracy (e.g. Bach and Huang, 2019; Jamshid Lou and Johnson, 2020; Rocholl et al., 2021). These models operate non-incrementally using whole sentences as inputs, often with a view to remove the disfluencies from transcripts all together.

This is also the case for research on disfluency detection in learner speech, which has been applied to improve the downstream tasks of grammatical error detection and correction using bi-directional LSTMs (Lu et al., 2019) as well as end-to-end mod-

Proceedings of the 17th Workshop on Innovative Use of NLP for Building Educational Applications (BEA 2022), pages 272 - 278

els (Lu et al., 2020). Approached as a sequence labelling task, disfluencies are flattened and models are trained to detect the reparandum phrase. This approach is not suited to spoken dialogue systems, however, which benefit from word-by-word processing and the retention of all parts of the disfluency in order to generate meaningful and timely responses (Schlangen and Skantze, 2009). In a language learning context, such capabilities would not only enable conversational systems to better employ incremental feedback strategies such as prompting but also provide insight into the nature of individual learners' disfluency behaviours.

Incremental disfluency detection addresses the issues described above and forms a smaller subsection of research. Restricted by their left-to-right operability, incremental systems detect disfluency at the point of repair onset and subsequently 'look-back' for the reparandum phrase. To date, there has only been one research paper related to incremental disfluency detection for learner speech, where Moore et al. (2015) reported poor performance when using an incremental dependency parser trained on native data. Various approaches have been tested using the Switchboard Corpus (Godfrey et al., 1992), however. These are described below.

Following a noisy channel approach, Hough and Purver (2014) implemented a pipeline of Random Forest classifiers detecting interregna, repair and reparandum phrases separately using input features derived from trigram language models for words and POS tags. Simplifying the task to a one model, multi-class sequence labelling problem using deep neural networks, Hough and Schlangen (2015) successfully applied a RNN using only word embeddings and POS tags as input features. This approach was extended further, using LSTMs for the joint tasks of utterance segmentation (Hough and Schlangen, 2017) as well as multi-task learning with utterance segmentation, POS tagging and language modelling (Rohanian and Hough, 2020). Current state-of-the-art performance is achieved by Rohanian and Hough (2021), who incrementalised a BERT-based disfluency detector by using utterance predictions from a GPT-2 language model as inputs to the model.

With the exception of word timings (Hough and Schlangen, 2017; Rohanian and Hough, 2020, 2021) the incremental approaches outlined above have yet to explore the impact of non-lexical features on disfluency detection, despite having been successfully integrated into non-incremental settings (Zayats et al., 2016; Lu et al., 2020). Considering the fact that incremental detection begins at repair onset, it seems likely that leveraging paralinguistic information associated with the interruption point will be beneficial to detection. Approaches to such integration are explored in this work.

3 Disfluencies in Learner Speech

On average, disfluencies occur at a higher rate in learner speech compared to native speech (Hilton, 2008; De Jong et al., 2013). Learner speech disfluency datasets also contain longer reparandum phrases compared to native equivalents (Lu et al., 2020). This is in part thanks to language learners having a lower degree of 'automatisation' in the language they are learning (Temple, 1992) and is cited by Moore et al. (2015) as the reason why disfluencies in learner speech are more difficult to detect automatically.

Another artefact of learner speech disfluencies is their co-occurrence with learner errors. The examples below highlight how errors interact with disfluencies in the NICT-JLE Corpus used for this study. The disfluency phrases are labelled and words in bold indicate learner errors.

(1) My computer [**use** + {er} is used] by [**all family** + my family]

(2) She [[**wanted shopping** + **wanted shop**] + {er} wanted to go shopping]

(3) [[I don't + **I'm not have watching movie**] + I don't have **no** time to **watch movie**]

As the examples show, learner errors can occur in the reparandum phrase, the repair phrase, or both. The first example shows an instance where the learner error occurs in the reparandum phrase and is then subsequently repaired to its correct form. The second example shows how this can occur in a nested disfluency, where the inner disfluency instance contains learner errors in both the reparandum and repair phrases, with the outer disfluency instance being without error. The third example shows an instance where the initial reparandum phrase is correct but the subsequent repair phrases both contain errors.

The presence of learner errors is often cited as a contributing factor to the difficulty of other NLP tasks for learner language data such as parsing

(Napoles et al., 2016) and POS tagging (Nagata et al., 2018). With this in mind, it was hypothesised that learner errors would have a similar negative effect on disfluency detection and so their impact was tested as part of this experimentation.

4 Silence and Laughter

Incorporating instances of silence is a successful method of increasing model performance in non-incremental disfluency detection research. Silence has been encoded explicitly using its presence or absence as an input feature (Liu et al., 2005; Ferguson et al., 2015), implicitly through the inclusion of audio features such as filter banks (Lu et al., 2020) and even as a prediction of prosodic cues from text (Zayats and Ostendorf, 2019). Research into the nature of silence in learner speech has shown that non-native speakers are more likely to pause mid-clause than native speakers during linguistic processes such as repair (Tavakoli, 2011). With this in mind, it seems likely that including silence features will have a positive impact on the model performance and so is tested here.

Language learners use laughter as a 'trouble management device' during uncertainty (Looney and He, 2021), when pre-empting a problematic action (Petitjean and González-Martínez, 2015) and after making an error (Gao and Wu, 2018). In an analysis of UK university English proficiency interviews of 23 Chinese students, Gao (2020) found that laughter co-occurs with disfluencies in three ways: *(i)*, on its own between the reparandum and repair phrase, *(ii)*, alongside indicators of an interruption point such as pauses and word cutoffs, and *(iii)*, simultaneously as laughed speech either during the repair phrase or the whole disfluency. Laughter has been shown to improve performance of models for other dialogue processing tasks such as dialogue act classification (Maraev et al., 2021) but as of yet, has not been applied as a feature to detect disfluencies in learner speech.

5 Experimentation Set Up

5.1 NICT-JLE Corpus

The National Institute of Information and Communications Technology Japanese Learner English (NICT-JLE) Corpus is a transcription-only corpus of 1,281 English oral proficiency tests (approximately 300 hours of speech) of Japanese speaking learners of English (Izumi et al., 2004). The test,

total words	1,165,785
disfluency instances per 100 words	7.54
edit terms per 100 words	11.55
learner errors per 100 words	11.10

Table 1: Dataset statistics for the NICT-JLE Corpus.

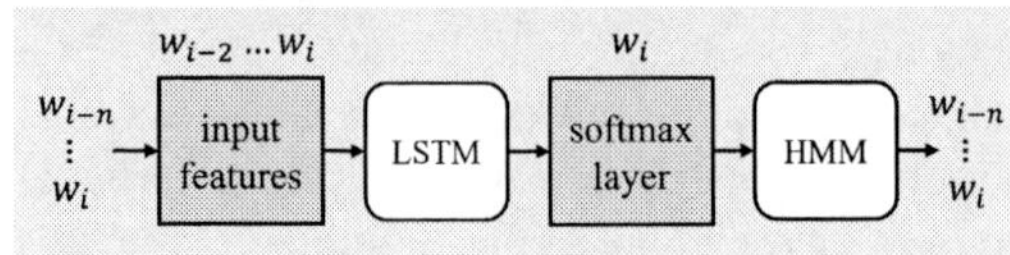

Figure 1: Diagram of the model structure used for experimentation.

known as the Standard Speaking Test (SST) is carried out in an interview style between learner and assessor, where the learner is asked to perform a selection of various tasks. These include engaging in open dialogue, a role-play scenario and a picture description task. Each transcribed interview contains labels for edit terms and disfluencies, 'non-verbal sounds' (including silence and laughter), as well as meta-data such as the learners' SST level, gender and nationality. 167 of the interviews contain additional labels for learners' morphological, grammatical and lexical errors.

For experimentation the corpus was lemmatized using the NLTK WordNet Lemmatizer (Bird et al., 2009) and POS-tagged by the Stanford POS-tagger (Toutanova et al., 2003). Learner utterances (excluding those that contained Japanese) were extracted from the transcripts and split with 80% of the data for training, 10% for heldout and 10% for testing, ensuring that each dataset had an equal distribution of SST levels and that all transcripts in the test set were taken from the subset that contained tagged learner errors. Dataset statistics are summarised in Table 1[1]. Note that the figure for learner error rates reflects the test set only.

5.2 Model

Following Hough and Schlangen (2017), the approach used for experimentation combines an LSTM model with an HMM decoder. As visualised in Figure 1, the model processes sequences incrementally in a maximum window of nine words to accommodate the repair start and the eight words prior. Features are extracted from the trigram $w_{i-2}...w_i$ and used as inputs to the LSTM. The

[1]GitHub repository of adapted dataset: `https://github.com/lucyskidmore/nict-jle`

Model	F_{rpS}	F_{rm}	F_e
baseline	0.757	0.723	**0.982**
+ silence	0.759	0.726	0.981
+ laughter	0.754	0.719	**0.982**
+ silence and laughter	**0.766**	**0.732**	**0.982**

Table 2: F-score results of the baseline compared to silence and laughter models for repair start, reparandum phrase and edit term detection.

LSTM network contains a hidden layer of 50 nodes and an output layer of size ten, reflecting the size of the tag set. Negative log likelihood is used as the cost function, as well as stochastic gradient descent over the parameters, including the word embeddings. The learning rate is 0.005 and L2 regularisation is applied to the parameters with a weight of 0.0001. The LSTM softmax output layer is used as an input to the HMM where outputs are updated incrementally with the best sequence hypothesis from Viterbi decoding.

5.3 Input Features

The baseline model uses trigrams of POS tags and fastText word embeddings (Bojanowski et al., 2017) of size 50 as input features. Silence and laughter features were derived directly from the NICT-JLE transcripts. Each word was assigned a vector, indicating the presence or absence of a preceding short pause, long pause, laughter, or if the word itself was laughed for the current word and previous two words.

5.4 Disfluency Tags

Following Hough and Schlangen (2015), disfluencies are labelled at repair onset as `rpS-n` as illustrated below, where `n` denotes the distance to the reparandum start from the repair start.

I'd	like	a	[coffee	{uh}	tea]	please
`f`	`f`	`f`	`f`	`e`	`rpS-2`	`f`

This approach allows for both incrementality and the labelling of nested disfluencies. Edit terms are combined with interregna and labelled as `e` and 'fluent' words are labelled as `f`. The maximum length of a disfluency is cut off at `rpS-8` which results in a total tag set size of ten.

6 Results

Table 2 reports the F-score results of the baseline model compared to the models with additional non-lexical features. F-scores are reported for repair start as well as reparandum phrase (commonly used to measure non-incremental performance) and edit term detection. Despite individually having little impact on baseline performance, when combined, the features of silence and laughter lead to an improvement in both repair start and reparandum phrase detection. Edit term detection performance remains high across all model variations.

Error Pos.	Model	P_{rpS}	R_{rpS}	F_{rpS}
rpS	baseline	0.730	0.757	0.744
	+ S&L	0.749	0.759	0.754
rpS-1	baseline	0.398	0.713	0.511
	+ S&L	0.432	0.726	0.541
rpS, rpS-1	baseline	0.481	0.768	0.592
	+ S&L	0.518	0.773	0.621

Table 3: Precision, recall and F-score results for repair start detection of disfluency phrases with co-occurring learner errors.

Model	Inc.?	Corpus	F_{rm}
+ S&L	✓	NICT-JLE	0.732
Moore et al. (2015)	✓	BULATS	0.478
Lu et al. (2019)	-	NICT-JLE	0.798

Table 4: Reparandum phrase F-score results of the final model compared to existing approaches with varying corpora and incrementality.

Table 3 reports the precision, recall and F-score results for repair start detection of disfluencies that co-occur with learner errors. Reflecting the three scenarios described in Section 3, disfluencies that co-occur with an error at repair onset (*rpS*), an error immediately preceding the repair phrase start (*rpS-1*) and errors occurring both immediately before and at repair onset (*rpS-1* and *rpS*) are reported. Firstly, comparing the baseline performance of all three scenarios with the overall baseline performance reported in Table 2 reveals the extent to which learner errors impact model performance — this is especially true for disfluency instances that are preceded by a learner error. In turn, it is these instances that show the most improvement in performance when silence and laughter features are included, with precision being particularly boosted.

Table 4 compares the performance of the adapted model with two existing approaches to disfluency detection in learner speech: an incremental model tested on the BULATS Corpus[2] (Moore et al., 2015) and a non-incremental model tested on the NICT-JLE Corpus (Lu et al., 2019). Neither approach reports repair start detection so only reparandum phrase detection is compared here. Although not directly comparable due to the mismatches in corpora and incrementality, the results from this paper significantly outperform Moore et al. (2015), setting a new benchmark for incremental disfluency detection for learner speech. As expected, performance does not reach the level of current state-of-the-art non-incremental approaches.

7 Discussion

The results from this experimentation give support to the integration of paralinguistic features for incremental disfluency detection in learner speech. The impact of silence and laughter on the detection precision of disfluencies that co-occur with learner errors highlights the value of such features in settings where lexical data is 'non-typical'. This is of particular importance in incremental approaches where detection occurs at repair onset, with a reduced reliance on the syntactic parallelism between reparandum phrase and repair phrase often exploited by non-incremental systems.

Despite the improvements described above, overall performance gains are small and remain lower than non-incremental approaches. However, there are further approaches to model improvement worth exploring. Firstly, following the recent work of Rohanian and Hough (2021), it would be of interest to test the impact of an incrementalised BERT-based detector on learner speech. Secondly, using a POS-tagger specifically for learner speech such as that developed by Nagata et al. (2018) may help boost performance. It would also be beneficial to investigate the impact of these adaptations on other aspects of learner speech that inform disfluency behaviour, including learners' first language, task type and proficiency level.

Another limitation of the study is that the NICT-JLE Corpus is a transcription-only dataset with limited features. Without audio files available, instances of silence and laughter are derived directly from transcripts. In the same way that ASR output deteriorates disfluency detection performance compared to transcribed data (Lu et al., 2019), it is likely that automatic laughter and silence detection derived from audio would have a similar effect and may not be as impactful for model improvement. In addition, it would be interesting to investigate the relationship between learner errors and disfluencies by modelling these features jointly. However, in the NICT-JLE Corpus, learner error tags are only available for the test set and so cannot be used as features in training. Furthermore, the performance boost shown when combining laughter together with silence provides the motivation to explore additional paralinguistic features in combination, such as gestures and gaze, both of which have been shown to be used in conversation to signal disfluency (Chen et al., 2002; Radford, 2009). Finally, as the NICT-JLE Corpus is a collection of assessor-learner conversations, it is not clear if learners would still enact the same strategies of laughter to indicate disfluencies when practising with a dialogue-based CALL system.

8 Future Work

To the best of our knowledge, there is currently no publicly available resource that addresses the limitations of the NICT-JLE Corpus outlined above. With this in mind, there is a strong case to be made for the development of a multimodal corpus for use in dialogue-based CALL applications, collected by means of a 'Wizard of Oz' experiment with language learners and human language tutors. Audio, video and transcript files annotated with disfluencies, edit terms, learner errors as well as paralinguistic information would provide ample opportunity for research into both incremental disfluency detection and also other dialogue processing tasks.

9 Conclusion

In conclusion, this work tested the impact of laughter and silence as features for incremental disfluency detection of learner speech. When combined, these features show an overall improvement in model performance, increasing precision for disfluencies that co-occur with learner errors. To date, this is the first work to use laughter as a feature for disfluency detection in a language learning setting, with the resulting model significantly outperforming previous incremental approaches for learner speech. These findings act as a starting point for the further integration of paralinguistic features for incremental disfluency detection and help make the case for the development of a multimodal corpora for dialogue-based CALL applications.

[2]This corpus was provided to the researchers by Cambridge Assessment English and is not publicly available.

References

Nguyen Bach and Fei Huang. 2019. Noisy BiLSTM-Based Models for Disfluency Detection. In *Proceedings of Interspeech 2019*, pages 4230–4234.

Serge Bibauw, Thomas François, and Piet Desmet. 2019. Discussing with a computer to practice a foreign language: research synthesis and conceptual framework of dialogue-based CALL. *Computer Assisted Language Learning*, pages 1–51.

Steven Bird, Ewan Klein, and Edward Loper. 2009. *Natural Language Processing with Python*. O'Reilly Media Inc.

Piotr Bojanowski, Edouard Grave, Armand Joulin, and Tomas Mikolov. 2017. Enriching word vectors with subword information. *Transactions of the Association for Computational Linguistics*, 5:135–146.

Lei Chen, Mary Harper, and Francis Quek. 2002. Gesture patterns during speech repairs. In *Proceedings of the 4th IEEE International Conference on Multimodal Interfaces*, ICMI '02, page 155, USA. IEEE Computer Society.

Nivja H. De Jong, Margarita P. Steinel, Arjen Florijn, Rob Schoonen, and Jan H. Hulstijn. 2013. Linguistic skills and speaking fluency in a second language. *Applied Psycholinguistics*, 34(5):893–916.

James Ferguson, Greg Durrett, and Dan Klein. 2015. Disfluency detection with a semi-Markov model and prosodic features. In *Proceedings of the 2015 Conference of the North American Chapter of the Association for Computational Linguistics: Human Language Technologies*, pages 257–262, Denver, Colorado. Association for Computational Linguistics.

Yan Gao. 2020. Laughter as Same-Turn Self-Repair Initiation in L2 Oral Proficiency Interview. *Open Journal of Social Sciences*, 8(4):479–494.

Yan Gao and Yaxin Wu. 2018. Laughter as Responses to Different Actions in L2 Oral Proficiency Interview. *Open Journal of Modern Linguistics*, 8(6):199–220.

John J. Godfrey, Edward C. Holliman, and Jane McDaniel. 1992. Switchboard: Telephone speech corpus for research and development. In *Proceedings of the IEEE International Conference on Acoustics, Speech, and Signal Processing*, volume 1, pages 517–520. IEEE Computer Society.

Heather Hilton. 2008. The link between vocabulary knowledge and spoken L2 fluency. *Language Learning Journal*, 36(2):153–166.

Julian Hough and Matthew Purver. 2014. Strongly incremental repair detection. In *Proceedings of the 2014 Conference on Empirical Methods in Natural Language Processing (EMNLP)*, pages 78–89, Doha, Qatar. Association for Computational Linguistics.

Julian Hough and David Schlangen. 2015. Recurrent neural networks for incremental disfluency detection. In *Proceedings of Interspeech 2015*, pages 849–853.

Julian Hough and David Schlangen. 2017. Joint, incremental disfluency detection and utterance segmentation from speech. In *Proceedings of the 15th Conference of the European Chapter of the Association for Computational Linguistics: Volume 1, Long Papers*, pages 326–336, Valencia, Spain. Association for Computational Linguistics.

Emi Izumi, Kiyotaka Uchimoto, and Hitoshi Isahara. 2004. The NICT JLE Corpus: Exploiting the language learners' speech database for research and education. *International Journal of the Computer, the Internet and Management*, 12(2):119–125.

Paria Jamshid Lou and Mark Johnson. 2020. Improving disfluency detection by self-training a self-attentive model. In *Proceedings of the 58th Annual Meeting of the Association for Computational Linguistics*, pages 3754–3763, Online. Association for Computational Linguistics.

Willem JM Levelt. 1983. Monitoring and self-repair in speech. *Cognition*, 14(1):41–104.

Yang Liu, Elizabeth Shriberg, Andreas Stolcke, and Mary Harper. 2005. Comparing HMM, maximum entropy, and conditional random fields for disfluency detection. In *Proceedings of Interspeech 2005*, pages 3313–3316.

Stephen Daniel Looney and Yingliang He. 2021. Laughter and smiling: sequential resources for managing delayed and disaligning responses. *Classroom Discourse*, 12(4):319–343.

Yiting Lu, Mark J. F. Gales, Katherine M. Knill, Potsawee Manakul, and Yu Wang. 2019. Disfluency Detection for Spoken Learner English. In *Proceedings of the 8th ISCA Workshop on Speech and Language Technology in Education (SLaTE 2019)*, pages 74–78.

Yiting Lu, Mark J.F. Gales, and Yu Wang. 2020. Spoken Language 'Grammatical Error Correction'. In *Proceedings of Interspeech 2020*, pages 3840–3844.

Vladislav Maraev, Bill Noble, Chiara Mazzocconi, and Christine Howes. 2021. Dialogue act classification is a laughing matter. In *Proceedings of the 25th Workshop on the Semantics and Pragmatics of Dialogue*, pages 120–131.

Russell Moore, Andrew Caines, Calbert Graham, and Paula Buttery. 2015. Incremental dependency parsing and disfluency detection in spoken learner english. In *International Conference on Text, Speech, and Dialogue*, pages 470–479. Springer.

Ryo Nagata, Tomoya Mizumoto, Yuta Kikuchi, Yoshifumi Kawasaki, and Kotaro Funakoshi. 2018. A POS tagging model adapted to learner English. In *Proceedings of the 2018 EMNLP Workshop W-NUT: The*

4th Workshop on Noisy User-generated Text, pages 39–48, Brussels, Belgium. Association for Computational Linguistics.

Courtney Napoles, Aoife Cahill, and Nitin Madnani. 2016. The effect of multiple grammatical errors on processing non-native writing. In *Proceedings of the 11th Workshop on Innovative Use of NLP for Building Educational Applications*, pages 1–11, San Diego, CA. Association for Computational Linguistics.

Cécile Petitjean and Esther González-Martínez. 2015. Laughing and smiling to manage trouble in french-language classroom interaction. *Classroom Discourse*, 6(2):89–106.

Julie Radford. 2009. Word searches: on the use of verbal and non-verbal resources during classroom talk. *Clinical linguistics & phonetics*, 23(8):598–610.

Johann C. Rocholl, Vicky Zayats, Daniel D. Walker, Noah B. Murad, Aaron Schneider, and Daniel J. Liebling. 2021. Disfluency Detection with Unlabeled Data and Small BERT Models. In *Proceedings of Interspeech 2021*, pages 766–770.

Morteza Rohanian and Julian Hough. 2020. Re-framing incremental deep language models for dialogue processing with multi-task learning. In *Proceedings of the 28th International Conference on Computational Linguistics*, pages 497–507, Barcelona, Spain (Online). International Committee on Computational Linguistics.

Morteza Rohanian and Julian Hough. 2021. Best of both worlds: Making high accuracy non-incremental transformer-based disfluency detection incremental. In *Proceedings of the 59th Annual Meeting of the Association for Computational Linguistics and the 11th International Joint Conference on Natural Language Processing (Volume 1: Long Papers)*, pages 3693–3703, Online. Association for Computational Linguistics.

David Schlangen and Gabriel Skantze. 2009. A general, abstract model of incremental dialogue processing. In *Proceedings of the 12th Conference of the European Chapter of the ACL (EACL 2009)*, pages 710–718, Athens, Greece. Association for Computational Linguistics.

Elizabeth Ellen Shriberg. 1994. *Preliminaries to a theory of speech disfluencies*. Ph.D. thesis, University of California, Berkeley.

Parvaneh Tavakoli. 2011. Pausing patterns: Differences between L2 learners and native speakers. *ELT journal*, 65(1):71–79.

Liz Temple. 1992. Disfluencies in learner speech. *Australian Review of Applied Linguistics*, 15(2):29–44.

Kristina Toutanova, Dan Klein, Christopher D Manning, and Yoram Singer. 2003. Feature-rich part-of-speech tagging with a cyclic dependency network. In *Proceedings of the 2003 Human Language Technology Conference of the North American Chapter of the Association for Computational Linguistics*, pages 252–259.

Vicky Zayats and Mari Ostendorf. 2019. Giving attention to the unexpected: Using prosody innovations in disfluency detection. In *Proceedings of the 2019 Conference of the North American Chapter of the Association for Computational Linguistics: Human Language Technologies, Volume 1 (Long and Short Papers)*, pages 86–95, Minneapolis, Minnesota. Association for Computational Linguistics.

Vicky Zayats, Mari Ostendorf, and Hannaneh Hajishirzi. 2016. Disfluency Detection Using a Bidirectional LSTM. In *Proc. Interspeech 2016*, pages 2523–2527.

Author Index